From watching actual classroom video footage of teachers and students interacting to building standards-based lessons and web-based portfolios . . . from a robust resource library of the "What Every Teacher Should Know About" series to complete instruction on writing an effective research paper . . . **MyLabSchool** brings together an amazing collection of resources for future teachers. This website gives you a wealth of videos, print and simulated cases, career advice, and much more.

Use **MyLabSchool** with this Allyn and Bacon Education text, and you will have everything you need to succeed in your course. Assignment IDs have also been incorporated into many Allyn and Bacon Education texts to link to the online material in **MyLabSchool** . . . connecting the teachers of tomorrow to the information they need today.

PEARSON
A B

VISIT www.mylabschool.com **to learn more about this invaluable resource and Take a Tour!**

Here's what you'll find in mylabschool™

Where the classroom comes to life!

VideoLab ▶

Access hundreds of video clips of actual classroom situations from a variety of grade levels and school settings. These 3- to 5-minute closed-captioned video clips illustrate real teacher–student interaction, and are organized both topically *and* by discipline. Students can test their knowledge of classroom concepts with integrated observation questions.

Becoming a Teacher

First year teacher Penny Brandenburg talks about why she became a teacher. Her philosophy of teaching is to encourage the students to take ownership of their learning.

00:22/4.53 sec

◀ Lesson & Portfolio Builder

This feature enables students to create, maintain, update, and share online portfolios and standards-based lesson plans. The Lesson Planner walks students, step-by-step, through the process of creating a complete lesson plan, including verifiable objectives, assessments, and related state standards. Upon completion, the lesson plan can be printed, saved, e-mailed, or uploaded to a website.

Lesson & Portfolio Builder

New Lesson Plan | New Portfolio | Copy | Open | Print | Delete

Type ▾ Name | modified ▾
New Lesson Plan | 11/20/06
social s
MCC
UNM L
The leg
reading
New Le
The Ca
Countin

Lesson & Portfolio Builder

New Lesson Plan (Basic Info)

- Basic Info
- Objective
- Academic Standards
- Rationale Statement
- Materials and Resources
- Procedures
- Assessment
- Style and Export
- Export Instructions

Lesson Title: What do you call this lesson?
New Lesson Plan

Area of study: What is the subject area? (e.g. Social Studies, English, Math)

Teacher Name: Enter your professional name here

Grade Level: For what grade levels is this lesson plan designed (e.g. 6th)

Duration of Instruction: How long will it take to conduct this lesson?

Here's what you'll find in mylabschool™

Where the classroom comes to life!

Simulations ▶

This area of MyLabSchool contains interactive tools designed to better prepare future teachers to provide an appropriate education to students with special needs. To achieve this goal, the IRIS (IDEA and Research for Inclusive Settings) Center at Vanderbilt University has created course enhancement materials. These resources include online interactive modules, case study units, information briefs, student activities, an online dictionary, and a searchable directory of disability-related web sites.

◀ Resource Library

MyLabSchool includes a collection of PDF files on crucial and timely topics within education. Each topic is applicable to any education class, and these documents are ideal resources to prepare students for the challenges they will face in the classroom. This resource can be used to reinforce a central topic of the course, or to enhance coverage of a topic you need to explore in more depth.

Research Navigator ▶

This comprehensive research tool gives users access to four exclusive databases of authoritative and reliable source material. It offers a comprehensive, step-by-step walk-through of the research process. In addition, students can view sample research papers and consult guidelines on how to prepare endnotes and bibliographies. The latest release also features a new bibliography-maker program—AutoCite.

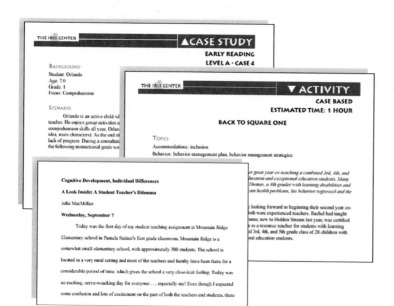

◀ Case Archive

This collection of print and simulated cases can be easily accessed by topic and subject area, and can be integrated into your course. The cases are drawn from Allyn & Bacon's best-selling books, and represent the complete range of disciplines and student ages. It's an ideal way to consider and react to real classroom scenarios. The possibilities for using these high-quality cases within the course are endless.

SECOND EDITION

All Children Read

Teaching for Literacy in Today's Diverse Classrooms

Charles Temple
Hobart and William Smith Colleges

Donna Ogle
National-Louis University

Alan Crawford
California State University, Los Angeles

Penny Freppon
University of Cincinnati

PEARSON
A and B

Boston | New York | San Francisco
Mexico City | Montreal | Toronto | London | Madrid | Munich | Paris
Hong Kong | Singapore | Tokyo | Cape Town | Sydney

Executive Editor: Aurora Martínez Ramos
Development Editor: Alicia Reilly
Editorial Assistant: Lynda Giles
Production Editor: Janet Domingo
Editorial-Production Service: Kathy Smith
Executive Marketing Manager: Krista Clark
Composition and Prepress Buyer: Linda Cox
Manufacturing Manager: Megan Cochran
Cover Administrator: Linda Knowles
Photo Research: Kathy Smith
Interior Design: Carol Somberg
Electronic Composition: Publishers' Design and Production Services, Inc.

Between the time Website information is gathered and then published, it is not unusual for some sites to have closed. Also, the transcription of URLs can result in typographical errors. The publisher would appreciate notification where these errors occur so that they may be corrected in subsequent editions.

ISBN 10: 0-205-51731-5
ISBN 13: 978-0-205-51731-2

Printed in the United States of America
10 9 8 7 6 5 4 3 2 1   RRD-OH   11 10 09 08 07

About the Authors

CHARLES TEMPLE stays busy teaching education courses at Hobart and William Smith Colleges in Geneva, New York; and writing books for children. Dr. Temple studied with the late Edmund Henderson at the University of Virginia, where he explored reading instruction, reading disabilities, invented spelling, and what was to become emergent literacy with many others who have gone on to do good work in the literacy field. He has written books on emergent literacy, invented spelling, writing instruction, language arts, diagnosis and remediation of reading disabilities, and children's literature. He is a director of Critical Thinking International, Inc., (**www.criticalthinkinginternational.org**) a non-profit corporation that develops materials and fields mid-career professionals for teacher training projects around the world. Temple has most recently offered literacy workshops in Haiti, El Salvador, Argentina, Romania, and the Republic of Georgia.

DONNA OGLE is Professor of Education at National Louis University in Chicago, Evanston, Illinois, and is actively involved in staff development projects work in the Chicago Public Schools, the Reading Leadership Institute, and in other U.S. districts. She also serves as a literacy consultant internationally, including Critical Thinking International and as a part of the editoral review boards of Lectura y Vida and the Thinking Classroom. She recently finished her term as the president of the International Reading Association (IRA). Donna also conducts research on visual literacy and content comprehension, having developed both the K-W-L and PRC2 (partner reading in content, too). She is the author of many books, book chapters, and professional articles and continues to give workshops around the United States and the world on teaching for comprehension and higher order thinking, as well as using the arts in teaching. Her K-W-L procedure has become so recognized and popular that teachers all over the world use it.

ALAN CRAWFORD is Emeritus Professor of Education at California State University, Los Angeles. He is Past President of the California Reading Association and has done extensive teaching, consulting, and writing on teaching reading in the elementary school, especially for English language learners. Alan has written curriculum for teaching reading in Spanish and serves on the Editorial Review Board of Lectura y Vida. He served as IRA's representative to UNESCO for many years, and was a Senior Literacy Specialist at UNESCO in Paris during International Literacy Year (1989-90). He is a director of Critical Thinking International. He frequently presents workshops on a volunteer basis for international development projects in Latin America, Europe, Asia, and Africa.

PENNY FREPPON is professor of education at the University of Cincinnati. Her professional work has focused on workshop-based and literature-rich instruction that attends to children's skill development, as well as working with teachers of young children, especially in urban classrooms. She works with Ohio teachers in a state-wide professional development project and is a member of Critical Thinking International. Those who are afraid that current trends in reading instruction run the risk of dismantling much that is good in child-centered instruction will be much encouraged by Dr. Freppon's thoughtful attention to skills in the context of meaning-centered instruction.

Brief Contents

Contents

PART 1
The Processes of Literacy

CHAPTER 1

Approaches to Teaching Reading
page 1

CHAPTER 2

The Social and Cultural Contexts for Teaching All Children to Read

page 30

CHAPTER 3

The Language Basis for Literacy

page 70

PART 2

Aspects of Reading

CHAPTER 4

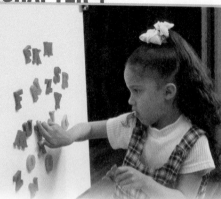

Emergent Literacy

page 104

CHAPTER 5

Phonics and Word Knowledge

page 136

CHAPTER 6

Helping Readers Build Fluency and Vocabulary
page 166

CHAPTER 7

Comprehension: Understanding and Responding to Narrative Texts

page 200

CHAPTER 8

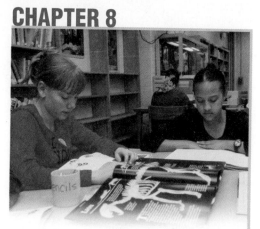

Comprehension: Understanding and Learning with Informational Texts

page 238

CHAPTER 9

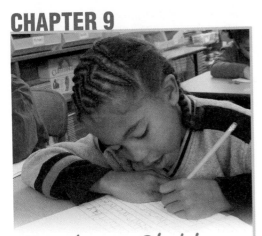

Teaching Children to Write

page 278

CHAPTER 10

Assessing Literacy
page 312

CHAPTER 11

Putting Effective Literacy Instruction into Practice: Grades K to 2

page 350

CHAPTER 12

Putting Effective Literacy Instruction into Practice: Grades 3 to 5

page 388

CHAPTER 13

Putting Effective Literacy Instruction into Practice: Grades 6 to 8

page 430

CHAPTER 14

Models and Strategies for Teaching ESL and for Teaching Reading in the Mother Tongue: A Focus on Spanish

page 472

Features

The World of Reading

Assessment: Focus on Instruction

SIOP®
Sheltered
Instruction
Observation
Protocol*

Differentiated Instruction

Being a Professional Reading Teacher

Preface

Teaching all children to read is the greatest challenge facing elementary schools in the United States. Reading instruction takes the most time and easily commands the most public scrutiny of any school subject. With the greater diversity of our schools, especially in terms of the home languages of the children, the challenge of helping all children succeed in reading will only increase. As authors of *All Children Read*, we accept this challenge and are dedicated to helping you help all children read. As you read these words:

- Making all children readers has become a primary concern not just of teachers and parents but of the President of the United States, the U.S. Congress, and the daily news.
- In country after country, an unprecedented emphasis is being placed on making all children readers through UNESCO's worldwide initiative called "Education for All" [See **http://www.unesco.org/education/efa/index.shtml**]. Diplomats from around the world gather to talk about ways to extend quality primary school instruction—and especially literacy—to every child on the planet.
- The major professional associations and the state education departments have passed learning standards that specify what children should know about reading and writing, and what teachers should know about teaching to make all children readers and writers.
- Scholars in the evolving field of literacy studies are sharing fascinating insights on the way reading and writing influence how people think and learn. New scholarship is changing our understanding of the ways members of different cultural groups use language, and how they respond to language and literacy instruction in the classroom. These insights have direct consequences in the classroom.
- American classrooms are inhabited by children who speak many languages other than English, and whose ancestral cultures come from every corner of the world. Legislation affecting children with special learning needs requires that children be educated in the "least restrictive environment." Children who were formerly educated in separate special education classrooms are now taught in inclusive classrooms, often with teams of teachers present. The task of making all children readers now means working effectively with children with different languages, different cultural backgrounds, and different learning needs.
- Disagreements among educators over approaches to teaching reading—beginning reading, in particular—have led to the formation of a national commission to study the issue. But attempts to settle disagreements among educators with appeals to science have raised new questions. What constitutes the scientific study of literacy, and who has claim to expertise in the field?
- The past decades have been a wonderfully inventive time for new insights into children's literacy learning. Our knowledge of emergent literacy, developing word knowledge, the writing process, literature-based instruction, strategic instruction, workshop approaches to teaching, and teaching for comprehension have both expanded and matured.
- We also have a richly supplied "tool kit" for teaching. A host of approaches exist for encouraging children's emergent literacy, promoting language development, teaching word recognition in ways that honor children's developmental processes, teaching comprehension, encouraging and teaching thoughtful and critical reading, and teaching students to use strategies for reading, writing, and learning.

How This Book Is Organized

Incorporating a "whole-part-whole approach," *All Children Read* is organized in three parts. Part 1 helps you develop a broad understanding of the processes by which students learn to read and write. Part 2 looks in depth at the different aspects of reading and writing. Finally, Part 3 describes, level by level, how to put all of this information together into an effective reading program that helps all children become readers and writers.

Part 1: The Processes of Literacy

The three chapters in the first section of the book set the stage for teaching reading and writing. Chapter 1, "Approaches to Teaching Reading," describes aspects of literacy that must be taught and stages of reading development before discussing the main approaches to literacy instruction. Chapter 2, "The Social and Cultural Contexts for Teaching All Children to Read," carefully describes the cultural and linguistic diversity of America's students, and lays out guidelines for making literacy instruction work for all of them. Chapter 3, "The Language Basis for Literacy," provides a background in the sounds, rules, and meanings of the English language, so the reader can successfully help learners navigate its challenges.

Part 2: Aspects of Reading

The chapters in Part 2 of the book focus on the key aspects of literacy. Chapter 4, "Emergent Literacy," details the early concepts about language and print that lay the basis for learning to read and write. There are many ideas, systematically arranged, for helping children get off to a successful start in literacy. Chapter 5, "Phonics and Word Knowledge," covers phonics and word recognition. The chapter begins by exploring what children need to know in order to read words, and the phases through which that knowledge develops. It then presents a host of strategies for teaching children to read words and build sight vocabularies. A **NEW Chapter 6, "Helping Readers Build Fluency and Vocabulary,"** summarizes our current understanding of reading fluency, the "neglected skill" in reading, and then presents best practices in teaching children to read fluently. The chapter uses the same theory and practice approach for teaching vocabulary. Chapter 7, "Comprehension: Understanding and Responding to Narrative Texts," explores the nature of reading comprehension and response to literature, and then helps the reader build a repertoire of teaching techniques that work with fictional texts. Chapter 8, "Comprehension: Understanding and Learning with Informational Texts," extends the discussion of comprehension to teaching students to understand and learn from informational texts. Chapter 9, "Teaching Children to Write," presents the components and phases of the writing process and then explains the writing workshop approach as well as other approaches to teaching writing in many genres. The methods include those that offer more support to beginning writers, and others that give the students more leeway to create in print. A **NEW Chapter 10, "Assessing Literacy,"** explains a host of procedures that can be used in four "moments" of assessment: screening, diagnosing, monitoring, and outcomes-based assessment.

Part 3: Organizing and Managing the Literacy Program

The last section of the book weaves together the concepts and strategies that were presented earlier and shows how to organize instruction for different levels of learners. Three chapters in this section share approaches to teaching reading in different grade level spans, and the fourth shows how to work with English language learners at all levels. Chapter 11, "Putting Effective Literacy Instruction into Practice: Grades K to 2," explains how to set up and manage a literacy program for emergent and beginning readers. Chapter 12, "Putting Effective

Literacy Instruction into Practice: Grades 3 to 5," shows how to build reading and writing fluency, and how to help children in the upper elementary grades read for meaning and learn from texts. Chapter 13, "Putting Effective Literacy Instruction into Practice: Grades 6 to 8," continues with middle school students and adds a strong emphasis on reading and writing to learn. Chapter 14, "Models and Strategies for Teaching ESL and for Teaching Reading in the Mother Tongue: A Focus on Spanish," shows you how to set up instructional programs in reading and writing for English language learners. The chapter puts primary emphasis on teaching Spanish speakers, since they constitute the majority of our English language learners, but addresses other English language learners, as well.

Content Changes in The Second Edition

The literacy field has seen significant developments in the few years since the first edition of *All Children Read* appeared. This new edition acknowledges many of these developments.

- *Chapter 1: Approaches to Teaching Reading* chronicles recent changes in the field, including government initiatives such as *Reading First*, that are affecting classroom practice, a new section on the major approaches to reading instruction, including Basal Reading Programs, Individual Reading Instruction, and Reader's Workshop, and new discussions of Guided Reading and the Four Block Model.
- *Chapter 2: Social and Cultural Contexts for Teaching All Children to Read* includes new demographic information about diverse learners, updated information about the legal aspects of No Child Left Behing (NCLB) and Reading First, and updated information about the Individuals with Disabilities Education Act (IDEA) and its ramifications for students with disabilities and their teachers.
- *Chapter 2: The Language Basis for Literacy* provides an even stronger background for understanding phonics and spelling, with particular attention to speech sounds, phonological awareness, and phonics, as well as a new emphasis on *morphophonemics*, the interface between sounds and meanings in words.
- *Chapter 4: Emergent Literacy* contains a new and extensive section on teaching phonological awareness.
- *Chapter 5: Phonics and Word Knowledge* has many more strategies for teaching phonics and word recognition, and enhanced coverage of the stages of word recognition (logographic, transitional, alphabetic, orghographic, and derivational reading).
- *Chapter 6: Helping Readers Build Fluency and Vocabulary*—NEW CHAPTER— offers an extensive discussion of reading fluency … the "neglected skill" … and a plethora of research-based approaches for teaching reading fluency and vocabulary.
- *Chapters 7 and 8, the Comprehension chapters,* differentiate strategies for understanding and learning from fictional and informational genres.
- *Chapter 9: Teaching Children to Write* includes a new emphasis on encouraging teachers to write themselves.
- *Chapter 10: Assessing Literacy*—NEW CHAPTER—reflects the expanded role of measuring, examining, and monitoring students' learning in contemporary classrooms.
- *Chapters 11 through 13, the Instructional Strategies chapters,* provide updated informaton about research-based approaches to teaching students at the different grade levels.
- *Chapter 14: Models and Strategies for Teaching ESL and for Teaching Reading in the Mother Tongue: A Focus on Spanish* includes new research and updated information about legal policies for English Language Learners as well as a new section on Sheltered Instruction Observation Protocol (SIOP).
- Students from California who use *All Children Read* will find that key terms from the **Reading Instruction Competence Assessment (RICA)** are fully developed in the text and also appear in the index. In addition, major concepts related to the assessment of students are also developed to support our readers in other aspects of the RICA.

Special Features

Throughout the book, special features focus on issues of recurring importance to reading teachers and extend understanding of key concepts in reading instruction.

TECHNOLOGY

Look up *Fluent Reader* online. How much of the needed interaction is the computer program providing to build a child's fluency?

Technology

The National Reading Pane[...] to read fluently: modeling [...] and feedback offered to the [...] one attention from a comp[...] provide much of this supp[...] ing (**http://www.renlearn.c**[...] offered texts to read from fi[...] ganized at seventeen difficulty levels. While rea[...] dent clicks on each difficult word and also cli[...] The program then computes the student's read[...] Both the student's present score and the tar[...] graph. Then the student reads the text aga[...] ent reader. On the screen the lines are [...] recorded voice can be set to different[...] slowly and clearly at first, and then[...] text several times, the student c[...] and accuracy scores are re[...] a version of the text t[...] reading the [...]

- Central to this text are **six overriding themes** interwoven throughout the book that are critical in reading instruction today. Special marginal icons call your attention to points in the text that specifically address these themes. NEW to this edition are critical thinking questions attached to each icon.
- A **graphic organizer** and **anticipation guide** at the start of each chapter provide readers with an overall perspective of the chapter and the opportunity to assess their level of understanding prior to reading the chapter.

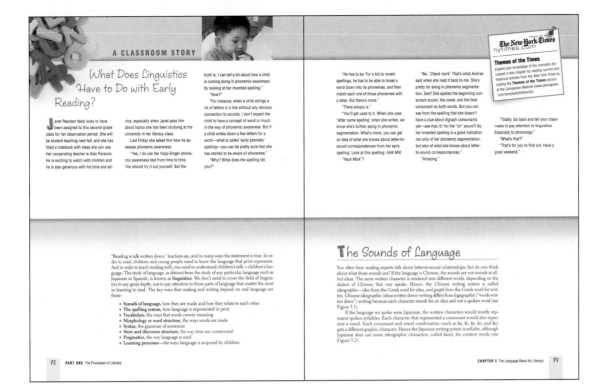

- Every chapter begins with a narrative **vignette** that shares a reading teacher's experience in an active classroom. Each vignette models key concepts from the chapters and demonstrates the challenges of today's classrooms and considerations for addressing children's needs.

- **Themes of the Times** are special Internet connections at the beginning of each chapter that encourage you to go beyond the text to learn all that you can about literacy via a direct link to specially selected *New York Times* articles, which present differing perspectives on contemporary topics on literacy and education.

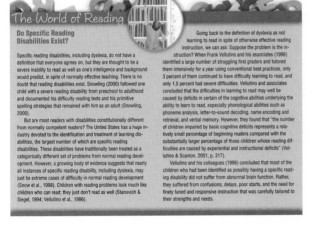

- **World of Reading** boxes investigate a wide array of subjects as they pertain to the field of reading.

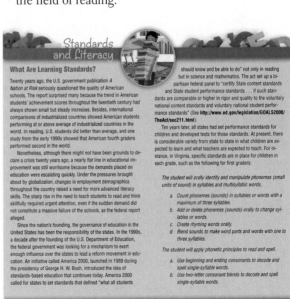

- **Standards & Literacy** boxes explore standards from an objective perspective and openly discuss the pros, cons, and considerations surrounding their use in literacy education.

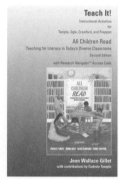

TEACH IT! **9**
First Day of First Grade

In addition, the book includes a special **Standards** appendix outlining the IRA Standards for Reading Professionals-Revised 2003, including a discussion of how these new standards differ from the previous IRA standards and how *All Children Read, second edition,* perfectly correlates to these changes. This special appendix also includes a table of the NCTE Standards for Language Arts (similar to the IRA table located on the inside cover of the book) and a correlation of where those standards are addressed within *All Children Read.*

- **TEACH IT!** boxes provide readers with ready-made teaching tips for skill development, as well as for introducing new approaches to the teaching of literacy.
  TEACH IT! BOOKLET—
Back by popular demand, and significantly updated and expanded for the second edition, this booklet accompanies each copy of *All Children Read.* As you read through the text, look for *Teach It!* margin icons that identify correlating activities from the *Teach It!* booklet that can be used to teach the concepts discussed. It is perfect for your field experience.

FOR REVIEW sections conclude each chapter and offer a convenient study tool in the form of a brief recap of the most important topics covered.

- **For Your Journal** sections offer ideas for using material learned in each chapter to inform development of a personal teaching journal.
- **Taking It to the World** exercises challenge readers to apply chapter material to authentic classroom situations
  - **Technology Connections** offer a selection of relevant websites and advice for using them to benefit professional development.
  - **Connect with Research** sections guide readers to the rich online resource **Research Navigator**™, a powerful online research tool that connects readers to a continually updated supply of mainstream news and journal articles.

New Features in the Second Edition

- **Differentiated Instruction** features in every chapter highlight ways to differentiate instruction so that all students are engaged positively and productively, acknowledging the increasing diversity of today's students. Several of these features also include a **Sheltered Instruction Observation Protocol—SIOP** component, highlighting ways to differentiate reading instruction for English language learners.

- **Assessment: Focus on Instruction** features in every chapter highlight practical aspects of information and formal assessment approaches related to chapter topics.

- **Being a Professional Reading Teacher** activities help future teachers explore their own thoughts about teaching and begin to prepare their own professional portfolio. Formerly included at the end of each chapter in the first edition, this feature has been integrated within each chapter.

- **Advice to Beginning Teachers:** First-year teachers, prospective teachers, as well as highly experienced teachers share their personal reflections and advice about what to expect during one's first year of teaching.

- **MyLabSchool** activities conclude each chapter with a variety of activities and assignments that take advantage of assets available in this rich online resource, including classroom video cases, lesson planners, licensure information, and more.

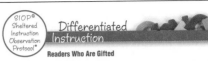

SIOP® Sheltered Instruction Observation Protocol®

Differentiated Instruction

Readers Who Are Gifted

Gifted children are usually not an instructional challenge for classroom teachers. Many have learned to read at home as a result of being read to, and most others very quickly learn to read in kindergarten or the first grade. But teachers often make four erroneous assumptions about gifted children:

- That gifted children don't have reading problems.
  The gifted child who is reading on grade level may have a reading problem that should be diagnosed and addressed. Ordinarily, gifted children will be reading above grade level, often several grades above their age-expected level. Teachers should identify the levels at which they need instruction and at which they can read independently without great effort, and then provide appropriate books at those levels.
- That all children will benefit from the same reading program.
  Children who already read, often far above grade level, will be bored if required to proceed laboriously through instructional content designed for children who are on grade level, or even below. Teachers should challenge such children, usually by differentiating the reading program for them and certainly by providing alternative activities when other children are learning something mastered long ago by children who are gifted or advanced in their reading abilities. This includes helping them find books of interest. Gifted children will often persevere even with difficult materials if they are of great interest.
- That gifted children have already mastered all of the basic skills.
  The fragmentation of basic skills is not unusual among gifted children. They can be integrated into reading groups that are addressing related areas of weakness at the time an appropriate lesson or lessons are offered, even though those groups are usually working below the levels of these otherwise more capable students.
- That all gifted children speak English well.
  We should search for gifted children among English language learners and other marginalized groups of children as diligently as we search among advantaged children. Gifted English language learners and children who speak African American Vernacular English will benefit greatly from language-rich strategies such as those found in the Sheltered Instruction Observation Protocol (SIOP) (Echevarria, Vogt, & Short, 2004).

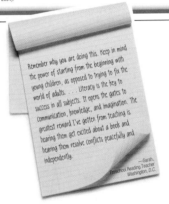

Remember why you are doing this. Keep in mind the power of starting from the beginning with young children, as opposed to trying to fix the world of adults. . . . Literacy is the key to success in all subjects. It opens the gates to communication, knowledge, and imagination. The greatest reward I've gotten from teaching is hearing them get excited about a book and hearing them resolve conflicts peacefully and independently.

—Sarah, Preschool Reading Teacher
Washington, D.C.

Assessment
Why We Assess

Assessment is a vital part of teaching reading and writing. Assessment allows teachers to determine how well a particular child is learning and how well an individual lesson succeeded and to evaluate the effectiveness of the whole program of instruction. Assessment enables children to see for themselves how they are performing as they learn to read and write and what they can do to improve. It helps school administrators to make decisions about the placement of individual children in special assistance, about the design of a curriculum, and about the in-service training needs of their faculty. Assessment also provides parents with feedback on their children's progress and identifies areas where they can provide support. It can even help parents and communities to know how their schools are performing in comparison to other schools. With the advent of the No Child Left Behind legislation of the past decade, assessment is also being used in an effort to determine which schools are performing satisfactorily in teaching children to read.

Assessment can take many forms, including testing. Although some formal and informal tests of reading and writing ability can be useful, some of the most informative kinds of assessments involve watching very carefully as children read and write under natural circumstances. The type of assessment that is used depends a great deal on what needs to be known and who needs to know it.

In this book, the topic of the assessment of literacy is covered extensively in Chapter 10. It is also integrated within each chapter. Suggestions for assessment are provided for emergent literacy, word recognition, fluency, [...]

at every [...]

mylabschool
Where the classroom comes to life!

Go to Allyn & Bacon's MyLabSchool (www.mylabschool.com), enter Assignment ID RMV2 into the Assignment Finder. Watch the video, *Teaching Phonics*, in which a first grade teacher works with small groups to teach vowels, diphthongs, and diagraphs.

Question: How would you incorporate phonics as part of the reading program? You may also answer the questions at the end of the clip and e-mail your responses to your instructor.

Being a Professional Reading Teacher

Changes in the Reading Field

If you are a new teacher just entering a school with many experienced teachers on the faculty, the conversations about changes in the teaching of reading could be puzzling to you, even unsettling. You could easily get the impression that the focuses of educational research and teaching are as changeable as the preferred colors of kids' T-shirts or brand of their sneakers. We hope the discussion you just read did not add to that impression. The truth is, things are moving forward in literacy education. The students we teach are far more diverse, and as great as the challenge of serving each of them well may be, our society as a whole is much more committed to helping every child become a success than it was a generation ago—ask your grandmother. Our knowledge base for teaching has grown tremendously. Although the disagreements among theorists and practitioners have been shrill at times, we do know much more about teaching reading than we did a generation ago. Our understanding of emergent literacy, the nature of language, comprehension, the development of word knowledge, the importance of fluency and how it is learned, the way children learn to write, and they way they learn literature; ways of serving children with special needs, ways of conducting assessment, ways of teaching—these have all advanced tremendously. Things are moving forward. Keep your eyes open. Hold on to your hat. Be part of the change.

Your Professional Portfolio

Most college and university teacher preparation programs now require that candidates prepare portfolios that reflect their professional development. In addition, many principals and school district personnel directors make new teachers' portfolios a focus of their preemployment interviews. Finally, your portfolio can be a means of self-evaluation, a record of past achievement, and a plan for future professional development.

As you begin this course, begin thinking about your own portfolio. Because reading instruction is such an important part of your new career, it should be highlighted in your portfolio. There are

many formats for teacher portfolios. Most include some or all of the following:

- Sample lesson plans
- Thematic units
- Videotapes of lessons
- Descriptions of cooperative learning activities used in your lessons
- Photographs or hand-drawn plans of your classroom environment
- Student, teacher, and participant products, such as writing assignments, self-evaluations, projects, lesson plans, maps, experiments
- Plans for and evidence of continuing education or professional development, such as courses, workshops, conference attendance, and activities in professional organizations
- Descriptions of mentoring activities, both as mentee and mentor
- Peer observations and evaluations
- Letters of reference, commendations, and recommendations from supervisors
- An essay about your teaching philosophy (how you teach and why)
- Written reflections about planning (why artifacts are included in the portfolio); many teachers write them on stick-on notes that can be attached to items in the portfolio. Your portfolio is a dynamic, living document. It should change over time. It should reflect you as you are, which means you should periodically remove items that no longer reflect your current status, interests, and capabilities. How large should your portfolio be? Only you can answer that. But it should be functional and useful, not a burden to you or to the person reviewing it.

Two final cautions:

- Ensure that all examples presented in your portfolio are your own original work. If you use or adapt the work of someone else, be sure to give credit.
- Proofread everything carefully; you are presenting your best face in your portfolio, including your ability to write and spell in English.

For more about portfolios, see McLaughlin and Vogt (1996).

Supplements and Learning Aids

To get the most use of *All Children Read: Teaching for Literacy in Today's Diverse Classrooms, second edition,* a number of useful supplements are available for students and instructors. Speak with your representative about obtaining these supplements for your class!

For the Instructor:

- **Instructor's Manual and Test Bank.** The Instructor's Manual includes a wealth of interesting ideas and activities designed to help instructors teach the course. Each chapter includes a chapter-at-a-glance grid, key concepts, student objectives, activities and discussion questions, and vocabulary and key terms. There is also a test bank for each chapter. (Available for download from the Instructor's Resource Center at **www.ablongman.com/irc**.)
- **Computerized Test Bank.** The printed Test Bank is also available electronically through the Allyn & Bacon computerized testing system, TestGen EQ. Instructors can use TestGen EQ to create exams in just minutes by selecting from the existing database of questions, editing questions, and/or writing original questions. (Available for download from the Instructor's Resource Center at **www.ablongman.com/irc**.)
- **PowerPoint™ Presentation.** Ideal for lecture presentations or student handouts, the PowerPoint™ Presentation created for this text provides dozens of ready-to-use graphic and text images. (Available for download from the Instructor's Resource Center at **www.ablongman.com/irc**.)
- **Allyn & Bacon Digital Media Archive CD-ROM for Literacy, 2002.** This CD-ROM offers still images, video clips, audio clips, web links, and assorted lecture resources that can be incorporated into multimedia presentations in the classroom.
- **(mylabschool** Available as a value-package item with student copies of *All Children Read: Teaching for Literacy in Today's Diverse Classrooms,* second edition, MyLabSchool is a collection of online tools for student success in the course, in licensure exams, and their teaching career. Visit **www.mylabschool.com** to access the following: **video clips** from real classrooms, with opportunities for students to reflect on the videos and offer their own thoughts and suggestions for applying theory to practice; an extensive archive of **text and multimedia cases** that provide valuable perspectives on real classrooms and real teaching challenges; Allyn & Bacon's **Lesson and Portfolio Builder** application, which includes an integrated state standards correlation tool; help with research papers using **Research Navigator™,** which provides access to four exclusive databases of credible and reliable source material including EBSCO's ContentSelect academic journal database, the *New York Times* On The Web subject archive, the "Best of the Web" Link Library, and FT.com business archive. MyLabSchool also includes a **Careers Center** with resources for Praxis exams and licensure preparation, professional portfolio development, job search, and interview techniques.
- **Professionals in Action: Literacy Video** (© 2000, 90 minutes in length). This Professionals in Action video consists of 10- to 20-minute segments on Developing Phonemic Awareness, Teaching Phonics, Helping Students Become Strategic Readers, Organizing for Teaching with Literature, and Reading Intervention, plus discussions with experts on literacy and brain research. The first four sections of each segment provide narrative along with actual classroom teaching footage. The final section presents, in a question-and-answer format, discussions by leading experts in the field of literacy. Please consult with your Allyn & Bacon representative for details and conditions on how to obtain this video.
- **Allyn & Bacon Literacy Video Library.** This selection of videos features reading experts such as Richard Allington, Dorothy Strickland, and Evelyn English, and addresses core topics covered in the literacy classroom. Videos include *Classroom*

Insight II, Developing Literacy in the Multiple Intelligences Classroom (featuring Evelyn English); *Professionals in Action: Children's Literature: Meet the Authors* (featuring Joseph Bruchac, Alma Flor Ada, Pat Mora, Carmen Lomas Garza, Walter Dean Myers, Patricia Polacco, Robert Sabuda, John Archambault, Barbara Park, Gerald McDermott); *Professionals in Action: Literacy* (featuring Phyllis Hunter and Donna Ogle); *Reading Strategies* (featuring Donna Ogle); *Reading and Writing: The Pathway to Meaning* (featuring Dorothy Strickland); or *Thoughtful Literacy: The Key to Student Achievement* (featuring Richard Allington). Please consult with your Allyn & Bacon representative for details and conditions on how to obtain this video.

- **VideoWorkshop for Reading Methods, Version 2.0.** An easy way to bring video into your course for maximized learning! This total teaching and learning system includes quality video footage on an easy-to-use CD-ROM plus a Student Learning Guide and an Instructor's Teaching Guide—both with questions and activity suggestions. The result? A program that brings textbook concepts to life with ease and that helps students understand, analyze, and apply the objectives of the course. VideoWorkshop is available for students as a value-pack option with this textbook.
- **Course Management.** Powered by Blackboard and hosted nationally, Allyn & Bacon's own course management system, CourseCompass, helps you manage all aspects of teaching your course. For colleges and universities with WebCT™ and Blackboard™ licenses, special course management packages can be requested in these formats as well, and the Test Item file for this text can be prepared in the appropriate format for importing into your system. Allyn & Bacon is proud to offer premium content for Elementary Reading in these platforms. (Your sales representative can give you additional information.)
  - Allyn & Bacon Blackboard for Elementary Reading (Open access)

For Students:

- **Teach It!** The *Teach It!* lesson plan booklet, written by classroom teacher and author Jean Gillett of the Orange County Public Schools in Virginia with Codruta Temple, doctoral student at Syracuse University, contains a wide variety of ready-to-use, classroom-tested activities for teaching critical concepts in Literacy Education. All activities are correlated to lessons in the text itself. This free supplement, packaged with the book, is the perfect resource for first time and experienced literacy teachers. The *Teach It!* booklet also contains students' personal access codes and instructions for gaining access to Research Navigator.

- **mylabschool** is a collection of online tools for student success in the course, in licensure exams, and the teaching career. Visit **www.mylabschool.com** to access: **video clips** from real classrooms, with opportunities for students to reflect on the videos and offer their own thoughts and suggestions for applying theory to practice; an extensive archive of **text and multimedia cases** that provide valuable perspectives on real classrooms and real teaching challenges; Allyn & Bacon's **Lesson and Portfolio Builder** application, which includes an integrated state standards correlation tool; help with research papers using **Research Navigator™,** which provides access to three exclusive databases of credible and reliable source material including EBSCO's ContentSelect Academic Journal Database, New York Times Search by Subject Archive, and "Best of the Web" Link Library; and **The New York Times Education News Feed.** MyLabSchool also includes a **Careers** center with resources for Praxis exams and licensure preparation, professional portfolio development, job search, and interview techniques.
- **Companion Website.** Created to accompany *All Children Read: Teaching for Literacy in Today's Diverse Classrooms, second edition,* this online site offers **tools and**

activities to help students understand and extend the text discussion and study more effectively. It includes for each text chapter an overview, learning objectives, web links, practice tests, flash cards, and study aid activities. Visit www.ablongman.com/templeallchildren2e

- **Themes of the Times for Literacy.** Available as a value-package, this collection of 50 *New York Times* articles provides students with real-world information about literacy.

Acknowledgments

The four of us have enjoyed writing this book, although we have to confess, this manuscript probably set a record for miles traveled before completion. We were brought together in the first place in Brasov, Romania, several summers ago by the Reading and Writing for Critical Thinking Project, which was facilitated by the International Reading Association and funded by the Open Society Institute. The authors would like to thank the RWCT volunteers and overseas partners who helped us lift up this great enterprise, Liz for believing in us, and G.S. for being so generous. We learned a ton from all of you.

We thank all teachers, educators, researchers, and our students who contribute so much to this team of authors' learning. In particular, we'd like to recognize the professional contributions of four people without whom this project would not have been complete: Jean Gillet, a long-time friend, author, and reading specialist in the Virginia school system who compiled the *Teach It!* booklet that accompanies *All Children Read* as well as the Instructor's Manual and Test Bank; Codruta Temple, a doctoral student at Syracuse University who revised the *Teach It!* book for this edition; Dr. Darlene Michener at California State University, Los Angeles and Sue Kawell, Director of the California State, Los Angeles RICA Rescue project, for their specialized efforts on the compilation of the special RICA material packaged with the book for California educators.

We also would like to thank the reviewers who took time out from busy schedules to share with us their support and expertise and provided us with the valuable feedback that helped to shape this project: Rebecca S. Anderson, University of Memphis; Diane Barone, University of Nevada-Reno; Marian S. Beckman, Edinboro University of Pennsylvania; Charlotte Black, California State University, San Bernardino; Melise Bunker, Palm Beach Atlantic College; Margaret Bell Davis, Eastern Kentucky University; Deborah Doty, Northern Kentucky University; Mary Ann Dzama, George Mason University; Callie L. Fortenberry, Texas A&M Texarkana; David Landis, University of Northern Iowa; Darlene Michener, California State University, Los Angeles; Michael Moore, Georgia Southern University; Kathleen R. Murphy, Clarion University of Pennsylvania; John Savage, Boston College; Corlis Snow, Delta State University; Kim Truesdell, State University College at Buffalo; Marion P. Turkish, William Paterson University; Debra Whitaker-Volturo, Ocean City School District; Clairin DeMartini Wilson, Nevada State College; Valerie Wright, Saint Leo; James Zarrillo, California State University, Hayward.

Charles Temple wants to thank his colleagues and students at HWS for good cheer at all hours, the International Reading Association and the Open Society Institute for all their support over the years, and his (oh so) extended family. Donna Ogle wants to thank her husband and her colleagues for their contributions to this book. Bud has provided incredible support for their project and takes ideas right into the field, testing them in his work in Good News Ministries and as a part of the Reading and Writing for Critical Thinking Project. The teachers with whom Donna works in Chicago and in international contexts energized her to share their ideas and hers in this book. Special thanks to Debbie Gurvitz, Marge Harter, and the rest of the RLI team, and to colleagues on the faculty at NLU. Alan Crawford thanks his colleagues and students in the public schools of Los Angeles and Cal State Los Angeles for inspiration over the years; the teachers with whom he's worked—in California, Latin America, Central Asia, Central Europe, and Africa; good friends at

UNESCO, the International Reading Association, and the Open Society Institute; and of course, Linda. Penny Freppon wishes to thank Dr. Jill Dillard and Linda Headings for their friendship and professional guidance. Penny also thanks her family, in particular, Don, her husband and intellectual partner with whom all things are possible.

Last but not least, a special thank you to everyone at Allyn & Bacon for working so hard to create this beautiful book out of our humble parts and for remaining so steadfastly cheerful and encouraging throughout: Executive Editor, Aurora Martínez Ramos; Senior Development Editor, Alicia Reilly; Senior Production Editor, Janet Domingo, for her project coordination; Sara Holliday for her assistance with the standards correlations, and to Kathy Smith for her good eye and detailed oversight.

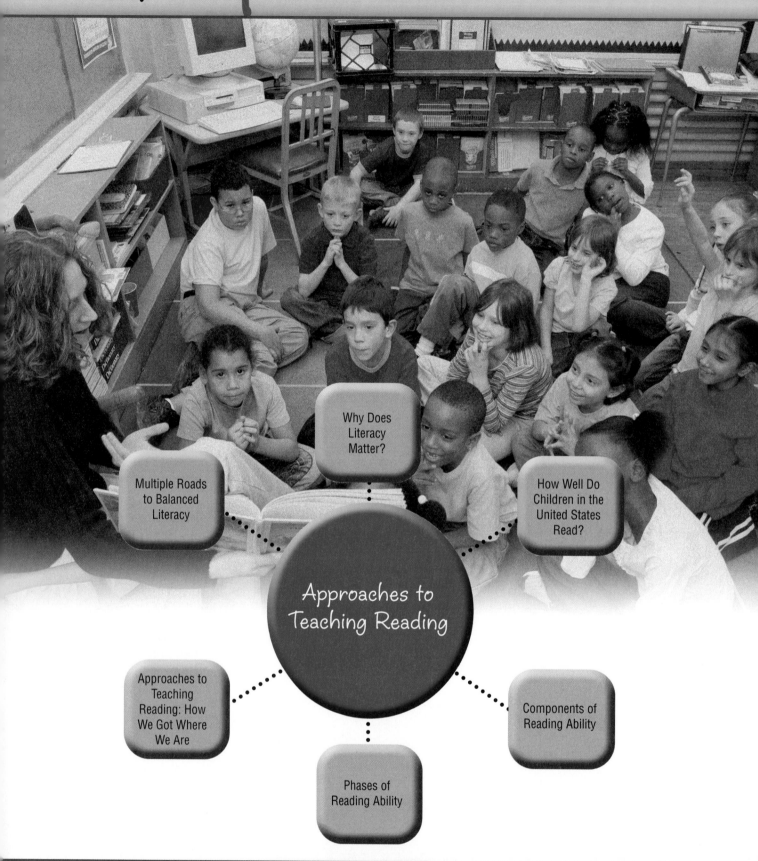

chapter 1

Multiple Roads
to Balanced
Literacy

Why Does
Literacy
Matter?

How Well Do
Children in the
United States
Read?

Approaches to
Teaching Reading

Approaches to
Teaching
Reading: How
We Got Where
We Are

Phases of
Reading Ability

Components of
Reading Ability

Approaches to Teaching Reading

Anticipation Guide

The following statements will stimulate your thinking about the topics of this chapter. Answer true or false in response to each statement. As you read and learn more about the topics in these statements, double-check your answers. See what interests you and prompts your curiosity toward more understanding.

_____ Literacy makes you smarter because the vocabulary, the information, and the habit of learning from text make you better able to learn new things.

_____ Among adults, there is little correlation between people's level of reading ability and their income level.

_____ American children read fairly well. Nine-year-olds scored second in the world on one recent international comparison of basic reading skills.

_____ Most reading disabilities are caused by malfunctions of the brain, and children with reading problems need a wholly different kind of teaching from what normally developing readers need.

_____ Research shows that more than 86 percent of the children who get a poor start in learning to read do not catch up with their peers.

_____ Differences in the amount of reading children do are not significant. What matters in teaching reading is the skill.

_____ Giving parents ideas for helping their children at home with literacy experiences makes a considerable difference in the children's success in school.

_____ Reading ability develops through stages in this order: beginning reading, emergent literacy, reading to learn and for pleasure, building fluency, and mature reading.

_____ The debate in the United States between advocates of phonics instruction and advocates of whole-word instruction began in the 1980s during the Reagan administration.

_____ Testing is the only worthwhile means of assessing children's literacy.

What Makes a Good Teacher of Reading and Writing?

Good teachers of reading and writing are multitalented people. They do know a great many teaching methods, but they also have a solid background in the science of language and literacy, and they manage to keep up with new developments in their field. They are keen observers of children's learning and inventive designers of lessons and techniques. They can connect with children, and children of all backgrounds like them, trust them, and are inspired by them. They make unusual efforts to connect with their students' families and help the families feel comfortable with the school environment and process. Good teachers of reading and writing love to read and write, and they gladly demonstrate their enthusiasm and share their knowledge with their students.

Good teachers of reading and writing are everywhere—in classrooms from Los Angeles to New York City, from the Rio Grande Valley to the fields of Saskatchewan, and all around the world. Some work in carpeted classrooms equipped with gleaming rows of computers, but just as many make cheerful places out of storage rooms, hallways, or even tropical shelters with rattling tin

Teaching every child to read and write is the most important mission of the elementary and middle school teacher. Science, mathematics, and social studies; art, physical education, and vocational preparedness; antidrug abuse and conflict resolution education; civic education and education for self-awareness—all contribute to the making of the well-rounded child. But teaching children to read and write and to use the thinking processes that go with literacy prepare them to learn their other school subjects and to educate themselves for the rest of their lives. The skills of literacy are centrally important for other reasons, too: Being able to read and write makes children smarter and ultimately makes their lives better.

Why Does Literacy Matter?

Teaching children to read not only gives them access to knowledge from print, but it also makes them better able to use that knowledge. Children who read store up background knowledge about the things they read about, whether it be nature, science, history, current events, or geography (Stanovich, 1992). This knowledge helps them make sense of the new things they read (Anderson & Pearson, 1984; Hirsch, 1987). Children who read gain bigger vocabularies, too (C. B. Smith, 1997), and having bigger vocabularies enables them to roofs and open walls—always thoughtfully orchestrating the learning of an individual child or of many different children. You will find them teaching in English, Spanish, French, Tagalog, Arabic, or many languages at once. You will find them in the offices of school principals and district-wide administrators, pondering the best ways to help all the children make progress in reading; you will also find them huddled in deliberations with a parent and a school psychologist, trying to unlock the puzzle of a child's reading difficulty. You will find them in a school or community library, sharing just the right book with a child who is on the threshold of becoming a reader. You will find them creating a lesson without books or paper in a classroom in any one of scores of developing countries for children whose parents never knew the craft of literacy, or strategizing in a committee room at the United Nations to help spread literacy to all of the children in the world.

The authors of this book hope that you will share with those good teachers a passion for bringing the gift of literacy to young people, that you will have a fascination for the intricacies of the task and an appreciation of the scholarship necessary to understand how reading works and how it is taught, and that you will continue to grow in your knowledge of reading and reading instruction.

notice things (R. Brown, 1955) and to make finer distinctions in their perceptions of the world (Beck, McKeown, & Kucan, 2002).

Literacy helps children to think in more sophisticated ways. Studies show that being readers makes profound differences in people's reasoning, their awareness of language, their awareness of themselves, and even their ability to formulate questions and learn about things they didn't know (Luria, 1976). Children who read and talk about books with others show greater self-awareness and critical thinking (Almasi, 1995), tend to engage ideas more deeply (Eeds & Wells, 1989; Goatley, Brock, & Raphael, 1995), and are more likely to perceive themes in stories: That is, they are more likely to get the message (Lehr, 1988).

Among adults, literacy is associated with better health, better jobs, and better income (National Adult Literacy Survey, 1992). Surveys show that people who can read and write well tend to have a wider range of options in life. This fact is important to teachers of the lower grades because students' early experiences as readers will probably have a determining effect on their eventual success or failure to learn to read and write.

Those of you who are fortunate enough to be teachers are in a privileged position to make sure your students have better choices available to them. You can teach them to read and write. But be aware that people with limited literacy do not usually see themselves as having a literacy problem (National Center for Education Statistics, 1993). The task of a teacher of reading, then, will not only be to teach, but also to motivate. Even though reading ability is a ticket to a better future for all students, they might not know that, and their families might not know it either. The teacher will have to make special efforts to encourage every child to want to be a reader.

How Well Do Children in the United States Read?

For years, the media have clamored about the poor state of reading in American schools. But the critics have mostly gotten it wrong. They have missed both the considerable achievements as well as the most serious challenges in the nation's efforts to teach all children to read (Klenk & Kibby, 2000). In a nutshell, three things are true about the way children read in the United States:

- On average, American students excel at basic reading skills. In terms of basic reading (that is, reading text with essential understanding) taken as a whole, American schoolchildren do very well. On the International Educational Achievement study done in the early 1990s (Elley, 1992), American nine-year-olds scored second in the world, surpassed only by children from Finland. Fifteen-year-olds performed respectably: They tied for fifth place, behind New Zealand, France, Sweden, and Finland.

- Success in reading is spread unevenly, however. The most successful American students do well in basic literacy tasks, but there are many students who do not perform well. The National Assessment of Educational Progress (NAEP) defines fourth graders with a "basic reading level" this way: These readers should "demonstrate an overall understanding of what they read. . . . [T]hey should be able to make relatively obvious connections between the text and their own experiences, and extend the ideas in the text by making simple inferences" (National Center for Education Statistics, 1994, p. 42; quoted in Snow, Burns, & Griffin, 1998, p. 97). But in 1996, 40 percent of U.S. fourth graders could not read on this basic level, even in narrative texts under the supervision of the teacher. For black students and Hispanic students, the results were even worse: 69 percent of black fourth graders and 64 percent of Hispanic fourth graders could not read on a basic level. At higher grades, the numbers for the total student populations are still disturbing: 30 percent of the eighth graders and 25 percent of the twelfth graders on the 1996 NAEP survey lacked basic reading ability.

- Differences in reading achievement are often related to economic circumstances. Schools in the United States fare worse than those in two thirds of the countries in the industrialized world when it comes to helping all children succeed regardless of their family income (Organization of Economic and Community Development, 2000; Willms, 1999). This fact is especially significant because, with a poverty rate of over 21.5 percent, American schools have by far the highest proportion of children living in poverty—twice as high as children's poverty rate in the United Kingdom (9.9%), and eight times as high as that in Sweden (Economic Policy Institute, 2007). Poorer children may be harder to educate:

  > As a result of their living in poverty, children may bring a variety of challenges to the classroom that necessitate the provision of additional services such as remediation or after school tutoring programs. These children may require basic provisions from the school, such as breakfast and/or lunch, and may lack essential supplies such as pencil and paper. (National Center for Education Statistics, 2000, p. 14)

- American students do not excel at thinking through reading. American students score right at the international average when asked to do higher-order thinking with what they read: to reflect on it, interpret it, or evaluate it drawing on their own prior information. In a recent international comparison of life-skills reading (reading and reasoning for everyday life outside

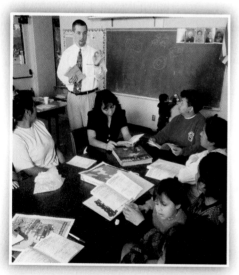

Because literacy is associated with better health and better socioeconomic standing, English as a Second Language (ESL) programs for adults are important services in all communities.

of school), American fifteen-year-olds scored sixteenth out of thirty-two countries, midway between Finland and Brazil (Organization of Economic and Community Development, 2000). Students from Canada, by contrast, ranked in third place, behind Finland and Korea. Results like these matter for many reasons, especially because the job market is increasingly requiring people with skills in communication, problem-solving, and analytical skills (Organization for Economic Co-operation and Development, 1995).

STRUGGLING **READER**

How will you recognize a student who is struggling with reading?

Who Are the Struggling Readers?

If success in reading in the United States is spread unevenly, how many of our children have "reading disabilities"? A reading disability is said to be present when a child with normal intelligence who has had adequate instruction fails to learn to read. By this definition, experts have estimated that 10 to 20 percent of all schoolchildren have specific reading disabilities (Shaywitz et al., 1992). Some researchers suggest that the figure might be much lower and that deficiencies can be overcome or prevented through appropriate reading-related experiences at home and proper instruction in kindergarten and first grade (see The World of Reading box).

Why are such early reading experiences so important? The importance of a good beginning in reading—and the damage that can be done by a poor beginning—was underscored by Connie Juel (1988). Juel surveyed a group of first graders in a Texas public school,

The World of Reading

Do Specific Reading Disabilities Exist?

Specific reading disabilities, including dyslexia, do not have a definition that everyone agrees on, but they are thought to be a severe inability to read as well as one's intelligence and background would predict, in spite of normally effective teaching. There is no doubt that reading disabilities exist. Snowling (2000) followed one child with a severe reading disability from preschool to adulthood and documented his difficulty reading texts and his primitive spelling strategies that remained with him as an adult (Snowling, 2000).

But are most readers with disabilities constitutionally different from normally competent readers? The United States has a huge industry devoted to the identification and treatment of learning disabilities, the largest number of which are specific reading disabilities. These disabilities have traditionally been treated as a categorically different set of problems from normal reading development. However, a growing body of evidence suggests that nearly all instances of specific reading disability, including dyslexia, may just be extreme cases of difficulty in normal reading development (Snow et al., 1998). Children with reading problems look much like children who can read; they just don't read as well (Stanovich & Siegel, 1994; Vellutino et al., 1996).

Going back to the definition of dyslexia as not learning to read in spite of otherwise effective reading instruction, we can ask: Suppose the problem is the instruction? When Frank Vellutino and his associates (1996) identified a large number of struggling first graders and tutored them intensively for a year using conventional best practices, only 3 percent of them continued to have difficulty learning to read, and only 1.5 percent had severe difficulties. Vellutino and associates concluded that the difficulties in learning to read may well be caused by deficits in certain of the cognitive abilities underlying the ability to learn to read, especially phonological abilities such as phoneme analysis, letter-to-sound decoding, name encoding and retrieval, and verbal memory. However, they found that "the number of children impaired by basic cognitive deficits represents a relatively small percentage of beginning readers compared with the substantially larger percentage of those children whose reading difficulties are caused by experiential and instructional deficits" (Vellutino & Scanlon, 2001, p. 317).

Vellutino and his colleagues (1996) concluded that most of the children who had been identified as possibly having a specific reading disability did not suffer from abnormal brain function. Rather, they suffered from confusions, delays, poor starts, and the need for finely tuned and responsive instruction that was carefully tailored to their strengths and needs.

found the 20 percent who read least well, and carefully tracked the reading progress of fifty-four of them for three years. At the end of the study, 86 percent of those children were still in the bottom half of the class. Although reading problems had not been severe in first grade, they were serious by fourth grade. There was little reason to hope that these children would close the gap in later years. Why?

Stanovich (1986) has shown how relatively mild deficits in the early years are compounded and grow into severe reading disabilities after three or four years. It is known that the more children read, the better they get at reading. The reverse is also true. Whatever mild deficit a child has makes reading difficult, and the difficulty breeds aversion. When Juel asked a fourth-grade subject whether he would rather do chores than read, he responded, "Lady, I'd rather scrub the mold around the bathtub than read!" (Juel, 1988). Children learn to read by reading. But studies of reading habits show huge differences in the amount of reading children do. One study showed that the most prolific three or four readers in a fifth-grade classroom read 100 times as much as the least prolific did (Anderson, Wilson, & Fielding, 1988).

Family and Community Involvement

FAMILY **LITERACY**

In what ways is family involvement so important to reading and writing development?

Families make a difference in children's preparation to learn to read and write. On the average, children from poor families with little education have more difficulty learning to be literate than children from middle-class homes do (Vernon-Feagans et al., 2001). But the exact reasons for this can be difficult to tease out. If a family is poor—and a fourth of America's children live in families that are poor—then poverty itself presents a complex set of stress factors (Ehrenreich, 2001). If you are poor, it is hard to raise a healthy and competent child. It is hard to buy and prepare nutritious food. It is hard to afford good-quality child care. It is hard to find the time and energy between jobs to spend time with your child.

Nonetheless, researchers have identified family literacy practices related to children's success in learning to read and write. Many of these may be influenced by the school or by the school working in concert with community partners. Here is a set of factors that the National Research Council (Snow et al., 1998, p. 123) has identified:

1. Value placed on literacy: By reading themselves and encouraging children to read, parents can demonstrate that they value reading.
2. Press for achievement: By expressing their expectations for achievement by their children, providing reading instruction, and responding to the children's reading initiations and interests, parents can create a press for achievement.
3. Availability and instrumental use of reading materials: Literacy experiences are more likely to occur in homes that contain children's books and other reading and writing materials.
4. Reading with children: Parents can read to preschoolers at bedtime and other times and can listen to schoolchildren's oral reading, providing assistance as needed.

Family literacy projects that encourage families to read to children and talk with children can have success (Vernon-Feagans et al., 2001). But helping families nurture their children's literacy is not a simple matter. Communication patterns in families are hard to change, even if we agree that educators have a moral right to try to change them! Poor families offer children less verbal interaction than middle-class families do, and the shortage of interaction has a strong effect on the children's vocabulary size (Hart & Risley, 1995), which in turn affects learning how to read and write. Here is another problem: It is known that children's preschool experiences with books and print also contribute to their success in learning to read once they arrive in school (Snow et al., 1998; Teale & Sulzby, 1987). But low-income families visit the library half as often on average as middle-class families do (Baker, Serpell, & Sonnenschein, 1995). Purcell-Gates (1997) writes of an illiterate mother of an illiterate son living in Cincinnati who didn't realize there were places in the city where they would lend you books for free.

Nearly all families in the United States have some contact with literacy materials (Teale, 1986), but many low-literacy families really do not seriously engage with print enough to provide experiences for children that teach them (Purcell-Gates, 1995). Even when low-income families visit libraries, the visits don't necessarily result in their finding materials to read (Neuman & Celano, 2006). Family literacy work is not always easy, but the title of Purcell-Gates's book about the illiterate mother and the semiliterate son—*The Cycle of Low Literacy*—underscores how important it is for educators to include families in their plans for promoting literacy.

Components of Reading Ability

What goes into teaching a child to read? At its simplest, reading is the act of getting meaning from a written text. To read successfully, readers must be able to collect or construct meaning through written symbols. Readers recognize squiggles of ink on a page as letters and words. This activity is called **word recognition**. To become skilled at word recognition, readers need to be aware of the smallest sounds in language, called **phonemes**. In turn, **phonemic awareness**, as this aptitude is called, prepares readers to look for matches between sounds and letters. Learning letter-to-sound correspondences is the study of **phonics**.

Readers work with the words they recognize, and somewhere in the interplay between what they see on the page and what they expect from what is in their heads, they construct an understanding of what they read. This activity is called **comprehension**, which is made up of several processes and kinds of knowledge, including knowledge of **vocabulary** and the pronunciation and meaning of words.

Readers eventually come to recognize words quickly and accurately while comprehending. This activity is called **reading fluency**. It is hoped that as they have learned to read, they have made books a part of their lives and found authors they especially enjoy and have developed a habit of reading. Eventually, they may learn to hone their minds by weighing an author's words, reflecting on arguments, and coming up with their own interpretations of what they have read, a skill known as *interpretation*, or **critical reading**.

Here is an illustration of these components in action. Suppose a fifth grader is asked to read this passage:

> *"Come quick," whispered Mother, from across the street. "The guard is looking the other way."*
>
> *Rebecca clutched her doll close to her chest, crouched low, and scrambled across the empty street toward the lamppost that hid her mother. Just then a searchlight from atop a darkened building swept the street she had just crossed.*
>
> *"Gestapo," said her mother, hugging the panting child. "They're everywhere." Rebecca squeezed the Star of David around her neck and trembled.*

A number of things have to happen for this passage to be read successfully.

Word Recognition

Of course, readers have to recognize most of the words for the meaning of the passage to be easily available to them. If they are reading the passage on their own, they should find no more than four words in this passage that they did not recognize (that is, they should easily recognize at least 95 percent of the words). If they are reading the passage with the support of a teacher, they would be expected to find no more than eight unknown words (a 90 percent recognition rate), according to many reading specialists (e.g., Gillet, Temple, & Crawford, 2004). As you will see, understanding a passage is much more than the sum of understanding the words. Nonetheless, if readers have to pause and puzzle over the meanings of more than a few words in a passage, their comprehension will be impaired.

How is this word recognition done? By the time they have reached fifth grade, children will have stored thousands of words in memory that they can recognize instantly. Read-

PHONICS and PHONOLOGICAL AWARENESS

How are sight words and phonemic segmentation related to phonemic awareness?

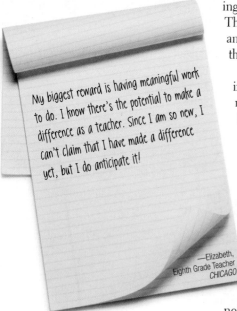

ing specialists call this store of instantly recognized words their **sight vocabulary**. These readers have been accumulating these words since they were in kindergarten, and as they progress through the grades, they will be learning more new words—thousands more new words—every year.

How do readers go about learning new words? In several ways. For example, if a child failed to recognize *clutched* on a first exposure, the teacher would remind the child to break the word into parts: *cl + utch + ed*. A fifth grader would be highly skilled at **phonemic segmentation** and would have no difficulty breaking the words in her speech into separate sounds, and she would be able to find matches between letters on the page and speech sounds. But also because she is a fifth grader, her knowledge of phonics would be a matter not just of matches between individual letters and sounds, but also of matches at the level of patterns of letters combining vowels and consonants. Therefore, she would be able to find the pattern *-utch*, which she would be able to pronounce by relating it to a word she knows: *Dutch*. She would know the *cl-* consonant blend from many words she can read, such as *clap, click, clock,* and *cloud.* She would also know the past tense ending *-ed* from her past reading and study of words. Once she worked out the pronunciation of this unfamiliar word, *clutched,* she would recognize it as a word that she has heard and used in speech but not read before. A third grader would be using phonics, but her word knowledge would include not just letter-to-sound relationships, but also knowledge of larger spelling patterns and even of grammar as a factor in word structure. The word *Gestapo,* however, would present a different problem. Here she would have to work out the pronunciation of this unfamiliar word, but once she could pronounce the word or an approximation of it, she still would not be able to associate the written word with a word she uses in speech. She would have to use other strategies—in this case, context clues—to decide what the word means. The sentence in which the word appears is

"Gestapo. . . . They're everywhere."

She would know that Gestapo are referred to as "they," meaning that Gestapo are most likely people. From the context of the passage, she would know to equate Gestapo with the guards who were scanning the street with their searchlights. Having surmised that the girl in the passage with the Star of David was Jewish, this reader would reason that Gestapo were guards or police who hunted Jews at some time in history. Perhaps they were German soldiers or police, and perhaps the setting was the time around World War II. In this second example, this reader not only learned to pronounce a previously unfamiliar word but also derived an approximation of its meaning. From the context of the passage, she learned a new item of vocabulary.

This example illustrates how recognizing words is a complex business involving several strategies. The example features a fifth grader who is a reasonably successful reader; when younger children are just beginning to recognize words, still more strategies enter the picture.

Comprehension

Look again at the passage on page 7. How would readers go about understanding it?

First, they would be helped by their knowledge of vocabulary (Pressley, 2000). They use their knowledge of words such as *guard, searchlight,* and *Star of David* to help them construct the meaning of the text; as was just seen, one reader reasoned that the word *Gestapo* provides a new name for a concept she already had: the Nazi police. Knowing vocabulary provides readers with building blocks to help them construct their understanding of the passage. But readers must also create a context in which choices among competing meanings of words can be made. Without a context to give these words meaning, a reader does not know whether a *chest* refers to a box or a rib cage, whether *scrambling* is a way of preparing eggs or of moving our bodies, whether *post* refers to a job or a pole, or whether *sweeping* is an act of cleaning or a kind of motion across a surface. So knowing the vocabulary helps a reader to construct a meaning for the text, but the meaning that is constructed for the text also helps the reader to understand the words. Thus a web of meaning is woven.

Second, readers have background knowledge or **cognitive schemes** that help them to understand the passage. Words such as *whispered, guard,* and *searchlight* are more than vocabulary items. Together, they help young readers to construct mental frameworks for understanding that the situation described in the passages is one of danger, of stealth, of the necessity to avoid detection. It is important that readers be able to supply this framework themselves because the situation of needing to avoid detection is not stated explicitly by the text. From the mention of Star of David, readers might also suppose, without being told explicitly, that the passage has to do with the flight of Jews from persecution by the Nazis during World War II, something they know about because they have read about it in other books, such as Lois Lowry's *Number the Stars* and Carol Matas's *Daniel's Story.*

Third, readers make **inferences** about what is going on in the text. Although the text never said that Rebecca was a young girl, a reader might notice the details of Rebecca's clutching her doll and depending on her mother for guidance and infer that Rebecca was young. And although the text left a gap between Rebecca's scrambling across the dangerous street and her being hugged by her mother, a reader can infer that she made it safely across the street into her waiting mother's arms.

TEACH IT! 28
Save the Last Word for Me

Fourth, young readers can visualize, or form mental images of, what the words in the text describe. They can picture a darkened street (even though the text never said explicitly that the street was dark), with silent, unlit buildings on each side. They might imagine a nearly silent scene. If they were asked, they could draw a picture of the street.

Fifth, if the teacher asked the young readers to say what they had read, the readers would be able to say, "A young Jewish girl snuck across the street and got away from the guards." In other words, they were able to find the **main idea** of the passage.

Sixth, in retelling what they just read about, our young readers make it clear that they think the girl was the main character—the hero, or the protagonist—of this text and that the rest of the text might tell about her attempts to escape from the Gestapo, the Nazi police. In other words, readers assume that they are reading a story, and they use their knowledge of the structure of stories to make predictions about what will follow in the coming pages. Their knowledge and use of the structure of the text make up one more important part of their comprehension of it.

Reading Fluency

Another aspect of reading related to word recognition and comprehension together is reading fluency. A child would not be considered a competent reader of this passage unless he or she could read it fairly quickly and accurately and with some **inflection**, some changes in the tone of voice that roughly paralleled the emotional or meaningful contours of the text. Reading fluency is both an indicator of and a contributor to successful reading. If you hear a child reading smoothly and accurately, you can infer that the child recognizes the words efficiently. If the child also reads with appropriate inflection, you can also infer that the child is comprehending the text to some degree (although occasionally a child will concentrate on rendering a text aloud with accuracy and pay little attention to the meaning). In this case, fluency is an indicator of the child's ability to recognize words and to comprehend text. It is also known that if readers read the text fluently, their fluency will contribute to their understanding. That is because having the ability to read strings of words smoothly and accurately leaves the mind plenty of capacity to appreciate the meaning of the text (Perfetti, 1992; Pressley, 2000). To illustrate this point, imagine two bicycle riders, one to whom riding comes naturally and a novice who is still struggling to balance, pedal, and steer the bicycle all at the same time. Which one do you suppose will enjoy the scenery?

TEACH IT! 24
Choral Reading

Reading experts have found it worthwhile to give children practice in reading for fluency because a well-developed capacity for relatively fast and accurate reading facilitates understanding. It is also a transferable ability: Becoming a fluent reader carries over from one text to another. That is why thoughtful teachers provide children plenty of opportunities to read texts that are fairly easy for them.

Critical Literacy

Critical literacy is another aspect of literacy that our fifth graders might or might not call into play. Critical literacy means reading with polite skepticism, examining a text's hidden assumptions and bringing to light the devices by which the text might be intended to work its effects on the reader (Luke & Freebody, 1999).

Critical reading leads us to ask questions such as the following:

- Why is the author telling us this?
- Whose voices are left unheard?
- What is this text trying to do to me?
- What questions can be asked about the message?

Critical insights that our young readers might reach could include some like these: Just as Indians used to be commonly portrayed as riding on horseback and shooting arrows at wagon trains, Jewish children are frequently and stereotypically portrayed as trying to escape persecution. Surely there are other interesting things about their lives that could be written about. Also, in American children's books, the example of ethnic persecution that is most often given has to do with Jews more than fifty years ago. Of course, the Holocaust was consummately important and should not be forgotten. But cases of ethnically motivated persecution going on in the world in our own time get much less attention, particularly children's attention. Shouldn't the focus on issues of justice be broadened to include contemporary problems that one can still do something about?

In summary, the act of reading has several components and each of them has its own complexity. To read, readers must recognize words, and word recognition entails not only having words stored in memory for instant recognition, but also knowing how to pronounce a word from its sequence of letters and word parts and being able to infer the meaning of words from their context. Reading also involves comprehension, which in turn includes knowing vocabulary, having and appropriately calling to mind frameworks of prior knowledge, making inferences, visualizing, getting main ideas, and knowing and making use of the structure of the text. Furthermore, skilled reading also includes fluency: reading quickly, accurately, and with appropriate inflection. Fluency is a sign of skilled reading, and the ability to read fluently also enables meaningful reading. Finally, reading ability can include critical reading. In the chapters that follow, you will see all of these aspects of reading in more detail. But first, it must have occurred to you that the issues involved in reading might look different if one were describing youngsters just learning to read or middle school students using their reading ability to study a science text. Now look at the way reading ability develops as children progress through the grades.

Phases of Reading Development

Using the word *development* to describe reading implies that the learner doesn't simply wait passively to take in reading instruction from a teacher, but rather, undertakes the interaction among growth, experience, and discovery that can be called **developmental learning**. Developmental learning proceeds according to these factors:

- Cognitive growth of learners, which opens up capacities for learning
- The provision of relevant models of skilled performance and challenges in learners' own performances from their surroundings
- Active discoveries initiated by the learners themselves

To say that learning to read is developmental implies that all children go through roughly the same set of stages as they learn to read. It implies that their maturation plays a part, but the stimulation, encouragement, and modeling of reading and writing behavior they receive are important, too. It also implies that, although the teaching that learners experience can be beneficial, teaching alone will not result in meaningful learning without the learners' reorganizing and expanding their own powers through activities of discovery. Developmental learning follows predictable pathways, although a learner's development along those pathways is more predictable in the early stages than in later ones.

Emergent Literacy

The earliest period or stage of learning to read and write has come to be called **emergent literacy.** In early childhood, before children enter formal instruction, they discover useful insights about literacy, and these insights become the basis on which their later learning can be built, even the learning that is orchestrated by their teachers in school. In the emergent stage, learning about literacy involves the following:

- Learning about the nature of reading
- Learning what books are, what kinds of experiences come from them, and how they are put together
- Learning about language itself, that it comes in patterns like stories and poems, and that even though you cannot see it, it is real enough to be captured in books and re-visited again and again
- Learning that language comes in units of words and even smaller units and that the language one speaks while reading bears some kind of relationship to marks on a page.

As awareness of emergent literacy has grown, teachers have promoted practices among families that help children's literacy to emerge. Head Start, the federally funded early child-hood education program for disadvantaged children, now includes as part of its program-ming both reading to children and other literacy activities that are embedded in children's daily play and learning activities. In order to underscore the importance of reading to chil-dren and to make the point that it is never too early to begin reading to a child, parents in some communities are given a children's book when they leave the hospital with a newborn.

With their growing awareness of emergent literacy, teachers have developed means of observing and assessing children's early concepts of literacy. These include approaches such as Marie Clay's *Concepts about Print* test, Elizabeth Sulzby's *Emergent Storybook Reading Inventory,* Darrell Morris's *Early Reading Screening Inventory,* and studies of invented spelling, as described by Richard Gentry or Temple, Nathan, Burris, and Temple. (You will see all of these presented in detail later in the book.) Using these investigative approaches yields often amazing profiles of what children have discovered about literacy. However, they also give cause for concern when they show that important concepts about literacy have not yet emerged in a child because it is known that those concepts will be important to the child as he or she learns to read. That point leads to the third contribution of our under-standing of emergent literacy.

Learning to read in school without a fully developed foundation of emergent literacy concepts has been likened to trying to climb stairs when the first several steps are missing. Because teachers are aware of the importance of emergent literacy, they are now able to teach all children in a way that gives them another chance to develop emergent concepts about literacy. They can also provide finely tuned tutoring to children who need it so that more children can get off to the best possible start in learning to read and write.

Beginning Reading

In late kindergarten and first grade, most children enter the phase of beginning reading. Most prominent in this stage is their learning to read words, but children are also learning to un-derstand what they read. The task of learning to make words emerge from different combi-nations of letters on the page is so challenging that teachers often must remind children to "go back and read that line so it sounds like talk" or ask them, "Does that make sense?"

That children are ready to learn words and coordinate reading them with making sense of what they read shows that this stage of beginning reading comes after much prior learning. After all, emergent readers must come to understand that print, and not pictures, talks (Clay, 1985), and a reader is not free to say just any words when paging through a text, but must come up with pronunciations of the words whose representations are printed there (Sulzby, 1985). They have a sense of the patterns of stories and poems, and they know how to follow them to make meaning.

With these understandings in place, children are able to concentrate on words and develop strategies for sounding them out, as well as develop sight vocabularies (stores of words in memory that they can recognize at sight or without having to work them out letter by letter). They are ready, although they often need reminding, to find humor, suspense, and surprise in what they read—in other words, to make meaning.

Building Fluency

Repeated Reading

By late first grade or early second grade, children have enough experience in reading words and following messages that their reading is becoming fluent: more rapid and more accurate. For children who have often been read to, this period can be a joyful affirmation of their own competence. After a period of struggling to read texts that were far simpler and less meaningful than the stories they had long heard read to them, children are at last able to do for themselves what adults had to do for them. For children who are not so lucky, however, this period can be a hard trek through unfamiliar territory because the fascinations of reading materialize only gradually. For the first type of child, teachers will find that their main task is to keep providing more books to a hungry reader. For the second type of child, the teacher will have to celebrate gains, but also gently and insistently push the child to read—and to read more challenging texts.

If the teacher is successful, then both types of children will rapidly amass sight words and steadily increase both the quantity and speed of their reading. They will be preparing themselves for the next stage of reading, which is called *reading to learn and for pleasure*. Even so, wide differences will begin to open up here in the amount of reading children do and the size of their sight vocabularies.

Reading to Learn and for Pleasure

By the beginning of third grade and increasingly in fourth grade, a threshold is crossed, and the emphasis shifts from learning to read to reading to learn—and, one might add, reading for pleasure. By now, children will be expected to read and follow directions and to gain information from texts. At the same time, they may be expected to read chapter books and novels and have something to say about them in their response journals and in their book clubs or whatever their discussion groups are called.

A period for reading and writing instruction is still provided every day, but more and more time is given to free reading and discussion, as well as to writing workshops. These activities are useful, even essential, because children must practice literacy to develop it. Nonetheless, a place for teaching the students how to comprehend, interpret, and compose still exists. There is also still a need to make students aware of the structure of written words and the way our English vocabulary works. This is because word knowledge is not gained in the early years and then is done with. On the contrary, because the collection of words children encounter in texts changes significantly at around fourth grade (from mostly words derived from Anglo-Saxon to words derived from Latin and Greek), there are new concepts to be learned about words though this period.

It is in fourth grade that problems in reading have traditionally become obvious. That is because reading shows up as a problem that is affecting students' learning in other subjects. It is also because the unsuccessful struggles to learn to read well have led children to frustration and poor motivation. Indeed, children's self-esteem might have begun to suffer because they haven't

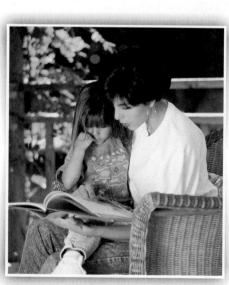

Reading for pleasure opens up a child's world and encourages imagination and inquiry.

succeeded in a skill that is highly valued in school (Stanovich, 1986). Although troubled readers can and certainly should be helped to overcome their difficulties, doing so is time consuming at this stage, especially because there is much content to be learned by now throughout the school day. Because they now understand how earlier experiences contribute to children's reading abilities, many teachers, and whole programs such as Reading Recovery, are placing their greatest emphasis on getting children off to a good start in reading, so that the problem of the so-called fourth-grade slump can be avoided wherever possible.

Mature Reading

After fifth grade and certainly by sixth grade, children who have made normal progress as readers have gradually shown other abilities that are characterized as mature reading. They read with an appreciation of the author's style, and they enjoy reading passages aloud to friends or try to imitate an author's style in their own writing. They read with an awareness of issues and themes and see a novel not only as a series of events but also as a metaphorical commentary on life. They might read several books on a theme and talk perceptively on the ways the authors' views affected the different presentations. They might practice critical literacy, argue back against the theme of a book, or be offended by its sexist or racist overtones. In any case, they are more analytical and more philosophical in what they look for in texts and in the ways they respond to them.

They are also more strategic. They can read for information, and they have strategies for previewing, questioning, marking, note taking, reviewing, and studying books they read for information.

As we noted at the outset of this section, one characteristic of developmental learning is that the earlier periods of development are more predictable and more commonly experienced than the latter ones. That is certainly true with respect to mature reading. Some readers show evidence of mature reading by the time they enter fourth grade. Many more show it by seventh or eighth grade. But many others rarely do this kind of reading.

In summary, so far we have discussed reading in terms of some of its core processes: word recognition, comprehension, fluency, and critical literacy. We have also looked at reading in terms of the stages children pass through: emergent literacy, beginning reading, building fluency, reading to learn and for pleasure, and mature reading. Later sections of this book will revisit each of the aspects of reading that must be developed. Then you will see how teachers help children learn to read and write at every grade level.

Approaches to Teaching Reading: How We Got Where We Are

Early Modern Descriptions of Reading

Early in the twentieth century, Edmund Burke Huey (1908) chronicled the major approaches to teaching reading that were practiced in American schools in his time. He found an unreconciled difference between teachers who preferred to emphasize words as wholes and teachers who taught students the relationships between letters and sounds. As Huey noted, this distinction was already very old—perhaps 350 years old, according to one of his sources. Huey offered research—his own and that of others—that showed that the eye and brain take just as long to recognize a single letter as they do a whole word. This finding, building on a reaction to the heavy drill orientations of reading approaches in the late nineteenth century, encouraged a movement toward whole-word teaching approaches that lasted through the mid-1960s. Even then, the issue was not settled, and between Huey's time and ours, there has been an intense outpouring of research on the issue and hundreds of conferences have been attended by thousands of educators, yet the tension between different approaches to teaching beginning reading remains.

Phonics versus Whole-Word Reading

In the 1960s, Jeanne Chall (1967) reviewed the available research on the question of the best approaches to beginning reading. She found that in the decades leading up to the time when she was writing, most children in the United States were taught to read in basal reading programs, that is, in textbooks composed of short reading passages with graduated difficulty levels. For the most part, the basal reading programs, such as the popular Dick and Jane series, used whole-word approaches (what Chall called a "meaning emphasis") and did not teach phonics (what she called a "code emphasis"). According to the studies Chall reviewed, however, reading approaches that did use phonics showed better results than programs that did not. Following the publication of Chall's influential book, publishers began to include phonics instruction in their basal reading programs. But that did not settle the matter. Many teachers, such as New Zealander Sylvia Ashton-Warner (1963), continued to favor whole-word approaches and argued that their use emphasized meaning, whereas the phonics approaches could lead children to focus on the small parts of reading—the letters and sounds—without an adequate appreciation of what the letters were supposed to add up to. Indeed, some of the reading materials that came into use during the 1960s focused so much on letter-to-sound regularities that they left very little meaning to be pursued. "Linguistic readers" contained text like this: "A man had a tin pin. It's a pin for a cap. It's a cap for Dan." Advocates of meaning-centered reading instruction worried that if children mostly read text as pointless as this, they could easily become confused about the true purpose of reading: to construct meaning from print.

Cognitive Revolution

The 1970s saw a revolution in the way scholars thought of language learning. The field of psycholinguistics was developing, largely under the influence of an ingenious linguist named Noam Chomsky. The researchers whom Chomsky inspired began to accumulate evidence that children learn language by exercising a built-in capacity for discovery. As long as they are in the company of people who talk to them and who model language, and as long as those around them honor children's own needs to communicate, children will learn to talk. Gradually, by stages, through an amazing exercise of finely tuned linguistic discovery processes, children learn language.

Almost immediately, theorists began to see applications of psycholinguistic theory to the acquisition of reading. Frank Smith wrote an influential book called *Psycholinguistics and Reading* (1973), in which he and others argued that children could learn to read, in large part, by discovery and encouragement. One of the contributors to that book, Kenneth Goodman (1967), had offered a conception of reading as "a psycholinguistic guessing game." Goodman's work, along with that of some imaginative Australians, such as Don Holdaway (1979) and Andrea Butler and Jan Turbill (1985), gave rise to what came to be known as the **whole-language movement**.

Whole Language

Whole-language advocates embraced many child-centered approaches to teaching. The **writing process approach** popularized by Donald Graves (1982) and Lucy Calkins (1996) was taken up by whole-language advocates and became part of the movement. So did the literature-based approaches of Dorothy Strickland (1991) and Nancie Atwell (1989). Whole-language classrooms were (and are) bursting with children's creativity as children have rich experiences that stimulate talk, as they read and listen to much good literature, and as they write out and act out their own ideas.

On the psychological front, the new field of cognitive psychology yielded studies of comprehension that were relevant to reading. A U.S. government grant to the University of Illinois created the Center for the Study of Reading, where Richard Anderson and David Pearson (1984) and others elaborated a theory of comprehension called **schema theory**. As we saw in the example of children reading the passage on pages 7–10, schema theory stresses the reader's active role in making meaning. Schema theory was highly compatible with the work of both the psycholinguists inspired by Noam Chomsky and the constructivist theories of intellectual development inspired by Swiss psychologist Jean Piaget and others. The theory found ready acceptance in the 1970s and 1980s, and most reading experts still accept it today in some form or another as our guiding theory of how comprehension works. Like psycholinguistic research before it, schema theory seemed to lend support to the child-centered, discovery-oriented beliefs of the whole-language movement.

Research-Based Emphasis

Still, the disagreements between the meaning-centered advocates and the code-centered advocates continued. In the late 1980s, the U.S. Department of Education commissioned another examination of beginning reading instruction. The resulting work was *Beginning to Read* by Marilyn Jaeger Adams, a psychologist. In it, Adams (1990) concluded that exposure to print and enthusiastic encouragement might work in some cases, but that they were not sufficient to teach all children to read. Like the evidence Chall had reviewed twenty years before, the evidence Adams collected led her to conclude that reading approaches that explicitly and systematically taught children the code that links speech sounds to patterns of letters in words were more successful than those that did not. Adams urged teachers to give primacy to teaching children to decode and recognize words, even as they immersed the children in print and encouraged them to write.

Adams also passed along another finding from late twentieth-century research on reading: the importance of children's awareness of phonemes, the smallest sound units in words. In a host of studies, phonemic awareness in first grade was found to make a critical difference in whether or not children learned to read successfully, and Adams made a strong suggestion that teachers emphasize phonemic awareness and letter-to-sound correspondences in their early reading instruction. She said in her conclusion,

In summary, deep and thorough knowledge of letters, spelling patterns, and words, and of the phonological translations of all three, are of inescapable importance to both skillful reading and its acquisition. By extension, instruction designed to develop children's sensitivity to spellings and their relations to pronunciations should be of paramount importance in the development of reading skills. That is, of course, precisely what is intended of good phonics instruction. (Adams, 1990, p. 416)

In 1989 President George H. W. Bush assembled fifty governors at the University of Virginia to work out a plan that would use U.S. schools to make American students more competitive in the world. In an initiative called Education 2000, led by their chairman, then-Governor Bill Clinton of Arkansas, the group agreed to specify explicit performance standards for reading and other subjects at intervals throughout the grades and to test students' abilities to meet those standards. Many states added standards for what schools of education should instruct new teachers to teach (see the Standards and Literacy box that follows). As individual states designed their standards, many drew on the work of Marilyn Jaeger Adams and like-minded writers and called for the teaching of

Programs such as Head Start and Jumpstart help prepare children for learning by promoting an interest in reading at a very young age.

Standards and Literacy

What Are Learning Standards?

Twenty years ago, the U.S. government publication *A Nation at Risk* seriously questioned the quality of American schools. The report surprised many because the trend in American students' achievement scores throughout the twentieth century had always shown small but steady increases. Besides, international comparisons of industrialized countries showed American students performing at or above average of industrialized countries in the world. In reading, U.S. students did better than average, and one study from the early 1990s showed that American fourth graders performed second in the world.

Nonetheless, although there might not have been grounds to declare a crisis twenty years ago, a nearly flat line in educational improvement was still worrisome because the demands placed on education were escalating quickly. Under the pressures brought about by globalization, changes in employment demographics throughout the country raised a need for more advanced literacy skills. The sharp rise in the need to teach students to read and think skillfully required urgent attention, even if the sudden demand did not constitute a massive failure of the schools, as the federal report alleged.

Since the nation's founding, the governance of education in the United States has been the responsibility of the states. In the 1990s, a decade after the founding of the U.S. Department of Education, the federal government was looking for a mechanism to exert enough influence over the states to lead a reform movement in education. An initiative called America 2000, launched in 1989 during the presidency of George H. W. Bush, introduced the idea of standards-based education that continues today. America 2000 called for states to set standards that defined "what all students should know and be able to do" not only in reading but in science and mathematics. The act set up a bipartisan federal panel to "certify State content standards and State student performance standards . . . if such standards are comparable or higher in rigor and quality to the voluntary national content standards and voluntary national student performance standards" (See **http://www.ed.gov/legislation/GOALS2000/TheAct/sec211.html**).

Ten years later, all states had set performance standards for children and developed tests for those standards. At present, there is considerable variety from state to state in what children are expected to learn and what teachers are expected to teach. For instance, in Virginia, specific standards are in place for children in each grade, such as the following for first graders:

The student will orally identify and manipulate phonemes (small units of sound) in syllables and multisyllabic words.

    a. *Count phonemes (sounds) in syllables or words with a maximum of three syllables.*
    b. *Add or delete phonemes (sounds) orally to change syllables or words.*
    c. *Create rhyming words orally.*
    d. *Blend sounds to make word parts and words with one to three syllables.*

The student will apply phonetic principles to read and spell.

    a. *Use beginning and ending consonants to decode and spell single-syllable words.*
    b. *Use two-letter consonant blends to decode and spell single-syllable words.*

---

letter-to-sound correspondences and the development of phonemic awareness. In 1996, for example, the California state legislature passed a bill that specified that the training of all elementary teacher certification candidates include:

    (i) *The study of organized, systematic, explicit skills including phonemic awareness, direct systematic, explicit phonics, and decoding skills.*
    (ii) *A strong literature, language, and comprehension component with a balance of oral and written language.*
    (iii) *Ongoing diagnostic techniques that inform teaching and assessment.*
    (iv) *Early intervention techniques.*
    (v) *Guided practice in a clinical setting. (quoted in Snow et al., 1998, p. 302)*

Also in the late 1990s, a study of early reading difficulties was undertaken by the Committee on the Prevention of Reading Difficulties in Young Children, a group of reading experts assembled under the auspices of the National Science Foundation. The resulting report, entitled *Preventing Reading Difficulties in Young Children* (Snow et al., 1998), recommended that teachers encourage students' growth in language and general knowledge,

c. Use beginning consonant digraphs to decode and spell single-syllable words.

d. Use short vowel sounds to decode and spell single-syllable words.

e. Blend beginning, middle, and ending sounds to recognize and read words.

f. Use word patterns to decode unfamiliar words.

g. Use compound words.

h. Read and spell common, high-frequency sight words, including the, said, and come. *(Virginia State Department of Education, 2002, pp. 6–7)*

In New York State, by contrast, the standards are specified only for students at "elementary," "intermediate," and "commencement" levels. They are expressed in broad terms that leave more to the teacher's discretion than Virginia's standards do. For example, the New York standard for reading and decoding that parallels the standard from Virginia simply states that the "elementary" student should be able to:

> Make appropriate and effective use of strategies to construct meaning from print, such as prior knowledge about a subject, structural and context clues, and understanding of letter-sound relationships to decode difficult words. *(New York State Education Department, 2002, p. 2)*

Reading Proficiency.

Average reading proficiency on a scale of 0–500 for various age groups, 1971–1999, based on nationwide tests given by the National Assessment of Educational Progress.

Source: "The Condition of Education 2001." June 2001. National Center for Education Statistics.

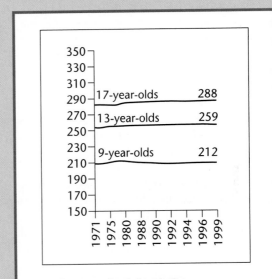

Performance level descriptions

150: Simple, discrete reading tasks
200: Partially developed skills and understanding
250: Interrelate ideas and make generalizations
300: Understand complicated information
350: Learn from specialized reading materials

their exposure to and appreciation of literature, and their opportunities to write while also providing instruction to boost phonemic awareness, knowledge of letter-to-sound relationships, fluency, vocabulary, and comprehension.

In 1997, Congress commissioned yet another group of experts to "assess the effectiveness of different approaches used to teach children to read" (National Reading Panel Web site, 2003). This was the National Reading Panel, organized by the National Institute of Child Health and Human Development (NICHD) at the National Institutes of Health. After reviewing what they considered to be evidence-based studies of reading over a two-year period, the National Reading Panel (2000) published their findings in *The Report of the National Reading Panel: Teaching Children to Read.* In it, the panel made a number of recommendations, including a strong push for skills instruction, especially in the recognition of words and the skills that support word recognition: awareness of speech sounds and knowledge of phonics. (See the Web site of the National Reading Panel at **www .nationalreadingpanel.org.**)

With the reauthorization of the Elementary and Secondary and Education Act (U.S. Department of Education, 2001), called No Child Left Behind (signed into law on

Being a Professional Reading Teacher

Changes in the Reading Field

If you are a new teacher just entering a school with many experienced teachers on the faculty, the conversations about changes in the teaching of reading could be puzzling to you, even unsettling. You could easily get the impression that the focuses of educational research and teaching are as changeable as the preferred colors of kids' T-shirts or brand of their sneakers. We hope the discussion you just read did not add to that impression. The truth is, things are moving forward in literacy education. The students we teach are far more diverse, and as great as the challenge of serving each of them well may be, our society as a whole is much more committed to helping every child become a success than it was a generation ago—ask your grandmother. Our knowledge base for teaching has grown tremendously. Although the disagreements among theorists and practitioners have been shrill at times, we do know much more about teaching reading than we did a generation ago. Our understanding of emergent literacy, the nature of language, comprehension, the development of word knowledge, the importance of fluency and how it is learned, the way children learn to write, and they way they learn literature; ways of serving children with special needs, ways of conducting assessment, ways of teaching—these have all advanced tremendously. Things are moving forward. Keep your eyes open. Hold on to your hat. Be part of the change.

Your Professional Portfolio

Most college and university teacher preparation programs now require that candidates prepare portfolios that reflect their professional development. In addition, many principals and school district personnel directors make new teachers' portfolios a focus of their preemployment interviews. Finally, your portfolio can be a means of self-evaluation, a record of past achievement, and a plan for future professional development.

As you begin this course, begin thinking about your own portfolio. Because reading instruction is such an important part of your new career, it should be highlighted in your portfolio. There are many formats for teacher portfolios. Most include some or all of the following:

- Sample lesson plans
- Thematic units
- Videotapes of lessons
- Descriptions of cooperative learning activities used in your lessons
- Photographs or hand-drawn plans of your classroom environment
- Student, teacher, and participant products, such as writing assignments, self-evaluations, projects, lesson plans, maps, experiments
- Plans for and evidence of continuing education or professional development, such as courses, workshops, conference attendance, and activities in professional organizations
- Descriptions of mentoring activities, both as mentee and mentor
- Peer observations and evaluations
- Letters of reference, commendations, and recommendations from supervisors
- An essay about your teaching philosophy (how you teach and why)
- Written reflections about planning (why artifacts are included in the portfolio); many teachers write them on stick-on notes that can be attached to items in the portfolio. Your portfolio is a dynamic, living document. It should change over time. It should reflect you as you are, which means you should periodically remove items that no longer reflect your current status, interests, and capabilities. How large should your portfolio be? Only you can answer that. But it should be functional and useful, not a burden to you or to the person reviewing it.

Two final cautions:

- Ensure that all examples presented in your portfolio are your own original work. If you use or adapt the work of someone else, be sure to give credit.
- Proofread everything carefully; you are presenting your best face in your portfolio, including your ability to write and spell in English.

For more about portfolios, see McLaughlin and Vogt (1996).

January 8, 2001), the administration of President George W. Bush insisted that every state develop learning standards in the basic subjects, including reading, and test every child annually from third grade up. (Testing was phased in over a four-year period.) The act requires that schools receiving federal funding use "evidence-based" instructional practices, and for its source of evidence, the administration embraced the recommendations of the National Reading Panel, with special focus on five particular recommended areas of focus: phonological awareness, phonics, fluency, vocabulary, and comprehension.

Armed with the No Child Left Behind legislation, the U.S. Department of Education has been aggressive in its insistence that schools receiving federal funds use methods and materials that are backed by "SBRR," or "scientifically based reading research." Too aggressive, it turns out. In September 2006, the General Accounting Office reported that the U.S. Education Department had ignored the recommendations of its own scientific review panels and had unfairly favored some approaches to reading instruction over others. Some of the country's most vocal proponents for SBRR instruction were caught in the glare of the scandal, and the credibility of the department's version of "evidence-based" approaches to reading instruction was challenged. Nonetheless, both sides of the aisle in Congress and a majority of the American people continue to support the emphasis on helping struggling readers, along with the use of state learning standards measured by end-of-year tests.

As noted in the Committee on the Prevention of Reading Difficulties in Young Children (Snow et al., 1998) recommendations, teachers need to take care to "develop children's language" and help them gain "a holistic understanding of reading." The research of Vellutino and colleagues (1996) and Dahl and Freppon (1995) lends weight to those recommendations. The committee urged that renewed efforts be made to involve families in their children's literacy and called for teachers to understand and accommodate cultural and linguistic differences in literacy learning. In addition, many teachers and specialists worry that teaching reading skills without immersing children in plentiful opportunities to speak, listen, read, and write could be unproductive. Children need skills, but they also need to understand the purposes of reading and writing and to be practitioners of both.

Balanced Reading Instruction

Today, many reading educators speak of the need for **balanced instruction** (Raphael, 1998) in teaching literacy. The term refers to an approach that, on the one hand, pays due attention to the need for giving children meaningful encounters with written language so that they will understand its purposes and forms and come to enjoy it. On the other hand, balance also means that teachers must ensure that children learn skills that make reading possible.

Multiple Roads to Balanced Literacy

The No Child Left Behind Act of 2002 established Reading First as a "high-quality evidence-based program for students" (ED.gov, 2004). Balanced literacy is widely viewed as an outgrowth of the National Reading Panel report of 2000, combining a literature-based focus on comprehension instruction with a strong explicit phonics component. Balanced literacy consists of five major elements (National Reading Panel, 2000):

- **Phonemic awareness:** teaching children "to focus on and manipulate phonemes in spoken syllables and words"
- **Phonics:** teaching children "letter-sound correspondences and their use in reading and spelling"
- **Fluency:** teaching children "to read orally with speed, accuracy, and proper expression" (expression referring to prosody, pitch, and intonation that indicates comprehension during oral reading)
- **Vocabulary:** helping children build knowledge of word meanings so that they can make sense of print
- **Comprehension:** teaching children the "active process that requires an intentional and thoughtful interaction between the reader and the text"

According to Strickland (1998), teachers can ensure maintaining balance in their reading programs by

- Teaching reading skills with a focus on meaning, not as ends in themselves.
- Providing daily instruction guided by the teacher and also independent work to enable students to internalize reading skills.
- Helping students build knowledge as the result of a process, not by filling them up as empty receptacles.
- Integrating print and electronic materials to reflect the modern multimedia world.
- Interpreting standardized test scores in terms of informal assessment.

Several major approaches to reading instruction provide these elements and also meet Strickland's criteria for a balanced literacy program. Some of these approaches incorporate the balanced literacy elements in their basic forms, and sometimes one or more approaches are combined to address all of them. We present a basic overview of these major approaches here in Chapter 1 to place them in context with the elements of Reading First and with balanced literacy. In subsequent chapters, you will find more specific and detailed treatments about how to implement these approaches in the classroom.

Basal Reading Programs

Certainly the most frequently encountered approach to reading instruction is the basal reading program, quite likely the kind of reading program that your teachers used when you were in elementary school. Most basal reading programs address all five elements of Reading First, and they are stand-alone, that is, they provide all of the materials needed for a complete reading program. Even so, most classroom teachers supplement a basal reading program with a classroom library of outstanding children's literature on a variety of levels and topics.

The typical basal reading program consists of reading textbooks sequenced by grade level for increasing difficulty. The difficulty of vocabulary is usually carefully controlled, as is the pace of introduction of new words. Basal reading programs contain narrative stories, expository text from science, social studies, and other areas of the curriculum, poetry, plays, riddles, jokes, song lyrics, and other types of text to read. There may be four or five small reading books at the kindergarten and first-grade levels, two to four at the second-grade level, often two at the third-grade level, and one larger textbook at grade levels 4 to 8.

Most modern basal reading programs are anthologies of original children's literature, often in complete form and with original illustrations. Vocabulary is not controlled in these programs. Some basal readers contain excerpts of longer pieces of children's literature. Often, selections of children's literature will not have all illustrations from the original work, or some illustrations may be partial renditions of the original. There may be simple text at the lowest levels that is designed for the teaching of reading skills. This text is usually not what we would characterize as authentic children's literature.

Lessons in basal reading programs are sometimes conducted with the entire class, although teachers that differentiate instruction according to children's needs may have two or more groups working on different levels and out of different books.

Basal reading programs also provide workbooks from which teachers typically teach such skills as phonemic awareness, phonics, comprehension, and vocabulary. They also provide opportunities to practice writing. These may be supplemented with large charts that can be used with easels or on word walls.

Basal reading programs also incorporate assessment tools that can be used to identify children's reading levels, their strengths, and their needs. These are frequently designed to be administered at regular intervals through the school year. Publishers of basal reading programs also often provide audiotapes, videotapes, and CD-ROMs that can be used for listening centers in the classroom.

A teacher's manual always accompanies each reading textbook. This provides information about how to use the program lesson by lesson, how to use assessment measures, and other suggestions for strengthening the reading/writing program. The instructions in the manuals range from suggestions and recommendations from which teachers can choose to highly scripted programs in which every word the teacher should say to the children in teaching the lesson is provided in the manual.

Basal reading programs can vary greatly in how they are used according to the philosophy of reading instruction promoted. In some programs, it is assumed that children must master the sound system early, and these are characterized as part-whole programs. In others, children are learning more holistic skills and whole words early in the program, along with the sound system, and these are characterized as whole-part-whole programs.

Individualized Reading Instruction

As structured and all-inclusive as a basal reading program is, an individualized reading program is at the other end of the continuum. There are no textbooks—the children select their own children's literature to read. There is a need for a large variety of outstanding children's literature at different levels and on different topics to reflect the varying and changing interests of children through a school year.

Whole class lessons are rarely seen in individualized reading programs. The main instructional interaction between teacher and child is the individual conference, which may occur every week or two. Teachers will occasionally form interest groups—children reading different books on the same topic. They may meet periodically to share their reading and their ideas about what they are reading. Teachers may also form interest groups around one story, and children reading at different levels can read the same basic story written at different levels.

Individualized reading programs require some extra effort to incorporate the five elements of Reading First, especially in the areas of phonemic awareness and phonics. For that reason, individualized reading programs are more often found in middle and upper grades than in the primary grades. Children are more independent readers at those levels, and there is not the problem of teaching word recognition skills without a textbook or workbook. Teachers who do implement an individualized reading program in the first grade will often use a stand-alone word recognition program in addition. A highly skilled and experienced teacher will be able to teach word recognition skills out of the context of the children's reading.

An individualized reading program can also be used in conjunction with a basal reading program. For example, a teacher may designate every Friday as an individualized reading day in which that approach is used instead of the regular basal program. A teacher who differentiates instruction may have one or two groups working in a basal reading program and another group working in an individualized reading program, usually a more capable group of fluent readers.

Reader's Workshop

Reader's Workshop is a more structured version of individualized reading that addresses the five elements of Reading First more routinely and transparently than individualized reading. Self-selection of authentic text in the form of children's literature and informational text is a parallel feature, but small-group lessons often resemble the basal reading approach (Atwell, 1998).

A typical reader's workshop time block might begin with a read-aloud in which the teacher, as an outstanding model of reading, shares different genres of children's literature for about ten minutes. There may be an interval of shared reading in which the entire class reads together with the teacher from a single text. This provides opportunities for work with fluency, word recognition skills, comprehension, and literary genres.

Guided reading (see the Teach It! box) is a lesson stage that may occupy thirty minutes or more. While some children have a guided reading lesson on their level, other children are completing independent work, writing, reading independently, and working in

Guided Reading

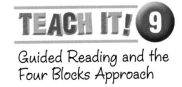

Guided Reading and the Four Blocks Approach

TEACH IT!

Refer to your **Teach It!** booklet for further activities you can use to reinforce concepts discussed in this chapter.

Guided Reading and the Four Blocks

Guided reading is "a context in which the teacher supports each reader's development of effective strategies for processing novel texts at increasingly challenging levels of difficulty" (Fountas & Pinnell, 1996). These are the key elements of guided reading:

- The teacher works with small groups.
- The children in each group are reading at about the same level.
- The teacher introduces stories and support children's development of independent reading strategies.
- Each child reads the entire text.
- Independent, silent reading is the goal for each child.
- Over time, the teacher focuses on increasing the levels of text provided.
- The children are grouped and regrouped in accordance with outcomes observed and assessed by the teacher.
- Books are carefully leveled. That is, the difficulty levels of books available to the children are precisely determined so that they can progress in an orderly way.

Guided reading lessons are conducted in three essential stages. "Before the Reading" is a stage in which the teacher introduces a new and appropriate text, and the children converse with the teacher about the text, asking questions and building expectations. "During the Reading" is the stage in which the teacher observes problem-solving strategies used by children. The children read the entire text, or a unified part of it, to themselves silently (or softly in the case of younger readers) and ask for help when needed. "After the Reading," the teacher involves the children in responding to the story through such activities as writing, discussion, paired reading, and sharing personal responses. The children talk about the story, verify predictions they made before reading, and respond, usually through writing or perhaps drama (Fountas & Pinnell, 1996).

Guided reading is often combined with the structure of the Four Blocks approach (Cunningham, Hall, & Sigmon, 1999). Together, the four blocks address the five elements of Reading First and also combine many of the strengths of the basal reading program, individualized reading, and reader's workshop while avoiding most of their limitations.

The four blocks are guided reading, as just described; writing; self-selected reading; and working with words. Teachers can implement the multilevel aspect of the four block approach by teaching a lesson to the entire class, making the text accessible to all students with multiple readings involving read-aloud, shared reading, and paired reading in small flexible groups. They can add the writing and self-selected reading blocks of the approach as after-reading activities from the guided reading approach.

Although children in Reading First classrooms are often doing word study as a whole group, with all working on the same skills, teachers may find it more useful to teach appropriate skills in smaller groups tailored to the needs of children. For example, some children are more advanced and may not need to work with skills already mastered, and other children may lack prior knowledge needed to achieve some skills, such as children trying to work with three-letter consonant blends such as *str* and *spl* before they have mastered two-letter consonant blends, such as *st* and *tr.* In order to decide which child needs what instruction, a teacher must become adept at using assessment.

As you can see, there are several roads to balanced literacy that also address the five major elements of Reading First: phonemic awareness, phonics, fluency, comprehension, and vocabulary. As you proceed through the chapters that follow, you will see more specific ways to apply these approaches and many others.

learning centers. This is often followed by a mini-lesson that addresses a need of many of the children, perhaps to decode three-letter consonant blends or to make inferences. Children may then have a guided writing activity, again accompanied with mini-lessons for some children, such as how to use the comma in a series of nouns or how to use adjectives correctly. Time for independent reading is also provided during the school day, often in the form of silent sustained reading (SSR). For a designated interval, often from ten to twenty minutes, everyone in the classroom reads a book, magazine, material from the Internet, or whatever else they might choose, including the teacher.

The popularity of guided reading comes from just this recognition of differences in students' reading development. Within a classroom teachers can gather together groups of students with common reading skill development needs and monitor their engagement during reading. For example, there may be students who hardly ever select informational texts for their independent reading. A teacher may create a group of these students, find some engaging informational text on a topic of high student interest, and help students become familiar with the different features and internal organization of this genre. The teacher can

Assessment is a vital part of teaching reading and writing. Assessment allows teachers to determine how well a particular child is learning and how well an individual lesson succeeded and to evaluate the effectiveness of the whole program of instruction. Assessment enables children to see for themselves how they are performing as they learn to read and write and what they can do to improve. It helps school administrators to make decisions about the placement of individual children in special assistance, about the design of a curriculum, and about the in-service training needs of their faculty. Assessment also provides parents with feedback on their children's progress and identifies areas where they can provide support. It can even help parents and communities to know how their schools are performing in comparison to other schools. With the advent of the No Child Left Behind legislation of the past decade, assessment is also being used in an effort to determine which schools are performing satisfactorily in teaching children to read.

Assessment can take many forms, including testing. Although some formal and informal tests of reading and writing ability can be useful, some of the most informative kinds of assessments involve watching very carefully as children read and write under natural circumstances. The type of assessment that is used depends a great deal on what needs to be known and who needs to know it.

In this book, the topic of the assessment of literacy is covered extensively in Chapter 10. It is also integrated within each chapter. Suggestions for assessment are provided for emergent literacy, word recognition, fluency, vocabulary, comprehension, response to literature, and writing. Suggestions for assessment are given at every level of schooling, from lower primary to upper elementary to the middle grades.

begin introducing students to informational texts by modeling with a text walk highlighting significant features. The lesson continues as students read sections of the text as the teacher monitors their progress in making sense of the content. By creating a small-group reading experience based on students' needs, the teacher recognizes the importance of providing instruction and practice with informational texts. The format of a small guided reading group permits the teacher to address specific needs while permitting other students to work on other aspects of their reading development. This is an important aspect of differentiation: targeting students' literacy development needs.

Students also differ considerably in their *reading interests*. In the intermediate grades, particularly, there is a huge range of types of reading students prefer. From humor, comics, and manga (illustrated books) to realistic fiction, biography, fantasy, sports, and informational books and magazines on particular topics and the wide range of Web-based information, children's interests and preferences keep expanding. This is one of the reasons individualized reading is popular: Students can self-select the materials they want to read. Teachers need to be responsive to students' interests in selection of books and materials for guided reading and whole-group modeling. They also need to ensure that classroom libraries are developed with a range of books and magazines so all students find materials they want to read. With so many women as elementary classroom teachers, the need to stretch and include books that boys, in particular, are interested in reading creates a more inviting time for reading. Opportunities for students to engage in self-selected silent sustained reading as part of a basal or four-block instructional program respects these differences, too. Teachers can interview students, create periodic surveys of interests, provide book talks, and watch students' self-selection of materials to guide them.

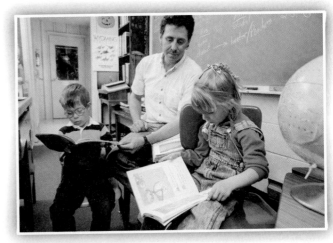

Students differ considerably in their reading interests.

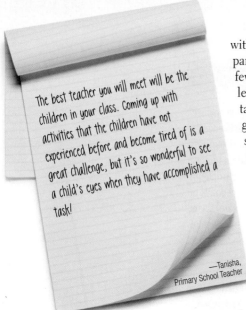

Students also differ in the *support they need in learning*. Some children come with little preparation or experiences needed for school activities. As a teacher prepares a group lesson on a topic like polar bears or fall holidays, it is likely that a few students may need more instructional attention up front before whole-group lessons so they can participate fully. This jump starting of instruction is important for many. Other students need more time to practice new concepts and strategies. Providing a range of ways they can reinforce learning permits them to be successful. Giving students opportunities to draw or act out scenes from stories they are reading may be essential reinforcements for their learning. Some learn well when put in small groups to discuss and deepen their understanding of texts together. Others need time alone to reflect and write about their responses to texts. Some work well with partners in making content and strategies their own. English language learners, in particular, benefit from opportunities to work with a same-language partner so they can process new content in their own language and clarify any confusing content or vocabulary. It is valuable to provide students a choice in the types of learning activities and settings that will help them be successful.

Accommodations for English language learners in the regular classroom can be made at many points. These students benefit when teachers become knowledgeable about their needs and ways to support their learning with comprehensible and responsive classroom activities. A good lesson framework that helps teachers be cognizant of learner needs and is used widely across the United States and internationally is based on the Sheltered Instruction Observation Protocol (SIOP) developed by the Center for Applied Linguistics (Echevarria, Vogt, & Short, 2004). It includes guidance in developing both content and language objectives for lessons, activating students' background knowledge, providing appropriate language so that directions and content are comprehensible to English language learners, and engaging students actively as learners. One section provides strategies that are most appropriate for English language learners. This model can serve as the foundation for professional development in schools with increasing numbers of English language learners. We elaborate on the SIOP instructional model later in this book.

Students, like adults, differ in interests, levels of reading ability, competence with the components of reading, and their preferences in learning. As a new teacher you will learn to make your instruction responsive to these differences and accommodate the English language learners by providing differentiated support through a multicentered classroom organization and by developing flexible instructional routines and lessons. Orchestrating all of the variables that make classrooms exciting learning environments is challenging, but the rewards are clear!

SIOP®
Sheltered
Instruction
Observation
Protocol*

Differentiated Instruction

What Is Differentiated Instruction?

The increasing diversity of students provides a visible reminder of how important it is that teachers provide appropriate, differentiated instruction so that all students can be engaged positively and productively each day they are in school. Students come with different background experiences and language, they come with different interests and ways of engaging in learning activities, with varied levels of knowledge of print and written language skill, with different levels of content knowledge and vocabulary, and they come with different home experiences and attitudes toward teachers and school. Creating classrooms where all students can learn means that both the classroom environment and the instructional program need to be designed to accommodate the range of interests and skills of students. Differentiation means taking into account all of these factors on which there are significant differences among the students and planning instruction so all students can be successful and enjoy their experiences.

It is important to start with students' strengths and help them develop the knowledge, skills, and strategies they need to become mature readers. The phrase "differentiated instruction" is used to encompass these varied ways to tailor classroom experiences so all students can be productively learning. Tomlinson (2000), who has worked extensively in differentiation, defines it well:

> In the context of education we define differentiation "as a teacher's reacting responsively to a learner's needs." A teacher who is differentiating understands a student's needs to express humor, or work with a group, or have additional teaching on a particular skill, or delve more deeply into a particular topic, or have guided help with a reading passage—and the teacher responds actively and positively to that need. (p. 4)

How can new teachers become this kind of responsive teacher and still meet the needs for student growth in determined areas of study? Knowing both students and curriculum is the key. Teachers begin the year by finding out as much as they can about the students under their care. Individual interviews with the children, interviews and informal conferences with parents, and ongoing communication with the home help teachers learn more what the students are like in their out-of-school lives where they spend most of their time and energies.

Knowing the curriculum and what students need to be learning is the other starting point. Teachers need to become well versed in the content that is to be taught. They need to know the skills that students should be developing. With this understanding, the next step is to collect information about the students' levels of knowledge and skill with that content. The teacher's task is to plan and develop appropriate instructional activities that will help students focus on what is important and that are also motivating and engaging. This means that teachers need to know students well so they can build classrooms that reflect their needs, interests, and preferences in learning activities.

Differentiation involves providing appropriate reading materials to students so they can be successful readers. This is one of the most important starting points in differentiating instruction. Within one classroom the range of reading levels can be substantial. Some estimates are that there is likely to be a range of two to four years in reading levels in the primary grades and from four to eight years in the intermediate and upper grades. Knowing that students should read materials that are at their instructional levels for guided reading and whole-class lessons, it is essential that teachers provide different texts to students, that materials are differentiated. Luckily, many publishers in the United States are now producing materials on varied levels but with similar content. There is also a rich array of materials from which teachers and schools can select so students can be placed in appropriate texts as they learn to read and as they learn content in the other academic areas.

Differentiation also involves knowing students well enough to *adjust strategy and skill instruction* to particular levels of need. Knowing and adjusting to reading levels is only the starting point. Students differ in their command of the components of good reading, too, and need appropriate instruction. For example, some students enter kindergarten knowing how to discriminate the important phonemes in English. They benefit from some oral rhyming activities with poetry. Others need to focus more attentively to develop discrimination of key sounds. For these students some daily teacher-guided discrimination activities are important. Rather than expect all students to complete the same auditory phonemic discrimination activities, differentiation is the responsive approach to these differences in students' development. With students who are non-native English speakers and those who speak dialects of English, modifications of phonemic discrimination activities and sensitivity in evaluation of students' level of mastery are needed.

Reading and writing are important parts of the school curriculum. They are tools that help students learn nearly everything else in the school day and continue to learn when they leave school. However, literacy is valuable as something far more than a school subject. Literacy leads to habits of language and mind that take readers beyond what they would find it natural to notice, think about, and communicate if they were not literate.

International comparisons show that U.S. students read fairly well—second in the world, according to one recent study. But another international comparison finds that they do not do as much deep thinking or problem solving with what they read. The benefits of literacy are not shared very equitably among students from different income groups or ethnic groups. When the National Assessment of Educational Progress has assessed reading ability, unacceptably high numbers of elementary age students have been found not to read with adequate comprehension. At the same time, studies show that few readers with disabilities have problems related to cognitive function. Ninety-seven percent or more, according to one study, could be remediated with appropriate instruction, although that instruction should be judiciously planned and intensively applied when necessary. These findings cast doubt on the still-continuing practice of treating so many children with "specific reading disabilities" as if there were something wrong with their brains.

The history of research on reading instruction is nearly as old as the scientific study of psychology. But debates over instructional methods in literacy—such as the whole-word versus phonics debate—have lasted for many generations. Arguments between advocates of holistic approaches and skills-based approaches have been heated in the past decade but appear to be easing with the emphasis on a balance of both. Research supports holistic instruction so that children see that literacy is meaningful; it also supports instruction in the alphabetic writing system—in phonics and the awareness of the sound system that underlies it.

The components of reading are interrelated, but reading can be viewed in terms of word recognition, comprehension, reading fluency, and critical literacy. Reading develops normally through stages: emergent literacy, beginning reading, building fluency, reading to learn and for pleasure, and mature reading.

To teach reading well requires that the teacher keep several things in mind. Effective reading instruction means immersing children in real literature, teaching decoding skills and coaching children in their use, attention to comprehension and to higher-order thinking skills, teaching learning strategies to children, frequent assessment, involving parents in their children's learning, and respecting cultural differences. Assessment of reading and writing ability is done for external and internal audiences. External audiences include parents, school administrators, and the general community, all of whom have a stake in knowing how well the literacy instruction program is working. External audiences usually want results from standardized tests. Assessment is also done for internal audiences, who are the children themselves and their teacher. Assessments for internal audiences typically include careful observations of children's reading and writing performance at real tasks and are intended to shed light on what learners are doing well and what aspects of their literacy need improvement.

For Your Journal

Go back to the Anticipation Guide that opened this chapter, and consider your answers to the questions posed. Divide a page of your journal with a vertical line. On the left side, write down one of your answers that you want to think about more. On the right side, write what you think about that topic now. Repeat the exercise with at least two more questions. Take your journal to class with you, and share your comments with your classmates.

Taking It to the World

1. Interview three primary grade teachers, and ask them how they have seen the emphases in reading instruction change in the past ten years. What aspects have stayed the same? What changes have they witnessed?

2. Many adults who have poorly developed reading skills don't see their limited literacy as a problem. Call the local chapter of Literacy Volunteers of America, and ask whether this is their experience. Do many of the adults in the community who need help with literacy seek help? (A class might choose to appoint a committee to do this so as not to inundate the chapter with phone calls.)

3. The National Adult Literacy Survey noted that prisoners are more likely than the rest of the population to have reading problems. Have a member of your class interview the person in charge of education at a local or regional prison. To what extent are literacy issues tied up with the problems the inmates have faced?

Technology Connections

1. On the Internet, log onto the Web pages of the International Reading Association (**www.reading.org**) and the National Council of Teachers of English (**www.ncte.org**). From what they say on these pages, can you tell what the emphases of these two organizations are?

2. The International Reading Association publishes an electronic journal called Reading On-Line. Log on and read an issue. What topics are of most interest to the readership at the moment?

Connect with Research

Review the following key words from the chapter and then connect to Research Navigator (**www.researchnavigator.com**) through this book's Companion Website to conduct a search into research on each of the various topics as they relate to reading and literacy education today.

balanced instruction	inferences	reading fluency
cognitive schemes	inflection	schema theory
comprehension	main idea	sight vocabulary
critical literacy	phonemes	vocabulary
critical reading	phonemic awareness	whole-language movement
developmental learning	phonemic segmentation	word recognition
emergent literacy	phonics	writing process approach

Companion Website

To access chapter objectives, practice tests, weblinks, and flashcards, visit the Companion Website at www.ablongman.com/templeallchildren2e.

mylabschool
Where the classroom comes to life!

Go to Allyn & Bacon's MyLabSchool (www.mylabschool.com), enter Assignment ID LAV4 into the Assignment Finder. Watch the video, *Teaching with Literature,* in which a teacher uses guided reading to enable various levels of readers to participate in the process and to make literature meaningful.

Question: What are some of the benefits of teaching reading through literature? What guided reading practices can you identify in this video? You may also answer the questions at the end of the clip and e-mail your responses to your instructor.

chapter 2

The Social
Contexts of
Literacy

Implications
of Current
Assessment
Practices for
Diverse Learners

The Social and
Cultural Contexts
for Teaching All
Children to Read

The Need for
a Learning
Community:
Linking Home,
School, and
Community

Find the Books
and Materials
They Want to
Read

Meeting the
Literacy Needs
of All Children

The Social and Cultural Contexts for Teaching All Children to Read

Anticipation Guide

The following statements will stimulate your thinking about the topics of this chapter. Answer true or false in response to each statement. As you read and learn more about the topics in these statements, double-check your answers. See what interests you and prompts your curiosity toward more understanding.

_____ ● Reading and writing are both social and individual forms of communicating.

_____ ● Differences among students in classrooms have little effect on how teachers work with children.

_____ ● Cultural groups have distinct values regarding the importance of reading and writing.

_____ ● Almost all English language learners are found in large urban centers.

_____ ● African American Vernacular English is a dialect of English.

_____ ● Children's culture is reflected in their body language, the way they manage time, and the distance they maintain between themselves and others.

_____ ● A gifted child who is reading at grade level probably has a reading problem.

_____ ● Boys tend to have more reading problems than girls do.

_____ ● Some children begin school without knowing how to handle a book.

_____ ● Children with special needs benefit from being in regular classrooms for part of the school day.

Getting Parents and the Community Involved in the Classroom

Marguerite has been teaching seventh grade for several years. Recently, she has begun to follow the new state standards for her reading and language arts classes. Just this last year, her state, Pennsylvania, provided a model unit on community biography that integrates language arts and history as students study their own community members. Knowing that her students always seemed to do better when there were connections between what she did in her classroom and what they did outside of school, she found this to be a natural way to get students more interested in developing their oral and written language skills and processes in interviewing, collecting data, and writing biographies. She got the CD-ROM that provides ideas for how to develop the unit and found a great deal of useful information and many teaching suggestions.

After reviewing these and thinking of her other plans for the fall, she decided to try this new unit, which involves students selecting a special person about whom they will write a biography. To complete the project, they need to select the special person, develop questions to use in their interview, conduct the interview, and write up their findings. In addition, they conduct research on the national and international events that occurred during this person's life, create a timeline of important events that correlate with the person's life, collect pictures and other artifacts that pertain to the report, and then represent the results on a three-part bulletin board to be shown at the Special Persons' Fair, which will be open to the public. Doing this unit permits students to use their language arts skills in reading, writing, and oral communication, as reflected in state standards.

Marguerite decided to check with some of her students before putting too much time into planning the unit, just to be certain that the idea of doing this elaborate unit would appeal to them. After she explained the basic structure of the unit, the students gave her very enthusiastic feedback, and she proceeded with the planning. As she read more and began to organize the time frame for this unit, she visited with the school librarian to see what resources were available to help students gain more information about local

Most people spend a great deal of time trying to do the things that family, friends, and those considered important are doing. Think of how you, as an infant and young child, learned to speak by following the models of those who nurtured you or how, as a teenager, you watched and then tried to dress and look just like your friends. The power of the social context is also very strong as people develop their literacy interests and behaviors. Children who come from families in which reading is a part of the fabric of their lives—in which family members keep books by their beds to read in quiet moments, newspapers arrive daily and are read avidly, and even bathrooms have piles of magazines that can be picked up for short periods—know that reading is important. They come to school with the expectation that they will become readers like the rest of their family members. Some children, however, come to school without a strong social foundation for becoming literate; this can occur in all socioeconomic, linguistic, ethnic, and cultural groups. No one might ever have read to them, there might be no books and magazines in their homes, and their family members history and community leadership. The librarian introduced her to the collection of local newspapers on file and suggested that the public library also had a wealth of materials that students could use.

Because this was a new unit, Marguerite decided to follow the unit through the experience of one student in each of her sections of language arts to ensure that she was clear and that the activities were appropriately explained and taught. She didn't want just to assign and test, but really to develop students' competence. The guide materials suggested that teachers introduce the skill of interviewing in this unit as part of meeting the state standards. Marguerite knew that this would be a new skill for her students, and she decided to emphasize it in her teaching. She looked through the materials for how to introduce the process, what steps were involved, and how to give students some practice before hav-

ing them conduct their actual project interviews. She decided to conduct a demonstration interview for students and began to think of whom she could ask to help her with this demonstration. This strategy fit into the planning model Marguerite preferred to follow: Anticipating Content and Activating Students' Prior Knowledge, Building Knowledge, and then Consolidating their new learning with activites that encourage higher-level thinking and applications in new contexts. As she thought more about the project, she decided that she would create her own community biography with her students so that she could share the experience and fun of the project.

With her planning done and with resources well organized, she was able to begin the unit with a sense of confidence. The students benefited from her careful preparation and became very excited about what they learned about their own

community during their research and interviewing. In fact, by the third week, Marguerite had allotted time for students to share what they were learning. The enthusiasm and insights gained by one student often sparked new ideas and questions from others. By the special community night when students shared their displays of their community subjects, the success of the project was clear. Both students and community members were proud of the students' accomplishments. The activity created a positive connection between the various parts of the community—those in leadership roles and many less noticed, but important, contributors.

might never read or write in their presence. It is particularly important to ensure that these students become part of a social network of children and adults who value literacy and who use it for a variety of purposes.

Teachers also need to be cognizant of the importance of the social nature of literacy as they deal with the impact of the range of literacy experiences and abilities of the children when they are in the classroom. Children continually compare themselves to those around them. Just ask students who the best readers are in their class—they know. Ask who should write the letter of thanks to the author who visited the school, and they will direct you to the best writer. Teachers must be sensitive to all the children so that each one gains confidence in being a capable part of the literacy community. All children have strengths that can and must be celebrated so that they will continue to put their energies into the challenges of developing as readers and writers. The social context of the classroom becomes more and more important as students develop many levels of social comparison. Even the positive small-group learning opportunities that teachers suggest can lead to domination of the less assertive students if care is not taken. Teachers therefore need to be aware of how powerful the social forces are in the participation in school life of students and families and in their sense of self-confidence and willingness to take risks in the classroom.

At the start of the new century, fewer and fewer classrooms are composed of children from one ethnic or cultural group who all speak English as their mother tongue and who are otherwise similar to each other. As cultural and linguistic diversity are increasing, most schools are now finding ways to make the regular classroom the center for the diverse universe of children. This chapter highlights the research and best practices that emphasize the importance of reading and writing as social activities, not just as individual skills to be acquired. Literacy happens in cultural contexts, and awareness of the power of these contexts is basic to creating the kinds of settings that support literacy efforts.

FAMILY   **LITERACY**

How were parents and community members involved in the schools you attended?

The Social Contexts of Literacy

Communities and families vary in their approaches and orientations to literacy, and many of these variations are grounded in historical and cultural circumstance. Not all Americans value literacy in their lives. Not all use reading and writing in the same ways. Research in mainstream American communities, as well as in varied cultural settings, has highlighted both the commonalities and differences across families and communities.

A classic study of variations in literacy is that done by Heath (1983) and reported in her book *Ways with Words.* In this comparison of literacy in three different cultural groups in Appalachia, Heath illustrates how the two working-class communities, Tracton and Roadville, provided their children with different cultural experiences related to reading and writing from those of the townspeople, whose use of literacy was more compatible with that of the schools. Roadville families saw literacy as very concrete and functional, and the students from this community had difficulty with more abstract learning. Tracton families viewed literacy as important for real, practical tasks. In neither of these communities was literacy important for the residents' jobs, yet the parents did want their children to read and would often help with the worksheet and skill assignments teachers gave the children. Reading for enjoyment and pleasure as a family event, however, was not part of these cultures.

Since that early work of Heath, others have explored underlying values and styles associated with literacy. Delpit (1995) has provided insights about African American cultural variations in literacy. She argues that African American children are accustomed to a more direct form of teaching and discipline and that they need that kind of clarity for all to succeed. According to Delpit, the more indirect forms of teaching and discipline preferred by many middle-class teachers leave some students out. They often don't understand the cues that teachers provide about what is important and what the students' roles should be.

Research by Kelly (1999) on a group of Mexican American mothers revealed the high level of respect they accord teachers and schools. Even when they have had few opportunities for formal schooling themselves, they want their children to succeed. Their high regard for teachers, however, has a potential negative effect. They do not want to interfere with the teachers' role by helping their children learn to read before going to school. Because of this respect for teachers and their lack of a tradition of home literacy, their children often do not enter school with the same story reading and writing experiences that other children have. These families also thought that their children could learn English in school but that Spanish would remain the language used at home. This has both advantages and disadvantages. It poses a problem in giving English language learners enough opportunities to speak and use English to become proficient. It also means that the language of intimacy and familiarity is not English, so the school associations with English need to be very positive if students are going to learn it easily. Students who speak languages other than English can be encouraged to work and talk together so that they can practice English more regularly.

Because students are coming from increasingly diverse cultural traditions with varying literacy experiences, it is valuable to try to understand something of their family and cultural values, particularly those related to literacy and schooling. It is also important to find good ways to communicate with the parents and adjust to their needs. For example, some Hispanic parents feel intimidated when asked to come to school for parent conferences. They are unfamiliar with the traditions of U.S. schools and the customary relationships between teachers and families. In an attempt to honor the different experiences of the parents, one school district in California changed its format for parent nights. Instead of having each family come alone for conferencing, the schools have small-group conferencing. After the teachers lead a discussion of students' work and curriculum expectations, they answer questions from the parents. The teachers then make themselves available to individual families who wish to talk privately. This format has worked very well. The parents feel much more secure discussing issues of school learning in a group setting rather than alone with a teacher. Instead of creating high levels of anxiety among the parents, there is much more comfort and willingness to participate.

The more teachers learn about the social contexts of their community, the better able they are to respond appropriately to their students and to build new expectations and competence so that all students can attain the levels of literacy needed today. Despite the traditional values that many communities place on literacy, all teachers need to expand their horizons and become versatile in their use of literacy in a wide variety of settings.

The Need for a Learning Community: Linking Home, School, and Community

Becoming aware of the relationship between community values and students' motivation and focus is a starting place for understanding the setting in which one teaches. The cultural importance of literacy activities and the ways adults and children communicate affect how teachers can help their students most effectively.

New teachers should think of themselves as working in a community, not just in a school. Before entering the school door and closing out the rest of the world, take time to become acquainted with the resources around you. For example, are there libraries you can link with to help provide the variety of reading materials you will want your students to have available to them? What resources are particular to the families you will be working with, such as community clubs, religious and ethnic centers, and local leaders?

Your most powerful opportunities, however, come within the school. As a teacher, you have a very important role for the parents and families of the children in your classroom. How you meet and relate to them is critical. Understanding the families' attitudes and values will help you work with the parents as partners in developing children's literacy. You want to know them as well as possible to communicate effectively with them. Think of their needs and ways to build bridges between the school and their homes. What do they want to know? How can you support them in their efforts to help their children? Think of how you can involve them in the life of the school and the classroom. What is appropriate and beneficial for both you and them?

As a teacher, you will be part of a school community, too. The more you can participate as part of the professional team, sharing your own literacy and learning and growing with others in the building, the more successful you will be as a teacher. Do not wait until you have your classroom under control before you think about building your roles within this larger support team. Begin to envision yourself as a committed professional sharing with others.

Inside the Classroom

Along with the variation among communities in how they express the values and functions of literacy, there is also great variation within schools in how the value of literacy is expressed. A part of creating a community is creating an inviting and purposeful space in the classroom, one that maximizes the possibilities for creating a real literacy community among students. Whether adjusting the physical environment or adapting the structure of reading and writing activities, each teacher can do a great deal to contribute to a school culture that stimulates literacy and honors students' contributions.

CREATE A LITERATE CULTURE.   One of the first statements you make to students about what is important in school is what they see in the classroom. Are desks grouped together? Are books and print materials displayed and easily accessible? Think about the classroom environment you want to create during your first year of teaching. What will the classroom look like? Remember, you will have a great deal to do in determining what kind of context you create for your students. Think of your classroom space as a visual and physical opportunity to invite your students to enjoy reading and writing. Think about some of the classrooms you have visited in recent years. How did the teachers make a clear statement that they valued reading and writing? Table 2.1 identifies things teachers can use in their classrooms to enhance the value of literacy.

One of the easiest and most important ways in which you can invite your students into literacy is by providing them with places where they can participate with others in literate activities. Every classroom with a library of appropriate books, magazines, and newspapers encourages the habit of reading. As you begin to create a library, identify the range of reading levels likely among the students, identify key themes and authors that children of this age enjoy, and begin building the collection. Many schools provide sets of books for each classroom. However, you will still want to evaluate the collection and make it as appealing as possible. It should contain material on a wide range of topics of interest to your students,

TABLE 2.1

Visual Survey of a Literate Classroom

The classroom contains:

1. A special place for reading and writing—a reading corner, a writing corner, etc.
2. A classroom library of books students can use regularly
3. A collection of books students have written either individually or in groups (these could be big books, bound books added to the classroom library, etc.)
4. A rack with magazines and newspapers appropriate for the students
5. An author's chair and/or a reader's and writer's chair from which the students read to the rest of the class
6. Books and magazines the teacher is reading, both professional and personal
7. Examples on the walls or ledges of students' responses to materials they are reading—reviews of books, story maps of key points, sketches of interesting parts of stories, shared responses, etc.
8. Charts and other visuals that serve as strategy guides for students learning to read and write—reading strategies, fix-up strategies, steps in writing, word walls to guide spelling using key patterns, etc.
9. Visual "in process" charts of students' work—I-charts, matrices of learning, K-W-L charts, responses to questions for reflection, etc.
10. Illustrations of what students are studying and learning in content areas—science process journals and social studies artifacts
11. Books, magazines, and other materials that reflect cultures represented in your class or school
12. Examples of writing in different orthographies so that students can explore the varieties of written languages

and some of the collection should connect to the science, social studies, and special topics that the children will study. Ensure that there are books representing the various cultures from which students in the school come. All students deserve to find and see themselves in the books and magazines in their classrooms.

Another important step is to create an attractive place for literacy activities. If space is available, create both a reading corner and a writing corner. In the reading corner, house the classroom library and additional inviting reading materials in a space where students can browse through the books and curl up on the floor or in comfortable chairs to read. Some teachers find soft chairs, pillows, or even bathtubs in which children can relax and read. You can add a small paper bin for students to make notes about special ideas they find while reading and for stick-on notes so they can mark places for sharing with each other. Some teachers involve students in creating bookmarks so they can easily access their point of reading and have extra bookmarks available in the reading center.

The writing space needs a table and comfortable chairs. The space becomes more attractive when students can enjoy a range of writing tools and a supply of writing materials. Depending on the students' age, these will vary, but a selection of colored pencils and pens, some wooden ink blocks with special designs, and a variety of kinds of paper, some with designs, make writing more fun. Computers in this area can be used for writing and editing support by parents and volunteers in early primary classes and by students as they become adept in using computers. In addition, dictionaries, thesauruses, and other writing aids should be displayed prominently for students' use. This area can house students' writing folders so that when they are ready to write, they can enter the process easily and, when finished, can refile their works in process.

WRITING and READING CONNECTIONS

What kind of writing center would you like to create for students?

ENSURE THE SHARING OF LITERACY. A key to helping students become lifelong readers and writers is to develop the social nature of literacy by providing regular opportunities for children to engage with each other around literacy events. Too often, as students move up in the grades, opportunities to talk with others about what they are reading and writing disappear. Yet it is through the sharing with others that students realize how central literacy can become in their own lives as part of their own enjoyment and learning. As you begin to plan for your literacy program, think carefully about including regular opportunities for students to engage with each other without the teacher dominating the discussion or exchange. Students need opportunities to work in paired reading and writing activities. They need to learn how to function as part of small cooperative literacy groups, knowing that they should be prepared with their own ideas to share and willing to listen and link to what others say. They also need to have experiences in larger groups and whole-class discussions that build from their partner or small-group experiences.

For many students who are new to this country, talking in a whole-class setting is extremely difficult because they lack confidence in their command of English and of the culture of the school. Teachers can ease these students into the classroom academic life by using paired reading and talking as a first step before involving the students in larger group activities. One variation of this is called Think-Pair-Share (McTighe & Lyman, 1988). As you think about all the literacy learning activities you will structure for your students, make sure students have frequent and regular opportunities to talk and share with their peers in nonthreatening settings. Don't assume that students know what it is like to discuss a book or piece of text. You might need to spend a significant amount of time getting students familiar with "talk about text." One way to develop more book discussion is to begin a Great Books program. There is full training for teachers and group leaders in this program and materials that guide students' thinking about the rich stories and texts that are included at each grade level (Plecha, 1992). Many teachers now use some form of book club (Raphael & McMahon, 1994) or literature circle (Daniels, 2002) as a way of involving students in focused talk about what they are reading. (Strategies for engaging students are discussed in Chapter 7, "Comprehending and Responding to Literature.")

Another support for book talk is to help parents learn how to elicit reflection from their children. Some school districts have developed videotapes of the kinds of questions and follow-up comments that parents can use to help children talk about their reading. Others have prepared guides for parents to follow. One example is shown in Figure 2.1.

FIGURE 2.1

Tips for Reading
with Your Child.

TIPS FOR READING WITH YOUR CHILD

1. Find a relaxed time and setting.

2. Talk about the book as you read.
   * Look over the cover, title, author, and picture and predict what you think may happen and why you like the book.
   * As you read, share connections to your life.
     "Doesnt this seem like Aunt Dorothy?"
     "This picture reminds me of our trip!"
     "Oh, I remember feeling like this!"
   * Ask questions of your child. For example:
     "Do you know anyone like this?"
     "How would you feel?"
   * After reading, share your favorite parts. For example:
     "I really liked . . ."
     ". . . was so funny!"

3. Reread favorite books.

4. Read many kinds of books—real world, poetry, folktales, humor, & fiction.

Reciprocal Teaching

Making and Breaking Words

It is useful to help students share literacy with each other at all ages and grade levels. In this way, the shared, cultural aspects of reading and writing can become more alive for all the students in the school. A very simple way to do this is for two grades to become partners in which students form buddy pairs for reading and writing and meet regularly (e.g., weekly, every two weeks, monthly). The children begin to share their literate activities with children older and/or younger than they are. The older readers help the younger ones as they read from books they want to share; the older students might also help write responses to the reading—what the two like about the story, characters, or information. When the younger students write their own descriptions of a trip to the nature center, the older student buddies take dictation and help to create personal accounts of the experiences.

In some schools, the students who struggle with reading also get help from older students who are trained in some basic reading strategies. In this way, both groups of students gain, and the shared understanding of literacy develops naturally. One particular program, Tall Friends, pairs middle-grade, below-level readers with second graders who are also having trouble. The reading teacher helps the older students develop some activities to help the second graders focus on the phonic regularities of English by doing controlled word sorts and by learning to listen to and support students as they read orally from their instructional-level materials.

If a school does not have a vibrant, shared literacy culture, think about how to bring in some new focus to stimulate students' attention to reading and writing. There are many ways in which this can be done. One is to celebrate special days, from International Literacy Day, September 8, to Dr. Seuss's birthday in March. Some states have their own awards for good children's books. Illinois holds a contest each year to select students' favorite books as part of the Rebecca Caudill Awards Program. California's Young Reader Medal, sponsored by the California Reading Association, is similar. School participation in the selection of these books creates a new focus for the celebration of books. Other programs that recognize student writing can also help to add emphasis to school literacy. Inviting authors to visit the school and speak with different groups of students can make literacy and the process of writing and reading very real. Most states have some beloved and respected authors who are willing to visit schools, and bookstores will often help to bring authors to area schools.

Each of these examples highlights the importance of thinking of literacy as a community activity in the school. The more there is a climate of support for and interest in how students read and write, the more all students benefit. In addition, the more students talk with each other about their reading, the more they identify with books and reading.

START THE YEAR OUT RIGHT.   Just as teachers can do much to create a warm, supportive literacy climate in the classroom, what they do even before students start the year can help to model the importance and joy of literacy. Consider writing a letter to each of your new students before the year begins, introducing yourself and telling a little about your expectations for the fall. You can suggest that students bring with them an example of their own writing (if they are beyond the second grade) or a favorite book or poem. Some teachers ask students to bring pictures of themselves doing something they enjoy to put on a board for the first day. Each of these activities is an example of using literacy as a bridge to building relationships. Students love to receive mail, and some of the apprehension of starting a new year can be melted away with such simple, yet profound, gestures.

Teachers can also involve parents in events at the start of the year. By sending a letter home during the first week explaining who they are and what they will be doing in the classroom, teachers can build a bridge from school to home. Parents respond positively to an introduction from the teacher explaining what to expect for the fall. After an initial letter, the teacher might publish a weekly or monthly newsletter of the class events, with explanations of aspects of the reading and writing programs. Parents need to know how they can contribute. Figure 2.2 shows an example of a home-school letter that a multiage team sent to help parents understand their approach to reading development. Figure 2.3 provides an example of a letter a kindergarten teacher sent to parents and children asking them to identify favorite poems and bring them to class for all to share. This simple activity set the stage for monthly units that involved some parent participation. Knowing that they were important and were helping their children extend the resources of the class, most parents participated eagerly.

During the first week of school, literacy activities can also help the class to become better acquainted. Ask each student to bring a favorite book or magazine to share, give the students time to explain why they have selected the particular material, and listen carefully to them. This can be a good way to find out even more about the students' personal and home uses of literacy. For students for whom such selection and sharing might not be comfortable, conduct a book talk about several books and magazines in the classroom library and ask students to select the one they think they will like most. Having time to scan the materials gives each student an opportunity to share responses.

Getting to know the students quickly is important. Asking them to draw or write something about themselves is another way to elicit shared literacy activity. The bulletin board that can be created from this activity then becomes an invitation to read and learn about classmates. In one school, parents created the covers for the writing journals that the kindergarten and first-grade children were given the first week of school. Imagine the children's surprise when they realized that they would be holding a creation of their parents each time they wrote! Parents knew their children would be using their developmental spelling abilities as well as drawing to write messages each day when they spent time at the writing table.

Involving Parents in the School

It is impossible to discuss social contexts of literacy without focusing on parents, for they are the children's first and most important teachers. Teachers need to know as much about

> **"Research is an effort to do things better, it is the problem-solving mind—it is the tomorrow mind, it is a natural extension of good teaching."**
> (Hubbard & Power)

Welcome to the *Research to Practice* segment of our bi-monthly class news. This is the place where we hope to clarify terms, strategies, theory, research, district expectations and how it connects to what we do in our classrooms. Each newsletter will focus on a particular area of instruction, learning, and/or curriculum. It is our professional obligation to not only keep you abreast with current research, but also to align it to what we do in our classrooms. We hope that you find this portion of the newsletter informative and helpful.

Rainbow Reading

Reading Levels (Jerry Johns, 2001)

Independent   The Independent reading level is the level at which the student can read fluently without teacher assistance. Materials should be read with near perfect accuracy (95–100%) and 90% comprehension.

Instructional   The instructional reading level is the level at which the student is <u>challenged</u> but not <u>frustrated</u> with teacher guidance. The student can read accurately (90–95%) with 75% comprehension.

Frustration   The frustration level is the level at which the student should not be given materials to read. Students at the frustration level (<90% accuracy and <50% comprehension) are unable to read the materials even with the support of the teacher.

Rainbow Reading

Rainbow Reading is one component of our Balanced Reading Program.* The Rainbow Reading books in our classroom are grouped into four colors: <u>Red</u> (Beginning), <u>Orange</u> (Developing), <u>Yellow</u> (Transitional), and <u>Green</u> (Fluent).

During Rainbow Reading (independent reading) students choose books from one of the four levels that are at their **independent** (95% accuracy, 90% comprehension) level. "Independent reading is essential for the development of fluency. Fluency comes from the ability to immediately and automatically identify most frequent words. This is key to the success of a life-long reader." (Cunningham, 1998)

During Reading Workshop, students are placed in materials at their **instructional** (90–95% accuracy) level. Teacher guidance provides a scaffold where students are challenged but not frustrated.

*A Balanced Reading Program provides opportunities for pleasurable, independent reading (Reading Rainbow), reading for a specific purpose (Reading Workshop, learn content, skill, strategy), and interaction through discussion, response to literature, research and inquiry. (Pinell & Fountas, 2000)

<u>AT HOME ...</u>

Continue to set aside a special reading time. During that time your child might be reading from the Rainbow Reading collection from school, reading a library book or other book of choice, reading to another child, or listening to you read. It is extremely important that children **hear** the language and pattern of text in the higher-level books adults read to them. Remember that reading should be pleasurable. Allow time for "easy"reading!

Happy Reading!

FIGURE 2.2

Home-School Newsletter.

the parents' cultural values and styles of communicating with their children as possible so that the adjustments to the school culture and style of each teacher can be made. Even the ability to talk about different ways of thinking, talking, reading, and writing can be useful to students, parents, and teachers. For example, you might suggest to a parent, "At school, we are trying to get the children to be independent in their reading by giving them time to

March

Dear Parents,
      March is poetry month. In celebration of our featured genre of literature, please complete the following "Literature Link".

                              Thank you,
                              Debbie Gurvitz

DIRECTIONS FOR MARCH LITERATURE LINK

1. Together, choose or write a poem to be shared with our class.

2. Print the poem in the area provided.

3. Have your child illustrate his/her poem.

4. Return to school at your earliest convenience.

POEM	ILLUSTRATION

POEM:

When I Was One

When I was One,
I had just begun.
When I was Two,
I was nearly new.
When I was Three,
I was hardly Me.
When I was Four,
I was not much more.
When I was Five,
I was just alive.
But now I am six,
I'm clever as clever.
So, I think I'll be six now
forever and ever.

                    A.A. Milne

Name ___SY___

FIGURE 2.3

Home-School Letter.

figure out unfamiliar words for themselves. We ask them to look for three sources of information: visual, grammatical, and meaningful. Of course, you want them to read perfectly and fluently. Giving them the correct pronunciation of words helps this. However, right now we are trying to get the children to be more independent. If you could help reinforce our teaching strategy for the next few months, your child will feel more comfortable and, I think, reach the goal we both share." Accept that what the parents value and think is important, and then help them understand how they can assist the instructional program.

As already mentioned, relationships between parents and schools vary tremendously. In some communities, parents feel too intimidated to join the school culture. They want teachers to do their jobs and will support this as best they can. In other communities, parents are very involved in the schools, serving on curriculum committees, working on standards development, and visiting classrooms regularly. They might want to know a great deal about how reading is taught and might have a wealth of experience themselves guiding their own children's literacy development. In this situation, the teacher will want to give parents some in-depth explanations. Figure 2.4 shows an example of a home-school letter that explains the importance of spelling and word study for primary students. Creating videotapes and programs that explain how literacy develops can help to build good communication in these situations. Even sharing some of the current research reports, such as *Preventing Reading Difficulties* and the National Reading Panel report, can be useful to knowledgeable community members. Dealing with the variations depends on the school and should be a shared decision of the faculty and administration. A key in all situations is being open to, and interested in, the parents' perspectives and concerns.

FAMILY **LITERACY**

What does this phrase mean: "Parents are a child's first teachers"?

Become Part of a Professional Community

Teaching is challenging work and can be exhausting, especially for new teachers. One of the best ways you can help yourself is by seeking out opportunities to become part of the multilevel professional community of educators.

WITHIN THE SCHOOL. At the most immediate level is the community within the school. If you are fortunate, your school will have some structured times for professional development when the faculty meets regularly to discuss issues of common concern and to learn together. New teachers might also have the option of working with a mentor teacher in an induction program as they begin their teaching careers. This can be a helpful way to get to know the specific culture of the school and district and can prevent many frustrations. The school district or the larger county or service center might also have an optional set of good activities that can be used to increase our effectiveness as teachers. Ask about these resources, and watch for special programs that are advertised. Many new teachers feel too busy to add another commitment, but the rewards can outweigh the time demands.

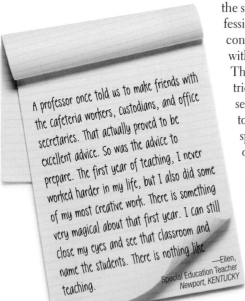

A professor once told us to make friends with the cafeteria workers, custodians, and office secretaries. That actually proved to be excellent advice. So was the advice to prepare. The first year of teaching, I never worked harder in my life, but I also did some of my most creative work. There is something very magical about that first year. I can still close my eyes and see that classroom and name the students. There is nothing like teaching.

—Ellen, Special Education Teacher Newport, KENTUCKY

OUTSIDE OF SCHOOL. Outside of school, teachers can seek out groups that meet regularly for discussions both of adult recreational books and of professional ones. Some book clubs also read and discuss new children's books, which can help teachers become aware of new possibilities for students. With so many new books published each year, it is difficult to keep up with the ones that might be appropriate for your students. You can attend book discussions hosted by bookstores and distributors with your teaching colleagues as well. They can help to identify special books and upcoming events to link into the classroom. If teachers share their search for books, magazines, and computer materials with each other, they can enjoy learning together as they find materials that are of interest to a wide variety of young people.

As you begin your journey of professional growth, share what you are doing with your students, who might not think of teachers as learners, too. Children might be intrigued to see the professional journals and books that help their teachers evaluate their own teaching and that encourage them to stretch in new directions. Keep some of your professional

Learning and Growing Together at Home

Word Study

"The purpose of word study is two-fold. Through active exploration, word study teaches students to examine words to discover regularities, patterns, and rules of English <u>orthography</u> needed to read and <u>spell.</u> Second, word study increases specific knowledge of words—the <u>spelling</u> and meaning of individual words." (Bear, Invernizzi, Templeton, Johnston, 2000)

<u>Educators in District #34 conducted year long spelling study (1999–2002) . . .</u>

After a comprehensive review of the research in spelling, the committee recommended **Word Study** as a method to study spelling. While memory does play an important role in learning to spell, it does not play the *only* role. (Henderson, 1990). Learning to spell should *also* be a process of coming to understand how words work—the conventions that govern structure and how their structure signals sound and meaning. (Berninger, 1994, 1995; Brown & Ellis, 1994; Read & Hodges, 1982; Templeton & Bear, 1992; Templeton & Morris, 2000)

<u>The goals for our District Word Study Program are:</u>

- **Students will learn spelling strategies to assist in spelling unknown or unfamiliar words.**
  - We want your child to be able to rely on "sounding it out" as ONE of several strategies to use when writing a challenging or new word. Additional strategies that will be taught are using word sorts, other references, applying knowledge of vowel patterns, and discovering how our alphabetic system works (Cunningham & Cunningham, 1992) and decoding by analogy (Goswami & Bryant, 1998).
- **Students will learn how to memorize words. Each grade level has identified words that should be memorized.** (See attached grade level list.)
  - Expecting students to memorize every word **just does not work.** However, there are key words from our Word Wall that we call the NO EXCUSES LIST! These are words that may not follow a spelling pattern and are words that we use in our daily writing. These words are like math facts—they need to be practiced and memorized. (Routman, 1999)
- **Students will learn common patterns used in spelling.**
  - Word sorts and make a word are strategies that reinforce vowel and blend patterns. (Cunningham, 1998)
- **Students will develop a spelling consciousness and competence.**
  - As your child explores words through spelling and meaning, your child will develop a curiosity and interest in words that will carry over into reading and other academic areas. Students gradually will move from inventive spelling to traditional spelling.
  - Good spellers attribute their spelling proficiency to reading and writing, not to spelling lessons or tests. Good spellers are more likely to conceptualize how words look and think about what they mean. (Hughes & Searle, 1997)

<u>At Home . . .</u> **Encourage your child to "Do What Good Spellers Do"** (Routman, 2000)

- Read a lot, enjoy reading, have a fascination with new words
- Integrate sound, visual, and meaning to words
- Use what you already know about words to find out new words . . . utilize strategies and resources
- PRACTICE often—learn 5 words from the Grade Level Spelling list, then learn 5 more and so on . . .
- Take pride in doing your best work!

FIGURE 2.4

Home-School Letter.

materials in the classroom as a visible reminder that adults are readers and learners, too. Talk about your own reflection and questions.

PROFESSIONAL ORGANIZATIONS. New teachers are also nurtured when they join professional organizations that hold conferences and publish journals and books designed to help them become better teachers. For literacy teachers, that means becoming a member of the International Reading Association (**www.reading.org**) and/or the National Council of Teachers of English (**www.ncte.org**). These organizations have local and state groups that meet periodically to bring speakers to the area and sponsor special events; they also may offer grants to teachers wishing to attend a conference or develop some special student project. These professional organizations also provide many opportunities for teachers to develop leadership skills by speaking, being an officer, and working on advocacy when the need arises. Teachers enjoy their challenges most when they become part of the larger professional community. At a personal level, membership often results in new friends and a valuable support network. Local affiliates can be found by checking the Web sites of the national groups. Participation with other teachers in the building or district can help to create a strong professional learning community.

Meeting the Literacy Needs of All Children

An Urban Classroom

Farah Al Jabar's fourth-grade class is located in a low-income area of a major urban center. Her thirty-six students represent, in about equal numbers, four major ethnic groups: African American, Asian, Hispanic, and Anglo. Almost half entered kindergarten speaking another language or dialect of English. Although all are at least minimally proficient in English now, many have gaps in their oral language vocabularies and in the background knowledge that corresponds to that of the middle-class children for whom the school curriculum and textbooks are typically designed. According to the results of informal reading inventories that she administered in the fall, many are reading below grade level, and a few are reading markedly below grade level.

Being a Professional Reading Teacher

Your Professional Portfolio

An important dimension of your professional development will be diversity. Potential employers want to know how you will address diversity in their classrooms. How can you use your portfolio to document your experiences with the diversity of students we have in our classrooms now? Here are some ideas that you might consider:

- Thematic literature units that reflect diversity
- Photographs of children in the classroom where you might complete a practicum or student teach, volunteer, or work as a paraprofessional
- Lesson plans that reflect gender equity, cultural sensitivity
- Descriptions or journal accounts of community experiences
- Descriptions of workshops and university classes about multicultural issues that you have completed

- Photographs of bulletin boards you have prepared that reflect diversity in the classroom where you volunteer or work as a paraprofessional
- Evidence of participation in the International Reading Association (IRA) through subscribing to their publications, participating in their conferences, and other activities, including state and local affiliates of IRA (**www.ira.org**)

Teaching Resources

This is a good time to begin reading and evaluating children's books that reinforce multicultural themes. Make a list of books appropriate for the grade levels you are interested in. Start looking for these books at swap meets, garage sales, used bookstores, and thrift shops. Building your own classroom library is a good way to ensure that children have easy access to good literature.

Today, one group of ten children, all reading at grade level, is beginning to read a novel by Spinelli (1990a) entitled *Maniac Magee*, which was awarded the prestigious Newbery Award. It is not a particularly difficult story, but many vocabulary words are new to the children. In addition, some lack background knowledge about substantive issues that underlie the story. As Farah planned this lesson and several to follow, she had in mind the state reading standards she would be addressing, the California State English–Language Arts Standards (California State Board of Education, 1997):

Reading

2.3 Make and confirm predictions about text by using prior knowledge and ideas presented in the text itself, including illustrations, titles, topic sentences, important words, and foreshadowing clues

3.3 Use knowledge of the situation and setting and of a character's traits and motivations to determine the causes for that character's actions

Writing

1.1 Select a focus, an organizational structure, and a point of view based upon purpose, audience, length, and formal requirements

In addition, Farah ensured that she was incorporating the elements of the four-block guided reading model she applies in her classroom: guided reading, writing, working with words, and self-selected reading. Before the children read, she leads them through several brief anticipatory reading activities that prepare them to read the story with good understanding. First, she says, "Let's read the title of the book and look at the illustration on the cover," demonstrating and modeling how she makes predictions about text she will read. She asks, "What predictions can you make about this book?" One child tries to sound out the word "maniac," saying "m-m-maniac—What does it mean?" Another child quickly responds, "It's a word for a crazy person, somebody out of control." Another notices the shoes on the cover and asks, "Do those shoes belong to a boy or a girl?" Farah says, "Let's find out." She reads the two-page foreword of the book aloud to the children; it ends with a short poem:

> *Ma-niac, Ma-niac*
> *He's so cool*
> *Ma-niac, Ma-niac*
> *Don't go to school*
> *Runs all night*
> *Runs all right*
> *Ma-niac, Ma-niac*
> *Kissed a bull.*

She then explains, "The main character is Jeffrey Magee, but they call him 'Maniac Magee.' He's a boy about your age. Now what do you think the story might be about?"

Farah has already prepared the beginning of a semantic map to introduce the term *dump*, which the children will encounter early in the story. She asks, "What do you know about this word?" The children share the information they already have, and Farah records it in appropriate categories on the graphic organizer.

She then has the children close their books with their finger in place at the first page of the first chapter, and she asks them a question that will guide their silent reading of that page, beginning the guided reading part of her lesson where they will build knowledge through reading. She asks, "How does Jeffrey's life suddenly change?" They listen to the question, then open their books and begin reading silently. (Jeffrey is orphaned when his parents are killed in an automobile accident. He lives with an aunt and uncle for a short time and then runs away to live in a dump.)

As they read, Farah circulates around the group, motivating them by touching shoulders, smiling, and offering encouraging comments. Some children ask for assistance with words that are unfamiliar, even after the anticipatory reading activities. She quickly provides that help so that they can maintain their comprehension. This activity also provides an opportunity for her to briefly circulate around the classroom and supervise the work of other children who are working independently as they wait for their own small-group lessons.

TEACH IT! 19

Semantic or Concept Web for Upper Grades

WRITING and READING CONNECTIONS

How can writing be incorporated into a reading lesson?

Story Maps

As the children finish reading the page and begin to raise their hands to respond to the question, Farah returns to her seat. She repeats the question and calls on a child who says, "He went to live with his aunt and uncle—they weren't too cool." Another adds, "His mom and dad were killed in a car accident." Yet another says, "He ran away." Other children add new information and share other points of view. Finally, Farah asks one student to read aloud the sentence that provides evidence for the answer that all the students finally agreed on. She then asks another comprehension-level question about the same page, following this procedure through the three pages of this first chapter of the story.

In a consolidation activity at the end of the lesson, Farah asks, "How did the story begin?" A child responds, "Jeffrey's parents were killed, and he went to live with his uncle and his aunt." She asks, "What happened next?" The children continue to retell the story up to that point in their own words. Farah then says, "Write a short paragraph, and predict what you think will happen in the next chapter of the story. While I teach the other group's lesson, please read from your library books." As they begin to think about that, she moves on to work with another small group of children that is reading from an anthology.

Farah has exhibited many behaviors that tell us she is an outstanding teacher, some of which relate to her strong instructional program, one that uses teaching strategies that support or scaffold their comprehension and that help them build confidence. In reading aloud the preface of the book, she provided a model both of fluent reading and of thinking about what she read, as revealed in her follow-up question. She gave attention to working with words in analyzing a crucial word in the story, *dump*, whose meaning was a key to understanding the circumstances in which Maniac Magee was living. She provided guided reading in the silent reading that was directed and scaffolded by the higher-order questions she asked before they read. She provided an application and extension activity: writing a short paragraph to predict what might happen in the next chapter. And, finally, she provided time for self-selected reading.

Equally important are aspects of her approach that motivate the children, that indicate her high expectations and affection for them, and that demonstrate her deep understanding of the cultures from which they come. Choosing literature for the children's lessons is an important part of her planning. The main character of *Maniac Magee* is a boy who has very positive interactions with African American children in the story. She has also provided a large-print version of the book from LRS Large Print Publications (Spinelli, 1990b) for a partially sighted student in the group. Farah's next literature choice for this group is *By the Lake of Sleeping Children: The Secret Life of the Mexican Border* (Urrea, 1996), about life in a dump in Tijuana, Mexico, which parallels and connects with the setting of *Maniac Magee*. She takes much care to ensure that all children in her class see themselves in many different roles in the literature she provides for them. She directs the major part of her small discretionary budget each year to the purchase of sets of trade books to supplement her basal reading program.

Valuing Diversity or Coping with Differences?

We can view the diversity in Farah's classroom, and in most American classrooms, from at least two perspectives. On the one hand, teachers can consider that associating with people who are different enriches everyone. On the other hand, because diversity means that differences between children are greater than just the ordinary individual differences found among homogeneous groups of children, some teachers see it as a problem. Different languages can make it difficult to meet needs, group students efficiently for instruction, and provide materials that are appropriate for all children. Cultural differences arise, making teaching a complex and demanding act. These are legitimate concerns, but they should be viewed as challenges instead of problems. Teachers who take the first perspective, the positive one, see diversity as an asset to be exploited for the benefit of the children, an asset that enriches the learning of all—the students and the teacher.

CULTURAL DIVERSITY, BACKGROUND KNOWLEDGE, AND LITERACY. The pervasive culture in U.S. schools, according to Gollnick and Chinn (1998), is essentially "based on the knowledge and perspective of the West (Northern and Western Europe)." Many believe that this culture is apparent in textbooks and curricula and in the cadre of teachers that staff most schools. It characterizes what teachers expect students to know when they come to school, and it serves as the basis for teachers' assessment of student outcomes. It often characterizes how teachers reinforce children's behavior, both positively and negatively; how they ask children questions and accept their responses; how they correct children; how they do, or do not, make the classroom safe for children; and how they use gestures and time. Clearly, schools cannot adopt the culture of each and every child, but they can accept the culture of every child, accommodate that culture, and use its presence and teachers' knowledge of it to help teach all children. According to Fitzgerald (1995), teachers must make reading instruction congruent with the background culture that children bring to their lessons.

Creating an inviting environment in your classroom can help promote a literacy community for all students.

THE ZONE OF PROXIMAL DEVELOPMENT.   The work of Vygotsky (1978) provides another view of social constructivism that underlies children's cognitive development, with particular applications to the teaching of reading and language. The learning community includes culture, language, and important adults who guide children in their learning.

Vygotsky's concept of the **zone of proximal development** is especially important. According to his view of learning, certain tasks can be performed by a student independently, others cannot be performed at all, even with help, and some fall within the "zone," which can be performed with help from others. Those others in the classroom are usually adults, such as teachers, paraprofessionals, and parent volunteers, but they can also be other more capable students in cooperative learning group settings.

Many implications for the classroom emerge from these concepts:

- Teachers need to design instruction that is at an appropriate level for each child—not so difficult that they fail, not so simple that there is no gain, but at a level where, with **scaffolding** (i.e., a support system), they can learn. A one-size-fits-all approach is not appropriate.
- Learning activities need to be done in meaningful contexts, not in isolation.
- Children need to construct their own meaning with the help of the teacher and other adults and peers in the role of facilitators.
- Children need to see relationships between what they are learning and the communities in which they live.

CULTURALLY RESPONSIVE CLASSROOM COMMUNICATION.   Children's language develops in a sociocultural context. How children use language in their homes and communities also has important effects on their use of language in classrooms, especially when they are learning to read and write. Although language arts and reading curricula often reflect a linear assumption about the development of language and literacy in all of its forms, ethnographers remind teachers that they must view how parents use language in rearing their children, the range of types of language use in the home, and the amount of exposure that children experience with respect to the diversity of languages, to the diversity of speakers of languages, and to the diversity of ways of using language outside of their homes (Heath, 1986). Culturally responsive teachers apply their knowledge of the many cultures in their classroom to how they address children and how they respond to them, both verbally and nonverbally.

Verbal communication.   Providing feedback to students is a vital teacher activity. When feedback is provided across cultures, there is always potential for misunderstanding. Scarcella (1990) provides several categories of feedback behavior:

- Interpreting student feedback (how they indicate that they are paying attention). Most Americans nod their heads to indicate that they are listening. Asian students often nod to indicate that they are listening, but this does not necessarily indicate understanding.
- Complimenting and criticizing (how this is interpreted from both perspectives). Asian students might reject too many compliments as being insincere, whereas Hispanic students usually welcome praise.
- Teacher correction of student errors (how students view the way the teacher corrects errors). Students from some cultures want to be corrected and are concerned at a lack of correction. In other cultures, correction can be a humiliation for the student. It is important for the teacher to consider how to treat this issue with each student in the classroom.
- Student requests for clarification (how, or if, students ask for help and how teachers interpret these requests). Teachers should carefully monitor the comprehension of their students, checking for understanding and watching for nonverbal behavior that might indicate a question that has not been expressed.
- Spotlighting, or calling attention to a student's behavior in front of others. Many children do not appreciate having attention called to them, especially from across the room. Teachers might be more effective if they walk over to students and softly give instructions, especially if student misbehavior is involved or even praise for older students. The teacher can avoid turning a small problem of inattention into a major problem of defiance.
- Questioning and answering (the purpose of questions). Asking questions is an important teacher instructional behavior. American teachers tend to ask many questions for the purpose of motivating critical thinking on the part of the students. But Heath (1983) has found that African American children are often confused by the way teachers ask questions when the teachers already know the answers to them. She recommends that these children be asked questions of the type they are asked at home, such as "What's that like?" or "What's happening?" To promote higher-order thinking, teachers often ask for opinions about what a character did in a story or how an author expressed an idea. Children from some cultures are uncomfortable in offering opinions; they can gain experience and confidence in acquiring this ability in small-group work before they express themselves in front of the entire class.
- Pausing (wait-time). Teachers tend to provide insufficient wait-time for students. They need to allow students time to think about their responses before going on to another student or accepting a response from students who always seem to know the correct answer before anyone else. According to Rowe (1974), teachers usually wait little more than one second. She found that when children were provided with at least three seconds of undisturbed wait-time, they responded more completely and correctly, the number of nonresponses decreased, and the number of volunteered responses increased.

Nonverbal communication.　Communication is often thought of only as a verbal process, but the important impact of nonverbal communication should also be considered, especially when teachers work with children from many different cultures. For example, a frequent type of interaction between teacher and child is the teacher's need to correct the inappropriate behavior of a child. To show respect, an Anglo child usually looks in the teacher's eyes when being corrected. The same child shows defiance by looking at the floor instead of looking the teacher in the face. Conversely, a Hispanic child often shows respect to the teacher by looking at the floor, whereas defiance is shown by looking the teacher in the eyes. What message does the teacher send by saying to the Hispanic child, "Look me in the eye when I talk to you"? In this case, the teacher might be asking the student to demonstrate defiance. This is only one of many examples of the potential for cross-cultural misunderstandings between teacher and child, even when both are behaving appropriately for their own cultures.

These nonverbal aspects of communication are a form of **paralanguage,** which includes many aspects of nonverbal behavior that are very useful for teachers to understand (see Table 2.2). These behaviors are the clues that tell us someone is from another culture, sometimes even what country they are from, although we might not be able to hear them speaking. You cannot be expected to be familiar with all of the nonverbal behaviors of all of the cultures of the children in your classroom, but you can begin to reflect about the reactions of children to your own nonverbal behaviors and about your own reactions to puzzling nonverbal behaviors of students. When student reactions to a teacher's behavior are counterintuitive, there is often a cultural explanation.

As children's experiences with life in the United States expand, they also begin to learn the appropriate nonverbal behaviors of the new language and culture they are acquiring. When they are successful, they are able to function comfortably in two cultures, making them **bicultural.** Teachers need to be sensitive to children as they go about the complicated task of becoming bicultural.

TABLE 2.2

Selected Components of Paralanguage

COMPONENT	OBSERVABLE BEHAVIORS	SELECTED CLASSROOM EXAMPLES
Kinesics (Pennycook, 1985)	Gestures and other movements of the body, including facial expression, movements of the eye, and posture	American children often show respect with eye contact; other cultural groups of children frequently show respect by looking down.
Proxemics (Hall, 1966)	Social distance	Hispanic children often cling closely to the teacher and like a hug; Asian children tend to maintain a greater social distance and are less comfortable with touching.
Haptics (Pennycook, 1985)	Arm and hand movements	Americans indicate the height of a person with the hand held horizontally at the appropriate level; Hispanics hold the hand vertically for people, but horizontally for animals.
Paraverbal features (Pennycook, 1985)	Nonlexical aspects of verbal communication, such as pitch variation, the use of silence, how space is filled in a conversation (e.g., *uh* in English, *este* for many Spanish speakers)	Asian children often giggle when embarrassed, such as when they are caught misbehaving.
Chronism (Hall, 1983)	Monochronic use of time in a linear mode in Western cultures, with sequential scheduling and tasks completed one at a time; polychronistic use of time in a cyclical mode in non-Western cultures, with less precise time commitments	*Monochronic:* Western children tend to line up to be helped by the teacher one at a time. *Polychronic:* Non-Western children often gather around the teacher's desk, all wanting to be helped at the same time, unconcerned that the teacher helps each one a little bit so that everyone is eventually completely helped.

Linguistic Diversity: Today's Classroom Demographics

Who are the English language learners? Where are they? Everywhere! The 2000 census revealed a significant and growing diversity in American classrooms in almost all parts of the country. Perhaps the most important aspect of this change is the number of children classified as **English language learners,** children who arrive in American classrooms with

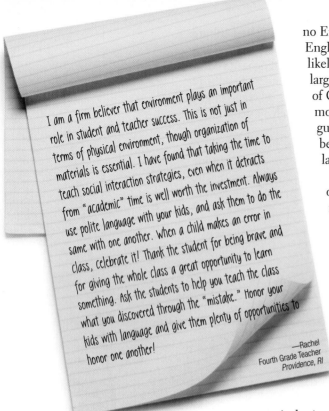

I am a firm believer that environment plays an important role in student and teacher success. This is not just in terms of physical environment, though organization of materials is essential. I have found that taking the time to teach social interaction strategies, even when it detracts from "academic" time is well worth the investment. Always use polite language with your kids, and ask them to do the same with one another. When a child makes an error in class, celebrate it! Thank the student for being brave and for giving the whole class a great opportunity to learn something. Ask the students to help you teach the class what you discovered through the "mistake." Honor your kids with language and give them plenty of opportunities to honor one another!

—Rachel
Fourth Grade Teacher
Providence, RI

LANGUAGE and DIVERSITY

How is the distribution of English language learners in the United States changing?

no English or insufficient English for learning to read and write in English. When teachers think of English language learners, they likely think of Hispanic children; indeed, Hispanics make up the largest population of English language learners. They also think first of California, Texas, Florida, and New York as the states that are most affected by the presence of Spanish-speaking English language learners. But schools in most areas of the country are now beginning to experience an influx of Spanish-speaking English language learners.

According to the 2000 U.S. census, the Hispanic population of the United States has nearly doubled since the 1990 census, rising from 9 percent to 12.5 percent of the total population (Campo-Flores, 2001; U.S. Census Bureau, 2000). Some of the largest percentage increases have occurred in surprising areas of the country. The meatpacking and -processing industry has attracted many Spanish-speaking workers and their families to such states as Nebraska, Iowa, Minnesota, Arkansas, Kentucky, Tennessee, the Carolinas, Alabama, and Georgia, accounting for major changes there.

The most dramatic difference in the growth of Hispanic populations in the 2000 census, however, was the rapid dissemination to smaller population centers and suburbs (Suro & Singer, 2002). Almost half of Hispanic population growth was in fast-growing Hispanic hubs and new Hispanic destinations; the other half occurred in established metropolitan areas.

Similar growth is seen in other language groups as well, and not only are these groups growing, but they are also appearing in states where they were not as numerous in previous years. For example, most Hmong immigrants from Laos began their American experience near Fresno, California, but many of them have moved to Minnesota and Wisconsin (University of Wisconsin–Eau Claire, 2000).

According to the National Clearinghouse for English Language Acquisition and Language Instruction Educational Programs (NCELA, 2006), almost ten million children don't speak English at home, and about half of those don't have sufficient English-language proficiency to succeed in English in our schools. Although the vast majority of these children speak Spanish (see Table 2.3), more than 100 languages are represented.

English language learners are not a monolithic population. Some are very proficient in speaking and understanding their mother tongue, and some are literate in that language. Some became literate in their home countries; others do so in programs of bilingual education here in the United States. As a result of living in refugee camps, some upper elementary and adolescent children have arrived in this country with little or no school experience at all. Some English language learners are migrant children from rural areas without educational opportunities, and others were working and contributing to the family income. Some English language learners have limited proficiency even in their mother tongue, just as some native English speakers are limited in their English proficiency. As teachers consider the challenges today's students represent, they also must think in terms of possible solutions.

BILINGUAL EDUCATION.   Perhaps the most sweeping policy change to affect the education of English language learners in recent years was the 1974 *Lau* v. *Nichols* decision of the U.S. Supreme Court, which ruled that equal education did not result from providing exactly the same education to all children (*Lau* v. *Nichols*, 1974; J. Crawford, 1989). It required that school districts take positive steps to overcome the educational barriers experienced by students who did not speak English. Soon afterward, the Elementary and Secondary Education Act was amended with Title VII to make limited English proficient students eligible for federal funds and to permit their enrollment in **bilingual education** programs.

TABLE 2.3

Language Backgrounds of Limited English Proficient (LEP) Students

LANGUAGE	RANK	PERCENTAGE OF LEP STUDENTS
Spanish	1	79.0%
Vietnamese	2	2.0%
Hmong	3	1.6%
Cantonese	4	1.0%
Korean	5	1.0%
Haitian Creole	6	0.9%
Arabic	7	0.9%
Russian	8	0.8%
Tagalog (Philippines)	9	0.75%
Navajo	10	0.6%
Others	—	11.45%

A 1981 court decision (*Casteñeda* v. *Pickard,* 1981) established three criteria for determining how programs of bilingual education were to be held accountable for meeting requirements of the Equal Education Opportunity Act of 1974. The criteria included the following:

- The program must be based on sound educational theory.
- The program must be effectively implemented with adequate resources for personnel, instructional materials, and space.
- Following a trial period, the program must be shown to be effective in overcoming language handicaps.

Although the *Lau* v. *Nichols* decision did not mandate bilingual education as a remedy, school districts did find it to be one of the few ways to ensure that English language learners had equal access to education, that is, education in their mother tongue while they were learning English. The No Child Left Behind Act of 2001 replaced the earlier Elementary and Secondary Education Act (ESEA) Title VII, which formerly funded programs of instruction for bilingual children and was rescinded (García, 2005). The new law, Title III, continues to provide resources for what are called English language learners. Annual assessments of English-language proficiency are mandated, as well as requirements that these children meet state academic content and student achievement standards in English (Office of English Language Acquisition [OELA], 2004). The term *bilingual* does not appear in the new law, which now stresses skills in English only. There is no federal interest in the development of academic bilingual education programs for these children.

In late 2006, the Department of Education released new regulations concerning English language learners (Federal Register, 2006). They have the effect of allowing school districts to delay the testing in reading of English language learners who have been in the United States for less than a year. Unfortunately, no evidence indicates that these children can learn English in one year, so the effect will be minimal.

ENGLISH LANGUAGE LEARNERS AND LITERACY. Bilingual education, however, is a subject of much controversy. In recent years, initiatives in a number of states, including California, Arizona, and Massachusetts, have discouraged most bilingual education in those states. They require instead a one-year period of **immersion instruction** in English as a second language, although the efficacy of this approach is not supported in the literature. In fact, abundant evidence indicates that children need two to five years

TEACH IT! 50

Using Questions to Teach English Language Learners

Because of the changing demographic of the U.S. population, strategies for meeting the needs of non–English-speaking students have become a focal point of discussion in many communities.

of instruction in English as a second language before they are ready to learn to read in English (Thomas & Collier, 1997). An analysis of test scores from the 2002 California Stanford 9 test scores reported by the influential League of United Latin American Citizens (LULAC) (O'Leary, 2002) suggested that English language learners were not developing English fluency and that many were falling further behind in academic subjects. O'Leary reported that four years after the passage of California's Unz English Initiative, Proposition 227, more than a million limited-English immigrant students in second through eleventh grades in California still had not been mainstreamed in English-only classes, an indication of the failure of the policy.

Goodman (1986) reminds us that bilingual children are not disadvantaged in some academic way. They are disadvantaged only if their linguistic strengths are not appreciated and if schools fail to build on their strengths. The International Reading Association (IRA) has recognized the efficacy of teaching children to read in the mother tongue while they learn to understand and speak English and before they begin learning to read in their second language, English. The IRA's resolution of support includes three major elements: (1) initial literacy instruction should be provided in the child's native language whenever possible; (2) although initial literacy instruction in a second language can be successful, there is a higher risk of reading problems than beginning with a child's first language; and (3) instructional decisions should support the professional judgment of the teachers and administrators who are responsible for teaching students whose first language is not English and oppose any restrictive federal, state, or local initiatives (International Reading Association, 2001).

Dialects of English and Literacy

English language learners, those whose mother tongue is not English and whose English proficiency is limited, are not the only children whose reading instruction is affected by linguistic factors. African American Vernacular English is a dialect of English that is spoken by many urban African American children in the United States. There are other dialects, including southern regional dialect, a mostly rural dialect of both Anglo and African American children.

AFRICAN AMERICAN VERNACULAR ENGLISH. African American Vernacular English, also known as black dialect and ebonics, is the dialect of the English language that is probably most frequently encountered in American classrooms. According to Labov (1970, 1972), African American Vernacular English is as logical and consistent as standard English, it can be reproduced, and it makes sense. It is merely different from standard English. A policy statement of the TESOL (1997) board of directors stipulates that African American Vernacular English has been demonstrated in research to be a rule-governed linguistic system that has its own lexical, phonological, syntactic, and discourse patterns and that it therefore deserves pedagogical recognition. It is not a substandard dialect of English, and it is not poor English. It is a dialect that is widely understood and spoken among many inner-city African Americans.

There are many phonological and syntactical differences between African American Vernacular English and Standard American English. Some of those identified by Johnson and Simons (1974) are presented in Table 2.4.

These characteristics of African American Vernacular English appear so consistently that they occasionally appear in the oral reading of children who superimpose their dialect over the words written on the page (Johnson & Simons, 1974). Teachers must consider whether or not there is a negative effect on reading comprehension or only on oral reading accuracy because both are possible, even in a single reading episode by an individual child.

The World of Reading

Children's Secret Languages

Most people remember the joys of confounding their childhood friends, or perhaps being confounded by them, when they first encountered Pig Latin. It was a secret language that we easily learned, once the principle of moving the first letter to the end of the word and adding the sound of "ay" was grasped. When the skill was shared with friends, it allowed them to communicate with each other while leaving adults perplexed.

Children are intrigued with the possibilities of understanding, speaking, reading, and writing in another language, although they often do not have the opportunity until secondary school. Today, more and more children across the country encounter classmates who speak another language in addition to English. Sometimes the other language is that person's only language. Children who speak only one language might not have an appreciation of the advantages of speaking another language or of the disadvantages of not speaking English. Teachers can gently address both issues by using secret languages as an example.

Children's secret languages are a nice language play activity that often has the added bonus of providing practice in syllabication and letter-sound correspondence.

If you have children in your class from other countries, you could ask if they have a secret children's language and if they would teach it to the class. This activity places them in a position of leadership that they might not often have, so you need to be sensitive to their comfort level in front of groups and help them with the process. If you do not have children in your class from other countries, or wish to explore a variety of secret languages, you could use Alvin Schwartz's book *The Cat's Elbow and Other Secret Languages* (1982), a collection of thirteen secret children's languages, including Pig Latin.

TABLE 2.4

Some Differences between Standard American English and African American Vernacular English

LINGUISTIC FEATURE	STANDARD AMERICAN ENGLISH	AFRICAN AMERICAN VERNACULAR ENGLISH
Phonological Features		
Initial and final sounds of /*th*/ (modified)	that, these	dat, dese
	both, breathe	bof, breave
Medial /*v*/ (modified)	seven	seben
Medial or final /*r*/, /*l*/ (deleted)	door	doe
	help	hep
Consonant clusters (deleted)	desk	des
	told	tol
Syntactical Features		
Past tense marker	I talked to him.	I talk to him.
Copula (deleted)	She is tall.	She tall.
Use of verb *be* (habitual)	Julie reads every day.	Julie be reading.
Subject-verb agreement	We were there.	We was there.
Double negative	Henry doesn't have a football.	Henry don't have no football.
Possessive (deleted)	The girl's dress	The girl dress
Question (reversal of subject and verb)	What is that?	What that is?

Source: Based on Johnson and Simons (1974).

ADDING STANDARD AMERICAN ENGLISH. Teachers demonstrate that they value the language of children when they accept the way the children communicate with each other and with members of their families and communities. In classrooms, however, teachers also need to help students add a second dialect of English: standard American English, a dialect that supports the children's continuing academic learning and offers access to higher education and desirable employment opportunities. The resulting bidialectical children resemble bilingual children in that they can readily switch back and forth between dialects according to the educational or social situation in which they find themselves. Part of the process of being bidialectical is knowing when and where to use each dialect.

Where an ESL program is already in place for English language learners, many ESL activities will be of value for children whose home and community language environment is African American Vernacular English. Teachers can use many intermediate and advanced ESL instructional strategies to add standard American English to the children's repertoire. The children will not require instruction at the basic stages of the natural approach for English language learners (described in Chapter 14), but participation in activities at the third stage of the natural approach will be helpful because they focus on communication, not on grammar. In addition, the activities described for "sheltered English" in Chapter 14 will support and enhance the children's development of **background knowledge** and vocabulary needed for effective reading comprehension. Where such a program is not in place because there are no English language learners, an oral language development program should be provided to help children acquire standard American English in much the same way that English language learners acquire English. This is not an ESL program, but rather a program of oral language development.

Rickford and Rickford (1995) suggest a very direct approach, beginning with an agreement among students that standard American English is appropriate for classroom interaction and writing. With that understanding, teachers should provide focused activities based on language needs that children demonstrate. Delpit (1990) suggests that these include dialect contrast activities in which students and teachers agree that learning standard American English is a goal, probably in the upper elementary grades and beyond. These dialect contrasts can be incorporated into dialogue journals, class logs, and student portfolios.

LITERACY ISSUES FOR AFRICAN AMERICAN CHILDREN. The issue of mother tongue instruction has important implications for children who speak African American Vernacular English. If learning to read in Spanish while learning to speak English is the most effective program for Spanish-speaking children, then it could follow that speakers of African American Vernacular English should learn to read from materials written in that dialect while they are acquiring standard American English as a second dialect (Simpkins, Holt, & Simpkins, 1974). Indeed, some educators have advocated for this approach. There are, however, some significant barriers:

- There is not broad acceptance in the African American community for the use of African American Vernacular English as a language of instruction.
- Although some reading instructional materials have been written in African American Vernacular English through the years, they have not been broadly or systematically used.
- Limited research evidence at present supports the use of reading materials written in African American Vernacular English (Simpkins et al., 1974).
- There is a sense among some African Americans and others that the use of African American Vernacular English might be a tool for minimizing opportunities for success among African American children. (Williams, 1991)

Given the highly controversial nature of the issue, there are several ways in which teachers can make effective and positive use of the presence of African American Vernacular English—and other dialects of English—in American classrooms:

- Value and accept positively the communication efforts of children who use African American Vernacular English in the classroom.

- Avoid correcting pronunciation and syntactical structures from African American Vernacular English and other dialects of English used by children in their ordinary classroom discourse; such attempts betray a negative valuing of the way the children speak and, by implication, of the children themselves and of their family members and communities.
- Demonstrate valuing of the dialect by accepting it in the dictations of children in key vocabulary and language experience approach activities.
- In addition to using children's literature in which dialogue is in standard American English for read-aloud activities, incorporate children's literature that includes dialogue in African American Vernacular English and other dialects spoken by children in the classroom (Brooks, 2005).
- In activities that are designed to help children acquire the standard American English, avoid references to the standard dialect as the "correct" or "better" way to speak.
- Use storytelling (Sanacore, 2004) and traditional cultural literary structures of the African American community, such as the praise song and the praise poem (Johnson-Coleman, 2001), and trickster tales, which are also a part of the Native American oral tradition. An Internet search at **www.google.com** will yield dozens of praise song, praise poem, and trickster tale resources.
- As an important part of the literacy program for African American children, include Afrocentric children's literature that reflects the culture and linguistic traditions of children who speak African American Vernacular English (Brooks, 2006; Sanacore, 2004).
- Ensure that phonological, morphological, lexical, and syntactical features of African American Vernacular English and other dialects of English are not used to penalize children in assessment activities, especially those that are not related to the purpose of the assessment (see Chapters 11 and 12).

Delpit (1991) offers suggestions for teachers to consider in educating children of color who are too often failed by our schools. She recommends that teachers do the following:

- Teach these children more, not less.
- Provide critical thinking experiences for them (also Sanacore, 2004).
- Challenge the racist view of some that these children are incompetent.
- Recognize and build on the children's strengths.
- Use metaphors, analogies, and experiences that are familiar to the children to connect them to school knowledge.
- Ensure that the children feel cared for, as in a family (also Sanacore, 2004).
- Identify the children's needs and meet them with a variety of strategies.
- Honor and respect the culture the children bring to school.
- Connect the children to their community, something that is greater than themselves.

Differentiating Instruction for At-Risk and Struggling Readers

Another aspect of diversity in American classrooms is a more generic category that incorporates children from all groups, that of the student who is at risk of not learning to read. Through the years since the Coleman Report (Coleman et al., 1966), many terms have been used to describe students whose school achievement is below expectation, including at-risk, disadvantaged, low-income, and others. The constellation of factors often associated with **at-risk students** includes the following: low income; inner city or rural; ethnic and/or language minority; non–English speaking; nontraditional family structure, including frequent absence of father; and high rate of school dropout.

Many students who exhibit the characteristics just listed have satisfactory or above-average achievement in school, and some students who exhibit none of the characteristics

TEACH IT! 46

Language Experience for English Language Learners

TEACH IT! 23

Readers' Theater

TEACH IT! 24

Choral Reading

PHONICS and PHONOLOGICAL AWARENESS

Why do teachers need to take care that pronunciation differences among children are not penalized in assessment activities?

STRUGGLING   READER

What are some of the factors associated with children who struggle learning to read?

do experience failure in school. But it is fair to say that these factors are strongly associated with low school achievement.

As a result of the Coleman Report (Coleman et al., 1966), a variety of federally funded efforts were initiated to alleviate the effects of these factors on low school achievement, especially in reading. These included Head Start, Title I and Title VII of the Elementary and Secondary Education Act (ESEA), and the Reading First and Early Reading First Programs. The most recent of these federally funded programs is the five-year Striving Readers Program, which sponsored eight research projects to determine what can work to lower the numbers of struggling middle and secondary readers.

The rapidly increasing influx of English language learners and other so-called disadvantaged students in U.S. schools provides a greater challenge than ever before to teachers whose charge is to promote the equitable access of all students to high-quality instruction in reading and writing. These students have generally been placed in compensatory or remedial programs, where they are expected to learn to read and write by acquiring isolated skills through interaction with incomplete fragments of language. Rarely do they emerge successfully from these programs into the mainstream; instead, often they leave the programs only when they leave school—all too often as early leavers or dropouts (A. N. Crawford, 1993).

COGNITIVE, AFFECTIVE, AND PSYCHOMOTOR FACTORS. Cultural and linguistic diversity are major factors for teachers to consider in planning reading instruction

TEACH IT!

Refer to your **Teach It!** booklet for further activities you can use to reinforce concepts discussed in this chapter.

Incorporating Authentic Children's Literature

The language-experience approach (LEA) to reading is a powerful tool for addressing culture and beginning reading that is based on the oral language of children. The approach centers on language as the vehicle for communicating thoughts and ideas. This Teach It! explores the approach with a lesson that incorporates authentic children's literature.

The first step is for the teacher to conduct a read-aloud of a piece of children's literature that is culturally appropriate—in this case, for a group of African American first graders—and that is also ideal as a stimulus for a language experience dictation. The book in this example is Patricia McKissack's *Ma Dear's Aprons* (1997), about a little boy living with his mother in a single-parent situation. In the story, David Earl's mother has a different apron for each day of the week, and David knows which day of the week it is by observing the apron his mother is wearing. Although there are seven days and seven aprons, the teacher might decide to read only up through the first three days and aprons. During the read-aloud, share the wonderful illustrations by Floyd Cooper, asking questions about the activities of the three days and the aprons that Ma Dear wears.

Then have the children dictate their brief version of the story. They might come up with something similar to the example seen in the figure. Accept the dictations of the children as stated, regardless of any cultural affectations.

In this collaborative chart story strategy, children negotiate with each other about what they want to dictate on the chart. Some children might suggest changes that result in a dictation reflecting more Standard American English than the original version. The example shows two past tense verbs, "wash" and "iron," that were written as dictated by the children because no child suggested a change. The word "next" was pronounced as "nex"; the teacher should spell it correctly according to best practice in the language experience approach. The children should have many opportunities to read the text in a shared reading mode as the dictation is recorded and after the children's rendition of the story is completed.

> On Monday, Ma Dear put on the blue apron.
> She wash the clothes.
>
> The next day she wore a yellow apron.
> She iron the clothes on Tuesday.
>
> David likes the green apron on Wednesday.
> It had a treasure pocket.
> There was candy in it.

for children. But cognitive, affective, and psychomotor aspects of diversity also have an effect on reading.

The increasing diversity of our classrooms seems to bring with it an increase in the numbers of children who are struggling to read. Duffy-Hester (1999) examined several model reading programs for such children and found common guiding principles that should serve teachers well in working with troubled readers. Among these guiding principles are the following:

- Reading programs should be balanced, drawing on more than a single theoretical perspective. A one-size-fits-all approach to reading instruction inevitably seems to miss meeting the needs of some children. A balanced program touches on all of the learning modalities that diverse groups of children bring to the classroom.
- There should be a well-supported role for every element in a balanced reading program. Several currently popular direct instruction reading programs, for example, make heavy use of decodable text, fragments of unconnected text in which the students are to practice word recognition elements they have been studying. Yet little research supports the use of such text, whereas abundant research supports the use of connected text, especially in the promotion of reading comprehension (Allington, 1997).
- Word recognition, comprehension, and vocabulary development should be taught in the context of authentic reading and writing activities, not in isolation.
- Teacher read-aloud activities serve to build background knowledge and vocabulary, preparing children to understand their own reading of the text later.
- Authentic assessment provides valuable information that teachers can use to inform their instruction. Some assessment does not provide this type of information and takes up valuable time that could be used for children to read and write. We are reminded of a traditional dictum about assessment: "You don't fatten a pig by weighing it."
- Teachers should use their professional preparation to make instructional decisions about reading programs they use.
- Staff development activities should provide time for reflection and opportunities to share experiences about best practices.
- The learner-centered goals and strategies that are most effective for troubled readers will serve other children well, too.

Other factors can affect the plight of troubled readers. Allington (2001) offers several research-based accommodations that relate to the organization of the school. Class size is an important factor, with research demonstrating that achievement is higher when classes are smaller, especially with children from low-income families (Achilles, 1999). Allington recommends a class size of twenty. Access to appropriate instructional materials is also important. In agreement with Duffy-Hester, he feels that programs should be designed to fit children, not force children to fit into programs. He recommends that no more than 20 to 30 percent of instructional time be devoted to single-source materials, that is, materials that all children in the classroom use in common. A third factor is that of honoring instructional time. No interruptions of the period for teaching reading should occur, not even public address announcements from the principal's office.

Allington then turns his attention to the question of access to intensive, expert instruction. He suggests that one-on-one tutoring is the most intensive type of instruction, but that real small-group instruction (four to seven students) is much more effective than traditional large-group or whole-class instruction. He further observes that pullout remedial reading programs, such as those underwritten by federal funds, frequently offer instruction for too short a time, but over too long a period. He recommends offering a semester of very frequent and intensive support instead of a year of

Inclusion for students with Individual Education Plans (IEPs) is one strategy for addressing the needs of at-risk students.

less intensive support. Finally, Allington suggests expanding instruction time for troubled readers. This can be accomplished by adding a second daily lesson, providing extended-day reading instruction through after-school programs, and providing summer school reading support to minimize summer reading loss.

INCLUSION IN REGULAR CLASSROOMS.   Federal law calls for inclusion for many children identified for special education services; many are now placed in regular classrooms, although sometimes for only part of the school day. They are educated, to the maximum extent possible, in the same setting as their classmates without disabilities. This means that regular classroom teachers must address the needs of some children who are physically disabled, mentally retarded, visually or hearing impaired, emotionally disturbed, and from other special needs categories.

Under provisions of the law, students are identified as requiring assessment if they have a disability such as mental retardation; a hearing impairment, including deafness; a speech or language impairment; a visual impairment, including blindness; a serious emotional disturbance; an orthopedic impairment; autism; traumatic brain injury; a specific learning disability; deaf-blindness; or multiple disabilities. These children's needs must be assessed, and an Individual Education Plan (IEP) must be developed for each student (Individuals with Disabilities Education Act, 1997). The plan must include the following elements:

- Current levels of educational performance
- Annual goals and short-term objectives
- Need for special education and related services
- Explanation if the child cannot be mainstreamed in the regular classroom
- Description and schedule of special education services provided
- Description of transition services provided
- Assessment of student progress, including needed accommodations

Support services from experienced special education teachers are often provided to the regular classroom teacher who is working with mainstreamed children, but they are often not sufficient or timely.

The Individuals with Disabilities Education Improvement Act of 2004 (IDEA) is carefully aligned with provisions of NCLB (NEA, 2004). Special education teachers are required to be "highly qualified," students with disabilities are required to be assessed annually in NCLB-required assessments, with some accommodations, and students must meet the same state standards as all other students, including English language learners, with some exceptions for students with severe cognitive disability. Needless to say, these provisions in the law are the subject of much discussion in all school districts as they attempt to meet these new requirements.

There is also great concern about the overrepresentation of children from linguistic and ethnic minorities in special education (Hill et al., 1993). Historically, children were often assigned to special education classes on the basis of supposed language disorders and/or mental retardation that might be nothing more than limited English proficiency. Under provisions of *Diana* v. *State Board of Education* (1970) and subsequent special education legislation, such as P.L. 94-142, this is no longer permitted. Damico (1991) suggests that care be taken to ensure that referral to special education is not based on the following:

- Other factors that might explain the child's learning and language difficulties, including lack of opportunity to learn, cultural dissonance, and stressful life events, for example, among refugee children
- Language difficulties that the student has at school, but not at home or in the community
- Ordinary needs of children to acquire English as a second language or the standard American English dialect
- Cross-cultural interference
- Bias in the assessment process, including data analysis that does not take into account the child's culture, language, and life experiences

Many strategies can be used very effectively in teaching children with these needs. According to Gersten and Baker (2000), teachers should do the following:

Differentiated Instruction

Readers Who Are Gifted

Gifted children are usually not an instructional challenge for classroom teachers. Many have learned to read at home as a result of being read to, and most others very quickly learn to read in kindergarten or the first grade. But teachers often make four erroneous assumptions about gifted children:

- That gifted children don't have reading problems.

    The gifted child who is reading on grade level may have a reading problem that should be diagnosed and addressed. Ordinarily, gifted children will be reading above grade level, often several grades above their age-expected level. Teachers should identify the levels at which they need instruction and at which they can read independently without great effort, and then provide appropriate books at those levels.

- That all children will benefit from the same reading program.

    Children who already read, often far above grade level, will be bored if required to proceed laboriously through instructional content designed for children who are on grade level, or even below. Teachers should challenge such children, usually by differentiating the reading program for them and certainly by providing alternative activities when other children are learning something mastered long ago by children who are gifted or advanced in their reading abilities. This includes helping them find books of interest. Gifted children will often persevere even with difficult materials if they are of great interest.

- That gifted children have already mastered all of the basic skills.

    The fragmentation of basic skills is not unusual among gifted children. They can be integrated into reading groups that are addressing identified areas of weakness at the time an appropriate lesson or lessons are offered, even though those groups are usually working below the levels of these otherwise more capable students.

- That all gifted children speak English well.

    We should search for gifted children among English language learners and other marginalized groups of children as diligently as we search among advantaged children. Gifted English language learners and children who speak African American Vernacular English will benefit greatly from language-rich strategies such as those found in the Sheltered Instruction Observation Protocol (SIOP) (Echevarria, Vogt, & Short, 2004).

- Build children's vocabulary and use it as a curricular anchor.
- Use visual representations to reinforce major concepts and vocabulary.
- Use the children's mother tongue as a support system.
- Adapt cognitive and language demands of instruction to the children by using sheltered English strategies.

It is not only the physical needs of these students that should be addressed in inclusion efforts, but also the content of the curriculum. If students of color or girls need to see themselves in the literature they read, then so should students with disabilities. According to Landrum (2001), this benefits not only those students, but also students without disabilities, who need to learn about and accept differences. Landrum has developed a set of criteria for the evaluation of novels that feature characters with disabilities. Among her criteria are the following:

- Plot: Story events are realistic, not contrived; disabled characters are active participants.
- Character development: Disabled characters are presented as strong and independent, not passive and dependent; the focus is on what they can do, not on what they cannot do.
- Tone: The text avoids using such terms as *retarded, handicapped,* and *crippled.*

READERS WHO ARE BOYS.   Much attention has been given to the roles of girls in literature for children in recent years—and with good effect. Whereas stories in basal readers and current literature anthologies tended to focus on boys in the most active roles in past years, there is now balance in the stories that the children read, not to mention representation of major cultural and linguistic groups as well. You might wonder why boys would be listed as a category of diversity among readers, but boys continue to have problems in reading that are out of proportion to their numbers in the population. Why do boys make up an almost overwhelming proportion of troubled readers? Among the many factors associated with this finding are the greater frequency of left dominance; lack of physical and emotional maturity compared to girls; greater frequency of attention deficit disorder; different cultural expectations for boys, including more physical activity and action; fewer positive reading models for boys; interest levels of books for boys; and female-dominated environment in schools, with teachers also favoring realistic fiction and character-related stories.

Teachers can take steps to ensure that boys do not continue to be overrepresented among the ranks of troubled readers:

- Provide more time in the initial stages of reading instruction for immature boys, especially those who exhibit signs of left dominance.
- Provide positive role models for boys: men and older boys who read.
- Provide books of interest to boys, such as the highly irreverent Captain Underpants series (Pilkey, 2000) and nonfiction informational books about nature, history, biography, and sports.
- Provide magazines and newspapers that have more real-world interest and shorter texts.
- Permit more physical movement, for example, letting the children sprawl out on the floor when reading.
- Provide structured opportunities for children to discuss the text they are reading and writing about. (Young & Brozo, 2001)

Finding the Books and Materials They Want to Read

Diversity is important with respect not only to the learning characteristics of all students, but also to their need for appropriate texts to read and from which to learn to read.

The Print Environment of Students at Home

As might be expected, the print environment of the home and community is closely related to the factors of diversity described in this chapter. The newspapers, magazines, books, calendars, checkbooks, notes on the refrigerator door, Web site pages on the computer screen, and instructional manuals found in most middle-class homes may be absent from or less frequently encountered in the homes of children from low-income families. There might not be a tradition of reading and writing in the family, or perhaps a Bible or other religious book is the only representation of print in the home.

In a study by Halle, Kurtz-Costes, and Mahoney (1997), they found that access to print was an important factor related to the reading achievement of African American children. In an international study of the relationships among reading achievement, home literacy environment, and school and public library availability of reading material in several countries, Elley (1992, 1996) reported that access to print was the most powerful factor associated with reading achievement, including the size of the school library. He found that frequent silent reading was the next most significant variable affecting reading achievement.

Beyond the presence of text to read, the need for models reading in the home is also of great importance, especially when it is recognized that men and older boys are often less likely to read than are women and girls in the family.

Besides often being a factor in the low-income home, the absence of text also characterizes the low-income communities in which the homes are located. In a study of print resources in two low-income and two middle-income neighborhoods, Neuman and Celano (2001) surveyed the availability of reading materials for purchase, such as newspapers, magazines, and children's books; the quantity of signage; public places where reading took place, such as laundromats and bookstores; the availability of books in child care centers; and the quality of services and materials provided by school and public libraries. They found an overwhelming advantage of print resources in the middle-income neighborhoods, and they concluded that children in the low-income neighborhoods would have difficulty finding books of good quality, whereas those in the middle-income neighborhoods would have difficulty avoiding them.

In addition, the provision of a full-time or even part-time librarian is often related to the income levels of students in the schools. Neuman and Celano (2001) found that there were no trained school librarians in the low-income communities they studied, whereas the schools in the middle-income communities had well-trained and highly experienced school librarians. School libraries in the middle-income communities were also open more days and hours per week than those in the low-income communities. The same disparities were found in public libraries in the communities studied.

They concluded, as did Cunningham and Stanovich (1997), that the children who are most in need of a print-rich environment are the least likely to encounter it, resulting in a spiraling down of environmental opportunities for reading in the community, which in turn results in less motivation to read and yet fewer opportunities to read. Allington (1983) adds that this is aggravated when these same children are enrolled in public schools in which low-level programs are provided to address the reading problems of the children, resulting in these children doing less reading of text than do children who read well. These programs involve major time commitments to studying about reading instead of time devoted to reading connected text.

Getting Books, Magazines, and Newspapers into Children's Hands

Given the diversity of children in our schools, especially children who are at risk of being troubled readers, teachers should take special pains to find books and other print materials that they will enjoy, books with characters and settings with which they can identify, books in which they can see themselves in positive roles, and materials that are of high interest and have visual appeal. A valuable resource of books and other sources of connected text that reflect cultures of diversity is found in Banks's *Teaching Strategies for Ethnic Studies* (2003). Banks categorizes many dozens of books in English for teachers and for children in the following groups: First Americans (American Indians, Native Hawaiians, and African Americans); European Americans (European ethnic groups and Jewish Americans); Hispanic Americans (Mexican Americans, Puerto Rican Americans, and Cuban Americans); and Asian Americans (Chinese Americans, Japanese Americans, Filipino Americans, and Indochinese Americans).

An abundance of books available in Spanish exist for children who want and need to read in that language (Schon, 2000, 2001, 2004; Schon & Berkin, 1996). Even when children do not have the opportunity to learn to read in the mother tongue, those who learned to read in the mother tongue in another school or country should be provided with opportunities to read more books in that mother tongue. It improves self-concept, offers evidence that the school and teacher value that mother tongue, and provides practice in reading that

TECHNOLOGY

How can teachers use technology to help address the needs of children who range from the gifted to the struggling?

builds background knowledge and skills that transfer positively to reading in English later. Teachers should also be very careful about the use of so-called bilingual books that are written in two languages, usually with English and Spanish versions on facing pages. This practice ensures that children will acquire English in terms of Spanish, that is, a very ineffective translation approach. It is better for children to read a story in Spanish from one book and then read the same story in English from another book, as elaborated in later chapters. The children can use their background knowledge from the first experience to support their comprehension and learning of English in the second book.

Gifted children require a rich variety of books and other text materials to maintain their many and changing interests. They will often tackle books at a much higher level than the level at which they are reading because of their motivation and willingness to persist. Given good guidance, they can use the Internet very productively, too. Many sites are now available that are geared to younger children's reading abilities. Teacher sites like MarcoPolo (see **www.marcopolo-education.org**) can also help teachers locate stimulating project ideas and resources for them. This is less of a problem for children in the lower grades of a multi-graded school because they will find reading resources for older children in the school library. But it can be a problem for the sixth-grade gifted child in a K–6 school. This child needs access to a middle or secondary school library or an understanding teacher who is willing to check out books at the public library.

Finding materials that are high interest and low vocabulary enough for troubled readers, especially for boys, is a perennial problem for teachers. The teacher who is always conventional might have difficulty finding books that meet both criteria. A good resource for magazines is *Magazines for Kids and Teens* (Stoll, 1997), which provides descriptions of the content and the reading and interest levels of over 200 magazines on a wide variety of topics, including some that publish students' own writing.

In addition, as noted earlier, boys will enjoy recent offerings in the immensely popular Captain Underpants series (Pilkey, 2000): *Captain Underpants and the Invasion of the Incredibly Naughty Cafeteria Ladies from Outer Space, Captain Underpants and the Wrath of the Wicked Wedgie Woman,* and *Captain Underpants and the Attack of the Talking Toilets.* Teachers who understand and appreciate the sense of humor of nine-year-old boys will recognize the appeal of these titles and the opportunities for stimulating those boys' creative writing instincts.

School budget problems are often a factor that affects the numbers of books, magazines, and newspapers available to children in the classroom. Some sources of text that teachers can exploit to augment those supplied by the school district are the following:

- School storage rooms, where surplus books are often hidden away
- Secondhand stores, public library book sales, yard sales, and swap meets, where teachers can often negotiate low prices with vendors "for the children"; returning to vendors at the end of the day and offering to buy all remaining books for a bulk price is often an effective way to maximize scarce teacher resources (many teachers spend much of their own money on books for children)
- Child-made books that result from collaborative chart stories, language experience approach activities, and other student writing activities
- Local public libraries that are usually available for walking field trips and that permit children to request library cards so they can check out their own books
- Commercial book clubs, which offer children's books at quantity discounts, usually with paper covers instead of hard covers. Depending on the number of books ordered by the children, many book clubs provide additional books for the teacher's classroom library.
- Newspapers that often sponsor programs to adopt a classroom and also often provide newspapers at no cost
- Support from parent groups, service clubs, and other community sources
- Reading Is Fundamental (**RIF.org**), which provides sets of books to schools at no cost

Finally, teachers should ensure that a wide variety of text is readily available for children to take home to read. Too many resources are so protected from loss or abuse that they are never used.

TECHNOLOGY

What is the effect of poverty on student access to libraries and technology?

Equity and Access to Computers

As was noted, library resources for children from low-income neighborhoods are limited, and certainly the same is true with respect to access to computer technology. According to Becker (2000), only 22 percent of children of low socioeconomic status have a computer at home; 91 percent of high socioeconomic status children do.

Access to the Internet at school has improved dramatically during the past several years. According to the National Center for Education Statistics (1999), 95 percent of all public schools provide Internet access, including 90 percent of those where 71 percent of students are eligible for free or reduced-price school lunch, a frequently used measure of a school's socioeconomic status.

When utilized properly, specially designed educational software or access to the Internet can offer a variety of opportunities for working with all children, regardless of their needs.

Even as the gap in providing access to computer technology and Internet access to all students is closed, teachers should consider the value of this access in terms of instruction in reading and writing. According to Krashen (1997), computer technology and the Internet might not have a great deal to offer in teaching children to read. He found no evidence that computer-based reading management programs such as Accelerated Reader or the IBM Writing to Read program provide any benefits to children. He concluded that funds should instead be directed to trade books for free voluntary reading, as time invested in this activity is very effective in increasing reading achievement. Becker (2000) reported that, in elementary grades from 4 to 8, most teachers who used computers in the classroom used them for skill practice games, for word processing, and to access CD-ROMs. He also reported that computers were used slightly more frequently in low socioeconomic status schools than in high socioeconomic status schools, but that their use in low socioeconomic status schools involved more traditional drill and practice activities, whereas their use in high socioeconomic status schools reflected teaching strategies that are more constructivist and innovative.

Children who surf the Net are reading, usually with high motivation. Children without access to the Internet are probably not reading something else instead of surfing the Net, the result being less practice in reading for those children, another example of the Matthew effect, according to which the rich get richer, and the poor get poorer (Stanovich, 1986). This could be a motivation to ensure that all students have access to computers with

Standards and Literacy

Finding Resources

There is a tendency in some areas of the country to limit what is taught to only the standards that are assessed. As you think about how to motivate students and engage them in becoming independent learners, ensure that your classroom activities are rich in complexity and challenge and continue to broaden children's interest in and understanding of the world. There are ways to achieve these goals while meeting most states' standards. You will need to think carefully about what you know about students' motivation and ways of learning so that your classroom is both structured and goal oriented and also stimulating to all students. Many positive resources have been developed to help teachers implement the state standards. You saw one example in the vignette about Marguerite, a Pennsylvania teacher, at the beginning of this chapter. The integrated unit on community biography comes with a rich set of resources for teachers to use in making this unit come alive. You need to find the resources and support available in the state in which you teach and within your school district and use them well.

focused purposes so that even the least affluent have opportunities to sample the wealth of information on the Net.

As noted earlier, boys are much more likely to experience difficulties in learning to read than girls are. A helpful source of ideas for boys, and for other identifiable groups of children, is the List category on the Amazon Web site (**www.amazon.com**), which recently included a Gross-Out Books for Boys list. Among the irreverent books listed there were *Dragon's Fat Cat* (Dragon Tales); *Pigs Aplenty, Pigs Galore!*; *Dogzilla*; *Kat Kong*; *Captain Underpants Boxed Set* (Four Books and a Whoopie Cushion); and *Dog Breath: The Horrible Trouble with Hally Tosis*.

Teachers need to know the community of which they are a part and respect the values parents hold. Always check with other teachers and the school librarian, when there is one, before recommending any books. The lists of books recommended by the International Reading Association, the National Council of Teachers of English, and the American Library Association are good places to start. Give a book you are unsure of to some parents to review as a way of gauging their feelings. Usually, when people read the books that might be in question, the concerns dissipate.

Implications of Current Assessment Practices for Diverse Learners

Tests and Standards

In recent years, calls for increased accountability of schools for academic achievement have resulted in a number of reforms, some with positive outcomes and some with negative ones. In almost all states, standards for reading achievement have been established, usually according to expectations for grade level. Some states have also established standards for English-language proficiency. The establishment of standards can be a positive step in that teachers, school administrators, and the school board are provided with a clear vision of what children should accomplish. Schools are held accountable for meeting children's needs. Tests are developed and adopted to assess progress in achieving established standards. But some states even adopt the dubious practice of financially rewarding schools and districts that are successful and penalizing those that are not.

Because of the priority placed on standards and the assessments derived from them, teachers need to be familiar with the standards in their states and know how their districts have designed the instructional program to reflect those standards and benchmarks. Teachers also need to review the state assessment tests and become familiar with what will be asked of students when they have to take these tests. The more teachers can help students feel comfortable with the language used in the state programs and the format of testing, the less they have to focus on specific lessons targeted to outcomes or do practice testing. It is helpful to think through your own experiences and ideas with state or professional standards and assessments because parents will also probably involve you in conversations about them. Both positive and negative outcomes are associated with the standards and assessment movement. Positive outcomes of such practices include a clear focus on educational goals; staff development based on those goals; high motivation to improve; and the provision of data to support changes in curriculum, staff development, instructional materials, and funding. Negative outcomes include extraordinary pressure to raise test scores at all costs, dishonesty in testing programs in some areas, instruction focused on fragments of language instead of on reading connected text, and narrowing and dilution of the curriculum to teach only what is tested.

McPhail (2005) makes a very compelling recommendation about teaching African American children to read and write. He expresses his concern about teaching low-level, basic skills and in that way placing what he calls a ceiling on their learning, however unintended. He sees great danger in the current practice of aligning the curriculum directly to the test and then teaching to the test.

Effects of a Diluted Curriculum

With respect to the last outcome, a particular concern relates to the development of students' vocabulary. When areas of the curriculum are eliminated because they are viewed as less important, students are deprived of the rich vocabulary associated with these areas. In this way, the more school-dependent students are deprived of a key tool in their own learning: vocabulary knowledge. Their knowledge of vocabulary is limited by the elimination of areas of the curriculum that are sometimes viewed as less important than reading and mathematics, and sometimes even as frills.

There are two important aspects of vocabulary development for English language learners and speakers of African American Vernacular English. One is the richness—or, often, the lack of richness—of the language that surrounds them. Students become familiar with the meanings of words when those meanings are highly contextualized, not when they are studied as isolated vocabulary words. It follows, then, that a richer language environment should result in increased exposure to contextualized vocabulary and therefore to understanding of their meanings. Teachers are often obligated to cut back or even eliminate instruction for these students, however, in the very areas of the curriculum where new vocabulary words will be offered in the most highly contextualized ways, such as science, social studies, art, music, physical education, and health. Teachers must ensure that these areas of the curriculum are present for at-risk students and presented in such a way that contextualized exposure to a rich vocabulary is promoted, including such strategies as cooperative learning, problem solving, and critical thinking.

In a related vein, Nagy, Anderson, and Herman (1987) found that a major factor in vocabulary development by third-, fifth-, and seventh-grade students was the sheer volume of reading that students did and the amount of vocabulary they were exposed to, even though the proportion of words learned was low. Stanovich (1986) elaborates this idea further in his treatment of individualized differences and the Matthew effect, the idea that those who read more (the rich) read better (get richer). Smith (1986) has added that good readers read, and poor readers take tests and do drill sheets.

This chapter considered the social and cultural contexts of literacy for children in grades K through 8. Different social and cultural groups have views of literacy that reflect their own realities and needs, which might vary from the mainstream view. It is important to acknowledge the validity of the various views of literacy as instruction is planned for children from these social and cultural groups.

Teachers can often create their own cultures of literacy within their classrooms by the way they value those points of view and by the way they organize the physical environment of the classroom and select instructional materials and trade books for their students. A shared literacy environment creates the most effective tone for extending literacy to all.

To involve parents and extended families in our shared literacy community, teachers must begin early in the school year with communications that welcome families to the classroom and request their support for classroom efforts. Teachers should also become a part of the professional community through induction activities, professional meetings, and involvement in major professional organizations in our field, such as the International Reading Association and the National Council of Teachers of English.

Because of the diversity that is found in U.S. schools today, it is the rare classroom in which the children all come from a single cultural, ethnic, or linguistic group. A typical classroom in the coming years will have children from several cultures and ethnic groups; most will have some children who speak another language at home, usually Spanish. Most classrooms will have mainstreamed children with special needs for at least part of the school day. This diversity can be viewed as a problem, but a more healthy viewpoint is to appreciate the richness of the diversity and use it as an asset in teaching.

This diversity also provides many challenges for teachers. They must be aware of cultural differences far beyond holidays and foods. Aspects of nonverbal communication are particularly important in determining how teachers relate to their students and their families. Teachers will encounter children who speak another language or dialect of English at home and who might not be able to communicate effectively in standard American English in the classroom; recent demographic trends indicate that teachers who have not yet encountered these children in their classrooms will find them there soon.

It is clear that many children struggle to learn to read in our classrooms. Some of them are at risk of failure because of environmental factors, such as living in low-income inner-city or rural areas and coming from ethnic or linguistic minority groups. It is sometimes tempting to address the needs of these children with one-size-fits-all approaches to literacy instruction, but their strengths and needs vary greatly, and so should the programs that are provided to teach them to read and write. Some children struggle with reading because of cognitive, affective, and psychomotor factors. Teachers must be flexible about children with needs for accommodations that are new to them and also to the need to work closely with colleagues from special education so that these children can have a school experience that is as similar to that of most students as possible.

In addition, it is necessary to find print materials for children to read that are interesting and culturally appropriate for them. Children need to see themselves in what they read. They need large numbers of books and other sources of text at many levels. This includes access to computer technology resources and the Internet for the children from many groups who have very limited access to technology.

Finally, assessment is important for planning instruction, selecting instructional materials, and making adjustments in our instruction when needed. But it is also necessary to be cautious about letting assessment become the tail that wags the dog. Assessment should emerge from the curriculum, which should in turn emerge from the needs of students and the standards established by state and local governing authorities.

For Your Journal

1. Now that you have read Chapter 2, return to the Anticipation Guide at the beginning of the chapter. What differences are there in how you would answer the open-ended questions now?

2. The true-false questions in the Anticipation Guide addressed many myths about the demographics of children in our schools and about children's learning. After you read and found answers to the questions, which one(s) surprised you the most? Why?

Taking It to the World

Now that you have considered the implications of classroom diversity, think about your classmates when you were in the third grade. In terms of diversity, how does the student population of the classroom to which you are assigned now compare to that of your own third-grade classroom? Make a list of positive outcomes that the children of today exhibit as a result of the increased classroom diversity they experience.

Technology Connections

1. Literacy Access Online offers connections to book and electronic initiatives for literacy access, including assistive devices and low-vision aides for the impaired. Visit their Web site at **http://chd.gse.gmu.edu/LiteracyAccess/prototype/resources/** and explore at least two of the listed resources. What is the primary focus of each site, and how might each help you as a teacher?

2. Visit the "Guys Read" Web site (**www.guysread.com**), a Web site that focuses on supporting boys' reading. How does this Web site help to encourage guys to explore connections to feelings through reading? Identify three books recommended by other guys as appropriate for early readers.

Connect with Research

Review the following key words from the chapter and then connect to Research Navigator (**www.researchnavigator.com**) through this book's Companion Website to conduct a search into research on each of the various topics as they relate to reading and literacy education today.

at-risk students
background knowledge
bicultural
bilingual education

English language
  learner
gifted
immersion instruction

paralanguage
scaffolding
zone of proximal
  development

Companion Website

To access chapter objectives, practice tests, weblinks, and flashcards, visit the Companion Website at www.ablongman.com/templeallchildren2e.

Go to Allyn & Bacon's MyLabSchool (www.mylabschool.com), enter Assignment ID CRV5 into the Assignment Finder. Watch the video, *Teaching to Diverse Learners,* in which a teacher discusses and demonstrates various techniques for improving reading comprehension with a diverse population of students.

Question: What are some of the ways to teach reading to students of various abilities? You may also answer the questions at the end of the clip and e-mail your responses to your instructor.

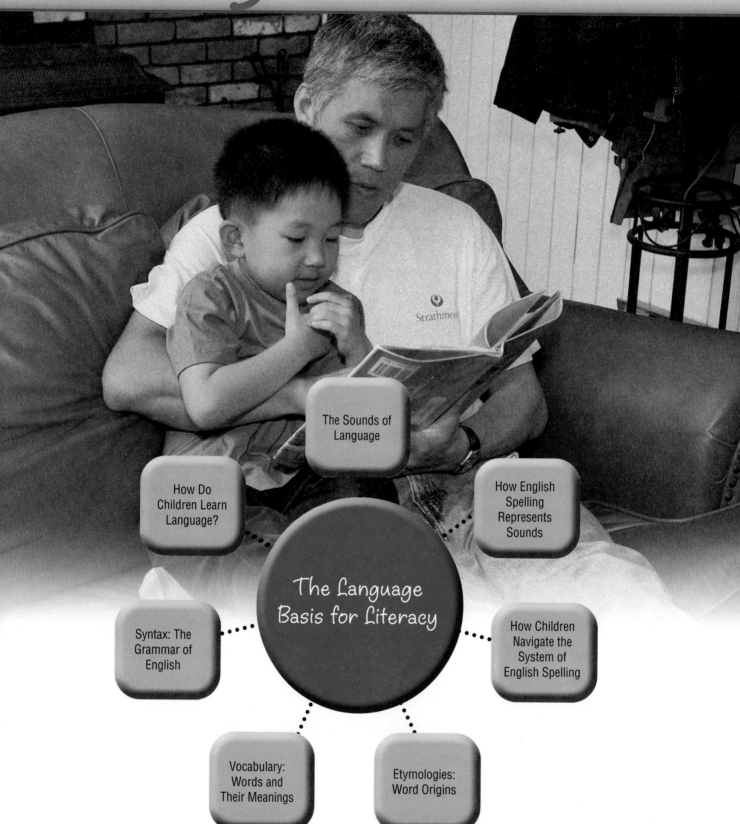

chapter 3

The Sounds of Language

How Do Children Learn Language?

How English Spelling Represents Sounds

The Language Basis for Literacy

Syntax: The Grammar of English

How Children Navigate the System of English Spelling

Vocabulary: Words and Their Meanings

Etymologies: Word Origins

The Language Basis for Literacy

Anticipation Guide

The following statements will stimulate your thinking about the topics of this chapter. Answer true or false in response to each statement. As you read and learn more about the topics in these statements, double-check your answers. See what interests you and what prompts your curiosity toward more understanding.

_____ ● You study French to learn about the French language and Spanish to learn about the Spanish language. The study of languages in general is known as linguistics.

_____ ● Chinese has an ideographic writing system; written characters relate to ideas. English has a syllabic writing system; written characters relate to spoken syllables. And Japanese has an alphabetic writing system; alphabetic letters relate to small sound units called phonemes.

_____ ● Over the centuries, the pronunciation of English sometimes has changed more than the writing system. Many English words are spelled the way they used to be pronounced.

_____ ● Morphemes can only be purchased with a prescription from licensed pharmacies.

_____ ● Rimes and phonogram patterns are the same thing.

_____ ● The words *elect* and *college* are related to each other. Both came from a Latin word meaning "to choose."

_____ ● Vocabulary words face two ways: they are a record of what you have learned in the past, and they enable you to learn more in the future.

_____ ● Syntax, also called grammar, cannot be learned without direct instruction.

_____ ● We usually think of grammar at the level of sentences, but longer texts like stories have grammar, too.

_____ ● There is remarkably little variation in the amount of language that is directed to children in families from different socioeconomic groups.

What Does Linguistics Have to Do with Early Reading?

Janet Reardon feels lucky to have been assigned to this second-grade class for her observation period. She will be student teaching next fall, and she has filled a notebook with ideas she can use. Her cooperating teacher is Alan Parsons. He is exciting to watch with children and he is also generous with his time and ad-

vice, especially when Janet asks him about topics she has been studying at the university in her literacy class.

Last Friday she asked him how he assesses phonemic awareness.

"Yes, I do use the Yopp-Singer phonemic awareness test from time to time. You should try it out yourself. But the

truth is, I can tell a lot about how a child is coming along in phonemic awareness by looking at her invented spelling."

"How?"

"For instance, when a child strings a lot of letters in a line without any obvious connection to sounds, I don't expect the child to have a concept of word or much in the way of phonemic awareness. But if a child writes down a few letters for a word—what is called 'early phonetic' spelling—you can be pretty sure that she has started to be aware of phonemes."

"Why? What does the spelling tell you?"

"Reading is talk written down," teachers say, and in many ways the statement is true. In order to read, children and young people need to know the language that print represents. And in order to teach reading well, you need to understand children's talk—children's language. The study of language, as distinct from the study of any particular language such as Japanese or Spanish, is known as **linguistics**. We don't need to cover the field of linguistics to any great depth; just to pay attention to those parts of language that matter the most in learning to read. The key ways that reading and writing depend on oral language are these:

- **Sounds of language,** how they are made and how they relate to each other
- **The spelling system,** how language is represented in print
- **Vocabulary,** the ways that words convey meaning
- **Morphology or word structure,** the ways words are made
- **Syntax,** the grammar of sentences
- **Story and discourse structure,** the way texts are constructed
- **Pragmatics,** the way language is used
- **Learning processes**—the ways language is acquired by children

"He has to be. For a kid to invent spellings, he has to be able to break a word down into its phonemes, and then match each one of those phonemes with a letter. But there's more."

"There always is."

"You'll get used to it. When she uses 'letter name spelling' when she writes, we know she's further along in phonemic segmentation. What's more, you can get an idea of what she knows about letter-to-sound correspondences from her early spelling. Look at this spelling: *HAK MIK*."

"Hack Mick"?

"No. '*Check mark.*' That's what Andrea said when she read it back to me. She's pretty far along in phonemic segmentation. See? She spelled the beginning consonant sound, the vowel, and the final consonant on both words. But you can see from the spelling that she doesn't have a clue about digraph consonants yet—see that /ĉ/ for the "ch" sound? So her invented spelling is a good indication not only of her phonemic segmentation, but also of what she knows about letter-to-sound correspondences."

"Amazing."

"Totally. Go back and tell your classmates to pay attention to linguistics. Especially to phonology."

"What's that?"

"That's for you to find out. Have a great weekend."

The Sounds of Language

You often hear reading experts talk about letter-to-sound relationships, but do you think about what those sounds are? If the language is Chinese, the sounds are not sounds at all, but ideas. The same written character is rendered into different words, depending on the dialect of Chinese that one speaks. Hence, the Chinese writing system is called *ideographic—ideo* from the Greek word for idea, and *graph* from the Greek word for written. Chinese *ideographic* (ideas written down) writing differs from *logographic* ("words written down") writing because each character stands for an idea and not a spoken word (see Figure 3.1).

If the language we spoke were Japanese, the written characters would mostly represent spoken syllables. Each character that represented a consonant would also represent a vowel. Each consonant and vowel combination (such as *ka, ki, ke, ko,* and *ku*) gets a different graphic character. Hence the Japanese writing system is *syllabic*, although Japanese does use some ideographic characters, called *kanji*, for content words (see Figure 3.2).

FIGURE 3.1

Chinese Ideographs.

愛	財	德	吉	美
Love	Wealth	Virtue	Lucky	Beautiful

FIGURE 3.2

Japanese Hiragana, Syllabic Characters.

sa	shi	su	se	so
さ	し	す	せ	そ
ta	chi	tsu	te	to
た	ち	つ	て	と
na	ni	nu	ne	no
な	に	ぬ	ね	の

The English language represents sounds at a level that is one step finer than syllables. Alphabet letters represent individual *phonemes*, small pieces of vowel or consonant sounds. Phonemes are the three sounds that make up the word *cat*—/k/, /æ/, and /t/.

If English used ideographs instead of letters of the alphabet, we would need to learn *a half million* characters for all the words in the *Oxford English Dictionary*, which is the language's largest. If English used a syllabary instead of an alphabet, we would still need to learn around 2,700 characters to represent all of our words (Barker, 2006). Because we use an alphabet, we can get by with twenty-six characters, or fifty-two, counting uppercase and lowercase letters. That's a big advantage. But there is a price to pay.

Matching a graphic image with an idea is easily done. Even animals can do it: That is why cut-out profiles of chicken hawks keep sparrows away from plate glass windows. Small children recognize the logos of their favorite soft drinks and fast foods. Matching characters with syllables is harder, but still not so very difficult. Even illiterate adults can do it (Morias & Alegria, 1987). And middle school students with severe disabilities can be fairly easily taught to read syllabaries (Gleitman & Rozin, 1973). But reading alphabetic writing—matching a character with a single speech sound at the level of a phoneme—is far more challenging. Many children struggle to separate out phonemes in words, and this difficulty causes problems in reading words (Snow, Burns, & Griffin, 1998). That is why we say that the economy of having relatively few graphic symbols in our writing system comes at the price of having to look at smaller bits of language. Teachers can help children cope with the difficulties if they themselves become familiar with some of the details of the spelling system of English.

PHONICS and PHONOLOGICAL AWARENESS

How do we make the two kinds of phonemes: vowels and consonants?

Phonology: The Sounds of English

Because English is an *alphabetic language*, words are presented by matches between small speech sounds or **phonemes** and letters of the alphabet. So let's take a closer look at how we make the two kinds of phonemes: **vowels** and **consonants**.

HOW ENGLISH VOWELS ARE MADE.　Vowel sounds are the sounds you produce when you vibrate your vocal cords and breathe across them. But what makes the difference between one vowel sound and another? That is, what are you doing when you produce the sound of "*eeee*" as opposed to "*ahhh*"? Say those two sounds aloud, one at a time. The answer is in how and where you hold your tongue in your mouth while you breathe past your vibrating vocal cords. The sound of "*eeee*" is made with the tongue high in the front of the mouth, while the sound of "*ahhh*" is made with the tongue low in the back of the mouth. But there is more.

Vowels: Long and short or tense and lax?   Teachers use the terms *long* and *short* to refer to the sounds represented by the letter *i* in *kite* (a long vowel sound) and the sound represented by the letter *i* in *kit* (a short vowel sound). But those terms do not really describe what you do when you make those sounds.

Say *feet* and *fit* aloud and stretch out the vowels as you pronounce them. Notice what your mouth does when you say each. If you can't tell the difference, then poke your finger firmly into the muscle under your jaw and say them again, very slowly. This time you should feel your tongue muscle tense up when you say the vowel in *feet* and relax when you say the vowel in *fit*. Because of the tensing and relaxing of the tongue muscle when you make the sound of *ee* and *ih*, linguists call these vowels *tense* (for the long vowel sound) and *lax* (for the short vowel sound).

The sounds of the vowels in <u>*fee*</u>*t* and <u>*fi*</u>*t* might seem completely unrelated, but that wasn't always true. During the fourteenth century, the time when Geoffrey Chaucer wrote *The Canterbury Tales*, the vowel sounds of *ee* and *ih* were spelled with the same letter. So were the vowel sounds *ay* and *eh*. These sounds, linguists would say, are tense and lax variations of each other.

But after Chaucer's time, the way people pronounced English words changed, so the vowel sound that used to be pronounced *ay* changed its pronunciation to *ee*, but the sound that was pronounced *eh* stayed the same. Also, the sound that had been pronounced *ee* was pronounced *iy* (as in *my*), while the sound that had been pronounced *ih* stayed the same. Those changes resulted in the situation we have today. Now the letters *a*, *e*, and *i* each represent pairs of sounds that do not sound much like each other, and that is because the pronunciation of the tense vowels changed, but the pronunciation of the lax vowels did not. This change is so important in the history of the English language that it has earned a name with capital letters: the **Great Vowel Shift**.

The results of the Great Vowel Shift cause confusion when young children try to discover how to spell vowel sounds. Children find it natural to spell the sounds of *ay* and *eh* with the same letter, and also to spell the sounds of *ee* and *ih* with the same letter, so they tend to write spellings like *MI FEH ES RAD* for "My fish is red." We will say more about this in Chapter 4 of this book in the discussion of **invented spelling**. Reading English vowels is also puzzling to speakers of many other languages, especially Spanish, Portuguese, French, Italian, and Romanian, where vowels are grouped the way they were in Middle English, before the Great Vowel Shift.

Diphthongs and monophthongs.   Listen to the vowels in *smooth* and *boil*. *Smooth* contains a single vowel sound and *boil* contains a double vowel sound. The technical term for a single vowel sound is **monophthong,** and for a double vowel sound it is **diphthong**. The vowel sounds in *out* and *soil* are diphthongs.

HOW ENGLISH CONSONANTS ARE MADE.   We saw before that vowels are produced when you vibrate your vocal cords while you are breathing out. Consonants are made when the flow of breath is interrupted in some way. There are many ways to interrupt the breath flow. If you stop the flow momentarily, you produce what are called *stop consonants*, such as the sounds represented by *p, b, d, t, k*, and *g*. If you buzz the breath slightly, you produce the *fricative consonants* represented by the letters *s, z, th, f*, and *v*. If you stop the air flow and then hiss it, you get *affricate consonants*, such as the sounds represented by the letters *ch* and *j*. And if you direct the airflow out through the nose, you get *nasal consonants*, such as the sounds represented by the letters *m, n*, and *ng*.

Which consonant sound you produce depends on two more things: where in the mouth you produce the interruption and whether the vocal cords are vibrating when you make it.

Let's illustrate. If you stop the airflow through your mouth with the back of the tongue raised against the top of the mouth toward the rear, you get the sound of *g* or *k*. If your vocal cords are vibrating while you do it, you get the sound of *g*. If they are not vibrating, you get the sound of *k*. Similarly, *b* and *p* are made by closing the lips. The *b* sound is *voiced* (that is, the vocal cords vibrate the whole time it is made), and *p* sound is *unvoiced* (the vocal cords don't start vibrating until forty thousandths of a second after you start producing the sound).

Teachers of primary grades should be aware of the ways speech sounds are made, because as children begin to experiment with spelling, you will see that they listen very carefully to speech sounds and their similarities, even when they can't talk about what they are hearing. For example, young children often spell the sound represented by *th* with the letter *v*. It helps to know that the name of the letter *v* is a buzzed (fricative) and voiced sound that's made in the front of the mouth, just as is the sound *th* in *then*. (The only difference is that the sound of *v* is made with the upper teeth on the lower lip, and the *th* sound in *then* is made with the tongue on the fleshy ridge behind the upper front teeth.)

Consonant blends and consonant digraphs.   **Consonant blends** are two or more consonants pronounced closely together, like the first two letters in *slip*, the first three letters in *split*, and the last two letters in *help*. In these words, each of the consonants can be heard distinctly if you pronounce the word slowly.

Consonant digraphs are single consonant sounds that are spelled with two letters. The beginning consonant sounds in *then*, *chip*, and *shirt* are consonant digraphs. (The word *digraph* comes from two Greek words meaning double writing.) To repeat, the difference between blends and digraphs is that in consonant blends, each of two or more consonant letters can be pronounced distinctly, but the two consonant letters in digraphs cannot be pronounced separately without distorting the words in which they occur.

Why do we have digraph consonants in English? They came about because the Roman alphabet, originally built to represent the sounds of Latin, was used to write English. But English had some sounds that did not occur in Latin. The Roman alphabet had no letters to stand for the English sounds of /sh/, /ch/, or /th/. To indicate when those sounds were intended by writers, early scribes came up with the convention of writing an *h* after certain Roman letters: *sh*, *ch*, and *th*. The spelling of *wh*, though, is a strange exception. The sound represented by *wh* is really a consonant blend and not a digraph: You really do hear two consonant sounds but the sounds are heard as *hw*, which is the reverse of how they are written. *HW* is the way that sound was originally spelled, until scribes in the twelfth and thirteenth centuries reversed the order of the letters, to make them look like *ch*, *sh*, and *th*. Findings like these were brought to us by linguists (see the World of Reading box).

Consonants and phonological awareness.   The recognition that spoken words consist of phonemes is called *phonemic awareness*. Phonemic awareness normally shows up in late kindergarten and early first grade (Goswami, 2000). However, some children have trouble with **phonological awareness** even into the first and second grades, and this difficulty can complicate learning to read. Why is phonemic awareness challenging for children? It is probably because words cannot be spoken so slowly that all of their phonemes are distinctly audible. If you tape-record someone reading the word *cat* into a microphone, you cannot cut the tape into segments in which each phoneme can be recognized. The vowel can be recognized by itself, but the consonant can be identified only when it is pronounced together with a vowel. That's not surprising, really. The term *consonant* comes from two Latin words, *sonare* (to sound) and *con-* (together).

Adults and older children know that the phonemes exist in words, but you know it by inference rather than direct perception. You know it because you can substitute a /b/ phoneme for the /k/ phoneme in *cat* and get *bat*, and you can substitute an /n/ phoneme for the /t/ phoneme and get *can*. Once you began to read, you saw that letters tend to be matched with phonemes in words such as *cat*, and that reinforced the idea that phonemes can be heard separately. But a young learner without that experience in reading is often challenged by the task of separating or *segmenting* phonemes in words.

TEACH IT! 15

Making and Breaking Words

Bring on the Linguists!

Scholars of linguistics have contributed a great deal to our knowledge of reading and writing. For instance, Professor Catherine Snow of the Harvard Graduate School of Education, has authored many important works on children's language development in home and school settings. She chaired the National Research Council that produced the influential work, *Preventing Reading Difficulties in Young Children* (Snow et al., 1998).

Charles Read, who trained in linguistics at the Massachusetts Institute of Technology, is often credited with bringing to light the fascinating practice of invented spelling in children (Read, 1975).

But Read had a great deal of help from another linguist and educator, Carol Chomsky (1971). Carol Chomsky's husband, Noam Chomsky, is the most influential linguist of the past century, and he, too, has contributed to our thinking about children's word recognition and comprehension—especially the idea that there are processes occurring "beneath the surface" of children's understanding of written language.

Michael Halliday, a linguist from Scotland, charted his son's use of **functions of language**, and contributed a very useful menu of ways to help children develop their ability to communicate, and later to read.

One more point: We are not saying children cannot hear the phonemes. Of course they can. Most English-speaking three-year-olds can correctly show you the _cat_ and show you the _bat_. It's the comparatively artificial task of saying slowly the three sounds in *cat* that many children find difficult.

Developmental Milestones in Phonological Awareness

Hall and Moats (1999) present the following as the phonological abilities of normally developing children in kindergarten and first grade:

At the end of kindergarten

- At the syllable level: Most children can distinguish single-syllable words from words with two syllables when they hear them.
- At the onset and rime level: Most children can match a target word with a rhyming word.
- At the phoneme level: Most children can pick out words that begin with the same sound as a target word and can tell you the odd word out, the one that does not begin with the same sound as the others.

Two months into first grade

- Given two letters on cards, most children can combine them and pronounce the word they spell (*in, on, at, it, up*)
- Given a three-phoneme word, most children can say the word that is left when the beginning consonant is deleted: *bat/at, sit/it, cup/up*.

By the end of first grade

- Most children can pronounce two-phoneme words slowly and separate the phonemes: /t/ - /oo/; /b/ - /y/.
- Given longer words, most children can leave off the first consonant and pronounce what is left: *b/utterfly*.
- Given three isolated phonemes, most children can combine them to make a word: /s/ /æ/ /t/ = *sat*.

Syllables, Onsets, and Rimes

Syllables are rhythmic pulses in words. The word *final* has two of them, *fi* and *nal*, while *awareness* has three: *a + ware + ness*. In the example of the word *awareness*, you can see that a vowel can stand alone as a syllable but consonants cannot (at least not in English). Some languages such as Spanish, Japanese, and Kiswahili have relatively few syllables. In Spanish, roughly fifty different syllables can be combined to make most of the words in the language. The English language, however, is made up of perhaps 2,750 different syllables (Barker, 2006). Few teachers of English would bother to have students learn groups of syllables, as teachers of Spanish, Portuguese, and Kiswahili regularly do.

English syllables can be open or closed. An *open syllable* ends in a vowel, and a *closed syllable* ends in a consonant. All three syllables in *banana* are open syllables, and both syllables in *problem* are closed syllables. When these words are divided at the end of a line of print, the hyphen goes after the vowel in words with open syllables like *final* (*fi-nal*) and *recess* (*re-cess*), and after the consonant in words like *picnic* (*pic-nic*) and *knapsack* (*knap-sack*). The vowel in an open syllable often has its long sound, and the vowel in a closed syllable usually has its short sound. Compare *cable* and *cabin*, *meter* and *metric*, *human* and *humble*, *open* and *offer*.

Syllables can be broken into smaller units that Rebecca Trieman (1985) has called **onsets** and **rimes**. The onset is the initial consonant sound of a syllable, if there is one; and the rime is the vowel plus any consonant sound that comes after it. For example, in *cat*, the sound of *c* is the onset and the sound of *at* is the rime. But *at* only has a rime. Children who have experienced playing with onsets and rimes—which is what we do when we recite nursery rhymes—have been shown to have an easier time learning to read words (Bradley & Bryant, 1985).

Rimes are also known as *phonogram patterns*. They are the rhyming portions of families of words such as *bug, dug, rug, tug,* and *mug*. As it turns out, the English language makes repeated use of a relatively limited set of phonogram patterns or rimes. Wylie and Durrell (1970) found a group of thirty-seven phonogram patterns that make up many hundreds of English words (see Table 3.1).

Because English has these common phonogram patterns, children who learn a few words with a given pattern can easily read and spell words that share that pattern. The activities such as word sorting and word making help children work with phonogram patterns. You will read about those and other related activities in Chapter 4.

TEACH IT! 15

Making and Breaking Words

TABLE 3.1

Phonogram Patterns, or Rimes

b<u>ack</u>	m<u>eat</u>	n<u>ice</u>	cl<u>ock</u>	d<u>uck</u>
m<u>ail</u>	b<u>ell</u>	st<u>ick</u>	j<u>oke</u>	r<u>ug</u>
r<u>ain</u>	cr<u>est</u>	w<u>ide</u>	sh<u>op</u>	j<u>ump</u>
c<u>ake</u>		l<u>ight</u>	st<u>ore</u>	j<u>unk</u>
s<u>ale</u>		<u>ill</u>	n<u>ot</u>	
g<u>ame</u>		w<u>in</u>		
pl<u>an</u>		l<u>ine</u>		
b<u>ank</u>		br<u>ing</u>		
tr<u>ap</u>		th<u>ink</u>		
cr<u>ash</u>		tr<u>ip</u>		
c<u>at</u>		f<u>it</u>		
pl<u>ate</u>				
s<u>aw</u>				
st<u>ay</u>				

How English Spelling Represents Sounds

Sometimes on a grocery store intercom you may hear advertisements for learning aids that promise to "teach your child to read simply by showing how letters spell sounds." The ads are usually accompanied by happy music and cheerful voices. But the relationship between letters and sounds in English is not a simple matter. Unlike languages such as Finnish and Spanish, in which the relationships between letters and sounds is nearly one-to-one, in English writing a single letter may relate to several different sounds, and a single sound may be spelled several different ways. For that reason, we say Spanish and Finnish have **shallow orthographies** and English has a **deep orthography** (Katz & Feldman, 1981). An orthography is a spelling system. A shallow orthography is a system that relates letters to sounds in a straightforward way—one letter usually represents one sound and one sound is usually spelled by one letter. A deep orthography has complications that keep letters from representing sounds in a straightforward way.

Vowels in English have much variation between letter and sound. First, there are long and short pronunciations. The short vowel sounds are spelled most consistently as in *get*, *got*, *fit*, *cut*, and *cat*. The long vowel sounds are spelled many different ways (note the way the long *a* sound is spelled in *way*, *straight*, *bait*, *fate*, *weigh*, and *fiancée*). But there are also combinations of vowels that produce different diphthongs—two vowel sounds run together—as in *brow* and *oil*.

Consonants in English are pronounced more consistently than vowels.

- Consonants *d, f, j, k, m, p, r, t, v,* and *z* are nearly always pronounced only one way each (although *f* sounds like *v* in *of*).
- *B* is usually pronounced as in *bet*, although it is silent in a few words like *debt*, *doubt*, and *subtle*.
- *C* and *g* have both hard and soft sounds. *C* can sound like /k/ in *cat* or like /s/ in *cent*. *G* can sound like /g/ in *gun* or like /j/ in *gentle*.
- *H* usually has the sound /h/ as in *hot*, although it is silent in *oh*, *ah*, and *honest*, and it forms part of a digraph—a single consonant sound formed by two letters—(see page 76) in *chip*, *ship*, and *thin*.
- *K* is usually pronounced /k/ as in *kit*, although it is silent in *knife* and *knot*.
- *L* is usually pronounced /l/ as in *loose*, but it is silent in *half* and *salmon*.
- *N* is usually pronounced /n/ as in *not*, but it combines with *g* to form a digraph in *sing* and *long*.
- *Q* is always followed by *u*, and together they have the /kw/ sound of *quick* or the /k/ sound of *unique*.
- *S* usually has the /s/ sound as in *sun*, but it also has the /z/ sound in *eyes*.

The letters *w* and *y* are called *semivowels* because they can function as consonants at the beginning of a word (for example, *way* and *year*), but can form diphthongs with other vowels in words such as *now* and *boy* to make vowel sounds. The *w* is silent in *whole* and *answer*, but it is also used in the consonant blend /hw/ that is spelled the reverse of the way it sounds (*wh*) in *which*, *where*, and *whirl*.

Complications in the English Spelling System

Here are the most important complications in the relationships between letters and sounds:

- Long and short sounds of vowels and systems for marking them
- Soft and hard sounds of consonants and systems for marking them
- Consonant blends and consonant digraphs
- Reduced vowels

- Family connections between words
- Historical oddities in spelling
- Syllables, onsets, and rimes
- Homophones and homographs
- Loan words

MARKING VOWELS LONG AND SHORT.   Teachers often tell children, "When two vowels go walking, the first one does the talking." That is often true, because the second vowel in words like *coat*, *boat*, *beat*, and *seat* is often a silent letter that indicates the sound of the first vowel is long. This rule works even when a single consonant comes before the first and second vowels, especially if the second vowel is *e*, *i*, or *y*, as in *wade*, *trading*, and *spicy*. A silent *gh* is another marker for long vowels, as in *high* and *fight*. However, this rule does not hold true for words like *look*, *eight*, *tool*, and *trout*, which account for more than half the words with pairs of vowels in them (Clymer, 1996).

In words like *get* and *it*, a single vowel coming before a consonant with no letter after it usually has its short sound. English has grammatical endings like *-ed*, *-er*, and *-ing* that would mark the preceding vowel long if something weren't done to insulate the preceding vowel from the lengthening effect of the following vowel. So words like *bat* and *fib* double their final consonants before adding the endings *-ed*, *-er*, and *-ing*: *batted*, *batter*, and *fibbing*.

MARKING CONSONANTS SOFT AND HARD.   The consonants *c* and *g* change their pronunciations between hard sounds and soft sounds. In *rag*, the *g* has its hard sound, but the following *e* (or *i* or *y*) indicates that its sound is soft in *raging*, *cagy*, and *paged*. If a word has the soft *g* sound before the vowels *a*, *o*, or *u*, the consonant is usually *j*: *jam*, *jog*, and *jug*. If a word has the soft *g* sound at the end of a word, the *g* usually occurs in the cluster *dge*, as in *badge*, *ridge*, and *fudge*. If a word has the hard *g* sound before *e* or *i*, the *g* is usually flowed by *u*: *guide*, *guitar*, *guilty*.

The sound of the letter *c* is soft when it is followed by *e*, *i*, or *y*. So we have *cent*, *dice*, and *lacy*. The sound of the letter *c* is usually hard when it comes before *a*, *o*, or *u*, as in *cat*, *cot*, and *cut*. A word normally does not end in *c* in the English language, so the hard *c* sound is spelled *ck* in *pack*, *pick*, and *lock*.

CONSONANT BLENDS AND CONSONANT DIGRAPHS.   Consonant blends, as we saw previously, are two or more consonants pronounced closely together, like the first two letters in *slip*. Consonant digraphs are single consonant phonemes that are spelled with two letters, like the beginning consonant sounds in *then*, *chip*, and *shirt*. Beginning readers are challenged to read two consonants together in consonant blends, and they may be baffled by consonant digraphs that can never be sounded out no matter how slowly they are pronounced. In their early spelling, children often write one letter for a consonant blend (writing SAP for *step*, for instance). They often write a single letter with a similar sound for a consonant digraph (writing VE for *the*, for instance).

REDUCED VOWELS.   One more thing that English speakers do with sounds that complicates reading and spelling is **vowel reduction**. In words of more than one syllable, vowels in the unstressed syllable are pronounced with an indistinct sound called *schwa*. Schwa occurs, for instance, in the second syllable of the word *fatal* and in the final syllable in *syllable*. The vowel in those unstressed syllables is reduced, and the reduction presents big difficulties to spellers. How would you spell the second syllable of *fatal*? It might be spelled *-le* as in *simple*, *-ile* as in *futile*, *-ol* as in *idol*, or *-el* as in *label*.

The trick is to think of a word related to the one with the unstressed syllable, in which the unstressed syllable is stressed. For example, you know that *simple* probably ends in *-le* if you think of the related word *simply*. You know that *futile* might end in *-ile* if you think of the related word *futility*. You know that *idol* might end in *-ol* if you think of the related word *idolatry*. For *fatal*, we can think of *fatality*.

To repeat, English has long and short vowel sounds spelled with the same letter, and also the phenomenon of vowel reduction makes us pronounce syllables with many different vowels by the same sound, schwa. It will require a fairly complicated set of rules to relate letters to sounds in English, because the sound system itself is so complicated.

MORPHOPHONEMICS: FAMILY CONNECTIONS BETWEEN WORDS. The spelling of the word *sign* makes no sense unless you consider the related words *signature* and *signal*. Then you become aware that the spelling preserves the relationship between words that have different pronunciations but common origins and related meanings and share a common **morpheme** or meaningful word part. Being aware of such morphemic or family relationships is especially useful in spelling, where the phenomenon of vowel reduction (discussed earlier) throws the spelling of unstressed syllables into doubt.

If a child is unsure how to spell the final syllable of *simple* (is it *-ol*, *-al*, *-ile*, or *-le?*), remembering the related word *simply* can provide a helpful clue. If a child is unsure of the second vowel in *photograph*, which is unstressed and reduced to schwa, it may help to remember the related word *photography*, in which that same vowel is stressed and therefore recognizable.

HISTORICAL ODDITIES. Some words defy simple spelling-to-sound relationships because of spelling changes that happened over the years. For example, many words from Anglo-Saxon with *o* before following consonants pronounce that vowel as a short *u*: *brother, mother, son, love, cover*. The letter *o* was substituted for the original letter *u* in many of those words by scribes in the tenth and eleventh centuries, to make them easier to read when they appeared in Gothic scripts (Scragg, 1974). Medieval scribes also inserted the *b* in *doubt* to make the word resemble the Latin word *dubere*, which had a related meaning.

HOMOPHONES AND HOMOGRAPHS. Mostly because of changes in pronunciation over the years, there are some pairs of different words like *deer* and *dear*, *bare* and *bear*, *waist* and *waste*, and *steer* (a bovine animal) and *steer* (to aim a car) that may have either the same or different spellings but are pronounced the same. They are called **homophones** (from *homo-*, meaning the same, and *phone*, meaning sound). **Homographs** like *lead* ("I will lead you to your table") and *lead* ("I put a lead weight on the line") have the same spellings but different pronunciations. Looking up the etymologies of homophones and homographs in a dictionary will show that these words came from different sources.

LOAN WORDS. English contains many loan words from different languages, and most of them are pronounced according to the rules of the original languages: *taco, filet, wiener, fuselage, macho, chassis*.

How Children Navigate the System of English Spelling

Invented Spelling

Understanding speech sounds and how words are constructed helps us to understand how children make sense of these sound patterns and how they incorporate that information into their reading and writing. One of the most fascinating discoveries in the past century with regard to literacy has been children's ability to invent and discover the ways in which letters represent sounds in print. This discovery of invented spelling was a natural extension of the research on children's spoken language acquisition: Children see people around them communicating in some medium (in this case, print); decide to try out their own versions of such communication; organize their versions according to rules or patterns that are logical, although incorrect by adult standards; and gradually, stage by stage, modify their strategies so they grow closer and closer to the versions they hear and see adults using.

WRITING and READING CONNECTIONS

Why should teachers of reading understand speech sounds and how words are constructed?

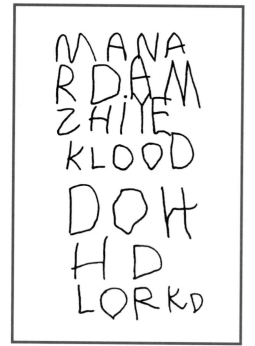

FIGURE 3.3

Prephonemic Spelling.

Jessie, Age 4

Source: Temple, Nathan, Burris, and Temple, 1992.

Sure enough, children appear to go through stages as they experiment with invented spellings for words (Gentry, 1989; Temple et al., 1992). Progress through the stages depends on two things: children's own developing concepts of how the English spelling system works (what we call their **word knowledge**) and the levels of challenge that system presents to them as they move through the grades. The stages of spelling development that we examine, modified from Gentry (1989) and Henderson (1990), are the **prephonemic** stage, the early phonetic stage, the **letter name** stage, and the **transitional** stage. Looking at children's progress through stages of invented spelling shows us a great deal about children's knowledge of words, which is important to their learning to read.

SPELLING AT THE PREPHONEMIC STAGE. When children first begin to write, they often fill entire pages with a lot of unconnected letters (see Figure 3.3). Although what the child has written has no meaning, the child has demonstrated prephonemic spelling. It is a kind of writing that uses letters without regard to their sounds. In this stage, children write down letters at random or possibly with some early notion of how they might represent ideas.

Children at the prephonemic stage of spelling know how to make many letters (and often many more pseudoletters). They know what writing looks like and might know how it is arrayed on the page. But children at this stage have not yet discovered the **alphabetic principle**: the understanding that spelling represents words by relating written letters to spoken phonemes. If this is the case, this means that much reading instruction in which children are expected to learn to recognize words by being exposed to them will not be effective yet. Neither will phonics instruction that focuses on learning particular letters and sounds, which requires an understanding of the fundamental idea that words are real, they consist of phonemes, and those phonemes are represented by letters.

SPELLING AT THE EARLY PHONEMIC STAGE. Figure 3.4 represents a child in the early phonemic stage of spelling. This child has used letters to represent some of the sounds in words but not all of them. That is why we call this stage early phonemic: The child is just beginning to represent words by their phonemes. Children at this stage typically represent only the first and last and possibly a middle consonant in the word. They usually leave out vowels unless the whole word is a vowel, such as *a*. Children who spell in the early phonemic stage sometimes spell the first sound in a word with a sensible choice of a letter, then add random letters to make the word longer and hence make it look like a word (Ferreiro & Teberosky, 1982). But note carefully what we mean by a sensible choice. When children do use letters to represent sounds, rather than to use letters for sounds in conventional ways, they spell intuitively, matching as best they can a letter with a letter name that sounds closest to the sound they want to spell. Thus, for example, they are likely to choose the letter *h* to spell /*ch*/, and the letter *y* to spell /*w*/.

If children are spelling in the early phonemic stage, we know they have discovered the alphabetic principle. They are not yet very proficient, however, at breaking words into phonemes and matching them with letter sounds. Matching letters to sounds contains at

FIGURE 3.4

Early Invented Spelling.

Daryl, Grade 1

Source: Temple, Nathan, Burris, and Temple, 1992

ILnglEADTXS

least four operations: making the word hold still in the mind, breaking it down into phonemes, matching each phoneme with a letter, and writing down that letter. All of these steps may be difficult for a beginner.

Determining the number of sounds children can represent in their spelling yields important diagnostic information. Bear in mind Ehri's hypothesis that a child's memory for storing images of written words for later recognition consists of a number of "slots" (Ehri, 1991, 1997). A child with more memory storage slots for word recognition will store a more complete memory of that word and will recognize it more accurately when seen in print. The number of slots a child has available seems to correspond to the depth to which that child can segment a word into its phonemes.

Examining a child's invented spelling is a good indication of his or her ability to segment words into phonemes. A child who writes *HK* for truck (that is, the early phonetic speller) shows a limited ability to segment phonemes in words. When it comes to recognizing words in print, that child will try to say the word on the basis of very shallow processing, typically looking at the first letter and calling out a word the child knows that begins with that letter. Because the child does not yet focus on all of the letters and phonemes in the word (Morris, 1998), he or she can easily confuse the words being read with other words that share one or two of the same letters.

SPELLING AT THE LETTER NAME STAGE. At a slightly more advanced stage, a child offers spelling like that in Figure 3.5. This child is in the **letter name stage** of spelling. Here, the child represents all or nearly all of the phonemes in a word, but does so intuitively. Logical judgments were made in choosing letters to represent sounds, but that logic still diverges quite a bit from the conventions of English spelling.

Children use names of the letters of the alphabet as if they were building blocks of sound out of which words can be constructed. In the case of some sounds, the letter name strategy results in spellings that look conventional; in others, the spellings can look bizarre. Especially in these cases, examining children's letter name spellings gives us a window into the ways children think about words and into the eccentricities of the English spelling system.

YUTS A LADE YET FEHEG AD HE KOT FLEPR

FIGURE 3.5

Letter Name Stage of Spelling.

No Name, Age 4 From Carol Chomsky.

Translation: "Once a lady went fishing and she caught Flipper."

Source: Temple, Nathan, Burris, and Temple, 1992.

- **Spelling Most Consonants.** As the sample in Figure 3.5 shows, many consonant letters are spelled intuitively in ways that look conventional. Note the use of *F, L,* and *P* in *FLEPR* (*Flipper*) and of *D* in *AD* (and). The letter *K* in *KOT* (*caught*) could be correct. The names of these letters are close enough to their corresponding phonemes to make the letter name strategy successful or nearly successful.
- **Spelling Nonintuitive Consonants.** The use of *Y* for the /w/ sound in *YUTS* (*once*) and *YET* (*went*) reveals very clearly that the child has chosen the *Y* for the sound of its name, rather than for its conventional value. But the letter name for W ("double U") doesn't sound at all like /w/, while the name of Y (wye) is close, so this choice of *Y* for the /w/ sound is not surprising for the child who is using the letter name strategy.
- **Spelling Digraph Consonants.** Young spellers are troubled by the spellings of digraphs, because they do not know about the conventions for spelling them. Note the

invented spelling of the *SH* digraph is *FEHEG* (*fishing*) and *HE* (*she*). In both cases, the letter *H* was chosen because the name of that letter sounds closest to the phoneme that is usually spelled by *sh*. The letter *h* is often used by children in the letter name stage of learning to spell the sounds of /*sh*/ and /*ch*/.

- **Spelling Ns and Ms before Stop Consonants.** As we see in the spellings of *YUTS* for *once* and *AD* for *and*, letter name spellers often leave out the letters *n* and *m* when they come before other consonants, especially before what are called **stop consonants** (so called because they briefly stop the flow of air through the mouth) such as /*p*/, /*b*/, /*t*/, /*d*/, and /*k*/. The problem is not that children don't know how to spell the /*n*/ and /*m*/ sounds. It is rather that they are used to feeling the consonants produced in the mouth as they sound out the word in order to spell it (Read, 1975). When *n* and *m* are pronounced before stop consonants, you cannot feel them in the mouth, because the tongue goes to the same position to form the stop consonant anyway. Say the words *wet* and *went* aloud, and you will see what we mean: The activity of the tongue in the mouth is the same in both cases. What is different when *n* or *m* is present is that the whole syllable is pronounced through the nose. The omission of *n* and *m* in this position is prevalent in the spellings of kindergarten and first-grade children and in older children who are advancing slowly as spellers.

- **Spelling Word-Final R, L, M, and N: "Syllabic Sonorants."** The spelling of *FLEPR* for *Flipper* shows another common feature of children's letter name spelling. Unstressed syllables ending in *r*, *l*, *m*, and *n* often lack vowels when they appear at the ends of words. Thus it is common to see *TABL* for *table*, *LEDL* for *little*, and *BIDM* for *bottom* in the writing of children in the letter name stage of spelling. English has a convention that all syllables must be spelled with vowels. Even though children in the letter name stage represent most vowels, they leave them out of these words, presumably because they expect every letter they write into a word to be clearly sounded, but in these syllables, no distinct vowel sound is heard (Read, 1975).

- **Spelling Long Vowels.** As the spelling of *a* for *a*, *LADE* for *lady*, and *HE* for *she* shows, long vowels in words usually "say their names"; that is, the sound to be spelled sounds much like the name of the letter we would use to spell that sound. As in the spelling in *LADE* for *lady*, the spelling of the second vowel makes it clear that the child intends for the *E* to "say its name."

- **Spelling Short Vowels.** Spelling short vowels presents problems to letter name spellers. As was discussed earlier, short vowels do not sound very much like the long vowels spelled by the same letter. There are no vowel letter names that have short vowel sounds so the speller must choose the letter name that is the best fit with that short vowel. This in practice is the long vowel sound that sounds the most like, or is produced in the mouth in the manner most like, that short vowel sound. This principle explains the spelling of *E* for the short vowel /ĭ/ in *fishing*. It also explains why children write A for /ĕ/ and I for /ŏ/.

Children who are letter name spellers represent nearly all of the phonemes (the smaller speech sounds) in words. But they represent those speech sounds intuitively, using a letter name strategy, rather than conventionally, using the kinds of spellings for sounds that are seen in books. Letter name spellers' ability to segment words into all of their phonemes gives them many corresponding slots in word memory storage for the parts of the words they see in print. Letter name spellers are usually beginning readers who are making progress acquiring sight words.

Letter name spellers have a means at their disposal to write many words, and children enjoy this freedom to create. Their spelling ability is still limited, of course. Because they spell words by relating letters to their individual sounds, they are not yet taking advantage of onsets and rimes and phonogram patterns. Nor are letter name spellers yet aware of the conventions for marking vowels long or short. They also are not aware of the standard spellings of grammatical endings such as *-ing* or *-ed*, which explains why *fishing* was spelled *FEHEG* in Figure 3.5.

When it comes to recognizing words, because letter name spellers look for matches between letters and phonemes, they often use a strategy that some researchers call *sophisticated guessing*. Letter name spellers try to sound out all of the letters in a word and sometimes produce bizarre readings such as /ree add/ for *read* and /lie vee/ for *live*.

Research shows that the practice of invented spelling is good for kindergarten and first-grade children. Children who are encouraged to invent spellings learn to recognize more words than do children who do not use invented spelling. But children should not persist in letter name spelling much beyond the end of first grade. To help them make progress, teachers need to be careful to remind children that invented spelling is temporary spelling, the way that they write some words before they learn the way words are spelled in books. They also need to be careful to give students correctly spelled material to read and take opportunities to call children's attention to standard spelling patterns in print.

SPELLING IN THE TRANSITIONAL STAGE. Spellers in the transitional stage are beginning readers who are becoming aware of conventional spellings for sounds. They are learning phonogram patterns (onsets and rimes) and are trying to master the marking systems for long and short vowels, although not always correctly, as seen in Figure 3.6. Transitional spellers may be keen observers of the English spelling system, and the difficulties they face in spelling correctly often reflect the eccentricities of the system. For example, transitional spellers may write LUV and ABUV. The correct spellings, *love* and *above*, thwart their expectations.

Transitional spellers have learned the common patterns of spelling, but some words don't conform because they aren't pronounced the way they are spelled, such as NACHER and GROSHRY for *nature* and *grocery*. In casual speech, we often say, "Dincha?" for "Didn't you?" The /t/ and /y/ sounds between those two words get run together as /ch/. Exactly the same thing happened to the pronunciation of *nature*, which went at some point from a pronunciation like /natyur/ to /nachr/. *Special, initial, grocery*, and many other words go through similar sound changes, which linguists call *palatalization*. It is no wonder children grapple with these phenomena!

What children who spell in the transitional stage show us, however, is that they have learned many things about the way the English writing system works, and this knowledge can help them both in writing and in reading. These children show a grasp of common onsets and rimes in their writing, indicating that they should be able to use knowledge of these patterns to read unfamiliar words. Children who are aware of onsets and rimes can see the strategy of reading by analogy. For example, if they encounter the unknown word *sill*, they can recognize its similarity to the known word *pill* and will read *sill* by mentally taking away the /p/ sound and substituting the /s/ sound in front of the *-ill* rime. Such reading by analogy leads to more rapid and accurate deciphering of words than does puzzling out words letter by letter.

Spelling in the transitional stage presents challenges, though, that many students never move beyond. A student who has learned to spell *gate*, for example, might still be unsure how to spell *great, bait, straight*, or *eight*. It will take a habit of studying words carefully plus an act of memory to master these challenges. Of course, encouragement and reminders from the teacher don't hurt! Spelling instruction should be guided by assessment.

> Stella
>
> We went to the park
> we went on a nacher
> chrl They hid The
> eggs I fond 7 eggs
> I fond candy we ate
> bobyQ we had fun
> We playd basball.

FIGURE 3.6

Spelling in the Transitional Stage.

Stella, Grade 1. Note spelling of "nature trail"

Translation: We went to the park. We went on a nature trail. They hid the eggs. I found 7 eggs. I found candy. We ate barbeque. We had fun. We played baseball.

Source: Temple, Nathan, Burris, and Temple, 1992.

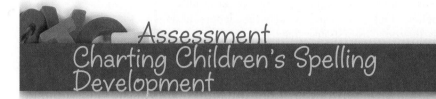

You are in your first year of teaching second grade, it's September and you know you need to find out where your children are in their spelling development. Instruction needs to get really focused, and the time is now. To do this you've already done several things.

Things Accomplished

- Started a writing workshop—children are writing nearly every day and they are using invented spelling.
- Collected several writing samples of invented spelling from each child and have written hunches about spelling on them—samples are in children's files.
- Given the children a quick five-word spelling test from my undergraduate textbook (Bear et al., 2005).

Plans

- Study the writing samples and the results of the spelling test for three to five children each night beginning on Monday and finishing the class by Friday.
- Using this assessment data write up a profile for each child making a decision about approximate spelling stage. Provide two or three reasons for the decision.
- Review the assessment profiles and organize two or three small groups according to spelling development, plan at least one data-driven lesson for the coming week for each group.

Celebrate a job well done! (Make more lesson plans, keep collecting samples.)

Morphology: How English Words Are Built

The study of the ways words are built is called **morphology**. In English, words are built in several ways. They can stand alone, like *cat*. They can be made up of two or more separate words, like *firehouse*. They can have prefixes and suffixes added to them, like *unforgettable*. And they can be built out of ancient parts, like *biology* and *biography*.

COMPOUND WORDS.   When two or more root words are combined, as in *houseboat* and *lawnmower*, they make compound words. Dictionary writers have three different ways of writing compound words:

1. *Houseboat:* Words that are frequently spoken together are joined without a space. Those words are made plural by adding *-s* at the end of the last word: *houseboats*.
2. *Mother-in-law:* Other compound words are joined with hyphens. When these words are made plural, the *-s* is added to the most important word: *mothers-in-law*.
3. *Boa constrictor:* Some words, although often said together, are written separately.

PREFIXES AND SUFFIXES.   All of us are aware that we can add an *-s* or an *-ed* or an *-ing* onto a **root word** in English to change its meaning. Those that are added before the root word are called *prefixes*, and those added after the root word are called *suffixes*. The general name for both of them is affixes. Some suffixes mark the person, number, or tense of a verb, like *fished* and *thinking*. Others mark the plural form of nouns, like *cats*. Both of these are called grammatical inflections. Other prefixes and suffixes can also change the meanings of words, like *unkind, retie, underestimate,* and *likeable*. Table 3.2 shows some prefixes and suffixes that are found in children's vocabularies.

TABLE 3.2

Prefixes and Suffixes

PREFIX	MEANING	EXAMPLES
sub-	under	submarine, subway, substandard
dis-	not	distrust, disrespect, distasteful,
mis-	not	misunderstand, misguided, mislead
inter-	between or among	interstate, international, intercity
pre-	before	preschool, pretest, preview

SUFFIX	MEANING	EXAMPLES
-er	more than	taller, shorter, quicker
-ful	containing	hopeful, wishful, bountiful
-ly	in the manner of	beautifully, miserly, shortly
-ness	state of being	goodness, highness, badness
-less	without	painless, toothless, penniless

WORDS FROM ANCIENT PARTS. Both prefixes and suffixes have forms that are less obvious and that attach to parts of words that are less obviously root words. For example, *gradual* and *annual* appear to share the suffix *-al*, that has the meaning *in the manner of*. But what do *annu-* and *grad-* mean? Both are ancient root words that came down from Latin. Annus meant *year*, and gradus meant *step*. So today, *annual* means *year by year*, and *gradual* means *step by step*. Ancient root words like these are called *historical morphemes*. A morpheme is a word or a meaningful part of a word.

There are many ancient prefixes and root words contained in thousands of English words. Most come from Latin and Greek. They are usually found in the vocabularies of children above third grade. Knowing them can expand children's vocabularies, and can help them read and spell more words (see Being a Professional Reading Teacher box).

In Table 3.3 are some common historical morphemes. More will be found in Chapter 6.

TABLE 3.3

Prefixes and Word Roots from Latin

PREFIX	MEANING	EXAMPLES
com, con, col, cor	together	collect, contract, correct
e-	out of	elect, eject, emigrate
ab	from, away from, by	abstract, abrupt
ad—, al—, ac—	to, toward	admit, accord, ally

ROOT WORD	MEANING	EXAMPLES
-lect, -lege	choose	elect, collect, college
-ject, -jac	throw	inject, reject, eject, adjective
-rupt	break	interrupt, abrupt, disrupt, erupt
grad-	step	graduate, gradual, grade

Morphemes and Reading

Being aware of morphemes helps a person read. Even third graders use word parts to recognize a word—especially in words like *hilly* and *helpful,* where the original word part is easily visible, or "transparent" (Carlisle & Stone, 2005). To read words that are typically encountered from the fourth grade up, it is more useful to be aware of the morphemes that make up words than to try to match letters with individual sounds (Reichle & Perfetti, 2003). Being aware of morphemes makes it possible to identify as many as 60% of unknown words that are encountered in the middle grades and above (Nagy et al., 1989). So, for example, a reader who knows that *inter* means *between* and *planetary* refers to *planets* can figure out that *interplanetary* means *between planets*. And children beyond the early elementary years who are aware of morphemes in words register better comprehension (Carlisle, 2000).

The strident emphasis on phonics—letter-to-sound correspondences—that the No Child Left Behind legislation ushered in might distract teachers from the realization that there are other important things to know about words, especially beyond the primary grades. Some of those things are the parts that make up words and where those words came from.

Etymologies: Word Origins

In many dictionaries, you will find listings for words that look like this:

give. (giv). Vt gave, giv'en, giv'ing. [OE giefan]

What do these notations mean? The part in parentheses is the pronunciation; *vt* means that the word is a transitive verb—that is, a verb that takes an object to complete the meaning. *Gave, given,* and *giving* are the past, past participle (the form used in compound verbs like *have given* or *had given*), and present participle (the form used in compound verbs like *is giving* and *were giving,* respectively). The part in brackets means that the word came down to us from an earlier word, in this case from Old English (OE). Words in English are derived from many sources. Nonetheless, it is possible to map out a rough lineage for a great many of the words used in English. Tracing the origins of words or looking at their histories reveals their **etymologies**.

The English language traces its origin to Anglo-Saxon. In the fifth and sixth centuries, Germanic peoples from northern Germany and the Netherlands invaded England and pushed the indigenous Celts north into Scotland and west to Wales and Ireland. They brought their Germanic language with them, and it came to be called Anglo-Saxon (Anglo comes from Angles, the name of one of the Germanic tribes, and Saxon comes from another of those tribes). In the eighth and ninth centuries, Vikings raided from Scandinavia, and Old English became a mixture of Germanic, Norse, Danish, and Dutch words.

In 1066, the Normans from France conquered England and brought with them not only an early version of the French language, but also Latin, which became widely used in the church, the government, and other places of higher culture—to the exclusion of English, which remained the language spoken around the hearth, on the farm, and in the market. Hundreds of words from Latin and Greek (Greek was read in the monasteries), as well as French, were absorbed into English in this period.

In 1477, William Caxton brought the first printing press to England and began printing books in English, giving an enormous boost to the language. The language he wrote, Middle English, had a sort of dual structure, consisting of Anglo-Saxon words and Latinate words. You can see this duality in the English words for food. The animal you call a *pig* (an Anglo-Saxon word) on the farm is called *pork* when it reaches the dining room table. *Pork* is a French word, from Latin. The *cow* (Anglo-Saxon) in the pasture became *beef*

(French and Latin) in the dining room. *Sheep* on the farm (Anglo-Saxon word) became *mutton* (French and Latin) in the dining room. This all came about because English was spoken on the farm by farm workers but French was spoken in the dining rooms of the ruling class. To this day, our language has a core of words that came through Old English from Anglo-Saxon. These are very often the common, basic items in our vocabulary; the words children learn first, the words you use when you are being most direct. But other words from Latin and Greek are more specialized, more scientific, and more limited to educated usage. Thus, you find the Anglo-Saxon words *cat* and *dog* and the corresponding Latin words *feline* and *canine*; you also find the Anglo-Saxon word *feel*, the related Latin word *sensitive*, and the related Greek word *sympathy*. Today the English language can be described as having an Anglo-Saxon base and a Latin vocabulary. Approximately a third of our words are Anglo-Saxon and the majority of the rest are from Latin (and through Latin, from Greek). Also, many words are borrowed from Spanish, modern French, German, and other languages.

Vocabulary: Words and Their Meanings

Another aspect of spoken language that is important for reading is **vocabulary**. The more words children have in their spoken vocabularies the easier it will be for them to learn to read. This is true for three reasons:

1. **Having a word in the spoken vocabulary makes it possible to recognize that word in print.** Having the word in their vocabulary allows children to confirm more quickly if they have deciphered the printed word correctly. It is frustrating for beginning readers who struggle to decipher a word from its letters, only to realize that they don't know the word anyway. Having the word in their vocabulary allows children to use meaning-based strategies for word identification strategies, such as, "Think of a word that begins like this one that would make sense in this sentence."
2. **Having more words in the spoken vocabulary boosts children's language awareness.** The more children are aware of language, the better able they are to read words and to be aware of their parts and their sounds (Wong, Fillmore & Snow, 2000).
3. **Having words in the spoken vocabulary boosts reading comprehension.** Words are tokens for concepts. They are units of meaning. The size of children's vocabulary is a measure of their knowledge of the world. It is also a measure of their potential for understanding new information. Let's elaborate on these issues now.

Vocabulary is important in reading. As Carl Smith puts it, "Most people feel that there is a common sense relationship between vocabulary and comprehension—messages are composed of ideas, and ideas are expressed in words" (Smith, 1997, p. 1). Vocabulary development interacts with word recognition as children try to recognize in print words they already know or partially know in speech. But, although younger children have most of the words in their spoken vocabulary that they are likely to encounter in print, many words occur in young children's picture books that they don't hear in speech (Stanovich, 1992). If you need convincing on this point, reread William Steig's *Sylvester and the Magic Pebble*. By fourth grade, the vocabulary found in books is considerably richer than the words children use in speech.

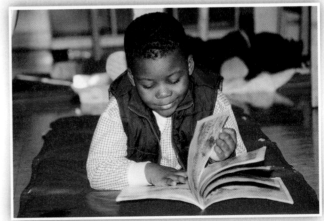

As children explore words on their own, they begin to find meaning in the words and to learn how to use words for different purposes.

Certainly, children can grow larger vocabularies from doing wide reading (Stanovich, 1992). As Nagy et al. (1985) point out, however, readers who encounter a hundred unknown words will perhaps learn five of them. Children must do a great deal of reading in at least moderately challenging texts to learn large vocabularies from reading. But there are huge disparities in the amount of reading children do. In one study (Wilson, 1992), the top 20 percent of a fifth-grade class read twenty times as much as the bottom 20 percent. The bottom 20 percent read very little. If we count on children to learn vocabulary from reading, we will surely continue to see huge disparities in vocabulary size.

Levels of Vocabulary Knowledge

What do we mean by *knowing* vocabulary? Beck, McKeown, & Kucan (2002) suggest a continuum of word knowledge that looks like this:

- No knowledge
- General sense, such as knowing *mendacious* has a negative connotation
- Narrow, context-bound knowledge, such as knowing that a *radiant* bride is a beautifully smiling, happy one, but unable to describe an individual in a different context as radiant
- Having knowledge of a word but not being able to recall it readily enough to use it in appropriate situations
- Rich, decontextualized knowledge of a word's meaning, its relationship to other words, and its extension to metaphorical uses, such as understanding what someone is doing when they are *devouring* a book (p. 10).

Knowing vocabulary well means not just understanding what words in a particular book mean, but knowing words in a range of contexts, in associations with other words, and in connection with one's experience—to have words as one's own.

Exploring Children's Vocabulary

The job of teaching vocabulary seems truly immense. Nagy and Anderson (1984) estimate that by ninth grade, students are having to cope with a written vocabulary of 88,500 words. If we to try to teach all those words, the prospect of teaching children nearly 10,000 words per year would be daunting indeed. But Beck et al. (2002) have found a useful way to break down those numbers into tiers:

- *Tier One Words:* There are many thousands of words already in children's spoken vocabulary that we don't usually have to teach. Beck et al. call these words tier one words, and they include examples such as *mother, clock,* and *jump.*

- *Tier Three Words:* Then there are many more thousands of words that are so highly specialized that they are almost never used outside of the disciplines where they are encountered. These tier three words—such as *monozygotic, tetrahedron,* and *bicameral*—are best learned in the science, social studies, and other classes where they are tied to the content under study.

- *Tier Two Words:* That leaves the tier two words, the words with wide utility that most children don't have in their spoken vocabularies—words like *dismayed, paradoxical, absurd,* and *wary.* Beck et al. (2002) estimate that approximately 7,000 words are tier two words, and even if we teach children half of them, or about 400 words per year, we will have gone a long way toward growing children's vocabularies and equalizing children's access to learning.

In Chapter 6 of this book, we describe ways of teaching tier two vocabulary, the general-purpose words many children do not know. In Chapters 7 and 13, we share ways of teaching tier three, content-specific words.

Syntax: The Grammar of English

Syntax, another term for *grammar,* refers to the set of rules that order words and their inflections meaningfully in sentences. Syntax is what enables you to read the sentence "The veterinarian bit the dog" and understand who was bitten and who did the biting. Syntax can be thought of as a kind of code that enables speakers to encode meaning and for hearers to decode meaning. The working parts of syntax are *parts of speech, word order,* and *inflections.*

Parts of speech are the different grammatical functions that different words serve; *but, run, dog, the, and, across, should, a, green, very,* and *slowly* are all different parts of speech and do different things in sentences. *And* and *but* are conjunctions; they connect things. *Run* is a verb and names an action or a state of being. *Dog* is a noun and names a person, place, or thing. *The* and *a* are articles (definite and indefinite, respectively) and introduce nouns. *Across* is a preposition and shows relationships. *Should* is a modal verb and shows fine shades of action or states of being. *Green* is an adjective and describes a noun. *Very* is an adverb and further defines an adjective. *Slowly* is also an adverb and further describes a verb. Your mind automatically knows these facts without your having to think of them. So, most likely, does whoever programmed the word processing software on your computer, which is why it lights up funny if you happen to write, "I have a very dog big."

We saw *word order* in action before. For example, the noun that comes before the verb is usually the subject, and the noun that comes after the verb is usually the object. *Grammatical inflections* include the past tense marker, *-ed,* and the number marker, *-s,* in sentences like, "Yesterday the wind how*led,* but today it whispers*.*"

Syntax occurs on two levels. At the conscious level, we think of syntax as the common set of rules of grammar taught in school such as, "A verb must agree with its subject in person and number." But conscious syntactical knowledge is only a fraction of what you know that enables you to produce and understand sentences. Consider, for example, the following sentences:

- *I would go bike riding if I weren't tired.* (But I won't go bike riding because I am tired.)
- *I will go bike riding if I'm not tired.* (I don't know yet if I will go bike riding.)
- *I go bike riding if I'm not tired.* (When I'm not tired, I usually go bike riding.)
- *I'm going bike riding, and I'm not tired.* (I expected to be tired, but I'm not.)
- *I did go bike riding, and I'm not tired.* (Somebody asserted that I didn't go bike riding.)

If you had ever taught English as a second language, you would have surely found that although the differences in the meanings of these sentences were clear to you, it was very difficult to tell non-native speakers how to produce sentences that convey those shades of meaning. That means you have knowledge of grammar, but you cannot easily explain what you know. Linguists call this *tacit knowledge*—we have it, but it's not conscious—and the lion's share of children's knowledge of syntax is tacit.

Syntax and Reading

Syntax is important in reading. First, and most obviously, syntax is needed to make meaning from text. In the sentences above, a reader needs to understand the syntax to create the right shade of meaning. Syntax matters in word recognition, too. A teacher will ask a reader who struggles over an unknown word, "What would make sense here?" And if the child is reading the sentence, "The mother hoped the jar would contain money, but it d_____," the word *but* will help the reader figure out that the next word should say *didn't.* The conjunction *but* tells the reader to expect those words to convey a meaning counter to the beginning phrase. So the syntax of the sentence is a strong clue to the identity of the unknown word.

Syntax at a Larger Level: Story and Discourse Structure

Syntax helps children learn organizing principles for longer units of language as well. Stories have been shown to have a particular order that is called **story grammar.** Other kinds of discourse, from social chatter to classroom lectures to persuasive arguments, also have their own structures.

STORY GRAMMAR.   The most thoroughly studied of the structures of discourse (discourse roughly means "a body of talk") is story grammar. Consider the story "The Frowning Princess" in Figure 3.7.

Stories such as this one have a set of identifiable elements, or slots, into which the particulars of the story are placed. These slots are almost always organized in a particular order. (The terms *identifiable elements* and *particular order* are signs that one is talking about grammar or syntax.) For example, a story consists of a setting, one or more episodes, and a consequence. An analysis of the story "The Frowning Princess" using this story grammar model is found in Table 3.4.

Children as young as kindergarten age have a sense of story grammar, and they appear to use it to comprehend stories (Stein & Glenn, 1979). Teaching children story grammar improves their comprehension (Olson & Gee, 1988). Such instruction has been found to be especially helpful for children with learning disabilities (Gersten, 1998).

Social Variations in Language Use

**LANGUAGE
and DIVERSITY**

What are three ways in which language use differs in social situations?

The focus in this chapter has moved from understanding language as a way of making meaningful utterances toward language as it is used in social situations. Three ways in which language use differs in social situations is in the use of dialects, registers, and social languages or discourses.

DIALECTS.   Members of different geographic, social, and cultural groups use language in unique ways. Part of the uniqueness is captured in dialects that the groups use. Geographic dialects are reflected in the differences in the word pronunciations, word choice, and conversational styles of speakers from northern Minnesota; Goliad, Texas; or Ocracoke, North Carolina. Social dialects are reflected in the speech of people from different social classes. Ethnic dialects are reflected in the speech of people from different racial groups. Of course, all these dialects overlap, as in the speech of a professional African American family from the southern Appalachian Mountains. Differences in dialects can result in children experiencing difficulties learning to read, especially if they aren't aware of sounds in the standard pronunciations of words reflected in the spellings.

From the choice of words and the structure of sentences to the patterns in which information is presented, written language differs significantly from spoken language—so much so that the language of print has been called the *grapholect*. The language of books is probably closer to urban-educated, middle-class speech than to any other dialect. Therefore, when it comes to reading and writing, that gives an advantage to people who already speak that dialect and a disadvantage to those who speak a different regional or social dialect.

REGISTERS.   Another way speakers use language differently is the many social registers all people employ when talking to people they hold in different degrees of intimacy and respect. Even a kindergarten child uses different forms of address when she is talking to another child, her mother, or her teacher. In English, different degrees of intimacy and formality are signaled by the amount of indirection that is used. Compare the following sentences:

"Hey, open the window!"

"Please open the window."

The Frowning Princess

In a faraway time and a distant place, there lived a king and his daughter. She frowned. From morning to night, she frowned and frowned and frowned. Even if you saw her in her sleep, she would still be frowning.

The royal advisor worried. "This is terrible, your majesty. A frowning princess is like a cloudy day," he said. "The people will think there is something wrong with your kingdom if the princess doesn't stop frowning."

"I pay you well, so I guess you are right," said the king. "We must find a way to make my daughter stop frowning."

The king and the royal advisor told the princess every joke they knew. But kings and royal advisors are not funny people, and after they had told both of their jokes, the princess was still frowning.

They brought a dozen monkeys and three trained hyenas to the palace. Nobody got any sleep for days. The princess frowned even harder.

Then it happened that a chambermaid put her head between her legs to clean under the princess' bed. Seeing the princess from this odd position, the chambermaid discovered something. "The princess is smiling," she thought. She told the princess to stand on her head and look into the mirror. When the princess saw her reflection, she tried to turn her upside-down frown right-side up. So, of course, she smiled.

Now the princess smiles all the day long. The king, his advisor, and the people are happy. It may be that the princess is still trying to frown, but I won't tell if you won't.

FIGURE 3.7

The Frowning Princess.

"Would you mind opening the window?"

"Don't you think we need some fresh air in here?"

Other languages signal these differences with grammatical forms. Spanish has the familiar form of the pronoun *tu*, used with close friends and family members, and the formal *usted*, used with socially distant adults. Romanian has *tu*, which is familiar, but also *dumnea voastra*, which is more formal and distant, and *dumneata*, which, as one Romanian explained, is "so polite that it's insulting." Linguists use the term *registers* to refer to the ranges of speech speakers have for expressing themselves in different social situations:

- A *ceremonial register*, used in religious functions and formal affairs such as school graduations

TABLE 3.4

Story Grammar Applied

ELEMENTS OF STORY GRAMMAR	EXAMPLES
The **setting,** a place and time	"In a faraway time and a distant place. . ."
There are **characters**	". . . a king and his daughter. . ."
An **initiating event**—something that creates a problem to be solved, and sets further events in motion.	"She frowned. From morning to night, the princess frowned and frowned and frowned."
There is one or more **episodes** that contain. . .	
An **attempt** to solve the problem	"The king and the royal advisor told the princess every joke they knew."
Which has an **outcome**	". . . the princess was still frowning."
Possibly another **attempt**	"They brought a dozen monkeys and three trained hyenas to the palace."
Which has an **outcome**	"Nobody got any sleep for days. The princess frowned even harder."
Possibly another **attempt**	"A chambermaid put her head between her legs to clean under the princess' bed. Seeing the princess from this odd position, the chambermaid discovered something. 'The princess is smiling,' she thought. She told the princess to stand on her head and look into the mirror."
Which has an **outcome**	"When the princess saw her reflection, she tried to turn her upside-down frown right-side up. So, of course, she smiled."
There is a **resolution**	"Now the princess smiles all the day long."
There is a **consequence**	"The king, his advisor, and the people are happy."

Source: Stein & Glenn, 1979

- A *professional register,* used in giving an explanation at school such as discussing a lesson in science or language arts
- A *polite register,* used in informal situations with people the speaker does not know well
- A *casual register,* used for sharing jokes with close friends.

Functions of Language

The Scottish linguist M. A. K. Halliday (1975) studied what his young preverbal son Nigel seemed to be trying to do with his unconventional utterances and gestures and identified seven functions of language that were obviously present before the child could utter recognizable words or use syntax (see Table 3.5). These seven functions grow with the child and remain the areas of language use in which children continue to develop competence. Thus, even after developing a vocabulary of conventional words and a grasp of syntax and beginning to learn various verbal strategies for addressing different audiences, a child will continue to add skills at using language to get things, to regulate others' behavior, to build relationships, and so on. Table 3.5 identifies activities language arts teachers can utilize to encourage language development.

TABLE 3.5

Functions of Language at Home and in School

LANGUAGE	CHILDREN USE UTTERANCES—	CLASSROOM PRACTICE ACTIVITY
Instrumental	as if they were extensions of their arms, to get things for themselves, such as to be handed something or to be lifted up	Students write letters to agencies such as state chambers of commerce requesting information to use in a report.
Regulatory	to control other people's behavior, such as to get someone to stop playing with a toy	Students explain to others how to do a procedure through verbal and written exercises.
Interpersonal	to set up and maintain relationships with other people, as in face-to-face play with a mother, or in teasing the family dog	Students are given training for working together in cooperative groups; students take turns being the class or school hosts, to greet and escort visitors.
Personal	to express how they are feeling, whether it is joy or loneliness	Students write in personal journals.
Heuristic	to express curiosity and to find things out, such as to find out where an absent parent went or what a noise was	Students keep learning logs; students write KWL charts.
Imaginative	to play with language and create sounds	Students write poems, songs, stories, and plays for their own and others' enjoyment.
Representational	to communicate knowledge about the world, such as to announce that a guest has arrived	Students give oral reports; students write reports; students use the I-Search Procedure.

Children develop their language along different tracks according to the different functions or purposes for which they use it. This is an enormously powerful idea. Developing different functions of language surely plays into children's ability to read in different genres of text (narrative, persuasive, expository, etc.). But it is also important in children's lives. What happens if a child is strong on the language of controlling behavior, but short on language to build social relationships? What happens if a child is long on language to describe the world outside, but short on the language to explore and understand personal feelings? It is hardly an exaggeration to suggest that our psychiatrists' couches and our jail cells are populated in no small part by adults who failed to develop all of their functions of language as children—especially the language of personal reflection and sociality. One language teacher, Brazilian linguist Francisco Gomes de Matos, has urged teachers to cultivate in their students the language of peace, through explicitly teaching (role playing, literature discussions, vocabulary teaching) the language of building up another person's self-respect, of emphasizing cooperation, of making apologies, of exploring another's experiences, and, above all, of demonstrating empathy (Gomes de Matos, 2002). (See the Teach It! box.)

TEACH IT!

Refer to your **Teach It!** booklet for further activities you can use to reinforce concepts discussed in this chapter.

The Language of Peace

Assign children to groups of four. Read this passage to the whole class:

Last Wednesday I was shopping at the grocery store. I reached up to a high shelf for a box of cereal. When I turned around, my shopping cart was gone! It only contained groceries that I hadn't paid for, but still I wanted to get it back. I noticed another cart near where I had left mine, and I saw a short elderly lady pushing a cart down the aisle. So I hurried after her and I said,

_____.

Give each group three minutes to discuss what they would say. Call on the different groups to share. Call special attention to the phrases that show tact and politeness.

Discourse

Families put language to different uses, and some of those uses can lead to mismatches in children's accommodation to the routines of classroom reading instruction. James Paul Gee (1999, 2000a, 2001) points out that all real uses of language occur in a social setting. Discourses—forms of language that are used in social situations—involve a *who* and a *what*. The *who* refers to the socially recognized role people play at the time they use language. The *what* refers to the thing they are trying to accomplish when they use language. In any setting, speakers and listeners use a discourse, a form of language that occurs within the boundaries of shared understandings of what roles they are playing and what they are trying to accomplish. Classroom instruction is a special kind of social setting that uses its own discourses, such as when a teacher asks children questions about readings, even when it is obvious the teacher knows the answers. But the questioning is a method of instruction, and the children quickly learn to play along with this "game." Teachers need to be aware of the special demands that learning school discourse places on students. Such awareness allows them to help their students learn the "language of school" while also helping them to learn the content (see the following Differentiated Instruction box).

SIOP® Sheltered Instruction Observation Protocol*

Differentiated Instruction

The Language of School

English language learners and other students who need extra support in the classroom can be helped to learn the content of the curriculum if the right kind of scaffolding is supplied. Sheltered instruction requires that the teacher carefully think through the demands that the language of the lesson, the content of the lesson, and the learning tasks will place on the student. Then the teacher takes steps to make all three accessible. As California teacher and professor Mary Ellen Vogt (2000) writes,

> For ELLs [English Language Learners] to become successful in learning content, they need to learn not only English grammar and vocabulary, but also "the language of school." . . . What we have learned from these students is that they need assistance with all three knowledge bases: knowledge of English, knowledge of the content topic, and knowledge of how tasks are to be completed. Together, these are the key components of academic literacy. (pp. 335, 336)

Vogt goes on to recommend the following:

- Make the objectives of the lesson—for both the language to be used and the content to be learned—very explicit, including writing it on the board.
- Engage the students in active and meaningful activities (not just seatwork), and use various means to communicate information: graphic organizers, examples, analogies, repetitions. Communication between teacher and student and among students is frequent.
- Relate the lessons to the students' prior experiences and background knowledge.
- Choose key vocabulary for the lesson and introduce it in advance, highlight it during the lesson, and review it at the lesson's end and periodically thereafter.
- Word lessons carefully and speak clearly and distinctly.
- Explain how tasks are to be carried out, then give examples of the kinds of responses that are expected, and explain why.
- Scaffold writing assignments with graphic organizers and other outlining aids; scaffold reading assignments with study guides, written questions, and outlines for note taking.
- Encourage higher-order thinking by means of many techniques.
- Use group work, including paired work.

How Do Children Learn Language?

As children learn to talk, they gain much of their power to use language through their own discovery processes, aided by the special support, but not the direct instruction, of the adults and older speakers around them. As they learn to use language, children infer the patterns of regularity or "rules" that govern speech, and gradually construct their own versions. Do children learn to read and write in the same way? Clearly, discovery helps, but because written language is a deliberate contrivance that bears peculiar relationships to speech, several conventions of reading and writing need to be taught.

Learning language relies on some things that are innate. Babies appear to come into the world "pretuned" with a set of capacities that makes it virtually inevitable that they will learn language. For example, newborn babies just a few days old do the following:

- Turn their heads and look toward the source of a sound
- Prefer patterned and varied sounds, such as human voices, to random noises like buzzes and clicks
- Synchronize the movements of their bodies so that they track along with the rhythms of the speech they hear
- Perceive extremely subtle distinctions in speech, such as the difference between the beginning consonant sounds in *bat* and *pat*—a difference that equals 40/1,000ths of a second delay in the vibration of the vocal cords
- Prefer high-pitched voices to low-pitched voices

Babies may even be "prewired" with a basic grammar, or system of order for language. Noam Chomsky (1973) argues that infants understand on some deep level that meaningful utterances should have a subject and a predicate (or a *topic* and *comment* or a *noun phrase* and a *verb phrase*).

Infants and older children are equipped with one other essential capacity: They can examine the language they hear around them, tease out its patterns, and use those patterns to shape their own utterances. This is not the same thing as imitating what they hear adults say, because children often say things that adults wouldn't say, and that is when their ability to discover patterns in language is revealed. For instance, a six-year-old boy says, "Don't worry, Mom. I'm hold-onning," after his mother told him to "hold on" during a windy sailboat ride. He is aware that verbs add *-ing* to show that action is going on in the present, and he has figured out a rule of grammar all on his own. This act of discerning and learning patterns of grammar is a significant achievement, and it is accomplished by virtually all children.

Children begin to hear speech patterns from early on and benefit greatly when adults make an effort to speak with them directly and often.

It is no wonder that literacy educators come back to children's amazing language-learning ability and look for its contributions to children's learning to read. Children possess the following abilities that allow them to learn language:

1. They are born with a highly developed set of sensory capacities that pre-adapt them to perceive and respond to human language.
2. They might also be equipped with a rudimentary grammar for language. (This claim is still controversial, as the evidence for it is indirect.)
3. They have the ability to analyze language for its features and for its patterns and to construct an organized understanding of those findings.

Linguist Steven Pinker (1994) writes,

The complexity of language, from the scientist's point of view, is part of children's biological birthright; it is not something that parents teach their children or something that must be elaborated in school—as Oscar Wilde said, "Education is an admirable thing, but it is well to remember from time to time that nothing worth knowing can be taught." A preschooler's tacit knowledge of grammar is more sophisticated than the thickest style manual or the most state-of-the-art computer language system, and the same applies to all healthy human beings, even the notorious syntax-fracturing professional athlete and the you know, like, inarticulate teenage skateboarder. (p. 6)

Direct instruction or not, however, adults must provide some kind of support for their efforts to learn language, or children will not learn to talk and listen. History has horrifying examples of children reared in isolation from adults who never really learned to talk, even after being placed later in normal environments. Children need us, or they will not learn language. But what do they need from us?

How Adults Support Children's Language Learning

When adults help infants learn to talk, it is remarkable how much of this "help" comes naturally and unconsciously. Take the case of a mother engaged in face-to-face play with a six-month-old child. The mother gazes into the child's face and raises the pitch of her voice to a high register. She makes swooping changes from low to high, from soft to loud. She exaggerates consonant sounds and stretches out vowel sounds. She speaks in sentences with few words and simple structures. She leaves pauses in her utterances: She speaks and waits, speaks and waits, as if she were inviting the baby into a conversation and demonstrating where to slot utterances. In short, she is speaking **Motherese** (Newport, Gleitman, & Gleitman, 1977).

When a parent speaks with a toddler, similar interactions take place that help the child learn language. A parent might read a book to a young child, turn to a picture of a dog, point to it, say to the child, "What's that?," and wait for the child to answer, "Dog!" (although the response more likely sounds like "Dock" because young children's speech usually gives voiced consonants at the beginning of a word and unvoiced consonants at the end of a word). Like Motherese, this book-reading exchange teaches the child important lessons about language: that words are names for things, that the same thing is labeled by the same word each time it appears, and that words are real and can be represented in print (Bruner & Ninio, 1978). This insight will be helpful as the child begins to wonder about printed language and how it works.

Children benefit from having adults talk to them. The more adults talk to children, the greater their development of syntax (McCartney, 1984). And the syntactic complexity of young children's sentences is borrowed from their caregivers (Hart & Risley, 1995). The impact of adults speaking to children also has a great impact on their development of vocabulary (Hoff-Ginsburg, 1998). This finding is doubly important because the amount and quality of language support that young children get from their families differ tremendously. One research team (Hart & Risley, 1995) found that three- and four-year-old children in professional families had twice as many words spoken to them as children from working-class families, and nearly four times as many words as children in families on welfare. Children in working-class families received three times as many verbal encouragements ("Good girl! See? You could do it!") as children from families on welfare, and children from professional families received 7.5 times as many verbal encouragements as children from families on welfare. Rates of prohibitions that children received from their parents ("Stop!" "Don't do that!" "Quit!") were just the reverse. Children in families on welfare received nearly twice as many prohibitions as children in working-class families, and almost three times as many as children from professional families received. Children from families on welfare were discouraged three times more often

Focus on "hopes and dreams": The hopes and dreams you have about yourself as a professional and the hopes and dreams of your students. Stay the course and even in your trying moments, remember hopes and dreams. . .

"The wash will wait while you show your child the rainbow but the rainbow won't wait while you do the wash!"

—Kathy,
6th Grade
Language Arts Teacher
Portland, MAINE

FAMILY LITERACY

What are some ways in which adults support children's language development?

What You May Be Expected to Know about Language

There are many reasons why teachers of reading need to know about language development. The ways in which children learn to talk—the efforts they contribute themselves and the help they need from others around them—are similar in many respects to what happens when they learn to read and write. Also, because reading involves understanding the ways that written symbols represent spoken language, it is helpful if the teacher has a sophisticated understanding of spoken language. Third, much of what native speakers know about their language is unconscious: Speakers just talk and understand without knowing how they do it. When teachers are helping English-language learners, however, they often need to know how to explain the fine points of grammar and pronunciation of language and the ways in which language is used. Some states have incorporated such knowledge into their state standards for assessment.

One such state is California, where the state competency test for future teachers of reading, known as RICA (Reading Instruction Competency Assessment), includes several standards that require teachers of reading to have deep knowledge of the structure of the English language in addition to knowing how all children learn to read, including those who are native speakers of other languages, that is, English language learners:

7A(a)—Each candidate participates in intensive instruction in reading and language arts methods that is grounded in

methodologically sound research and includes exposure to instructional programs adopted by the State Board of Education for use in California public schools. This instruction enables her/him to provide a comprehensive, systematic program of instruction to students. The reading and language arts instruction for students includes systematic, explicit and meaningfully applied instruction in reading, writing, and related language skills, as well as strategies for English language learners and speakers of English, all of which is aligned with the state-adopted academic content standards for students in English Language Arts and the Reading/Language Arts Framework.

7A(d)—For each candidate, the study of reading and language arts methods includes instruction and experience in teaching organized, systematic, explicit skills that promote fluent reading and writing, including phonemic awareness; direct, systematic, explicit phonics; and decoding skills, including spelling patterns, sound/symbol codes (orthography), and extensive practice in reading and writing.

7A(f)—For each candidate, the study of reading and language arts includes the phonological/morphological structure of the English language, and methodologically sound research on how children learn to read, including English language learners, students with reading difficulties, and students who are proficient readers (California Commission on Teacher Credentialing, 2001).

than they were encouraged. Children from working-class families were encouraged twice as often as they were discouraged. And children from professional families were encouraged six times as often as they were discouraged (Hart & Risley, 1995, pp. 252–253).

Less talk between adults and children means less-developed vocabulary. By the age of six, children from low-income undereducated families come to school with well below half the vocabulary as those from middle-class families, and the differences continue to grow after that (Beck et al., 2002). Having a limited vocabulary (and limited structures for language) limits children's concept formation and their "world knowledge," and it certainly creates problems for children learning to read and write (Droop & Verhoeven, 2003; Snow, Tabors, & Dickenson, 2001).

For Review

If reading is making sense of talk written down, then children need a healthy level of language development in order to read, and teachers need more than a passing acquaintance with linguistics, the study of language, to teach reading well.

In this chapter we explored the main areas of language knowledge, including the sound system of language, or phonology, the grammar of language, or syntax, and the meaning system or semantics. We also looked at social variations in language as well as the uses to which language is put. English uses an alphabetic writing system, so the letters of the alphabet relate to individual speech sounds. But morphemes, or meaningful word roots, and affixes are also important both in the structure of words and in the act of reading them.

English spelling relates to the spoken language in interesting and often vexing ways. Watching children trying to discover the patterns and rules of English spelling—that is, their invented spelling—is not only fascinating but important if we are going to understand how they are thinking about words, and help them advance their knowledge.

Teachers need to be aware of the varieties of registers and dialects of language. Dialects and registers are a great part of the richness of language; but we need to make sure all children have control of the grapholect, the dialect of written language. The functions for which language is used should be practiced in all their diversity. This will not only help children read a variety of genres, but also increase their awareness of things and their ability to reflect on themselves and relate to others.

For Your Journal

1. Review the answers to the anticipation guide on the first page of this chapter. What answers would you give to those questions now that you have read this chapter?

2. If you still need proof that you have *tacit* knowledge of English grammar, that is, knowledge that enables you to talk and listen but of which you are largely unaware, try this exercise. Explain what is wrong with this sentence: *Ignacio is playing with a red big ball.* State the rule that you would use in writing the sentence correctly.

3. Families from different social backgrounds think of literacy in strikingly different ways. How did you use literacy in your family when you were growing up? What materials did the people around you read? Did they share or discuss them with each other? If so, how? Was there bedtime reading? If so, what was it like?

Taking It to the World

1. Look up your own state's standards for elementary and reading teachers' knowledge of language. You can find them on your state department of education's Website, usually by using the key word *standards*. What do you think teachers need to know about language besides what is mandated in the state standards?

2. Halliday's functions of language constitute a menu of ways in which people of every age need to learn to use language. Interview a kindergarten or first-grade teacher and ask whether he or she consciously tries to help children develop their ability to talk and listen for different purposes—that is, to use language for different functions. If so, what purposes should the teacher emphasize? How does the teacher help children learn to use them well?

3. Interview a guidance counselor at a middle or high school or a counseling psychologist who treats adults. Interview a foreman or manager at a business or manufacturing plant. With regard to their clients or the people they supervise, to what extent do these professionals find that people's problems are related to their difficulties in using language for different purposes—for self-awareness, for getting along with others, for giving and receiving directions clearly? Do these people believe that schools have a role in teaching communication for different purposes?

4. After you have written in your journal about your own family's uses of literacy, interview a first- or second-grade teacher. What differences does that teacher notice in different children's expectations of and approaches to literacy tasks? That is, what do different children do when they are asked to make up a story or to discuss one?

Technology Connections

The Internet has many excellent sites with information on language.

Lily Fillmore and Catherine Snow have an excellent summary of language concepts for the teacher available online at **http://www.cal.org/ericcll/teachers/teachers.pdf**. The work, entitled *What Teachers Need to Know about Language*, was originally published in August 2000, by the U.S. Department of Education's Office of Educational Research and Improvement. This fifty-page monograph is written in a question-and-answer format with chapters on oral and written language, and language and diversity. It's an excellent summary of essential knowledge about language by two distinguished scholars.

Several sites on the Internet provide rich examples of how sounds are made, including diagrams of the mouth, recordings of sounds, and even spectrographic displays of sound waves produced with sound:

1. Professor George Dillon at the University of Washington has a wonderful site (**http://faculty.washington.edu/Dillon/PhonResources**) that provides information about speech sounds and also links to numerous other sites that provide detailed information and tutorials.

2. Visit the "Vocal Vowels" exhibit at the San Francisco Museum of Science's online Exploratorium (**www.exploratorium.edu/exhibits/vocal_vowels**) to see how a duck call can be made to produce human vowel sounds by modifying the production chamber.

3. Noted linguist Peter Ladefoged provides a comprehensive site devoted to speech sounds at **http://hctv.humnet.ucla.edu/departments/linguistics/VowelsandConsonants**.

Connect with Research

Review the following key words from the chapter and then connect to Research Navigator (**http://www.researchnavigator.com**) through this book's Companion Website to conduct a search into research on each of the various topics as they relate to reading and literacy education today.

alphabetic principle
consonant blends
consonant digraphs
consonants
deep orthography
diphthongs
etymologies
functions of language
Great Vowel Shift
homophone
invented spelling

letter name stage
linguistics
monophthong
morpheme
morphology
Motherese
onset
phonemes
phonological awareness
phonology

rime
root word
shallow orthography
stop consonants
story grammar
syntax
vocabulary
vowel reduction
vowels
word knowledge

Companion Website

To access chapter objectives, practice tests, weblinks, and flashcards, visit the Companion Website at www.ablongman.com/templeallchildren2e.

mylabschool™
Where the classroom comes to life!

Go to Allyn & Bacon's MyLabSchool (www.mylabschool.com), enter Assignment ID RMV2 into the Assignment Finder. Watch the video, *Teaching Phonics,* in which a first grade teacher works with small groups to teach vowels, diphthongs, and diagraphs.

Question: How would you incorporate phonics as part of the reading program? You may also answer the questions at the end of the clip and e-mail your responses to your instructor.

chapter 4

Language-Based Learning

Involving Families in Emergent Literacy

Emergent Literacy

Learning about Print

How Does a Teacher Nurture Emergent Literacy?

Emergent Literacy

Anticipation Guide

The following statements will stimulate thinking about the topics of this chapter. Answer true or false in response to each statement. As you read and learn more about the topics in these statements, double-check your answers. See what interests you and what prompts your curiosity toward more understanding.

_____ When you get right down to it, learning to read is "natural."

_____ Children's scribbles are a window into their thinking about how print works.

_____ Concepts about print, such as the arrangement of print on the page or the fact that people read the print and not the pictures, rarely need to be taught.

_____ Children should never be allowed to write words incorrectly.

_____ Invented spelling provides teachers with insights into children's knowledge of phonics.

_____ We can teach children a lot about reading and writing through passive means, such as labeling items in the classroom.

_____ When children imitate adults reading storybooks, they teach themselves important concepts about the way reading works.

_____ Reading aloud to children is a waste of valuable instructional time. If it is to be done at all, it should be left up to parents.

_____ Teaching reading is such a complicated undertaking that parents should be discouraged from taking any part in it.

_____ There are no significant differences in the amount of time that parents from different social groups spend reading to their children.

A Kindergarten Classroom

It is the second Monday in November, and Ignacio Diaz's kindergartners know the morning routine very well. As they enter, they take off their coats, stuff their lunch boxes into their cubbies, then check the job board to see who will give the weather report, who will lead the Pledge of Allegiance, and who will line the children up to go to lunch. Then they go to the task board and see what their rotations are for the language block. Their names are pasted in quadrants with symbols, indicating who will go to the independent study center, who will work with the teacher in the reading circle, who will write, and who will have reading time. Charmaigne enters the room and hands her teacher a book baggie, a plastic bag that holds a book and a group of games and activity sheets. "Mama said she liked the drawing I did of Toad. Or maybe it was Frog. . . . How do you tell them apart again?" she says. "And she said to tell you we finally figured out how to do the alphabet game."

Ignacio laughs and puts the book baggie into a bin to be repacked for another child to take home.

As children come in from various buses, Charmaigne wanders to the library corner and begins reading a little book about frogs. It is one of her favorites, written by Henry, the boy who taught them all to draw cartoons. Henry's penciled letters make dubious spellings that flow across the page, but Charmaigne focuses on the neat black letters her teacher has written with a felt-tipped pen. She can read some of the words, and she likes finding the ones she knows. Henry's drawings always make clear what is going on in his books, so when Charmaigne wants to, she can hold the book up and tell the story aloud as if

In science, observations often follow theory. As you saw in Chapter 3, through their own efforts at discovery children learn to talk (Pinker, 2000). Shortly after psycholinguists began to publish their studies of children's language acquisition, researchers began to take a close look at children's literacy learning, too. They wondered whether children might learn about the features of written language and how reading and writing work by being immersed in an environment of readers and writers. These assumptions turned out to be largely true. Children learn a great deal about reading and writing years before they enter school and even before they are taught to recognize their first letter (Clay, 1975; Neuman & Dickinson, 2003; Teale & Sulzby, 1986; Temple, Nathan, & Burris, 1982). They learn many of these insights by their own efforts, but they learn better with the support of adults who orchestrate opportunities for discovery. We call this **emergent literacy**, which refers to the following:

- The period in children's learning to read and write that begins when children first notice print and wonder what people are doing when they work with it.
- Early instruction that children receive in preschool and kindergarten at the hands of careful teachers who make sure that all children gain the insights about literacy they will need in order to profit fully from formal reading instruction once it begins.

she were reading it, even though she does not yet know many of the words.

The class is all here, and Charmaigne's time has come to lead the Pledge of Allegiance. She knows what a flag is, but the word *flag* is taped underneath it anyway. It begins with *F*, just like the title of Henry's book, *Frogs*. Now Mr. Diaz calls the children to the rug in front of the chart stand.

"Who knows what today is?" he asks.

"Monday," says Henry.

"Right," says Ignacio. "And I'm going to write '*Today is Monday*' right here on the chart. Let's say that sentence: '*Today is Monday*.'"

"Today is Monday," chants the class.

"What's the first word I need to write?"

"*Today*," Charmaigne offers.

"Good. I'm going to start writing up here," and he points to the upper left-hand corner of the sheet. "What's the first sound we hear in '*Today*'?" Some children, including Charmaigne, chant the *tuh* sound, over and over. After a moment's hesitation, other children join them.

"Aw, you're champions. Now, what letter will we use to spell the *tuh* sound?"

With the children and Mr. Diaz taking turns offering up sounds and naming letters to spell them with, the morning news is written on the chart. It covers four lines. Ignacio is careful to show the children that he begins writing over on the left side, then writes across to the right,

then returns to the left but down one line, and continues writing to the right again.

The children read the sentences through three times as Ignacio points to every word with his Harry Potter wand, the stick he uses for pointing to words.

Because print represents spoken language, learning how to read requires that children simultaneously understand print and be conscious of the features of language that it represents. Learning about language, learning about print, and learning how reading and writing work are the main aspects of emergent literacy that will be explored in this chapter.

Language-Based Learning

With speech, we can pledge love, declare war, and forecast blizzards—all without being conscious of the language we use to do these things. When children learn to read, however, they have to be conscious of language. Because print represents spoken language, emergent readers need to be aware of the words from which language is built. They also need to be aware of the sounds. If their language is Japanese, emergent readers need to be aware of sounds at the level of syllables. If their language is English (or German or Finnish), readers must be aware of sounds at the level of onset and rimes and phonemes.

Short periods of dedicated instruction can help struggling readers improve their reading skills.

The Concept of Word

The first unit of language of which young readers need to be aware is the word. Distinguishing words in speech is not a simple matter, because speech usually comes to us all run together. We more often hear someone say "Whuzapnin?" than "What is happening?" If we can sort an utterance into individual words, it is because, as experienced learners, we can already think of those words in units. For children in kindergarten and even first grade, separating speech into word units is not so simple. Not being aware of words in speech puts children at a disadvantage when they are learning to read. Suppose a teacher teaches the children the song "The Corner Grocery Store" and then writes the words on chart paper. The teacher then asks the children to look at the printed words as they sing the words from memory. Children who are aware of word units—who have a **concept of word**—can look at the word *corner* at just the instant they sing it. Children who do not have the concept of word might scan their eyes across a whole line of text as they sing the word *corner*, or they might look at only a single letter. In either case, at the conclusion of the activity, a child who lacks the concept of word is unlikely to have learned to recognize any new words from it. The child who has the concept of word, who looks at the written word at the instant each is sung, will be in the position to associate the written version of the words with the spoken versions and is likely to learn to read several of them from the activity.

Phonological Awareness

PHONICS and **PHONOLOGICAL AWARENESS**

Why must emergent readers be aware of syllables, onsets and rimes, and phonemes?

Beyond the level of words, there are other levels of speech of which emergent readers must be aware. These are syllables, onsets and rimes, and phonemes. **Syllables** are the "pulses" of language. They are the "beats" we hear in *elbow* (two syllables), *love* (one syllable), and *popsicle* (three syllables). As was discussed in Chapter 3, onsets and rimes are two parts of most single syllables: The *onset* is the beginning consonant sound (if the syllable has one), and the *rime* is the vowel sound plus any consonant sound that follows. In *cat*, the onset is *k* and the rime is *-at*. In *step*, the onset is *st-* and the rime is *-ep*. As the smallest speech sounds in language, phonemes roughly correspond to letters. *Dig* has three phonemes: /d/, /i/, and /g/. *Clam* has four phonemes: /k/, /l/, /æ/, and /m/. (Note that we conventionally represent phonemes with slashes on either side.)

As a good deal of research has shown (e.g., Adams, 1990; Snow, Burns & Griffin, 1998), children who are aware that words can be broken into onsets and rimes and phonemes are more likely to learn to read words successfully than those who are not. If children are aware of sounds in words, they will have an easier time matching letters and sounds when they begin to read. Moreover, reasonably short periods of exclusive phonemic awareness instruction embedded in reading, writing, and oral discussions improve children's phonemic awareness learning. Several exercises to help emergent readers become aware of language—from words to syllables to onsets and rhymes to phonemes—are presented later in this chapter.

Learning about Print

Children's emergent literacy involves both the development of language and of the awareness of language. Simultaneously, children also gain awareness of aspects of print. Print awareness includes the following:

- *Graphic principles*: a set of discoveries about the features of print that are often displayed in children's scribbles

- *Awareness of the alphabetic nature of writing:* the idea that, in languages such as English, German, Spanish, and Kiswahili (but not Japanese or Chinese), writing works by using units of letters to represent language at the level of phonemes
- *Concepts about print:* a constellation of realizations about what print is and how it works
- *Alphabet knowledge:* being able to recognize and produce many letters of the alphabet
- *Orthographic concepts:* an understanding of the particular rules and relationships that relate letters to sounds

Graphic Principles

When examining the scribbles of four-year-old children from literate families whose languages were English, Arabic, and Chinese, educator Jerry Harste and his colleagues (Harste, Woodward, & Burke, 1984) found that they could easily tell which scribbles came from which child.

Even though the scribbles did not use any actual letters or characters from any of the languages, the children's scribbles nonetheless looked like their parents' writing and not like those of the other children. Although the children did not yet know how to make any graphemes from their languages, the children nonetheless managed to capture many of their visual features.

Marie Clay (1975) carefully examined the patterns in children's scribbles and identified **graphic principles** that emerge as they begin to experiment with writing. Understanding these principles will not necessarily tell you what to teach next, any more than listening to a child's baby talk will. Nonetheless, following the emergence of these graphic principles will increase your appreciation of a preschool and kindergarten child's growth in emergent literacy.

THE RECURRING PRINCIPLE. As the scribbles in Figure 4.1 make clear, a young child's mock-writing is often composed of the same mark, roughly the same size, repeated again and again, usually in a linear arrangement. Children whose language is English will sometimes show a preference for linked and continuous marks that resemble cursive writing or for discrete marks that resemble print. Children who are used to other writing symbols might produce recurring marks that resemble those.

THE GENERATIVE PRINCIPLE. When children realize that they can add some variety, but not too much variety, to their mock-writing, they have discovered the generative principle: the idea that a few marks or characters can be combined and recombined in different orders to produce a whole page or more of writing. We often see children taking advantage of the generative principle when they have learned to write a few letters, such as those that spell their own names. Then they combine and recombine those letters to generate many lines of text (see Figure 4.2).

The generative principle, of course, is real. It is a key advantage to alphabetic writing. Whereas speakers of Chinese must learn to write and read some 6,000 characters by the time they finish grade school, speakers of English need only twenty-six letters (fifty-two counting the uppercase ones) to write. Don't be surprised if a child who has generated a page of mock-writing shows it to you and asks, "What did I write?" As Marie Clay observed in her book by that title (1975), children at this stage believe that they can now generate writing, but because they cannot yet read, they rely on the adults around them to tell them what their creations mean.

FIGURE 4.1

The Recurring Principle.

Carlene, Age 4

Source: Temple, Nathan, Burris, and Temple. (1992). *The beginnings of writing.* Boston: Allyn and Bacon.

FIGURE 4.2

The Generative Principle.

Age 4

Source: Temple, Nathan, Burris, and Temple. (1992). *The beginnings of writing.* Boston: Allyn and Bacon.

THE FLEXIBILITY PRINCIPLE. To a child, letters must be arbitrary-looking things. Some have straight lines, and some have curves. Some have loops that flop to the left, and some have loops that flop to the right. Some are vertical staffs with one, two, even three horizontal arms. To adults, the combinations of lines that make up letters, with their straightness or their curves, with the directions of their slants and their slopes, with the numbers of their parts, constitute the closed system of the alphabet. To children who do not yet know the system, these variations in lines are an open field of possibilities. Consider that children are trying to learn the set of features that make up particular letters. What makes matters confusing is that often even letters they know are sometimes being presented to them in forms they do not yet recognize, as occurs when they see new words in different typefaces.

good	good	*good*	**good**	good	*good*
good	*good*	good	good	good	

It should not be surprising, then, that children experiment with the forms of letters and sometimes produce original forms. A strategy that many children seem to use is to take a letter they know how to make and add things to it to make letters they never made before (see Figure 4.3). Sometimes this works: An *L* with two extra arms becomes an *E*. But suppose we add *five* extra arms? What letter will that be?

DIRECTIONAL PRINCIPLES. A particular instance of the flexibility principle is the set of *directional principles.* Directional principles have to do with learning to associate the identity of letters with the directions they face. We refer to "principles" because they include the horizontal orientation of both individual letters and of words.

Letters are nearly the only things in children's experience whose identity changes with their orientation in space, so it is not surprising that children find it hard to remember what direction they should face. What is surprising, from an adult point of view, is how easily children can shift from one orientation to another. As you see in Figure 4.4, a five-year-old child who starts writing on the right-hand side of the page might find it natural to reverse the letters and write a whole line of text from right to left.

In past years, children's tendency to reverse letters was taken as a sign of a dysfunctional brain, but now it is seen as a sign of intellectual immaturity and inexperience with print. Reversing letters and whole lines of print is natural for kindergartners and first graders who are learning the directionality principle (Temple et al., 1992). In the writing of older students, whose literacy is not advancing as quickly as their classmates', reversals can still appear, but they are evidence of delayed literacy development rather than neurological problems. Students who are diagnosed with dyslexia make no more reversals of letters than do normally developing younger children who read at the same level (Vellutino, 1979). Kindergarten and first-grade teachers need to take every opportunity to remind children of the orientation of letters and avoid materials, like the one shown in Figure 4.5, that aren't sensitive to the challenges directionality poses to children.

FIGURE 4.3

The Flexibility Principle.

Carlene, Age 4

Source: Temple, Nathan, Burris, and Temple. (1992). *The beginnings of writing.* Boston: Allyn and Bacon.

Concepts about Print

New Zealander Marie Clay has long been the literacy field's favorite example of a *kidwatcher,* Yetta Goodman's term for a teacher who observes children very, very carefully and appreciates how they see the tasks of learning and what they do to learn. Kidwatchers make good teachers because they help children solve puzzles, and they adjust their instruction to fit nicely with children's own efforts to discover how literacy works and how to become good at it. Clay offers us this account of a novice teacher giving a reading lesson to a group of beginning readers:

> Suppose the teacher has placed an attractive picture on the wall and has asked her children for a story, which she will record under it. They offer the text, "Mother is cooking," which the teacher alters slightly to introduce some features she wishes to teach. She writes:
>
> Mother said, "I am baking."
>
> If she says, "Now look at our story, 30% of the new entrant group [children who are just beginning reading instruction] will attend to the picture. If she says, "Look at the words and find some that you know," between 50 and 90% will be looking for letters. If she says, "Can you see Mother?" most will agree that they can, but some see her in the picture, some can locate M, and others will locate the word Mother.
>
> Perhaps the children read in unison, "Mother is . . ." and the teacher tries to sort this out. Pointing to said, she asks, "Does this say is?" Half agree that it does because it has s in it. "What letter does it start with?" Now the teacher is really in trouble. She assumes that the children will know that a word is built out of letters, but 50% of the children still confuse the verbal labels word and letter after six months of instruction. She also assumes that the children know that the left-hand letter following a space is the "start" of a word. Often they do not. (Clay, 1975, pp. 3–4)

As this example makes clear, there are many concepts about print that children must have in place so that in a reading lesson, they can orient themselves properly to a book and direct their attention appropriately. These concepts include understandings of the layout of books; the relative roles of print and pictures; the orientation of print on the page; the

FIGURE 4.4

Directionality.

Annabrook, Age 5

Writing backwards was easy for her.

Source: Temple, Nathan, Burris, and Temple. (1992). *The beginnings of writing.* Boston: Allyn and Bacon.

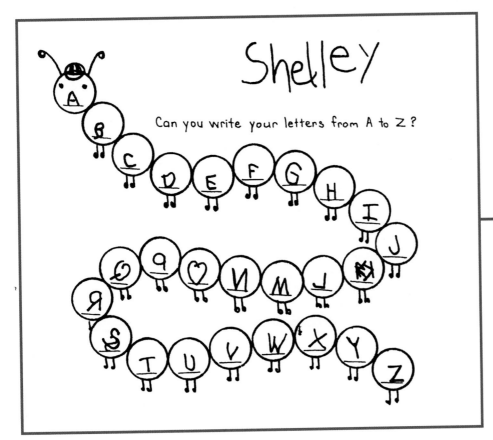

FIGURE 4.5

The Snake Picture.

Shelley, Kindergarten

The "A" and "Z" were already printed.

Source: Temple, Nathan, Burris, and Temple. (1992). *The beginnings of writing.* Boston: Allyn and Bacon.

A child's knowledge of concepts about print can be tested by showing the child a book that contains both pictures and print and asking a series of questions to probe the child's ability to orient to the book and the print it contains. You will need a book that has the following features:

- A double-page spread with print on one page and a picture on the other
- A page with a single line of print
- A page with two or more lines of print
- A page that has both uppercase and lowercase versions of two different letters
- Several punctuation marks, including periods, a question mark, an exclamation point, and quotation marks

You will also need two index cards. It is advisable to prepare a record sheet ahead of time for keeping track of the child's responses.

Concepts to Be Tested:

- **Knowledge of the layout of books:** Hold the book out to the child so that the child is looking at the spine. Say, "We're going to read this book. Show me the front of the book." Note whether the child lays the book in front of himself or herself so that the front of the book is properly facing up.
- **Knowledge that print, not pictures, is what we read:** Show the child a double-page spread with text on one page and a picture on the other. Say, "Show me where we read. Point to the spot where we begin reading." Note whether the child points to the text or to the picture.
- **Directional orientation of print on the page:** Show the child a page with at least two (and preferably three) lines of print. Say, "We're going to read this page. Show me where we begin reading. Point to the place. Show me where we go after that. Now show me where we go after that." Note whether the child points to the upper left-hand word, then sweeps across to the right, then goes the whole way back to the left and down one line, then across to the right. (A correct response will include this entire Z-like pattern.) Then you read the page.
- **Knowledge of the terms, *beginning, end, first,* and *last* with respect to words on a page:** Turn to a new page and say, "Show me the *beginning* of the story on this page. Show me the *end* of the story on this page. Show me the *first word* on this page. Show me the *last word*." Note if the child points to the appropriate words. Then read that page.
- **Orientation to *top* and *bottom* of a page:** Turn to a new page. Say, "Point to the *top* of this page. Point to the *bottom* of this page." Note whether the child points to the right places. Then read the page.
- **Understanding of the terms *word* and *letter:*** Turn to a page that has one line of print. Take an index card in each hand and say, "Look. I can hold these cards so you can only see one or two words or one or two letters. Here. You try it." Hand the cards to the child and say, "Show me one word. Now show me two words. Show me one letter. Now show me two letters." Note whether the child responds correctly. Then read the text.
- **Knowledge of uppercase and lowercase letters:** Turn to a page that has uppercase and lowercase versions of two different letters. Point to an uppercase letter and say, "Find me a little letter like this." Then point to the lowercase version of the other letter. Say, "Find me a big letter like this." Note whether the child responds correctly. Then read the text.
- **Knowledge of punctuation:** Find a page with a period on it. Say, "What is this? What are we supposed to do when we get to it?" In turn, find quotation marks, a question mark, and an exclamation point. As you point to each one, say, "What is this? What does it tell us?" Note which ones the child understands.

meanings of terms used in reading instruction, such as *beginning, end, first,* and *last*; where to find the "top" and "bottom" of a page; the terms *word* and *letter*; uppercase and lowercase letters; and at least a beginning understanding of punctuation. The Assessment box identifies some ways in which you can assess students' knowledge of the concepts of print.

Alphabet Knowledge

Alphabet knowledge is considered part of a child's emergent literacy because a great many children learn to recognize and even produce letters of the alphabet before they enter first grade. Children's knowledge of the alphabet is both an indicator of their exposure to print (Walsh, Price, & Gillingham, 1988) and a facilitator of learning to read (Morris, 1999). Although children can start learning to read and write without knowing all of the letters of the alphabet, they do need to know most of them to make progress. Thoughtful teachers will want to know how many letters each of their students can recognize and produce, especially when they are concerned about a particular student's progress.

An inventory of children's letter knowledge should be taken from one child at a time. Show the child a set of randomly ordered letters, such as the one given in Figure 4.6. Prepare a sheet on which to record the child's responses. To administer the inventory, point to each letter and ask the child to name it. Go through the uppercase letters and the lowercase letters. Record the child's responses by circling letters the child does not know and write in letters the child substitutes above the appropriate letters. Then give the child a blank sheet of paper and ask the child to write the letters as you call them out. For scoring purposes, accept both uppercase and lowercase letters. Tally the responses on the record sheet.

New teachers should ask a lot of questions. Remember that every teacher has been in your shoes at one point in their career. Don't be afraid to ask for help and take their advice. Rely on the teachers around you; they are an invaluable wealth of experience and information.

—Theresa Morris,
Sixth Grade Teacher
Monroe, OHIO

LETTER-TO-SOUND CORRESPONDENCE: LEARNING PHONICS. A child realizes that language is real and comes in units of words, syllables, and phonemes. The child can now produce not just letterlike forms, but also many actual letters. The child has learned to orient himself or herself to books. The child realizes that ours is an alphabetic writing

A	F	P	W	K	Z	B	C	H	O	J	U	Y
M	D	L	Q	N	S	X	I	G	R	E	V	T

+++

a	f	p	w	k	z	b	c	h	o	j	u	y
m	d	l	q	n	s	x	i	g	r	e	v	t

_____ Uppercase Recognition

_____ Lowercase Recognition

_____ Production

FIGURE 4.6

Alphabet Inventory.

Invented Spelling

The International Reading Association (IRA) and the National Council for Teachers of English (NCTE) have developed a set of standards for certifying reading specialists. The standards are quite specific with regard to what reading professionals should know about invented spelling.

According to Standard 3.3, teachers should

understand that spelling is developmental and is based on students' knowledge of the phonological system and of the letter names, their judgments of phonetic similarities and differences, and their ability to abstract phonetic information from letter names (National Council for the Accreditation of Teacher Education [NCATE] 2000).

This is a tall order, but you should be able to master it from studying this chapter and the previous one. The idea that "spelling is developmental" has just been covered, and you know what language development means: children's discoveries, finding patterns in the language they hear used around them, positing invented rules for language use that unfold in stages. These things occur as children learn to talk as well as write. The *phonological system* is the system of meaningful speech sounds of words: syllables, onsets and rimes, and phonemes. It also includes the ways consonants and vowels are produced, including digraph consonants and tense and lax vowels. *Judgments of phonetic similarities and differences* is what children are making when they spell a lax vowel like the one in *pet* with the acoustically most similar vowel letter name *A* (as in *PAT* for *pet*), or the consonant phoneme that is conventionally represented by the digraph *sh* with the single letter *H* (as in *HEK* for *chick*).

system that works not by showing pictures of things, not by representing syllables, but by matching letters with phonemes. Now what?

Now comes the process of discovering the system by which writing spells words and letters and clusters of letters represent sounds or groups of sounds. This kind of knowledge is called *phonics*. It is also called *orthographic knowledge* and *letter-to-sound relationships*. The patterns that relate letters to sounds are complex. They come in layers that are peeled back, essentially in stages, by the child who is encouraged to be an active explorer of written language. Teachers need to be aware of them; and they are written into many states' learning standards for teachers (see the Standards and Literacy box).

TEACH IT! 15

Making and Breaking Words

INVENTED SPELLING AND WORD KNOWLEDGE. One of the best ways to observe children's growth in their orthographic knowledge—that is, knowledge of the spelling structure of words—is through their invented spelling (see Chapter 3). As Gill (1992) and others (Mann, Tobin, & Wilson, 1987) have noted, when children spell words they have not been taught, that is, when their spelling is the result of invention and not of memorization, their invented spelling gives us a window into the complicated issues of how children understand the relationships between spoken words and written symbols, also known as their **word knowledge**. Word knowledge consists of more than the sum total of correct spellings the child has memorized. It more accurately refers to their awareness of the units of language such as words, syllables, onsets and rimes, and phonemes and of the many ways in which words are represented by letters and groups of letters.

Research and experience show that it can be useful to encourage even beginning readers to venture their own ideas of how letters can represent sounds. This practice helps in several ways:

1. It leads children to focus carefully on the spoken language they want to write down and practice finding its units of sound.
2. It challenges children to think of the relationships between letters and sounds.
3. It provides useful diagnostic information to the teacher about the children's growth as writers and even as readers.

Looking at children's invented spellings can help to answer questions like these:

- Does this child appear to have a concept of word? Can the child make words "hold still" in his or her mind while the child examines their parts and decides how to spell those parts?
- Can this child segment words into phonemes?
- Can this child match letters to phonemes? Which ones?
- Which principles of the English writing system does this child understand? Letters-to-sounds? Onsets and rimes? Marking of long and short vowels? Grammatical endings? Word families?

The World of Reading

The Development of Storybook Reading: Language and Print Together

A line of development that combines both language awareness and concepts about print is children's progress in storybook reading. Researcher Elizabeth Sulzby (1985) has shown us that having children pretend-read a favorite storybook can be a very useful way to observe their concepts of what reading is about and how language is captured in print. When we read a storybook to children at the age of four or five, they often ask to have it read again. A storybook that is read to a child three or more times, especially when it is requested, can be said to be a favorite storybook. What happens if we ask the child to read that favorite storybook back to us? With a little encouragement, most children will pretend-read the book; when they do, they are demonstrating for us their conception of what reading is. Sulzby has observed hundreds of children rereading favorite storybooks and has documented stages or advancing strategies that children use to read books. Her stages are repeated by other children so reliably that watching for them can give us a developmentally based assessment tool.

- **Picture naming.** At the earliest of the book-reading strategies, the child points at the picture, shouts the name of the depicted object, then points to the next page and does the same thing. As Sulzby notes, such a child is repeating a ritual he or she has been through many times with a parent or other adult reader, who often opens a book, points to a picture, says, "What's that?" waits for the child's answer, then says, "Right! That's a _____!"
- **Verbal storytelling with conversation.** Slightly later, some time around the age of four or five years, the child will point to the pictures and then weave an oral story around them in a conversation with the adult. This is not a stand-alone story yet, as it still relies on an adult for support. It also is cued by the pictures rather than by the print on the page or the exact words the child remembers from the adult's reading.

- **Verbal storytelling without conversation.** At a slightly later time, often around age five, a child will tell a story while paging through the book from picture to picture. The story is clearly a told story, and if the child pretend-reads this book more than once, no attempt will be made to keep the wording the same.
- **Talking like a book.** Still later, the child will use a singsong, rather distant voice that sounds like a reader's—sometimes even complete with stumbling over words—while creating a monologue to accompany the pictures. Amazingly, the child is still not actually reading the words, which you will note when the monologue bears little resemblance to what is on the page.
- **Refusal to read.** At a still later stage when asked to read the book aloud, the child will become troubled by the request. Why? Because the child doesn't know how to read the words. This is actually a breakthrough. Not knowing the words did not prevent pretend-reading of the book before. But now the child seems to have realized that to read a book, one has to look at the print and know how to pronounce it as spoken language.
- **Reading a word or two.** Still later, when asked to pretend-read the book, the child will look for known words and read them aloud.

This fascinating sequence of strategies shows the child moving from a series of isolated verbal responses to pictures to a woven verbal text—first with the support of conversation and then without support, followed by a phase of talking like a book and then leading to the realization that to truly read, one must know how to bring to life exactly the words that are written on the page. Once that last discovery has been made, the child is ready to match the expected words with the words on the page (and doubtless bringing into play other knowledge, such as the concept of word and knowledge of letters) and read a few words aloud. The child has gone from playful imitation of the whole of reading to a careful study of the details. Bit by bit, especially if given books written on an accessible level, the child will be able to return to the whole while reading the entire book aloud.

How Does a Teacher Nurture Emergent Literacy?

Classrooms where literacy emerges are set up and managed by thoughtful teachers who understand how children learn to read and write and who carefully follow each child's development and provide each child the opportunities to learn what she or he needs to know at a given time. These teachers make literacy—listening, reading, and writing—a rich part of every school day. Let us look at a few active and passive ways in which you can help literacy grow in an early childhood classroom.

Arranging Classrooms for Literacy Learning

To promote literacy, reading and writing must be made part of the classroom environment. The classroom itself should demonstrate both the importance of literacy and the way literacy works while also providing many opportunities for children to observe and use written language. There are many ways in which classrooms can be arranged passively to immerse children in print.

LABELS.   Label objects around the classroom with written letters that are readable from far off. Every several days, take time to "read the room" with the children together (Fountas & Pinnell, 1996) as you or a student points to the labels with a pointer or ruler. Remind students to listen for the first sounds in the words, such as in *door*, and point out that the first letter in *door* is D.

LITERACY PLAY.   Make props readily available to support children's dramatic play. Some of these props might include reading and writing. For example, the doctor's office has an eye chart and a pad for the doctor to write prescriptions. Shelves in a grocery store might have labels (*fruit, soup, bread*) where the grocer would stock the items and pads handy for the customers to use for writing grocery lists.

Allowing children to act out stories encourages interpretive imagination, and the active involvement adds fun.

CLASSROOM LIBRARY.   Create a classroom library in a corner of the room. It should have a carpet and comfortable chairs (such as beanbag chairs) for creating an inviting reading environment. Include a space for displaying books so that children can see their covers, and change the books on display every few days to catch the children's eyes. Books should accommodate a range of tastes, from informational books with bright illustrations to simple patterned books. On a regular basis, read a book or part of a book aloud and then place it on display in the library corner to entice children to look it over. The classroom library should include books written by individual classroom authors and books written or dictated by the whole class—perhaps books of favorite jokes and riddles, books about animals, and books about the seasons.

CHARTS AND POSTERS.   Display on the walls around the classroom posters of children's books and pictures of authors. You can solicit these directly from children's book publishers. Children know authors such as Rosemary Wells, Dr. Seuss, Arnold Lobel, Cynthia Rylant, and Alma Flor Ada, and the children are excited when the teacher announces that the class has a new book by one of these or other authors they know and like. You can also display charts of interesting things, such as volcanoes and maps of the town or neighborhood with the children's street names labeled. You could also include autobiographical posters with each child's name and something special that each child has dictated. Children love to see their own works posted.

CLASSROOM POST OFFICE.   Include in your classroom a post office where children can mail letters. Each child could have a mailbox (constructed from three-inch cardboard tubes) for receiving mail. Have children write each other letters at least once a week; the teacher should also make a point of writing something to put in each child's box every few days.

WRITING CENTER.   Create a writing center with paper, markers, and pencils. Include magazines as sources of pictures that can be cut out and glued to attach them as illustrations for children's compositions.

Reading Aloud to Children

Reading aloud is one of the most useful, active things adults can do to nurture children's literacy growth. Many of the abilities that are considered essential to literacy can be developed as children listen to a book read aloud by a parent or teacher. Among the benefits of being read to are the following:

Big Book Lesson: Five-Day Plan for Using a Big Book

- *It expands their vocabulary.* As Stanovich (1992) has pointed out, there are words that are more commonly encountered in books—even children's books—than in conversation or from watching television. Listening to books being read aloud helps children learn a literate vocabulary.
- *It develops their ability to comprehend written language.* Research on reading comprehension tells us that it involves component skills that include perceiving main ideas and supporting details, making inferences, venturing predictions and confirming them, and visualizing in the mind's eye what the words suggest. Children have the opportunity to develop all of these abilities from listening to a book being read aloud and discussing it.
- *It encourages enthusiasm for literacy as they participate in the teacher's excitement.* When children first learn to talk, parents slow down and exaggerate their speech and their gestures as if to say, "This is how language works. This is how we show excitement and interest. This is the way we soothe each other." Similarly, when adults read books aloud with expression, they have the opportunity to show children how written language conveys the full range of emotions. This not only will make literacy appealing to children, but also will show them how to derive meaning and associate emotions with the language of print.
- *It makes them aware of the structure of stories and of other kinds of texts.* Skilled readers learn to find questions and pursue answers according to the structure of whatever text they are reading. A story shows characters in settings, the problems they have, and how those problems are solved. Expository writing frames questions about topics and goes about answering those questions. By reading texts aloud and commenting on them, a careful teacher can help students to become aware of the recurring structures of different texts and use them to guide their comprehension.

Reading aloud at least twenty minutes each day should be a regular feature of every classroom from preschool through the primary grades and on through the elementary grades. Even when children are learning to read, it is not until fourth grade that many children's reading ability approaches the speed and fluency with which teachers can read to them. Many children's reading rate will take much longer to develop. Therefore, the teacher's reading aloud is a necessary source of language, of stories, and of information for children (see the following Teach It! box).

TEACH IT!

Refer to your **Teach It!** booklet for further activities you can use to reinforce concepts discussed in this chapter.

Reading Aloud

You certainly do not need advanced training to read a book aloud successfully with children! Nonetheless, good preparation is rewarded by a more satisfying experience all around. We suggest following these steps when reading aloud to children:

1. **Prepare to read the book.** Read the book through yourself before you read it to children. Decide whether it is suitable for this group. Does it have enough excitement or depth to hold the interest of a whole group? If it is suitable, decide how you want to read it—with humor, with drama, with questions to whet curiosity? If there are voices to bring to life, decide how you want to make each one sound. If you decide to stop reading to ask for predictions or discussion, decide where the stopping places should be. If there are any words or ideas that will be unfamiliar to the children, make a note to pronounce them carefully and explain them to the children.

   If the book has illustrations large enough for the children to see, practice reading the book through while you hold it in front of and facing away from you, where the children will be able to read it.

2. **Prepare the children.** Make sure the children are seated comfortably where they can see and hear you. Most teachers prefer to have the children sit on a carpet or cushions in front of them. Remind the children, if you need to, of the behavior you expect of good listeners: hands to themselves, eyes on the teacher, and ears for the story.

3. **Begin to read.** Show the children the cover of the book. Ask them what they know about the topic. If you want to arouse more curiosity, quickly show them some other pictures in the interior of the book (but not the last pages, keep the children in suspense about those). Ask the children to make predictions about what will happen or what they expect to find out in the book.

   Turn to the title page. Read the author's name and the illustrator's. Talk about what each contributed to the book. It might help to point out that if only one name is given, then the illustrator and author are the same person. Otherwise, the children should know that the author and illustrator both have important things to do to bring the book into being. (Publishers usually pay authors and illustrators equally and usually encourage them to work independently of each other.) Remind the children of any other books they know by this author or this illustrator.

4. **While reading.** As you read the book through the first time, ask for comments about what is going on. How is the character feeling? What is the character's problem? What do they think the character can do to solve the problem? Ask the students to predict what will happen. Read a few pages, then stop again. Ask how things look for the character now. What is the character doing to solve the problem? How is it working? What do the children think will happen now? Why do they think so? Stop right before the end and ask for last predictions. You can add to the suspense if you take an obvious quick look at the last page, but don't let the children see it. Then ask the children to predict what will be on the last page.

5. **Follow up the reading.** Ask the children whether the book turned out the way they thought it would. What made them think it would turn out that way, or why were they surprised? What did they like about the book? How did it make them feel? Why?

6. **Reread the book.** Read the book a second time through. This time, you might want to take more time to look at the ways the illustrator pictured the action. If there are any chants given in the book, ask children to repeat them. If there is time, ask questions about characters, motives, and other things you and the students find interesting about the book.

7. **Leave the book available to the children.** Put the book on display in the library corner, and encourage children to read it later during scheduled time in the reading center or between other activities. The children might especially enjoy taking turns reading it to each other.

Extending Reading Experiences for Younger Children

The meanings of books can loom larger in children's imaginations by providing them opportunities to respond to the books in various ways. Although children of all ages can talk about what they read (Martinez & Roser, 1991), younger children find it most natural to respond to books with their whole bodies: by getting up and moving around, by chanting chants, by acting out parts, and by drawing key scenes (Hickman, 1992). English language learners have more opportunities to participate if meaningful responses to stories are encouraged through drama, music, and art rather than through discussion only.

USE CHANTS. A very engaging form of response to a story is to repeat a key phrase or chant every time it occurs in a book. English language learners profit from repeating shorter chants, which become nuggets of remembered language that are useful models of grammar and good for pronunciation practice. Children listening to the traditional English tale, "The Little Red Hen," love to repeat the animals' refrains:

> *"Who will help me plant the wheat?"*
> *"Not I," said the Duck.*
> *"Not I," said the Cat.*
> *"Not I," said the Dog.*
> *"Then I will plant it all myself," said the Little Red Hen. And she did.*

USE DRAMA. Many children's books have clear patterns of actions that are easy for children to act out. Some books, such as Michael Rosen's *We're Going on a Bear Hunt* (2003) and Frances Temple's *Tiger Soup* (1992), are already scripted for children to act out. Both have chants and movements that the children will enjoy. *The Three Billy Goats Gruff* is not scripted as a play, but it has simple, repeated actions and chants that are easy for children to practice and perform. The whole story can be rehearsed and staged in a single class period. If time is short, single scenes of longer stories can be acted out, too.

Acting involves interpretation. You can encourage children to interpret stories imaginatively as they rehearse the dramatizations: "How does the little goat feel when he sees the troll? How might he look at that point? What would his voice sound like?" Props help children get into character. In *The Three Billy Goats Gruff*, horns made of construction paper bring the goats to life, and a robe and a club add to the troll's fierceness. Construction paper masks indicate which character is Tiger and which one is Anansi, the Spider in *Tiger Soup*.

USE ART. Drawing is a favorite way for children to respond to a story. The drawings may be extended by asking the children to leave space at the bottom of their papers and think of one line they want to dictate to the teacher. The children can rehearse reading these lines and then take them home to read to family members. Another activity, "Sketch to Stretch" (Short, Harste, & Burke, 1996), is a wonderful way to add interpretation when children draw in response to a story. After they have listened to a story, the children draw their favorite part or the most important part. Then one child is invited to be the artist and display his or her work for the critics (classmates) to interpret. After the critics have noted the features in the drawing and commented on what they think each one means, the artist then gets to interpret his or her own work, telling the critics why the story was depicted as it was.

Dialogic Reading

When working with individual children, one approach to reading with children, called **dialogic reading**, helps put the child in the active role as a storyteller and not just a listener. Dialogic reading results in gains in children's language acquisition and growth in concepts about print (Whitehurst & Lonigan, 2001).

Dialogic reading is intended to be used by parents, teachers, and volunteer tutors (including college students working in special literacy programs such as America Reads or Jumpstart). In some communities, training in dialogic reading is available through family literacy programs offered by public libraries. The training is supported by twenty-minute videotapes (Whitehurst, 1994). Adult readers are taught to read interactively with the child. Two acronyms, PEER and CROWD, are used to remind the adult readers of the steps. PEER is a mnemonic for a strategy used to nurture language development with younger children as they read a book together with an adult. The letters stand for:

Prompt the child to name objects in the book and talk about the story.

Evaluate the child's responses and offer praise for adequate responses and alternatives for inadequate ones.

Expand on the child's statements with additional words.

Repeat by asking the child to repeat the adult's utterances.

For more advanced children, a more advanced form of dialogic reading called CROWD is used. The acronym CROWD identifies five kinds of questions adults ask:

Completion prompts. Ask the child to supply a word or phrase that has been omitted. (For example, "I see a yellow duck looking at _____.")

Recall prompts. Here the child is asked about things that occurred earlier in the book. ("Do you remember some animals that Brown Bear saw?")

Open-ended prompts. Here the child is asked to respond to the story in his or her own words. ("Now it's your turn: You say what is happening on this page.")

Wh- prompts. The adult asks *what*, *where*, *who*, and *why* questions. ("What is that yellow creature called? Who do you think Brown Bear will see next?")

Distancing prompts. Here the child is asked to relate the content of the book to life experiences. ("Do you remember when we saw a yellow duck like that one swimming in the lake? Was it as big as this one?")

Dialogic reading can be carried out by trained volunteers (see the Differentiated Instruction box).

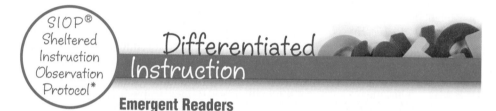

SIOP® Sheltered Instruction Observation Protocol*

Differentiated Instruction

Emergent Readers

Emergent literacy faces in two directions. In one direction, it focuses on the concepts about reading, writing, and written language that children have acquired at home. The teacher can build on those and make a bridge that connects what children are figuring out for themselves with the formal reading curriculum. In another direction, emergent literacy helps us realize the concepts and abilities that some children have not developed yet—concepts and skills they will need to be successful in learning to read and write. These children will need to

- Be read to, to boost their vocabulary and their familiarity with books.
- Explore print, as in giving dictations and having someone read them back.
- Learn the letters of the alphabet.

These are critical experiences, but fortunately it is not such a long list. One way to make sure children get these experiences is to recruit and supervise volunteers. The U.S. Department of Education provides funding for college students to be paid from work-study funds to serve as tutors. Many colleges and high schools have service learning classes in which students are required to perform some kind of community service. Student volunteers can offer effective help to young readers who need it. The key to the success of such efforts is the teacher's supervision. Tutoring is far more effective when a teacher assesses the children in advance to see exactly what they need, and orients and supervises the tutors to make sure they provide the right help (Morris, 2005).

PHONICS and **PHONOLOGICAL AWARENESS**

How is awareness of the sound constituents of language an advantage to children's reading development?

Teaching Phonological Awareness

As noted earlier in this chapter, children who are aware of the sound constituents of language have an advantage when it comes to reading words because they will sense the elements of words that are matched with letters. The National Reading Panel (NRP) (2000) recommends that teachers teach phonological awareness in kindergarten through second grade. This teaching may occupy a short part of each day—six or seven minutes—to yield the twenty hours a year of phonological training that the NRP recommends. Activities to boost phonological awareness can take place at several levels.

LISTENING GAMES FOR LANGUAGE AWARENESS.   Children need to pay attention to language—to listen for words, to move their bodies in response to words, to clap along with the rhythm of language, and to notice rhymes. A number of enjoyable listening activities can help them develop these skills.

Games that play on deleting words.   Folk singer John McCutcheon (**http://www.folkmusic.com/**) taught us this gesture song, which is popular with young children. The verse is sung to the tune of *The Battle Hymn of the Republic.*

John Brown's Ford.

John Brown's (Stroke your chin, indicating a beard.)

Ford (Turn an imaginary steering wheel with both hands.)

Hit a bump (Smack the palm of one hand with the palm of the other.)

Upon the road (Move your hand in front of you, palm down.)

John Brown's (Stroke your chin, indicating a beard.)

Ford (Turn an imaginary steering wheel with both hands.)

Hit a bump (Smack the palm of one hand across the palm of the other.)

Upon the road (Move your hand in front of you, palm down.)

John Brown's (Stroke your chin, indicating a beard.)

Ford (Turn an imaginary steering wheel with both hands.)

Hit a bump (Smack the palm of one hand across the palm of the other.)

Upon the road (Move your hand in front of you, palm down.)

But he went rocking right along (Rock back and forth in your seat.)

The second time through, don't sing "John Brown's" but just stroke your chin. The third time don't sing "John Brown's" or "Ford" but do both gestures, and keep dropping out words until the whole song is done in mime.

Listening games with gestures.   The following poem (by Bucksnort Trout, in Temple & MaKinster, 2005) is recited by the teacher or the tutors numerous times until the children learn it. Then they recite it, complete with finger gestures.

My ears can hear the baby cry	(Cup ear, as if listening.)
My nose can smell the bacon fry	(Touch nose.)
My tongue can taste the toast and jelly	(Point to your tongue.)
My hands can feel my happy belly	(Lightly rub your belly.)
My eyes can see my Mama smile	(Put hands on both sides of your eyes.)
Because she looooves to feed this child	(Fold arms, smile, and rock.)
And every day goes mighty well	(Throw your arms wide.)
'Cause I see, hear, touch, taste, and smell.	(Point to your eyes, ears, fingers, tongue, and nose.)

Listening for special words.   "Magic Words" are target words to listen for. Say a word like *hotdog*, and tell the children that you are about to tell a story that will have the word *hotdog* in it—they should clap their hands when they hear the word. Start telling the story. For instance, you could say,

> *Last summer I went down to the park. I was really hungry, so I walked up to the food counter and ordered a —— hamburger. The waitress said "We don't have hamburgers. I'll have to make you a hotdog."*

Make up several stories with the word *hotdog*. Later ask the children to give you a new magic word, and then you make up a story that has that word in it. The children can take turns making up stories of their own with magic words in them and tell them to others.

Next, you can raise the level of challenge of the magic word game by asking children to listen for two words together. If those words are *ironing board*, for instance, you might say,

My father was ironing his shirt. He was ironing it on the table, but the table got too hot. He was ironing it on the floor, but the floor was too dirty. "Daddy," I said. "I know. Why don't you try ironing on the ironing board that's in the closet?"

You can also have children listen for one word repeated two times, such as *short short*.

There was a girl named Short. But Short wasn't short. Short was tall. Her friend Gladys was short. One day Gladys asked Short, "If you were short, Short, your name would match you better." (Temple & MaKinster, 2005)

Clap out words.   You can make clapping games that range from the simple to the elaborate. Clapping their hands to the words you pronounce is an easy game for young children. Clapping in a sequence adds more challenge: hands together, hands on knees, hands on chest, hands on sides of thighs. Have children clap to these words as you say them with emphasis:

When—I—go—to—Lu's—big—house
I—like—to—play—with—Lu's—pet—mouse.

SONGS, CHANTS, AND POEMS.   Songs, chants, and poems are a natural way to get children to pay attention to rhymes and to memorize words, phrases, and sentences that will aid language development. They are also a lot of fun to learn and repeat.

A song like this one invites hand claps and close attention to the rhymes:

Miss Mary Mack

Dressed in black

Silver buckles

Up and down her back

The lyrics are available in book form. Tutors and new teachers are advised to seek out collections of songs, especially those with tapes. The following are good bets:

Cole, J. (1990). *Miss Mary Mack.* New York: Morrow.

Beall, P., Nipp, S., & Klein, N. (2002). *Wee sing 25th anniversary celebration.* New York: Price Stern Sloan.

Fox, D. (1987). *Go In and Out the Window.* New York: Henry Holt.

Jenkins, E. (1997). *Ella Jenkins songbook for children.* New York: Music Sales Corp.

Krull, K. (1995). *Gonna sing my head off.* New York: Knopf.

Milnes, G. (1999). *Granny, will your dog bite?* Little Rock, AR: August House.

Orozco, J-L. (1994). *De Colores and other Latin American folk songs for children.* New York: Dutton.

———*Diez deditos and other play rhymes and action songs from Latin America* (1997). New York: Puffin.

———*Fiestas: A year of Latin American songs of celebration* (2004). New York: Puffin.

Crawford Seeger, R. (1993). *American folksongs for children.* New York: Linnet Books.

All of these are valuable additions to a teacher's personal collection. Also, experienced teachers know many other songs that you can learn from them. Songs for transitions, songs that introduce tasks, songs to celebrate special people—all of these are essential for a teacher's repertoire. When you find a teacher who knows these songs, write them down! And also, bring along a small tape recorder so you can capture the tunes.

Other activities that boost phonological awareness at various levels include the following:

At the syllable level:

- Children can clap along to the syllables in their names—"*Bet-ty*," "*Ta-kee-sha*," "*Da-vid*."
- Children can raise their hands when the teacher says a word with one syllable, two syllables, or three syllables.
- When the teacher says "One syllable!" a child must say a one-syllable word; when the teacher says, "Two syllables!" and calls on a child, that child says a word with two syllables; and so on.

At the onset and rime level:

- Children are asked to supply rhymes to complete couplets such as the following:

    Ding, dong, dell
    Kitty's in the _____ (*well*)
    Ding, dong, dasement
    Kitty's in the _____ (*basement*)
    Ding, dong, dimming pool
    Kitty's in the _____ (*swimming pool*)

- When the teacher says a target word, such as *boy*, the children raise their hands when they hear a word that rhymes with it when the teacher says a list of words such as "*tea, tock, tack, toy*."
- When the teacher says a word such as *bat* and then pronounces the sound /k/, the children say a new word that begins with the sound /k/ and rhymes with *bat: cat*.

At the phoneme level:

Three kinds of tasks are generally used to increase children's awareness of phonemes: One is **phoneme segmentation**. Segmentation means to break something into small parts. Phoneme segmentation tasks have children take spoken words and break them into their individual sounds.

- A spoken exercise goes like this: "If I say *dog* /d/ /o/ /g/, you say *cat, ball,* and *foot* the same way."
- The children place letter markers into boxes as they pronounce each letter sound. Then they say the word that is formed by the sounds (Elkonin, 1973) (see Figure 4.7 and Chapter 11).
- Once children begin to learn letter sounds, they can practice pushing tokens marked with letters. For example, given a card marked with three boxes, and the three letter chips, *l, e,* and *t*, the child places each letter into the box, pronouncing its sound at the same time: *ull, ehhh, tuh,* and then saying the whole word *let*.

    A second way children become aware of phonemes is to combine phonemes into words. For example,

- the teacher asks, "What word do I get if I add the sounds of *ih* and *tuh*? or *suh* and *ay*? or *cuh, uh,* and *puh*?

TEACH IT! 15

Making and Breaking Words

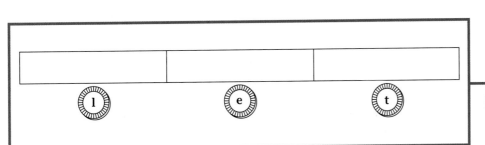

FIGURE 4.7

A third way that children become aware of phonemes is to delete a phoneme from a word and say what word is left over. For instance,

- The teacher asks, "What word do I get if I take off the sound *suh* from *slot*? Or if I take off the sound *duh* from *find*?

Games that work with phonemes can be playful, of course. For example, the children can sing a song that substitutes the vowel sounds:

I like to eat, eat, eat, apples and bananas.
I like to eat, eat, eat, apples and bananas.
I like to oot, oot, oot, ooples and bonoonoos.
I like to oot, oot, oot, ooples and bonoonoos.
I like to oat, oat, oat, oples and bononos.
I like to oat, oat, oat, oples and bononos.

Teaching the Alphabet

Children pay closer attention to the letters of the alphabet after they have come to notice writing as a holistic display (Gibson & Levin, 1975). That means, as we saw earlier in this chapter, that children will spend considerable time doing pretend-reading of books and producing scribbles and mock writing before they come to focus consistently on individual letters. Nonetheless, teachers can encourage children's learning processes by pointing out individual letters and by making displays of letters prominent in the classroom. If teachers hold off teaching children letters of the alphabet until they show readiness to learn, they might inadvertently penalize children who have not been given alphabet books or taken to the library. Children will undeniably learn the alphabet more quickly and easily when they have pretend-read and scribbled their way to the point at which they are paying close attention to letters. Nonetheless, it is important to show all children the letters anyway, as this kind of learning is too important to delay.

DISPLAYING PRINT. Even as you invite children to write inventively, including mock-writing, or read to them and show them print, you also need to show them individual letters and demonstrate how the letters are formed. There are many ways of doing this:

- Alphabet letter cards can be posted around the room, with pictures of objects that feature that letter.
- Letter-sorting and letter-matching games can be arranged for children to play with at center time.
- Children can practice writing letters at their desks as the teacher writes a model. They may use large-ruled paper for this or individual slates and chalk. Later, they may practice writing letters with a grease pencil on a transparency film overlaid on sample words with large letters.
- Alphabet strips can be taped to children's desks. A strip of tagboard with the letters of the alphabet carefully printed in lowercase can be attached to each child's desk in front of the pencil tray. Such strips are available commercially, or they can be produced by the teacher or by an aide.
- The alphabet song can be taught, with the teacher pointing to the letter cards as the children sing the song slowly.
- Children's names can be written on cards and taped to their desks, with the first letter of the first name written in a bright color. Then the children can practice saying, "A is for *Ana*, B is for *Bart*," and so on.
- Plastic letters can be placed in centers to match with printed letters to form words.
- Sandpaper letters on cards can be used in centers for children to trace with their fingers.
- Letter cards can be sent home so that parents can play letter recognition games with the children.
- Alphabet books can be made. Prepare a blank book for the class and print a letter on the top of each page, A to Z. The children think of objects that begin with the sound of that letter and take turns drawing pictures of those objects on the appropriate page.

TEACH IT! 12

Beginning Sounds
Picture Sorting

TEACH IT! 46

Language Experience
with English Language
Learners

Encouraging Early Writing

The practice of writing can and should begin well before children know how to spell words or even to form letters. When children produce their own versions of writing and when they invent spellings, they are led into exploring how the writing system works and putting forth their own hypotheses about what writing looks like, how it is arranged on a page, how writing represents ideas, and how the spelling system works. The child who is actively investigating these questions is alert to the ways the system actually works. With encouragement and some lessons from the teacher, that child should progress step by step and stage by stage to standard writing and spelling and fluent and meaningful reading. Teachers can encourage early writing in several ways.

WRITING WORKSHOP.   Beginning in kindergarten, many teachers conduct writing workshops three or four days per week. (Writing workshops are described in greater detail in Chapter 8.) For emergent readers and writers, teachers begin by reminding children of the topics they want to write about. Children who are reluctant to begin writing immediately might draw a picture of their topic. The teacher reminds the students to leave space at the bottom of the drawing for their writing. The children then have a period of ten to fifteen minutes for writing and drawing at their seats. Those who have drawn pictures write captions underneath their drawings. Then, one at a time, they take the page to the teacher and read it aloud to her or him. The teacher writes the words correctly above the child's words and might take this opportunity to show the children how letters represent sounds. During sharing time, children share their works with the rest of the class.

The writing workshop should have a period of time set aside for focused lessons that show students how to handle particular aspects of writing. A very useful focused lesson for young children is shared writing, an effective strategy for demonstrating how spoken words are broken into sounds and spelled with letters and for encouraging writing (Tompkins, 2000). A sample lesson in shared writing might go as is shown in the Teach It! box.

DICTATION.   Taking dictation from children, long considered part of the language experience approach (Stauffer, 1975), is one of the most effective techniques for teaching children about literacy. The technique is especially useful for English language learners because it provides an opportunity to attach language to meaningful concepts and then shows how that talk can be represented in print.

LANGUAGE and DIVERSITY

Why are dictations particularly useful for English language learners?

Using the dictation method can demonstrate very directly the whole purpose of writing and reading: to encode and decode meaningful messages and to help record experiences that can be retrieved and reviewed later. Taking dictation enhances children's language awareness by slowing down their words and capturing them in print. The teacher can show children how print is laid out on the page, that language comes in units of words, and that words come in phonemes. The teacher can also show how letters represent sounds and words. In short, using dictation teaches language awareness, phonemic segmentation, and phonics. Taking and rereading students' dictations also teach them to recognize words.

Dictated experience accounts have the advantage of recording children's own experiences in their own words, which is a source of excitement and motivation for many children (Ashton-Warner, 1963). But dictated accounts have the drawback of being disjointed and unpredictable, as might be expected of a text dictated by a group. Young readers like to read predictable and patterned text, and they find such text easier to read. A compromise approach is to have children learn a patterned text orally and then dictate that text to the teacher and proceed with the steps outlined above.

Two sources of patterned texts for dictation are songs and poems. Children can learn song verses, dictate them for the teacher to record, and then sing them as the teacher points to the words. Children can make up their own verses to songs, too; songs like *Down by the Bay* and *Corner Grocery Store*, with their highly patterned verses, are easy and inviting to innovate on. Another source of patterned text is retold stories. After the children have heard

Sample Writing Lesson

After discussing an exciting event with his students, a teacher gathers kindergarteners around an easel and invites them to help write about the event. First they agree on a short sentence they want to write:

A fireman came to school.

They practice saying the sentence several times so that everyone is aware of the words. The teacher then tells the students that they will write the first word and asks, "Who can tell us what letter we need to write?"

A child suggests the letter *A,* and the teacher accepts it, writes it slowly on the easel, and then says, "We wrote *A.* Now what's the next word we want to write?"

After someone says, "*Fireman,*" the teacher says, "Right. It's *fireman.* That's a new word, so I'm going to leave space between the word *A* and the first letter of this new word."

The teacher puts his finger after the *A* to identify the space and says, "What is the first sound we hear in *fireman?*"

When the students identify the first sound, the teacher asks, "What letter are we going to use to write the *fuh* sound in *fireman?*"

The teacher pauses for responses and then says, "Right. It's *F.* Who can come up and write the letter *F* for me?"

This process continues as the group works through the entire sentence. When they are finished, the teacher might end up with

A FIRMN CAM TO SKOL.

The teacher concludes by saying, "This could say *A fireman came to school.* Later on, I will show you another way to write it."

The teacher recognizes that these kindergarten children—most of whom are prephonemic or early phonemic spellers—will not be ready to focus on the silent letters in *fireman* and *came* or on the uncommon spelling of *sch* in *school.* Later, when the children can produce letter name spellings, the teacher will show them where silent letters and other conventional spellings would be added to these words to show the students the next challenges they will need to master. But for now, matching letters with phonemes is a sufficient challenge for these children. Shared writing lessons can be conducted almost daily with a class. In the meantime, children should be encouraged to use writing every chance they get.

TEACH IT! ③
Language Experience or Group Dictated Story

a story read aloud to them a couple of times, they can retell a short and memorable version for the teacher to record and read back with them. Following a group dictation, the teacher can prepare smaller versions of texts to give to each student for individual reading. These texts, typed by the teacher or a parent volunteer on a word processor and photocopied, can be used in many ways. Pairs of students might "buddy-read" two copies of the text with each other. Children might take the texts home with them, with instructions to the parents such as those found in Figure 4.8 on page 131. Children's collections of readings can be put on loose-leaf paper and clipped in a binder. Children enjoy rereading songs, poems, and stories together well after they were originally dictated, and this repeated reading makes the words more familiar to the children.

Using Books

USING BIG BOOKS. Big books were the brainchild of New Zealand educator Don Holdaway (1979). Holdaway wanted to be able to teach children to read from well-composed, patterned texts, yet have texts that were big enough to allow the teacher to guide the children's attention to features of the text as they read them. At first, Holdaway produced his own versions of big books, and many teachers still make their own; but now trade book publishers and textbook publishers alike are producing big-book versions of many simply written picture books, especially those with highly patterned texts that are especially good for emergent and beginning readers.

Big books can be used to show children the layout of books and also to practice reading and rereading text. In a typical lesson with emergent readers, the teacher reads the book twice.

On the first reading:

- Put the big book on an easel, and call the children's attention to the cover. Point to the title, and have the students read it aloud with you. Ask the students to say what they think the book will be about, given the title, and invite their ideas and predictions.
- Point to the cover illustration, and invite the students to say what they see. When they think of the title and consider the picture, what do they think will happen in the story?
- Open to the title page, and point to the author's name. Make sure the children understand that this is the person who wrote the book. Do the same with the name of the illustrator. Do the children know any other books by either one of them?
- Now turn to the first page of text, and read it aloud, pointing to the words as you go. Read several more pages this way, pausing to discuss a picture or to comment on an action.
- Ask the children to make predictions, even predictions about what will happen on the other side of a page. Sometimes rhyming books have a phrase on one page that ends in a word that is matched with a phrase on the next page ending in a rhyming word. You might pause at the page turn and ask the children what will come next. For example, on one page of John Langstaff's *A Hunting We Will Go* are the words:

> *A hunting we will go*
> *A hunting we will go*
> *We'll catch a fox*

Before turning the page, pause and ask the children to predict what comes next. The text continues:

> *And put him in a box*
> *And then we'll let him go.*

Using big books is a valuable way to introduce students to reading and to help them become familiar with all the elements in books.

On the second reading:

Follow the process described for dictation:

- Go back to the beginning of the book, and invite the children to read it again with you. Using a stylus or something similar, **choral-read** a page with the children.
- Still pointing to the words, **echo-read** the next page with the children.
- Silently point to the words in a repeated phrase, and invite the children to read them.
- Finally, invite individual children to come up and read a line of text as you point to the words.

Following the reading with the group, leave the big book available for children to read individually and to each other.

USING LITTLE BOOKS. Little books are short, patterned, and predictable texts supported by pictures and written at carefully graduated levels of difficulty. The lowest difficulty levels include one or two words on a page, with an illustration that strongly suggests what the words might be. Several titles are available on each level so that child readers can practice reading in material that is accessible. The difference in challenge between levels is so slight that children can find progressively more difficult material within their reading competence.

Reading levels of little books. Publishers of little books provide their own system of levels. The Wright Group/McGraw-Hill, publisher of the Story Box and the Sunshine Series, has twenty levels of books, ranging from "Early Emergent" through "Upper Emergent"

TABLE 4.1

Systems of Leveling Books for Young Readers

BASAL READING LEVELS	SUNSHINE BOOK STAGES	SUNSHINE BOOK LEVELS	READING RECOVERY LEVELS
PP–P	Early emergent	Levels A B C D	1–10
1–2-1	Upper emergent	Levels E F G H I J	11–12
2-2–3-1	Early fluency	Levels K L M N	13–20
3-2–4	Fluency	Levels O P Q R S T	

and "Early Fluency" to "Fluency." These levels would cover most children from kindergarten through late second or early third grade, and they are designated by letters.

The Reading Recovery Program (Clay, 1993) makes regular use of little books and has identified twenty difficulty levels from late kindergarten to late second grade. **Reading Recovery** levels are given in numbers and not letters, and they roughly correspond to the Wright Group/McGraw Hill levels. Reading Recovery levels are widely accepted by teachers in organizing their books by difficulty level.

To complicate matters further, Informal Reading Inventories and basal reading textbooks report reading levels as grade equivalents: PP (preprimer), P (primer), 1 (second half of first grade), 2-1 (first half of second grade), and so on. Table 4.1 provides a rough correlation of these leveling systems.

Matching children with little books.   The first point in using little books with children is to match the child with the proper level of book. To make sure the book matches the child's reading level, preview a book with a child and then ask the child to read it through. If the child misses at least one but no more than two words in twenty, the book is at the right level for the child to read with supervision. That is, the book challenges the child at an appropriate **instructional reading level**, the level at which the child experiences moderate challenges and learns to read new words and practice new strategies without being overwhelmed by difficulty. (See the Being a Professional Reading Teacher box.)

STRUGGLING   READER

Why are little books so useful for struggling readers?

Teaching with little books.   Using little books helps children to learn concepts about print, strategies for reading, and sight words. Because little books are real books—complete with text, pictures, pages that turn, author, and illustrator—and because they are written simply at the lower levels, with graduated degrees of complexity, they make it easy to call children's attention to the features of text and to practice a few reading strategies at a time. Typically, a teacher has a child read a little book three or more times:

- The first time, the child reads to preview the book to reduce the difficulty of reading it. With the teacher, the child pays attention to the title and the cover illustration, sampling pictures inside and reading a few words and repeated phrases.
- On the second reading, the child grapples with the text, attempting to read the words and derive meaning from the words and the pictures. The teacher provides scaffolding to support the child's reading and teaches and reinforces the child's use of strategies for reading (see below).
- On the third (and possibly fourth and fifth) reading, the child, alone or with minimal support from the teacher, reads the book for pleasure, for practice, and to gain fluency.

Little books are designed to make children successful readers at some level from their very first encounter. To support a child's success, the teacher can use several strategies to scaffold the child's reading activity—that is, to provide just enough support to make it possible for the child to make sense of the book but not so much as to stifle individual motivation for learning. One scaffolding technique that has already been mentioned is to preview the book: to page through and look at the pictures, reading aloud any repeated phrases so

Being a Professional Reading Teacher

Children's Reading Levels

The point of providing children with little books on many levels of reading difficulty is to invite them to "ramp up" their reading skills gradually and even delightfully, with colorful and fun books that are just within each child's level of competence. There are a couple of issues here for the teacher to be mindful of, however.

One concern is that the teacher should be aware of each child's instructional and independent reading levels. The instructional level, which will be discussed at length in Chapter 10, is the level of challenge that is just hard enough, but not too hard for a child. This is the level of text that is recommended when the child is working with the support of a better reader. The independent level, as the name implies, is the level where the child can read on his or her own without support. Even when they are reading at their independent levels, it is recommended that children read the highest-level books that they can read independently.

The other issue is that children be given books that are as substantial as possible, even when they are written on low levels. With a little searching, a teacher can find simply written books that give students something to talk about: such as Chris Rashka's *Yo, Yes!*, Arnold Lobel's *Frog and Toad* stories, and Nancy Shaw and Margot Apple's *Sheep in a Jeep.* Learning to read fluently is important, but children should also learn from the very beginning that the point of reading is to explore meaning.

Your Portfolio

What happens in children's lives before they go to school is a very important determiner of their success in reading years later. Consider writing an advice column for a parent newsletter in which you make recommendations about what they can do at home to support reading for their younger children. It can be a publication suitable for inclusion in your portfolio.

Teaching Resources

Begin to accumulate chants, finger plays, stories that lend themselves to dramatization, puppets, and other resources that you can use to support emergent literacy. Even if you do not teach in a primary grade, they will be useful with your own children or those of friends and relatives. You might expand on some of these in a regular feature for the parent newsletter. Your principal will definitely mention this positively in your annual review.

---

that the child will come to expect them. Another kind of scaffolding is to take turns reading parts of the text. For example, the teacher reads a line and the child reads a line; the teacher reads a passage and the child reads a passage; the teacher reads a page and the child reads a page. As the child gains confidence and ability to read on his or her own, the teacher reduces the scaffolding by taking a lesser role in reading the text.

At the same time, children should be taught to use helpful reading strategies, such as the following, and should be praised when they use those strategies correctly:

- Reading an unknown word by sounding the first letter and thinking of a word that begins with the letter and that would make sense in the passage
- Skipping an unknown word, reading to the end of the passage to get the meaning of the sentence, and then going back and reading the unknown word
- Using the grammatical context of the sentence to narrow down the choices of an unknown word

CLASSROOM-PRODUCED BOOKS. Classroom-produced books provide a useful and enjoyable way to showcase children's authorship and to share their works with each other. Single-author books typically are written or dictated by a child (if written, they have corrected text pasted or written in by the teacher or parent volunteer) and, of course, are illustrated by the child-author. Composite books are collections that all of the children in a class contribute to. The range of such books is very broad; but for emergent readers, the following are recommended. These can be written by the children themselves (with corrections written in darker ink) or simply dictated. Remember that because the books are intended to be read repeatedly by children, the text should be spelled correctly.

Alphabet books: Every child is assigned a letter and writes a word that begins with that letter and draws a picture of it.

Counting books: A group of children are assigned numbers 1 through 10. They draw pictures of 1, 2, 3 (and so on) of something and then write the name of the things (e.g., birds, pennies, cars) next to or under each drawing.

Riddle books: Children contribute individual riddles. The riddle is written on one side of the page and the answer on the other.

Joke books: The jokes of five- and six-year-old children are funny, if only for their lack of obvious humor. Individual children can contribute jokes to a whole-class book.

Concept books: Concept books focus on one or a few specific topics, such as kinds of animals, sports, famous people, things to be thankful for, or images we associate with each season. Ideas for topics are limitless.

FAMILY   LITERACY

Why are kindergarten and first grade important times for connecting with parents and families?

Involving Families in Emergent Literacy

The day a child leaves home to enter kindergarten is a poignant one for families. Many parents feel the shock of having well-meaning strangers take over the intellectual and social parts of their child's upbringing; for parents who feel "different" from the school because of language, culture, or income, the feeling of estrangement can be particularly pronounced. Kindergarten and first grade are especially important times for teachers to reach out and invite parents to take part in their children's education.

Keeping parents involved in their children's education is important for the children, too. Parental involvement in school is positively associated with everything from children's academic achievement to good behavior (they will be less likely to be disruptive) and even eventual resistance to using drugs (National Center for Educational Statistics, 1999, 2002). The amount of time parents devote at home to reading to their children, telling them stories, and teaching them songs is clearly related to the gains children make in literacy. Likewise, a child's level of reading ability in English is related to the mother's reading ability in English.

Not surprisingly, parents' involvement in their children's education and their practice of literacy at home increases with the income and the educational level of the parents. In 1996, at least 80 percent of three- to five-year-old children were read or told stories in the past week by a parent or family member. Children whose parents had a bachelor's degree or more education were more likely to read to their children than were parents whose highest educational level was a high school diploma or less. Also, white children were more likely to have been read to in the past week (approximately 90 percent) than were African American children (approximately 75 percent) and Hispanic children (approximately 65 percent) (National Center for Educational Statistics, 1999).

For emergent readers, families can be involved in their children's literacy instruction in two ways: in the school and at home.

In the Classroom

TECHNOLOGY

There are many excellent on-line resources for teacher-family partnerships.

First, it is desirable for parents to come into the classroom and take part in activities. They can help move instruction forward by reading to children, taking dictation, and helping publish and bind books. They can also tell stories, especially family stories; and they can demonstrate family traditions and crafts. In this latter way, they can make their families' lives part of the curriculum.

Some parents might be more willing than others to come into the class and participate. Parents of children who have been through Head Start might well have been involved in classroom activities already and might have been trained to conduct activities such as reading aloud. For other parents, special invitations and special orientations will probably be required. The National Center for Family Literacy has developed a program to recruit and orient parents to help out in classrooms. A description of the program, called PACT (Parents and Children Together), can be found on the center's Web site at **www.Famlit.org**.

At Home

Family literacy initiatives can also be reinforced at home by sending home to parents materials and ideas for helping develop their children's literacy. Two good examples of home-directed family literacy initiatives are home books and book baggies.

HOME BOOKS.   Simple books with very short and predictable texts can be written and sent home for children to read aloud to their parents. Eight-page home books can be made from one sheet of paper, printed on both sides, and assembled with the two double pages stapled one inside the other. Pictures are added to remind the children of what the text says. A sample text for a home book is shown in Figure 4.8.

   The teacher reads the book through twice with the children before they take it home so that they will be able to read it on their own. Instructions go home with the book for parents to read the book with their children, many times if possible. Home books can go home once a week. They provide useful practice in reading and help children to acquire concepts about print and even sight words.

BOOK BAGGIES.   A book baggie consists of a simple paperback book in a bag with an accompanying activity sheet (such as instructions to draw a favorite character, a word hunt, or an alphabet matching game) and perhaps a recording of the book on tape. Parents are encouraged to read the book with the child and take time to do the accompanying activity. Children should be told how to take care of the book bags when they go home. A book bag may spend several days at a time with each child and then be repacked with a new activity sheet and passed along to a different child.

FIGURE 4.8

A Sample Home Book.

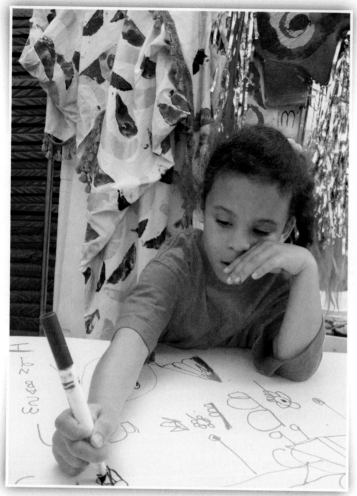

Family involvement in education is associated with children's academic and social success on many levels.

Help with Family Literacy

A parent who was a regular volunteer in a Head Start classroom worried aloud because her child was going into kindergarten the next fall.

"But you can still volunteer in the kindergarten," the teacher pointed out. "They will be happy to have you."

"Me? Suppose they hand me one of those school books to read?" the troubled mother said.

Like this mother, there are parents who do not volunteer to help in school and do not read to their children because they cannot read well themselves. For those parents, the agencies that used to provide adult literacy services are now offering family literacy programs, in which parents who are English language learners are taught basic English and parents who need help with reading are taught to read to their children. These programs can be quite successful because the imperative of helping the children can serve as a motivation for parents to improve their own literacy skills, and the stories they practice to read to their children can be appropriate fare for developing their own reading fluency. For information on programs that offer literacy services to parents, contact the following organizations:

- Literacy Volunteers of America at **www.literacyvolunteers.org**
- The Barbara Bush Literacy Foundation at **www.barbarabushfoundation.com**
- The National Center for Family Literacy at **www.famlit.org**
- The Even Start program at **www.evenstart.org**

For Review

Children's literacy begins to emerge at home, well before they enter school. Once they enter kindergarten and first grade, their literacy develops through a combination of children-driven discoveries and experiences orchestrated by a teacher. A successful teacher of reading and writing in the early years must be part psychologist—a kidwatcher (see Chapter 10), a careful observer of what children have discovered and are discovering for themselves—and part bridge builder, carefully constructing experiences that will lead children from where they are to where they are going as readers and writers.

Although all children develop concepts about print before they enter school, the amount of experience they have with literacy varies widely. A teacher of kindergarten and first grade must both provide lavish opportunities for children to learn about print and target help for children to learn what they need to know. The teacher can also reach out to the home, both to invite families to contribute material from their lives—family stories and traditions, for example—and to enlist the help of parents in helping children practice their literacy.

Emergent literacy refers to the period from early childhood through the first year of school in which children learn about language and print and about reading and writing. In recent years, scholars have come to recognize the role of the child's own discoveries in learning to read and write, and research in literacy has identified aspects of literacy that teachers can help children to develop.

Children must learn about the features of print and how print works. Marie Clay has provided a set of concepts about print that children must honor in their reading. She has also described a set of graphic principles that children try to master in their writing even before they can form recognizable letters. The English writing system is alphabetic—letters of the alphabet represent words by their smallest sounds, called phonemes. This concept, too, must be discovered or otherwise understood by children. Once children recognize the alphabetic principle, they are ready to figure out how letters represent sounds, or phonics. On the writing side, they may discover the mirror image of phonics as they invent ways to use writing to represent words. Understanding children's invented spelling yields valuable insights into their word knowledge, the knowledge they use to read and to spell words.

Teaching for emergent literacy should support and encourage children's processes of discovery, call children's attention to details, and give them guided and independent practice in reading and writing. Parents are children's first teachers, and careful teachers include parents in the school's efforts to help children's literacy emerge.

For Your Journal

1. Take a moment to review your answers to the questions on the Anticipation Guide that opened this chapter. Has your thinking changed? If so, write about the changes in your journal.

2. Recall the discussion in Chapter 3 of children's language learning, and consider those points along with the discussion about emergent literacy. What are two ways in which learning to read and write is like learning to talk? What are some ways in which the processes are different?

3. Teachers and literacy experts differ in the degree to which they expect children to learn about literacy from being immersed in print—that is, being read to and having chances to read and write on their own level—and from being taught the skills of reading. Where along this continuum would you place yourself?

Taking It to the World

1. What are your first memories of reading and writing? Can you remember not being able to read and write? Were you curious about these activities? What things did you do to teach yourself about them?

2. Visit a preschool—a Head Start program, if possible. Ask the teachers what they do to support children's early literacy. How and when are reading and writing used during the day? How have their approaches to supporting children's early literacy changed over the last ten years?

3. To learn about efforts to involve parents in supporting children's literacy, interview an elementary school teacher or administrator. How are parents' ideas and volunteer efforts brought into the classroom? What things are sent home to help parents help their children? What special efforts are being made toward increasing family literacy?

4. Continuing with the interview in item 3, how are English language learners being supported as they learn to read and write? How is the school working with its students' parents?

5. Ask a teacher of kindergarten or first grade to show you samples of children's mock-writing and invented spelling. Using the discussion in this chapter of graphic principles and invented spelling, do a careful analysis of two writing samples from children who appear to be at different points of development.

6. Speak with a kindergarten or first-grade teacher about how he or she assesses students' concepts about print and what types of screenings are used to assess students' reading skills.

7. Visit the Jumpstart Web site (**www.jstart.org/about/**) to determine whether there is a Jumpstart program near your community. What are some possible ways in which you might be able to volunteer some time?

8. Big books are quite expensive. What are some of the advantages of using big books over regular-sized books that make the extra expense worthwhile?

Technology Connections

1. Visit the literacy homepage of the North Central Regional Educational Laboratory at **www.ncrel.org/litweb** and do a search for "emergent literacy." Examine the numerous articles and connections to useful information and materials. A search for "Elizabeth Sulzby" on this Website leads to evaluations of children's emergent writing.

2. The National Right to Read Foundation (**www.nrrf.org**) provides thorough information and support on phonics instruction. The site also raises a number of concerns about issues such as emergent literacy and invented spelling. Visit the "Topical Essays" page to read the critiques of these and other topics.

3. The University of Idaho's Center for Disabilities and Human Development provides training materials for promoting emergent literacy in Head Start centers. The center's Web page can be found at **www.idahocdhd.org/cdhd/emerlit**.

4. Investigate the "Read to Me" program run by the Idaho State Library (**www.lili.org/read/readtome/index.htm**). What programs do they offer to promote family literacy?

5. The Center for Research in Early Reading Achievement is a federally funded consortium of five universities. Its website (**www.ciera.org**) might be the single best site on emergent literacy, with research reports, book reviews, news of conferences, and links to other sites.

Connect with Research

Review the following key words from the chapter and then connect to Research Navigator (**www.researchnavigator.com**) through this book's Companion Website to conduct a search into research on each of the various topics as they relate to reading and literacy education today.

choral-read
concept of word
dialogic reading
echo-read

emergent literacy
graphic principles
instructional reading level
phoneme segementation

Reading Recovery
syllables
word knowledge

Companion Website

To access chapter objectives, practice tests, weblinks, and flashcards, visit the Companion Website at www.ablongman.com/templeallchildren2e.

Go to Allyn & Bacon's MyLabSchool (**www.mylabschool.com**), enter Assignment ID LAV3 into the Assignment Finder. Watch the video, *Contextual Analysis and Story Dramatization,* in which a first-grade teacher conducts a read-aloud activity.

Question: What strategies does this teacher use to promote her students' comprehension of the story? You may also answer the questions at the end of the clip and e-mail your responses to your instructor.

chapter 5

Children's Knowledge of Words

Helping Students Read Words in Context

Phonics and Word Knowledge

Stages of Children's Development of Word Recognition

Alphabetic, Orthographic, and Derivational Readers

Teaching Word Recognition

Phonics and Word Knowledge

Anticipation Guide

The following statements will stimulate your thinking about the topics of this chapter. Answer true or false in response to each statement. As you read and learn more about the topics in these statements, double-check your answers. See what interests you and what prompts your curiosity toward more understanding.

_____ ● Teaching children to read words in English is much harder than teaching them to read in Japanese.

_____ ● *Sight words* are words that are not decoded, but that are recognized instantly.

_____ ● As they learn to read words, children most naturally learn first to read letters, then syllables, then whole words.

_____ ● *Phonics* is an umbrella term for a variety of explicit, implicit, and systematic ways to show children how the print-to-speech/speech-to-print system works.

_____ ● Decoding requires the skill of transforming written words into spoken words. Spelling requires exactly the same thing.

_____ ● If you pronounce any English word slowly enough, you can distinctly hear each one of its constituent sounds, its phonemes.

_____ ● A consonant digraph is a single sound—one in which two separate consonant sounds cannot be heard—that is spelled with two consonant letters.

_____ ● Knowing where a word came from makes little difference in reading that word.

_____ ● Word walls are groups of words, usually arranged in columns, written on chart paper and hung on the wall.

_____ ● The English spelling system is so irregular that looking for patterns in it is a complete waste of time.

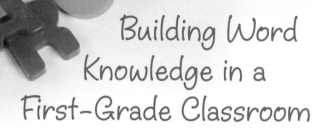

Building Word Knowledge in a First-Grade Classroom

First-grade teacher Ms. Gupta has students who range from emergent to beginning readers. This afternoon she sits at her desk planning a lesson on word recognition for some of the children who are struggling to read beginning consonant blends. The lesson will use words from the book *The Eensy Weensy Spider* (Hoberman, 2000) to focus on a limited number of initial blends. She gathers sets of "/g/ /l/ *gl* as in *glue*" word cards she made for a previous lesson and constructs a set of cards featuring "/s/ /p/ *sp* as in *spider*" so that the children can compare and contrast the different blends. She also sets aside some of the more challenging cards such as /s/ /t/ /r/ for the more advanced readers. She makes matching target word cards on small pieces of acetate to show on the overhead projector. She sets up two large charts and puts the book *The Eensy Weensy Spider* on her desk. Now she is ready.

The next morning, Ms. Gupta calls the children who will *not* take part in her phonics lesson to the writing center and helps them get started on their choice of two writing activities. She then asks the others to turn around in their chairs so that they can see the overhead screen clearly and says, "Children, do you remember reading the *The Eensy Weensy Spider?*"

Nodding yes, the children read along as Ms. Gupta points to each of the words in the poem on the "spider chart," a 3-foot-tall version of *The Eensy Weensy Spider* text. She does this because she knows the importance of fluent reading.

She pauses at the end of lines and then asks the children to practice reading fluently as they read the poem. Following the reading, the children and Ms. Gupta sing the poem and do the finger-play for *The Eensy Weensy Spider*.

Ms. Gupta then calls the children's attention to the words *water* and *spout*. "If you think you know what a *spout* is, whisper it in your neighbor's ear," she says. The children do so with plenty of interaction. With a vocabulary teaching point in mind, Ms. Gupta goes to the chalkboard and sketches a waterspout pipe that carries rain away from a house. The children whisper their ideas to one another and then state their guesses aloud.

"Did you picture in your head what it would look like for a spider to climb up a pipe? Good readers make pictures in their minds when they read; they really think about what they are reading."

"Here is something else I've noticed about some of the words in the spider poem," Ms. Gupta continues. "With what two letters does the word *spider* begin?"

Children's Knowledge of Words

In Chapter 4, you saw how young children sometimes pretend-read books. You saw that many preschoolers cheerfully chant their way through favorite storybooks, largely oblivious to the written words on the page—until they reached the moment when they could not.

"I can't read this," a child may say, even though for weeks before she had happily rendered aloud her version of that very book.

"Why not?" asks her teacher.

"Because I don't know the words."

Ms. Gupta writes the word *spider* in large letters on the board and points to the *sp*-blend as children say the letters. "And how about *spout*?" She writes, points, and the children respond again. Ms. Gupta draws a line under the *sp-* in each word and says, "This *s-p* is a blend. Blends are letters that work together to make a beginning or ending sound in a word. When you say the blend, *sp*, it sounds like /*sp-*/. Try it with a partner—remember to whisper."

The children practice saying the *sp*-blend, and Ms. Gupta reviews. "Blends are interesting spelling chunks. Even though they work together, you can still hear each letter sound if you listen carefully. For today's word sort, we will work mostly on beginning blends, although some of you may have some ending blends, so watch carefully."

Ms. Gupta continues to talk as she puts the word *spider* on the overhead and underlines the *sp*. With several blank transparency cards nearby, Ms. Gupta asks the children to think of some words that begin with the *sp* sound. The chil-dren's responses, guided as needed by her prompts and questions, are written on the transparency cards and placed under the word *spider*.

Drawing the discussion to a close, Ms. Gupta reviews: "Excellent thinking. You've come up with *spell, spend*, and *spot*, and we found out that *see* and *snow* won't work. And why is that?" Children respond by talking about the differences, and Ms. Gupta confirms. She adds, "I also made the words *spill* and *space* [she shows each of these word cards on the overhead projector], and you have these words in your new word sort bags."

Ms. Gupta has some of the children help her make cards for each of the words the children provided and adds them to the word sort bags. She then has the children get started on word sorts by having them work in pairs to compare and contrast words, and to watch for the target blend.

As the children begin working on their word sorts, Ms. Gupta checks on the children at the writing center and then moves quietly around the room, speaking and questioning the children as she guides them toward success. To complete this lesson, she will have the children self-assess their consonant blend word sorts using classroom checklists that have the correct sorts listed. When the children are finished, Ms. Gupta will assign as homework fifteen minutes of reading for pleasure (or being read to) and a minimum of five to eight minutes of adult/child word sorts (or longer if the child is having a good time).

At various points throughout the lesson, Ms. Gupta jots down some assessment notes about the children's responses to the lesson. Later, she will elaborate on these notes and put them into the children's individual files.

As you could see in that chapter, this child has actually reached a developmental milestone. Not only is she aware that the language comes from a book, but also that it emerges from particular words in a particular order. And to be able to read the message, she must be able to read those words.

This chapter is about what that child needs to know to read the words. It assumes that the children have reached the point where that preschool girl is:

- They know that print talks and not the pictures.
- They know language is composed of words, although this concept might be a little shaky.

- They know most of the letters of the alphabet.
- They realize that spoken words can be broken down into smaller units of sound.
- They know that they should be looking for ways that print and spoken words go together.

This chapter focuses on children's word knowledge. The discussion begins with the words that are represented in print and the sounds that make them up. Then come stages through which children's word knowledge develops. We share many teaching strategies recommended for children at each stage, along with ways of building children's sight vocabulary. Finally, we share ways of helping children read words in context.

Word Recognition and English Spelling

In Chapter 3 with the example of the grocery store advertisement for the simple phonics program, we said that the relations between letters and sounds in English may be systematic and understandable, but they are certainly not simple. In the first years of school, teachers in countries with shallow orthographies can take students through an ABC book that shows them letters and sounds, and after that most children (but not all) are able to read on their own. But because English has a deep orthography, the study of the spelling structure needs to be spread over several years, emphasizing different aspects of the system at each level.

Let's look now at stages of word recognition and the kind of word recognition instruction that can help children at each stage.

PHONICS and PHONOLOGICAL AWARENESS

How would you describe the connection between word recognition and phonics?

Stages in Children's Development of Word Recognition

The stages of children's development of word recognition have been described by Frith (1985) and summarized by Goswami (2000). According to these scholars, children go through a set of stages of word recognition that can be called **logographic, transitional, alphabetic,** and **orthographic.** After explaining these stages, we lay out ideas for instruction that will help children at each stage.

LOGOGRAPHIC READING.   Young children—preschoolers and kindergartners—who are just beginning to see familiar words around them tend to recognize words as whole displays. Children recognize McDonald's restaurants by their golden arches. They may recognize the word *look* by associating the two O's with eyes. Children in this stage may call the same word with different but related names, calling a Crest toothpaste label at one time "Crest" and at another time "toothpaste" (Harste, Woodward, & Burke, 1984). They are not yet reading the letters in the words but are trying to find any identifiable feature that will help them remember the words, almost as if the words were faces. **Logographic** readers often give no response at all when faced with a word they do not know because they do not yet have a strategy for sounding out words.

Marsh et al. (1981) called this stage of word recognition "glance and guess" because children look at a word and call it by the few names of words they know, or say nothing at all. They have no way to begin to recognize words by working through their letters.

When they are writing with invented spelling, children who are logographic readers may produce one or two memorized words—usually their names—and also symbols such as heart shapes or sun shapes. They will also produce prephonemic spelling: strings of letters that might resemble words but whose letters have no phonetic value (see Chapter 3).

TEACH IT! 7

Modified Reading Recovery Lesson

TRANSITIONAL ALPHABETIC READING.   More advanced children—usually in early first grade—begin to read words by their letters, but not by very many letters. The **transitional** reader might read the first consonant of a word and call it by the name of another word she or he knows that begins with that sound. It is as if a word such as *ball* appeared to children like this: bxxx. They might correctly read the word, especially if they are helped by the context, but they might readily confuse it with *bat, bark,* or *beep* (Morris, 2006).

As writers using invented spelling, alphabetic readers produce what we call early phonemic spelling (see Chapter 3); that is, they write a few letters to represent only the most salient sounds, usually consonant sounds. Thus they might write LDL for little and BT for boat.

ALPHABETIC READING. By the middle of first grade and into early second grade, most children begin to read more and more letters in words. When they attempt to read a word, rather than calling out the name of another word that begins the same way, a child might sound out every letter, even if it means pronouncing something that doesn't make sense. A child might say, "We went to the fire sta-ty-on" instead of "fire station." With practice, students produce fewer nonsense word readings and read words more accurately.

Children are acquiring a growing body of sight words, words they can read accurately and quickly without having to decode them. This rapid word identification occurs after a period of sounding out the words, or **phonological recoding,** as linguists call it. Ehri (1991) suggests that the earlier practice of reading words alphabetically—figuring them out letter by letter—lays down pathways to the memory that makes it easier for children to recognize the words when they see them later. She explains,

> When readers practice reading specific words by phonologically recoding the words, they form access routes for those words into memory. The access routes are built using knowledge of grapheme-phoneme correspondences that connect letters in spellings to phonemes in the pronunciation of words. The letters are processed as visual symbols for the phonemes, and the sequence of letters is retained as an alphabetic, phonological representation of the word. The first time an unfamiliar word is seen, it is read by phonological recoding. This initiates an access route into memory. Subsequent readings of the word strengthen the access route until the connections between letters and phonemes are fully formed and the spelling is represented in memory. (Ehri, 1991, p. 402)

As writers using invented spelling, **alphabetic** readers produce examples of what we call letter name spelling or phonemic spelling. Now children's spellings represent all or most of the phonemes in a word. Yet, because they focus on matching one letter to one sound at a time, they are not aware of silent e's or other ways of marking vowel letters long or short. Thus BET can spell either *beat* or *bit.* Children usually do not spell consonant digraphs either; they might write IHOVER for *each other.* In fact, because their reading exposure is still very limited, they are only gradually noticing conventional ways in which letters represent sounds in spelling.

ORTHOGRAPHIC READING. By late first grade to the middle of second grade, most children are moving into another stage. Now they are looking at words in terms of spelling patterns—not just one letter to one sound, but also familiar patterns such as *-ake, -ight,* and later *-tion.* Children who can separate words into **onsets and rimes** and who are taught by means of word sorts (Bear et al., 2004; Gillet & Temple, 1978) can read by analogy; that is, if they can read *bake* and *take,* they can also read *rake* and *stake.* As they move further into the **orthographic** phase, children read not just by **phonogram patterns,** or onsets and rimes, as Trieman (1985) calls them, but increasingly by root words and even historical morphemes.

Children's spelling now passes through the transitional spelling stage. They are spelling words in conventional ways, although not always correctly. For example, they might write *baisball, fase, trane,* and the like.

DERIVATIONAL READING. From about fourth or fifth grade and up, normally advancing readers enter a phase of word recognition that we call **derivational** reading. (This term is not from Frith, but derived from Chomsky and Halle, 1970, and Templeton, 1991.) Readers from late first grade and second grade recognize that words like *firehouse* and *groundskeeper* contain other words they know within them. From fourth grade and later, more proficient readers recognize that words like *telegraph, telephone, biology,* and *biography* also contain word parts that they recognize: *-graph,* from a Greek word meaning "to write;" *tele-* from another Greek word meaning "at a distance." They recognize that *sanity* is related to *sane* and that *sign* is related to *signal.* Derivational reading thus combines something of word recognition and vocabulary.

Teaching Word Recognition

In the sections that follow, we make suggestions for teaching word recognition. Before we begin, note that children at different phases in their development of word recognition need different kinds of instruction. When it comes to teaching word recognition, one size does not fit all. In word recognition, as in other aspects of reading instruction, children need differentiated instruction.

Children at the earliest phase of word recognition—the *logographic phase*—need to learn many words as wholes. They can also benefit from being reminded of the sounds that make up words and of individual letter-to-sound correspondences. But it is important that they practice reading words in meaningful contexts (National Reading Panel, 1998), and also that they learn to read plenty of words (Cunningham & Stanovich, 1998; Juel, 1988; Lehr, Osborn, & Hiebert, 2006).

Children in the *transitional* and *alphabetic phases* of reading need to learn to see patterns in the ways letters and sounds relate to each other. They may have naïve notions of these relations that need to be redirected toward correctness (Read, 1975; Temple et al., 1992). But they still need to read connected text and to see how texts make meaning, words make texts, and letter combinations make words.

Children at the *orthographic phase* of reading have moved beyond concern with simple letter-to-sound correspondences. They need to know the most productive phonogram patterns in English, such as *-it, -at, -ick*, and *-ock*; *-ight, -ain*, and *-oat*, and also be aware of the words that are exceptions to those patterns, like *love, though*, and *women*. They need to pay attention to what happens at the boundaries of syllables when endings are added to words, as in *bat/batting*. They need to be careful with homophones, like *waste* and *waist* and *reed* and *read*.

Readers at the *derivational phase* of reading words have moved beyond a focus on letters and sounds, even at the level of orthographic patterns. Now they are concerned with a word's grammatical function, its origin, and the family relations among words to both pronounce them properly and to know something of their meanings.

Teaching the Logographic Reader (K–Grade 1)

Children at the logographic stage of word recognition are emergent to beginning readers. They are just learning to recognize words as wholes, so we encourage that. As children learn to recognize several dozen words as wholes, they will pay more attention to the letters that make up those words.

WHOLE-PART-WHOLE TEACHING. Begin word study at all levels by paying attention to words in the context of meaningful sentences before you focus attention on individual words and their parts. The few minutes of extra time that are required to pay attention to the context may well keep some children from becoming confused and will make it more likely that children will apply what they learn from the word study sessions when they are reading words in connected text. Several models of whole-part-whole teaching follow here: shared reading, the language-experience approach, and guided reading.

Shared reading. Shared reading (Holaway, 1979) is a justly popular method to teach children about words and other details of reading at the same time you introduce children to reading in a holistic way. Shared book reading requires that you have a **big book**, a three-foot-tall version of an illustrated text written in simple patterned language. You may create your own big book on large sheets of paper or use a commercially prepared version.

Here are the steps to shared book reading. Put the big book on an easel so that your hands are free to point to the words. Get a pointer stick to point to the text. Invite the children to sit close to the text so that all can see and all may feel involved.

First, *preview the book*, to show the children what they are about to hear and see. Show them what they will need to pay attention to in order to find their way around in a text. You may show them the title, the author's name, the cover illustration, and the first few lines of the text. You may also show illustrations in the body of the text. Do a *picture walk* through the text; that is, point to the pictures and have the children help you weave a story across them. Say, "Oh, look. What do you think is happening here?" Wait for responses and then say, "We'll have to read to find out, won't we?"

Then read the text aloud. Read the words fluently, clearly, with enthusiasm. Run the pointer under the words, phrase by phrase, as you read. Read in an animated voice—not too fast, and not too slow. The students should follow along with their eyes. Pause occasionally to ask students to supply a predictable word or a phrase, or to ask them to make predictions about what will happen next, before you turn the page.

On a second reading, you and the students may take turns reading lines from the text. *Choral-read* a page: that is, you and the children read the words together as you point to them. Then *echo-read* a page. That is, you read a line and then the students read the same line together while you point to the words.

Talk about the text. Ask questions. Invite comments. Ask the students to talk about the most interesting parts of the story or about the pictures.

After a second or third reading, you can use it to teach words. Try these strategies:

- Cover a word with your hand or with a piece of tag board, and ask students to guess it from context, or with only the first letter showing, or the first two letters showing, and so on. If the children cannot do this readily, "think aloud" and model it for them. Say, "The sentence up to this point says, 'Oh, no! what a . . .' and the picture shows things piled up in a messy way. Our mystery word begins with M, which makes the 'muh' sound. Let's see. What would make sense here? 'Oh, no! What a muh, muh, muh . . . *mess!*'"
- Write three or four sentences from the text on strips of paper, and have students arrange them in order in a *pocket chart*.

> Don't be afraid to ask for help from other teachers, administration, support staff, and counselors. Remember that your staff was in your shoes at one point in their career. Always remember to try different approaches if something isn't working.
>
> —Kate Wood,
> Kindergarten Teacher
> Monroe, OHIO

A teacher using a pocket chart in class.

- Cut apart a sentence, scramble the words, and have a student or students arrange the *sentence strips* in the proper order on the pocket chart. For an easier task, keep another version of the sentence intact, and have the students arrange the cut-apart words underneath. For a harder task, have the children arrange the cut-apart words without a model.
- Pass out word cards and have students come forward and match those words to words in the text.

Word banks.   Once a student has demonstrated she has learned to recognize a word that is separated from other words, write that word on a piece of thick paper or tag board and give it to the student to put into her **word bank**, a personalized collection of words in a container such as a coffee can, zip-lock plastic bag, or an index card box. Students should practice reading the words in the word bank every day or every other day. They can

- Read the words to partners or to parent volunteers.
- Group the words into categories, such as things, actions, animals, etc.
- Group all the words that begin with the same letters.
- Do "word hunts": look for the same words in children's books.

Try to find time to review each child's word bank every week or ten days. If there are words the child cannot read correctly, take them out of the word bank and put them in a special envelope inside or beside it. The child can practice reading those words later, and if they are read correctly, the words go back into the bank.

Morning message.   As a technique for getting students to understand written language and focus on words, morning message (Kawakami-Arakaki, Oshiro, & Farran, 1989) gets high marks. Use chart paper or a pocket chart, and write the words in handwriting large enough for all of the children gathered in front of you to see. A typical morning message says,

> *Today is Wednesday, February 17.*
> *The weather is snowy.*
> *We have art today.*
> *Surprise! Today is Janisha's birthday!*

Ask the students what words you should write. If a child says "Today," ask which letter it should begin with. If she volunteers "T," ask if it will be an uppercase or a lowercase T. A child can come forward and write some of the letters for you. The other children can "air write" (make gestures of writing in the air) while one child writes on the chart.

Write some of the words that are often repeated on separate pieces of thick paper. Either tape them to the bottom of the chart or arrange them in a lower pocket of the pocket chart. Invite children to come forward, find the proper word, and either tape it onto the chart (the tape is already placed on the back of the word) or place it where it should go in the pocket chart. Have the child read the sentence aloud before placing the word in the sentence, then read the sentence with the word in place.

Next, have all of the children practice reading the lines of print as you follow along beneath the words with the pointer: First they read the lines aloud as you point, then they choral-read the text, then they echo-read, and then different groups of children are invited to read.

Finally, ask individual children to come forward and point to any words they can read alone (that is, in isolation). Bracket each word with your hands as the child reads it. If he or she is successful, write the word on a small piece of thick paper and present it to the child. The word then goes into the child's word bank for later practice.

Labeling the room.   Each child's name should be printed in big letters on her or his desk. The important items around the classroom should be labeled, too—the blackboard, the clock, the door, the window, the books, science center, the sink—with cards bearing letters 3 inches high so they can be read from anywhere in the room. In time children can write or trace the labels you prepare. Take time every other day to "read the room": first as a whole class, then in small groups taking turns to read the signs together. Every few weeks, change some signs around (so that the label "sink" is over the door, for instance) and ask who notices anything wrong. Ask the children to move the words to the correct locations.

Words that are used as labels can be put in students' word banks, too, if the students can read them correctly.

Teaching the Alphabetic Reader (Grades 1–2)

Once children are becoming alphabetic readers, they are beginning readers who have learned several dozen words and are paying attention to the letters in words and associating them with sounds. The goal of our instruction with these children should be to help them notice more and more letters and the sounds with which they are associated. It will also help to call students' attention to sounds in words.

PICTURE SORTS. Make sets of 1 × 2-inch cards with pictures on them, depicting objects that begin with different sounds. For example, *sun, sandal, sail, sand, soda; can, candy, cat, cart, calendar; dog, dart, dish, diaper, diamond; goat, girl, gorilla, guitar, gun.* Place one member of each group side by side on the table. Scramble the rest of the pictures, and then ask a child to name the picture aloud and then place the picture cards one at a time in a column below the appropriate picture. Once children become proficient at this, substitute a card with a letter as the guide card at the top of the column.

Commercially prepared picture sort cards are available from these companies:

- Teaching Resource Center (**http://www.trcabc.com/**)
- ReallyGoodStuff.Com (**https://www.reallygoodstuff.com**)

WORD WHEELS. On a piece of thick paper or tag board, write a phonogram pattern like *-an, -it,* or *-ock.* Leave space to the left of the pattern. Then cut out a round piece of the same material, and write consonant letters such as *f, s, h,* and *p* (for *-it*) facing outward around the edges of the circle. Attach the circle to the slip of paper with the phonogram pattern using a brad, as shown in Figure 5.1. Children can rotate the circle until a beginning consonant lines up with the phonogram pattern and then pronounce the resulting word.

FLIP CARDS. Instead of a circle with consonants as in the word wheels, cut out a set of short cards, write consonant letters on them, and staple them to a longer card with a phonogram pattern written on it, as shown in Figure 5.2. Children can fold back the short cards to pair up different beginning consonants with the phonogram pattern and then read the resulting word.

FIGURE 5.1

A Word Wheel.

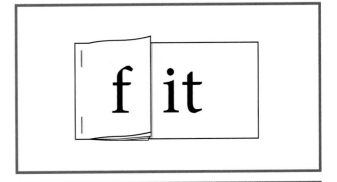

FIGURE 5.2

Flip Cards.

PLASTIC LETTERS. Gather two to five students in front of you. Using sets of plastic letters (some are sold in toy stores with magnetic backs to stick to refrigerators), make a word like *band*. Say the word aloud, and then take the letter *s*. Exaggerate the sound of /s/, and tell the students to watch what happens when you substitute the *s* for the *b*. You get *sand*. Demonstrate this several times, and let some of the children make the same substitution. Then hold up the letter *h* and ask who can tell what word we will have when we substitute the letter *h* for the *s* in *sand*. Then follow with *l*. Pairs of children can follow up by playing this game themselves. On other days you can introduce other phonogram patterns and other beginning consonants.

RHYMING GAMES. Chants and songs are good for rhyming games, and rhyming games help call children's attention to sounds in words. The Mother Goose rhyme, "Ding, dong, dell/Kitty's in the well," can be used to play with rhymes:

> Ding, dog, doset
> Kitty's in the _____ (closet)
> Ding, dog, dimming pool
> Kitty's in the _____ (swimming pool)
> Ding, dog, didewalk
> Kitty's on the _____ (sidewalk)

Or try the popular children's song, "Willaby, Wallabee, Woo":

> Willabee, Wallabee, Woo
> An elephant sat on you,
> Willabee, Wallabee, Wee
> An elephant sat on me.
>
> Willabee, Wallabee, Wonna
> An elephant sat on _____ (Donna)
> Willabee, Wallabee, Walan
> An elephant sat on _____ (Alan)

WORD WALLS. Word walls (Cunningham, 1995; Cunningham, Hall, & Sigmon, 2007) can provide strong support in children's learning and teachers' systematic instruction. Word walls consist of words that children are learning arranged alphabetically on the walls of the classroom in ways that allow the words to be easily seen and accessed. Word walls should be interactive, made and used by the teacher and the children. Much good instruction can spring from various kinds of words on walls, including serving children's self-assessment needs. Here is a brief description of two types of word walls and how they be might be used (see also Bear et al., 2000; McGee & Richgels, 2003; Pinnell & Fountas, 1998):

- A picture-word wall: Post the words from favorite books, inquiry units of study, and words and pictures with the letters of the alphabet. It is nearly always best if words are put on the wall during the teaching process.
- A literature-based picture-word wall: This example can be applied with young children and older children. Picture having read *Lilly's Purple Plastic Purse* (Henkes, 1996) or *Lily's Big Day* (Henkes, 2006). You introduce the word *wall* by showing an enlarged picture or colorful sketch of Lilly on the wall with Lilly's name under it. Next you ask for suggestions about other words children want to add from the book. You write their words in full view, leaving space for the pictures that will come. The children are asked to remember their favorite word. Next, they are asked to draw a picture that depicts or explains their word and write the word and explanation. The teacher talks the children through some examples of what they might write.

As children's development progresses, word walls change from picture-word walls to word-only walls. Word hunts and word sorts expand the word study. Books are reread to keep a focus on meaningful reading and for enjoyment. Imagine the word walls on science and other inquiry work you can have with middle and upper grades.

The World of Reading

Synthetic Phonics and Spelling

Synthetic phonics was described by Jeanne Chall in her book *Learning to Read: The Great Debate* (1967), which, along with Rudolf Flesh's book, *Why Johnny Can't Read* (1956), is often cited as part of the great debate over reading and spelling instruction. This debate has raged for years and continues today.

For years, the "look-say" method of learning words dominated the teaching of reading in the United States. The best known look-say reading series was the Dick and Jane series. These texts helped millions of children learn to read by repeating words in stories until children learned them as sight or known words. However, although these children demonstrated good comprehension and vocabulary in first grade, they were not as accurate in word recognition as the children taught with a phonics approach. Some children picked up enough knowledge to become good readers and spellers for life, but many did not.

Some teachers of the look-say approach included a phonics component, teaching parts of words (letter/sound relationships) after the children knew them on sight. However, some teachers included no phonics component in their instruction. Fewer still taught phonics that connected children with the English-language spelling patterns, let alone with their teaching of reading or writing. Spelling was a subject unto itself. Historically, spelling instruction has gone through several notable shifts. From the 1920s to the 1960s, spelling was a process of rote memorization. Learning to spell depended on word memorization and weekly tests prescribed by the spelling book. It was not grounded linguistically and had nothing to do with language learning. In the 1960s and 1970s, spelling was seen as a language-based process that involves abstracting, or learning, regular sound/spelling patterns. Beginning in the late 1970s and continuing today, spelling has been seen more as a developmental process, one in which there are definable patterns of learning, and spelling is taught based on those developmental patterns (Templeton & Morris, 2000).

None of these approaches was totally wrong. In fact, the memorization and abstraction approaches laid the groundwork for the developmental recommendations in this book. The period of linguistic abstraction showed that spelling was a language process (including memory) that is involved in all learning. We now know better how to implement synthetic phonics in language-centered and developmentally appropriate ways that make sense to children. We know that spelling instruction supports orthographic knowledge and that spelling and word recognition are important to reading comprehension (Perfetti, 1985; Stanovich & Cunningham, 1993). Thus attention to spelling instruction should not be left to be done on an as-needed basis (Templeton & Morris, 2000, p. 537). Spelling and phonics should be viewed as a means of studying and seeing words as tools that serve reading, writing, and vocabulary development (Templeton, 1991). Research continues to search for more understanding of how children learn to spell and read and how we can improve all children's literacy instruction.

SIGHT WORDS. **Sight words** are learned primarily through sheer exposure. Repeated readings are key. Children should reread their favorite books while they also select challenging books from several the teacher recommends. Importantly, sight word knowledge helps children progress in reading to the point that reading is easy and joyful. With enough sight words students read with less effort and are able to better concentrate on meaning and reading comprehension.

Sight word walls contain high-frequency words that are posted as the children encounter them in their reading and in lessons. The teacher should engage children in doing sight word walls regularly (Cunningham et al., 2007). When word walls are used daily in the course of reading, writing, and spelling, they are embedded in authentic literacy practice. This is how you can create and use a sight word wall:

- Add words gradually (about five per week).
- Make words highly accessible by putting them where all students can see them, writing them in large print with big black letters, and using colors for words that are often confused, such as *for, from, that, they,* and *this.*
- Select only the words children encounter most frequently in their reading and the words they use most frequently in their writing. Do not overwhelm them or yourself with too many words. Nothing succeeds like success!
- Practice the words by saying, spelling, and writing them ("do the wall").

Standards and Literacy

Standards for the English Language Arts

Much stress is put on word knowledge—particularly phonological awareness and phonics—by the U.S. government and many state departments of education these days. But it is worthwhile to note that the two largest national professional organizations that concern themselves with reading—the National Council of Teachers of English and the International Reading Association—treat reading much more holistically. Here are the twelve Standards for the English Language Arts that were created by both groups.

Sponsored by NCTE and IRA

The vision guiding these standards is that all students must have the opportunities and resources to develop the language skills they need to pursue life's goals and to participate fully as informed, productive members of society. These standards assume that literacy growth begins before children enter school as they experience and experiment with literacy activities—reading and writing, and associating spoken words with their graphic representations. Recognizing this fact, these standards encourage the development of curriculum and instruction that make productive use of the emerging literacy abilities that children bring to school. Furthermore, the standards provide ample room for the innovation and creativity essential to teaching and learning. They are not prescriptions for particular curriculum or instruction. Although we present these standards as a list, we want to emphasize that they are not distinct and separable; they are, in fact, interrelated and should be considered as a whole.

1. Students read a wide range of print and non-print texts to build an understanding of texts, of themselves, and of the cultures of the United States and the world; to acquire new information; to respond to the needs and demands of society and the workplace; and for personal fulfillment. Among these texts are fiction and nonfiction, classic and contemporary works.
2. Students read a wide range of literature from many periods in many genres to build an understanding of the many dimensions (e.g., philosophical, ethical, aesthetic) of human experience.
3. Students apply a wide range of strategies to comprehend, interpret, evaluate, and appreciate texts. They draw on their prior experience, their interactions with other readers and writers, their knowledge of word meaning and of other texts, their word identification strategies, and their understanding of textual features (e.g., sound-letter correspondence, sentence structure, context, graphics).
4. Students adjust their use of spoken, written, and visual language (e.g., conventions, style, vocabulary) to communicate effectively with a variety of audiences and for different purposes.
5. Students employ a wide range of strategies as they write and use different writing process elements appropriately to communicate with different audiences for a variety of purposes.
6. Students apply knowledge of language structure, language conventions (e.g., spelling and punctuation), media techniques, figurative language, and genre to create, critique, and discuss print and non-print texts.
7. Students conduct research on issues and interests by generating ideas and questions, and by posing problems. They gather, evaluate, and synthesize data from a variety of sources (e.g., print and non-print texts, artifacts, people) to communicate their discoveries in ways that suit their purpose and audience.
8. Students use a variety of technological and information resources (e.g., libraries, databases, computer networks, video) to gather and synthesize information and to create and communicate knowledge.
9. Students develop an understanding of and respect for diversity in language use, patterns, and dialects across cultures, ethnic groups, geographic regions, and social roles.
10. Students whose first language is not English make use of their first language to develop competency in the English language arts and to develop understanding of content across the curriculum.
11. Students participate as knowledgeable, reflective, creative, and critical members of a variety of literacy communities.
12. Students use spoken, written, and visual language to accomplish their own purposes (e.g., for learning, enjoyment, persuasion, and the exchange of information).

Source: http://www.ncte.org/about/over/standards/110846.htm

WORD WALL CHANTS.   From Joe Fuhrmann's amazing Web site (**http://www.k111.k12.il.us/lafayette/fourblocks/word_wall_chants.htm**) come these suggestions for word wall chants. As the children and the teacher review the words on the word wall, they use different and engaging ways to spell out the letters and then read the word. Some of the chants can be done with the children at their seats:

- "The chicken": Flapping your arms up and down as you say each letter
- "The movie star": Blowing kisses, like a starlet on awards night as each letter is said

- "The opera singer": Singing each letter, and finally the word, in an operatic voice
- "The volcano": Saying each letter louder and louder, until you shout the word
- "The nose": Holding your nose as you say the letters and the word

Other chants can be done standing up and moving around:

- "Dribble and shoot": Dribbling each letter and shooting the word
- "Mexican Hat Dance": Chanting letters as each foot goes forward
- "Pumping iron": Pretending to hoist a heavy weight as you say each letter. Then pretending to put the bar back on the frame as you say the word with an exhausted voice.
- "Frog jump:" Beginning standing up, and crouching a little lower as you say each letter. Then leaping as you say the word.

SHARED WRITING.   Shared writing is a way for the teacher to demonstrate how spoken words are broken into their sounds and spelled with letters, and also for engaging children's participation in writing. After sharing a poem or discussing an event that is exciting to the children, the teacher gathers students around an easel and invites them to help him write about what they just heard. First children agree on a short sentence they want to write: for example, "A firefighter came to school." The children practice saying the sentence several times so that everyone is aware of the words. Then the teacher says, "Now we're going to write the first word, 'A.'" Who can tell us what letter we need to write? A child suggests the letter A. The teacher accepts it and writes it slowly on the easel. Then he says, "We wrote A. Now what's the next word we want to write? Right. It's 'firefighter.' That's a new word, so I'm going to leave space between the word A and the first letter of this new word (He puts his finger after the A to demonstrate the space). What is the first sound we hear in 'firefighter'? Right: it's 'fuh.' What letter are we going to use to write the 'fuh' sound in 'firefighter'? Right: It's F. Who can come up and write the letter F for me?" A child comes up and writes the letter. The teacher proceeds in this way, having the children supply the letters they can, and adding the sounds himself that the children do not hear. If a child makes an error in writing, the teacher puts a piece of wide correction tape over the error and helps the children write the correct letter.

Conduct shared writing lessons with the class almost daily when children are in the alphabetic stage of writing. In the meantime, encourage the children to use writing every chance they get.

GUIDED READING.   As you saw in Chapter 1, guided reading is done with a small group of children or as few as two children to support children's progress in reading development, including fluency, comprehension, and word knowledge. The texts used in guided reading gradually become more and more challenging (Fountas & Pinnell, 1996). Even when you want to use guided reading to emphasize word study, it is important to create a meaningful context for the words. Thus you begin the lesson with a focus on meaning before proceeding to word study. Here is an example of how to do this.

Each child has a copy of the story or informational text that is "leveled," written in ways appropriate to the children's reading development. This text is at the children's instructional level and might be a basal excerpt or a little book. In ways similar to shared reading, you introduce the book and in doing so build on the children's prior knowledge. "Hmm . . ." you might say, "This looks like a story that could be about a friendship, see it says (pointing to the text) *Lost and Found* by Oliver Jeffers (2005) and if we look at the picture, the boy and the penguin are hugging. What do you think it's about?"

After children have the opportunity to talk with you and one another, you may then shift to looking at some key vocabulary words you have prepared in advance. These are words you have taken from the text and put on word cards. Remember, too many words can overwhelm children, so just do a few, perhaps only two. As you show the words, pronounce them and discuss their meanings. This is an opportunity for word study to begin, but don't focus yet. Rather the next step is to read the story.

Because this text is written at their instructional level, you guide children to *whisper read*—read in a low voice to themselves—the first few pages. As this happens you listen carefully so you can intervene and help as needed. Next, you encourage them to take turns and read out loud in their "quiet voices" in pairs with your support. Then you might invite volunteers to read on their own while others run their fingers under the text watching the words carefully. Take time to enjoy reading and discuss what has happened so far to continue to build understanding.

Although the main focus of guided reading is on reading fluency and comprehension, it also affords a fine opportunity to draw attention to key vocabulary words in the text. Again, prompt the children's thinking and engagement by saying, "Nice reading. I heard you work! You self-corrected and tried to read fluently with expression. Let's look at these pages now. Do you see any key vocabulary words we have here [referring to the word cards]?" As children chime in, finding text words and key vocabulary matches, draw their attention to word recognition skills, such as letter-to-sound correspondences. Then move on to more reading and thinking. This process of reading and thinking and then attending to some key vocabulary words may continue to the end of the story.

After they have finished reading, guide the children to closure by discussing the text they've read and making connections to what they know. Following this attention to words, you may include a review of the key vocabulary words, and give the children copies of the word cards for later practice at their tables or desks when they can reread the book. A short writing and drawing activity may also be included. Children thrive on writing about their favorite part, and writing supports word learning.

Teaching the Orthographic Reader (Grades 2–3 to 3–5)

Children in the orthographic stage of word reading are beginning to pay attention to spelling patterns, or what linguists call *onsets* and *rimes*. At the beginning of this period, that means they are ready to understand that if they can read *hit* and they know the sound represented by the letter *s*, they can also read *sit*. Toward the end of this period, they must learn how to cope with two-syllable words, homophones, and other challenges English orthography poses to the reader. Teaching activities at the orthographic stage work extensively with patterns of spelling.

TEACH IT! 13
Word Sorting Activities

WORD SORTS.   **Word sorts** have been a favorite teaching practice for decades at the McGuffey Reading Center of the University of Virginia (Bear et al., 2005; Gillet & Kita, 1979; Gillet & Temple, 1978; Henderson, 1995). They were an extension of the language-experience approach developed by Russell Stauffer in the 1960s and 1970s (Stauffer, 1975). Word sorting activities include sorting words by spelling or phonogram patterns—for example, words that are spelled like *rock*. Word sorts also may focus on the concepts that words represent—for example, sort all the weather-associated words in one row (*rain, snow, . . .*), and sort all the cooking-associated words in another row (*stove, bowl, . . .*). Word sorting by affixes and word provides sound practice and the kind of hands-on activity that older children appreciate.

Sorting instruction encourages children to see words as objects that they manipulate and own by organizing and classifying them. Jerry Zutell (1999, p. 105) notes, "Organizing objects, events, and experiences into categories and classes is a fundamental way we make sense of the world around us. The act of sorting makes words concrete objects of study."

SMALL-GROUP DEMONSTRATION.   After children have had a lively experience with a text—whether by reading a big book, or from a dictated story, or reading a trade book—the teacher calls attention to a couple of individual words. These words are chosen because they exemplify a pattern that can be generalized to other words. By generalized, we mean that once children have noticed a pattern in one word, they can apply that pattern to help them read other words. For example, the words *sit* and *cub* can be chosen for children who are early orthographic readers. These words are written on cards of thick paper or tag board. If they will be used in front of a small group of children, use 3 × 5 cards.

Now the teacher writes on more cards several words that share the same phonogram patterns as *sit* and *cub*. For example, he writes *fit, bit,* and *kit*; and *tub, rub,* and *sub*.

The teacher then puts the two original cards on the table or in the top pocket of a pocket chart, side by side. He reads both words several times, pointing to each word, to make sure that all of the children can read them. Next the teacher scrambles the remaining cards. Then he draws one of the remaining cards—let's say it is *rub*—and holds it up for the children.

"Where does it go?" he asks. Should I put it in the columns with *sit* or with *cub*? Note that he doesn't read the word he drew yet.

The children say it goes in the column under *cub*. Then the teacher says, "Let's read down the column. *Cub* and *rrrrrrr*—. . ."

The children say "*Rub!*" The teacher congratulates them, and then he stresses the point that once they could read *cub*, and they saw that the new word began with *r*, they could read it: "*rub.*"

Now he invites children to come up one at a time to choose words from the scrambled set and place them under the guide words, *sit* or *cub*. Later the teacher can add another group of words to the sets: *dad, sad, mad,* and *had.*

PRACTICE IN PAIRS.   Once the procedures for word sorts have been taught to the class, pairs or trios of students can play word sort games with groups of words that have been prepared in advance. The procedures for the game work the same as in the group lesson just described.

- Prepare groups of words on 1 × 2-inch cards, about the size of a business card.
- There should be four to five examples of each spelling pattern.
- Make sure that each student can read at least one word from each group. These words should be used as the guide words. They should be placed at the top of the column, and during the word sorting game, the other words should be placed one at a time underneath them.
- The other cards are left face up and scrambled.
- One at a time, a child chooses a card from the scrambled pile, places it in the column beneath the guide word, and reads down the column of words.

MEMORY GAME.   Once the students have sorted the words into their respective columns, they can put the cards face down on the table in front of them, arranged in rows (see Figure 5.3). Taking turns, one student turns over two cards. If they match (that is, if

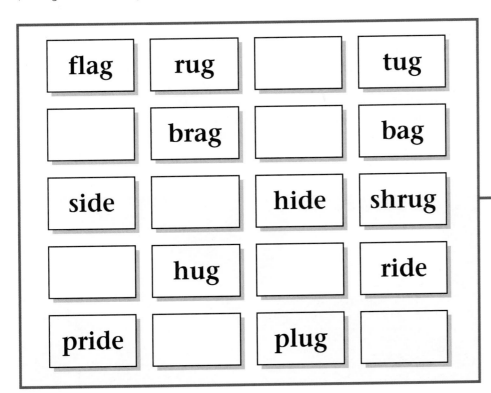

FIGURE 5.3
The Memory Game.

they share the same phonogram pattern), that student gets to keep those cards. They continue playing in turns until all of the cards are paired with other cards and taken off the table.

BOARD GAMES. Groups of cards arranged into patterns make good board games. In the "Race Track" game, a board with fifteen to twenty blank spaces is drawn up. Sets of word cards that share spelling patterns are shuffled and dealt to two to four payers. One player rolls one die and moves her marker piece (similar to marker pieces in a Monopoly game) the number of spaces showing on the die. If she is the first to land on a space, she may put down one card on the space. The next player who lands on that same space must put down a word with the same spelling pattern or forfeit a turn. The game continues until all cards are exhausted. Note: It can add a welcome element of chance if you add some wild cards to the stack: "give two cards to the person to your right" etc. (see Figure 5.4).

SPEED SORTS. After children become accurate with word sorts, they can extend their expertise by seeing how quickly they can sort. This activity supports fluency and healthy competition in a gamelike task. (Sixth to eighth graders really like them.) Like so many developmentally appropriate activities, speed sorts build intrinsic motivation and provide that all-important sense of satisfaction!

A speed sort is done as follows:

- Use a timer of some type. Egg timers really help and are quiet!
- Children sort as fast and as accurately as they can.
- Children self-assess the sorts with a rubric alone or with another child. If they encounter any uncertainty, they skip the word and later get help with it.
- Children may chart the number of words sorted correctly in N minutes. Once the activity has been taught well, a teacher-made charting sheet aids children's independent charting. Learners thrive on healthy competition with themselves.

The Order of the Patterns for Word Study

The order of words used in word sorts matters. We work in this order:

- **Start with single beginning consonants.** For demonstration purposes, we can begin with *m* and *s*. Why those two? Because you can stretch out the pronunciation of the sounds (try stretching out the sound of *t*, if you don't believe us!), and also the two sounds are nicely contrasted. Then you can add **l** and **n** because those, too, can be stretched out. Later, you can add **b, d, f, h, p,** and **t**. Those letters usually represent a single sound each. Choose the most different letters to introduce together.

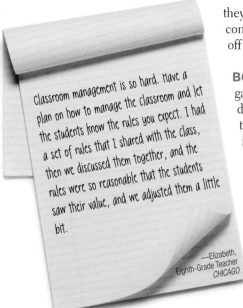

Classroom management is so hard. Have a plan on how to manage the classroom and let the students know the rules you expect. I had a set of rules that I shared with the class, then we discussed them together, and the rules were so reasonable that the students saw their value, and we adjusted them a little bit.

—Elizabeth, Eighth-Grade Teacher CHICAGO

FIGURE 5.4

Board Games for Word Sorts.

Avoid grouping **b** and **d** because they look similar; and also avoid **d** and **t** because they sound similar. Beginning consonants are introduced with picture sorts, and later you can substitute letters on cards for the pictures.

- **Then introduce short vowel phonogram patterns.** Use words with these short vowel patterns:

  -an, -ad, -ap, -at
  -ed, -et
  -it, -ip, -id
  -ot, -ob, -op
  -up, -ub
  -ill, -ell
  -ack, -eck, -ick, -ock
  -ank, -ink, -ump

- **Now make groups of words with the same short vowel, in different spelling patterns:**

  For example, *cap, bad, sack, stab,* and *sank* as a group contrasted with *jump, pup, cut, stub, rut,* and *duck.*

- **Introduce *r*-controlled vowels:**

  -ar, ur, -ir, -or

- **Introduce words with** *-all.*
- **Introduce consonant blends at the beginning of words:**

  dr-, tr-, cl-, pl-, st-

- **Introduce long vowel patterns:**

  -ate, -ake, -ail, -ame, -ain, -ay
  -eat, -eal
  -ice; -ide
  -ool

- **Introduce patterns with** *-ook* and *-ull*; and *wa-.*
- **Then two-syllable words,** such as *mother, table, kitten,* and *happy.*
- **Then compound words,** such as *into, cowboy, steamboat,* and *football.*
- **Then words with inflectional endings,** such as *-er, -est, -ing,* and *-ed.*

WORD HUNTS. Word hunts help children make connections between spelling words and reading them. This is important because some children do not automatically apply what they learn in word study activities when they are trying to read words in texts (Ehri, 1997). Word hunts also incorporate children's literature, poetry, or other whole texts. The Teach It! box shows a sample lesson that uses a word hunt based on a poem.

Word Sorting with Two-Syllable Words

Learners in grades 2 through 4 must learn what happens when syllables meet. This is more of a challenge for spelling than for reading, but readers must be aware of the problems raised by the vowel *marking systems of English.* For example, the spelling pattern of *bat* is fairly easy to learn. But when *bat* adds the grammatical ending *-ed* or *-ing,* the consonant must be doubled. If it were not doubled, the *e* or the *i* would have the effect of marking the vowel in *bat* long, giving it the pronunciation *baited* or *baiting.* Conversely, the final two consonants in *sing* are enough to insulate the vowel from the lengthening effect of *-ing,* so nothing need be added to its final consonants. And here is an oddity: Because the *x* in *ax* is made up of two sounds, it insulated the vowel from the lengthening effect of any following vowel, so we write *axes* and *axing.* But words that contain a long vowel already do not need to double the final consonant: *dream, dreaming; cool, cooled.*

Children can be taught when and when not to double consonants when endings are added to single-syllable words. To teach children to sort for two-syllable words, begin by

TEACH IT!

● Refer to your **Teach It!** booklet for further activities you can use to reinforce concepts discussed in this chapter.

Word Hunts

In the fifth week of school, student teacher Breanna demonstrates a word hunt for her children. She works with eight to ten children at a time. Breanna reads the poem "Books, Books" by Ritsa Tassopoulos (Personal communication, April 10, 2002) to the children from a large chart and then says, "Now, let's read it together."

Books, Books

Books, books fun to read
Books, books just what I need
Books, books fill my head
Books, books in my bed
Books, books morning noon and night
Books, books make me feel just right.

The children follow along well. After reading, the children reread together in partner groups. Breanna, the teacher, says, "What do you notice about some of these words?"

Children talk. They share their observations and volunteer to read rhyming words (*times* and *rhymes*).

Breanna says, "Now I'm going on a word hunt. I want to find two words that <u>don't</u> rhyme."

Thinking out loud about rhyming and nonrhyming words and how they sound and look, she lists two words—*head* and *need*—in separate columns. Breanna organizes the group into pairs and asks them to work together. She says, "Copy these two words onto your papers and make them look like this (pointing to the columns). Find rhyming words to match the top word in each column. The words can be new ones you think of, words from our word walls, and words in this poem. Get ready to talk about what you've found. This is just practice. No one has to get everything right; it's practice. Don't worry, we'll have fun talking about what makes words rhyme."

making groups of words that double the final consonants before adding an ending *-er* or *-ing*. For example, the guide words might be *batted* and *dreaming*. The "scrabbled" words can be *call*, *steal*, *sit*, *start*, *run*, and *cut*. Children place each word under a guide word depending on whether the word doubles the final consonant when the ending is added.

FAMILY LITERACY

Suggest a lesson plan that might encourage support from families.

FAMILY AND COMMUNITY. Home support by families or caregivers can be built from nearly any lesson that is taught at school. For example, easy word sorts can go home for five- to seven-minute practice sessions; word sort games can be especially fun when played with a loved one. Simple turn-taking and charting progress or keeping score (with little ones winning!) create a game. Include for the adults one page of simple and limited suggestions for conversations about words with take-home sorts. Ask for a "read around the house" adventure. Adults help children read any and every word they find in the kitchen, bathroom, or elsewhere. Groups of parents, caregivers, and children who play together or attend community functions will benefit from getting together to support their children in literacy play. Some thoughtful adult structure and guidance can help regular play groups move into literacy games and activities.

TECHNOLOGY

Do an on-line search for good word recognition programs.

TECHNOLOGY CONNECTION. For home and school technology materials, look into word recognition software programs. A good program that is very popular with young children is Wiggle Works from Scholastic Publishing and the Center for Applied Special Technology. Wiggle Works focuses on emergent, early, and fluent language development using reading, writing, speaking, and listening. It contains a variety of creative activities that entertain while also building skills. Additional programs can be found online at Superkids.com (**www.superkids.com**), where teachers and parents can check out various programs and read reviews of their efficacy. For an up-close look at how two second-grade teachers have used technology in their classrooms, visit **http://buckman. pps.k12.or.us/room100/room100.html**.

Taking a Broad Perspective on Phonics

Phonics, the teaching of letter-to-sound relationships, has long been the most controversial aspect of reading instruction. As we saw in Chapter 1, over the past forty years, several large-scale summaries of research in reading instruction have tried to answer the question of which works best: teaching phonics explicitly or teaching phonics implicitly (by showing words that share spelling patterns and asking children to derive a generalization about the ways spellings represent sounds). Research has fairly consistently favored teaching phonics explicitly.

But that does not mean phonics instruction is all children need in order to read. Catherine Snow and her colleagues (2005) recently made that point very clearly: "A focus on phonological awareness, phonemic awareness, and phonics is essential for poor readers but not enough—instruction must also address key areas such as comprehension, vocabulary, the identification of irregular words, and fluency" (p. 166).

Teachers receive plenty of advice on teaching word recognition from all sides. Not only has the federal government come down firmly on the side of teaching explicit phonics, but many states have, too. Laypeople also offer plenty of advice on the subject, as we saw in the example of the phonics programs for sale in the grocery store.

Professional reading teachers should stay informed on this issue. One good way is to read the publications of the International Reading Association, especially *The Reading Teacher*, and to attend the regional and national conferences.

Your Portfolio

Including a statement of your philosophy about teaching beginning reading in your portfolio provides evidence of how you view children and reading. It also provides a window on your writing abilities. Think about including a reflection about why you incorporated such a statement into your portfolio. Supporting your views with scientific research evidence strengthens your statement. Among many possible sources of evidence are the following refereed professional journals: *Reading Research Quarterly, The Journal of Literacy Research, The Reading Teacher*, and the *Journal of Adolescent and Adult Literacy*. Additional sources are cited later in the chapter.

Teaching Resources

Word sorts are very useful activities for strengthening children's abilities in word recognition and spelling. Now is a good time to begin accumulating different kinds of prompts to use in word sorts at many levels and for a variety of purposes.

Teaching the Derivational Reader (Grades 3 or 4 and Up)

Derivational reading is just a five-syllable way of saying that by the middle elementary grades on up, the challenges of word recognition cease to be a question of identifying words from reading letters or even from reading letters grouped into patterns. Now the challenges of reading words has to do with how words are built from parts—combined into compound words or built from historical spare parts from languages that are no longer spoken. The challenges have to do with reading words whose spellings honor their histories rather than their present-day pronunciation. We use the term *derivational* for this stage because the most common challenge is reading words derived from other words.

STRUCTURAL ANALYSIS.   **Structural analysis** is examining the parts of a word to help arrive at the meaning of the whole word. This procedure works when (1) the word is a compound word, or is made up of root words and prefixes and suffixes, and (2) the students understand the meanings of those root words' affixes.

Helping with compound words.   As we pointed out in Chapter 3, English words are built from other words. Compound words are built three different ways. Knowing whether to write two words together, like *motorboat*, to join them with a hyphen, like *see-saw*, or write them separately, like *delivery boy*, is a challenge for spelling rather than for reading. But

Word knowledge instruction with older students focuses more on understanding things such as derivations and word analysis.

readers can find long words like *grandmother* or *grasshopper* to be daunting, so teachers often give the advice, "Find a little word that you know in that big word," and we hold our thumb over part of the word to focus their attention on the other part of the word.

Make 3 × 5 cards with these words on them: *foot, ball, basket, ball, rain, coat, lawn, mower, mother, in, law, see, saw, ninety, six, ice, cream, paper, boy, all,* and *right*. Also, make five hyphens ("–") on cards. Place these in the bottom rows of a pocket chart. Have the students help you assemble words to make compound words. Which ones are joined together without spaces? Which ones are joined with hyphens? Which ones are written separately?

Working with prefixes and suffixes. Make 3 × 5 cards with these prefixes and suffixes on them: *dis-, inter-, re-, un-, under-, -able, -al, -ant.* Place these on the bottom row of a pocket chart. Make another set of cards with these root words: *trust, do, act, stand, nation, contest,* and *consider.* Place these word cards on the next-to-bottom row. Then have the students help you combine root words, prefixes, and suffixes into words that you place on the upper rows of the pocket chart. (As an alternative, you can write the prefixes, suffixes, and root words on small pieces of acetate and have the students build words on the overhead projector.) For follow-up, make a word wall of words with prefixes and another word wall of words with suffixes.

Word journals. A useful way to have students record and recall words from word sorting and word-building exercises is to have them keep a word journal. A word journal is a medium-size spiral notebook, with sections labeled according to the groupings of words it contains. These groupings might contain all the categories into which words have been sorted during word-sorting activities. To record compound words, have the students divide a page with two vertical lines to make three columns. In the left-hand column, they can write compound words that have the parts written together, in the central column, words joined with hyphens, and in the right-hand column, words written separately. For words with prefixes and suffixes, students set aside half a page each for words with *un-, re-, inter-,* and *-dis, -ant, -ful,* and *-able.* They add words to those pages from time to time as they come across them from their reading. The teacher reminds the class to share aloud some of their new entries. These also can be added to the word wall.

WORKING WITH WORDS WITH PARTS FROM ANCIENT SOURCES. Most of the words in the English language are made up of ancient parts from Latin and Greek. We mean words like *fortunate, masculine, ignition, sensitive, symphony,* and *microscope.* As you can see from the examples, those words are considered more mature vocabulary items, though, so children don't read very many of them before fourth grade, unless they are precocious readers. From that point on, however, readers encounter more and more of them, and it is very useful for students to recognize their parts, know their range of meanings, and be able to figure out at least roughly how the words should be pronounced as well as what they mean.

Structural analysis with Latin and Greek parts. Make 3 × 5 index cards of the Latin and Greek prefixes in Table 5.1. Display them in a pocket chart for the students. Explain they came from two languages, Latin and Greek, that are no longer spoken, but that contribute to most of the words in the English dictionary. Then discuss their meanings.

Then make 3 × 5 index cards of the word roots in Table 5.2. Display them in a pocket chart for the students, and discuss their meanings, too.

Have the students help you join prefixes and stems to make words. Discuss what you think the words mean. Then check the meanings in a dictionary to be sure. (Note: Some possible words are *collect, college, elect, object, dejected, eject, reject, conjecture, abrupt, erupt,*

TABLE 5.1

Prefixes and Suffixes of Latin and Greek Origin

PREFIX OR SUFFIX	MEANING
con-, com-, col-, cor-	together
ab-	from, away from, by
ad-, al-, ac-, at-	to, toward
de-	down from, off
dis-	lack of, not
e-	out, out of
ortho-	straight
photo-	light
re-	back, or again
tele-	far, far off
-ure	state of

disrupt, corrupt, revolve, evolve, devolve, contain, detain, retain, attain, contort, distort, retort, torture.)

Make smaller sets of word cards and have pairs build words with them. Make a word wall on which to display sets of these words. Have students record them in their word journals.

FAMILY AND COMMUNITY. As we stated earlier, the importance of family or caregiver involvement in children's word learning does not decrease with the child's age. An easy and interesting mall walk creates a discovery game for older students. It involves giving the child a list of Greek root words: *aero* (means "air"), *bio* (means "life"), *geo* (means "earth"), *log, logy,* or *logue* (means "word" or the study of something), *meter* (means "measuring"), *phone* (means "sound"), *therm* (means "heat"), *photo* (means "light"), *hydro* (means "water"), and so on. The child and adult(s) identify words in the mall signs that have a Greek root and do a structural analysis of the word. For example, a father spots "log" in a word on a store sign, the child reads "logo," and the father and child read the sign: "T-Shirt Logos in One Hour." Many word games are created once adults and older children begin to play them. For example, consider the derived, polysyllabic, and plural words seen on driving trips. Work in the community might well be part of the literacy activities of the middle and upper elementary student. Volunteer work provides many opportunities for literacy and its authentic use.

TECHNOLOGY. A brochure from the International Reading Association (IRA) on family literacy is available at **http://bookstore.reading.org**, and the Public Broadcasting Ser-

FAMILY   LITERACY

How is family involvement important to older children's literacy development?

TECHNOLOGY

Do an Internet search for reading programs geared to children aged 9–12.

TABLE 5.2

Roots of Latin Origin

ROOT WORD	MEANING
-lect, -lege	choose
-ject, -jac	throw
-rupt	break
tort	twist
-volt, -volve	turn, roll
-tain	have, hold

vice (PBS) offers educational television programs for children ages nine to twelve. Online, the Corporation for Public Broadcasting offers information about new, safe, engaging, and educational programming on television and the Internet for this age group (**www.cpb.org/ ed/5**).

Helping Students Read Words in Context

When teaching children to learn and recognize words, it is very important to help them connect the words they've studied with similar words they come across in reading various texts. You can help children of all ages become more keenly aware of this in many ways.

Effective teachers know that demonstration and modeling provide a good beginning. For example, recall the opening classroom story of this chapter that featured Ms. Gupta's lesson with the words *spider* and *spout* and the focus on *sp* blends. In this lesson the children studied several words including *spider, spout, spell, spend,* and *spot.* They also generated words such as *see* and *snow* that didn't work for *sp* blends. This was a way to model and demonstrate connecting "studied words" with new ones.

Now picture Ms. Gupta's extending her teaching by presenting a lesson that used a sample of new text with similar words (e.g., some new *sp* blend words and some that did not fit the *sp* blend pattern). In such a lesson Ms. Gupta builds on the previous lesson and even more explicitly shows students that they can and should pay attention to words in their reading that are similar to words they know and are studying.

In conducting such demonstrations you model your thinking out loud to show the children that this is the kind of thinking they should also do. Imagine yourself reading a text on a large chart or in a big book in view of the children. The conversation goes something like this.

> **Teacher:** Humm. . . . I'm not sure about this word (silently draw your finger under the word *motorcar*), but it looks like one I know because we did a word sort with *motorboat* in it. And this story is about driving to the store. What do you think, children?

A few children respond that they see c-a-r and almost immediately some respond in unison saying, "car!"

> **Teacher:** Nice observation! I like the way you watch carefully and connect words you know with new words. And you are thinking about what is going on in the story. Good thinking, you used the context!

Once children have been taught through teacher modeling, remind and support them by teacher talk to connect known words to unknown words using everything they know to learn more and more words. Watch like a hawk and seize opportunities to affirm children's accomplishments in acquiring word knowledge in their reading.

Word learning strategies discussed in this chapter such as word hunts can also be adapted and expanded. Rather than hunting for the same studied words in books, children hunt for words that are similar to those in a list of known words given to them by their teacher or that they write on their own.

Also, as noted earlier in this chapter, word walls built from social studies, science, or literature units provide words that are similar to studied words. Call children's attention to comparing and contrasting such words to their studied word walls and invite them to find similarities.

A powerful teaching tool for any instruction is your classroom talk and use of language (Johnston, 2004). Often, rather than directly telling students something, asking them questions provides strong motivation. Consider a seventh-grade teacher observing a student puzzling over the word *periscope* in a book about submarines. Because in this class they study Greek and Latin roots, the teacher initiates the following conversation.

> **Teacher:** Is there a word you know that looks like this one?
> **Student:** It looks a little like *telescope*.

Good teachers use a variety of informal assessment strategies that are systematic and provide evidence-based information on children's learning. These assessments are not produced for thousands of children, as are standardized, formal assessments; they are not created to yield a comparison of one child to all other children at the same grade level. Rather, most informal assessments are carried out daily in teaching.

For example, you can observe children's word-reading errors in texts to infer the stage of word recognition they are in or the strategy they are using. Use Table 5.3 as a guide. The table offers suggestions for inferring a word-reading strategy from a child's error. It also suggests teaching strategies you might use. Of course, these categories are meant to be suggestive because one reading error is not sufficient evidence that a child is using a strategy. If you see several errors that fit a single category, you may infer that the child is using the corresponding strategy. Then try the suggested teaching approach and see if it helps.

TABLE 5.3

Word Knowledge Levels by Error Type

LEVEL OF WORD RECOGNITION	TARGET WORD	TYPICAL MISCUE OR READING ERROR	DESCRIPTION OF THE ERROR TYPE	TEACHING FOCUS
Logographic Reading	plant right	papa road	Student typically looks at one letter and calls out any word it reminds her of.	The student should continue to learn more sight words as wholes. Word study should focus on parts of words beyond the initial letter and also explore letter-to-sound correspondences.
Alphabetic Reading	plant right	pee lay night rye gut	Student reads through words one letter at a time, making a sound for each letter.	The student should continue to learn more sight words as wholes. Word study should point out conventional spellings for sounds and also begin to introduce common spelling patterns.
Orthographic Reading	plant right	pl, pl, ant, plant! ruh, ruh, -ight, right!	Student sees words as patterns of *onsets* and *rimes*.	Word study should introduce more spelling patterns (onsets and rimes).
Derivational Reading	assign	Assigg—No, assign!	Student recognizes that the target word is derived from a familiar word.	Word study should focus on derivational relationships between words.

Source: Temple, Crawford, and Gillet (in press). *Developmental literacy inventory*. Published by Allyn & Bacon, Boston, MA. Copyright © 2008 by Pearson Education. Reprinted by permission of the publisher.

Differentiated Instruction

SIOP®
Sheltered
Instruction
Observation
Protocol*

The Language-Experience Approach for English Language Learners and Struggling Readers

The Language Experience Approach, or LEA (Crawford et al., 1995; Stauffer, 1975), works for people of all ages who are learning to read and need additional support. The LEA is unique in that it uses the student's oral language to teach written language, that is, to teach reading. There are several cumulative steps to take when teaching with the LEA and many variations of it. The following is a step-by-step process we recommend. Use it with a small group or in working with one child.

First Lesson

In the first twenty- to thirty-minute lesson, complete these three steps.

STEP 1: DISCUSSION   Talk with students about their experiences (e.g., their favorite foods or birthday parties). Respond positively, be curious about their stories, and value their input. Let the children know that you will write down some things from their stories that they can all read together. In later LEA lessons the discussion topics could be about science or current events.

STEP 2: DICTATION   Ask the children what to write, select some of their responses, and write them on large chart paper, an overhead, or a computer screen. Be sure everyone can see your writing. Make teaching points about where to begin writing as you think appropriate. Read each sentence and ask them to read it back to you.

STEP 3: READING THE TEXT   Now it's time for the children to read their text. But first read it to them again and guide them to watch the words as you run your finger or pointer under them. Then have the children read along with you, and finally they read on their own.

To extend the lesson give the children copies of the text and have them practice in pairs or alone. Emphasize that this is just practice; give the children time and support to engage deeply in reading their own language.

In this initial two-day cycle of LEA, the first lesson consists of motivation and discussion, dictation and reading, and shared reading, as just described. On the following day, there are several additional steps.

Second Lesson

STEP 1: READING THE TEXT   Read the text again and prompt careful watching of the words as you point to them. Then have the children read with you. Practice this as much as needed. When reading sounds somewhat fluent, have the children take turns reading on their own. Include everyone. Every child can read even if it is only a word or two with your support.

STEP 2: REASSEMBLING THE TEXT   Before step 2, make copies of the sentences on sentence strips in the order they appear on the original text. Begin the lesson by having the children look at the whole text and then have them look for the first sentence. As children point out each sentence, put them in a sentence strip holder or adjustable pocket chart one at a time and practice reading them together. Each time read the sentence and then read the entire text. Again, children can take turns reading individually as they are able. You can also ask children to point at the sentence that tells [fill in blank].

Teacher: Yes. We've had that one. Do you know any other words that are similar to this one (pointing to periscope)?

Student: Well, we also had *microscope* in science the other day.

Teacher: Hmm. . . . what's this book about?

Student: Submarines. Is it periscope?

Teacher: How did you know?

This two-day cycle is repeated once or twice every week with a new theme for each set of lessons. Children will not learn all the words at first, but keep developing new charts for them to maintain interest. Be sure to keep copies available so children can practice. When you notice that children have learned a number of words, you can add a third lesson on sight vocabulary and move on to a three-day LEA cycle.

Third Lesson

STEP 1: REASSEMBLING THE WORDS INTO SENTENCES   Before step 1, cut each sentence strip made for the second lesson into individual words. Place the words in the pocket chart or even on the chalk rail. Place them in a random order and support the children in reassembling the words into sentences. Have the original story nearby so they can refer to it as needed. Build independence by asking children, "If you don't know a word, can you find it in our story? Now read the sentence. Can you read the word?" As sentences are reassembled, guide the reading of the whole text from time to time. Finally, you can implement other word activities. Here are a few ideas:

- Give word cards from the sentences to the children, and ask them to find the words in the text.
- Say, "Here is the word _____. Find the same word in the text."
- Make a large chart paper copy of one of the texts with some words left out. Tell the children that some words are missing and ask if they can identify them. Read with the children, pausing when you come to a missing word. Support them in "guessing the missing word" and write it in.
- Guide the children to write and keep a personal file collection of the words they learn. Begin with a few words and encourage building the collections and game playing with the word cards.

For further support of word recognition, you might color code sentence strips and word cards. Or various colors might be marked on the back of cards. Word cards are inevitably mixed up as children work with them at their desks or tables. They are easily sorted back into word groups of original sentences according to the colors on the reverse side.

Several weeks or even months after the third lesson activities, children will likely show signs of recognizing using letter/ sound correspondences in words. This is a signal to add a fourth day to the cycle, a day for word analysis using the context of words the children now recognize at sight.

Fourth Lesson

STEP 1: WORD RECOGNITION STUDY   The children read the story, they find words that begin alike, and you support their learning to associate letters and sounds using words they already know. Guide the children to draw conclusions, that is, phonic generalizations out of their observations of letters and corresponding sounds. Continue to use the written language, the words, sentences, and whole texts that have evolved from the children's oral language dictations. This makes powerful use of their background knowledge and helps them to extend their knowledge of sounds and letters in known words to new words. You can also bring out old LEA charts from time to time for review lessons and practice.

Repeated readings develop fluency and automaticity (when children recognize words automatically). As word recognition becomes easier and easier, they are able to focus attention on comprehension (Samuels & Farstup, 2006).

Student: I remembered the scope part. And the "up periscope" I saw in a movie.
Teacher: Great thinking!

Here you saw the teacher guide the student to use multiple cues to get the unknown word. As so often is the case, use of multiple cues supports children's literate thinking. Importantly, this teacher's talk attributed competence to the student. This is a wonderful way of building independence and students' awareness that they are in charge of their word learning.

For Review

Throughout the elementary grades, children need systematic, frequent, and flexible opportunities to learn words. They must have word recognition instruction that is grounded in reading as a sense-making and meaningful activity. Many word-learning activities may be used successfully from grades 1 to 8 in exclusive practice time periods of about ten to fifteen minutes. About thirty minutes of word work in context and in exclusive teaching and practice usually works for most children. Use a whole–part-whole approach in highly contextualized word instruction, especially in exclusive word study. That is, always return to word, sentence, and whole text meaning. It is recommended that you teach children the relationships between letters and sounds, beginning with individual letters and individual sounds and soon moving to groups of letters that spell parts of syllables, that is, onsets and rimes.

This chapter focused on word recognition, what it contributes to the reading process, and why it is important. It highlighted phonics and how to handle teaching word recognition, how much phonics to teach and for how long, and how to conduct word and phonics assessments. Ongoing assessment, an inseparable part of instruction, was emphasized. English language learners and struggling readers were given specific attention.

For Your Journal

1. Imagine a grade level you wish to teach or are teaching. Make a list of what you need to know about teaching words. Jot down any related concerns or frustrations you have at this point or anticipate.

2. Try this on your own, or work with a partner. Review the "Eeensy Weensy Spider" lesson described in the chapter-opening classroom story. Consider the levels of word knowledge in this chapter: logographic, transitional, alphabetic, and orthographic. What stage or stages were Ms. Gupta's children in? Why do you say so?

Taking It to the World

The debate about whole word versus phonics instruction as ways of teaching children to read has never been as simple as people often make it sound. Virtually all teachers read to children, invite children to write, and give them opportunities to explore meaningful print; and virtually all teachers point out letter-to-sound relationships to children. But there are differences in the emphasis that teachers put on these activities.

Either alone or with a partner, interview two or three first grade and two or three second grade teachers about their approaches to teaching reading. What things do the teachers at the same grade level have in common? What aspects of teaching are approached differently?

Ask them, too, to what extent their reading approaches are left up to their own decisions and to what extent their approaches are guided by reading coaches at the school level or district level.

Technology Connections

1. The International Reading Association holds that it is the responsibility of teachers to prepare students for a future that will require new literacies. These include becoming users of computers, high-quality software, and word processing. Visit the association's special Focus on Technology Website at **www.reading.org/focus/tech.html**, and investigate what the IRA is doing to help reading teachers incorporate technology into their classes.

2. Visit Learning Media at **www.learningmedia.com**, and click on the "Literacy and Media" button to learn more about key areas of literacy. Investigate the menu options at the left of the page. What can you find out about guided reading? What are the steps to guided reading? What other key topics in literacy education does this Website cover?

3. Many useful articles are available online through the IRA. The following Websites offer additional information on some of the major topics in this chapter:

   - Using think-alouds to analyze word sorts: **www.readingonline.org/articles/fresch**

   - Effects of traditional versus extended word study spelling instruction on students' orthographic knowledge: **www.readingonline.org/articles/abbott**

4. Visit the Scholastic Software Club Website (**http://teacher.scholastic.com/clubs/**) to investigate some of the various software options you can use in the classroom. Conduct your own review of materials you think might be helpful when you teach.

Connect with Research

Review the following key words from the chapter, and then connect to Research Navigator (**http://www.researchnavigator.com**) through this book's Companion Website to conduct a search into research on each of the various topics as they relate to reading and literacy education today.

alphabetic reading	sight word
big book	structural analysis
logographic reading	synthetic phonics
onsets and rimes	transitional reading
orthographic reading	word bank
phonogram patterns	word sorts
phonological recoding	word walls

Companion Website

To access chapter objectives, practice tests, weblinks, and flashcards, visit the Companion Website at www.ablongman.com/templeallchildren2e.

Go to Allyn & Bacon's MyLabSchool (www.mylabschool.com), enter Assignment ID LAV4 into the Assignment Finder. Watch the video, *Phonics Instruction*, in which a teacher conducts a lively sight word lesson.

Question: You may also answer the questions at the end of the clip and e-mail your responses to your instructor.

chapter 6

Fluency in
Reading

Using Online
Sources to Build
Vocabulary

Helping Readers
Build Fluency and
Vocabulary

Family
Literacy

How Do We
Teach
Vocabulary?

Helping
Readers Build
Vocabulary

Helping Readers Build Fluency and Vocabulary

Anticipation Guide

The following questions will stimulate your thinking about the topics of this chapter. Answer true or false in response to each statement. As you read and learn more about the topics in these statements, double-check your answers. See what interests you and what prompts your curiosity toward more understanding.

_____ ● Fluency and vocabulary are both considered key areas of reading ability by the U.S. government.

_____ ● Reading fluently consists entirely of reading quickly.

_____ ● Children who read fluently tend to understand what they read.

_____ ● Teachers should never model fluent reading for children, for fear of discouraging them.

_____ ● An average reading rate for a third grader is about thirty words per minute.

_____ ● Vocabulary is knowledge of words and word meanings.

_____ ● All children enter school with very nearly the same number of words in their vocabularies.

_____ ● Having a word for something in your vocabulary makes it more likely that you will notice that thing.

_____ ● Vocabulary knowledge is one of the best predictors of reading comprehension.

_____ ● Research suggests that although it helps to teach vocabulary, we don't need to teach all of the words children need to know.

Volunteer Tutors Help Children Develop Fluency

Katie Flowers directs a tutoring project for a small liberal arts college. The program has worked continuously for thirteen years and is very popular with college students. Nearly a hundred of them volunteer each term to go out to a local school and work one on one with a first-, second-, or third-grade student who has been recommended by a teacher for extra help.

At the beginning of each semester, the students are given a couple of hours of training. Then the students go out to a local school two times each week, both before and after school. Each time the students go out, they follow a lesson plan with five parts. The lesson plan was borrowed from Darrell Morris's *The Howard Street Tutoring Manual* (2006):

1. Read an easy book to develop fluency.
2. Read a harder book to help the children learn new words.
3. Do a word study task—phonics or vocabulary.
4. Have the child write something.
5. Read aloud to the child.

Katie asks the teachers to fill out feedback forms at the end of each term. Last spring, one teacher reported that over the year a third-grade student progressed from 58 to 153 words per minute. Another teacher reported a big increase in

Both **reading fluency** and **vocabulary** are important areas of children's reading ability (see the Standards and Literacy box). As we demonstrate in this chapter, if children are to read well, they must read fluently: with appropriate rate, automatic word recognition, and meaningful phrasing. Reading fluency can be taught, and it should be. Vocabulary, which can be thought of as a growing storehouse of tokens of meaning, is also critically important for students of all ages to develop. Students must learn tens of thousands of words during their school years, and most of them will be learned through reading. There is much that teachers can do to help students learn words and their meanings.

Fluency in Reading

"Dance like nobody's watching, . . . sing like nobody's listening." That advice from Mark Twain is true whether we are dancing, singing, swinging at a baseball, or reading. Conscious attention to the act itself takes concentration away from the purpose of the activity and makes our performance stiff, self-conscious, and unsuccessful. With regard to reading, it has been demonstrated that those who are lacking in reading fluency have diminished comprehension: The more they're thinking about the words, the less they're thinking about the meaning (Foorman & Mehta, 2002; Perfetti, 1985; Samuels & Farstrup, 2006).

a child's Lexile score on a commercial reading test. These and other comments from teachers attest to the success of the students' tutoring, but they also reveal something else. The teachers' comments nearly all emphasize the aspects of reading stressed under the federal No Child Left Behind legislation: phonemic awareness, phonics, word recognition, fluency, vocabulary, and comprehension. Over the past dozen years, these aspects of reading have always been stressed in the tutoring program, just as all of them have been emphasized in Morris's Howard Street model. But Katie realizes she should adjust the emphasis of the tutoring on some of these aspects, at least to make sure the tutoring is coordinated with where the teachers are now placing their emphases.

Two areas that call for more attention are fluency and vocabulary. Katie sets about making sure her first training session this fall will show her student-tutors how to do repeated reading, readers' theater, and choral reading. She thinks to herself that the tutors and their young charges will need to work in groups some of the time to do these fluency activities, which will bring some welcome variety to the tutoring sessions. She also plans to show the tutors how to lead Word Conversations and also how to use semantic maps, semantic feature analysis, and some other vocabulary-building activities.

Thus reading fluency has two parts to it: effortless efficiency at word recognition and rendering the text expressively so it sounds like it makes sense. Here is the National Reading Panel's definition of reading fluency:

> *Fluency is the ability to read a text accurately and quickly. When fluent readers read silently, they recognize words automatically. They group words quickly in ways that help them gain meaning from what they read. Fluent readers read aloud effortlessly and with expression. Their reading sounds natural, as if they are speaking.* (National Reading Panel, 2000, p. 22)

Fluency is not mere word recognition. Children can score well on word recognition tests without being able to read smoothly, accurately, and with expression in connected text. Fluency is not mere comprehension. Children can demonstrate comprehension skills without performing the rapid acts of understanding that characterize fluency—although we do know that unless children read fluently, their comprehension is likely to be impaired (Pinnell et al., 1995).

Between the component skills of language and print concepts, word recognition ability, and comprehension skills, on the one hand, and the ultimate goal of successful reading, on the other, reading fluency stands in the middle—serving as the driving force that orchestrates those skills and puts them to work in reading text, so that with experience over time, learners will acquire the large vocabularies, the versatility with sentence and text structures, and the background knowledge they need to become successful readers. Samuels and Farstrup (2006) compare learning to read fluently with learning to drive a car. Fluent

Fluency and Vocabulary

Fluency and vocabulary are considered "building blocks for literacy" by the U.S. government's National Institute for Literacy. They constitute two of the five such building blocks. The others are phonemic awareness, phonics, and comprehension.

About **fluency,** the Institute's Web site says,

Fluency is important because it provides a bridge between word recognition and comprehension. Because fluent readers do not have to concentrate on decoding the words, they can focus their attention on what the text means. They can make connections among the ideas in the text and between the text and their background knowledge. In other words, fluent readers recognize words and comprehend at the same time. Less fluent readers, however, must focus their attention on figuring out the words, leaving them little attention for understanding the text. . . .

A recent large-scale study by the National Assessment of Educational Progress (NAEP) found that 44% of a representative sample of the nation's fourth graders were low in fluency. The study also found a close relationship between fluency and reading comprehension. Students who scored lower on measures of fluency also scored lower on measures of comprehension, suggesting that fluency is a neglected reading skill in many American classrooms, affecting many students' reading comprehension.

And about **vocabulary,** the Institute's staff writes,

Vocabulary refers to the words we must know to communicate effectively. In general, vocabulary can be described as oral vocabulary or reading vocabulary. Oral vocabulary refers to words that we use in speaking or recognize in listening. Reading vocabulary refers to words we recognize or use in print. . . .

Vocabulary . . . is very important to reading comprehension. Readers cannot understand what they are reading without knowing what most of the words mean. As children learn to read more advanced texts, they must learn the meaning of new words that are not part of their oral vocabulary.

Source: **http://www.nifl.gov/partnershipforreading/publications/reading_first1.html.**

reading, like fluent driving, requires the orchestration of many tasks at once. At first a student driver can only focus on one task at a time, but a fluent driver can change lanes, obey signals, watch for traffic, and choose which route to take, all while carrying on a conversation or listening to a talk show on the radio.

Drivers learn to drive with some training and a great deal of practice. Readers need practice, too. But most young readers don't get enough of that practice. One careful study of fifth graders' reading showed just how scant that practice can be (see Table 6.1).

According to this study, the average fifth grader reads less than five minutes a day. That prompted one of the researchers to observe, "If you walk into a typical elementary school today, you would have to say that you were among nonreaders" (Wilson, 1992). The good news is that fourteen minutes of reading per day amounts to a million words read in a year, so efforts to increase children's time spent reading need not change children's lives dramatically to have some results. But such efforts will not soon close the gap between good readers and poor readers. In one year, the top six readers read as much as the bottom six readers would read in fifty-four years, and the top three readers read as much as the bottom three readers would read in two centuries.

On the positive side, we know that some of children's favorite moments in reading instruction come as they listen to the teacher reading aloud to them fluently and with animated expression, and also when they themselves perform fluent reading aloud brilliantly in front of their classmates (Ivey & Broaddus, 2002). As a second grader who participated in a study of oral reading exclaimed to Martinez, Roser, and Strecker (1999), "I never thought I could be a star, but I was the best reader today."

Fluent reading was itself elevated to star status among the emphases in "scientifically based reading instruction," the approaches sanctioned under the federal No Child Left Behind Act. That means that reading programs that hope to receive government funding need

Plan well—the environment, the time, procedures, materials, and instruction. Read The First Days of School by Harry Wong. Take time to build community within the classroom. Greet and welcome every child every day. Listen. Remember—children need to know what is going to happen each day—don't keep it a secret.

—Barb,
First Grade Teacher,
Cincinnati, OHIO

TABLE 6.1

Differences in Amounts of Independent Reading by Fifth Graders

PERCENTILE RANK	MINUTES OF BOOK READING PER DAY	WORDS READ IN BOOKS PER YEAR
98	65.0	4,358,000
90	21.1	1,823,000
80	14.2	1,146,000
70	9.6	622,000
60	6.5	432,000
50	4.6	282,000
40	3.2	200,000
30	1.3	106,000
20	0.7	21,000
10	0.1	8,000
2	0.0	0

Source: Anderson, R.C., Wilson, P.T., & Fielding, L.G. (1988, Summer). Growth in reading and how children spend their time outside of school. *Reading Research Quarterly, 23*(3), 285–303. Reprinted with permission of the International Reading Association.

to show that reading fluency is a priority. It also means that reading experts consider an emphasis on reading fluency to be a best practice in reading instruction.

Tim Rasinski suggests that teaching reading fluency should include these four emphases:

1. Model good oral reading.
2. Provide oral support for readers.
3. Offer plenty of practice opportunities.
4. Encourage fluency through phrasing. (Rasinski, 2003)

Modeling Fluent Oral Reading

As a five-year-old, one of the author's daughters loved to pretend-read books. Once she picked up Bill Martin's *Brown Bear, Brown Bear, What Do You See?* and read, "Wuh, wuh, wuh once . . . thuh, thuh, thuh, there . . . wuh, wuh, wuh, was . . . a buu, buh, buh, bear . . ."

"Annabrooke," I said, "What in the world are you doing?"

She beamed and said proudly, "I'm reading like a first grader!"

The anecdote should make us pause to ask, do our students know what fluent reading sounds like? Annabrooke did, fortunately, because her parents had read to her since the time she would have fit in a shoe box. But other students may not, if most of the reading they hear around them is the word-by-word struggles of other neophyte readers.

Teachers should be careful to provide models of fluent reading for their students (see the Teach It! box). We mean this in two senses. First, teachers should actually demonstrate the concept of fluent versus disfluent reading. Second, teachers should frequently read aloud to students and entice them with examples of rich language read well.

Reading Aloud with Expression

When you read aloud to children, you are pointing out for them what is important and interesting in books. You convey enthusiasm and paint events with importance using your voice. Your voice is a marvelous instrument, capable of communicating joy, drama, humor,

Demonstrating Fluent Reading

To introduce the very concept of fluent reading, begin by reading a passage to the students two ways. First read it haltingly and uncertainly, in a voice that suggests you are concerned with slashing your way through the words and getting a disagreeable experience over with: In other words, read disfluently. Then read it again, but this time with your voice full of expression and interest, with pauses and emphases. Show that you are enjoying the message of the text and not simply struggling to pronounce the words: That is to say, read fluently. Then ask the students which reading they preferred and why. In the discussion that follows, call attention to the qualities of fluent reading:

- The reader is thinking about the message and not just about pronouncing the words.
- The reader varies her voice between loud and soft, and between faster and slower.
- The reader groups words meaningfully.
- The reader may show emotion—enjoyment, surprise, and excitement—as she reads.

Later, read aloud to the students again, reading as fluently as you can, and "thinking aloud" as you read: That is, pausing to explain to the students of a decision you just made—such as where to pause, what words to group together, or how to read a character's voice—in order to read fluently.

excitement, and importance. If you do not have very much experience reading to children, or even if you do, it is worth taking the time to develop your capabilities at reading aloud.

QUALITIES OF VOICE. Have you ever watched a golf coach demonstrate the proper way to drive a ball? The coach will slow down and exaggerate the swing, to give the learner time to watch the grip of the hands, the planting of the feet, the rotation of the hips, and the swing of the arms. Reading aloud to children is like that: You slow down and exaggerate the swings of the voice from fast to slow to high to low; you add pauses to create suspense, and you read the action as if you were seeing it and the dialogue as if you were hearing it. Listen to a recording of a professional actor reading a children's book. Note the way the actor gives life to characters, creates suspense, moves the story quickly along in spots and slows it down for dramatic effect in other places. All of these are techniques you can imitate, and they will add power to your reading aloud.

Try this exercise. Practice reading the following passage aloud several times through.

1. The first time through, decide where to place one-second pauses in your reading for dramatic effect.
2. Read it again, alternating between faster and slower pronunciation as the text suggests.
3. Read it a third time, making some parts quiet, and some parts suddenly loud, to raise suspense and surprise the listeners.
4. Once you have practiced those readings one at a time, read the passage a fourth time, and combine all three effects: pauses, fast and slow, and soft and loud reading.

On a dare, the girl went to the old dark house at midnight. Did ghosts really live there? She would find out. As she approached the shadowy front door through the overgrown weeds, she saw something gleaming. It was only the moon reflecting from a glass pane. But she could swear it looked like eyes. She found the knob and twisted. The door creaked open! She stepped inside. She found the staircase in the pitch dark, and climbed up, one creaky step at a time. She found the bedroom door, pushed, and swung it open. Nothing in here. Carefully she lay down on the floor, and was nearly asleep when she heard a scratching sound across the room. Her heart stopped beating in her chest. A MOUSE! That's what it was!

BRINGING CHARACTERS TO LIFE. When books have more than one character in them, it helps animate the reading if you read each character's lines in a different voice. Younger characters might get higher voices; older characters, lower ones; and wiser characters, slower, more thoughtful voices. As a rule of thumb, try to portray personality styles—

clever, lazy, humorous, haughty—in the different voices rather than the character's ethnicity or region of origin because doing the latter may be offensive to some.

Choosing Texts for Reading Aloud

Your school librarian, or the local children's librarian, will have good recommendations for read-alouds. There are printed sources you can rely on for suggestions as well. The International Reading Association annually sponsors the children's choice contest, in which teachers across North America ask children to select the books they enjoy most from each year's new publications. *The Reading Teacher* publishes the results. The American Library Association's monthly journal *Bookbird* publishes reviews of books with curricular tie-ins. And the *Hungry Mind Review* publishes suggestions of books for young people that are especially provocative and interesting.

When you read aloud to students, you can point out what is important and interesting in books, and convey enthusiasm, joy, drama, humor, and excitement.

Read books from parallel cultures often. American children are truly fortunate to have books available that reflect the lives of all children, from every cultural group. As Rudine Sims Bishop (1999) reminds us, books from parallel cultures can serve as *windows and mirrors*: as *windows* into other cultures that are different from the readers' own, and as *mirrors* of the readers' own culture, to give those readers reflections of their own experience. Best books each year about African American children's experience compete for the **Coretta Scott King Award**. Best books about Latino children's experience compete for the **Américas Award**.

Don't overlook informational books—especially books about science and social studies topics—when choosing books to read aloud. Children enjoy hearing about the real world, too. Informational books for young people are written with as much skill and artistry as fictional works, but listening to them and understanding them exercises different kinds of concentration and comprehension (Duke, 2000). The National Science Teachers Association's journal *Science and Children* recommends good titles for children in their field. The journal from the National Council for the Social Studies, *Social Studies and the Young Learner*, recommends good books for young readers as well on topics from the social sciences. Finally, articles from the excellent specialized journals on scientific, geographical, and historical topics—from *Ranger Rick*, *National Geographic World*, and *Cobblestone*—can make excellent read-alouds as well. Remember, a key to a good read-aloud is that you, the teacher, have surveyed the text and determined where to put emphasis and how to read orally.

Engaging the Students as You Read

When you read a text aloud to your students, take steps to call attention to your fluent reading. Make sure to point out to students how you

- Match the emotional qualities of the passages—serious, humorous, exciting, urgent—with your tone of voice.
- Stress the important words in the passages.
- Honor the punctuation—pausing at commas, stopping at periods, and raising your voice at the ends of sentences with question marks.
- Read the dialogues as if people were actually talking.

Also, the reading will be more successful if you take steps to engage the students as you read. These steps include previewing the text, pausing to raise suspense before important parts of the text, asking for predictions, inviting the students to read repeated parts of the text with you, and rereading the text to invite the students to read more of it with you (see the discussion of reading aloud on pp. 171–172).

TEACH IT! 1

Reading Aloud

TEACH IT! 4

*Language Experience
with Authentic
Children's Literature*

Extending the Meaning of the Text

After reading a text aloud to the students, you may further engage them with the meaning of the text with follow-up activities. These include dramatizing the students' favorite parts (see page 223 and the Teach It! on page 225), posing reader response questions (see pages 216–223), or having them do a "Sketch-to-stretch" activity (see pages 219–220) or fill out a four-way response chart (see next section).

FOUR-WAY RESPONSE CHART.   The students each take a sheet of paper and divide it into four panels. In one panel they write an important quote (younger readers write just a few words) they remember from the text. In another panel they draw a picture of an important character or scene. In a third panel they write or draw what the text reminded them of or made them think of. In the last panel they write what they liked about the text (adapted from Preece, 1998).

Supporting Children's Reading for Fluency

There are three general approaches to supporting children's reading for fluency:

- Sustained silent reading
- Directed activities, such as repeated reading
- Artistic means, such as readers' theater and choral reading with voice choirs

DROP EVERYTHING AND READ AND SUSTAINED SILENT READING.   Drop Everything and Read (DEAR) and **Sustained Silent Reading (SSR)** are reading activities that are scheduled during times set aside during the day for children—as well as teachers, school principals, librarians, custodians, and parents—to pick up a book or magazine and read it for a fixed number of minutes, usually fifteen to thirty minutes.

Teachers still may set aside time for sustained silent reading, especially if they take steps to keep the students on task and provide opportunities for students to report on what they have read so they encourage others to try those books (see the World of Reading box). Books read during sustained reading time should be those written at each child's independent reading level—that is, the children should be able to read them without a more fluent reader's help. Nonetheless, students can be encouraged to read more interesting and challenging materials within their independent reading levels.

There are few rules for sustained silent reading, except that

- Everyone should choose what to read—the material is not assigned—but students should choose material at their independent reading level.
- Games, television, videos, and similar distractions are out of bounds for students; grading papers and getting other work done is not allowed for teachers.
- The reading time should be followed with a discussion, such as having students give synopses of what they read and recommend it to others.
- Teachers may wish to keep track of what students read in the classroom. Students can write their responses, evaluations, and recommendations—or two or three students can be asked to share these orally at the end of each reading session. You can ask parents to keep track of what children read at home, when they are reading under the guise of DEAR or SSR. Students can write their responses to their independent reading in a reading journal.

Repeated Reading

Repeated reading is a method of having a child practice reading the same moderately challenging passage repeatedly up to four times until she or he can read it at a predetermined

Is Sustained Silent Reading Effective?

Because few experimental research studies have measured the effects of sustained reading, the National Reading Panel (2000) did not endorse this practice in its survey of recommended instructional strategies to improve reading.

The National Institute for Literacy discourages the practice of sustained silent reading because they don't find sufficient support for it in research. The NIFL Web site says,

No research evidence is available currently to confirm that instructional time spent on silent, independent reading with minimal guidance and feedback improves reading fluency and overall reading achievement. . . .

Research . . . has not yet confirmed whether independent silent reading with minimal guidance or feedback improves reading achievement and fluency. Neither has it proven that more silent reading in the classroom cannot work; its effectiveness without guidance or feedback is as yet unproven. The research suggests that there are more beneficial ways to spend reading instructional time than to have students read independently in the classroom without reading instruction.

The Institute's Web page goes on to make this recommendation:

Rather than allocating instructional time for independent reading in the classroom, encourage your students to read more outside of school. They can read with an adult or other family member. Or, they can read on their own with books at their independent reading level. Of course, students might also read on their own during independent work time in the classroom—for example, as another small group is receiving reading instruction, or after they have completed one activity and are waiting for a new activity to begin. **http://www.nifl.gov/ partnershipforreading/publications/reading_first1fluency.html**

What's wrong with sustained silent reading? Some critics worry that poor readers especially won't get much done during sustained silent reading time; they may need support from the teacher to stay on task and learn to read more fluently (Kuhn & Stahl, 2003). Others worry that, left to their own devices, students may choose material that is too easy to increase their fluency by much (Shanahan, 2002).

We would argue that to become fluent, students certainly do need to read material that is written at their **independent reading level** (see Chapter 10), material that they can read without help. And to learn new words and structures, and become able to read more challenging material, of course they also need to read materials at their **instructional reading level**—materials in which they encounter occasional words they don't know or structures that are less familiar, and for that they will need the support of the teacher or some other more fluent reader.

Given the amount of time children spend reading outside of school (see Figure 6.1) just fifteen minutes of sustained silent reading per day *triples* the average fifth grader's accomplishment. It amounts to *twenty times* the reading done by the least avid five readers, and *150 times* that of the two or three least avid readers. That's a lot of bang for fifteen minutes of instructional time.

Encouraging children to read outside of school is important to do, and all teachers should work with book clubs, participate in reading incentive programs, encourage children to get library cards, and make other efforts to get children reading outside of school (see later). But because we know from research that the average child does very little reading outside of school and some children do virtually none, we would not recommend giving up on encouraging reading during the school day, especially if it is well supervised and if children are given regular opportunities to talk about what they are reading and encourage other children to read what they did.

To improve their reading fluency, children need guided support in reading challenging texts, too—material written at their instructional reading levels. To read at those levels, the children will need the support of the teacher or some other capable reader. Techniques that provide that support include the method of repeated reading and similar strategies presented later.

---

level of speed and accuracy. To carry out repeated reading, select passages of between 50 and 500 words, depending on the reading rates of the children. The passages should come from different sources, but they should be running text and not poetry or lists. Informational text should be mixed in with fiction. Find a text written at each student's instructional level—that is, the student should be able to read the text with about 95 percent accuracy—making one error for each twenty words. If the text seems a little difficult for the student, offer support, such as *echo reading* (you read a line and the child reads a line).

Sit next to the student in a quiet place, and listen as the student practices reading the text repeatedly. Keep a copy of the text yourself on which you can mark the student's reading errors. Error are words that are omitted, or for which other words are substituted, or

TABLE 6.2

Average Reading Rates

GRADE LEVEL	TARGET NUMBER OF CWPM
Second half of first grade	60 CWPM
Second grade	90 CWPM
Third grade	100 CWPM
Fourth grade	110 CWPM
Fifth grade	120 CWPM
Sixth grade or higher	140 CWPM

Source: Rasinski, 2003

that are mispronounced. If the student does not say a word, wait two seconds and say the word yourself, and count that as an error. Time the student's reading for exactly sixty seconds, then stop the student, count the total number of words read, and subtract the errors from the total. The child should practice reading the text several times, preferably until she reaches the criterion score for her grade level (see Table 6.2). CWPM means "correct words per minute," that is, the total number of words read minus the words read incorrectly.

Once the child has reached the criterion score, assign her another text of equivalent or greater difficulty to practice reading. From time to time, ask the child to read a passage she has not prepared, and measure the reading rate for an independent comparison.

Keep a record of the child's efforts on a log such as the one in Figure 6.1.

FIGURE 6.1

A Chart for Recording Repeated Readings.

Child's Name:				
Name of Passage	Dates Read	Date Ended	CWPM	Comparison Text Rate

Instructions: Record the name of a new text the student is working on, and enter the dates that he or she reads the text. In a separate row, you may enter the date of each day the student reads the same text, and enter the CWPM ("Correct Words Per Minute") attained that day. When the child reaches the criterion score, enter the date of that achievement. Occasionally (at least every two weeks) have the child read a text of similar difficulty that she or he has *not* prepared. Enter the name and date in the first two columns, and enter the fluency score (in CWPM) in the right-hand column.

Practicing Fluency without the Teacher's Guidance

The method of repeated reading requires that the teacher set aside the time to listen to individual students reading. Rasinski (2003) recommends setting aside time each day for repeated reading instruction. If that recommendation is followed, the teacher of a moderate-size class might reach each child for a few minutes each week. What should the students do when they are not with the teacher? Four suggestions are *paired reading, buddy reading, recorded reading,* and *Radio Reading.*

PAIRED READING. In **paired reading** (Topping, 1987), a fluent reader is matched up with a less fluent reader. They work together on a passage that is chosen at the less fluent reader's instructional reading level. The more fluent reader begins by reading the passage aloud to the less fluent reader. Then the two read the passage through several times in unison. Then the less fluent reader takes over the reading while the more fluent reader monitors the other child's reading. The more fluent reader corrects the other's errors by saying the word correctly and by having the less fluent reader reread the sentence in which the misread word occurred. The fluent reader might say, "Read that sentence again and make it sound like you're talking to me." The "more fluent reader" in this method might be a parent volunteer, a tutor from the local university, or even an older student.

Labbo and Teale (1990) suggest having a less fluent reader from an older class pair up with a younger reader who needs support and carry out the paired reading procedure. Research shows that the activity can be beneficial to both.

FAMILY LITERACY

How will you persuade families to read daily with their children?

Family Literacy

The paired reading procedure and other related methods can be carried out by parents with their own children. During a parent night at your school, you can give parents an orientation in the method of paired reading. Begin by pointing out the importance of reading fluency. Show the parents the statistics on children's book reading (see page 171). Parents will be surprised to learn how even ten or fifteen minutes a day of support for their child's reading can greatly increase the amount of reading the child might otherwise do. Point out the benefits that can be gained from this: as many as a million words read, with accompanying boosts in vocabulary and understanding.

Show parents how to carry out the steps of the paired reading procedure. Remind them to keep the tone encouraging.

Send home passages for the parent to read with the child that you have found to be on the child's instructional level. Send notes of encouragement to the parents who carry out the procedure, and recognize them at school.

Some parents might be interested in offering to support students' reading fluency by using these methods with other students in the community, or they might be persuaded to come to school and volunteer to read with children in the classroom.

BUDDY READING. Buddy reading is another way for students to practice reading for fluency without the teacher's devoting time to individual students. At its simplest, two students take turns reading paragraphs of the same text to each other. A more elaborated version begins with the teacher reading from a big book or a text projected on an overhead projector while running his or her hand under the words and using a fluent delivery. Then pairs of students take turns reading passages from the text (Koskinen & Blum, 1986). How are the pairs formed? In one approach, the teacher divides the

In paired reading a fluent reader is matched up with a less fluent reader.

students into four groups of readers, from the most fluent (group 4) to the least fluent (group 1). Students from group 4 are paired with students from group 2, and students from group 3 are paired with students from group 1. Some teachers finds that students spend more time on task if they are allowed to choose their own partners.

FLUENCY ORIENTED ORAL READING (FOOR).   This strategy combines group instruction with paired study. FOOR (Kuhn, 2004) proceeds in a three-day cycle. The teacher assembles a group of students who are on roughly the same instructional reading level. Copies of the text are provided for the students and the teacher.

- Day 1: The teacher fluently reads a passage aloud to the students. The teacher may "think aloud" and call attention to the way he reads the words in groups and how he provides emphasis with his voice to important words. The teacher may discuss the meaning and invite comments. Then teacher and students echo read the text; that is, the teacher fluently reads a line, and the students read the same line. They take turns echo reading the entire text.
- Day 2: The students pair up and take turns reading the text, each one reading a sentence or a paragraph.
- Day 3: The students come back together in the original group with the teacher. Now they choral-read the text; that is, they all read the text as if with one voice. The students may take turns reading parts of the text in dramatic fashion, following the ideas of readers' theater (see later).

Technology

TECHNOLOGY

Look up *Fluent Reader* online. How much of the needed interaction is the computer program providing to build a child's fluency?

The National Reading Panel (2000) recommends two kinds of activity to help students learn to read fluently: modeling fluent reading and guided repeated reading, with monitoring and feedback offered to the student. The latter of these activities ordinarily takes one-on-one attention from a competent adult. But computer-based programs have been able to provide much of this support. Consider *Fluent Reader*, developed by Renaissance Learning (**http://www.renlearn.com**), for a good example. On a computer screen, students are offered texts to read from fiction, poetry, and informational genres, and the passages are organized at seventeen difficulty levels. While reading the passage for the first time, the student clicks on each difficult word and also clicks on the last word read after one minute. The program then computes the student's reading and accuracy rates and sets a target score. Both the student's present score and the target score are presented to the student on a bar graph. Then the student reads the text again while listening to the recorded voice of a fluent reader. On the screen the lines are highlighted as the recorded voice reads them. The recorded voice can be set to different speeds, so the student can listen to the words spoken slowly and clearly at first, and then again read at a normal speaking rate. After reading the text several times, the student can be tested again by the program, and again his or her speed and accuracy scores are recorded and presented on a bar graph. The teacher may print out a version of the text the student is working on, too, either to enable the student to practice reading the text at home or to free up the computer for another student to use while the original student practices reading the paper version. The program records the student's voice, so the teacher can listen to it later for assessment purposes. It also compiles assessment information for each student, including the passage she or he is working on, the student's speed and accurate rate, and the number of repetitions it has taken for the student to reach the target score.

Embedding Repeated Reading in Performance

Language education is about more than skill development. Teachers want to cultivate children's appreciation for language and broaden the variety of literature that children can enjoy. So it is recommended that teachers use literary performance as another approach to teaching children to read fluently. Two such activities are readers' theater and choral performance.

READERS' THEATER. **Readers' theater** combines an emphasis on fluency, meaning, drama, and rhetoric as students practice reading texts aloud and use their voices to convey the meaning of the text. Performing in readers' theater is much like acting on a stage, except that instead of speaking memorized lines, the students read them; and instead of moving dramatically around the stage, the students convey meaning with the sound of their voices and their facial expressions. Readers' theater is most commonly used with fictional works, and when it is, the readers must decide what the characters are like, what is at stake for the characters at each point in the text, and thus how the reading should sound. If the piece is informational or persuasive, however, the readers must decide what the text is saying, what the important points are, and what kinds of emotions the readers should convey. In either case, students need to practice reading the same passages many times to "get them right." Thus they are doing repeated readings naturally, with the emphasis on meaning.

As they prepare to read a fictional text with readers' theater, players should discuss the setting of the text, who the characters are, and what they are like. Then they should read portions of the text several times to read the lines fluently and with the expression called for. It helps if the teacher offers coaching, asking the students,

- "What is your character feeling right now? How do you sound when you feel that way? Should your voice be loud or soft? Fast or slow?"
- "What might your character think about what the other character is saying? How will your character sound then?"
- "What is going on at this point in the story? How is your character reacting to it?"
- "How is your character changing as the story proceeds?"

As they prepare to read an informational or argumentative text, readers identify the message of the text and how they feel about it. Then they decide what points to read with greater emphasis, where to put pauses for suspense, what parts should be said quietly, what parts loudly, and what parts to hammer home. They think about how the beginning and the end of their piece should sound. The teacher's side coaching helps the students make these decisions. Both the teacher and the other students can offer comments and suggestions after each practice reading.

Selecting texts for readers' theater. Fictional texts for readers' theater can be found in picture books and chapter books, and in the many commercial sets of readers' theater scripts now available. Some of these even have different levels of reading for particular parts so differentiation can occur within the same production. The best choices are those that contain a good deal of dialogue. For example, *White Dynamite and the Curly Kid* by Bill Martin, Jr., and John Archambault is written entirely as dialogue. Frances Temple's *Tiger Soup* contains a readers' theater script in the dust jacket. Chris Raschka's *Yo! Yes?* is a simple dialogue between two little boys with a multicultural theme. When using longer books, choose dialogues taken from pivotal scenes in the plot. *Roll of Thunder, Hear My Cry* by Mildred Taylor contains many scenes in which confrontations between people of different races is thoughtfully handled. Kate DiCamillo's *Because of Winn Dixie* contains many poignant encounters between characters. Informational or argumentative texts should be interesting and powerful. News stories of historical events make good texts for readers' theater. So do speeches, such as Martin Luther King Jr.'s "I Have a Dream" speech.

To prepare a text for readers' theater,

1. Make a photocopy of it so you can mark it up.
2. Decide how many readers you have, and then go through the text and divide up the lines that will be read by each reader.
3. Mark each reader's parts of the text by putting brackets around the words or lines and writing the initials of the character above those parts.
4. Remember the narrator! Since anything not already assigned to a character will be read by a narrator, you can divide the narrator's lines by as many readers as you need to accommodate, and mark their sections N1, N2, N3, etc.
5. Draw lines through any parts that do not need to be read, like "he said," "she said," etc.

6. You may photocopy the text as marked, or type out a clean copy with each reader identified before the lines.

Scripted texts for readers' theater are available in which roles are identified for readers of different levels of fluency. Books containing readers' theater scripts include these:

Braun, W., & Braun, C. (1995). *Readers' theater: Scripted rhymes and rhythms.* Calgary, Alberta: Braun and Braun Educational Enterprises.

Coleman, M., Farley, J., & Holliday, S. (2001). *Readers theater level 1.* Columbus, OH: McGraw-Hill. (grade levels 2–5)

Crawford, S. A., & Sanders, N. I. (1999). *15 irresistible mini-plays for teaching math.* New York: Scholastic.

Farley, J., & Sishton, J. (2001). *Readers theater level 2.* Columbus, OH: McGraw-Hill. (grade levels 3–7)

Glassock, S. (1995). *10 American history plays for the classroom.* New York: Scholastic.

Glassock, S. (2001). *10 Easy-to-read American history plays that reach all readers.* New York: Scholastic.

Hoberman, M.A. (2001). *You read to me, I'll read to you.* Boston: Little, Brown.

Haven, K. (1996). *Great moments in science.* Englewood, CO: Teacher Ideas Press.

Pugliano-Martin, C. (1999). *25 Spanish plays for emergent readers.* New York: Scholastic.

Pugliano-Martin. C. (2000). *25 just-right plays for emergent readers.* New York: Scholastic.

Worthy, J. (2005). *Readers theater for building fluency.* New York: Scholastic. (grade levels 3–6)

Here are some Web sites with scripts for readers' theater that are available for free:

Blau, L. *Monthly scripts readers' theater language arts ideas.* **www.lisablau.com/freescripts.html.**

Lansky, B. *Classroom theatre.* **www.fictionteachers.com/classroomtheatre/theatre.html.**

Shepard, A. *Readers theater (Readers' theater: Free scripts).* **www.araonshep.com/rt.rte.html.**

When you assign roles in readers' theater you can give all the students roughly equal chances to participate. There can be several narrators. Students can read the lines for more than one character (although if they do, they should read the same characters' lines consistently, and they might develop different voices for different characters). The same script can be read by more than one group, and the "readings" (as in interpretations) can be compared after. Another way to involve more students is to choose different scenes from a longer work and to assign each scene to a smaller group of students.

TEACH IT! 24
Choral Reading

CHORAL READING IN VOICE CHOIRS. Choral reading is another performance-oriented way of practicing reading for fluency. Like readers' theater, because readers are reading and rereading to get just the right sounds to convey meanings and emotions, the practice of repeated reading is imbedded in a meaning-driven activity. Choral reading can be done with poetry or with speeches or other texts. When they are choral reading poetry, readers should practice over and over again to get the sounds right. What are the possible variations of sound? Texts may be read

- By the whole chorus, by individuals, by pairs, or by two alternating sections.
- In loud or soft voices.
- Rapidly or slowly.
- Melodiously, angrily, giggling, or seriously.

Prepare the children to choral-read a text by discussing the circumstances or the context in which it might be said. For example, the following poem, "The Grand Old Duke of York," has a martial rhythm. Invite the children to imagine they are a platoon of soldiers marching along a road. From a single vantage point they are very quiet when they are heard from a distance, then louder as they approach, then very loud when they are right in front of the person, then quieter until they are very quiet. Have them practice reading the poem in unison, going from very quiet to *very loud* to very quiet again.

The Grand Old Duke of York (Traditional)

The Grand Old Duke of York
He had ten thousand men.
He always marched them up the hill
Then he marched them down again.
And when they were up they were up.
And when they were down they were down.
And when they were only halfway up
They were neither up nor down.

"Come Play Catch?" by Bucksnort Trout can be read by two individual children, or by two groups. One group takes the words on the left and the other takes the words on the right. The children should practice reading the poem until they can keep up the rhythm perfectly.

"Come Play Catch?"

Hey, Cousin Kenny, can you come play catch?
    Can you catch come, come? Can you come play catch?
Whatcha say, Cousin Kenny, can you come play catch?
    Can you come catch, come play catch—huh?
Hey, Aunt Jody, can you come jump rope?
    Can you rope jump, jump? Can you come jump rope?
Whatcha say, Aunt Jody, can you come jump rope?
    Can you rope jump, come jump rope—huh?
Hey, Uncle Harry, can you come hopscotch?
    Can you scotch hop, hop? Can you come hop scotch?
Whatcha say, Uncle Harry, can you come hop scotch?
    Can you scotch hop, come hop scotch—huh?
Hey, gorilla, will you put me down?
    Will you down, put, put? Pretty please, down, down?
Whatcha say, gorilla, will you put me down?
    Will you down put, put me down—huh?

This country poem, whose author is anonymous, can be said as a round, with up to three parts. When they are performing the poem, have each group begin reading right after the group before it completes the first line. Have each group read the poem through two times fully. On the second time through, the first group repeats the last line while the second group reads it, and then the first and second group repeat the last line as the third group reads it.

Can you dig that crazy music?

Can you dig it, Can you dig it, Can you dig it, Can you dig it?

Can you dig that crazy music?

Can you dig it, Can you dig it, Can you dig it, Can you dig it?

Oh, look. Here's a chicken come struttin' down the road.

Now, now. There's another on a barbed wire fence.

Ma-ma! Ma-ma!

Get that son-of-a-gun off my porch!

Encouraging Out-of-School Reading

Children need to read to become readers, and there is nothing quite so motivating as having their own book in their hand to take into a corner and read. Commercial book clubs like Scholastic (**http://teacher.scholastic.com/clubs/**) distribute catalogs periodically to classrooms (Scholastic's come every month), and children can choose to purchase books at below retail prices. Some companies also hold book fairs in the school, in which they make attractive displays of books that children can purchase.

Reading Is Fundamental (**http://www.rif.org/about/programs/default.mspx**) is a well-established program that gives new books for free to children and families, especially in lower income communities, including migrant workers' camps. RIF also sponsors community-based literacy activities.

Public libraries conduct many activities to interest children and their families in reading. The children's libraries often hold special events after school and on weekends and during the summer to get children in the habit of using the library. The American Library Association (**http://www.ala.org/**) is a valuable ally of reading teachers. Their Association for Library Services to Children (**http://www.ala.org/ala/alsc/alsc.htm**) links 4,000 children's librarians around the country. Their Web site gives a window onto their activities to promote reading among children.

Some community-minded organizations have put their resources behind the goal of encouraging children to read. Notable among these is Pizza Hut, whose Book It! program rewards millions of children across the United States who meet their reading goals with personal pan-sized pizzas and other prizes (see their Web site at **http://www.bookitprogram.com/**).

Helping Readers Build Vocabulary

Knowing vocabulary is essential to comprehending what one reads (Davis, 1944). For nearly a century, research has stressed the importance of knowing vocabulary to understanding text (Baumann, Kameenui, & Ash, 2003; Blachowicz & Fisher, 2000; National Reading Panel, 2000; Whipple, 1925). In this section we outline what research tells us about vocabulary and how it is taught and learned. The following sections describe the major components of good vocabulary instruction.

What Is Vocabulary?

Vocabulary is knowledge of words and word meanings (Lehr, Osborn, & Hiebert, 2006). This is not as simple as it sounds. That definition implies that vocabulary has two parts: the word and the meaning that the word stands for. Because a word is a sign for a concept, a student may or may not have the concept that an unknown word labels. For example, children may not know the word *interrogate*, but they do know what it is to have someone question them to find out if they did something wrong! But many children will lack both the label and the concept behind the word *ennui* because few of them will know what it is for a person to be sated over a long period of time to the point where nothing is capable of exciting him or her.

In addition to consisting of words and their meanings, vocabulary also varies between being either receptive or productive. **Receptive vocabulary** refers to the words students can understand when they hear or see them, and **productive vocabulary** refers to the words they can use themselves. And, of course, words can also be received and produced in speech or in print.

Receptive vocabulary is usually larger than productive vocabulary, either in speech or in print; that is, most people can understand more words than they feel confident enough

FAMILY LITERACY

Look at the Reading Is Fundamental website and describe how families can use it to support children's literacy development.

to use. And most students' spoken vocabulary is larger than the number of words they can recognize or use in print, at least until after fourth grade, when the gap is largely closed (Loban, 1976). That means that for teachers of the primary grades, "vocabulary" is as much an issue of helping students recognize the printed form of words they already understand in speech as it is of expanding children's knowledge of unfamiliar words and their meanings. For teachers of older students, the issue of "vocabulary" is particularly about helping students learn challenging content words that they neither know in speech nor in print (Lehr et al., 2006).

Besides consisting of signs and the concepts they represent, being receptive or productive, and occurring in speech or in print, words vary in some other ways, too. Many words have multiple meanings, like *bank, root, staff, vessel, glass, row,* and *star.* Some words have completely multiple meanings, like the bank of a river and a savings bank (although the meanings were originally much closer). And some words have much closer multiple meanings, like a *glass* window and a drinking *glass.*

Words have denotations and connotations, too. **Denotations** are the literal meanings of the words, and **connotations** are the associations we have for those words. So the word *tyrant* has the denotation of someone who governs with little regard for the governed and the connotation of a terrible, brutish person.

Words differ in their degree of *formality* and *informality,* as well as their *propriety* and *impropriety.* Informal and formal words with roughly the same meaning are "Hi" and "Greetings"; and "automobile" and "ride." Propriety adds a different dimension, referring to words that are not allowed to be used on the school grounds or for which our grandmothers sometimes threatened to wash our mouths out with soap. What does the research tell about vocabulary?

Over the last decade there have been several excellent reviews of the research on vocabulary. Together they make clear how important attention to vocabulary is and the contribution good vocabulary makes to reading comprehension.

Perhaps most importantly, vocabulary knowledge is one of the best predictors of reading comprehension (Davis, 1944, 1968). Why this is so may relate to the fact that vocabulary knowledge can be used as a measure of general verbal ability that underlies learning (Terman, 1916). It is also true that the ability to make inferences is a critical component both in reading comprehension and in learning the meaning of new words (Sternberg & Powell, 1983). Both explanations have strong support in the research literature.

We also know that students' vocabularies differ greatly. One factor contributing to these differences is related to economic conditions in the home. Hart and Risley's (1995) long-term study of vocabulary development in children during the first years of life revealed significant differences strongly related to parental income and welfare status. Children in economically disadvantaged households were exposed to significantly fewer words and to less oral engagement. These conditions affected the children's breadth of vocabulary use as well as their rate of vocabulary growth during these formative years. Hart and Risley found that when these economically disadvantaged children enter school, they possess only about half the vocabulary of their more advantaged peers and so begin their school careers at a disadvantage.

Another factor contributing to the size of students' vocabularies is the amount of reading they do. Keith Stanovich (1992) demonstrated that children who were avid readers had much larger vocabularies than children who did not read so much, even when the children had the same levels of general intelligence. Perhaps a big reason for this is that written language is a far richer source of vocabulary than either speech or television. As Figure 6.2 demonstrates, even a children's book has a richer vocabulary than a prime-time adult television show, and more sophisticated vocabulary than the conversation of college-educated adults. The best way to get a bigger vocabulary is to read.

Research studies have also demonstrated that vocabulary knowledge is a critical factor in the school success of English language learners (Carlo, August, & Snow, 2005; Folse, 2004; Nation, 2001). Knowledge of English vocabulary is one of the strongest correlates associated with the discrepancy between the reading performance of native English speakers and English language learners. This correlation remains despite the fact that many English language learners possess a large vocabulary in their native language (Garcia, 1991; Goldenberg, Rezaei, & Fletcher, 2005; Verhoeven, 1990).

FIGURE 6.2

On the "Richness" of Vocabulary from Different Sources.

	Rank of Median Word	Rare Words Per 1,000
I. Printed Texts		
Abstracts of scientific articles	4,389	128.0
Newspapers	1,690	68.3
Popular magazines	1,399	65.7
Adult books	1,058	52.7
Comic books	867	53.5
Children's books	627	30.9
Preschool books	578	16.3
II. Transcripts of Television Shows		
Popular prime-time adult shows	490	22.7
Popular children's shows	543	20.2
Cartoon shows	598	30.8
III. Adult Speech		
Expert witness testimony	1,008	28.4
College graduates, friends, spouses	496	17.3

The "rank of median word" refers to how common or rare the word is. For instance, "the" is common and has a low score. "Antidisestablishmentarianism" is a rare word and has a high score.

Source: Hayes and Ahrens (1988).

The impact of readers' vocabularies is most clear in the comprehension of academic content. Although most students, including the disadvantaged and those who are English language learners, do well with conversational English, it is when they engage in more academic topics that the differences emerge. Cummins (1980) describes these differences as basic interpersonal communication (BIC) and cognitive academic-language proficiency (CALP). For learners to be successful in school, they need to become increasingly competent with academic language. This is clearly an ongoing process. Teachers need to be sensitive to the fact that the more dense materials are with content-specific terminology, the more support students will need in making sense of the materials. Stories and literature are much less dependent on specific terms used by authors than informational texts used in science, social studies, and mathematics. The two kinds of academic terms essential for all learners are the procedural terms used to give directions and structure learning tasks and academic "content terms," words with precise meanings that are often central to content area understanding and differ from general meanings of even the same terms (e.g., "borrowing and sets" have very specific meaning in mathematics). These academic terms and their specialized meanings often pose the greatest challenges for English learners (Graves, 2006; Marzano, 2004).

Numerous studies indicate that vocabulary can be improved by good instruction. In their summary of this research, Blachowicz et al. (2007) explain that good vocabulary instruction

- Takes place in a language- and word-rich environment that fosters the word consciousness, the motivation, and the ownership that support incidental word learning.
- Includes intentional teaching of selected words that provides multiple sources of information and opportunities for repeated exposure, use, and practice.
- Includes the teaching of generative elements of words and word-learning strategies in ways that give students control over their own strategic behaviors.

How Do We Teach Vocabulary?

Efforts to teach vocabulary can be organized around these principles:

1. Motivate students to be open to learning words by promoting a respect for language.
2. Create a language-rich environment in which students can learn words through general acquisition.

3. Teach specific words (during language arts and during specific content study).
4. Teach students strategies for learning new words.
5. Use assessment to monitor students' vocabulary learning.

Promoting Respect for Language

A fire inspector for the Hartford Insurance Company and amateur linguist named Benjamin Whorf used to spend his summer vacations among Native American peoples of the southwestern United States, paying attention to the language they used and the ways they thought. Later, he announced a radical conclusion about thought and language that is nicely summarized in this quote:

> Every language is a vast pattern-system, different from others, in which are culturally ordained the forms and categories by which the personality not only communicates, but also analyzes nature, notices or neglects types of relationship and phenomena, channels his reasoning, and builds the house of his consciousness. (Whorf, 1964, p. 252)

Put simply, he meant that each culture makes sense of reality in its own way and uses language to pass on to its members its way of understanding reality. Put still more simply, language gives shape to thought.

Having a word in our vocabulary means we can notice something. Each word is a flashlight that illuminates another corner of our experience (Patterson, 1984). In psychological research, it was demonstrated years ago that we most readily recognize what we have a name for (Brown, 1958). This point was recently made in a classroom setting, too, by Mary Cowhey:

> During my first year teaching, I estimate I lost twenty to thirty minutes of instructional time each day dealing with post-recess conflicts, long tearful renditions of who did what to whom, fraught with passionate contradictions and denials. . . . The following summer I took a workshop in Second Step, a "violence prevention curriculum." . . . I was surprised when some students really couldn't identify emotions such as disgusted, scared, and angry in photos of children. Before I began teaching Second Step lessons, I observed a couple of boys "joking" with some other children. They didn't notice when one of the other children became upset, and continued "joking" even when the other child began to cry. When I intervened, the jokers said "We were just having fun." I asked if they thought Patrick, who was crying, was still having fun. They said yes. (Cowhey, 2006, p. 40)

As Cowhey's example makes clear, having a word in one's vocabulary means that one understands the word and can connect it to experience. Indeed, she goes on to say that her lessons about emotions

> explicitly teach children to read facial expressions, body language, and tone of voice to name the emotion being expressed, to recognize cause and effect, and to realize that two people can have very different feelings about the same situation. (Cowhey, 2006, p. 40)

But without the word, there is nothing to anchor the experience in consciousness, and nothing to enable one to communicate about it to others.

Creating a Language-Rich Environment

A cornerstone of classrooms rich in language is teachers reading aloud to students from a variety of books just beyond the students' own reading levels. Most of the vocabulary students will want and need to learn can be introduced naturally through the oral reading or read-alouds by the teacher. Teachers at every grade level can entice students into developing interest in words and language as they read aloud. Pausing over interesting terms and phrases, thinking aloud and elaborating on words, exploring the images created by text passages, and savoring particular words are all ways teachers can help students develop interest in words and build their vocabularies. Teachers can also ask students to listen for interesting, beautiful, curious uses of language and then take time after an oral reading to discuss what students noted. It is useful to write these words and phrases on the board so all students, particularly English language learners, have the advantage of both hearing and seeing the terms.

In the intermediate and middle grades, students also take great pleasure in word play and jokes. Reading humorous pieces and challenging students with riddles and jokes can connect with students' developing explorations of the richness and complexity of language (e.g., Nothing succeeds like success/no—recess.; I've heard of trade schools, and I'd like to.; What's black and white and red/read all over? The newspaper). Teachers often have bulletin boards devoted to multiple-meaning words or confusing phrases.

The classroom also is enriched when teachers make available a collection of books that explore and play with language. Students enjoy reading books like *Miss Alaneus* (Frasier, 2000), *A Chocolate Moose for Dinner* (Gwynn, 1988), and *Baloney* (Scieszka, 2001). In addition, books with puzzles and word games, rhymes and riddles, and magazines that introduce varied topics in inviting formats encourage language exploration (see the Being a Professional Reading Teacher box). Critical to these classrooms' collections on language is a good set of dictionaries. Students should have their own, and the classroom should contain more adult and larger dictionaries for reference. Making available and teaching students how to use both dictionaries and classroom thesauruses provides them independent tools for expanding their language. In classrooms with English language learners, some bilingual dictionaries are also important. The whole class can enjoy exploring how different words are expressed in each language and can gain when the different forms of the words are displayed in the classroom.

General Vocabulary Development and Content-Specific Terms

At the primary level, teachers informally expand students' vocabularies through their oral language use and their reading to students. By the time students are in the intermediate grades, teachers become more specific in their attention to vocabulary learning. Both in literature and in other content areas, specific terms are needed to ensure comprehension

Being a Professional Reading Teacher

Helping Children Explore Words

Teachers can entice children into exploring words in a variety of ways, one of which is with word games. There are many available commercially and also ones you can create yourself. Classrooms that have a collection of games and puzzles make play with words fun. As a new teacher you may appreciate help in building a collection of word-focused activities. This is a need that parents are often willing to fill by donating new games as birthday gifts in their child's honor. Then the "Word Wonder" corner in your room can be personalized by family contributions to the classroom. A collection of games may include Scrabble, Boggle, Fictionary, crossword puzzle books, word tiles, and poetry magnets. These can be used by children before school and during designated times.

There are several books or games about words you can add to your collection. For teachers of older students, Jack Umstatter's *201 Ready-to-Use Word Games for the English Classroom* (Jossey-Bass, 2001) and *Words, Words, Words: Ready-to-Use Games and Activities for Vocabulary Building, Grades 7–12* (Jossey-Bass, 2004) are both recommended. From Auckland, New Zealand, comes Allen Trussel-Cullen's *50 Wonderful Word Games (Grades 3–6)* (Scholastic, 1999). Then there is Lorraine Hopping Egan's *Best-Ever Vocabulary & Word Study Games (Grades 4–8)* (Scholastic, 2001).

Some Web sites also include frames for you to create your own games and crossword puzzles with words children need to review from your instructional program. FunBrain is one: **http://www.funbrain.com/words.html**. Vocabulary University is good for upper elementary and middle grades: **http://www.vocabulary.com/**. The PBS television series *Between the Lions* has put many word games online at **http://pbskids.org/lions/games/**. "Surfing the Net with Kids" keeps you up to date with new recommended links for word games: **http://www.surfnetkids.com/games/Word_Games/**.

Play with words is an important component in children's vocabulary development. Don't overlook it!

of text materials. By attending to specific terms, teachers can also build the vocabulary knowledge students will need for school success. The less students are stimulated at home with rich oral language contexts, the more important it is that at school teachers focus on and reinforce vocabulary development.

Teachers are often unsure about what words they should teach directly. Yet there are good sources of help in making those decisions. Most basal reading programs now include a vocabulary strand and highlight some key words that are essential to the selections. Focusing students' attention on a small set of words prior to reading a literature selection will help them notice these words as they read. They can then be discussed after the reading, and students can practice using the terms in their own speaking and writing. The same is true in most science, social studies, and other content area curricula. Textbooks often identify key terms that are basic to the content. Teachers can highlight these and ask students to Rate Your Knowledge (Blachowicz, 1987). Look at the example shown in Figure 6.3 for a Knowledge Rating of terms that was used as a prereading activity.

If we were to teach all of the words children need to learn, we couldn't do it. Nagy and Anderson (1984) put the number of words in "printed school English" at 88,500! And that was just through ninth grade! There is no way to teach 10,000 words a year. Most of these words will have to be learned from experience, especially from reading. But teaching helps, too.

Beck and her colleagues have come up with a way of approaching the seemingly enormous task of teaching vocabulary (Beck, McKeown, & Kucan, 2002). As we saw in Chapter 3, they identified three "tiers" of words. The first tier are common everyday words that most of us know. The second tier of words are those we encounter frequently in school and in reading and that are used in a variety of situations; knowing these words provides a foundation for many kinds of learning. These are words worth teaching in language arts and reading. The third tier of words are the specialized vocabulary terms connected to particular content. They have specific meanings that need to be honored. These terms are only taught as they are needed for specific content development (see Chapter 3, pp. 88–90, for further discussion).

Another useful guide for content words is the one developed by Marzano (2004). He and his colleagues collected all of the academic terms needed for students to be successful with state and national standards and then sorted them by school levels. The Academic Vocabulary List includes key words for eleven subject areas including science, mathematics, language arts, history, social studies, the arts, and health. These words are then organized according to four levels (level 1 = grades K–2; level 2 = grades 3–5; level 3 = grades 6–8,

These are words we are going to be using during this unit. Mark how familiar you are with them as we begin. Those that are not so familiar are words to put in your learning journal so you can build your understanding of them during our study.

Key Words	New to Me	Have Seen	Know Well
mummy			
pyramid			
scribe			
artisan			
pharaoh			

FIGURE 6.3

Rate Your Knowledge Chart.

and level 4 = grades 9–12). These lists provide a good reference list for teachers wanting to assess and then develop students' vocabularies for academic reading and learning.

A final important source for words is the students themselves. Some researchers have demonstrated that involving students in selecting the words to be studied is a productive strategy (Fisher, Blachowicz, & Smith, 1991; Haggard, 1986). Students are able to self-select important terms that are similar to and equally valuable to those the teachers select. And, when students self-select terms, the involvement has the added benefit of motivating students to learn the terms more deeply.

Teaching Strategies for Word Learning

Students need to develop independent strategies for dealing with the new words they will meet in school and in other areas of their lives. The goal is that when they encounter unknown words, students can examine the context for general clues, look at the structure and morphology of the word itself (the internal context) for clues, or consult a reference if needed. They will also determine if the word is one they want to add to their general vocabulary. If it is, then they will employ a strategy to help them retain the word by creating a word card, making a personal association and practicing it, or using some other memory device.

Teachers can do a great deal to help students become active language learners. For students to maximize their opportunities to expand their vocabularies, they need to be actively engaged in their own learning. They need to be helped in developing some awareness of how they can learn new words and exploring strategies for attending to words and rehearsing them. It is important that teachers not give the false impression that word learning is memorizing definitions for terms on a list the teacher supplies. Teachers do a big disservice when they pass on this traditional and ineffective approach to word learning. Rather teachers need to guide students to understand that word learning is an ongoing and cumulative process. We start with a kernel of meaning for a new term and then keep expanding our understanding of how that term is used in varied situations. Each time the term is encountered in print or in oral language, learners can check out their own understanding against the new input and then modify their association network for the term.

A graphic format that helps students understand the ways an understanding of new terms is built is the "Concept of Definition" map (see Figure 6.4) that highlights the relations among words and their meanings (Schwartz & Raphael, 1985). On the Concept of Definition map, the new term is listed in the center. Above the term the student indicates the larger class of word to which the new one is related. Then the student elaborates the description of the term with more categorical and semantic information related to the word's definition along with examples and nonexamples. Some variations of the map also ask stu-

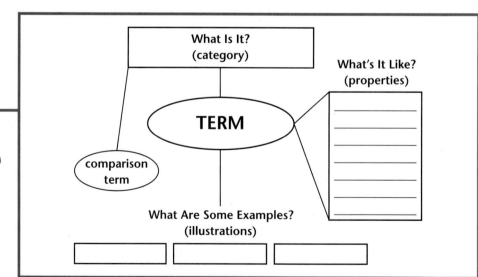

FIGURE 6.4

Concept of Definition Map.

Source: Schwartz, R.M. & Raphael, T.E. (1985, November). Concept of definition: A key to improving students' vocabulary. *The Reading Teacher, 30*(2), 198–205. Reprinted with permission of the International Reading Association.

	Bear live young	Have gills	Cold-blooded	Have milk
SHARKS				
DOLPHINS				

FIGURE 6.5

A Semantic Feature Analysis.

dents to draw an example of the term. By building this kind of association web around the new term, students can develop a better concept of what word learning entails.

Semantic feature analysis is another activity that helps illustrate semantic relationships among words. Semantic feature analysis provides a graphic display that focuses on the features that distinguish words in a particular category from one another, such as various types of vehicles or human relatives. The teacher creates the matrix either as a model or with students during a unit of study (see Figure 6.5 for an illustration).

The students then determine which features each of the terms possesses and finally can compare and contrast similar terms. In their research to determine the effectiveness of various approaches to vocabulary learning, Bos and Anders (1989, 1990, 1992) compared the effectiveness of three semantic relatedness techniques (mapping, semantic feature analysis, and semantic/syntactic feature analysis) to definition study with students of various ages and abilities. They concluded that all three of the interactive techniques were more effective than the traditional approach that has students write and study definitions.

More recently an added component has been included in word learning: having students create visual diagrams or pictures of the targeted terms. Marzano (2005) includes in his six-step process for helping students learn new academic terms the idea that "Students create a nonlinguistic representation of the new term." After the teacher provides a description of each term to be learned, students first write their own explanation of the term, and then they represent the term in a graphic organizer, picture, pictograph, or cartoon form. In this way English language learners and students with nonverbal strengths can build personal associations with new terms (see the Differentiated Instruction box).

Differentiated Instruction

English Language Learners

In a case study focused on using visual enhancements with English language learners and other reluctant readers (Ogle, 2000), struggling, less than enthusiastic science students became much more eager learners when their teacher developed a vocabulary card deck for her students. Each week there were eight terms to be learned for which students were given 4 × 6 note cards. On one side the student wrote the term and a description based on information from the teacher. On the other side the students drew what they thought represented that term. During the week students were given five minutes at the beginning of each science class to test their friends on the word cards. They would show the pictures to the other student, who would have to guess what term was being illustrated. The increased motivation and learning were apparent. Students who had barely contributed to class became eager to see if their drawings would elicit the accurate connection for the class terms. José turned out to be a fairly gifted artist, and soon other boys were calling on him to help them illustrate terms more creatively. He also provided suggestions for depicting some of the more abstract concepts. A nearly invisible student became a central resource to the class with this artistic talent; in the process the teacher also learned that he had more to contribute about science than she had expected. Although he hesitated to speak in class, he didn't hesitate to illustrate ideas.

TEACH IT! 15

Making and Breaking Words

Showing Relationships among Terms and Word Parts

Students benefit when teachers guide them to understanding the relationships among words and the various aspects and attributes of terms (see the Assessment box). The more students use new terms, the more likely it is that they will retain them and incorporate them into

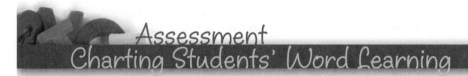

Assessment
Charting Students' Word Learning

Teachers have struggled with how to evaluate students' vocabulary learning because word learning is not a one-step process. Words are learned gradually over time as more and more associations with terms are experienced. Yet it is also important for teachers to find out how much of the vocabulary needed to comprehend particular texts is known by students before the texts or materials are used. If students lack a significant number of key terms, then more prereading and concept building needs to be done. Teachers also need to determine what strategies students possess so they can figure out new terms in context as they read. If students can use context effectively and know how to identify combining forms and affixes, they have good tools to help as they read.

However, teachers also need to know how supportive the texts are in helping students access new terms. Supportive texts will provide meanings for important terms through restatement, illustrations, and examples. The terms may be identified in boldface type or in italics. Some texts define terms in the margins. Other texts or text sections may not provide these scaffolds and key terms may remain opaque, so students will require outside support for the vocabulary to become meaningful.

Before asking students to read a text or begin a unit of study, teachers can easily identify students' familiarity with key terms. Several informal activities provide good starting points. Using a Rate Their Knowledge chart of the terms, students can indicate their levels of familiarity with them before reading. As students are completing the activity, teachers can move around the class making an informal assessment of how the students are responding. Teachers can also ask students to "Connect two or three of the terms" and write a sentence using the terms as an initial assessment. The students who struggle to create interesting and accurate sentences can be noted, and more vocabulary work can be provided. An alternative activity is to have students sort new terms into concept groups and then to label the groups. Each of these informal activities provides a way for teachers to get an initial assessment of students' familiarity with key terms and concepts needed for learning.

These same activities also can be used at the completion of the study. Changes in levels of knowledge of terms, ability to write using the terms accurately, and ability to cluster similar terms by concept are what is expected from focused learning. Both students and teachers can compare the beginning and ending knowledge levels and evaluate growth together.

If the study permitted focus on particular combining forms or affixes, the same kind of pre and post assessments can be given. Creating an activity in which students are asked to divide several key content words into their parts (prefix, base, and suffix) and providing meanings for each is a quick way to determine how comfortable students are in using word parts. Any unfamiliar word part can then be included on a study list, with students searching for other similar words, with groups creating lists of families of terms, and so on. At the conclusion of the unit, students can be asked to create a list of related terms, to define some unknown terms with the familiar parts, or to engage in using the word parts in some creative way.

By focusing assessment on specific terms used in the stories, informational texts, or general unit concepts, teachers and students can take the word-learning journey together. Specific targeted words and word-learning tools are valuble to monitor, and the concreteness of the gains motivates students to continue their learning.

The classroom is enriched when teachers make available a collection of books that explore and play with language.

their working vocabularies. You can give students points or credit when they use the new terms either in oral class discussion or in their written work to reinforce the continuing attention word learning requires.

Another important component of a word-learning strategy is for students to identify key word parts. The intermediate grades are the years to focus students' attention on how words are formed and modified. Identifying morphemes, particularly derivational morphemes (see pp. 86–88 in Chapter 3) and common affixes helps students determine word meanings. Activities that involve students in brainstorming and creating word splashes of related terms focus attention to related terms and how meanings can be deduced from partial knowledge (i.e., disrupt = *dis* (apart) + *rupt* (break up)). Then students can connect the morpheme—*rupt*—to other words they may know like *interrupt* and *corrupt*. Students can make charts of words that contain the same word parts, and discuss the meanings they have in common (see Figure 6.6).

Introducing and Focusing Attention on New Vocabulary

WORD CONVERSATIONS FOR KINDERGARTEN AND FIRST GRADE. When young readers (kindergarten and first grade) are learning new words, Beck and colleagues (2002) suggest that teachers conduct a rich discussion of words that includes these six steps:

1. Contextualize words, one at a time, within a story. For example, with kindergartners, the teacher could use Don Freeman's perennially popular *Corduroy* (1978) as a pre-text for introducing the words *insistent, reluctant,* and *drowsy.* The teacher says, "In the story, Lisa was reluctant to leave the department store without Corduroy [her new teddy bear]."
2. Ask the children to repeat the word so as to make a phonological representation of it.

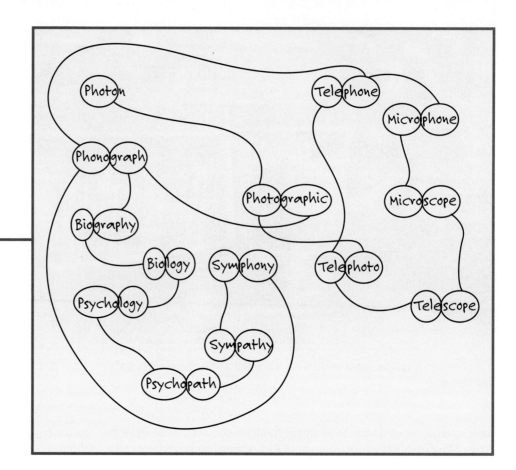

FIGURE 6.6

A Connected Word Web.

3. Then explain the meaning of the word in a child-friendly way: "*Reluctant* means you are not sure you want to do something."
4. Now provide examples of the word in other contexts: "I am reluctant to go swimming in the early summer when the water is cold."
5. Next ask children to provide their own examples: "What is something you would be reluctant to do?"
6. Finally, ask the children to repeat the word they have been talking about, to reinforce its phonological representation.

Word conversations are not as easy as they look. Teachers need to do the following:

- Choose books carefully to provide a meaningful context for introducing the vocabulary.
- Think carefully about the words, and formulate child-friendly explanations of the word meanings.
- Plan questions to relate the words to the children's experience.
- Remind the children of the words they are studying, giving them several opportunities to pronounce the words. (See Beck et al., 2002, for further discussion of this approach.)

Activities to teach vocabulary should relate words to a meaningful context, to other words, and to the students' own experiences. The following activities satisfy these requirements by making connections (to self, personal stories, and other books); collaborating with peers (interpersonal dynamics through all the language arts); exploring meaning (asking questions, making statements, interpreting higher-level thinking such as application, synthesis, and evaluation); and participating as an active reader (summarizing, predicting, confirming, and clarifying).

- **Vocab-o-gram:** Terms that are important to a piece of fiction can be highlighted for students through the use of a vocab-o-gram. The terms are listed and the students

Before we read the Japanese folktale, see what you can predict about how these terms will be used. Put each term in the box with which you think it is connected. Words: bitterly cold, weaving, reed hats, empty cupboards, New Year's Day, kind old man, stone statues, fortunate, Jizo, guardian god of children, old woman, hungry, no coal, sack of food, thank you, village, gift.

Characters	Setting	Problem
Feeling/Tone	Solution	Other Words

FIGURE 6.7

Vocab-o-Gram.

are asked to sort the terms according to the story elements of plot, setting (time and location), characters, conflict, and resolution. Words that just don't seem to be clearly identified with the elements can be placed in the mystery category (see Figure 6.7).

- **Semantic Webs:** A **semantic web** is a way to organize information graphically according to categories. There are several ways to use semantic webs. The most open-ended way is to draw a circle on a page and write a topic word in it. Then, together with the students, the teacher thinks of aspects of the topic and comes up with examples or aspects of that subtopic.

  One approach to semantic webs is the character web, in which the name of a character is written in the circle in the middle of the display. Then words that describe the character are written as satellites around the character's name. Examples that illustrate each attribute are then written as satellites around the descriptive words. Figure 6.8 depicts a semantic web on dolphins.

- **Webbed Questions:** Schwartz and Rafael (1985) suggest guiding the students' responses to a semantic web and asking them to offer answers to three questions asked about the target word, as shown in Figure 6.9:

  What is it?
  What is it like?
  What are some examples of it?

  This beginning web can then be turned into the more formal Concept of Definition Map in the upper grades (see Figure 6.4 for an example of a map). In creating the map, students extend their attention to new terms by asking themselves to describe the term and find examples of it. Some teachers have added a section for students to illustrate the term and/or use it in a sentence. In both the basic semantic webbing and in creating maps, students learn to think of words as related to larger concepts. They also begin to look for associations and attributes for the terms being learned.

- **Concept Ladders:** Concept ladders (Gillet & Temple, 2003) provide yet another way for children to organize their thinking and to categorize, thus supporting comprehension. The concept ladder shown in Figure 6.10, would be useful in a study

FIGURE 6.8

A Semantic Web.

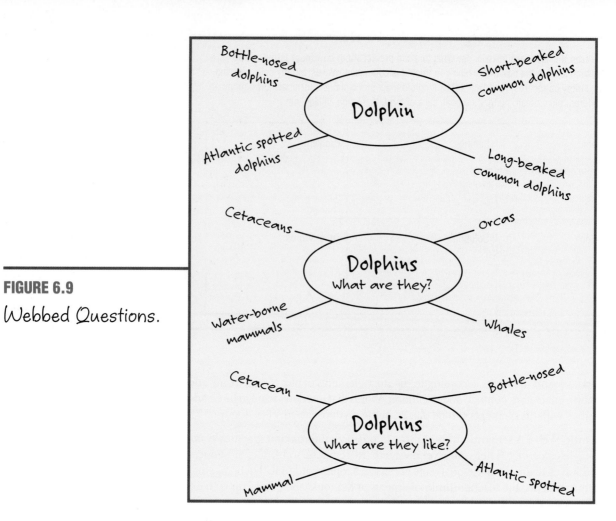

FIGURE 6.9

Webbed Questions.

on volcanoes and earthquakes. It also helps students think of new terms as having important attributes that distinguish each from other similar terms.

- **The Frayer Model:** Another graphic organizer for laying out words for a concept in relation to other words is the Frayer model (Buehl, 2001). **The Frayer model** directs students to think of essential and nonessential characteristics of a concept as well as examples and nonexamples of it. The model is best used to name a common concept that has many characteristics and examples. That way the students get to consider a larger number of words in context (see Figure 6-11).

What kind of thing is this?	What is it a part of?	What causes it?
What are the kinds of it?	What are its parts?	What does it cause?

FIGURE 6.10

A Concept Ladder.

Teachers can do a great deal to build students' interest in words and language by having newspapers, magazines, and books from other languages in the classroom and referring to them periodically. Listening to music from other countries and cultures is another way to develop sensitivity to languages and vocabulary different from our own. Because so many of our academic terms come from Latin and Greek origins, it is often interesting to compare forms of the words we use with those in Spanish and other languages of the students in the classroom. For example, during the political elections in the fall or during school elections it would be interesting to put the terms on the board and ask students to supply the equivalent terms in their home languages. What would *election*, *candidate*, *voting*, *campaigning*, and *party* look like in Spanish, French, or Farsi? Asking the question and taking time to compare languages is another way to expand students' flexibility with words and the ever-expanding corpus of words in English.

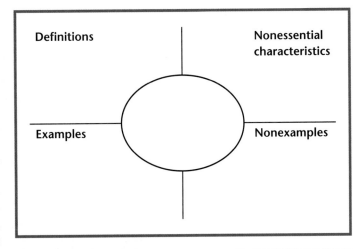

FIGURE 6.11

The Frayer Model.

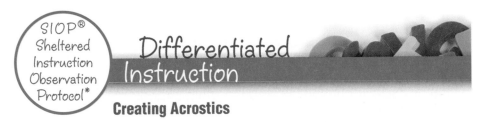

Creating Acrostics

Getting to know your students is made interesting and enjoyable by asking each student to create an acrostic poem of their name. Each letter in the student's name is written vertically down the left side of the page of paper. The students select descriptive words that begin with the letters of their name and these terms then create the poem. For example, Diedra created her poem in the following way:

Daring
Interested
Explorer
Doing
Rambunctious
Activities

It is very easy to identify some of the things that Diedra may be interested in doing given the window on her personality and interests she opens. Each student's poem is distinctive; even those who are shy generally reveal that aspect of their selves, too.

Teachers can use this activity as a way to build awareness among a class of the value of selecting words carefully. By involving students in several steps they are more likely to find good terms. Begin with brainstorming lots of words that begin with each letter of one's name. Then give students thesauruses and have them search for additional words that may be even more illustrative of what they want to say about themselves. Model this with your own name if they seem unsure of how to proceed. The dictionary can also be helpful in leading students to just the right words. These resources make it more likely that they will find just the right terms to describe themselves. Finally, before the poems are completed have students check their acrostics with a partner for a final review. The final poems can be read orally, posted in the room, and combined with lists of students' favorite music, books, and activities. It certainly is a good way to focus students' attention on the value of words and the connotations and nuances each word we use contains.

Students and teachers have many strategies to choose from for building vocabulary.

How can teachers stimulate students' interest in words by using online vocabulary resources?

Using Online Sources to Build Vocabulary

Teachers can stimulate students' interest in words by using the online resources of the vocabulary sites. Some have a new word each day that can be shared. Others are great for providing word histories and noting new words that come into our language. There are dictionaries so terms can be looked up and the definitions and references compared. One of the easy ways to help students explore language is to introduce them to the resources now available on the Web. The tools are particularly useful for English language learners because they can use the online resource to look up words that they don't know in English and get helpful hints on what other sites are useful. There are several fun sources for words. For general vocabulary and interesting information about words:

> www.eduplace.com/kids/hmsv/
> www.wordsmith.org
> www.vocabulary.com
> www.funbrain.com/words

Spanish-English dictionaries are available at these sites:

> http://www.spanishdict.com/
> www.yourdictionary.com
> http://www.my-spanish-dictionary.com
> http://education.yahoo.com/references/dict_en_es/

For Review

Traditionally, reading instruction focused on word recognition and comprehension. Now we realize that reading fluency needs our attention and so does vocabulary. These two aspects are included in the five building blocks for literacy identified for special attention by the National Institute for Literacy.

Reading fluency is not just reading rate. In fact, sometimes children read *too* fast. Reading fluency includes an easy and natural rate, appropriate to the material, along with intonation and proper phrasing. Fluency can be learned, which means that attention to teaching children to read this or that text fluently will carry over to their reading of other texts. Reading fluency aids comprehension: The more naturally and fluently a child reads, the more attention that child will have left over to think about the text.

Approaches to teaching reading for fluency include the following:

- Model good oral reading.
- Provide oral support for readers.
- Offer plenty of practice opportunities.
- Encourage fluency through phrasing.

In this chapter we showed techniques such as repeated reading and approaches imbedded in performance, such as choral reading of poetry and readers' theater.

Vocabulary, too, is getting more attention in reading instruction than in the past. Vocabulary is a big divider: Some children have at least twice as many words in their vocabulary as others, and the vocabulary size affects their understanding, not only of text, but of the world around them. Words are labels for concepts, and the more concepts we have, the more easily we can notice things and think about experience. There is a vast vocabulary to learn, so teachers must prioritize. One way is to focus on useful words that children don't yet know (as opposed to words they are learning anyway or words that are included in disciplinary study). Several suggestions for teaching vocabulary were included in this chapter, including encouraging respect for words, teaching relationships between them, and teaching their parts. Also, children can be helped to recognize words in context.

For Your Journal

Fluent reading means reading with expression and not just reading quickly. Fluent reading is a skill that many adults need to work on, especially if we are going to be models for children.

Find a well-known children's book with rich language. J.R.R. Tolkien's *The Hobbit* is a good choice. Or Kate DiCamillo's *Because of Winn Dixie*. Practice reading passages of it aloud. Then go to the library and check out the audio book versions of the books. Listen carefully to the professional readers.

Choose one reader and listen for two minutes. Then write in your journal: What makes this person's reading so interesting to listen to? How many of the qualities of reading fluency that were described in this chapter are present in the readings? How does the reader group words? How does the reader use intonation—make his or her voice rise or fall at certain points? How does the reader bring characters to life?

Finally, try reading the text yourself the way the professional reader did it. Try tape recording your reading, and analyze it the same way you did the professional reader's. Afterward, decide what aspects of good oral reading you do well. Decide what aspects you want to work on. Write these things in your journal. And be sure to practice.

Taking It to the World

How much does vocabulary matter to people? Sit down with two or three classmates and make a list of as many ways as you can that vocabulary matters in people's lives. It might help get the conversation going to recall the self-help books published for adults that promise them more successful careers if only they will master a larger vocabulary or the vocabulary items on the SAT test.

Think also of times—in films or in the discourse of our politicians—when having a larger vocabulary is held up as a sign of snobbery.

After making a list of both kinds of situations, try to reach a conclusion. What are the advantages of having a large vocabulary? What caveats should be kept in mind about using the right words at the right time? How will you use these conclusions in your teaching?

Technology Connections

1. Many software packages are now available that purport to help build children's reading fluency. Consider the aspects of reading fluency we have explored in this chapter—automatic word recognition, reading rate, and expressive reading. Then look up "reading fluency software" on a search engine. Review the descriptions of three or four programs. How many of the above-mentioned aspects of reading fluency are built into them?

2. Go to the SuperKids! Website at **http://www.superkids.com/aweb/pages/reviews/vocab/** and look up several of the vocabulary building software programs that are reviewed there. To what extent are the five principles of vocabulary listed in this chapter (please see pages 184–185) taken into account in these programs?

Connect with Research

Review the following key words from the chapter, and then connect to Research Navigator (**http://www.researchnavigator.com**) through this book's Companion Website to conduct a search into research on each of the various topics as they relate to reading and literacy education today.

choral reading	instructional reading level	semantic feature analysis
connotations	paired reading	semantic web
Coretta Scott King Award	productive vocabulary	sustained silent reading
denotations	readers' theater	vocabulary
fluency	reading fluency	voice choirs
the Frayer model	receptive vocabulary	webbed questions
independent reading level	repeated reading	

Companion Website

To access chapter objectives, practice tests, weblinks, and flashcards, visit the Companion Website at **www.ablongman.com/templeallchildren2e**.

Go to Allyn & Bacon's MyLabSchool (**www.mylabschool.com**), enter Assignment ID RMV3 into the Assignment Finder. Watch the video, *Teaching Vocabulary,* in which a middle school learning coordinator discusses techniques for teaching content area vocabulary to her students.

Question: Why is knowledge of technical and non-technical language so important in content area learning? You may also answer the questions at the end of the clip and e-mail your responses to your instructor.

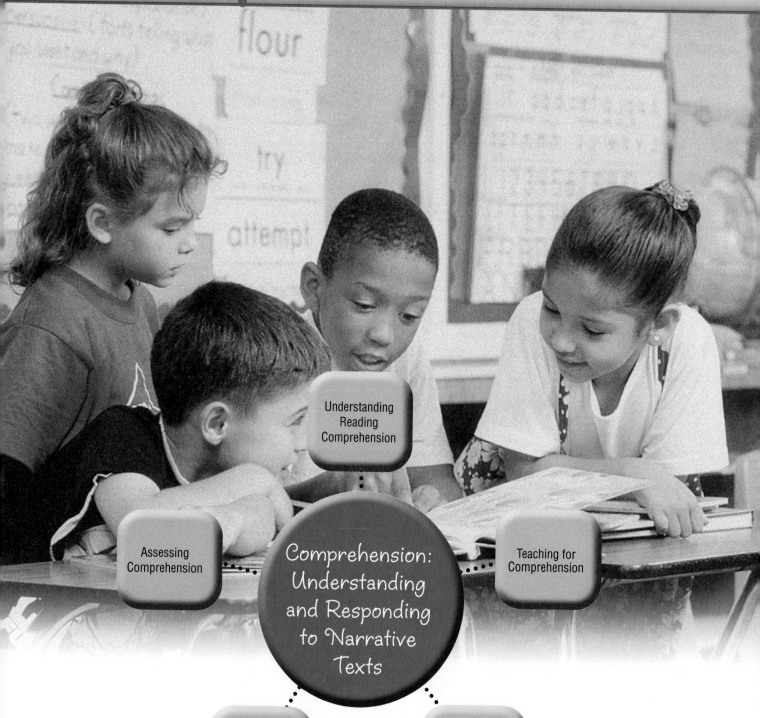

chapter 7

Understanding
Reading
Comprehension

Assessing
Comprehension

Teaching for
Comprehension

Comprehension:
Understanding
and Responding
to Narrative
Texts

Building
Knowledge,
Consolidation,
and Shared
Reading

Organizing
Instruction for
Comprehension
and Response

Comprehension: Understanding and Responding to Narrative Texts

Anticipation Guide

The following questions will stimulate your thinking about the topics of this chapter. Answer true or false in response to each statement. As you read and learn more about the topics in these statements, double-check your answers. See what interests you and what prompts your curiosity toward more understanding.

_____ ● Comprehension, or understanding what you read, is mostly a process of memorizing the details of the author's message.

_____ ● Schema theory holds that readers understand what they read by using what they already knew to interpret the new information.

_____ ● Readers vary considerably from one another in what they understand and take away from a text.

_____ ● Comprehension is the aspect of reading that has traditionally gotten the most attention in classrooms.

_____ ● Good teachers show how readers read with comprehension, by "demonstrat-

ing their own thought processes when they read."

_____ ● Good comprehension lessons have three parts: consolidation, building knowledge, and anticipation, in that order.

_____ ● The structure of the text helps the reader make sense of what is written.

_____ ● Struggling readers need an entirely different kind of instruction in comprehension than more able learners.

_____ ● Drama has no place in the teaching of reading comprehension.

Reading Activity in a Fourth-Grade Classroom

The students in Hank da Silva's fourth grade at North Street Elementary School can predict the day's events in broad outline but not completely. They know that after the morning class meeting, they will talk about their topics in social studies. They have been reading about the settlement of the Great Plains in their social studies text. At the same time, they have been reading Patricia McLachlan's *Sarah,*

Plain and Tall and Laura Ingalls Wilder's *The Little House on the Prairie.* Mr. da Silva reads to them from *Letters from a Woman Homesteader,* a work of nonfiction told in the form of letters home from a feisty single woman in the 1880s. He has also bookmarked and assigned three Internet sites where students will find information about the settlement of the Great Plains by European Americans.

The class has written dual-entry diaries every day about their readings. They have also created a Venn diagram comparing what skills people have to have if they move to a new place now compared to what skills people needed in the days of the homesteaders. Figure 7.1 shows what the class has come up with.

This morning, Mr. da Silva is conducting a discussion of a couple of pages of the social studies book. He begins by pointing out that sometimes textbooks do not make their meanings very clear.

"Take right here, for instance," he points out. "The text says, 'Westward expansion gave the new country a constant

FIGURE 7.1

What You Need to Live in a New Place.

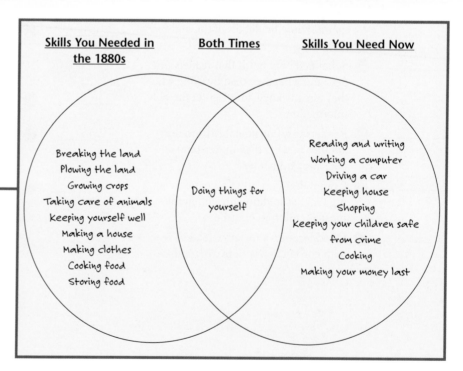

Skills You Needed in the 1880s

Breaking the land
Plowing the land
Growing crops
Taking care of animals
Keeping yourself well
Making a house
Making clothes
Cooking food
Storing food

Both Times

Doing things for yourself

Skills You Need Now

Reading and writing
Working a computer
Driving a car
Keeping house
Shopping
Keeping your children safe from crime
Cooking
Making your money last

sense of excitement, of new possibilities.' What do you suppose the author means by that sentence? Let's start with 'Westward expansion.' What do you suppose he means by expansion? If the author were here, what do you think he would say about that?"

After lunch, Mr. da Silva has reading workshop. According to the rotation chart on the wall, some students read independently. Today those students are doing something special: They are writing self-assessments about their reading comprehension, which they will later give to Mr. da Silva. A group of six students who are reading Phyllis Reynolds Naylor's *Shiloh*

meet with Mr. da Silva for a literature circle; each of the six students is conducting a part of the discussion, according to a role she or he has been assigned. Mr. da Silva takes part in the discussion, but he also is taking occasional notes. He writes about how the discussion is going. He writes a note to remind himself to have the students to ask more questions of each other in the literature circle rather than just reporting on what they think. He also makes a note that four of the students do not seem to make the connection between the boy's asking the shopkeeper for stale bread to feed the dog he has hidden away and the food that people in the

community begin leaving for his father, a mail carrier. In other words, they are not making inferences. In the course of the next week, Mr. da Silva will make a point of reading with each one of these students to see what they know about reading comprehension. He will also teach a mini-lesson on making inferences during reading workshop tomorrow.

The goal of reading instruction is for all students to read with comprehension—understanding what they read. Comprehension in reading is also a sort of thermometer measuring the intellectual life of a classroom. True, teaching children to read with understanding is partly a matter of teaching them a special set of reading skills. But it is also a matter of exposing students to literature, cultivating their knowledge about a range of subjects, stimulating their habits of inquiry, helping them make connections between ideas, and inspiring in them a broad range of interests. Researchers tell us that reading comprehension has too often been left to chance, as if understanding would happen if only children could read the words. Surveys of reading instruction in elementary schools, from twenty years ago (Durkin, 1978–1979) and more recently (Pressley, 1999), have found that word recognition instruction is common enough, but it is rarer to find teachers trying to develop their students' comprehension. Reading comprehension is heavily stressed in state standards for literacy (see the Standards and Literacy box).

In this chapter, we talk about ways to help students understand narrative texts. Chapter 8 is devoted to teaching readers to understand informational text. But first, we set out some ideas about reading comprehension.

Texas Standards for Literacy Stress Comprehension

Many schools have not given students as much explicit instruction in reading comprehension as they need (Durkin, 1978–1979; Pressley et al., 1996). Such will not be the case in Texas as the state learning standards take hold there. The Texas standards for reading in elementary schools (Texas Education Agency, 1998) call for students to learn essentially the same subskills of comprehension and response discussed in this chapter:

Reading/comprehension. The student uses a variety of strategies to comprehend selections read aloud and selections read independently. The student is expected to:

(a) *use prior knowledge to anticipate meaning and make sense of texts (K–3);*

(b) *establish purposes for reading and listening such as to be informed, to follow directions, and to be entertained (K–3);*

(c) *retell or act out the order of important events in stories (K–3);*

(d) *monitor his/her own comprehension and act purposefully when comprehension breaks down such as rereading, searching for clues, and asking for help (1–3);*

(e) *draw and discuss visual images based on text descriptions (1–3);*

(f) *make and explain inferences from texts such as determining important ideas and causes and effects, making predictions, and drawing conclusions (1–3);*

(g) *identify similarities and differences across texts such as in topics, characters, and problems (1–2);*

(h) *produce summaries of text selections (2–3); and*

(i) *represent text information in different ways, including story maps, graphs, and charts (2–3).*

Reading/literary response. The student responds to various texts. The student is expected to:

(a) *respond to stories and poems in ways that reflect understanding and interpretation in discussion (speculating, questioning) in writing, and through movement, music, art, and drama (2–3);*

(b) *demonstrate understanding of informational text in various ways such as through writing, illustrating, developing demonstrations, and using available technology (2–3);*

(c) *support interpretations or conclusions with examples drawn from text (2–3); and*

(d) *connect ideas and themes across texts (1–3).*

Understanding Reading Comprehension

Our understanding of reading comprehension and literary response, and our techniques for teaching them, have grown tremendously over the last twenty years. With advances in cognitive psychology came the recognition of the reader's active role in comprehending. The reader is a sense-maker, one who works to construct meaning. What do people do when they understand something that they read? Many reading specialists' favorite explanation of the act of comprehension is schema theory, articulated by Richard Anderson and David Pearson (1984). But if we want to understand how readers create different meanings from texts, another theory comes into play: reader response theory. And if we want to take a somewhat skeptical stance toward what we read, we will need yet another way of thinking about comprehension: critical literacy. We talk about all three in this chapter.

One thing that is becoming clear about reading comprehension is that understanding fictional text is not quite the same thing as understanding and learning from informational text. For that reason, in this chapter we consider reading comprehension in general and understanding and responding to works of fiction in particular. In Chapter 8 we focus in detail on reading and learning from informational text.

Schema Theory

Schema theory (Anderson & Pearson, 1984) holds that readers understand what they read by finding clues in the text that lead them to summon up frameworks of stored knowledge from their memories. These frameworks have been called **schemas**. Once readers have a schema in mind, they use it to make sense of the other details. There is a complementary relationship between readers' schemas and the details on the page. Reading the details tells them what schemas to evoke, and evoking the schemas helps them to make sense of the details. Consider the following example:

Shawn's footsteps slowed as he approached the door to Belinda's apartment. Two children were ahead of him, already knocking on the door. They were dressed in the proper clothing. But Shawn had on his old jeans. Shawn was also embarrassed because he was empty-handed. His mother had been at work when he got home from school, and he hadn't any money of his own.

The door swung open, and there was Belinda in a nice dress and a party hat.

"Hi," she said. "Come on in."

"Hi," he said as he sidled into the apartment, his hands behind his back. Inside, the table was set for the celebration and piled high with the things other children had brought. Shawn avoided the table and slid into a corner.

Just then, Belinda's mother shouted from the kitchen, "Get ready to sing, everybody. Here it comes!" She marched ceremoniously in from the kitchen holding forth her beautiful creation, her face brightened by the nine tiny flames.

You probably worked out that the passage recounts a birthday party. Once you realized that, you evoked a cognitive scheme that helped you understand Shawn's embarrassment because he hadn't worn party clothes or brought what the other guests had piled on the table—a birthday present. You also knew what song would be sung ("Happy birthday to you . . ."), and what it was the mother proudly carried in from the kitchen (a birthday cake with nine candles). How much of what you understood about the passage was actually supplied by the text? And how much information did you yourself supply?

Schema theory is a powerful way of understanding comprehension. It shows us that students' prior knowledge (or their schemas) is very important to their reading comprehension. It also shows us that understanding is real activity. Readers do not passively absorb meaning from the page; they construct meaning by trying to make sense of details according to the schemas they already possess in their memories. Hence schema theory supports a **constructivist approach** to reading comprehension because it suggests that readers construct meaning.

Reader Response Theory

Different readers understand different things from the same text. The **reader response theory** provides some understanding of what happens when individual readers make meaning from texts (Bleich, 1978; Iser, 1978; Rosenblatt, 1978) (see the World of Reading box). As formulated by Louise Rosenblatt, reader response theory suggests that three considerations are involved whenever a fictional text is read meaningfully: the reader, the text, and the poem.

THE READER. The reader brings to the reading her or his knowledge of vocabulary; associations for words; experiences in the world with certain people, places, and things; and experiences in literature with certain authors, genres, plots, symbols, and themes. In the case of a birthday party, for example, the knowledge and associations would include the reader's experiences with birthdays, both as a member of a cultural group and as an individual.

THE TEXT. The text offers marks on the page put there by the author. Usually, the author is trying to orchestrate understandings and emotions in the reader. But the author's intended meaning might never be identical with the meaning that readers make for them-

Reader Response in Action

Diane Barone (1992) reports on a second- and third-grade class in which the teacher was having her students record their reactions to each chapter of Roald Dahl's *Danny the Champion of the World* (1998) in a kind of response journal called a *dual-entry diary* (see page 217). An early chapter in the book describes the cozy days enjoyed by Dahl's protagonist, living in a gypsy wagon with his father. After reading this chapter, a student in the class wrote that he was expecting the woman to come into the story at any time. The teacher was puzzled, because the only woman that had been mentioned in the book was the boy's late mother, who had died before he was born. But in entry after entry, her student registered his worry that the woman might come into the story on the very next page. As it turned out, this young reader had lived a cozy existence for some time alone with *his* own father—until the father found a female companion. For the little boy, the woman really did come along, and the boy no longer had an exclusive claim to his father's attention.

The boy created a poem out of *Danny the Champion of the World* that was about the almost-too-good-to-be-true bliss of a boy's living alone with his father and his feeling of dread at its loss. The boy's concerns had led him to write responses that seemed bizarre at first. Yet it serves as a good example of how stories can evoke different responses from different people, children included. Teachers need to be aware of this critical piece of information.

As the boy's reading of *Danny the Champion of the World* suggests, there can be striking variations in the interpretations or poems created by different readers. That is why David Bleich (1970) urges teachers to think of literature discussion groups as interpretive communities. *Interpretive communities* are places where readers share their responses to works of literature so that communities of understanding can be formed. The sharing of individual responses not only contributes to a larger understanding of a work, but also promotes students' awareness of each other's thinking. Becoming aware of others' thinking is of particular value when the students come from different social and cultural backgrounds.

It takes special approaches on the teacher's part to set up an interpretive community. Merely asking students to answer literal questions will not do it. What is needed is to create a risk-free environment and to conduct—or let students conduct—discussions that invite personal responses to questions such as, "What did you notice in the text? What did it make you think of? How did it make you feel?"

selves. The author's words are suggestions only. It is up to the readers to bring the words to life in their own way.

THE POEM.   From the reader's construction of the author's words is created the poem: a sort of virtual reality that comes into being in the reader's imagination as he or she reads and stays in memory after the reading is done. (Rosenblatt is using the historical sense of the word *poem*, meaning a "created thing," not necessarily something that rhymes!) The poem is what comes to mind when you think back on a book you have read. It is not just the author's exact words. It is not just your memories from your own life and your knowledge of word meanings and literary devices that you called to mind as you read. It is a construction that is made of both.

During the act of reading, the reader and the text transact as the poem is created, and the poem colors what the reader makes of the text. Once the reader has decided that a book is "about X," that interpretation will color what the reader selects for response from the author's words, from the text.

Rosenblatt made a distinction between what happens when readers respond to fictional texts and what happens when they respond to informational texts. When we read fiction, we take what Rosenblatt (1978) called an **aesthetic stance**. That is, we respond to the work with our feelings and thoughts as we create the poem. Most fictional works have meaning for us and tell us some kind of truth, but we take away the total or thematic meaning of the work and do not expect its parts to be literally true. In the real world, frogs and toads do not carry around picnic baskets, and hippopotamuses do not have loafers to pour pea soup into; but both Arnold Lobel's Frog and Toad books and James Marshall's George and Martha books tell children things about friendship that are arguably true in the real world.

When we read informational works such as an account of the geography of Ireland, we take a different stance and expect every detail in the work to correspond truthfully to details in the real world. Because we can carry away facts and knowledge from the work, Rosenblatt calls the typical stance to nonfiction the **efferent stance**.

Even within a single work, readers might move back and forth between the aesthetic and efferent stances. For example, readers of Katherine Paterson's historical novel *Lyddie* (1994) take an aesthetic stance as they construct the character of a brave young woman who tries to make a life for herself in oppressive circumstances; but they also take an efferent stance as they learn details about life in a nineteenth-century New England textile mill.

Based on observational studies of students reading and discussing literature, Judith Langer (1995) teased out a pattern of stances that describes what happens when readers create and work with the poems that Rosenblatt brought to our attention. Langer's **envisionment** is a virtual stage set constructed, with the help of the author's words, in the reader's imagination. Readers move in and out of several stances of the envisionment at different points in their reading. These are Langer's stances of envisionment:

- *Being out and stepping into an envisionment.* From the author's clues about setting, characters, and dramatic situation, the reader begins to create in the mind's eye the virtual stage set. The reader tentatively picks up and tries out more and more clues as to what this virtual world is like, until he or she is able to leave something from the literal world behind and step into the envisionment.
- *Being in and moving through the envisionment.* Having created or cocreated a mental image of the setting, characters, and dramatic situation, the reader now follows the logic of the plot forward while asking questions and seeking answers. At this point, the reader may feel completely absorbed in the moment-to-moment living of the fictional world of the text.
- *Stepping out and rethinking what is known.* Occasionally, the reader may pause to consider the text, wondering what will happen next or thinking about what the text means to the reader's own life.
- *Stepping out and objectifying the experience.* This fourth stance normally is taken after the reader has read the whole book. Reading through a text is a linear event, in which one thing leads to another, but when readers look back on the finished text the experience of it becomes whole and rounded. The reader objectifies the experience after reading the story.

Langer's concept of envisionments and the stances we take them toward is a helpful way of looking at the experiences of reading literature. This idea leads us to think of understanding literature as something different from understanding informational text. As other writers have pointed out, we understand literature not simply by comprehending and remembering the details. Rather, we use the details in a fictional text to create an imaginative whole and to comprehend and learn from fiction by relating that fictional whole to what we know about life.

Critical Literacy

If schema theory and reader response theory were the only relevant accounts of how texts have meaning, newspapers would not print editorial pages, politicians would not make speeches, and television and radio programs would not be interrupted by advertisements. The fact is that texts (including storyboards for advertisements) are written by someone for a purpose, and that purpose is usually to have an effect on the reader (or viewer). Especially because the purpose is not always transparent, readers need to exercise their critical faculties to filter what they understand and are asked to believe from texts. **Critical literacy** is an approach to reading that stresses the reader's exercise of constructive skepticism in the face of a text. Often it is the unquestionable text that passes on messages we might want to challenge. When reading a persuasive text or even an informational text that we have reason to doubt, readers might ask questions like the following (modified from Browne & Keeley, 2000):

- What is the question this text is answering?
- What answer does it offer?
- Does it give good reasons for that answer?
- What has the text left unsaid?
- What other answer might I give to that question? Which seems stronger: my answer or the one offered by the text?
- Are there "facts" in the text that I might have reason to doubt?
- Does the text use loaded language (terms such as *troublemaker* or *good citizen*) that smears or exalts what it is talking about without making a real argument against it or for it?
- Who wants me to believe this text? Why do they want me to believe it?

With the case of fiction, stories, as William Doty (1986) points out, usually pass on some attitude toward the social order—the rights, privileges, and relative worth of male and female, young and old, beautiful and unbeautiful, rich and poor, upper class and lower class, and so on. The story might do the following:

- Challenge the social order (as do Robert Munsch's *The Paper Bag Princess* (1992) and Jane Yolen's *Sleeping Ugly* (1997) with respect to sex roles)
- Affirm the social order (as do Frances Hodgson Burnett's *Little Lord Fauntleroy* (1906/1996) and the early Babar stories with respect to the stratification of social classes)
- Pass on assumptions about the social order without criticizing them (as do so many fairy tales, such as "Cinderella" and "Snow White" with respect to sex roles)

When reading a fictional text, readers can ask questions such as the following:

- Who "won" in this story? What did he or she do to win? Who lost? Why? What lessons might be drawn from the winning and the losing?
- What difference would it make to the outcome of the story if the sex of the characters was changed (or the income group, race, or physical characteristics)? Why?
- With whom does the author of this work seem to want the reader to identify? That is, who is the reader supposed to be "for" and "against"? How can the reader tell?
- How would this story sound if it were told from the point of view of a different character?

Asking questions like this often brings to light prejudices in works that children might not agree with if these prejudices were stated clearly. Children might wonder, for example, why it is usually the female character (as in "Beauty and the Beast") who must be selfless to gain a reward, whereas the males get to go after what they want, or they might wonder what would have happened if the ugly duckling had remained ugly (Biklen, 1981). Would his ugliness have been grounds for others to shun him?

Acts of Comprehension

What are key strategies and skills that children and other readers use to comprehend text? Researchers have agreed on several. This list, derived from Pressley and Afflerbach (1995), captures the issue nicely. Comprehending a passage well involves the following:

Engaging prior knowledge

Knowing vocabulary

Visualizing details and events

Following the patterns of texts

Asking questions and pursuing answers

Making inferences

Monitoring comprehension

Noting main ideas from supporting details

Summarizing and rehearsing main ideas

ENGAGING PRIOR KNOWLEDGE. When they begin to read, good readers focus on the topic of the text, decide what they already know about it, and make predictions about what they are likely to learn. As they read, they go back and forth between what they knew about the topic and what they are finding out. When they are finished reading, they might reexamine what they knew or thought they knew and take note of how their knowledge has changed on account of the reading they have done. Not all readers do this fully developed version of engaging prior knowledge and checking new information against it, but readers should at least sense the topic of the reading and be reminded of what they already know about it.

Families can support children's development of comprehension by keeping up their contributions to children's background knowledge and supporting children's voluntary reading. Teachers can remind parents of the importance of taking their children to the library and museums and of putting informative children's magazines on their children's gift lists. *Ranger Rick* (**www.nwf.org/rangerrick/index.html**), the nature magazine, features enticing photographs of animals in the wild and articles on wildlife that fascinate children ages seven and up. *Cobblestone* (**www.cobblestonepub. com**) magazine features interesting articles on historical topics that appeal to children ages nine and up. *National Geographic World* (**www.nationalgeographic.com**) features highly illustrated articles on everything from undersea exploration to mountain climbing, and *Sports Illustrated for Kids* (**www.sikids.com**) follows teams and players and talks about the basics of the sports.

For general reading, including stories to read, *Cricket* magazine (**www.cricketmag.com**) for children ages eight and up and *Ladybug* for slightly younger children feature work that makes good reading by well-known and aspiring children's authors. *Highlights for Children* (**www.highlights.com**) also features stories and interesting informational articles, as well as riddles and games.

Remember why you are doing this. Keep in mind the power of starting from the beginning with young children, as opposed to trying to fix the world of adults. . . . Literacy is the key to success in all subjects. It opens the gates to communication, knowledge, and imagination. The greatest reward I've gotten from teaching is hearing them get excited about a book and hearing them resolve conflicts peacefully and independently.

—Sarah,
Preschool Reading Teacher
Washington, D.C.

FAMILY **LITERACY**

How can families support children's development of comprehension?

VISUALIZING DETAILS AND EVENTS. In creating works of fiction, authors take pains to describe events so the reader can visualize them and be drawn into the scene, or in Langer's term, "step into the envisionment." Frances Temple begins *The Beduin's Gazelle,*

> *Halima sat with her chin resting on her knees, close enough to touch her kinspeople, yet with her mind far away. The singsong of the storyteller's voice lulled her. The lanterns threw a soft glow on the dark wall of the tent, on the red and brown embroidered cushions, on the familiar faces of the listening women and children. Halima played with her bangles, her mind drifting with the story.* (Temple, 1996, p. 1)

The author's appeal to sights, sounds, and touch leads a competent reader to create an image of the scene in a beduin's tent in North Africa, where the events of the novel will soon unfold.

KNOWING VOCABULARY. Knowing the words in a text is an issue both in word recognition and in comprehension. As an aspect of comprehension, vocabulary items can be considered building blocks of understanding. It is possible to understand a text without knowing all the words, by making inferences from the context surrounding the unknown word. But making such inferences ties up concentration that might otherwise be used to comprehend the larger meaning of the text. Whether by making important information unavailable or by distracting attention, a shortage of vocabulary makes comprehension harder. A good reader has a vocabulary available that is nearly equal to the vocabulary she or he encounters in reading.

FOLLOWING THE PATTERNS OF TEXTS. Texts come to us in **genres**, which are a combination of purpose and pattern. The narrative or story genre, for instance, has the purpose of relating fictional events in an entertaining or edifying way that usually evokes an emotional response. Stories follow structures or patterns called *story grammars*. A story usually introduces a main character and other characters in a setting, and engages that character in an initiating event that leads the character to set a goal; then there might follow a series of episodes in which the character makes attempts to reach the goal. Each attempt has an outcome, then follows a consequence, the state of affairs at the end of the story (Stein & Glenn, 1979). As we discussed in Chapter 3, research and experience have shown that even by the time they are in first grade, listeners and readers use their knowledge of story grammar both to understand and to produce their own stories (Temple et al., 1992).

Of course, texts have other kinds of structures, too. Patterns such as lists, **taxonomies** (hierarchical lists), descriptions, comparisons, and cause-and-effect and problem-and-solution explanations guide readers' understanding. Persuasive essays use the structure of claims, reasons for the claims, and evidence to support the reasons.

How is text on the Internet demonstrative of concatenated structure?

Text on the Internet has a sort of **concatenated** structure; that is, items are linked to other items, as in a chain or a web. Readers can click on a term within an entry and be taken at once to a new entry that explains the term. While reading the new entry, readers might be invited to click on another term within that entry and be taken to a new entry explaining that term. So an entry on mammals might allow readers to click and go to an explanatory entry about elephants. There they might be invited to click and go to another entry or even a whole new Web site on Tanzania because that country is home to many elephants. The challenge to the reader, of course, is to keep in mind the topic of the original search and the questions that guided that search.

Reading by the pattern can help to guide the reader's understanding below surface events toward the deeper logical structure of the text. Readers who know how to follow the patterns of text when they read learn to raise questions and search for answers according to the way the text reveals its contents. When they are reading a story, readers can identify the problem that the character has and try to anticipate the solution to the problem. When they are reading a problem-and-solution explanation, readers can identify the problem and look for solutions.

ASKING QUESTIONS AND PURSUING ANSWERS.   As they summon up ideas related to the topic of the text, good readers make predictions about what they will find out. Then they monitor what they are learning from the text to see whether those predictions are being confirmed. When good readers read a story, they can follow the outlines of the plot to generate predictions and experience satisfaction or surprise as those predictions are confirmed or not by what happens. In fact, authors count on readers' acts of prediction to evoke readers' emotional experiences of suspense, surprise, and completion as patterns of events raise expectations and sometimes thwart and sometimes satisfy them.

MAKING INFERENCES.   When readers have to piece together information themselves that is not directly supplied by the text, they are making **inferences**. Fiction writers often leave gaps in the text (Iser, 1974) that must be filled in by the reader's inferences, and readers experience the activity of filling those gaps as engagement. Even young readers make inferences. For example, kindergarten children enjoy listening to Harry Allard and James Marshall's popular picture book *Miss Nelson Is Missing* (1977), about a too-sweet school teacher who is replaced by a very mean substitute teacher. Most young children, but not all, can infer the substitute teacher's identity from the next-to-the-last page of the book. There, the illustration shows (but the text does not mention) an ugly black dress hanging in the sweet teacher's closet underneath a box with the word WIG written in upside-down letters.

MONITORING COMPREHENSION.   Good readers are aware when a text is making sense, and they are alerted when it does not. Perhaps they misread a word, or they assumed the text was going to say something that it does not. Then the breakdown in their comprehension leads them to go back and make a "repair." They reread the misinterpreted word or reconsider where the argument is going so that they again have the feeling they are understanding the text. Comprehension monitoring, then, assumes that readers think on two planes: They think about what the text means, and they are also aware of their own understanding or lack of it.

In the case of fictional or poetic texts, in which there is figurative language or symbols, or irony to be navigated, the reader has more interpreting to do.

NOTING MAIN IDEAS AND SUPPORTING DETAILS.   Readers who are aware of the argument of the text can distinguish main ideas from small details. Consider, for example, a child reading this passage from *Charlotte's Web*:

> *On foggy mornings, Charlotte's web was truly a thing of beauty. This morning each strand was decorated with dozens of tiny beads of water. The web glistened in the light and made a pattern of loveliness and mystery, like a delicate veil. Even Lurvy, who wasn't particularly interested in beauty, noticed the web when he came with the pig's breakfast. He noted how clearly it showed up and he noted how big and carefully built it was. And then he took another look and saw something that made him set his pail down. There in the center of the web, neatly woven in block letters, was a message. It said:*
>
> > SOME PIG!
>
> *Lurvy felt weak. He brushed his hand across his eyes and stared harder at Charlotte's web. (White, 1952/1980, p. 77)*

There are many details in this passage about the way the spider's web looked. But a reader who gets the main idea will focus on the fact that the spider has written words, they describe her friend Wilbur the pig, and they have been noticed with great surprise by Lurvy the farmhand. The child who has been following the plot of the story will realize that Charlotte's writing is a possible solution to the main problem of the book because it is meant to impress Wilbur's human owners so they will spare the little pig's life.

Readers who distinguish main ideas do so by following the argument of the text. They understand the problems the text is setting out to solve, and they are aware when information is significant as answers to questions or solutions to problems posed by the text: Such information is a main idea.

SUMMARIZING AND REHEARSING MAIN IDEAS.   Once they identify main ideas, good readers might slow down, reread the passage that contained them, and rehearse the ideas so that they will remember them later (Pressley & Afflerbach, 1995). Following the reading, the readers might retell the main ideas to themselves, or they might reread important passages aloud to a friend. Good readers might reread the key passages in the text to make sure the main ideas were stated the way they remembered them. In this way, good readers hope to store the main ideas in memory and learn from the reading.

Scaffolding: From Strategies to Skills

STRUGGLING   READER

Why might struggling readers need more support to use reading strategies?

Once you are aware of the component abilities that make for reading comprehension, you can deliberately and overtly teach readers to use those strategies until they become internalized, that is, until they become skills (Duffy & Roehler, 1989).

Skilled and struggling readers use the same processes to read with comprehension that we just described. But struggling readers might need more support to make sure they use all of these strategies and orchestrate them into fluent reading with comprehension. Kameenui (1998) recommends that teachers of struggling readers employ these steps:

1. *Make strategies explicit.* Through modeling, think-alouds, and regular reminding, show the students how to carry out each of the comprehension strategies we described in the previous sections.
2. *Supply scaffolding.* Scaffolding is temporary support for students as they learn to do a task or apply a skill. Scaffolding may be used temporarily and be withdrawn when students can function independently. An example of scaffolding is a story map, in which students are asked to identify the character, setting, problem, and solution in a story they are reading (see Figure 7.4 on p. 224).

3. *Connect ideas.* Remind students of ideas they find in a text that they have seen on a field trip or in a lesson in another subject. Struggling readers might be so preoccupied by the act of making sense of what they read that they do not think about the larger ideas. They need the teacher to point out to them the relatedness of ideas.

4. *Provide background knowledge.* Struggling readers might not have the background knowledge they need to make sense of what they read. A story about an early twentieth-century immigrant's journey from Europe to America will make little sense to a student who does not realize that Europe is a continent that lies thousands of miles across the ocean from America or that until a few years ago, travel from Europe was so difficult and expensive that people who made the trip could not go back.

5. *Review skills and ideas often.* Struggling readers need to be reminded of both the skills they have learned and the ideas they have gained. They need to be reminded of both, and they need to apply the tasks and ideas in new settings.

Teaching for Comprehension

Teaching for comprehension and response is not just a matter of teaching skills. Although it is important to develop children's reading strategies and support the strategies until they become skills, it is also important to develop children's familiarity with literature as well as their knowledge and interests. In the pages that follow we present several methods and strategies for teaching reading comprehension and response to text.

Organizing Instruction for Comprehension and Response: The ABC Model

Children should have many opportunities to read for meaning and for pleasure in personally chosen books that are not used for instruction by the teacher (Block and Pressley, 2001). Children should also have lessons in which the teacher guides them through aspects of comprehension so that the students will internalize those aspects and practice them when they are reading independently. Teaching comprehension successfully requires that teachers engage students' thinking and invite students to keep their minds appropriately active throughout the reading process. The ABC model offers instructional choices for guiding comprehension—for activities to be used before reading (in the *a*nticipation phase), during (in the phase of *b*uilding knowledge), and after reading (in the phase of *c*onsolidation) after Vaughn and Estes (1986) and Steele and Meredith (1997). The ABC model is flexible. Within its three parts or phases, the teacher can make many choices. So, eventually, can the students, because they need to internalize the pattern of thinking captured by this model and use it when they read independently.

ANTICIPATION.   Before they read, readers should think about the topic, then recall their prior knowledge about it. If they don't have very much prior knowledge about the subject or if their thoughts about it are disorganized, the teacher might want to spend some time telling the students more about the topic and organizing their thinking about it. Readers should wonder how their present knowledge about the topic might relate to the text they are about to read. If they are to read an informational text, what do they still want to know about the topic that they might learn from this text? If it is a fictional text, what other works do they know by this author or in this genre? What does their prior knowledge lead them to expect from this reading? This preliminary phase of the lesson is called **anticipation**.

Teaching goals in the anticipation phase are to prepare the students to read with comprehension. We want them to do the following:

- Connect the topic (or the genre, or the author) of the text they are about to read with their prior knowledge.

Think-Pair-Share

Anticipation Guide

- Raise questions about the text they are about to read and set purposes for reading.
- Know the vocabulary they will need to make sense of the text.

Several teaching approaches can be used to achieve these goals.

Focusing questions.   Questions that make a connection between what the students already know and what the reading will cover are valuable ways to prepare for a reading. In keeping with the goal of encouraging principled knowledge, it is advisable to steer questions toward the main ideas of the passage.

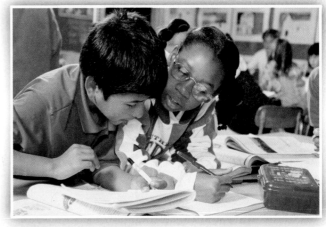

How does the think/pair/share activity encourage anticipatory reading?

For example, a group of fifth graders are reading Pam Conrad's *Pedro's Journal* (1992), a fictional account of Columbus's historic voyage. Before the students begin reading the first chapter, the teacher asks, "If you were about to sail three ships across the Atlantic Ocean in 1492, at a time when nobody knew for sure what was on the other side of the ocean, what three pieces of advice would you give yourself?"

The students might discuss the question as a whole group, or using the think/pair/share procedure (see below). Doing so activates thoughts and ideas that will help them make sense of and appreciate what they will encounter as they read the book.

Think/pair/share.   Focusing questions can be still more effective when a mechanism has been provided for all students to consider and answer them. Think/pair/share (Kagan, 1997) is a cooperative learning activity in which the teacher puts an open-ended question to the class, preferably by writing it on the chalkboard. Children are given two minutes to respond to the question individually. (Often they are asked to do this in writing.) Next, each child turns to a partner, and they share their answers with each other. Finally, the teacher calls on two or three pairs to share their answers with the class. Then the class begins reading the text. In a think/pair/share activity, every student—even in a class of thirty or more students—is motivated to think about the topic and to discuss it with someone else.

Anticipation guide.   Anticipation guides are used with fiction or with informational text. In using an anticipation guide (Vaughn & Estes, 1986), the teacher prepares a set of questions with short answers (usually true/false answers) that tap important aspects of the topic of the text. The questions are distributed to children on a worksheet, and the children are asked, individually or in pairs, to answer the questions as best they can before reading the assigned text. After reading the text, they return to the questions at the end of the class to see how their thinking has changed. Figure 7.2 provides an example of an anticipation guide.

Paired brainstorming.   When factual information will be shared, older students can be asked to make personal lists of the facts they know or think they know about the topic of the reading (Vacca & Vacca, 1986). After two minutes, they turn to a classmate and combine their lists. The teacher can make a master list of the class's ideas and leave their ideas on the chalkboard or on a piece of newsprint so that the students can compare them to the ideas they have after they have read the text.

Terms in advance.   A teacher may display a set of key terms that will be found in a reading and ask students to ponder their meanings as well as the relationships between the terms. The students are asked to predict how this particular set of terms might be used in the passage they are about to read. For example, if the book they are about to read is *Miss Nelson Is Missing*, the terms might be as follows:

Terms in Advance

kind teacher	mean substitute	police inspector	return
misbehave	make faces	homework	disguise

FIGURE 7.2

Anticipation Guide for Pedro's Journal.

Instructions: Before reading *Pedro's Journal,* answer these questions *true* or *false* on the left-hand side. After reading the book, enter new answers on the right-hand side.

Answer Before		Answer After
_____	1. Columbus was well liked by his crew.	_____
_____	2. Columbus prepared his ships to sail in front of the wind.	_____
_____	3. Columbus's captains were very loyal to him.	_____
_____	4. The first people Columbus met lived in a city.	_____
_____	5. Columbus was very respectful of the people he met.	_____
_____	6. Columbus seemed very interested in finding gold.	_____

BUILDING KNOWLEDGE.   Once students have had their expectations raised for what they are about to read, they are ready for activities that will help them construct meaning from the text or build their knowledge. As they read, students need to compare their expectations with what they are learning from the text. They should be able to revise their expectations or raise new ones as the text reveals more information, raises more questions, or plants more clues. They also need to think about what they are reading and be able to identify the main points. They will need to reflect on what the text is meaning to them personally and fill in any blanks in the text—that is, to make inferences about what the text says. Finally, they should be able to question the text, to argue with it. This phase of the lesson while children read is called **building knowledge**. Several strategies for helping students to build knowledge are described next.

GUIDED READING.   The guided reading procedure (Fountas & Pinnell, 1999) introduced in Chapter 5 provides an excellent opportunity to teach comprehension. Guided reading proceeds in three steps.

1. **Preparing the children to read with understanding.** Prepare the students to read and understand the book with some preliminary activities.
   - **Preview the text.** Show them the cover illustration, the title, some of the pictures inside. "Think aloud" and speculate on what the text might be about. You may discuss the author and the kinds of books she or he writes.
   - **Introduce the genre.** Whether the book is a folktale, a biography, tall tale, or a work of realistic fiction, you may expect different things to happen in the text.
   - **Go over vocabulary.** Tell the students that they will meet some interesting words in this text. Name them one at a time. If there is time, do a **word conversation** to introduce each word.
   - **Teach other skills.** Depending on your objectives for this lesson, teach a brief focused lesson on the skills you want the students to practice. For example, if you want the students to pay attention to the plot of the story, you can prepare them to fill out a **story map,** such as the one found in Figure 7.4 on page 224. Show the whole group how to fill out a story map, and later have them fill out a story map themselves after they have read the story.
   - **Read the story to them.** If the story is challenging for some of the students, you may choose to read it aloud to them first. If you have a big book version of the text available, they can read along with you.
   - **Begin a K-W-L (Know/Want to Know/Learn) or Directed Reading-Thinking Activity (DRTA).** Comprehension strategies that ask children to discuss what they know and what they think they will find out can be introduced now.
2. **The students read the text.** The students may read the text on their own or in pairs. A number of useful strategies for having them read with a purpose are found in the section called "Building Knowledge" later in this chapter.

- **If you are conducting a DRTA or a K-W-L,** they read to an assigned stopping place and have questions to guide their search for information.
- They may *buddy read*, that is, take turns reading paragraphs or pages.
- They may use the *Paired Reading/Paired Summarizing* technique (Crawford et al., 2005). That is, one student reads a paragraph aloud and summarizes it. The other student asks questions about the passage that both answer. Then they change roles with the next paragraph, and so on.
- They may read with *text coding* (Crawford et al., 2005). That is, the teacher helps students think of a set of four to six questions or issues they wish to track as they read the text. For example, if they are reading a passage about acid rain, they may be asked to look for passages that say where it occurs (W), others that say what its sources are (S), others that describe the chemical reactions that make it happen (CR), others that talk about the damage it does (D), and still others that talk about possible preventions of the problem (P). As they read, the students pencil in the letter indicating which kind of information they have found.

3. **The group reviews what they have learned.** After the students have read the text, the teacher brings them back together to discuss the text and to consolidate what they have learned.
- **Discussions** can use many of the formats described in this chapter. These methods include Sketch to Stretch, shared inquiry, dual-entry diaries, Save the Last Word for Me, the discussion web, and dramatization.
- **Revisiting the skills you introduced.** Assuming you began the lesson with certain skills in mind—understanding characterization, following the plot, getting the main idea, and so on—you will revisit those skills now. Have the students or pairs of students explain how they read and what they discovered, and make sure everyone understands and can carry out the practice you introduced.

Questioning the Author. The Questioning-the-Author technique, designed by Isabel Beck and her colleagues (Beck et al., 1997), rests on the realization that readers sometimes fail to understand what they read, not because they are incompetent, but because the authors haven't made their meaning sufficiently clear. When students listen to their peers reading their works aloud in a writing workshop, they don't hesitate to say, "I don't know what you mean right there. Help me understand." Yet when young readers come across unclear passages in a published text, they often assume that the problem is theirs for not understanding, rather than the author's. This focused reading technique encourages students to question what they don't understand in a text.

To prepare to conduct the Questioning-the-Author procedure, choose a portion of texts that will support an engaged discussion of twenty to thirty minutes. Read through the text in advance and identify the major concepts that the students should gain from the text. Plan frequent stopping points in the text to devote attention to the important ideas and inferences in the passage. Write some probing questions to be asked at each stopping point to motivate discussion.

Conducting the Questioning-the-Author lesson then proceeds in two stages:

Stage 1. Preparing the Students' Attitudes. Begin the discussion by reminding students that comprehension often breaks down because authors don't tell readers everything they need to know. Things may be unclear. Ideas may have been omitted or hinted at but not stated. A good way to comprehend is to think of questions you would ask the author if she or he were present and imagine what the answers might be. Because the author is not present in the classroom, the class will attempt to answer for the author.

Stage 2. Raising Questions about the Text. Now have the students read a small portion of the text. At a preselected stopping point, pose a question or query about what the students have just read. Early in the text, initiating queries might be:

- What is the author trying to say here?
- What is the author's message?
- What is the author talking about?

Later in the text, follow-up queries might include:

- So what does the author mean right here?
- Did the author explain that clearly?
- Does that make sense with what the author told us before?
- How does that connect with what the author has told us here?
- But does the author tell us why?
- Why do you think the author tells us that now? (From Beck et al., 1997)

As you ask these questions, ask several students to contribute ideas. Prod the students to clarify their thoughts, to elaborate their ideas, to debate each other's ideas, and to reach a consensus opinion.

Directed Reading–
Thinking Activity
(DRTA)

The Directed Reading-Thinking Activity.   The **Directed Reading-Thinking Activity** (Stauffer, 1975), or DRTA, uses the dynamic of prediction and confirmation to create interest and excitement around a reading assignment, provided that the text is a work of fiction with something of a predictable structure. The DRTA is normally done with a group of six to ten students; this size is large enough to yield a range of predictions but small enough for everyone to participate. It is advisable that the students be roughly matched for reading ability, because all students must wait for the slowest one to finish reading each section.

The DRTA can be used by itself, or it can follow one of the activities we introduced in the anticipation phase. Some teachers precede the DRTA with the terms-in-advance procedure or with the anticipation guide.

The teacher prepares for a DRTA by choosing four or five stopping places in the text, yielding more or less same-sized chunks of text. The stops should be placed right at points of suspense, places where the reader has been given some information and is wondering what is going to happen next (in other words, where the commercial break would be placed in a television thriller). One of these is normally right after the title. The Teach It! box demonstrates the DRTA process.

In a DRTA, the questions are worded in a very open way. The teacher asks, "What do you think will happen? Why do you think so?" More specific questions from the teacher would take some of the initiative for making predictions away from the children, and the point here is for children to learn to ask their own questions about what they are reading.

There are a number of ways to scaffold a DRTA to make it more accessible to students. One is to read the text aloud instead of having the students read it. This variation of the method goes by a different name: the directed listening-thinking activity. Another is to think aloud yourself. If the predictions are slow in coming or seem to be going too wide of the mark, the teacher can offer a choice. For *Miss Nelson Is Missing*, the teacher might say, "I'm wondering if Miss Nelson has gone away to teach in another school where the kids are better behaved, or if she'll come back to her same class. Which one do you all think will happen?" Finally, in third grade and above, instead of a teacher-directed activity, a DRTA can be done by individual students or pairs of students.

CONSOLIDATION.   By the **consolidation** phase, the students have gone through the text and have at least begun to comprehend it. They need to go further, though, and do something with the meaning. They need to summarize it and be able to interpret and debate the meaning while applying it to new situations and creating new examples of it.

Students need to practice higher-order thinking with the issues from the text. After they read, students should be able to think back over the material and summarize the main ideas. They should compare what they found out with what they thought about the subject when they first approached the reading. If the ideas are not transparent, students should be able to interpret them. If the text is evocative in some way, students might be able to make personal responses to the ideas, such as applying them to the way they normally think or to the realities of their own lives. Students should also be able to test out the ideas—using them to solve problems or think up other solutions to the problems posed in the text.

Several teaching approaches are available to assist teachers with guiding students to consolidate and extend their ideas about what they have read. For fictional texts, teachers can use activities that allow students fairly free responses, some techniques that guide their

TEACH IT!

Refer to your **Teach It!** booklet for further activities you can use to reinforce concepts discussed in this chapter.

Conducting a DRTA

The directed reading-thinking activity is a sound strategy for helping students build knowledge as it helps create interest and excitement around a reading assignment. Following are the steps in a DRTA:

1. Tell the students that you are about to read a story together, using the method of prediction. The activity should be enjoyable, but it is necessary that they follow your instructions closely. You will tell them to make predictions about what they are going to read. Then you will have them read short passages of the text and stop. It is very important that they stop reading where you tell them to and not read ahead until asked.

2. Tell the students the genre of the story: realistic fiction, tall tale, folk tale, etc. After naming the genre, ask them what kinds of characters they expect to meet. Ask what kinds of events they expect to happen.

3. Read the title, and show the students the accompanying picture, if there is one. Ask them what they think will happen. Remind them that it will not be possible to know for sure, but ask them to stretch their imaginations and take a guess. Press for the most specific answers you can get. Write some of these on the chalkboard. (Remember to leave room to write three more rounds of comments.)

4. Before the students read on, ask them to consider the predictions they have heard and silently choose the one they think is most likely to happen. Then ask them to keep their predictions in mind as they read to the next stopping place.

5. Now they should read (silently) to the stopping place and turn their books over when they have finished.

6. At the stopping place, review several of the predictions and ask the class whether the predictions are seeming to be borne out by the text or contradicted. Ask for proof from the text: Which predictions are coming true? What evidence do the students find in the text that makes them think so? You can put check marks on the board next to the predictions that are coming true, minuses next to those that are not, and question marks beside those that are uncertain. Ask the students how things look now in the story.

7. After some discussion, ask the students to make more predictions, choose the most likely ones, and read ahead as in step 4.

8. When the students have reached the end of the story, review the predictions, and ask the students what it was that made them guess what turned out to be the correct predictions. What was it about the characters, the plot, or the genre of the story that helped to guide their predictions?

---

attention to different aspects of the text, or for more analytic approaches that help to guide students in taking a close look at some aspect or aspects of the text. Table 7.1 identifies various activities with the appropriate approaches.

Dual-entry diary. The dual-entry diary (Berthoff, 1981) is a kind of journal students use to record responses to readings. To make a dual-entry diary, the students draw a vertical line down the middle of a blank sheet of paper. On the left-hand side, they write a passage or image from the text that affected them strongly. Perhaps it reminded them of something from their own experience. Perhaps it puzzled them. Perhaps they disagreed with it. Perhaps it made them aware of the author's style or technique.

On the right-hand side of the page, they write a comment about that passage: What was it about the quote that made them write it down? What did it make them think of? What question did they have about it?

There are a number of ways in which these journals may be treated next. Students can exchange them and comment on each other's quotes. The teacher can take them up (a few each day) and comment on them. Or the children can bring them to a discussion group in which the students are reading a common book and offer their comments to the discussion.

Save the Last Word for Me. Save the Last Word for Me (Short, Harste, & Burke, 1996) provides a framework for a small-group or whole-class discussion of a text. The procedure is especially good for encouraging children to take the lead in discussing their reading. The steps of the strategy are as follows:

1. After being assigned a reading to do independently, students are given note cards and asked to find three or four quotations they consider particularly interesting or worthy of comment.

TEACH IT! 27
Dual Entry Diary

TEACH IT! 28
Save the Last Word for Me

TABLE 7.1

Activities for Consolidation

TEACHING APPROACHES

Open Response	Focused Approach	Analytic Approach
"Save the Last Word for Me"	Shared inquiry	Story maps
Literature circles	Discussion web	Character clusters
Value line	Debate	Character maps
Sketch-to-stretch		Dramatic roles
Dual-entry diary		Structured opposites

2. The students write the quotations they have found on the note cards.
3. On the other sides of the cards, the students write comments about their chosen quotations. That is, they say what the quotations made them think of, what is surprising about the quotations, and why they chose them.
4. The students bring their quotation cards to discussion groups. The teacher calls on someone to read a card aloud.
5. After reading the quotation on his or her card, the student invites other students to comment on that quotation. (The teacher might need to help keep comments on the subject of the quotation.) The teacher also may comment on the quotation.
6. Once others have had their say about the quotation, the student who chose it reads his or her comments aloud. Then there can be no further discussion. The student who chose it gets to have the last word.
7. That student can now call on another student to share his or her quotation and begin the process all over again. Not all students will be able to share their quotation if the whole class takes part in the activity, so the teacher will need to keep track of who shared quotes and make sure other children get chances to share their quotes the next time.

Literature Circles

Literature circles. *Literature circles* (Short & Kauffman, 1995), *grand conversations* (Eeds & Wells, 1989), and *book clubs* (Raphael et al., 1995) are all terms for literary discussions in which students' curiosity about the text is allowed to play a directing role.

Students in such discussions typically have read the same work; that work might be a short text they have already read or heard, or it might be a longer work. That is discussed while students are still in the middle of it. The choice of texts for literature circles is critical because not all works are equally successful in evoking interested responses. Those that do often have a core mystery, elements that invite more than one interpretation, and a clear connection to issues that matter to the students.

These discussion groups may at first be conducted with the whole class at once until students have grown familiar and comfortable with the procedure. Then they may be conducted in smaller groups of four or five students meeting simultaneously. Literature circles are conducted several times a week. Early in the year, they might last no more than twenty minutes, but as students gain experience and confidence talking about literature, they might run for up to forty minutes, not counting the time it takes to read the text. Everyone is free to offer comments and questions in literature circles, and students are reminded that they are free to address their comments and questions to other students and not always to the teacher.

The role of the teacher in a literature circle is mainly to be a spirited participant; however, Martinez (in Temple et al., 2002) points to four additional roles teachers play:

1. The teacher is a model. The teacher might venture her or his own questions or responses to get a discussion going. The teacher is careful to speak as one seeking insights and not as a lecturer. The teacher's statements might begin, "I wonder about . . ."

2. The teacher helps students learn new roles in a literature circle. Although all students know how to have conversations, they might need reminding of ways to participate in conversations in a classroom. These include rules such as these:
   - Sit in a circle so that everyone can see each other.
   - Only one person speaks at a time.
   - Listen to each other.
   - Stay on the topic.
3. The teacher moves the conversation forward. Without dominating the discussion, the teacher might invite other students to comment on something one student has said. The teacher might ask a student to clarify an idea. Or the teacher might pose an interesting open-ended question that she or he has thought about in advance. (Such interpretive questions are discussed in the section on shared inquiry later.)
4. The teacher supports literary learning. Lecturing about literature is not an adequate substitute for having students think and talk about it; nonetheless, it helps if teachers supply students with concepts and terms they can use to give form to ideas they are trying to express or insights they are struggling to reach. A student might notice that there is a point in a story where tension is highest because the main question in the story is about to be answered. The teacher tells the student that this is a *climax*. Researchers have noted that students' discussions go deeper when they have literary terms available to them (Hickman, 1979, 1981).

When conducting cooperative learning activities, the teacher might need to assign students particular roles to play in a group. Over time, when individual students learn to play the many roles of encourager, timekeeper, facilitator, recorder, and summarizer, they eventually learn all of the aspects of a good participant in a group because a good participant may practice most of these roles at once.

Literature circles often function better when students have particular roles to play. Also, by performing designated roles, students may exercise the many tasks that are carried out by an effective reader and discussant of literature. Table 7.2 outlines roles that students may play in a literary discussion (Daniels, 1994, 2001). Five suggestions make the use of these roles more successful:

1. Teach the roles to the whole class, one at a time. The teacher might read or tell a story, then introduce one of the roles—for example, the connector. The teacher might then call attention to a connection between something in the text and something in real life. Then the teacher will invite several students to do likewise. Over several days, many of the roles can be introduced in this way before students use them in an extended discussion.
2. Encourage students to ask questions from their roles rather than to say what they know. For example, the character interpreter might invite the other students to construct a character map or a character web about a character and venture his or her own ideas only after the other students have shared their own.
3. Choose only the most useful roles for a particular discussion. Sometimes four or five roles are sufficient.
4. Rotate students through the roles. Each student should play many roles over the course of several discussions. The accumulated experience of playing many of these roles adds dimensions to each student's awareness of literature.
5. Be careful not to stress the roles more than the rich discussion of the literary work. Having students carry out the roles is a means to the end of sharing their insights about a work. Once the conversation is under way, the teacher should feel free to suspend the roles and let the conversation proceed.

Sketch-to-Stretch. An ingenious device for having students of all ages respond together to a literary work is Sketch-to-Stretch, from Short et al. (1996). After the students have read and thought about a poem or a story, they are invited to draw pictures that symbolize what they believe are the main ideas or central themes of the piece. One student shows his or her drawing to a group of students, and they interpret the picture, saying what they think

TABLE 7.2

Roles in a Literary Discussion Group

- *Quotation finder:* This student's job is to pick a few special sections of the text that the group would like to hear read aloud.
- *Investigator:* This student's job is to provide background information on any topic related to the text.
- *Travel tracer:* When characters move from place to place in a text, this student's job is to keep track of their movements.
- *Connector:* This student's job is to find connections between the text and the world outside.
- *Question asker:* This student's job is to write down (in advance of the discussion) questions for the group to talk about—questions he or she would like to discuss with the others.
- *Word finder:* This student's job is to find interesting, puzzling, important, or new words to bring to the group's attention and discuss.
- *Checker:* This student's job is to help people in the group do their work well by staying on the topic, taking turns, participating happily, and working within time limits.
- *Character interpreter:* This student's job is to think carefully about the characters and to discuss what they are like with the other students.
- *Illustrator:* This student's job is to draw pictures of important characters, settings, or actions so that the other students may discuss the pictures.
- *Recorder:* This student's job is to take brief notes on the main points raised in the discussion.
- *Reporter:* This student's job is to report on the group's discussion to the teacher or to the whole class.

it means and how its images relate to the literary work. After the other students have had their say, the student who drew the picture is invited to give his or her own interpretation of the picture.

Shared inquiry discussion.　The Great Books Foundation developed the shared inquiry method to accompany their literature discussion program (see Plecha, 1992), which has been conducted in thousands of schools and libraries for more than thirty years. Shared inquiry is a procedure by which the teacher leads a deep discussion into a work of literature. It is best done with a group of eight to ten students, to maximize participation but allow for a diversity of ideas. The procedure follows these steps:

1. Before the discussion takes place, choose a work or part of a work that encourages discussion. Such a work should lend itself to more than one interpretation (not all works do this well) and raise interesting issues. Folktales often meet these criteria surprisingly well.
2. Make sure that all of the students have read the material carefully. (The Great Books Foundation insists that students read material twice before discussing it. But in our experience, a reading using some of the comprehension methods just described can make the students very aware of the contents of the reading selection.)
3. Prepare four or five discussion questions. These should be what the Great Books Foundation calls interpretive questions, and they have three criteria:
   a. They are real questions, the sort of question you might ask a friend as you walk together out of a provocative film.
   b. They have more than one defensible answer. (This criterion guarantees a debate. If it is not met, the discussion won't be a discussion but a "read my mind" exercise.)
   c. They must lead the discussion into the text. (A question such as, "Why was the giant's wife kinder to Jack than his own mother was?" leads the children to talk about what is in the text first, even though they might then comment on what they know from experience. A question such as, "Have you ever done anything as brave as Jack?" leads the discussion away from the text and out into twenty-five different directions.)

4. Write the first question on the chalkboard, and ask the students to think about the question and then briefly write down their answers. (If the children are so young that writing answers is laborious, allow plenty of time before calling on anyone. This allows them time to think about their answers.) As you invite students to answer, be sure to invite reluctant speakers to read what they wrote as well. Encourage debate between students, pointing out differences in what they say and asking those and other students to expand on the differences. Press children to support their ideas with references to the text or to restate ideas more clearly. However, avoid correcting a child or in any way suggesting that any one answer is right or wrong. Finally, do not offer your own answer to the question. Keep a seating chart of the students' names with a brief record of what each one has contributed. When the discussion of a question seems to have run its course, read aloud your summaries of the students' comments and then ask whether anyone has anything to add.

5. Once the discussion gets going, follow the children's lead and continue to discuss the issues and questions they raise.

Even when they don't use the whole approach, many teachers use aspects of the shared inquiry procedure in conducting book discussions. For example, they might ask students to write down ideas to bring to a discussion, or they might take notes during the discussion, or they take care to draw out the students' ideas and not dominate the discussion themselves.

The discussion web.   The discussion web is a cooperative learning activity that involves all students in deep discussions of readings. The discussion web proceeds with the following steps:

Discussion Web

1. The teacher prepares a thoughtful binary question, a question that can be answered "yes" or "no" with support. For example, in discussing "Jack and the Beanstalk," a binary discussion question might be "Was Jack right to steal from the giant?" For Louis Sachar's book *Holes* (1998), the question might be "Did Stanley succeed in the end because of his personal qualities, such as being strong and good, or was it because the luck of his family finally changed?"

2. The teacher asks pairs of students to prepare a discussion web chart that looks like the one in Figure 7.3. Those pairs of students take four or five minutes to think up and list three reasons each that support both sides of the argument.

3. Next each pair of students joins another pair. They review the answers they had on both sides of the issue and add to each other's list. Then they argue the issue through until they reach a conclusion, that is, a position they agree on, with a list of reasons that support it.

4. At the conclusion of the lesson, the teacher calls on several groups of four to give brief reports of their position and the reasons that support it. The teacher can invite groups to debate each other if they took different sides of the argument.

Debates.   With students in third grade and up, it is often useful to follow the discussion web activity with a debate. The purpose of the debate is not to declare winners and losers but to help the students practice making claims and defending them with reasons, even when others defend different claims. Working with claims, reasons, and arguments and debating ideas without attacking people are key elements in critical thinking.

To have a debate, you need a binary question—that is, a question that has a yes/no answer (because the discussion web we saw above also uses binary questions, you can follow the discussion web with a debate). Here are the steps:

1. Think of a question you think will truly divide the students' opinions, and put the question on the chalkboard for all to see. If you are not sure the question will divide the students roughly equally, ask for a show of hands on each side of the issue before going forward.

2. Give students an opportunity to think about the question and discuss it freely.

YES		NO
_____	Was it wrong	_____
_____	for Jack to steal	_____
_____	from the giant?	_____
	CONCLUSION	
	_____	
	_____	
	_____	

FIGURE 7.3

A Discussion Web.

3. Ask students to divide up: Those who believe one answer to the question is right should go stand along the wall on one side of the room; and those who think the other is right should stand along the wall on the other side. Those who are truly undecided (that is, after thinking about it, they believe that both sides are partially right or neither side is right) should stand along the middle wall.

4. Explain or review the two ground rules:
   a. Don't be rude to each other. (You might have to explain and demonstrate what this means.)
   b. If you hear an argument that makes you want to change your mind, walk to the other side (or to the middle). Here is a hint to the teacher: As the debate proceeds, you can model the behavior of changing sides with a pantomime, by looking thoughtful for a moment after someone offers a good argument and moving to that student's side.

5. Give the students on each side three or four minutes to put their heads together and decide why they are on that side. Ask them to come up with a sentence that states their position. Then ask them to appoint someone to say that sentence.

6. Begin the debate by asking one person from each side (including the undecided group) to state that group's position.

7. Invite anyone on any team to say things (counterarguments or rebuttals) in response to what the other team has said or give more reasons in support of their own side.

8. Monitor the activity to make sure the tone stays away from negative attacks. Ask for clarification. Offer an idea or two as necessary from the devil's advocate position. Change sides. Encourage the students to change sides if they are persuaded.

9. When the debate has proceeded for ten or fifteen minutes, ask each side to summarize what they have said.

10. You may follow the debate with a writing activity: Ask each student to write down what he or she believes about the issue and why. (See Chapter 8 for suggestions of ways to structure this writing activity.)

Value line. A cooperative learning activity that is an extension of the debate procedure is the value line (Kagan, 1997). The value line is well suited for questions that have more than two good answers and students might have a range of answers along a continuum. Here are the steps:

1. Pose a question to the students on which answers may vary along a continuum. For example, after reading *Ramona and Her Father* (Cleary, 1997), you might ask the children, "Do you think Ramona's parents really understand her?"

2. Give the students three minutes to consider the question alone and write down their answers.

3. Now stand on one side of the room and announce that you represent one pole, or extreme position, on the argument. You might say, "Yes, I think Ramona's parents understand her perfectly, 100 percent of the time." Invite a student to stand at the other

end of the room to represent the other pole of the argument. The student might say, "No, I don't think Ramona's parents understand her. Not at all. Never."

4. Now invite the students to line up between the two of you in places along the imaginary value line between the two poles of the argument. Each stands at a point in the line that reflects his or her position on the question. Remind the students to compare their views with those of the students immediately around them to make sure they are all standing in the right spots. After hearing others' answers, some students might elect to move one way or another along the value line.

5. Students may continue to discuss their responses with the students on either side of them.

6. Identify three or four clusters of students who seem to represent different views on the question. Invite them to prepare a statement of their position and to share it with the whole group.

7. As an option, the formed line may be folded in the middle so that students with more divergent views may debate their responses.

8. You might want to follow this exercise with a writing opportunity in which students write down what they think about the issue and why. In this way, the value line serves as a rehearsal for writing an argumentative or persuasive essay.

Drama in response to stories. James Moffett (1976), a brilliant teacher of the language arts, pointed out many years ago that forms of literature differ in the degree to which they move closer to or further away from actual events. An essay about human nature is *abstract* (the word comes from two Latin roots that mean "drawn away from"), far removed from actual events. A story is more concrete, getting closer to events. Still, by putting events into story form, an author summarizes them, compresses actions, and leaves out much of what might really have happened. Drama, however, is live action: It is about as close to the real events as we can get because it plays the events out in real time for us so that we can see, hear, and feel them as they unfold. Here is Moffett's shorthand way of stating these points:

- Drama shows what is happening.
- A story tells what happened.
- An essay tells what happens.

Dramatizing a story, or a part of a story, can be a very effective way for children to unpack its meaning. Dramatization should be done after the children have read or heard a story and have had a chance to air their first thoughts about it. The Teach It! box on page 225 demonstrates a procedure for dramatizing a story.

The teaching approaches that we have considered up to now encourage discussions of stories or enactments of them. It is also useful to lead students in activities that teach them particular aspects of stories.

Story maps. As a rule, students read with better comprehension when they are asked questions that conform to the main arguments or developments of a text. When it comes to reading fiction, it helps if students are encouraged to raise questions along the lines that the stories are organized, and that usually means following the plot. The *plot* is a structured way in which authors organize places, people, actions, and consequences to make all of those things meaningful for the reader. The elements of a plot are as follows:

TEACH IT! 31

Story Maps

- *The setting:* the time and place the story happened
- *The main characters:* the persons the story is about
- *The problem:* the challenge the main character faces, which it is his or her goal to solve
- *The attempts:* the effort or series of efforts the character makes to solve the problem, along with their outcomes
- *The solution:* the attempt that finally pays off in solving the problem or the event that otherwise puts an end to the action
- *The consequence:* how things are for the characters at the end, including what the events of the story meant for them

What can students learn by acting out a story? What does it mean to "unpack" the meaning of a story?

Character Clusters and Character Map

For many years, researchers have noted that students down to age five and even younger use something like a plot or a story grammar to understand and tell stories (Stein & Glenn, 1978; Sutton-Smith et al., 1981). You can help students use the plot consciously in understanding a story by using a story map, a chart that invites them to identify the keys parts of a story (see Figure 7.4) The process builds their responsiveness to the structures of story plots. For students younger than second grade, it might be preferable to use a simpler version of a story map consisting of only the setting, the characters, the problem, and the solution.

Character clusters. Not only are stories developed through plots, but characters come to life in them, too. Literary critic Roland Barthes (1975) suggested that characters are mostly just bundles of attributes that authors put into situations and play off against each other to show us what happens. In essence, writers ask themselves, "What would happen if a person like X got stuck in a situation like Y with people like Z?" Children's comprehension and appreciation of stories can be enhanced by showing them some ways to think about characters.

One way is the **character cluster**, which is a kind of graphic organizer: a semantic web with the character's name written in the middle, main features of the character written as satellites around the character's name, and examples of those features written as satellites around the features. Figure 7.5 contains an example of a character cluster.

As when using other graphic organizers, you need to teach the whole class how to create a character cluster first. Then they can use it on their own as a guide to thinking more deeply about characters.

Character maps. When characters in stories interact with other characters (which is most of the time), students might need some way of keeping track of characters and the relationships between them. **Character maps** are a way to guide students' thinking about relationships between characters. In a character map, you write the names of two or more characters in their respective circles. The circles should be spaced widely apart on the page. Then draw arrows between the characters. Along the arrow that points from Character A to Character B, write about how Character A feels about Character B. Along the arrow that points

Setting	Characters	Problem	Attempts	Solution	Conclusion
In . . .	there was	who wanted	so she . . . , but . . . And she . . . but . . .	Finally, she . . . and . . .	In the end . . .

FIGURE 7.4

A Story Map.

TEACH IT!

Refer to your **Teach It!** booklet for further activities you can use to reinforce concepts discussed in this chapter.

Dramatizing a Story

Dramatizing a story allows children to take a closer look at a story by getting a real feel for the action. The procedure for dramatizing a story is adapted from the works of Spolin (1986) and Heathcote (Wagner, 1999).

Immerse students in the story. You need to make sure the students get the story on a literal level—that they know what happened. This might mean reading the story to them or asking them to reread the part you are going to dramatize.

Warm them up to do drama. There are many warm-up activities that work well to prepare students to act with more expression:

1. Stretches: Have the students stand in a circle. Now tell them to stretch their arms as high as they can as they spread their feet apart and make very wide faces. Now tell them to shrink up into tiny balls. Then stretch out big again. Have them do the same with their faces: Lion face! (expansive expression). Prune face! (shrunken expression).

2. Mirrors: Have students stand opposite each other. One is the person, and the other is the person reflected in the mirror. Have the person move (slowly) as the other mirrors the person's movements. Then switch roles.

3. Portraits: Have students get into groups of four or five. Have them think of something to depict that uses all of them as parts. For example, to depict a skier, children can act as poles, skis, and the person.

4. Superactions: This activity is more complex. Explain to the students that when we do things with other people, we often act on two levels: what we are doing and what we mean by what we are doing. For example, when we pass somebody we know in the hallway, having just seen the person a short time before, we might nod and say, "Hi." But when we see a friend in the hallway who has just come back to school after a long illness, we might say "HI!" with more exuberance. In both cases, the action is the same: to greet the friend. But the *superaction* is different. In the first case, it is just to show the person that we know he or she is there; in the second case, it is to show that we are surprised and delighted to see the person. Now practice dramatizing superactions by setting up brief situations, such as a waiter taking a customer's order. Write superactions on small pieces of paper, and give one privately to each ac-

tor. Have different pairs of students act out the same scene, with the same actions but with different superactions, leaving time for the other students to guess what they thought the superaction was and say why they thought so.

Choose critical moments. It can be particularly useful to dramatize just a few choice scenes from a story, especially the turning points when the most is at stake. In "Jack and the Beanstalk," such a scene might be when Jack first approaches the Giant's castle, knocks on the door, and is greeted by the Giant's wife.

Segment the Situation. Now assign students to take each of these roles. Invite other students to join them as they think about the situation from each character's point of view. What must be on Jack's mind when he approaches the huge door? What do the door and the walls of the castle look like? How large are they in proportion to Jack? What does Jack hear around the place? What does he smell? How does the place make him feel? What makes him pound his fist on the door? What is at stake for him? What are his choices? What will he do if he *doesn't* knock on the door? Why does he decide to do it?

Do the same for the Giant's wife. How does the knocking sound to her—thunderous or puny? What does she think when she sees the small but plucky boy at her door? What thoughts go through her mind, knowing what she knows about her husband? What are her feelings as she looks down at Jack?

Ask the actors to focus their minds on a few of these considerations as they prepare to act out the scene.

Dramatize the scene. Use minimal props and minimal costumes to help students think their way into their roles. Ask the other students to watch carefully and see what the actors make them think of.

Side coach. As the director, don't be passive, but take opportunities to make suggestions from the sidelines that will help children act more expressively. You might ask, "Jack, do you feel scared now or brave? How can you show us how you're feeling?"

Invite reflection. Ask the other students what they saw. What did they think was on the characters' minds? It is worthwhile to invite several groups of students to dramatize the same scene and have the class discuss the aspects of the situation that each performance brings to light.

---

from Character B to Character A, write about how Character B feels about Character A. An example of a character map for two characters in Mildred Taylor's *Roll of Thunder, Hear My Cry* (1997) is found in Figure 7.6.

Following dramatic roles. As French drama critic Etienne Souriau (1955) pointed out many years ago, a large part of the way we understand characters in stories is by the

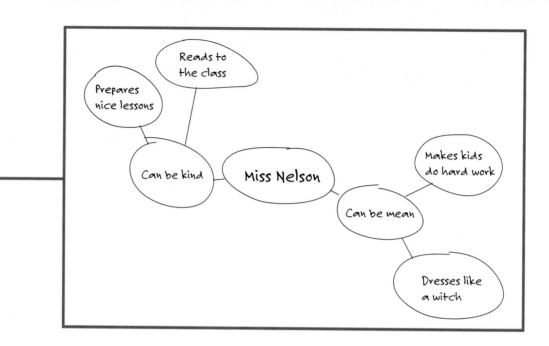

FIGURE 7.5

A Character Cluster.

symbolic roles they play in the plot. That is because whether we are watching sports or reading fiction, it is normal for us to cheer the hero, boo the rival, and have a warm place in our hearts for the trusty helper. Authors of stories wittingly or unwittingly use these propensities to shape the reader's reactions to characters: assigning one the role of protagonist or main character, another the role of helper, and another the role of rival or enemy.

Making children aware of the roles characters play in stories can help them interpret the stories and, eventually, to understand better how stories work. Following are common roles that occur in stories:

- The hero is the person whose desires and needs drive the story forward. In "Jack and the Beanstalk," to use that story as an example, the hero is Jack.
- The goal is the hero's main need or desire. In "Jack and the Beanstalk," Jack's goal seems to be to get money or to get some independence and not be thought of as a dolt.
- The rival is the person who stands between the hero and her or his goal. The rival in "Jack and the Beanstalk" is certainly the giant.

FIGURE 7.6

A Character Map for *Roll of Thunder, Hear My Cry*.

- The helper is a person or persons in a story who help(s) the hero achieve his or her goal. In "Jack and the Beanstalk," there are a couple of candidates for the helper: the mysterious old man who sells him the beans and the giant's own wife.

The teacher can use dramatic roles in several ways to think about stories. One way is to have students nominate candidates for each of the roles and discuss their choices in small groups or as a class. These discussions can become lively because not all role assignments are obvious. Is the helper in "Jack and the Beanstalk" the mysterious old man or the giant's wife? If it is the giant's wife (and the giant is the rival), why should she help the person who is striving against her husband? Is Jack's goal to obey his mother, to get money, to satisfy his curiosity, or to prove himself? Or is it all of these things? Discussing these issues takes students deep into the story.

Another way of using dramatic roles is to help students take different perspectives on a story. The teacher does this by asking students to take a character who seems to be playing one role and ask how the story would seem if we imagined that character playing a different role. For example, in "Jack and the Beanstalk," suppose the giant's wife were the hero; that is, suppose we saw things from her perspective. What is her goal? Who is her rival? Exploring these questions can lead to some very interesting discussions of stories and exercises the comprehension strategies of inferring and interpreting.

Reading for structured opposites.   People often find it most natural to think of extreme contrasts first, and then to think of things in the middle. For example, we learn hot and cold, huge and tiny, before we learn tepid and middle-sized. Storytellers also tend to use extreme contrasts. As Bruno Bettelheim (1975) observed, characters in fairy tales are very good or very bad; few are mixtures of the two. Stories tend to deal with the same great problems and urges again and again, as the folklorist Joseph Campbell (1968) brilliantly showed us. Thus we can see similarities in those things that are most starkly contrasted in stories, and then begin to ask what those contrasts remind us of in our own experiences. Claude Levi Strauss (1970) argued that a useful way of interpreting stories is to look for their contrasts, ask what things are similarly contrasted in other stories, and then find parallel contrasts and tensions in our own lives. This method is called **reading for structured opposites**. A folktale works very well for introducing this method and could be taught like this:

1. Ask the students to think of the two characters in the story they are reading who are most unlike each other or most opposed to each other. For example, if the story is "Jack and the Beanstalk," the two characters might be Jack and the giant.
2. Write the names of those two characters at the heads of two columns (see Figure 7.7). Ask the students to come up with contrasting descriptive words about those two

Jack	The Giant
Small	Huge
Young	Old
Poor	Rich
Uses wits and courage	Uses brute strength
On his way up	"Over the hill" and on his way down

FIGURE 7.7

Looking for Contrasts between Characters.

The Power of a Good Story

Some years ago we were conducting a workshop for a group of teachers in Virginia in which we were exploring ways to discuss stories. Toward the end of the day, one participant looked at us with an expression that was a mix of amazement and joy and said, "This stuff is about your whole life!" She was right. When you really think about a good story, even a seemingly simple story like "Jack and the Beanstalk," you find yourself peeling back layer after layer of meaning, and tracing connections to people and situations that are suddenly familiar. Why *was* the giant's wife kinder to Jack than his own mother was? What happened to her after the story was over? And why are we so focused on Jack's exploits that we don't give her another thought? Who else has kindly worked out of the limelight and out of our concern? Reading and reflecting makes children more thoughtful. It makes us more thoughtful, too. Good teachers of reading—good teachers—cultivate and value the habit of reading themselves. They make regular trips to the library and to bookstores. They have accounts with online booksellers who let them know when a new book comes out by a favorite author or about a topic of special interest They discuss books with their friends, either face to face or online. Their delight in reading undoubtedly rubs off on their students.

Reading comprehension is a process that takes students from their prior knowledge—the schema they already have—and leads them to construct new meaning from the new knowledge they gain by reading.

The Role of Questioning in Reading Comprehension

What kind of question do teachers ask most frequently? What kind should they ask? Provide an example of each type.

Schema Theory and Background Knowledge

We know that background knowledge is an important component of reading comprehension. Can you think of instances in the past year in which your background knowledge has helped you to understand something you were reading? Do you have an example where a lack of background knowledge about a topic made it difficult to understand what you were reading?

Story Grammar and Reading Comprehension

Knowledge of story grammar supports reading comprehension. How could knowledge of the story grammar of a fairy tale help a student write her or his own fairy tale?

Critical Literacy

We often think of critical literacy as a skill for upper-grade and secondary students and adults. How early can children be involved in critical literacy lessons? How would you make a case for beginning in kindergarten or first grade?

Your Portfolio

Be sure to include a lesson plan for reading comprehension in your portfolio. It should include higher-order questions that lead students to activate background knowledge and use it to assimilate and then apply new knowledge from their reading. Are your only classroom experiences with kindergarten or first grade? If so, use a listening comprehension lesson, in which, instead of reading themselves, the children listen to the teacher read aloud.

Teaching Resources

There are many very useful comprehension strategies in this chapter. As you read, make a list of strategies and how they are used most effectively in lessons—as anticipation activities, for building knowledge, or as consolidation activities. As you begin teaching, refer to the list, and make an effort to use each item. Your students will appreciate the variety of approaches because they can become bored after encountering the same strategy on many occasions.

characters. That is, ask for a word that describes one character; then ask for an opposite word that describes the other character.

3. Now create two new columns beside each of the original two. Use one pair of these columns to list other characters in literature or movies or on television who are contrasted much as the original characters are. Use the other pair of columns to list people in the real world—in history, current events, or in our personal experience—who are similarly contrasted (see Figure 7.8).

THE LANGUAGE CHART. As a way to motivate children to think more deeply about themes and other features of the book, you might choose three or more books that share similarities and construct a language chart as a means of comparing them. **A language chart** (Roser & Hoffman, 1995) asks the same question about all of the books, as shown in Figure 7.9.

In life?	In books and movies?	JACK	THE GIANT	In books and movies?	In life?
Serfs ...	David Tweety R. Runner Harry Potter Frodo The Logans	Small Young Poor Uses wits & courage On his way up	Huge Old Rich Uses brute strength On his way down	Goliath Sylvester W. Coyote Valdemoort Saran Harlan Granger	Medieval Barons ...

FIGURE 7.8

Looking for Contrasts between Characters—Detail.

Books by William Steig	What Was the Problem?	What Was the Solution?	How Were Things Different at the End?
Sylvester and the Magic Pebble	Sylvester got turned into a rock.	His parents found the magic pebble and wished him back to his old self.	Sylvester was happy to be normal.
Caleb and Kate	Caleb got turned into a dog.	Kate said the magic words and changed him back.	Caleb and Kate were glad to be together.
The Amazing Bone	Pearl was going to be killed by a fox.	The bone said a charm and shrunk the fox.	Pearl was glad to be home with her family.

FIGURE 7.9

A Language Chart.

Children discuss these and other questions at the time they read each book. Then the teacher records a summary of their answers in the space provided on the chart. After they have read two books, they compare them according to the questions. Using a language chart has been shown to lead even young children into more analytical thinking about what they have read.

We have seen in this chapter that reading comprehension is a complex activity that includes readers'

- Prior knowledge and their willingness to use it to generate questions about what they are reading.
- Activity to seek answers to questions and construct meaning.
- Ability to follow the pattern or structure of the text.
- Metacognition—thinking about their understanding and rereading to repair their understanding when it fails.
- Making mental images of what is described in the text.
- Getting the main idea and supporting details.
- Making inferences.
- Connecting the meaning to other texts and to issues outside of the text.

There is no simple way to measure all that. The most thorough approaches to the assessment of comprehension are observations of the reader's attempts to comprehend. In addition, you may wish to use a more quickly administered device, recognizing that such a device will yield an incomplete picture of a reader's comprehension.

Approaches to assessing comprehension include the following:

- *Observational assessments:* You observe and assess students' comprehension behaviors as students demonstrate them in real reading tasks.
- *Self-assessments:* You ask students to observe and critique their own use of comprehension strategies. Self-assessments have the advantage of teaching students to be mindful of reading strategies and deliberate about in their use when they read.
- Quantitative assessments: Periodically, you might gather data that allow you to compare students' performance against some standard, such as grade-level expectations.

Observational Assessments

One kind of observational assessment is simply to keep a folder for each student into which you place observations about each student that you write down every few days. The observations consist of whatever strikes you as being worthy of note.

A more systematic way of making observational assessments is to keep a checklist of reading behaviors—in this case, comprehension behaviors. Schedule an eight- to ten-minute period every week to read with each child, individually or in a group of no more than four, and record observations on a checklist such as the one shown in Figure 7.10.

Student Self-Assessments

Self-assessments (see Figure 7.11) are recommended because they not only give the teacher some information about how the child is reading but also make the child aware of what she or he should be doing while reading. In other words, self-assessments teach at the same time that they assess reading behaviors.

Students will need to be taught what each of the questions on the self-assessment instrument mean. Each question can be presented in a mini-lesson and added to the self-assessment instrument after it has been taught. This means that the self-assessment instrument will get longer and more elaborate as the year goes on and as more component strategies of comprehension are taught and then added to the instrument.

Students can be given self-assessments to complete every two or three weeks. It is helpful to review the assessment instrument with the students just before they complete a reading assignment and have them fill out the assessment afterward. Discuss with the students how the strategies they indicate they are using help them to understand what they read. Talk over the strategies they still need to learn to use, and teach those strategies if necessary.

Quantitative Assessments

Teachers and students also need to know how well students are reading in comparison with their grade-level group. As we noted in Chapter 1, teachers and grade-level teams can focus attention on aspects of teaching that need improving, but only if they have evidence that tells them where the strengths of their instructional program are as well as the areas in which they need improvement.

Several kinds of assessment devices are available. For the purpose of getting a close look at readers' strengths and areas of need, probably the most informative are informal reading inventories. Informal reading inventories must be administered one at a time, so they are time consuming. But the fact that they yield both quantitative results (in terms of reading levels) and detailed portraits of most areas of students' reading abilities makes them worth the investment of time.

Informal reading inventories (IRIs) are thoroughly discussed in Gillet, Temple, and Crawford's *Understanding Reading Problems* (2007).

Although teachers can make their own IRIs, most teachers prefer to use commercially available ones. Here are some recommended informal reading inventories:

Temple, C., Crawford, A., & Gillet, J. (in press). *Developmental literacy inventory: Emergent reading through high school.* Boston: Allyn and Bacon.

Lauren, L., & Caldwell, J. (2005). *Qualitative reading inventory-4.* New York: Pearson Education.

Burns, P. C., & Roe, B. D. (2006). *Informal reading inventory: Preprimer to grade twelve.* Boston: Houghton Mifflin.

Silvaroli, N., & Wheelock, W. (2003). *Classroom reading inventory.* New York: McGraw-Hill.

Applegate, M. D., Quinn, K. B., & Applegate, A. J. (2003). *The critical reading inventory.* New York: Pearson Education.

For more information on IRIs, see Chapters 10 and 12. Other procedures for assessing reading comprehension, including the Cloze procedure and the Lexiles Framework, are discussed in Chapter 10.

Student's name: _____ Date: _____ Observer: _____

Material read: _____ Level: _____

1. Before reading

a) The reader demonstrated familiarity with the topic (or the author or the genre) of the text before reading.

No prior knowledge shown	Some prior knowledge shown	Much prior knowledge shown

b) The reader raised questions about the content of the text before reading.

No questions offered even when asked	Vague questions raised when asked to by teacher	Precise and informed questions offered

c) The reader was able to make predictions about what was coming in the text.

No predictions offered even when asked	Imprecise or illogical predictions made when asked for by teacher	Made logical predictions spontaneously

2. During reading

a) The reader read aloud with animation that honored the meaning of the text.

Expressionless reading	Sometimes showed emphasis and drama	Consistently showed proper emphasis and reflected the dramatic contours of the text

b) The reader knew the vocabulary in the text.

Did not know many key words	Knew most key words; used context for some but not all others	Knew almost all key words and was able to use context to figure out others

(Continues)

FIGURE 7.10

Observational Checklist for Assessing Comprehension.

c) The reader continued to ask questions and make predictions.

No questions or predictions even when asked	Some questions and predictions when asked by the teacher	Asked insightful questions and made reasonable predictions

d) The reader found answers to questions or confirmed predictions.

Seldom	Sometimes, when asked	Consistently

e) The reader was able to make inferences.

Unable to, even when asked	Occasionally, when asked	Consistently, and picked up on subtle nuances

f) The reader monitored comprehension.

Frequently misread text without self-correction	Occasionally misread text and made some self-corrections	Rarely misread text or always self-corrected

3. After reading

a) The reader could retell or summarize the text.

The retelling had major gaps	The retelling was fairly complete	The retelling was complete, and the reader summarized the main points

b) The reader could interpret the text.

Offered limited response or interpretation when asked	Offered responses to aspects of the text	Offered personal response to or interpretation of the main point of the text

FIGURE 7.10

Continued

	Not at all	A little bit	A lot
Before Reading			
I thought about what I knew about the topic of the reading.			
I thought of things I wanted to find out.			
It was a story. I tried to predict what would happen.			
While Reading			
I read with expression to make it sound real.			
I thought about what I was finding out.			
It was a story. I predicted what would happen next.			
I was able to figure out words I didn't know from the words around them.			
I was able to tell what was going on, even when the author didn't come right out and say it.			
After Reading			
I thought back over what I had found out so I would remember it later.			
I thought about what it meant to me.			
I thought about why the author wrote this text and what he or she was trying to say.			

Your name: Today's date:

What you read: Pages:

FIGURE 7.11

Student Self-Assessment.

Differentiated Instruction

Placing Students in the Proper Level Material

If a student is especially interested in a topic, or if he already knows a lot about it, he will be able to read a more challenging text about that topic than he might otherwise. Nonetheless, a student's reading level is a normally good indicator of the level of text that student should be expected to read. Many times in this text we have referred to the independent level as the level of a text easy enough for a student to read with accurate word recognition and sufficient understanding that the student will not require help. In measurement terms, that means the child should read with 90 percent comprehension, which is to say that he can answer at least nine questions out of ten or retell nine important points out of ten. If she is to read a text with the support of a teacher, then a rate of comprehension between 70 or 75 percent and 90 percent would be expected.

Once students have been assessed, they should be placed in text material that is at the proper reading level for the instructional task, even if that means moving a student up to more challenging material or down to less challenging material.

For Review

Reading comprehension is using the knowledge we already have to understand the new information we find in the text. It is an active process in which we quest after new knowledge and make meaning in the process. Responding to literature, too, is an active process in which we bring our own expectations and associations to the words the author has strung along the pages of the text.

Comprehension has several components: knowing the vocabulary of a text and being able to follow the text's structure, visualizing it, making predictions about it, summarizing its meaning, getting the main ideas in it, making inferences within it, interpreting it, arguing with it, and monitoring one's comprehension of it.

To encourage students to carry out that activity, there are teaching techniques we can use before, during, and after the reading or during the phases of a lesson we have called anticipation, building knowledge, and consolidation. In the anticipation phase, we remind students to think of what they already know about a topic, raise questions about what they are about to read, and otherwise prepare for reading. In the building knowledge phase, we guide students in using strategies to set expectations and meet them and to clarify meanings. In the consolidation stage, we have a host of methods for having students think back over what they have gained from the reading, respond to it, interpret it, critique it, apply it, and debate it.

In this chapter, we also stressed the importance of assessing students' comprehension. The three general approaches we discussed were observations, self-assessments, and quantitative assessments.

For Your Journal

1. Return to your answers to the anticipation guide that opened this chapter. Look at the items for which your answers remained the same. In your journal, explain how you came to know the answers. Look at the items to which your answers changed, and explain how your thinking has changed.

2. This chapter explained how reading comprehension of fiction and response to literature work. Chapter 8 focuses on teaching students to comprehend and learn from informational text. What do you think the main differences are between teaching students to comprehend and respond to fiction and teaching them to do this for informational text?

3. Recall the vignette of Hank da Silva's classroom that began this chapter. He used a combination of strategies for teaching students to read with comprehension. Think of a class you have taught or might teach. Describe the combination you might choose from the reading comprehension strategies you have seen in this chapter. How would you make them work together?

Taking It to the World

1. When they observed skilled teachers teaching reading comprehension, Michael Pressley and his colleagues (1996) found that they usually taught their students to do the following:

   - Make predictions of what was to come in the text based on their prior knowledge

   - Generate questions about issues in the text

   - Seek clarification about confusing parts

   - Form mental images of what they read

   - Relate what they already knew to what they are reading in the text

   - Make summaries of what they have read

   Alone or with a group of your fellow students, observe three reading lessons in a primary grade school. Do these six activities capture what the teachers are doing by way of helping the children read with comprehension? Do they do other things as well, such as encouraging students to make inferences or debate about what they read?

2. Go to a school, and practice a shared inquiry lesson (see pp. 220–221). Make sure you use a text that has core of mystery to it (many folktales work fine), and prepare your questions carefully according to the criteria given on page 220. Before you put the questions to the children, though, write out your own best answers to your questions. How do the students' answers compare to yours? Are you surprised? If so, what surprises you and why?

3. Using the text you used with your shared inquiry lesson, try the dramatic activities described on page 225 with your classmates. Then try the activity out in an elementary school. What different insights about the text come to light when you dramatize it rather than discuss it?

Technology Connections

1. In 2001, the International Reading Association (IRA) issued a position statement on the use of information and communication technology (ICT). Visit the International Reading Association online (**www.reading.org**) and locate this position statement, entitled "Integrating Literacy and Technology into the Curriculum." Summarize the context of the statement. What are the six rights the IRA believes students have with regard to ICT? What will be teachers' primary challenges in addressing these rights?

2. The Great Books Foundation offers training in their methods, including the shared inquiry method, in many places in North America. Visit the foundation's Web site (**www.greatbooks.org**) to find further information. What materials or trainings are available through the organization?

Connect with Research

Review the following key words from the chapter, and then connect to Research Navigator (**www.researchnavigator.com**) through this book's Companion Website to conduct a search into research on each of the various topics as they relate to reading and literacy education today.

aesthetic stance
anticipation
building knowledge
character cluster
character maps
concatenated
consolidation
constructivist approach

critical literacy
Directed Reading-Thinking
   Activity
efferent stance
genres
inferences
language chart
reader response theory

reading for structured
   opposites
schema
schema theory
story map
taxonomies
word conversation

Companion Website

To access chapter objectives, practice tests, weblinks, and flashcards, visit the Companion Website at **www.ablongman.com/templeallchildren2e.**

Go to Allyn & Bacon's MyLabSchool (**www.mylabschool.com**), enter Assignment ID RMV7 into the Assignment Finder. Watch the video, *Literature and the Reading Process,* in which a teacher discusses how she uses fiction and nonfiction books and articles to promote steps in the reading process.

Question: How can teachers select and use literature as a supplement to text-books? You may also answer the questions at the end of the clip and e-mail your responses to your instructor.

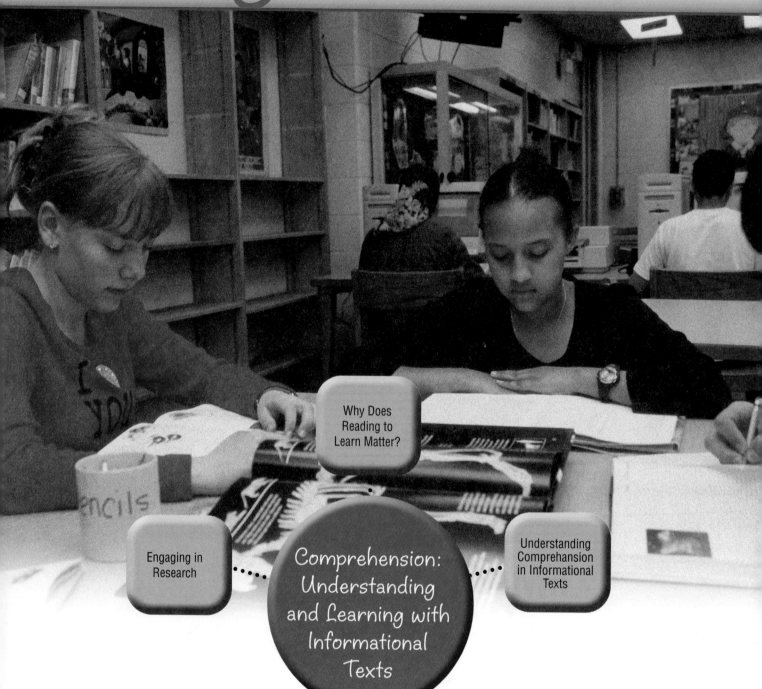

chapter 8

Why Does Reading to Learn Matter?

Engaging in Research

Comprehension: Understanding and Learning with Informational Texts

Understanding Comprehansion in Informational Texts

Strategies for Active Reading of Informational Text

The Nature of Informational Texts

Comprehension: Understanding and Learning with Informational Texts

 ## Anticipation Guide

The following statements will stimulate your thinking about the topics of this chapter. Answer true or false in response to each statement. As you read and learn more about the topics in these statements, double-check your answers. See what interests you and prompts your curiosity toward more understanding.

_____ There has been a big shift from fiction reading to informational reading by adult readers in the United States.

_____ Primary children get too confused with the different formats of nonfiction texts. Instruction in using nonfiction should wait for third grade and above.

_____ Teachers in the United States have changed their teaching practices to show students how to comprehend informational material.

_____ One of the best ways to show students how to read informational text with comprehension is to read an informational text yourself and discuss it with your students.

_____ Having prior knowledge helps students to comprehend, but one kind of prior knowledge is about as useful as another.

_____ Students who have had an extensive introduction to a topic are likely to be more motivated to learn about it than are those with only superficial knowledge.

_____ Just as stories have a "grammar" that readers can follow to understand the story, informational texts have recognizable structures.

_____ Reading strategies for informational texts are the same as those for fiction.

_____ Informational texts have so many different structures that there is little point in teaching students the parts of an informational text.

_____ When it comes to teaching vocabulary, teachers should stress only the words the authors of the text prioritize.

Reading to Learn in a Primary Classroom

Teacher Debbie Gurvitz likes to introduce her first- and second-grade students to informational reading through integrated units of study. In the spring, she develops an expanded science unit that involves real problem-based inquiry. It serves as a way of expanding students' reading skills in nonfiction and of teaching some science standards. Recently, Ms. Gurvitz focused the unit on pond life and the relationship between the quality of the water for animals and the human community. To introduce the unit, she invited a naturalist from the local nature preserve to speak to the students. When the naturalist showed the students some of the animals from the pond, they became fascinated with the mutant frog he included. "Wow, that's weird!" "That doesn't look like the frog I have at home. Who did that to it?" "What happened?" The children's questions came naturally and quickly. Garth, one of the first graders, expressed the feelings of the whole group when he said, "Ms. Gurvitz, we really have a problem!"

Ms. Gurvitz took her lead from the children and helped them to focus their study of the natural environment on the frog problem. They began by framing the problem—exploring what facts and information they already knew and identifying the questions they had. They made a list of what they knew about frogs on a large piece of chart paper. She helped them write questions for research; these also filled a sheet of chart paper and were hung on the wall. As a result of these discussions, she divided the class into smaller groups that searched for information to help solve the problem. In this case, it was a very real problem. Scientists do not understand why so many frogs in the area are being born with strange-looking body parts. This created an authentic study full of the kinds of ambiguities that are found in most scientific research.

Ms. Gurvitz was careful to make sure she could locate the kinds of reading texts the children could read. She wanted some that would be at an independent level for all the children and some that would be good instructional-level texts for her guided reading groups. After collecting the books, she leveled them to ensure that she could accommodate the whole class with appropriate materials.

In considering the language arts and reading objectives she wanted to address, Ms. Gurvitz focused instruction on helping students find answers to questions they posed. She wanted them to learn to use the table of contents and the index in books to locate the information they needed. She knew this would be a good opportunity for them to learn to make decisions about what sections of a text they would read and to gain control over information searching as contrasted with fictional reading. She also wanted the children to learn to make notes about what information they were collecting so that those notes could guide their reporting. To do this, she made copies of the Amazing Fact Sheet (see Figure 8.1) and put them in a shoe box on the inquiry table so students could take one whenever they wanted to save some interesting or important information.

As she introduced this way of making notes, Ms. Gurvitz used one child as a model. Side by side at the overhead transparency, Ms. Gurvitz and Andrew made a note card of the information he wanted to remember.

"Andrew, what do you want to write?" Ms. Gurvitz asked.

"It says that frogs lay lots of eggs in water," Andrew replied.

Ms. Gurvitz encouraged him, "So, can you write that on your Amazing Fact Sheet?" As Andrew began to write on a transparency, the other children watched. When he tried to write "water," he hesitated.

"What is giving you trouble with that word?" Ms. Gurvitz asked. "Can you find it written somewhere?"

With that nudge, Andrew turned to the book again and located the word; without any further help, he finished his writing. Ms. Gurvitz reminded him to list the book title, the author, and the page that contains the fact on his note. Finished, he then signed the note on the Reporter line.

Ms. Gurvitz praised his efforts: "Good work, Andrew."

She concluded the mini-lesson by reminding the children that when they found interesting information, they should write that on an Amazing Fact Sheet and put it in the Amazing Facts Box on the counter. Each morning, Andrew and other children read their cards during the morning share time and used them to build their knowledge.

When parents volunteered, Ms. Gurvitz gave them specific guidelines on how to work with the children. Some helped children to record information on their Amazing Fact Sheets. Ms. Gurvitz also asked parents to involve their children in talking about what they learned when they were at home. Some Home Links letters included specific questions parents were to ask their children and space for them to record what the children told them. These letters were sent home regularly to inform parents of what the children were doing and help them become part of the learning activities. The children would then return these links the next day to be shared in class.

The children got very involved in this unit of research, and so did several of the families. One family created a frog pond in their own yard, and the children loved

hearing about its progress. By the conclusion of the unit, each student had a report prepared by himself or herself and their research team report. Large murals the children created gave a focus for their presentations of results to the class and to visiting classes that came to learn from their study.

Assessment is an integral part of good instructional planning. In her work as a primary teacher, Ms. Gurvitz is always assessing her students' development as learners. She finds the integrated units a natural place to teach (attend to details of reading), provide guided practice, and then have opportunities to observe how the children apply her teaching of strategies in their individual work and in the group projects. During guided reading using the frog and pond texts, she monitored each child and periodically did a running record of the child's performance with attention to his or her strategy use. She had no problem in checking to see whether the students monitored their own reading for meaning. She knew that they were full of questions, and their Amazing Fact Sheets provided records of the information they gained. When they read their own fact sheets during the class share, she got another chance to watch them read their own writing and then explain what they knew in response to other students' questions.

Ms. Gurvitz noted that some children actually moved to higher levels of books as a result of their increased familiarity

with the words in the unit that occurred regularly. She monitored their reading carefully because she did not want to push students too quickly and knew that as they read in other materials, they might not have the same level of knowledge to support their reading. Yet the students gained real confidence in their reading as they explored many books and articles about frogs. As students worked in groups, Ms. Gurvitz was by their side, observing how they used the information they gathered to think about their aspect of the problem. Some children became good at locating facts in the books they read; others relied on the clear visual diagrams and photographs in the texts. All the children had their own responsibilities and also completed Home Links periodically, so she had ways of monitoring their independent work, too. At the end of the unit, as the groups presented the findings of their research, Ms. Gurvitz carefully recorded notes on each child's performance. When parents came in for conferences, she had a rich set of notes on what the children had read, their growth in reading and writing, and their part in the class learning experiences that she could share with the parents.

FIGURE 8.1

Amazing Fact
Sheet.

AMAZING FACT SHEET

An amazing fact about frogs is that

_____

_____

Found in (provide the source of your information)

_____

Written by _____ p. _____

Reporter _____

To be human is to be a learner. Young children are full of questions, so many that parents and teachers are sometimes amazed by the depth and breadth of children's curiosity. As we grow, we continue to be curious about the world around us and ask questions. To find answers to these questions, we read informational materials—from textbooks like this one to cookbooks, travel guides, biographies, self-help and diet books, and newspapers and magazines. To be successful learners in school, students must also learn to read and study about concepts that society considers important. These are generally elaborated on in textbooks and other reference materials. Therefore, it is important for teachers to prioritize helping young readers develop the joy in and ability to read a wide range of materials. They need guidance so they can become confident and flexible readers empowered by the variety of strategies they have developed to navigate the wide range of materials and formats in the informational materials they encounter daily. They also need to learn to study new material and find strategies that will help them retain that material.

Why Does Reading to Learn Matter?

Much of the reading we do is to learn. Schools require students to use textbooks and a wide variety of other resource materials throughout the grades. Unfortunately, too often we just assume that students will develop good strategies for using informational materials and knowing how to prioritize what they need to remember. Most schools also spend little time teaching students how to use informational materials effectively for answering their own questions and for creating reports. Yet this kind of reading becomes increasingly important as students progress through the grades. Most content courses still depend heavily on textbooks, but no one seems to take the responsibility to teach students to use these resources effectively. Most middle and secondary school teachers also expect students to engage in independent research and write informational essays and reports. The skills needed to be successful learners can be introduced in the primary grades and developed throughout the grades. (See the Standards and Literacy box.)

What we read outside of school also underscores the importance of knowing how to read and use informational materials. Recent research studies on the reading habits of adults reflect the shift away from fiction to informational reading and nonfiction sources (Smith, 2000). We read newspapers and magazines to find out about the world around us and our favorite activities. We browse the Web to gain in-depth information and alternative points

Content Area Standards

The standards of many states now include expectations that students be able to read and learn from informational texts. Although traditional reading instruction has focused on story reading, a real shift is occurring, and both fiction and informational reading are being highlighted. Standards such as the following are frequently found:

- Use information to form questions.
- Summarize content using text organization.
- Use table of contents.

- Use information presented in simple tables, pictures, and charts.

Standards for teachers also may specifically address the importance of teaching content reading. For example, Illinois now has a reading strategy standard for all content area teachers. Check to see what you will be expected to know and be able to do as a teacher helping students with reading to learn. Then examine the instruction provided to elementary students in your schools. Do students have regular opportunities to engage with informational texts and build their confidence by reading a wide range of materials?

of view. We read self-help books and books on health and fitness because we want to improve our health and lifestyle. We read spiritual and religious books to reflect on our beliefs and deepen our quality of living.

As a society, we are shifting from a nation of fiction readers to a people who read a preponderance of **informational texts.** We want to know as much as possible—about ourselves as well as the rest of the world. Publishers recognize this shift in interests and are publishing more and more informational texts, both printed and electronic. The wide range of magazines being published reflects the wide range of reader interests. Just check a magazine stand for the hundreds of specific topics that are available to address particular interests and tastes of readers. The best-seller lists generally have one section for fiction, another for nonfiction, and often a third for self-help books. One of the real transformations in the last decade has been the explosion of materials available for us to read on an enormous range of topics on the Web as well as in more traditional publishing venues.

Knowledge Standards and High-Stakes Assessment

The current focus on knowledge standards and measuring what students learn each year puts pressure on teachers to cover more content. This means that students are asked to read more and remember what they are taught. In this climate of rising expectations, students who have read widely possess the background knowledge that enables them to remember new material and deepen their knowledge schemata. (See Chapter 7 for a discussion of the role of schemata in reading and comprehending.) Instead of diminishing, the demands on learners as readers are increasing.

Another implication of the current accountability climate for teachers is that even the assessments of students' reading abilities are now much more balanced between reading for literary purposes and reading to learn. These newer assessments reflect the fact that for students to be successful as readers throughout schooling and life, they need to read for a variety of purposes from a variety of materials. Reading fiction for pleasure is only one of many forms reading takes. More important for school success across the curriculum is the ability to read informational texts and learn from them (Ogle & Blachowicz, 2001). Standardized tests, state performance assessments, and the current international tests (Donahue et al., 2001; Organization for Economic Cooperation & Development, 2000; Sainsbury, 2001) all incorporate a variety of materials and purposes. Reading for information is as important as reading for literary purposes. Many state standards tests balance fiction with informational passages. Standardized tests also include a range of reading passages and expect students to be able to read for literary purposes, for information, and to perform tasks.

Instructional Priorities

I've found that the hardest thing about teaching reading is incorporating strategies beyond the very structured reading program that they require me to use. Another is finding time to meet all of the standards while looking beyond reading and mathematics. My students know nothing about history and science.

—Mary,
First-Year Teacher,
Grades 4–5
Los Angeles

Despite the priority being placed on informational reading in society and in tests, the data collected recently in studies of classrooms (Duke, 2000; Pressley et al., 2001; Taylor, Graves, & Ven Den Broek, 2000) indicate that primary teachers have not shifted their teaching to reflect these higher expectations of students. Most primary teachers are still using fiction almost exclusively in their teaching. This is not adequate preparation for children who will live most of their literate lives in a culture of nonfiction with responsibility to learn from their engagements with texts of many types. Studies in intermediate classrooms replicating Durkin's early work (1978–1979) also indicate that little instruction is given to students on how to read informational texts (Pressley et al., 1998). Responsible teachers need to provide a broad range of instruction in reading strategies and purposes and make students comfortable negotiating a variety of text types. Students deserve this help so that they can be successful learners for life.

Because purpose has such a powerful effect on individual reading habits, it is important to provide opportunities for many purposes, from learning new information to performing tasks to recreating experiences and representing them in new ways. Teachers need to prioritize the importance of learning to read and remembering information in textbooks and the reference materials that are used heavily in schools. This kind of reading ability often determines whether students will be successful throughout their schooling.

Informational reading does not develop automatically and deserves concerted attention by teachers. In addition, teachers need to help students use a variety of materials as they engage in inquiry and report writing. Reading across texts, comparing authors and ideas, and evaluating materials are important priorities in many assessments. Students' abilities to read, write, and think critically will become even more important in the future, especially with the range of unedited ideas available on the Internet. Today's classrooms need to reflect the kinds of experiences that will help students develop these skills throughout their elementary and middle school years.

Teachers as Role Models

Teachers can help students become engaged readers of informational materials by modeling such reading themselves. They can use their own insights as a starting point in helping students; they can provide immersion in and demonstrations of a variety of informational texts. By sharing widely ranging forms of reading—from newspapers to professional books and articles, to biographies and autobiographies, and other materials—teachers can help students appreciate the breadth of what reading is and set the stage to help students develop the different strategies they can use in reading.

A natural starting place is to share some personal reading interests with students. You can talk about what you read, share some materials with them, and then read aloud from these materials and from good informational texts at the students' level. A good guideline is to read daily from a variety of informational materials. For example, read interesting pieces from the newspaper, perhaps about how to raise special flowering plants, about current music or entertainment, or something about the foods we eat. You and your students can learn together. This is often one of the gifts of reading to learn: With the changing nature of our world, we all can learn together. Later in the day, read aloud something related to a topic the class is studying, from a more difficult text than the students would be able to handle themselves—perhaps a biography or magazine article. This can be valuable in helping the students understand that their curriculum relates to what others know and care about and can help them develop a broader vocabulary and sense of how content is structured by adults.

Understanding Comprehension in Informational Texts

Learning from reading is an active, ongoing process that can be described by what we do before, during, and after engagement with a text. Just as we do with reading literature (see Chapter 7), we follow the simple ABCs of reading to learn. We begin by anticipating what we want and need to learn. Then we build knowledge as we read and engage with authors. Finally, we consolidate the ideas with what we previously knew, sometimes modifying those ideas and sometimes expanding on them. This ongoing process is also a recursive one. That is, with each new set of ideas we read, we rethink what we knew, ask new questions and set new purposes, and build on the ideas that are freshly ours. Some essential aspects that undergird active reading to learn include the following:

- Assessing schemata or prior knowledge
- Assuming a metacognitive orientation
- Setting one's own purposes and asking questions
- Actively seeking information and making notes so that it can be retained for connecting and organizing ideas
- Forming interpretations of what is read
- Consolidating new information and ideas
- Analyzing and evaluating the sources and adequacy of information
- Creating a synthesis and representation of the learning that can be shared
- Reaching conclusions about and finding applications of what has been learned

As students develop their own control over reading to learn, all of these aspects of the process need attention. How teachers introduce learning tasks to students and give students instructional tools to use as they learn will determine to a great degree students' success at becoming learners. Planning carefully across each year, beginning with initial assessment of what students already know and can do and then structuring good teaching and guided practice activities will lead both teachers and students to success.

The Importance of Background Knowledge

Reading is always an active, constructive process during which students need to activate what they know to make sense of text. As we noted in Chapter 7, readers comprehend by having the details in the material they are reading lead them to evoke relevant knowledge **schemata**. Then they use these schemata to give meaning to the details and, ideally, to understand the meaning of the whole passage. There are at least four kinds of background knowledge that readers need in order to comprehend well. The first is knowledge of the vocabulary. The second is knowledge of text structure. The third and fourth deal with content knowledge, both topical and principled.

VOCABULARY. One of the most important tools to understanding content is having a grasp of how the key terms are used in a

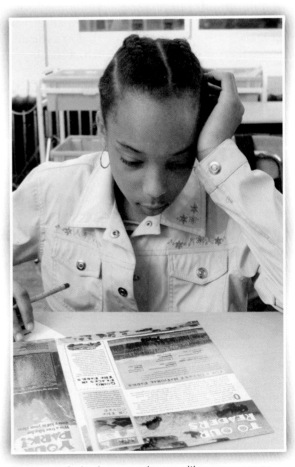

The layout of a book or magazine can either encourage or impede the understanding of the content. What would the design of a textbook need to look like to be attractive to middle school students?

specific content. Vocabulary represents the knowledge of words and their meanings. In reading, the issue of vocabulary knowledge ranges between word recognition and comprehension. In word recognition, children may labor to recognize a word in print, but once they recognize it, they know the spoken word and its meaning. On the meaning end, students might be able to recognize or sound out a word but not comprehend its meaning, or they might recognize a word and know some but not all of its meanings. Obviously, a reader must know the meanings of most of the words in a text to read it successfully.

KNOWLEDGE OF TEXT STRUCTURE.   The structure of a text is a little like the grammar of a sentence. Because you understand the grammar of a sentence such as "The man bit the dog," you know who was bitten and who did the biting. In the same fashion, if you understand the structures of stories, you know how to follow a plot. If you can understand the structure of explanations, you know how to find the questions and get the answers to them. If you understand the structure of persuasive writing, you know how to spot the claim and weigh the support for it (Goldman & Rakestraw, 2000). The more you know about the way informational articles and texts are generally organized, the more you will be able to predict and read actively. This knowledge of structure also helps you retain what you read, because you can organize the ideas into major categories for memory.

TOPICAL CONTENT KNOWLEDGE.   The term **topical content knowledge** represents a fairly shallow level of knowledge, consisting of little more than some passing familiarity with the subject of the reading. For example, assume that while reading a little girl is faced with a scientific passage about ducks. If she has seen a Donald Duck cartoon (and realizes that the character of Donald is based loosely on a real duck), she will have some topical knowledge about ducks. She will realize ducks have beaks, two wings, and two webbed feet and that they make quacking sounds. This amount of knowledge will not help much when reading a scientific text about ducks, but at least it will help the child picture what is being talked about.

PRINCIPLED CONTENT KNOWLEDGE.   In contrast to topical content knowledge, **principled content knowledge** is knowledge of a deeper kind. It consists of familiarity with the topic as well as an understanding of its parts, its causes and effects, and other issues related to it (Gelman & Greeno, 1989). For example, readers who have studied the lives of geese and know something of the lives of migratory aquatic birds will have principled knowledge with which to understand a scientific passage about ducks. Readers with principled knowledge are better prepared to understand challenging passages than readers who have only topical knowledge. Their curiosity is likely to be deeper, and their expectations will conform more closely to the unfolding presentation of information in the text. The reader with topical knowledge, by contrast, might recognize isolated parts of the information in the text but will be less prepared to make sense of the flow of information or the more important ideas in the text.

The Teacher's Role in Guiding Instruction

The choices teachers make in determining instructional focus and the kind of guidance they provide greatly influence how students think as they read and make a difference in the kinds of knowledge students gain about the subject matter in the curriculum. Too often, content reading becomes frustrating for both students and teachers. To prevent this, teachers need to take care to focus instructional time on the most important aspects of comprehension development. As we already noted, a key is to ensure that students have an understanding of how the content or text they are reading is organized. This framework provides a structure within which students can distinguish key ideas from those of lesser importance. During instruction, teachers have several important tasks. These include modeling and guiding engagement with text, teaching skills and strategies, eliciting students' own interests and motivation, and providing adequate time for students to explore ideas and concepts in depth.

DEVELOPING PRINCIPLED KNOWLEDGE. The kinds of knowledge students gain about the subject matter in the curriculum is very important. In reading to learn, the content-specific information needs attention, something that is not a priority when reading fiction. A key to comprehending a text is linking ideas presented within and across sentences to create a sense of a whole text. Teachers influence students' knowledge formation in two important ways: by the questions they ask and by the depth of study they encourage with their students.

The questions teachers ask. The ideas to which you call children's attention, by means of your questions or comments, influence the course of the children's thinking about what they read and study. You can direct students' attention toward important ideas or trivial ones. When reading a story, it makes a difference whether you dwell on minor details or ask questions that call attention to the deep structural elements of the story: the character's problem, goal, conflicts, and solutions to problems or the author's message or theme in the story. When reading informational text, it matters whether you call attention to minor details or to important ideas such as chronological development, cause and effect, or hierarchical relationships between ideas.

The depth to which teachers lead children to study a topic. You can encourage children to gain deeper knowledge about topics by staying with subjects for more than brief periods. You also can enhance children's understanding by looking at topics through many different disciplines. For example, look at a historical phenomenon such as immigration through fictional works in addition to the social studies text. By seeing phenomena through the eyes of fictional participants, students have more possibility of connecting with, visualizing, and interpreting the concept. Lengthy discussions, especially those that make connections between the subject of study and the children's own experience, also make it more likely that children will form deep, principled knowledge about a subject (see Allington & Johnston, 2002).

SKILLS AND STRATEGIES. In addition to some background knowledge with which to understand text, readers need skills and strategies. **Skills** are processes that readers use habitually. **Strategies** are the processes by which they use their skills under conscious control. Teachers need to know what skills and strategies students possess and consciously develop a strong repertoire in all students.

When children first learn to read, they may be taught to perform comprehension activities consciously as reading strategies. For example, when they come across a word they do not know, the teacher might urge them to read to the end of the line to get a sense of the meaning of the sentence, then go back and guess the unknown word. This strategy is known as the *reading ahead/reread activity*. Later on—possibly much later on and after continued support from the teacher—when the readers habitually use the context to figure out unknown words, the behavior has become a skill.

When readers are working with difficult material, however, or when they want to be especially careful in their reading, skilled readers often employ some reading strategies consciously (Pressley & Afflerbach, 1995). For example, even when their reading skills are adequate for comprehending a reading in a social studies text, readers might choose consciously to apply the strategy of summarizing and rehearsing main ideas to remember them for a discussion the next day.

INTEREST AND MOTIVATION. Performing acts of comprehension takes some effort, and exerting effort takes will. No wonder children are more likely to take the trouble to do what they need to do to understand what they read when the topic is interesting to them. This fact, although not always honored in school curriculum, has been recognized for the better part of a century (Beane, 2002; Dewey, 1913; Guthrie & Davis, 2003). But readers may be interested in a topic in different ways, and these differences have consequences. In the chapter-opening vignette, as Ms. Gurvitz began her unit on the pond, she had a naturalist speak with the children and show them samples of the frogs that were deformed. This piqued their interest. Readers might be interested in a topic because it has been presented in an engaging way—with exciting illustrations or dramatically written and with explanation points. Or they might be interested because they have some reason to find out more about a topic and they want to know more about the line of inquiry the text is following. For example, because you want to know how to help your present or future students read with comprehension, you might find this textbook of particular interest. You likely don't need movie poster–like illustrations to draw you into the ideas presented here. If you pick up the Sunday magazine in your newspaper, however, it might take an interesting picture with a curiosity-provoking caption to get you interested in reading about something that is new to you.

These individual **motivations** for learning correspond to the kinds of prior knowledge readers have about a topic. Readers who have principled knowledge about a topic tend to be interested in adding to and deepening that knowledge, whereas readers with the shallower, topical knowledge might not be motivated automatically to learn more about something through reading. Research has shown (Alexander, 1998) that readers with these different kinds of background knowledge notice different things in a text. Readers with only topical knowledge might focus on flashy or exotic details to the exclusion of main ideas and arguments, whereas those with principled knowledge might do just the opposite.

THE "MATTHEW EFFECT": ASPECTS OF COMPREHENSION ARE INTERRELATED.

What we have just considered as separate aspects of comprehension—prior knowledge, strategies and skills, and interest—are in fact interrelated. Although it is true, as Duffy and Roehler (1989) and others have shown, that children can profit from being taught to carry out comprehension strategies, it is also true that reading comprehension develops as a conglomerate of achievements (Alexander et al., 1994). For example, engaging prior knowledge can be helped along by teaching; however, for this teaching to be successful, children must have some prior knowledge of the topic to call on. Moreover, children are more likely to have deep enough interests in the topic to use the strategies of applying prior knowledge, making predictions, arguing with the text, or finding main ideas, unless their prior knowledge is deep and principled. To carry this point further, if their prior knowledge about a topic is deep and principled, then their interest in the topic will also extend below the surface to main ideas and structures of argument.

The process is cyclic and is an example of what researcher Keith Stanovich (1986) called the "Matthew effect" in reading. If young readers have deep and principled knowledge, they will have deep interest; if they have deep interest, they will use thorough-going strategies of comprehension; and if they use thorough-going strategies, they will gain more principled knowledge (see Figure 8.2). The cycle works the other way, too. A reader might lack deep knowledge, not habitually use thorough-going reading strategies, or have only superficial interest in the topics being read. These factors may interact to prevent satisfactory comprehension. The best teaching for comprehension, then, includes attention to all these aspects:

- Creating a learning environment in which students can become immersed in a topic over time and explore it deeply
- Guiding students' attention to the way the texts they read are organized
- Helping students develop principled knowledge by encouraging children to consider ideas deeply, and pointing them toward the main ideas and the underlying structures and issues
- Teaching thorough-going, powerful strategies for comprehending and remembering and then supporting and reinforcing these strategies until they become habituated into skills
- Engaging children in deep discussions of what they read and getting them to think about, write about, and respond to what they read so they will understand issues deeply and extend their curiosity about things in the world

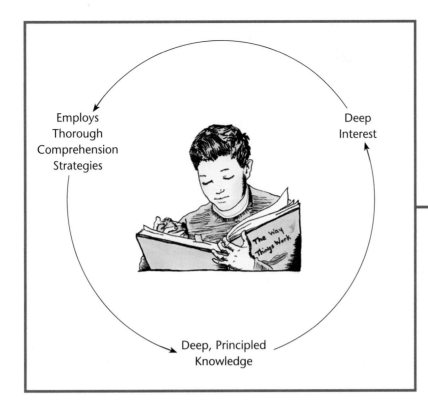

FIGURE 8.2

The Matthew Effect in Reading Comprehension.

- Focusing their attention on the vocabulary of the topic or area so they develop a more precise way of thinking and differentiating ideas
- Encouraging students' questions and taking their inquiry seriously, weaving their deep-seated interests into the very fabric of the school day

Student Engagement

Although the teacher's role in developing a thoughtful classroom is critical, students play equally important roles as learners. Right from the beginning of the school year, teachers need to take time to observe how students approach learning. How involved and aware are students of what learning entails? They need to be active—and interactive—if they are going to be successful learners. People learn best when they do so strategically. That means taking charge of their own reading with a clear purpose. Just as in reading fiction (see Chapter 7), students need to be actively engaged while reading and learning from nonfiction and other content materials. Because content material is usually dense with ideas to be learned, the following strategies are especially important.

ANTICIPATING. Students need to anticipate, to ask what they want to learn from the reading. They do this by first assessing what they know and what the task demands are and what needs to be accomplished. For young students, this initial orientation is modeled in the K-W-L framework discussed later in this chapter. As students begin their engagement with a new topic, watch them and discuss with them how they begin. Do they skim through the material and activate what they know and make connections with the text? Do they look closely at diagrams or pictures and think about their meaning?

Once students have assessed their starting point in learning, they then need to develop a plan for how to proceed to accomplish their goals. That means knowing that there are options for how to proceed. Students too often think that all they can do is read and then reread. Rather, they need to know they can use a variety of tools to guide their acquisition of knowledge. They are going to want to make notes when they encounter new information that is important or use some form of marginal notation if they can keep the

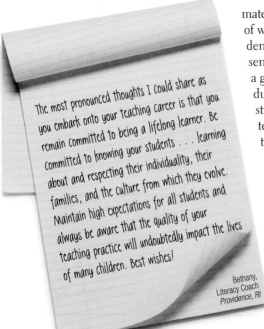

The most pronounced thoughts I could share as you embark onto your teaching career is that you remain committed to being a lifelong learner. Be committed to knowing your students . . . learning about and respecting their individuality, their families, and the culture from which they evolve. Maintain high expectations for all students and always be aware that the quality of your teaching practice will undoubtedly impact the lives of many children. Best wishes!

Bethany,
Literacy Coach
Providence, RI

materials. Stick-on notes serve wonderful purposes in helping students keep track of what they want to learn. These notes can then be grouped later by the student to chunk information in a way that will give the student a more coherent sense of what is to be learned. Some students learn best when they can create a graphic network of ideas or draw diagrams of what they learn. Being active during the process of learning is essential. It takes little time to check whether students have some active strategies they use when reading informational material that is full of important concepts and main ideas. (Several strategies that support students' active engagement are discussed later in the chapter.)

BUILDING KNOWLEDGE. Students build knowledge as they deal with the ideas they are reading about. That means monitoring what they are thinking and learning, asking questions as they go, and creating summaries of ideas for themselves. Some students like to think aloud, others make notes in the margin or on sheets of paper, some prefer drawing key ideas to represent the text's main ideas, and some like to share with another person what they are getting out of a text as they read. Teachers need to model each of these approaches to building new learning. Asking students to put stick-on notes in their text material as they read is an easy diagnostic of how they attend to important elements of these texts. As you expand their options for engaged reading and help them practice these strategies frequently, your students will become better equipped to make decisions about which work best for them in particular situations.

CONSOLIDATING WHAT THEY LEARN. As students continue to build their knowledge and understanding as a result of reading, they also consolidate what they are learning. That means going back and thinking again about how the ideas fit together and what they mean. Students can create a new graphic representation of what they have learned. They might write an outline and then elaborate on it in a summary, or they might want to talk to someone about the ideas they have gained. If students are using a textbook or a guide from a teacher, they can return to the questions or talk about the main objectives. If students are going to retain important ideas, they need to do something actively with them — by summarizing or extending what the authors have presented. Most elementary students need sustained teacher guidance and support to develop the habit of rehearsing what they are learning. Several graphic organizers discussed later in this chapter can help students to organize their thinking and provide good visual reviews of content. If they transform the ideas into a new form, students have a greater chance of remembering ideas. Simply asking the question "What did that mean to me?" helps students to stay active metacognitively. Strategies for working together to read, question, and reflect can be used with even the youngest students, who can learn to pair and ask each other what they have learned (Pressley, 2002).

Finally, good readers engage in evaluation of both the materials they read and their accomplishment. If the text seems unclear or lacking in information, they might decide to read other material to clarify ideas or to confirm accuracy and currency. Good readers also assess the achievement of their own purposes. Returning to their questions or categories that were unclear, good readers make sure they understand and have met their own purposes. They know that learning takes effort. Those who are not confident learners often feel disadvantaged when there are intense content expectations. You can help them to realize that they can learn new material but it is a process that takes time and active involvement on their parts. Giving insecure learners and second-language learners models of process learning and time to rehearse and clarify ideas is essential. They need to understand that reading a text once is never enough if the material is new and important. Studies of effective fourth-grade teachers (Allington & Johnston, 2002) revealed that they often help students to engage in rehearsing the same materials many times as a tool to their learning. Regularly modeling and reinforcing a process of anticipating, building knowledge, and consolidating learning will create active, confident readers (Pressley et al., 1998).

The Nature of Informational Texts

Reading to learn is linked generally to reading informational materials, not pieces of fiction or poetry. Successful reading for the sake of learning requires readers to develop specific strategies to use magazines, trade books, newspapers, primary documents, and Internet sites. For example, readers of informational texts will notice that they don't have to start on the first page and read to the end of the material. Rather, by using the table of contents and index, they can find a pertinent section without reading the whole text. Or they might be able to skip parts that are less essential to their purposes. The first thing they might observe about informational material is that it is organized differently from fiction both internally and externally.

Developing Familiarity with External Features of Informational Texts

One of the first things we notice when we pick up nonfiction or informational materials is that they generally have a format different from fiction, with many external aids to help readers negotiate them. These aids include the following:

Table of contents

Chapters

Headings and subheadings

Illustrations (e.g., maps, graphs, diagrams, pictures, cartoons)

Captions

Index

Vocabulary noted in italics or other graphic ways

Glossary of terms

References

In surveying the features of books, we note that in addition to a table of contents, these books generally include a glossary and index. The chapter titles are worth some attention because they are often key indicators of how the author has organized the information. Within each chapter, there is likely to be a further breakdown of information with headings and subheadings designed to guide our reading to important content or main ideas. Many books and articles also highlight key vocabulary with italic or boldface type or in marginal notes that provide explanations of the terms. A well-organized informational piece includes several of these external features that help us locate the part of the text we want to read when we have particular questions we want answered. In addition, because timely, accurate information is important, readers need to be aware of both the copyright date and the author's qualifications.

Books for very young readers are just now becoming more complete, so looking for chapter divisions is important before books are selected for primary students. Check to see whether the pages are numbered because it is hard to locate and return to information without some pagination. As you help children use informational books, be sure you have high-quality books available for them. Sometimes the color photographs are stunning, but the rest of the important book features are inadequate or missing.

Some books now display graphics in a wide variety of places on the pages and often on a two-page spread. The captions are often placed variously, too. Sometimes the captions are beneath the picture; at other times, they are beside or even above the illustrated material. Only by carefully studying the individual pages and mapping the positions of text, graphics, and captions can their relationships be determined. Then it is important to share with the children that process of exploration and what is learned about the text layout. Without support from teachers, young readers can overlook much of the richness of these new informational texts. When you introduce a new informational text or textbook, it is useful to do a picture and visual walk through the text. Each new text deserves attention because there are so many different formats and organization is highlighted in so many ways.

FOCUS STUDENTS' ATTENTION ON FEATURES.   As a way to reinforce the special nature of informational books, you could have students complete a nonfiction book report using the checklist shown in Figure 8.3. The book report might ask for what they liked, what they learned, and what would make the book better. When their attention is drawn to these features of the text, students begin to use them more regularly and think of them as resources (adapted from D. Gurvitz).

Intermediate-grade teachers also can have children preview expository texts they are using both as textbooks and as other resource materials. At the beginning of the year, it is always good to refresh students' use of all the ways information is available. Reading aloud to students from magazines and books and consciously thinking aloud provides further opportunity to focus attention on illustrations, captions, and other presentations of information. Making a transparency of the first one or two pages in a chapter or article lets you talk with the students about what they do when they navigate a page of informational text. In fact, informational texts are similar to the computer screens at which many students spend a great deal of leisure time. They can have fun exploring the similarities and differences in materials presented in these two formats. After such a comparison, encourage students to add diagrams and other visuals or links from their textbooks to other sources. They can become active in making materials more accessible to them. Rather than feeling overwhelmed

---

Title _____

Author _____

Nonfiction Book Checklist

_____   1. Table of Contents

_____   2. Index

_____   3. Photographs

_____   4. Realistic, accurate illustrations

_____   5. Maps

_____   6. Diagrams

_____   7. Captions – bold lettering

_____   8. Glossary – words and definitions

_____   9. Page numbers

_____   10. Other

Something I liked about this book:

Something I learned from this book:

FIGURE 8.3

Nonfiction Book Checklist.

by texts, students need to develop confidence in using texts and in going beyond single texts when these are not clear.

Predict tables of contents.   Intermediate-grade students should begin to anticipate how informative expository material is organized. By third grade, most students should be able to predict what might be in the table of contents of an animal book (e.g., description, habitat, food, family). Before studying regions of the earth in fourth grade, some students should be able to identify some possible topics that will reoccur with each region studied (e.g., plants, animals, geography, human life). Fifth graders need to know that biographies have some common topics that are used to organize information (e.g., early life, education, hardships, accomplishments). One way to assess students' awareness of these expert ways of organizing content information and then using it to prepare for reading and learning is to have them create a possible table of contents alone or with a partner. In this way, teachers can help students begin to think more deeply and begin to develop principled knowledge (see the Teach It! box).

Create chapter graphic organizers.   At the middle-grade level, some teachers have students identify and use the external structure of chapters in textbooks and magazines to make notes. They skim through the chapter and create a graphic organizer or map of the chapter with the title in the center and each of the main headings on one spoke of their spider map (see Figure 8.4). This graphic organizer is then used while students read to help them understand how the information is related. This mapping of the text can also be used as an interactive guide for reading. The students can brainstorm what they know about each section before reading; write those ideas on the map; highlight the areas that are least familiar and that will require slower reading, note making, and possible rereading; and then make notes on their map of new information as they read. This active engagement helps students to focus and retain information as they read.

Jigsaw text sections.   Another strategy teachers use to help students utilize the external structure of articles and chapters is to have a chapter read in cooperative fashion using a type of "jigsaw" cooperative learning strategy. The class first previews the text by identifying the major sections, and the teacher writes these on the board. Then the class

TEACH IT!

Refer to your **Teach It!** booklet for further activities you can use to reinforce concepts discussed in this chapter.

Using the Table of Contents to Predict

There are many ways to help students become familiar with the structure and organization of informational materials. One of the easiest is to predict what content a book might contain and then check the table of contents to see how the authors have organized the text. For example, before beginning an oral reading of a book on polar bears, a first-grade teacher asked her students what they thought they might learn as they listened to her read this interesting book. One eager boy blurted out, "How they fish for their food!" Soon other children volunteered their ideas: why they are white, how they take care of their babies, and more. The teacher praised the children for their ideas and then turned to the table of contents of the book. She ran her finger down the list of chapters or sections and said, "Um, yes, the book begins with 'An Arctic Home'—that

must tell about where they live. 'A Fight for Food'—that must tell us about how they get their food." In this way she modeled for the students the way they can begin to think like experts—and build the foundation for principled knowledge of polar bears.

With older students, skimming through the headings of an article or chapter can provide an overview of the authors' organization. When these reader aids do not indicate the text structure, students can do a quick read and use stick-on notes to label the text parts as they occur. Then students can create a graphic organizer to guide their reading of the material. Many teachers have found that having students learn to create graphic organizers of informational texts (articles, chapters, or books) provides a good road map for reading materials that might seem so dense that readers are in danger of getting get lost in details otherwise.

Refer to your Teach It! booklet for further activities you can use to reinforce concepts discussed in this chapter.

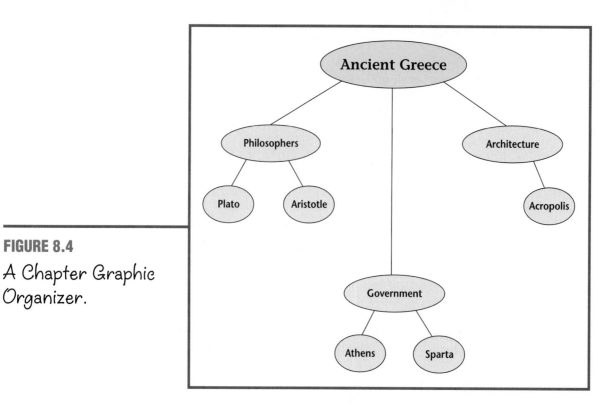

FIGURE 8.4

*A Chapter Graphic
Organizer.*

is divided into teams, one team per major section. Each team of students reads and creates a visual report of the key ideas of their one section of the text. Because many of the informational chapters and articles have such a heavy load of information, asking students to learn just one section from reading makes it manageable. Each group then reports on their section. Serving as "teachers" for the rest of the class both enhances the students' engagement in reading and creates a shared environment for learning.

USE VISUAL AND GRAPHIC INFORMATION.   Information presented visually in pictures, diagrams, and graphics is also critical in many informational texts. Think of an informational book you have recently read or a children's book such as *My Season with Penguins* (Webb, 2000) with its maps, drawings, and journal format. Today, good informational books, textbooks, and magazines use more pictures and visuals to enhance engagement and help readers understand the concepts than ever before. Much of the information, in fact, is often presented in the pictures, graphs, diagrams, maps, cartoons, and their captions. This visual information is often essential to understanding the content. Teachers need to help students read this information and integrate it into the rest of the narrative textual content.

There are several ways in which you can guide students' use of these texts to learn. First, you need to assess how students attend to pages of busy text. Informally ask students individually to describe how they read a two-page spread in a book or magazine. As they do, make notes of their approaches. Where do they start? Do they read the visually presented information? When do they read it? Do they integrate the visuals and the running text? Do they read captions on graphs and pictures? Are they aware of how they approach reading when the materials are presented in a variety of formats? Do they integrate these different sources in notes they make or in summaries they create?

Questions such as these can help you to assess students' engagements with text materials. From this assessment, you can develop your instructional focus. A good starting point is modeling how to approach busy text by doing think-alouds, such as the following, with groups of students. Make a transparency of one or two pages of text. Using an overhead projector, demonstrate how you survey the page, noting the different layout of information and graphics and raising questions that are stimulated by the text. Start by looking at the title of the chapter or section and note the way the sections are marked—with boldface print or words in capital letters, for example. Then focus on the visuals, such as pictures, diagrams, or notes in the margins. You might ask, "Why did the author/s use this cartoon? What is its role in this section? Let's see, the caption says . . . Oh, yes, I bet it is an example of . . ." You can also cover the text on the transparency and ask students to survey the graphic information. From this survey, ask them to predict what content they think is being highlighted and what questions they think will be answered on the next page or two. In this way, the importance of using the visually presented material may become clearer to them. In fact, sometimes this kind of preview can reduce the actual reading time considerably.

When you take time to think aloud about how to approach informational texts, students begin to think metacognitively about their own approaches to texts. Adults use many of these strategies automatically when appropriate. Students, by contrast, often need to hear another person's thinking before they understand how active they need to be as readers.

Developing Understanding of Internal Organization

TEACH IT! 35
Graphic Organizers

Another key to reading and learning from materials written to inform is becoming familiar with the way the writer has organized the ideas. As readers of narrative stories, we have learned—often first by listening to stories our parents read to us—that fiction has a predictable pattern. We read to find out who the characters are, what problem they encounter, and how they go about resolving it. Then we savor their victory at the end. No similar single pattern characterizes informational texts. They are written with different internal organization patterns. The most common ways of organizing ideas include the following:

Description (main ideas and details)

Compare/contrast

Problem/solution

Cause/effect

Sequence of events

These varying patterns can make predicting and organizing ideas more difficult for novice readers; therefore, it is all the more important that teachers provide guidance so students can learn to identify these internal structures. As they do, their ability to write informational pieces and reports more effectively also will improve. Here again, graphic organizers can help students recognize the underlying organization of texts. Figure 8.5 shows some simple models.

COMPARE TEXTS.   One way to introduce students to internal patterns is by collecting several books on the same topic and guiding students to compare their internal structures. By introducing the reading of the book in this way, you engage the students to think in terms of the big picture about what an author is trying to accomplish in a text. An easy way to create varieties of texts is to download articles from online encyclopedias and Internet articles and compare their organization. This can be a starting place for contrasting and comparing longer articles and books (see the Being a Professional Reading Teacher box on page 257).

WRITE TEXTS.   A good way to help students apply their knowledge of text organization is to have them write their own books using the structure of one they have studied. For example, during a unit on insects, third-grade students used Brown's (1949) *The Important Book* as a model for their writing. Each student wrote about his or her chosen insect and used the book structure as a guide. They took the text predictable pattern, The important thing about _____ is that _____. They have _____, _____, and _____, but the important thing about _____ is _____, and wrote about insects. One child had studied bees and wrote, "The important thing about a bee is that it stings. It is true that a bee has two pairs of wings and collects honey, but the important thing about a bee is that it STINGS!" Each child used this same pattern to write about their insect and the teacher then collected the pieces

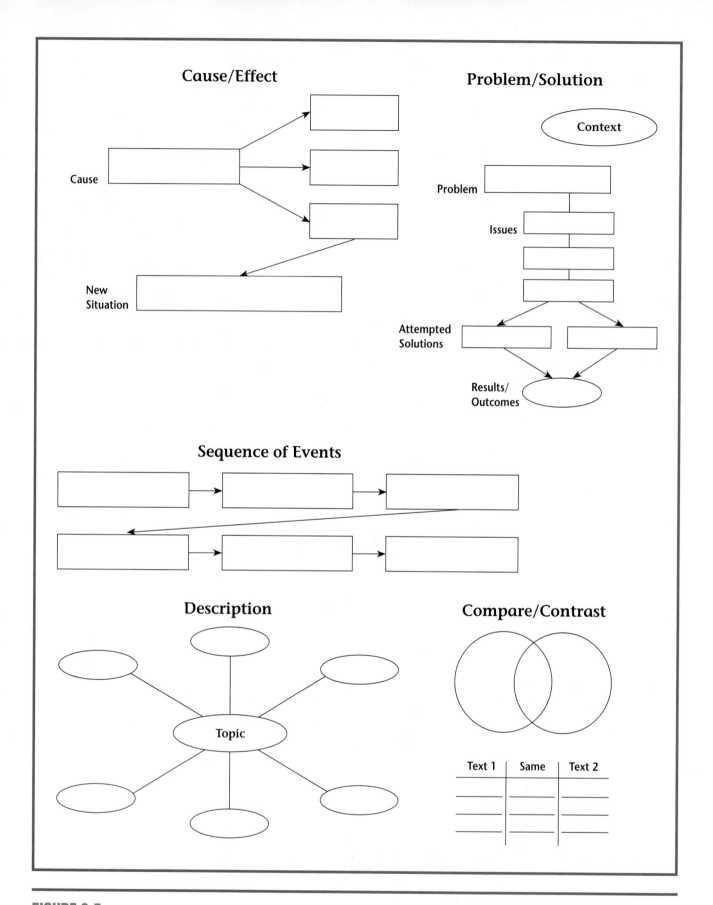

FIGURE 8.5

Graphic Organizer Models.

into a class book, *Important Insects*. This experience helped sudents focus their attention on simple, predictable text structures. Later the teacher introduced other structures used by authors of informational books they were reading. With this concrete experience in writing, the students were more attuned to organization and the structure of ideas.

ATTEND TO VOCABULARY AND CONTENT-SPECIFIC TERMINOLOGY. A key to learning content material is attention to vocabulary that conveys key concepts. Again, the differences between reading for one's own purposes and reading to learn are dramatic. When one reads for oneself, unfamiliar vocabulary can be ignored. In fact, good readers attend only to information that they know is helpful in comprehending. Therefore, they skip unfamiliar terms. In reading to learn, however, this practice can hinder comprehension. The unfamiliar terms are often exactly what the reader needs to attend to. Therefore, you need to help students develop the habit of attending to key terms that are content carriers. There are three important components to vocabulary learning in content materials:

TEACH IT! 20

Connect Two

- Words the authors prioritize (e.g., with boldface, italics, marginal definitions, or illustrations)
- Teacher-highlighted key new terms
- Students' own monitoring of what words are new and need to be learned

The first place to start in attending to vocabulary is by noting what the authors have already indicated as important. Students often overlook these aids without teacher guidance. Because authors often help readers by highlighting these terms, helping students to preview material to find these indicated words can be a great help to later reading and learning.

Teachers can help students note key words, too, by creating a list of key terms and then giving students some activities to focus their attention on these terms. One easy way to do this is to ask students to connect two (or three) of the terms and create new sentences using them (see Chapter 6 for an example of this activity). Even if the students do not know much about the words, they can have fun anticipating what they mean. Working with partners to create new sentences gives children a chance to use the words orally, too, thus increasing their awareness of the words both visually and orally. A more sophisticated activity is to ask students to chunk new words into categories and then label the groups and justify them to the class. The children now are attuned to these words and will definitely notice them as they read. (See the Differentiated Instruction box for ideas to use with English language learners.)

Students need to follow their initial search for terms with some active ways of retaining them. You can model this process by keeping a list of key terms on the board or on a word wall. This list can include both the words you introduced and ones the students identify as important. Then students can find more examples of these words being used in other places in their reading and listening and build a more elaborate meaning for the words. Asking students to draw their own images of the terms also helps to lock new words in place. Elaborating associations with new words through drawings and personal examples will help students to retain the words. Concept maps for the terms can also be used (see Figure 8.6). In this way, students learn that terms have meanings, associated examples, and attributes.

Specific terms are critical in content learning. Marzano (2004) has provided an excellent summary of the key academic terms students need to know and use to meet the content standards in each of eleven academic areas. Some school districts are now identifying key terms in each grade level that students should know and be able to use. This is one way they are highlighting the importance of specific academic language in learning. With the importance of vocbulary in informational

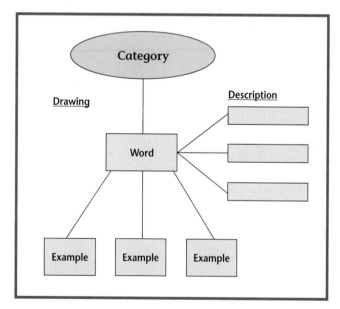

FIGURE 8.6

Concept of Definition Map.

SIOP®
*Sheltered Instruction Observation Protocol**

Differentiated Instruction

Reading Comprehension: Understanding and Learning with Informational Texts

Many students who speak languages other than English in their homes do very well with conversational English, and teachers may be unaware of the need to provide specific instruction when it comes to the academic vocabulary needed for content area reading and learning. Yet this is an area deserving particular attention. Research studies have highlighted the fact that there is a great difference between conversational English and academic English competence. Teachers can do a lot to help English language learners be successful in this area of academic learning by focusing on vocabulary development.

Begin by assessing students' depth of understanding of key academic terms. For example, if the unit in social studies is about the westward movement of European pioneers across the continent, then terms like *pioneer, covered wagon, wagon train, trails, obstacles,* and *hardships* will probably be needed. These are terms that students would not encounter in normal conversational contexts. They are academic terms needed for this particular unit of study. In a similar way, as a unit in science on light is initiated, teachers highlight terms that will be used and check to see if academic terms like *opaque, translucent, transparent, reflection,* and *refraction* are familiar to students. Because these are words not used in regular conversational English, they need to be highlighted and taught specifically.

It is often helpful to English language learners to make a list of key terms and then compare them with the same terms in their home language. Because there are many Latin-based cognates used in English, this can make the learning task much easier. For example, the science terms can be listed on one side and the Spanish terms on the other.

Opaque	opaco/a
Reflection	reflexión
Refraction	refracción
Translucent	translúcido/a
Transparent	transparente

English language learners will be much more successful if teachers focus on key academic terms and provide them with extended opportunities to practice these words and phrases. It is in academic English that these English language learners deserve our help.

---

materials, students need to develop their own metacognitive control over what words are new to them, and they need to develop ways to retain those particular terms. Using individual student vocabulary notebooks and word cards provide tools for rehearsing and practicing these words. Making new vocabulary a part of the oral talk of the classroom is an essential component in this process. Some teachers use a reward system to encourage usage, such as giving students points when they hear and note a new word being used by a fellow student. This highlights oral as well as written vocabulary recognition and provides an internal incentive as well.

LANGUAGE and DIVERSITY

How can you stimulate students' interest in how English adds words from so many languages?

Strategies for Active Reading of Informational Text

As students become familiar with the structure of informational text, they must develop ways to engage actively with the authors of those texts and think about the content. There are some basic strategies worth practicing to the extent that students can use them on their own. They have been developed independently but often work well when used together.

Prereading Preparation

Until students are able to take control of their learning by finding their own questions and level of knowledge, it is unlikely that they will retain much of what is studied. Therefore, the time spent activating personal and class interest is important.

K-W-L. Students become much more engaged in reading when they and their interests are the starting point for new inquiry and learning. K-W-L (Ogle, 1986, 1991) is a group process in which the teacher models and guides active engagement with informational texts. It uses the knowledge and information students bring to help each other build a better starting place for learning and for sharing the results of their reading. The adept teacher weaves together what some class members know (either topical or principled knowledge) and stimulates questions for all to pursue as they read to learn. The process also helps students who lack confidence in both reading and writing because the teacher is the first one to write on the board. This permits children to see the written forms of key terms they will encounter later in the text. It also models what the students will write on their own guidesheets (see Figure 8.7) or in their learning logs.

What we know. The teacher and students begin the process of reading and learning by brainstorming together what they *know* (the K in K-W-L) about the topic. The teacher guides students to probe their knowledge statements and find conflicting or partial statements of what they know. For example, as a group brainstorms what they know about the desert, one student says, "Nothing much lives there." Another volunteers, "That's not true! I know lots of insects live there. I just read a book about tarantulas." The teacher can encourage more student engagement by continuing the thinking: "Does anyone else know something about what lives in the dry, barren lands of the desert? Can anyone frame a question that may help us find out more?"

Another student chimes in, "We'd better find out what animals can survive there with little water or food." The teacher writes on the blackboard, overhead, or computer what the students ask as their own questions and what they volunteer they think they know, writing down their ideas just as the students volunteer them (see Figure 8.8). The teacher does not correct or evaluate but encourages and stimulates students to think broadly about what they bring to the study. Through this brainstorming process, some questions or uncertainties generally surface.

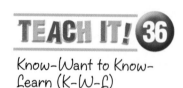

TEACH IT! 36

Know–Want to Know–
Learn (K-W-L)

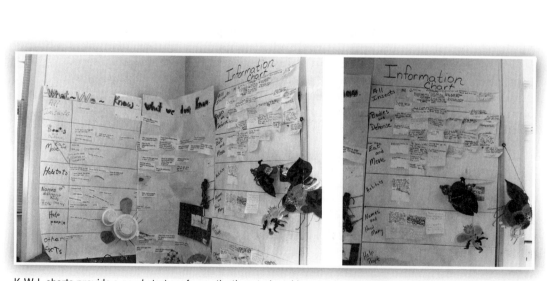

K-W-L charts provide a good strategy for motivating students' interest in new topics.

1. K – What We Know	W – What We Want to Learn	L – What We Learned and Still Need to Know

2. Categories of Information We Expect to Use:

A.   E.

B.   F.

C.   G.

D.   H.

3. Where We Will Find Information:

1.

2.

3.

4.

FIGURE 8.7

K-W-L Guide.

Source: Ogle, Donna M. "K-W-L: A Teaching Model That Develops Active Reading of Expository Text." *The Reading Teacher* (©1986), 36(6), pp. 564–570. Reprinted by permission of the International Reading Association.

WHAT WE KNOW

Lots of snakes
Sand and windy
Cactus
Road Runners
Tarantulas
Hot weather
No water
No rain
Gila monster
Lizards
Bats
Phoenix
Sun City
Oil under the ground
Utah and Arizona

FIGURE 8.8

What We Know about Deserts.

The teacher's role is to help students activate their knowledge and develop interest in the topic. Some basic rules are established at the beginning:

- All ideas are acceptable.
- Say what first comes into your mind. These ideas will be checked and edited or revised later.
- Listen to each other, but do not judge the quality of ideas.
- The goal is to get as many different ideas out as possible in the time allotted.

As ideas are voiced and written down, they might seem random and unconnected. At this point, you need to make a decision. If the group is engaged and ready to think a little more deeply, ask the students to think of ways in which the experts organize information on this topic. This move to a deeper level of thinking (to principled knowledge) can begin by first focusing on categories of information about which the children already have some intuitive knowledge. You can initiate reflection: "Look at what we listed in the 'Know' column. Are any of these items connected? For example, I see three items about animals that live on the desert. I also see some plants. Can you find other items that go together in a category? What are the basic categories of information we are likely to need to use?" In this case, the categories might be those shown in Figure 8.9.

The teacher might also begin simply by asking students to step back and think about the topic generally: "If you were going to write a table of contents on this topic, the desert, what would you include?" The ideas that students volunteer can be listed on the bottom of the "Know" column.

What we want to know.   With a variety of ideas being shared the teacher can easily ask what the students *want* (the W in K-W-L) to know. Again, it is the students' responsibility to think of real questions as you write down what they say. These questions form the second column on the worksheet or blackboard. If students are not familiar with the process of generating their own questions, you might need to model some questioning at the beginning. You might be able to extend comments made by class members into questions.

For example, if the class is beginning a unit on the desert region and someone has listed cactus as a plant in the desert, you can extend this by suggesting, "I wonder whether there are any uses people make of cactus in the desert?"

You can write this in the "We Want to Know" column and continue to guide students to find questions, suggesting, "Is there anything else we might want to learn about the animals that live on the desert? Do we have to be careful of any of them? If we were hiking, should we watch out?"

This process puts the students right in the center of any new study. Rather than beginning with a text and previewing it, the students and the teacher become active listeners and recorders. This group-focusing effort helps students think about the range of ideas that they and others already have on the topic. It should also help them make new connections and become intrigued by what they don't know. Listening to each other can stimulate new vocabulary and associations; the writing done by the teacher often helps more reluctant readers begin to make associations between oral language and the written forms of words they will encounter as they read.

Once the students have discussed the topic, they are more ready to begin their own reading. It might be useful to have students individually write down on their own worksheets or learning logs the pieces of information they individually think they know and the questions they want to know more about. In this way, both the group and the individual are respected. You could have students work in pairs to do both the writing and reading because this is more stimulating and supportive of some children who lack confidence in writing and taking risks.

What we learned.   You can diagnose from this discussion what texts will be most useful to the students. It might be that what you thought would be adequate turns out to be

---

Categories of Information:

A. animals   C. location   E. physical features

B. climate   D. plants

FIGURE 8.9

Categories of Information.

inappropriate. Rather than reading the planned text, the class can collect other materials and even write some of their own materials as needed. This is where the Internet can come in handy as a resource. Look up a few sites, and bookmark them for the class. If the text or texts in the classroom and school library are appropriate, students can read and make notes on their own of what they *learn* (the L in K-W-L)—both answers to their questions and unexpected information they think is interesting and/or important. Many teachers create large bulletin boards with sections for the "What We Know," "What We Want to Learn," and "What We Learned" sections of the K-W-L. Students can keep adding information and questions to the class chart as they study. Small index cards work well for this kind of class activity. You can also make photocopies of material or graphics that students find and want to have shared.

K-W-L+. After years of working with students in content areas, teachers know that even with motivation and engagement, students will not remember much of the new information the first time they encounter it. Therefore, the "plus" in K-W-L+ (Carr & Ogle, 1987) extends this learning process by asking students to do more reorganizing of what they have learned by making a semantic map or graphic organizer of the key information (see Figure 8.10). Students select the major categories and list facts under those categories, thus rethinking what they are learning.

Finally, they write what they have learned in an essay, summary, or more personal form (see the example in Figure 8.11). The cognitive activity needed to use ideas they have been learning in a new written format deepens memory and provides an additional opportunity to consolidate their learning. Engaging actively in this variety of learning gives the students a sense of how they can become active learners on their own, even when the teacher is not present. Reorganizing and rehearsing new knowledge and connecting it with what was previously known establishes for students the effort needed in learning and reinforces their personal self-esteem because they possess a productive process for school tasks (see the Assessment box).

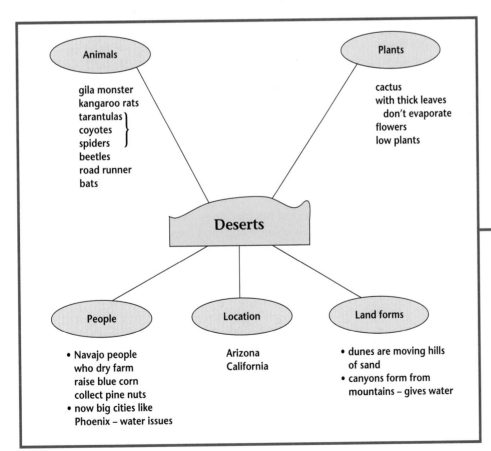

FIGURE 8.10

K-W-L+ Semantic Map.

Deserts

Deserts are interesting and hard places to live. They are very dry and finding water is hard. Deserts are made of dunes that are hills of moving sand. When water comes down from the mountains it creates canyons and these help streams of water come.

Navajo people have lived in the deserts for a long time. They know how to dry farm, and grow blue corn and squash. They collect nuts like pine nuts from trees. Now many other people live in the desert, too. This makes problems because people want too much water.

Animals know how to live on the desert. Many are small like the spiders, especially tarantulas and beetles. There are also roadrunners, coyotes and gila monsters. Bats and kangaroo rats are there, too.

The plants are small and have thick leaves that don't evaporate easily. There are cactus and small, low bushes.

If you want to visit a desert you can go to Arizona or California.

I-CHART. Using multiple sources of information is an important way to help students find texts that meet their own levels of knowledge and interest, find answers to their own questions, and compare and contrast authors' points of view. It encourages the critical thinking so needed in the world today. Yet many students have a difficult time using more than one source effectively. Hoffman (1992) has developed a very useful tool in the **I-Chart** (see Figure 8.12), which helps students take important questions, select three to four sources of information they want to use to explore those questions, and then come to their own conclusion about the questions they framed initially.

Once students have used the K-W-L process to activate their knowledge and interest, they select some key questions for more in-depth research they can do together. The class or small groups can decide on the questions they want to concentrate on and write these on the chart. Then the best sources of information for the questions are selected, usually with teacher help and guidance, and they are also listed across the top of the chart. This simple framework establishes that in seeking answers to questions, multiple sources are needed.

As children move into the intermediate and middle grades, they should be involved in monitoring their own growth as readers. Having students maintain Reading Logs of their reading helps them become more self-conscious about their habits, preferences, and strategies. Asking them to keep a record of all the books and articles they read along with their responses to the pieces is an easy starting place. Periodically, it is helpful to ask all students to record their responses to particular texts. In this way you can compare how students respond and what focus they reflect. Asking students to share their responses with each other is a good way to stimulate a discussion of the various ways readers attend and construct meaning from texts. Reading Logs can provide an ongoing record of engagement and help teachers know if students need to be encouraged to expand their range of readings. Some students tend to stay in one genre or with very easy books.

Another way learning can be made visible to students is to have them keep samples of texts that they have marked with marginal notes or sticky notes during the four quarters of the school year. They can return to earlier text notations and analyze changes. If students are engaged with several units and reading many informational texts over the course of the year, there should be changes in depth and range of responses they can look for. For example, students can track the number of times they make comparisons across texts, as well as the times they question authors' inferences, ask questions of a text, and visualize ideas presented. The KWL sheets can be a good component of this kind of activity, too. Students can evaluate the quality of their questions, the extent to which they fulfill their desires to learn new content, and the graphic organizers and summaries they create.

Questions	What We Know	Text 1	Text 2	Text 3	Summary
1.					
2.					
3.					
Interesting new info./ New questions					

FIGURE 8.12

I-Chart.

The practice of summarizing the information and answering their own questions scaffolds the process of inquiry well. Using the I-Chart establishes a simple framework for a systematic search for information. The chart also includes a column for interesting information, pieces that do not fit the basic questions but still are relevant to the students' inquiry. This often becomes an important way to take notes on ideas that can be shared with the class later—ideas that are full of potential for more reading.

Reading Strategies

STRUGGLING **READER**

How can students become engaged in learning using these strategies?

K-W-L and the I-Chart are frameworks through which teachers can engage students personally and cooperatively in thinking about their relationship to a content to be studied and in setting a course for learning. The frameworks do not show students how to actually engage with the text as they read it, however. That is where one of the following strategies is most useful.

RECIPROCAL TEACHING. One of the most researched strategies for engaged reading of informational text is **reciprocal teaching**. Developed by Palincsar and Brown (1984, 1986) to help less able readers handle the demands of expository texts, reciprocal teaching includes four different strategies that students learn to use. You first model each of the strategies and then turn the teacher's role over to the students. The students apply what they are learning by becoming teachers for their classmates and guiding the continued reading of small portions of text. The four basic strategies are as follows:

1. Summarize what has just been read.
2. Think of two or three good questions about the passage.
3. Clarify any ideas or information that was not clear.
4. Predict what you think will be in the next part of the text.

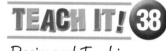

TEACH IT! 38

Reciprocal Teaching

In conducting a reciprocal teaching exercise, decide in advance how large the chunks of text will be that the students will read before you engage them in thinking about that portion. The text units should be short enough that the students can discuss each in five to seven minutes. Tell the students you will be the first discussion leader and that the students should pay attention to how you conduct the discussion, not just focus on answering the questions.

Model reading a short section of text and creating a summary of the main ideas. Depending on the group and the amount of time needed to teach each of the four strategies, you might spend several sessions on a single strategy, or you might model more than one at a time until all four strategies become part of the readers' response to each paragraph or segment. Students learn to ask good questions about the text through this process. They also learn to identify problems that hinder comprehension—vocabulary items that are unfamiliar, for example, or references that are confusing, or other unclear aspects—and ask questions to clarify these problems posed by the text. Finally, they learn to make predictions about where the text is leading. Students then assume the teacher role for each segment of text so that during a class period, many students have had the opportunity to lead their fellow students in considering the meaning of a common text. You could create a visible chart of the four strategies to help students understand the process. This becomes a guide for students when they lead the discussions.

This form of guided and shared reading has been effective in helping less able readers make sense of dense text material. The combination of good interactive strategies with group-oriented teaching and a shared learning approach helps students to maintain interest and focus on the material they are studying. The Teach It! box provides an example of how one teacher used reciprocal teaching in his classroom.

Increasing interest and giving students a sense of power when dealing with difficult and dense reading material are not easy. Both reciprocal teaching and the next teaching strategy—questioning the author—give teachers and students supportive alternatives to round robin reading, a still overused way to have students read content texts.

QUESTIONING THE AUTHOR.   Rather than having to memorize text content, with the questioning-the-author teaching strategy (Beck et al., 1997) students learn to think more about who has written a text and how successful the writer was in conveying the message to the reader. Students develop a dialogue with the author, just as they would with a person talking with them face to face. In classrooms where students write a lot, the analogy of having the textbook or text author in the "author's chair" helps the students to visualize the writer as a person. Students are encouraged to "query" the absent author, asking questions that explore the writer's decisions. It can be difficult initially to engage students in such an activity, so introducing it by having a small group model the process with the rest of the class observing can be useful. You can also work with students in small groups, as you do with literature discussion, to develop this habit of thinking. Following are some basic questions students might ask:

- What is the author trying to say?
- Why is the author saying this?
- What could the author have said instead?
- What was the intent of the author?
- What is the point of view?
- How could something be stated more clearly?

Students are led by their teacher in a discussion of short segments of text, just as they are in reciprocal teaching, but this time, they focus on the author, thinking about how the author has written for them as readers or learners. After reading a paragraph in a sixth-grade history text, students might begin by asking one or some of the following questions:

- Why do you think the author spent a paragraph explaining the religious beliefs of the Egyptians?
- What do you think it represents to the author?
- What else about the society might have been more important?
- Was it clearly written?
- Could something have been added to make it easier to understand?
- How would you have written this?
- Would a diagram or chart have helped you understand?

By questioning or querying the author, students take a different stance in relation to the text and begin to feel more active as participants in the process of communication about content topics. In classrooms where teachers use this approach, they have reported that the students seem to engage more deeply with the material they are asked to read and are more willing to read content textbooks.

METACOGNITIVE GRAPHIC ORGANIZER.   Although several variations have emerged in recent years (Caverly, Mandeville, & Nicholson, 1995), the key to the metacognitive graphic organizer strategy is that students create their own graphic organizer as they preview a chapter of text and use this visual as a guide for their reading. The term **metacognition** refers to the process in which learners are self-aware of their own learning needs and can monitor and adjust to the demands of the text. Students place the title of the chapter or article in the center of a sheet of paper and then add the major headings from the chapter as they survey the material. After doing this, they return to the text and look at the visual information in charts, diagrams, and the like. They put key ideas from these visuals on the graphic where appropriate under the headings. They can add subheads if necessary to make the flow of the text clear. Once the author's structure and visuals are clearly framed, students return and do the metacognitive check by asking themselves which sections are familiar (✓), which are unknown or unfamiliar (?), and which seem interesting (+). Sections that seem most necessary for the course, if that is the purpose of reading, can be highlighted with an asterisk (*). In this way, readers create a personal guide for reading and study. Then while reading, students can make additional notes on the outline or on stick-on notes.

When finished reading, students review the graphic and the notes made and decide whether to revise the graphic, add to it, or write some extended notes to rehearse the im-

TEACH IT!

Refer to your **Teach It!** booklet for further activities you can use to reinforce concepts discussed in this chapter.

Reciprocal Teaching

George Mead and five of his fifth-grade students are reading a short informative text on crocodiles and alligators. Mr. Mead is still modeling the reciprocal teaching process with these troubled readers because they have had only a few experiences with the process. He has decided in advance that this text is best read in units of paragraphs. These students are very unconfident about their abilities as readers and the text is dense.

Mr. Mead announces that he will be the discussion leader for the first paragraph. He advises students not only to pay attention to the paragraph and participate in the discussion, but also to observe carefully how he conducts the discussion. They know that each of them will play the role of the discussion leader when the next paragraphs are read. Mr. Mead has prepared a chart that lists the steps that are taken after each paragraph is read. He refers the students to the chart to help them follow the procedure he is using as he leads the discussion. Mr. Mead asks everyone to read the first paragraph silently. When they are finished, he gives a verbal summary of the paragraph and looks around at the students to ask if they would summarize the passage the same way or have something to add. Next, Mr. Mead formulates a question. He takes care with the question because as well as eliciting their ideas, he is demonstrating the art of questioning for the students. He asks, "What are the easiest ways to tell the differences between alligators and crocodiles?" He draws out the students' ideas on this question and affirms their suggestions. When Matt volunteers that the shape of the mouths might be easier to notice than either how their teeth fit together or

whether the animal has sensory pits, especially if one was coming at you, he gets a nod.

Next, Mr. Mead attempts to clarify parts of the paragraph that are unclear to the students. He notes that the word *crocodilian* is used for the whole group of reptiles that includes crocodiles, alligators, and caimans. He asks whether someone can clarify when to use crocodilian and when to use crocodile. As the students try to differentiate the uses of the terms orally, Mr. Mead knows that they are becoming more familiar with these words in both their reading and their speaking. To help them as they clarify, he writes the words on the chalkboard as one student explains that *crocodilian* should be above the other three words, *crocodile, caiman,* and *alligator,* because they are all examples of this group of reptiles. Then Mr. Mead goes on to make a prediction, suggesting that the text will probably tell how these different reptiles survive. Finally, he assigns the next section of the text.

After that paragraph is read, Mr. Mead takes another turn as discussion director to make sure the students fully understand how to carry out the steps in conducting a discussion before it becomes their turn. Mr. Mead often refers to the chart as he conducts each step in the discussion. He knows that if the students do not clearly understand how to conduct the procedure, he will have to intervene later, which will undermine the students' autonomy and confidence. Before the third passage is read, Mr. Mead points to the student on his left and asks her to lead the next discussion. After that student has had her turn, the role of discussion leader passes to the student on her left, and so on.

portant ideas. The final step of note making is designed to encourage student reflection and learning. What an individual student does depends on how much detail needs to be absorbed to achieve the learning goal. It might be that the actual organization of the text is different from what the student initially drew and requires creating a revised text graphic. It might be that there are many new ideas, and the student needs to write a summary explaining the meaning of the ideas. Students monitoring their own learning can adjust this final stage of learning to their own needs to retain the content.

Personal graphic guides are very helpful to many students. They combine attention to the text and to the learner at the same time. In longer chapters, they help students maintain their focus on how all the ideas and sections fit together. They also provide a great tool for review and rehearsal later.

Questioning

TEACH IT! 37

What? So What? Now What?

Before we close this section on learning, it is valuable to address the role of questioning for both teachers and students. Asking and answering questions are major parts of the life of schools. Each of the active strategies described here requires both teachers and students to become good at asking important and thoughtful questions. Questioning is an important active thinking activity that learners use while reading and trying to make sense of text. It is a central part of comprehension for students and teachers. Therefore, it is valuable to spend time both in analyzing the questions you ask and in developing students' sensitivity to what constitutes good questions and good questioning. A starting place is to discuss with students what role questioning plays in learning and what they think good questions are. Direct the discussion to include the realization that some questions ask for very specific and direct information (e.g., "What was the pharaoh's role in religion?"), some for more abstract interpretations or conjectures (e.g., "What effect did the caste system have on how people treated each other?" or "What similar situation have we had in our country?"), and some are very personal (e.g., "What do you think or how do you feel?").

You also need to analyze periodically how you use questioning and tape yourself during class discussions. Traditionally, and continuing into today, many teachers have used questions to find out how well students have comprehended what they read. The teacher asks the student a question, the student answers, and the teacher gives some evaluative feedback. Researchers (Mehan, 1979) refer to this form of school dialogue as I-R-E (initiation, response, evaluation) and conclude that the process helps teachers test students more than it aids student comprehension. To encourage students to ask good questions and engage in metacognitive self-monitoring, you need to model good thinking when sharing ideas out loud and questioning students.

You can use questioning to model the process of thinking before and during reading. Begin a lesson or introduce a story by asking students what they already know about a topic. This kind of questioning activates students' own thinking. Most teachers use questions to help students connect ideas, consolidate what they have read, and reflect on ideas. However, you can ask much more thoughtful and reflective questions by first considering how you want to focus students' reflections about what they have read. Think about how you can involve students in reflecting together to deepen their responses to questions you or texts pose.

Reading specialist Marge Harter (2000), who has worked with teachers in her school to develop better questioning, suggests making the process of questioning very explicit with teachers. In her teacher workshops, she has helped them to focus on and identify good questions and has developed a chart (see Figure 8.13) based on the reciprocal teaching strategies for teachers to use in planning lessons. One group of teachers developed their own guide called "Questions Teachers May Ask to Help Students Clarify Text." In the guide, they suggest these options:

- Does anyone need anything clarified?
- Please share words or phrases you're uncertain of.
- What do you think this means? Can anyone add to what has been given?
- What other resources might we use to help us clarify and answer our questions?
- Where did this information come from? If you used the textbook, what part was most helpful?

As Harter worked with the teachers, they also discussed ways to help their students become more aware of their questions. She encouraged the teachers to discuss with their students the role of questioning in thinking and learning. The students in one middle-level classroom made a chart of what they thought constitutes good questions.

A Good Question:
1. Cannot be answered "yes," "no," or ask for a one-word answer
2. Requires a researcher to give more information that is focused or directed to a concept
3. Possible beginnings—Describe, How, Why, Compare, Explain

The teacher then put this chart on the board so that the class could refer to it regularly. Both students and teacher became much more conscious of their questions as a result of this activity.

Some teachers extended their attention to questioning by engaging students in discussing what kinds of questions are most interesting to have answered and how much elaboration is needed in answering well. From an initial discussion of questions, teachers expanded students' understanding of kinds of questions and appropriate responses.

Writing questions on the board and making them visible led to a good discussion of the significance of the questions and helped students to understand the value of voicing their own uncertainties.

Many educators focus on the nature of the process of constructing meaning and argue that questions should ask students, "What do you predict will happen?," "What else could have been done?," and "What does this remind you of?" They argue that the reader–text interaction should be the focus of attention and that questions should de-

PREDICTING

What is your prediction for this passage?

What strategies will you use to help your students predict?

CLARIFYING

What words, phrases, or ideas do you need clarified?

What words, phrases, or ideas do you think your students may need clarified?

What strategies and responses will you use to help clarify those parts of the text?

SUMMARIZING

Write your summary for this passage.

How will you help your students summarize?

QUESTIONING

What "Quality Questions" are you asking your students?

1.

2.

3.

Why are these questions "Quality"?

Answer these questions on the back of this sheet.

FIGURE 8.13

Content Questions.

Source: Harter (2000).

rive from those interactions. Do readers connect and respond personally to what they read? Can they establish a purpose and fulfill their own purpose? This focus leads to another range of questions about text construction or engagement. Some students never seem to connect text to their own lives or to the reality around them. Thinking of this dimension of questioning can be helpful in planning for activities so that students see school learning as part of their own world (see the World of Reading box).

Because the process of asking and answering questions is a critical part of teaching and evaluation, some focused attention to questions is necessary. By considering the nature of the questions they ask and the questions in the materials they give students, teachers can make the questions as valuable as possible. Modeling and attending to questioning provides the context for students to become more aware of their own questioning and encourages them to develop questioning skills that

What can a teacher do to activate students' interest in a new topic and promote involvement by all students?

are useful to their own learning. Two strategies to use while students are reading that help them apply their knowledge of good questions are ReQuest and paired reading/paired summarizing.

REQUEST PROCEDURE. The ReQuest procedure (Manzo, 1969) is best suited for use with informational texts. In this procedure, two students read through a text, stop after each paragraph, and take turns asking each other questions about it, which the other student must try to answer. It helps if the teacher serves as a partner when the technique is first introduced. Because one goal for teaching comprehension is to develop principled knowledge of the topic, the teacher's questions serve as valuable models of ways to inquire about the important ideas in a text.

For an example of the ReQuest procedure in action, assume you have assigned the students in the class to pairs. Amalia and David are reading a text together. After they both read the first paragraph silently, Amalia asks David three good questions about that paragraph. She asks questions about main ideas. She asks questions that probe beneath the surface. She asks what importance some item in this paragraph might come to have later in the text. David answers those questions as well as he can. After David has finished answering Amalia's questions, they both read the next paragraph. Now it is David's turn to ask Amalia questions about the new paragraph, and Amalia has to answer them. When both students have brought to light the information in that paragraph, they read the next one, and Amalia gets the first turn at asking David several good questions about that paragraph, and so on.

The ReQuest procedure can be used well with a whole class, too. One way is for the class to read one or two paragraphs from the text. Then the students pause and close their books, and students take turns asking the teacher all the questions that come to mind. Following that, they read a new paragraph and the roles are reversed: The teacher asks the students several good questions, taking care to model not just factual questions but also those that probe concepts and implications. After several such exchanges, the teacher might shift the activity to ask students to predict what the rest of the assignment will be about and state why they think so (Vacca & Vacca, 1996). Another variation for a whole-class use of the ReQuest procedure is to assign students to teams of three and have them take turns asking and answering questions.

PAIRED READING/PAIRED SUMMARIZING. Paired reading/paired summarizing is an elaboration on the ReQuest procedure that introduces more comprehension processes into the mix. In paired reading/paired summarizing, students pair up and read a text together and then divide the text into chunks of one or two paragraphs. The first student reads a chunk aloud as the other student reads along silently. Then the first student summarizes what the passage said. The second student then asks questions about the passage to probe its meaning. Both students attempt to answer the questions. The students exchange roles

Using Taxonomies in Questioning

As we take time to consider the role of questioning in learning, we need ways to categorize and analyze the nature of our questions. There are some commonly used frameworks that can be used to help us in this activity. The most widely used is probably one developed by Benjamin Bloom and his colleagues in the 1950s. Bloom's taxonomy was not really developed for use by teachers but was developed as a taxonomy of educational objectives to measure school goals and assessment. However, teachers saw its value and have used it as a tool to help us reflect on our classroom questioning patterns. The taxonomy has seven levels of questions: memory, translation, interpretation, application, analysis, synthesis, and evaluation.

In research studies of classroom talk, it is not uncommon to see analyses of the levels of teacher questions. In some descriptions of reading comprehension and reading assessment, Bloom's seven levels have been chunked into three or four levels. For example, one common way of describing reading is by thinking of literal, interpretive, applied, and critical levels of comprehension to define kinds of questions in relation to text.

Raphael (1986) has helped students to think about sources of information for questions they are to answer by creating four categories:

- Right there: Questions that can be answered directly from the text
- Think and search: Questions that require more than one piece of information from the text
- Author and you: Questions that go beyond the text
- On your own: Questions that rely on the reader

The whole strategy is called Question-Answer-Relationships and provides very practical definitions that make it easy for students to become more involved in both planning their strategies for responding and becoming aware metacognitively of the range of responses they need to be able to make to the text.

Taxonomies provide a helpful language to think about questioning and the kinds of thinking we want to help stimulate in students. Some teachers keep the levels of questions in their teacher manuals or put them on the bulletin boards so that both they and students are more aware of the need to go beyond the literal or memory level. Other teachers do not like to use taxonomies to evaluate comprehension. Rather than conceiving of them as a hierarchy, these teachers see taxonomies as an array of options that are available to use as appropriate.

---

for the next passage. Like the ReQuest procedure and reciprocal teaching, students will play their roles more effectively if the teacher first demonstrates what is meant by making an effective summary and by asking good questions.

Engaging in Research

An important part of study reading is learning to conduct research and write reports. This skill is often left for the middle grades, where teachers teach a semiformal approach to research. However, when primary-grade teachers engage students in content reading and study, the process can be scaffolded so that by the time students reach the middle grades they are already confident in the skills that permit them to conduct good research. Think back to the activities that have been described already. Research requires the following:

- *Asking good researchable questions.* Learning to narrow one's topic is a basic skill that needs to be developed. When children use K-W-L and I-Charts, they become experienced in finding good questions.
- *Locating good sources of information.* Integrated units that are framed around students' questions develop their abilities to find the materials they need and to locate within the texts the sections that will answer their questions.
- *Making notes of important ideas.* Children who get in the habit of writing Amazing Fact Sheets have already learned how to make good notes. The use of graphic organizers and journals also helps students build good note-making skills.

- *Critically evaluating information.* Students who have regularly read several texts on the same topic know the importance of evaluating the sources of information they use and cross-checking them for accuracy and currency. They learn to check the authors of Web sites for their expertise and biases. They also know that textbooks and encyclopedias are good, reliable backup sources for their use.
- *Organizing information.* When students learn to chunk ideas as part of the K-W-L process, when they cluster new vocabulary, and when they learn to look for and use internal text organization in their reading and writing, they develop skills in organizing ideas into interesting and coherent texts. The more writing they do throughout the elementary grades, the more confident they become in creating interesting and meaningful texts.

Taking notes while reading can help the reader identify the details of information content and organize them for understanding.

- *Presenting information visually and graphically.* Students who have studied how authors and illustrators present visual information and weave it together with the connected texts are more able to create their own. The computer tools and digital cameras that schools now possess make this task an exciting one for young students.

Look back over the different strategies that help to engage students actively as learners across the content areas. All of these taken together prepare students to be active, thoughtful learners. With this foundation, doing research and writing reports and even creating a more formal research paper is not difficult.

As we think of learning new material and conducting research, writing becomes an essential part of the ongoing literacy curriculum. (Refer to Chapter 9 for many ideas on how to develop a good writing program in the classroom.) When children write regularly, they develop their skills and fluency as writers. Regular writing, just like regular reading in a variety of genres for a variety of audiences and purposes, creates confident and capable learners. The more students can engage in their own inquiry on topics and questions of their choosing, the more they will want to write and share what they learn. The more they write, the more comfortable they will become with informational texts and the more able they will be to consider alternative ways authors can present information to connect with their readers. These experiences also prepare them for the focus of most of the writing they will be asked to do throughout their schooling: reports, summaries, and expository and persuasive essays.

WRITING and READING CONNECTIONS

Compare short writes with more extended essays as tools for learning.

A Look at Classrooms for Learning

As teachers take seriously the importance of helping children become confident readers and learners with informational materials, the greatest challenges are finding the time and structuring the learning experiences properly. Two general approaches are often used. The first is to think of teaching reading as finding a balance between the reading of fictional literature (for literary purposes) and the reading of informational material (to learn). The second approach is to create integrated units of instruction and combine standards and strategies for both literacy and content learning. If your school has basal readers, then check to see that there is a balance of literary fiction and nonfiction and informational selections. Many of the newer basal reading programs include more varied selections, recognizing that students need to become familiar with these texts. You also need to provide experiences in integrated content units so students learn the value of using a range of informational resources in their learning.

LANGUAGE
and **DIVERSITY**

What extra resources do English language learners bring to the classroom?

Involving English Language Learners

Integrated content units provide an open framework in which teachers can involve students at all levels of language competence in classroom learning experiences. Because the unit model provides for a range of materials and activities, students with little English can participate using resources in their own language and can begin their learning in their first language. Helping English language learners to create vocabulary lists with words in both English and their first language makes their participation in the general classroom activities more possible.

Teachers and other students can often gain from the English language learners' knowledge about the topics of study. Often, their experiences have been rich in the content of focus. For example, students from South America might have personal experiences with some varieties of frogs we consider exotic and might have a sense of their value that is different from the sense of urban dwellers in North America. Children from North Africa can contribute much to the study of civilizations that have derived from ancient Egypt or of studies of deserts. All children bring with them their experiences, language, and folktales and stories that can enrich any unit of study. Think of the potential resources represented by diversity in the classroom, and seek out what your students and their families can bring to each other.

During the development of the units, English language learners also can participate in ways that go beyond verbal learning. They can take major roles in creating the visual displays and the graphic representations of the topics, as in the development of the murals of the frog issue. If some dramatic presentation of content is part of the unit, these students can build their English skills by memorizing parts and participating in group presentations.

Using Computer Resources

Units of instruction provide an ideal place to introduce the use of computer resources. A number of excellent Web sites exist that can be resources to learning. With the help of the instructional media or technical support team in a school, specific and appropriate Web resources can be bookmarked for a class, and students can participate in learning from these resources. Many also contain great visual content, so students with limited English proficiency can learn in easy ways.

The computer also makes the development of reports easier for all. Digital cameras make it possible to dress up reports (e.g., by importing pictures of direct explorations during science units). The ease with which corrections can be made on the computer gives students more freedom to compose their own reports and not fear misspelled words or poor handwriting. Students take great pride in producing reports with great graphics and print quality that reflect their best work. Knowing that their work can be turned into high-quality products serves as an incentive to many students. For primary students, the support of parent helpers or older-grade aides in the classroom can make the computer accessible and not consume all of the teacher's time.

Planning Instruction: A Reflection

You can build a strong reading to learn curriculum in both of these ways—with a balance between fiction and informational material in the reading block of the day or by integrating reading to learn instruction with content units. Our experience has been that for new teachers, it is easier not to do all the instruction through integrated blocks initially but to be sure there are resources for the range of reading and learning needs of students in your class first. What is critical is that you pay attention to what students bring with them in skills and strategies for reading informational texts and provide instruction so students develop increasingly sophisticated knowledge of how to read to learn in a variety of materials and for a variety of purposes. Reading to learn science content is different from reading to learn from social studies materials. Both are different from reading that is taught as if a selection of text was sufficient just to be read and enjoyed.

For Review

Students are eager to learn about the world around them. Your job is to provide the scaffolds so they can do so successfully. This chapter began with an explanation of why teaching students to use informational texts is so important. Then the ABC model of active reading was applied to reading for information. Four kinds of background knowledge were identified: vocabulary, text structure, and content knowledge, both topical and principled.

Many children have little experience with informational materials. Therefore, specific features were explained that you need to introduce to students. These include external features like chapter headings and subheadings, captions, illustrations, the glossary and index, and even the table of contents. The internal structures of informational texts are also important for students to identify so they can determine what is important information and retain it. The use of graphic organizers, having students jigsaw the reading of sections of texts, and having them write using the pattern of the authors were suggested as ways to highlight text organization.

This chapter introduced two frameworks and several instructional strategies that help students become aware of and utilize these features and become active questioners and thinkers. K-W-L and I-Charts help frame students' inquiry. Reciprocal teaching, questioning the author, metacognitive graphic organizers, and ways to develop good questioning through paired reading/paired summarizing and ReQuest help students build their knowledge as they engage actively with text ideas.

Finally, the chapter concluded by highlighting the importance of helping students develop their abilities to engage in research and establishing a rich classroom environment where students' inquiry can be nurtured with print and technological resources.

For Your Journal

Keep a record for one or two days of all the reading you do. Note the material you read, the time you spent, and how you engaged yourself in the materials, including what you thought and felt as you read. Try to remember your school experiences, and write about what kinds of materials you were taught to read. What tips did you learn for reading and comprehending informational material?

Taking It to the World

1. Most children are curious about the world around them. Yet sometimes teachers get very busy meeting all the curricular demands and overlook students' interests as a natural connection point to content. Visit a school library or a public library and become familiar with some of the excellent magazines available for young readers. Sit down and talk with some children about which of the magazines they enjoy most. Then see whether the library has a service that permits you to search the magazines by topic so you can use articles in the future as you develop your own teaching units and extend readings on key topics in the curriculum.

2. Try out your skills in eliciting from students what they know about a topic and helping them articulate good questions to extend their knowledge. The K-W-L process is an easy way to start. Ask a teacher to allow you to teach a lesson with a small group of students around some topic of current interest, an item in the news or some community event. Have two or three short texts with you so you can read to the students to

help them answer their questions after the first two steps in the K-W-L are complete. Keep a copy of the chart you create so you can reflect on the students' knowledge and interests after the session.

Technology Connections

Visit the National Geographic Kids Web site (**www.nationalgeographic.com/kids/**), and investigate what it has to offer young children. How does it utilize graphics to enhance the information? Is the layout organized in a way that is easy to follow? What options are available to help students search for more information about specific topics?

Connect with Research

Review the following key words from the chapter and then connect to Research Navigator (**www.researchnavigator.com**) through this book's Companion Website to conduct a search into research on each of the various topics as they relate to reading and literacy education today.

I-Chart
informational texts
K-W-L-+
metacognition
motivation to learn

principled content knowledge skills
reciprocal teaching strategies
schema
topical content knowledge

Companion Website

To access chapter objectives, practice tests, weblinks, and flashcards, visit the Companion Website at www.ablongman.com/templeallchildren2e.

Go to Allyn & Bacon's MyLabSchool (**www.mylabschool.com**), enter Assignment ID RMV6 into the Assignment Finder. Watch the video, *Reading a Textbook,* in which a middle school teacher discusses with her class how to read a science textbook.

Question: What are some strategies for reading and understanding textbooks? You may also answer the questions at the end of the clip and e-mail your responses to your instructor.

chapter 9

The Advantages of Promoting Writing Among Students

Using Technology in Teaching Writing

Writing in Different Genres

Teaching Children to Write

Involving Families in Their Children's Writing

Assessment of Writing

Teaching Children to Write

Anticipation Guide

The following statements will stimulate your thinking about the topics of this chapter. Answer true or false in response to each statement. As you read and learn more about the topics in these statements, double-check your answers. See what interests you and prompts your curiosity toward more understanding.

_____ ● In general, children never write until they have been carefully taught how.

_____ ● When we speak of a writing process, we mean a process by which many successful adult writers as well as schoolchildren produce written compositions.

_____ ● The goal of writing instruction is to teach children to write everything once and write it correctly.

_____ ● Children can help each other learn to write.

_____ ● It is generally better for teachers to assign writing topics than to let children choose their own.

_____ ● Children need different levels of support as they learn to write. Some children flourish in the open atmosphere of the writing workshop, but others need more explicit guidance.

_____ ● It is important for teachers to write in front of children and demonstrate writing as a studio craft.

_____ ● The difference between editing and revising is that editing is done only by professional writers.

_____ ● There is no such thing as different levels of support teachers give to writers at different ages. Writing is a sink-or-swim affair.

_____ ● Reading helps children learn to be writers because it shows them the choices that writers make in crafting language into print.

A CLASSROOM STORY

The Writing Process in a Third-Grade Classroom

At West Street School in Geneva, New York, Anne Bergstrom is trying a new approach to her third graders' study of African geography. The school's experience has corroborated what the National Assessment of Educational Progress has found: Not only do elementary students need to know more geography, but they also need to know how to think with geographical information. So this spring, because their student teacher from last fall, Sarah Barry, is studying in Dakar, the capital of Senegal, Ms. Bergstrom has arranged to conduct an inquiry lesson on Senegal via the Internet.

In the fall, the students located Senegal on a map and discussed its tropical climate and its history as a slave state and as a colony of France, and they read material about Senegal from the National Geographic Web site. They also did their best to make sense of the U.S. State Department's Web-based information. In December, the students thought of questions they wanted Sarah to investigate, wrote them on a piece of chart paper as part of a K-W-L chart (see Figure 9.1), and sent them to Sarah in an e-mail.

As you can see from the vignette, in Ms. Bergstrom's class, writing provided the third graders a valuable tool for finding out about their topic of West Africa. Because the students eventually had an audience for their findings—when they performed their class play for the school—having to write about Senegal gave the students a feeling of authority over their

FIGURE 9.1

The First Questions We Have.

The First Questions We Have

1. Do they go swimming?
2. What is the population?
3. Do they know about King's fight for freedom?
4. How do they talk?
5. What do they eat?
6. How hot does it get?
7. What are their houses made of?
8. What do they do in their spare time?
9. Was it a slave trading place?
10. What do they celebrate?
11. What games do they play?
12. What kinds of animals do they have?
13. What are their religions?
14. How do people treat each other?
15. What kind of jewelry do they wear?
16. Does anyone have piercings or tattoos?
17. Do they trade? What do they trade with other countries?
18. Does everyone have a job?
19. Are there homeless people?
20. How do they dispose of trash?
21. Do they brush their teeth, and if so, with what?

Sarah wrote the students an e-mail from Senegal and asked them how they wanted her to find answers to their questions: "Who do you want me to talk to? What do you want me to ask?" The students took turns writing e-mails to Sarah on the classroom computer. But Sarah realized that there are fascinating things about Senegal that the students did not know to ask about. So she sent them occasional transmissions that she called "mysteries," intriguing photographs with questions attached. The students took turns writing to Sarah about the mystery; they sent guesses or questions they wanted to ask her. In a way, Sarah became an extension of the class, their remote-control anthropologist.

In the spring, Ms. Bergstrom had the students prepare write-ups of what they had learned. The students used the writing workshop to focus on their topics, write a first draft, revise their drafts, edit them, and prepare them for publication. Later, the class collaborated on a joint composition: the script for a class play about aspects of life in the West African country of Senegal, which they performed for an audience of the whole school.

information and helped them to think about it all the harder. The tools of writing and reading worked together nicely in this project. The students needed to read about Senegal so that they would have a better idea what to ask, and they had to write out their questions, read the student teacher's responses, and write more questions. Because they had become inquirers about Senegal, they read material about that country with more interest.

Humans are the most communicative animals. Remembering, imagining, and communicating in words come naturally to us. If you take a stroll down the street or look around in the waiting area of any shop or business, you will see that we find it natural to communicate in print.

Even young children share the human fascination with print. By the age of two, children are making marks on things with pencils and crayons—and jelly and gravy and anything else they can lay their hands on! By age four or five, especially if they have a parent in the house who is also a writer or a student, children will imitate that parent and produce page after page of script (see Figure 9.2), show it to the parent, and ask, "What did I write? What does this say?"

With a little encouragement in kindergarten and first grade, children write inventively and sometimes voluminously. Children go through a golden age of creativity between the ages of four and seven that is manifested in their spontaneous poetry (Heath, 1984), in their playacting (Pellegrini & Galda, 2000), and most especially in their artwork (Gardner, 1980). The exuberance of young children's writing can be a joy to read (see Figure 9.3). When teachers structure environments for writing and give the proper kinds of instruction and encouragement, children's native creativity as writers can mature and be nurtured into a disciplined skill.

FIGURE 9.2

Iuliu's Script at Age 4.

No Geting
To eat turcky.
No Pillgrims.
No indeins
No inethang.
Like I say
if you Dont thqnk
that's Not Boring Whdt
                              IS

FIGURE 9.3

Early Writing.

Source: Temple, Nathan, Burris, and Temple, *The Beginnings of Writing.* Copyright © 1992. Allyn & Bacon Publishers, Inc.

Releasing children's writing creativity, however, is not always a simple matter of "just letting them write." For one thing, enthusiasm for writing differs among children. Because children differ in the amount and kinds of literacy encouragement that they receive at home (Heath, 1984), some will find writing—even the laborious efforts of writing by sounding out words and spelling them inventively—natural and even fun, whereas others will be puzzled by the whole business of writing and will expect the teacher to tell them exactly what to do (Delpit, 1996). Also, children might find writing natural at one age but difficult later. That might be because the cognitive changes children undergo beginning at the age of eight or nine make them more self-conscious and less spontaneously creative (Calkins, 1996; Winner, 1982). Thus children who with little prompting produced dazzling artwork and daring verbal creations with ingeniously original spelling at age six might worry about their lack of correctness by age nine and need careful instruction and a lot of encouragement to write more than a few safe but bland sentences. Moreover, schools escalate their expectations of children's writing as children progress through the grades, so by fourth grade, children must demonstrate correct spelling and grammar, stick to the point, and answer the assignment in addition to showing enthusiasm.

The task of kindergarten and first-grade teachers is to show children how to record thoughts on paper and then give the children many opportunities to write and share what they write. But the tasks of teachers of second grade and above are to teach writing in such a way that they keep alive children's enthusiasm and creativity while teaching them to use writing deliberately for many purposes and to honor the conventions of correctness and propriety.

The Advantages of Promoting Writing Among Students

WRITING and READING CONNECTIONS

What are some advantages of promoting students' writing?

Not that long ago, if you asked most teachers about writing, they assumed that you meant handwriting or possibly the format of a friendly letter. The idea had not yet dawned that young people had important things to say, that they could get their ideas elegantly onto paper, or that they would enjoy sharing their ideas with a wide and interested audience. Since the early 1980s, an outpouring of research—much of it based on studies of what competent writers do when they write and what happens when students are shown how to do those same things—has changed the thinking about young people's writing and has developed a framework for teaching young people to write using a process approach. The advantages of promoting writing among students turn out to be many:

- Writing makes students more observant, both of their own experience and of the outside world.
- Being writers makes students closer readers of other writers. It makes them more appreciative of words and builds their vocabulary and their skill at choosing just the right word.
- Writing makes students more reflective as they record an idea, examine that idea in print, and have a further idea in response to it.
- Writing builds community. As students work hard to capture and communicate their thoughts and experiences and as they listen to their classmates' efforts to do the same, students reveal themselves to each other and come to understand each other.
- Applied to literature and to other subjects in the curriculum, writing responses and other kinds of inquiry also serve as a powerful learning tool.

Those who have developed the process approach to teaching writing to children and young people have themselves had two main groups of teachers: professional writers and young people themselves. They studied what writers do when they write and the conditions they need. Then they have tried to set up circumstances for young people to carry out the same processes under similar conditions.

What Writers Need

If you were to study the work habits of professional writers, you would learn many secrets of the trade that help them work successfully. Young writers also can use these secrets to write well.

AUTHENTIC REASONS TO WRITE. Some writers write because readers love their stories. Others write because they know about something other people will want to read. Children may also write for these reasons. Or they may write because they want to compare their predictions about a story with those of their classmates. Or they may write because they want to compare their impressions of a book they have read with those of the teacher or a classmate. All of these are authentic reasons to write. As such, they are more motivating than random assignments by the teacher would be.

REGULAR CHANCES TO WRITE. Writers need to know that they will be expected to sit down and write something out. If they know that, they begin to think up ideas even when they are not writing. Regular chances to write are important for another reason. Because many of people's best ideas come while they are writing, writing regularly gives writers more time in which they are most open to new ideas, even ideas they never suspected they had.

TOPICS THAT ARE INTERESTING TO THEM.   Professional writers choose their own topics, and they decide what is most interesting about those topics and how to make readers interested, too. Unlike children who are given narrow assignments in school, professional writers usually write about things they know about and care about. Sometimes they write about things they want to know more about, and they enjoy using writing as a kind of inquiry.

COLLABORATION.   Many professional writers collaborate to present research results or to tell different parts of a story. Children enjoy writing with other children, too. They can help each other find the most effective ways of expressing something. They enjoy having each other for an audience.

MODELS AND DEMONSTRATIONS.   Most professional writers are intensely tuned into the writings of others. They pounce with delight on a phrase, a word, a technique, or a form that another writer uses successfully, and they frequently borrow the best ideas of others. The already-written serves as **static models** for what others might write.

Writers also need **active models** who demonstrate writing while explaining that even adults' writing often begins with brainstorms and doodles, includes false starts and reverses on itself, and is marked up many times and corrected before some fraction of the writer's output turns into the flawless flow of print seen in published books. Without this sort of modeling, where published writing came from would be mysterious. Donald Graves (1982) describes writing as a "studio craft," one that is best taught by example. The teacher must provide the model of what a writer does. The teacher must go first and provide direct teaching. Children need to be shown how to write—from thinking up ideas, to verbalizing sentences, to sounding out words and spelling their sounds, to composing in different genres.

PUTTING CONVENTIONS IN THEIR PLACE.   People who agonize over handwriting, spelling, and neatness on their first draft soon suffer from self-doubts and writer's block. The most confident writers are those who can write out a draft of an idea in the full knowledge that they will be able to come back later to make it neater, more grammatical, better organized, and correctly spelled. This is not to say that conventions are not important, but writers should consider conventions only after they have gotten out what they want to say. Current learning standards for writing stress compositional issues as well as mastery of conventions (see the Standards and Literacy box).

Standards and Literacy

Writing Process Requirements

The writing process is promoted in classrooms that follow what is called the *writing process approach* (Calkins, 1996; Graves, 1982). Not many years ago, this approach was used by the more innovative and adventurous teachers. Now the approach is widely accepted as a best practice of English language arts instruction. Indeed, many states are requiring that teachers instruct children in the writing process. For example, in Texas, the TEKS, or Texas Essential Knowledge and Skills (Texas Education Agency, 1998), calls for students in grades 1 through 3 to be able to do the following:

Writing/writing processes. *The student selects and uses writing processes to compose original text. The student is expected to:*

(A) *generate ideas before writing on self-selected topics (K–1);*

(B) *generate ideas before writing on assigned tasks (K–1);*

(C) *develop drafts (1–3);*

(D) *revise selected drafts for varied purposes, including to achieve a sense of audience, precise word choices, and vivid images (1–3); and*

(E) *use available technology to compose text (K–3).*

The Writing Process

The model of the **writing process** used here was put forward several years ago by Pulitzer Prize–winning journalist and writing teacher Donald Murray (1985) and language arts specialist and researcher Donald Graves (1982). According to their writing process model, thoughtful writers may go through five steps or phases as they produce their works: rehearsing, drafting, revising, editing, and publishing.

REHEARSING. Rehearsing is the act of preparing to write by gathering information and collecting one's thoughts. Student writers think of what they might like to write about, they survey what they know about the topic, and then they begin to plan a way to write about it. Several strategies are available that can teach students to rehearse their ideas before writing:

- *Brainstorming and clustering.* Children can jot down in list form their ideas about a topic before embarking on writing about it. As a more elaborate version of the brainstorm, you can have them create a graphic organizer, such as a cluster or semantic web, with the topic listed in the center connected to "satellites" around it (see Figure 9.4).

- *Interviewing each other to find the story.* Students can interview a partner. Whether or not a writer has already prepared a cluster, it often helps if another student asks the writer questions about the topic to help the writer "find the story." The student asks questions such as the following:

  "Why did you choose this topic?"
  "What most interests you about the topic?"

  The student also asks questions about details, things that the writer might not realize readers will want to know.

- *Making class collaborations.* In introducing a new kind of writing, such as a poem or a fairy tale, it might be best to ask the students to compose one work together

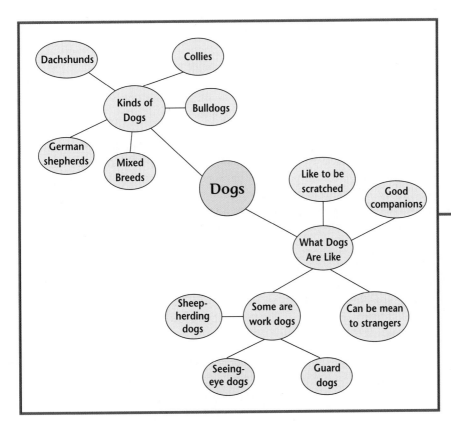

FIGURE 9.4

A Cluster.

before writing on their own. This is especially helpful for younger students. The teacher can contribute as well to help steer the work in positive directions. If the students have difficulty beginning, offer them a series of choices:

Where does the story take place? In a big city or a small village?
Who should be the main character? A young girl or an old magician?
A young girl? Okay. Then who can describe her? And what is her problem?

- *Researching the topic.* Students might be able to write stories or papers about personal experiences off the tops of their heads, but when they are writing about the world outside of themselves, they usually need to collect information about their topics. They might need to read up on it or interview experts about it, or they might observe carefully and collect details about it. Lucy Calkins and her colleagues in the New York City Writing Project (1992) suggest having students keep notebooks for gathering observations.

DRAFTING.   Drafting involves setting ideas out on paper. Drafting is tentative and experimental. Students write down their ideas so that they can see more of what they have to say about their topic; often their best ideas do not occur to them until they begin committing thoughts to paper. The phase of drafting is not the time to be critical about spelling and handwriting. Such mechanical concerns are better dealt with later; this is the time for students to focus on getting their ideas onto the page.

Most young writers do not have the habit of writing more than one version of a paper. Proficient writers, however, believe that good writing is rewriting. You can encourage students to think of writing as drafting in a number of ways:

- Stamp the papers DRAFT or use recycled office paper. Both means make it clear to everyone that these versions of their papers are not final.
- Have the students write on every other line. This leaves room for them to add material they think of later on.
- Show students how to use arrows, carets (^), and stapled-on sections to indicate on a draft how it should be rewritten. Unless they are shown, students will not know how to physically mark up and modify a draft and use it to plan the next version of the paper.
- Remind students not to worry too much about spelling, handwriting, and mechanics at the drafting stage. A large advantage to writing more than one draft of a paper is that it frees writers to concentrate on their ideas at first and worry about form and correctness later. This should be explained to students at the start, and the treatment of their early and later drafts should be consistent with it. Be careful, however, that you do not encourage students to be messy. Bromley (1999) advises against calling an early draft of a paper a "sloppy copy."

REVISING.   After their thoughts have been written out in draft form, students need to consider how the ideas can be stated more clearly. Most students need to be shown ways in which writing can be improved: by having clear beginnings, middles, and ends; by finding a topic and sticking to it; by showing and not telling; and the like. You can teach these points through focused lessons (discussed later) and help young writers internalize them by means of conferences. There are two main kinds of conferences in teaching writing.

Teacher-led conferences.   Conferences allow you to help students clarify their writing and also to model for the student ways to ask helpful questions that will help encourage other struggling writers, their peers. You need to ask questions that teach, pulling solutions from the students themselves and always respecting the students' ownership of their writing. Ask students questions to help them focus on areas to improve their writing, and provide checklists of things to watch out for.

Peer conferences.   Once you have modeled the process, students can hold conferences with each other. Because many conferences will be going on in the room at one time, it helps if students understand their tasks clearly. You might put together a checklist of good questions to ask as they review with each other, such as the following:

- Did my opening lines interest you? How might I improve it?
- Do I need more information anywhere? That is, where could I be more specific?
- Do you ever get lost while reading my draft?
- Do I stay on topic?
- Do I come to a good conclusion?

EDITING OR PROOFREADING.   Once a paper has been drafted and revised, it needs to be reviewed for mistakes. Of course proofreading is held off for last because paragraphs or even pages might be cut or added in the revising stage. The habit of proofreading must be taught; it consists of three things:

- Caring that the paper be correct
- Being aware of particular errors
- Knowing how to set them straight

A caring attitude toward their writing is probably best developed by publishing what students write. Students are most likely to care about correctness once they realize that writing is not simply done for a grade, but that their works must pass the scrutiny of others, who will be distracted from their ideas if the papers are marred by flaws in spelling, grammar, and handwriting.

Children should be made aware of errors through focused lessons that demonstrate one or two errors of writing at a time. Focused lessons treat errors that one or more students are actually making in their writing. Areas in which children make errors might include the following:

- Beginning each sentence with a capital letter and ending it with terminal punctuation (a period, a question mark, or an exclamation point)
- Making each sentence express a complete thought, avoiding sentence fragments and run-on sentences
- Spelling correctly

After clearly teaching students to be aware of different kinds of errors and how to repair them, the next step is to get the students to proofread their own work. Give them a checklist to guide their proofreading, such as the one shown in Figure 9.5. Each point on the checklist should be carefully introduced, explained, and practiced before students are sent off to use it on their own. Several versions of the checklist might be introduced during the year as new points for correction are added to the students' repertoires. Once the checklist has been introduced, students should practice using it with a partner to go over each other's papers before they are ready to use the checklists by themselves.

PUBLISHING.   Publishing is the final stage of the writing process and actually drives the whole endeavor. The prospect of sharing what they have to say with an audience makes many students want to write, rewrite, and smooth out and refine, especially if they have seen other students' work received with appreciation and delight. Publishing also lets students see what others are doing. A good idea is contagious; and anything from an interesting topic, to a plot structure, to a way to use dialogue, to the habit of taking risks with spelling may be shared from one student to another through the process of publishing.

How to Organize and Manage a Writing Workshop

A popular approach to teaching children to write is the **writing workshop**, in which students are taught to use the writing process and are given regular opportunities to use it to produce many different kinds of writing. Teachers who teach writing successfully work three elements into their teaching:

- *Time.* Writing workshops should be scheduled at regular intervals so students know when they will have opportunities to write. When students know that they will have

1. Did I spell all words correctly?
   (*Underline words you are unsure of. Try looking some of them up.*)

2. Did I write each sentence as a complete thought?
   (*This is an incomplete thought: "On the street." This is a complete thought: "The little puppy stood all alone on the street." Note: Sometimes writers use an incomplete sentence on purpose—to create a certain effect. For example: "Not me!"*)

3. Do I have any run-on sentences?
   (*Here is a run-on sentence: "The little puppy stood all alone on the street and he couldn't find his mother and he was so, so frightened that he thought he would die and so he looked around to find a friend and he didn't find one so he walked on and on." This is a run-on sentence, too: "I don't have a pet at home do you?"*)

4. Did I end each sentence with the correct punctuation?
   (*Here is a sentence that has the wrong punctuation at the end: "Could the puppy find his mother." The sentence needs a question mark, not a period.*)

5. Did I begin each sentence with a capital letter?

6. Did I use capital letters correctly in other places?
   (*Names, days of the week, months, titles, etc.*)

7. Did I use commas, apostrophes, and other punctuation correctly?
   (*Commas are used between words in lists, before a conjunction introducing an independent clause, after salutations, etc. Apostrophes are used with possessive forms [Jimmy's shoes, the boys' lockers] and in contractions [can't, it's — for "it is"].*)

8. Did I indent each paragraph?
   (*Whenever you start a new idea, you need a new paragraph. Dialogue [talk between two or more people] also requires a new paragraph each time a different speaker talks.*)

these opportunities, they are more likely to collect ideas during their daily lives that they can write about during writing workshop.

- *Emphasis on communication.* There is an important difference between writing for the teacher (to demonstrate skill or to get a grade) and writing because you want to say something to people who will be interested in hearing it. When writing is real communication, students engage their full powers of expression. Therefore, students should have opportunities to choose their own topics or—when the topic is assigned—to decide on their own approach to the topic. When conferences are conducted to help students improve writing, their ownership of the work—that is, their communicative intent—must still be respected, with freedom left for them to choose the advice they will follow.

- *Demonstration and direct instruction.* Teaching writing is a studio craft, with attention to the process of creating. The teacher should demonstrate every phase of the process so that students will know how writing is done. The teacher should also teach skills of writing, from organization to correct punctuation, but teach them in the context of writing for communication so that students will actually come to use them.

The length and frequency of writing workshops often varies from one teacher to another, but having a consistent plan will help each teacher to encourage student writing. Figure 9.6 shows one plan for managing the time in a writing workshop. This writing work-

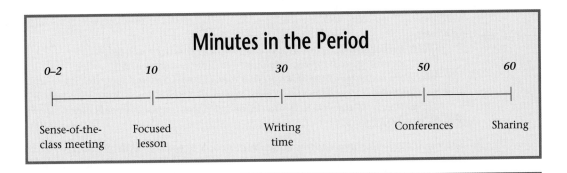

FIGURE 9.6

Daily Schedule of a Writing Workshop.

shop lasts an entire 60-minute class meeting, perhaps three days a week, with time set aside for five distinctive activities.

SENSE-OF-THE-CLASS MEETING. Assuming that the students are already engaged in writing tasks, the period begins with a brief sense-of-the-class meeting (Atwell, 1986) to find out who is working on what writing topic. Students keep a list of writing topics in a journal or a writing folder; if they do not have a work in progress, they should already have a topic ready to be written about. By finding out and recording several interesting things about each child at the beginning of the year, the teacher can have a lively suggestion ready if a student comes up empty.

FOCUSED LESSONS. The goal of writing workshops is to encourage students to write about things they care about to real audiences and to improve their writing so that it communicates more and more effectively. It is essential to give students time, models, and opportunities to write. But students also need careful instruction on all aspects of writing—from how one carries out the writing process to proper punctuation. Focused instruction helps children in the rehearsal and drafting stages by showing them strategies for writing, and it helps them in the revising and editing stages by giving them criteria or working standards for making their writing better. In the past, focused lessons were called mini-lessons, and teachers tried to hold their length to five to seven minutes; now the preferred term is *focused lessons*, to give due attention to the importance of writing instruction (Bromley, 1999; Routman, 1996).

Focused lessons may relate to any aspect of writing, from mechanical issues such as spelling and punctuation; to word-choice issues such as showing, not telling, to write vividly and clearly; to composition-related issues such as ways to write strong introductions and closings. Focused lessons also may highlight the writing process itself, showing students how writers get ideas and narrow them, how writers put ideas into words, how writers go back and make the work better, and how writers share their work and learn from their peers' comments.

The goal of all focused lessons is for children to internalize the main points and observe them while critiquing their peers' paper and their own. In other words, the writing teacher tries to work himself or herself out of a job. It is important to conceive of focused lessons not as teaching writing skills in the abstract, but rather as ways of adding information and guidance to the children's own writing and editing processes.

Focused lessons follow the same four-part model used throughout this book to teach skills in context: demonstration and immersion, attention to detail, guided practice, and independent use. In the writing workshop, focused lessons use those four parts in the following ways.

1. *Finding a text that demonstrates a point or skill you want to teach.* For example, if you want to show children how to write vivid beginnings to stories by jumping right into the action, read the beginning of *Charlotte's Web:*

"Where's Papa going with that axe?" said Fern to her mother as they were setting the table for breakfast.

"Out to the hoghouse," replied Mrs. Arable. "Some pigs were born last night."

"I don't see why he needs an axe," continued Fern, who was only eight.

"Well," said her mother, "one of the pigs is a runt. It's very small and weak, and it will never amount to anything. So your father has decided to do away with it."

"Do away with it," shrieked Fern. "You mean kill it, just because it's smaller than the others?" (White, 1952/1980 p. 1)

2. *Sharing the example and calling students' attention to the skill it demonstrates.* E. B. White could have begun his story by describing the setting and the characters, but he didn't. He started right in with the action. He decided to have Fern ask that question, hear that terrible answer, and get upset. After just these few lines, it is evident that the main problem of the story will be saving the little pig's life, and readers will want to know what can be done to solve this problem.

   You might ask the students how the beginning made them feel and what it led them to expect. What advice do they suppose E. B. White gave himself that made him begin the story that way? Discuss this example until the point is clear that a good way of beginning a story is to start right in with action that shows readers a problem and makes them care what will happen in the story.

3. *Providing the students with guided practice using the skill.* Ask the students to take out a draft of a story they are writing. Have them rewrite the beginning of the story so that it starts right in with action or dialogue that leads the reader right into the main problem of the story. Have the students pair up and take turns explaining to a partner the changes they made to their paper.

4. *Encouraging students to use the skill in their independent writing.* So that the points taught in the focused lessons enter students' repertoire of writing skills, you might add each point to a writing rubric or editing checklist or to your guidelines for good writing. You can also add that point into rubrics used to evaluate students' writing or into the checklists they use to edit their own and each other's drafts.

WRITING TIME. During much of the writing workshop, all of the students are writing. This is quiet time. The teacher writes for the first five minutes as well, to help establish an atmosphere for quiet independent work. For the next ten minutes, the teacher might move around to individual students, to encourage them as they write. Nathan and colleagues (1988) advise that the teacher go first to those who appear to be having trouble writing.

CONFERENCES. After the students have written, a period of conferences begins. The teacher can conduct a conference for the whole class, with one student, or with a small group.

Students may confer with a partner or with a small group. Conferences were discussed in detail earlier. Students who wish to continue writing during this time may do so.

SHARING. The last ten minutes of the workshop are reserved for sharing. The teacher should choose students to share who are far along in a draft or whose work displays an interesting issue. Different students should share each time because only one or two can normally share in a ten-minute period. Some teachers extend sharing time to get in three students a day; that way, every student gets to share every other week.

Different Levels of Support for Writing

The writing workshop model assumes students are capable of a fair amount of self-direction and that they understand at least the rudiments of how ideas are put down on paper. It is true that children as young as kindergarten age can participate in writing workshops in some fashion. But teachers find that many young writers—and not just the youngest—sometimes need more explicit support as they learn to write. Fountas and Pinnell (1996) and Tomp-

	High				Low
	←——————————— Teacher Input and Support ——————————→				

Kind of Support	Modeled Writing	Shared Writing	Interactive Writing	Guided Writing	Independent Writing
How many?	Group	Group	Group	Group	Solo or buddy activity
Whose ideas?	Teacher composes	Teacher and students compose	Teacher and students compose	Students compose	Student composes
Who writes?	Teacher writes	Teacher writes	Teacher and students write	Students write	Student writes
Sample activities	Demon- strations	K-W-L charts; dictations	Daily news; songs, poems	Class collaborations form poems; formula books; (concept books; riddles, etc.)	Writing workshop; journals; plays; free compositions

FIGURE 9.7

Writing Instruction with Different Levels of Support.

Source: Adapted from Tompkins, 2000.

kins (2000) suggest that teachers prepare to give different levels of support for young writers and provide a range of activities for doing so. Those that give higher levels of support put the teacher in the role of demonstrator and explainer.

Those that give lower levels of support maximize the children's initiative and put the teacher more in the role of coach and guide. Five kinds or levels of writing support are modeled writing, shared writing, interactive writing, guided writing, and independent writing. Figure 9.7 shows examples of the kinds of activities that are conducted at each level of writing support. Although some of the activities at the more highly supported end of the scale are intended for young children, it is not the case that only younger writers need more support and only older writers need less. At one time or another, writers of all ages can use both support and freedom to create.

MODELED WRITING.   In **modeled writing**, when students need to be shown some aspect of the writing process, the teacher models it for the class. For example, if you wish to introduce the writing process to young students for the first time, you might proceed as follows:

Gathering the children in front of you, announce that you are going to write about something important. Explain that you are first going to draw your ideas as you talk about them and that you will then write in a space below the picture. Take a piece of chart paper, and fold it horizontally so that the crease is about a third of the way from the bottom. When the paper is flattened out, the crease will mark off the space for writing. Now think aloud by naming and talking about your topic: your aging family dog. Using a page of chart paper, draw a picture as you talk, and demonstrate how you can use drawing as a way of rehearsing or thinking out your ideas. Then think of one line you want to write about the dog in the space you left for writing underneath the picture.

My dog is old.

You say the sentence to yourself several times and then announce that you're going to write the first word, "My," which you pronounce slowly.

"What sound does it begin with?" you ask.

"Muh," you say, "and what letter makes that sound?"

"M," you say and write M on the board.

You then pronounce the next sound and spell it, and you write the other words in the same way. When you are finished, you have the children read the sentence with you and discuss the picture. Ask the children to identify one thing that interests them about the picture and writing and to ask one question. Post the composition on the wall for the children to look at later, and remind the children that they can write down their ideas in the same way.

The road to literacy isn't just about learning to read. It involves using techniques that involve fostering communication skills, creativity, and problem-solving. The bond I've formed with my kids is great. To see their trust in me manifest itself in day-to-day events is wonderful.

—Bryan.
Head Start Teacher
Washington, D.C.

SHARED WRITING. In **shared writing**, the teacher not only models acts of writing but also engages students in composing the writing. When shared writing is used, the topic needs to be one that both the teacher and students know about and are excited about. Such a topic might be a shared experience such as a field trip, a story that all are reading, or a topic that is under investigation by the class. Completion of a K-W-L chart offers a natural occasion for shared writing. Another kind of shared writing activity is group dictation. Here the writing activity is preceded by some kind of activity that excites the students and stimulates talk about it. The teacher leads a discussion and helps students find things to say, then asks the students to offer comments about the topic and writes these down on a piece of chart paper. The teacher might lead the students to sound out some of the words and to offer spellings for them.

INTERACTIVE WRITING. **Interactive writing** is a procedure developed to help emergent and beginning readers and writers explore the writing system in its details. Developed in London by Moira McKenzie, the method has been incorporated into Fountas and Pinnell's guided reading program because "Interactive writing provides an authentic setting within which the teacher can explicitly demonstrate how written language works" (Fountas & Pinnell, 1996, p. 33).

Interactive writing works very much like taking a dictated account except that the teacher and the children "share the pen." The procedures follow these steps:

PHONICS and
PHONOLOGICAL AWARENESS

How do writing activities support development of phonemic awareness?

1. The teacher and a medium-size group of students share an experience and agree on a topic. The topic might be a retelling of a story or a poem or a song, the daily news, or an idea that the class is studying.
2. The children offer a sentence about the topic. The teacher has the children repeat the sentence many times and even count the words to fix them firmly in their minds.
3. The teacher asks the children for the first word, then pronounces that word slowly, writing its letters.
4. The teacher now asks for the next word and invites a child up to write the whole word, a few letters, or a single letter. The teacher fills in letters the children miss. Each time a word is added, the whole text is read back by the children, with the teacher pointing to the words.
5. To help the children orient themselves to the text and add letters, the teacher might write blanks where the letters should go.
6. The teacher uses correction tape to paste over letters that are poorly formed.
7. The teacher teaches about words and print as the lesson progresses, reminding children of words they know or almost know, reminding them of spelling patterns they have seen before, and reminding them to leave spaces between words and to add punctuation.

GUIDED WRITING. When teachers teach students to create a particular pattern of writing or use a particular strategy, compose a sample piece as a group, and then ask individuals or pairs of students to produce their own writings according to the form or the strategy, they are guiding student writing. **Guided writing** is used when students can handle the rudiments of writing—making letters and spelling words—but still need to know some strategies for organizing their ideas on the page.

Many kinds of the writing lessons described in the next section on writing in the genres lend themselves to guided writing. For example, the form poems of cinquains and list poems can be done as class collaborations and then individually by students as guided writing activities.

INDEPENDENT WRITING. **Independent writing** includes writing in journals, self-initiated writing of all kinds, and writing done in writing workshops. It is important that children of all ages have regular chances to write independently. Doing so allows children to exercise many of their ideas and strategies for writing—from letter formation, to the direction of print on a page, to spelling, to the use of illustrations, to the arrangement of ideas in a composition. Good writing ideas are contagious. If you observe children who have spent extended time in writing workshops, you will see that many more ideas emerge from the children and are passed from child to child than the teacher would have time to think up and teach them during more structured writing time.

Enthusiasm for writing differs among children, but it's an important part of literacy that goes beyond just learning how to put words on a page.

Some children will produce writing on their own, but many will not. That is why the writing workshop is so useful: It uses a combination of teacher example and direction with encouragement of children's peers to get them writing. What about children who find writing difficult? See the suggestions in the Differentiated Instruction box.

Writing in Different Genres

A writing **genre** is a form of writing related to a purpose. Writing expert Lucy Calkins (1994) suggests that teachers immerse students in genre study, in which they read several published works written in a particular genre and then try their hands at writing in that genre. The format for teaching lessons of genre study is similar to that of focused lessons and is demonstrated in the Teach It! box. Different kinds or genres of writing pose different challenges to writers. The main genres of writing include the following:

- *Journals.* These are personal accounts of events or ideas whose purpose is to record experiences and help writers remember them and think about them deeply.
- *Stories.* These are fictional accounts of characters in settings who attempt to overcome problems. The purpose of stories is to be outlets for writers' inventiveness and to entertain others.
- *Poems.* These are compositions that capture and convey emotions and insights while taking liberties with sentence and paragraph construction.
- *Expository accounts.* These are intended to be careful descriptions or explanations of things in the world.
- *Persuasive essays.* These convey writers' views of real issues in their lives and try to influence their readers' views.

TEACH IT! 43

Descriptive Writing

These genres include important subtopics: A play is a kind of story; a song is a kind of poem; an observation report in science is a kind of expository account, as are biographies and autobiographies; and an advertisement is a kind of persuasive essay. They may also be mixed with each other; sometimes writers describe or explain to persuade readers or to tell them a story. Fictitious journals can be a form of storytelling, as Pam Conrad (1992) ably demonstrated in her novel *Pedro's Journal*, a fictional day-by-day account of the voyage of Christopher Columbus.

Differentiated Instruction

Helping Struggling Writers

The writing workshop is a wonderful forum for many children's creativity, but it has not always served all children well. There are some students for whom the self-direction afforded by the writing workshop seems almost tantamount to neglect, particularly children whose home culture and language differ significantly from those of the school (Delpit, 1996). One explanation of the difficulty is offered by Collins (1998), who points out that writing is a secondary form of discourse normally based on speech, which is the primary form of discourse. If the kind of discourse a child sees in books and is expected to produce with a pencil fairly closely resembles the kind of discourse that is spoken, then the task of learning to write is largely one of discovering or acquiring the relations between speech and writing—that is, to figure out the strategies that enable us to put down on paper what we say in speech. The kind of writing workshop described earlier should serve this child well, for as Collins (1998) tells us,

> When literacy activities involve language forms and functions that are close to one's primary discourse, they can be achieved through a balance between acquisition and learning which favors acquisition. The typical writing workshop shows this balance in favor of acquisition, owing to its pronounced student-centered methods, including student-generated topics and genres for writing, multiple drafts to gradually improve writing, and supportive feedback from teachers and peers. When literacy activities involve ways of using language substantially different from one's primary discourse, the balance shifts in favor of learning. (p. 6)

As you might recall from the discussion of language acquisition and language learning in Chapter 3, learning refers to formal, teacher-directed, explicit instruction. Acquisition means learning by discovery and inference from being immersed in writing activities. Moving the balance toward learning means explicitly teaching students what they need to know to carry out the processes of writing. Struggling writers do not need to be taken out of writing workshops and given skill sheets to fill out. It is still possible for teachers to teach students strategies for writing that they can use to express themselves to an audience of their peers (Harris & Graham, 1996).

Strategies are explicit procedures. Strategies relate to every aspect of writing, from choosing a topic, to deciding which parts of the topic to include and which to leave out, to organizing ideas on paper. Strategies may be taught in two ways. One is by means of focused lessons. In a focused lesson, the teacher makes it very clear to the students when and how to use a particular technique in writing, whether it be a beginning + middle + ending organization for a paper or the way to punctuate dialogue. Another means of teaching a strategy is using writing guides or graphic organizers. For struggling writers, having a graphic organizer to follow, such as a story map or an outline for a persuasive essay, helps to make the writing strategy explicit. After the students understand the steps to the strategy, the teacher gives them guided practice using the strategy and provides feedback on their use of it. After they have learned to use the strategy, they will no longer need to use the graphic organizer.

Journals and Other Personal Writing

Journal writing consists of writing down thoughts, feelings, and impressions that are close to the writer and are addressed to the writer herself or himself as the audience. Such writing usually comes fairly naturally to young writers because it has few formal demands. Nonetheless, the kind of personal expressive writing used in journals is important for students to use because it serves as a sort of playground or laboratory for the imagination (Britton, 1970). Students may begin ideas in journals that they later turn into more formal pieces.

TEACH IT!

Refer to your **Teach It!** booklet for further activities you can use to reinforce concepts discussed in this chapter.

Teaching Students to Write in Genres: Descriptive Writing

Writing expert Lucy Calkins (1994) suggests that teachers immerse students in genre study, in which they read several published works written in a particular genre and then try their hands at writing in that genre. The format for teaching lessons of genre study is basically the same as that for focused lessons.

In the following sample lesson, teacher Paul Darion has decided to immerse his students in descriptive writing.

- *Sharing a sample of the writing form.* To demonstrate descriptive writing, Mr. Darion selects the opening paragraphs from Frances Temple's *Tonight, By Sea* (1995) and makes copies of them for his students. He plans to call the students' attention to the author's skill at writing vividly. In this case, the writer has carefully observed a process and shown it to the reader, step by step, and has put the reader in the picture by naming sights, sounds, smells, and tactile sensations.

- *Calling attention to the features of the writing form.* Mr. Darion reads the passage aloud as the students read along. Then he invites the students to say aloud what they experienced in reading the passage. He invites one student to retell the process of lighting a fire. Then he invites several more students, one at a time, to name a detail the writer has given and say whether that detail is a sight, a sound, a smell, or a feeling. Mr. Darion has also decided to pass out different colored pencils and ask students to use different colors for words that appeal to different senses. This part of the lesson ends with the students saying aloud how the writer achieved vivid descriptive writing: "Descriptive writing names things exactly, and uses words for sights, sounds, smells, tastes, and feelings."

- *Providing guided practice in using the writing form.* Sometimes, the next thing Mr. Darion does is to have the students observe something carefully in the classroom and describe it in writing. Today, however, he pulls out a mystery bag he created beforehand. It is nothing more than a paper bag containing an object (such as a chess piece, a spark plug, a sewing thimble, or a Christmas tree light bulb). Mr. Darion invites the students, one at a time, to reach into the bag and touch the object. The students then describe it on paper, with the understanding that they must thoroughly describe the object before they name it.

- *Make a poster explaining how to write in that genre.* Mr. Darion has the students create a poster that names the kind of writing,

provides an example of it, and includes a graphic organizer that makes clear the instructions for writing in that form or genre. The students will now be able to refer to the poster as they complete their own writing.

- *Encourage the students to write in that genre during their independent writing.* Mr. Darion reminds the students of what they know about descriptive writing and encourages them to describe things carefully with words that appeal to the senses. The term *descriptive writing* enters the students' vocabulary, and the reminder to "use words that name sights, sounds, smells, tastes, and feelings" is commonly heard among the students themselves.

> Kneeling in the sand, Paulie shredded dry seaweed and fluffed it into heap between the three black cooking stones, half forgetting that she had no food to cook. She broke palm fronds over the seaweed, then propped two pieces of driftwood with their tips just above the palm. Raking the sand together with her fingers, she built up a ring around the outside of the stones, careful to make room for the air to blow in and give life to the fire, a little and not too much.
>
> Paulie leaned back, still kneeling, circling her upper arms in her hands to warm them. Night had come. The tree frogs stopped singing all at once.
>
> "You got matches, Uncle?"
>
> Paulie's uncle was washing in seawater from a bucket, pouring it down his back to get off the sweat and the sawdust, rinsing his arms.
>
> "All the matches gone, Paulie."
>
> "Go see if you can borrow a coal," her grandmother said. Sitting on the steps of her house, a cloth around her thin shoulders, Grann Adeline leaned toward the fire as if it were already lit. She frowned, slapped at a mosquito on her ankle. "Go on, girl. Ask sweetly and somebody bound to give you an ember."
>
> Paulie wandered down the sand path. The small houses clustered under the trees were mostly dark. She could hear voices talking softly, a baby crying. A thin dog came out and sniffed at the backs of her knees. Paulie looked for the glow of a cook fire, smelled the breeze for one. She could feel the sea air, and hear the waves coming in, but it seemed like nobody was cooking.

Source: From *Tonight* by Frances Temple. Scholastic Inc./Orchard Books. Copyright © 1995 by Frances Temple. Reprinted by permission.

DUAL-ENTRY DIARY.   Journals have other important pedagogical uses, too. Response journals are used to encourage students to reflect on their reading and their learning. A simple but powerful approach to response journals is the **dual-entry diary** (Barone, 1992; Berthoff, 1981). In a dual-entry diary (DED), the students are asked to divide the page down the middle with a vertical line. On the left-hand side, they record phrases that they found striking, important, or puzzling. On the right-hand side, they write comments on the passages. DEDs can be used to respond to literature or a host of other topics. After the students have written their DEDs, the teacher may write comments in them or may ask the students to share their entries in a discussion group.

DIALOGUE JOURNALS.   In this form of response writing in journals, students are assigned to pairs by the teacher. After they have read a part of a book or participated in some other learning event, they write their impressions of it in their journals. Later, they have written conversations with each other. One makes a comment in writing and ends with a question for the other. The other answers the question, makes a comment as well, and writes another question for the partner, and so on.

Stories

Most students enjoy writing stories, and because they are surrounded by stories, they find it natural to do so. Yet the structure of stories is fairly complicated, so some instruction in writing stories is helpful. There are many ways to show students how to write stories.

IMITATING AN AUTHOR.   In the genre study approach, you might read the children several stories by the same author and then ask them to write a similar story. For example, second- and third-grade children delight in writing their own episodes about *Amelia Bedelia* (Parrish, 1992), James Marshall's character *Fox* (Marshall, 1994), or Russell Hoban's character *Frances* (Hoban, 1995).

USING STORY MAPS.   Story maps are outlines that give shape to stories. In Chapter 7, story maps were used as devices for calling children's attention to the parts of a plot. In writing, story maps can be used as frameworks like the one shown in Figure 9.8. In using a story map as a way of planning to write a simple story, students fill in the blanks on the right-hand side of the chart. The parts in parentheses are filled in when a story has more

FIGURE 9.8

A Story Map.

| There was a person . . . |
| who wanted . . . |
| So she . . . |
| but . . . |
| (and she . . .) |
| (but . . .) |
| And then she . . . |
| And finally, . . . |
| So . . . |

than one episode. After the students have filled in the chart, they write the story out, adding details and whatever other twists occur to them. No one would maintain that a story written to a formula will be interesting to read, but children can use story maps during the rehearsal stage of writing as they think and talk through—individually or with a partner—where their story might go.

DIALOGUE STORIES.   A simple but effective pattern for structuring stories is the dialogue story. Students can be shown an example of a dialogue story, such as John Archambault and Bill Martin, Jr.'s *White Dynamite and the Curly Kid* (Archambault & Martin, 1989). Then ask the students to write their own story in dialogue form. As a rehearsal step, have two students make up an oral story together and each write their own version of it later.

Poems

Form Poems

Styles of poems range from those that put an emphasis on form to those that stress ideas and let form take care of itself. Next are three different approaches to writing structured poems. Even though the form is tightly prescribed, children write poems that are lively and surprising with these frameworks to support them. To teach children to write a form poem, follow these steps:

1. Show the students an example of a well-written poem that follows the form. (You might need to write this yourself or save it from a previous class.)
2. Have the students help you create a poem as a group. Discuss each choice they make so they understand the process well.
3. Have individuals or pairs write their own poems.
4. Share several of the poems, and discuss their qualities. Also call attention to the ways in which the poems followed the structure.
5. Make a wall chart in which you feature several of the students' poems; also outline the procedures for writing a poem with the structure in question.

ACROSTICS.   These are probably the simplest form poems to use. Students write their names in capitals vertically down the left side of a page and then go back and insert a word that begins with each letter. For example,

Persistent

Energetic

Never dull

Native of the mountains—

Yes, you will like this person.

CINQUAINS.   Christmas tree–shaped poems that look like the following are called cinquains:

Harry

Young, charmed

Studying, flying, surviving

Ron Weasley's best friend

Wizard

Cinquains are surprisingly useful means of encouraging students to think about a concept and follow a simple pattern:

- The first line names the topic.
- The second line contains two describing words.
- The third line has three action words ending in *-ing*.

- The fourth line is four feeling words, which may be written as a phrase.
- The fifth line is a one-word synonym for the name in the first line.

LIST POEMS.   Throughout the ages, many fine poems have been developed around the idea of lists. Take this medieval prayer, for example:

> From Ghoulies
>
> And Ghosties
>
> And long-legged Beasties
>
> And Things that go bump in the night:
>
> Good Lord, deliver us.

Writers can use the idea by listing all of the things that are:

—dark
—lonely
—round
—scarce

The effect is heightened when writers include in their list both concrete and abstract things. For example,

> A pebble in the pond
>
> a policeman's beat
>
> the moon's halo
>
> subway tokens
>
> surprised eyes
>
> a ghost's mouth
>
> and the world—
>
> are round.

Expository Writing

This genre includes writings that describe or explain. Young writers can be helped to write expository works by focused lessons that share good examples from literature and encourage their imitation. Graphic organizers serve as valuable tools for helping to write descriptive and explanatory prose. A number of graphic organizers are popular with children from second grade up and have been discussed at various points in the book. As you might recall, graphic organizers are important learning aids in comprehension (Chapters 7 and 8) as well. This reinforces an important theme of this book about the close connection between the teaching/learning of reading and writing.

CLUSTERS.   Clusters, also called *semantic webs,* are linked circles that show relationships between ideas. The writer starts by naming the topic of the writing in a circle in the center of the page and then writes subordinate topics in satellite circles around the main circle. Aspects of each subordinate circle are written in still more satellites (see Figure 9.4).

VENN DIAGRAMS.   Venn diagrams are helpful planning aids when writers want to compare and contrast two items, and they consist of two interlocking circles (see Figure 9.9). In the outer left-hand circle is listed everything that is true about Topic X but not Topic Y. In the outer right-hand circle is written everything that is true about Topic Y but not Topic X. In the overlapping part in the middle is written everything that is true about both Topic X and Topic Y.

CAUSE-AND-EFFECT CHARTS.   When students plan to write about cause-and-effect chains, they may organize their ideas before writing using a cause-and-effect chart. A cause-

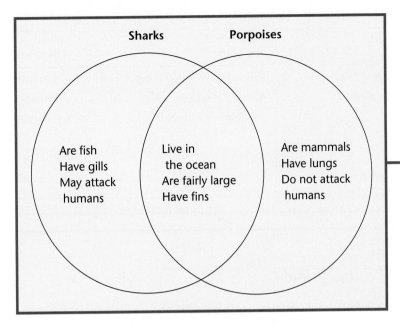

FIGURE 9.9

A Venn Diagram.

and-effect chart (Figure 9.10) may have few or many boxes. Causes are listed in separate boxes on the left-hand side of the chart with effects listed on the right. Several causes may contribute to a single effect, which may simultaneously be the cause of several other effects. The chart in Figure 9.10 shows the many causes of air pollution and their related effects.

Persuasive Essays

There are many ways to help students produce arguments and shape them on paper into persuasive essays. A popular procedure for helping students formulate their ideas for a persuasive essay is the K-W-L strategy (Ogle, 1984), discussed in Chapter 8. By constructing a K-W-L chart, students consider what they already know about a topic, formulate questions that say what they want to know about it, and later list what they learned about the topic. Having done this activity, you can then construct a new chart, labeled like the one in Figure 9.11, that will guide the students to think about and take positions on actions that should follow from those findings.

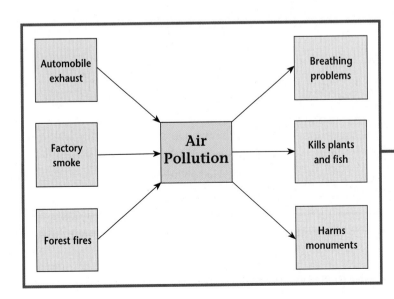

FIGURE 9.10

A Cause-and-Effect Chart.

What?	So What?	Now What?
Pollution from automobiles and industrial pollution causes global warming.	Global warming is bad for plants and animals, including humans.	We should reduce automobile pollution by driving less and reduce industrial pollution by using less fossil fuel.

FIGURE 9.11

What? So What? Now What?

What? So What? What Now?

After the students have completed the chart, they might think about ways to use their entries in an argumentative essay. One way in which the essay can be structured is to enter the information into another kind of format, like the one shown in Figure 9.12.

Writing should be integrated into the reading program early and children should write every day. How can we accomplish these two goals?

Creating a Supportive Atmosphere for Teaching Writing

- Why is it so important for students to have an audience in mind when they write? Why is it not so useful for that audience to be only the teacher?

What do you believe should be done about _____?	We should reduce automobile pollution by driving less and reduce industrial pollution by using less fossil fuel.
What is one reason why that should be done ?	Pollution from automobiles and industrial pollution causes global warming.
(What is a second reason why that should be done ?)	Global warming is bad for plants and animals, including humans.
(What is a third reason why that should be done?)	We are ruining our environment by warming the whole planet's climate.
So, say again what you believe should be done about _____ .	Therefore, we should reduce automobile pollution by driving less and reduce industrial pollution by using less fossil fuel.

FIGURE 9.12

Framework for a Persuasive Essay.

Being a Professional Reading Teacher

Modeling the Writer's Life

In Chapter 7 we suggested that if you are going to inspire children to read, you must be a reader yourself. So it shouldn't surprise you to hear us make the same point about writing. If you haven't participated in an adult writing group, you may not know how completely satisfying it can be to put your heart and soul into creating something meaningful on paper and to have other people be moved by it. The experience comes as close to genuine communication with yourself and others as anything we humans can do. Many communities offer writing classes for adults who want to be motivated to write and to have opportunities to share what they write with others. If you attend one you will quickly see that the point is not, as many believe, to see who has "true tal-

ent" as a writer. It is rather to help you *find your voice* as a writer. Finding your voice takes motivation, practice, and a little inspiration. Inspiration? The ancient Greeks believed in divine creatures called muses who blew ideas into people's heads (that is literally what "inspire" means). We advise our own writing students to assume that the Greeks were right. Think about it: If a divine creature were to blow an idea into your head, wouldn't you be more likely to do something with it if you were writing at the time, instead of watching television or listening to your iPod? So cultivate the habit of writing. Join a group if you can. You will quickly see what a marvelous activity writing really is, and you will motivate your students with your example. And, who knows? Like Regie Routman, Nancie Atwell, Will Hobbs, Paul Janezko, Cynthia DeFelice, Jim Burke, and countless other teachers who became writers, you may connect with a large audience.

- Describe how you might use an author's chair in your classroom to emphasize the importance of writing.
- How can teachers develop a community of writers? Why is the community aspect so important?

The Developmental Nature of Writing

- In a developmental view of children's writing, why is error correction such an important issue?
- Why is it important for a teacher to consider so carefully the issue of correct spelling at different points of a writing cycle?
- How can skills development be integrated into children's writing lessons in such a way that grammar or mechanics doesn't become the main focus?

YOUR PORTFOLIO Of course, it is always useful to include writing samples of your students in your portfolio. Sometimes it is difficult to convince students to part with their best work, but you might be able to photocopy pieces of writing that they want to keep in their own portfolios.

In addition, think about including samples of your own writing. Here are some examples that you might consider: a letter to the editor of your local paper or a magazine, a poem submitted for publication, or a short piece of work submitted for a university class. Your reflections about artifacts in your portfolio and your statement of philosophy of education are also examples of your own writing that might be included in your portfolio.

Finally, think about including a photograph of your author's chair. The more it looks like a throne, the more importance children will attach to it.

TEACHING RESOURCES There are many very useful writing strategies in this chapter. As you read the chapter, make a list of strategies and where they are used most effectively in lessons—as anticipation activities, such as quick-writes; as knowledge-building activities, such as constructing a story grammar while reading; or as consolidation activities, such as the written retelling. Of course, some writing activities are just that, opportunities to write using different styles and conventions. As you begin teaching, refer to the list and make an effort to use each strategy. Your students will appreciate the variety of approaches, and they will not grow weary of the same tired strategy used over and over.

Assessment of Writing

Various parts of this chapter have focused on teaching children to revise and edit their own work. Revising and editing are basic forms of assessment of children's writing. Assessing students' writing and providing ongoing feedback are critical in encouraging students to write. However, in assessing students' writing, keep in mind some valuable principles:

- Not everything should be assessed. Most of children's writing should be for communication and not be graded.
- Assessment should teach; that is, children should learn about writing from the assessment.
- The criteria for assessment should be explicit and clear.
- Children should be involved in their own assessment.
- Assessment should show strengths and progress as well as needed improvements.

Six Traits writing evaluation can guide you in evaluating and grading children's written works. But it has another, equally valuable purpose, which is to call children's attention to the things they are doing well and point the way toward improvement. One highly effective way of showing children what they are doing well and what they can do to improve is to use rubrics.

Six Traits Assessment, a popular evaluation tool, is featured in the Assessment Box.

Using Rubrics

Rubrics are detailed presentations of quality criteria. Rubrics address several aspects of writing at once, and they explain clearly what constitutes a good job. Rubrics may be constructed by the teacher or by the teacher and the students together. Rubrics should be closely connected to the qualities of writing that have been stressed in the focused lessons and any checklists that have been used to guide the students' revising and editing. Students should be fully aware of the meaning of each criterion (aspect of quality) on the rubric before they produce the work that will be assessed. Figure 9.13 illustrates a sample rubric for middle elementary grades, which was adapted from the Six Traits writing evaluation.

Following are the steps for using rubrics:

- Choose four to eight qualities of writing to assess. (Consider having the children suggest qualities of good writing.)
- Make sure the qualities of writing you assess have been carefully explained.
- Describe good work according to each quality. You may also describe fair and poor work.
- Share the rubrics with the students before they write the works that will be assessed.
- Use the rubrics often so that students learn what they mean and are able to use their criteria to guide them when they write.

Work Sampling

Another effective approach to evaluating writing is work sampling. One way to sample work is to choose representative pieces of each child's writings at intervals during the year but at least once per month. Sit down with the child, and discuss the improvements you both see. Ask the child to take the lead in pointing out the improvements. If the child needs help, you might comment on the following:

The Six Traits model for writing assessment meets all of the principles just identified. Developed by Vicki Spandel and her associates (1996, 2000) at the Northwest Regional Education Laboratory, the Six Traits model seeks to direct teachers' and students' attention to six aspects of writing: ideas and content, organization, voice, word choice, sentence fluency, and conventions.

1. *Ideas and content* amount to the quality of having something to say and saying it clearly to the reader. They include having found out something about the topic before writing about it and having an original point of view. They can include providing details that lend an eyewitness feel to the paper.
2. *Organization* refers to the paper's having a beginning, a middle, and an end. It may include supporting main ideas with details, sticking to the topic, and making clear transitions from one point to another.
3. *Voice* describes the quality of reaching for words that express ideas well, even when this means writing words one has not been taught to use or taught to spell. A paper with a well-developed voice approaches the writer's oral fluency and expressiveness.
4. *Word choice* is the quality of showing the writer's meaning with precise words and specific details, and using fresh ways of expressing ideas, avoiding clichés.
5. *Sentence fluency* means a reader can easily read the work aloud. There are sufficient numbers of sentences to convey the meaning, and the sentences are varied in their length and form.
6. *Conventions* include spelling, capitalization and punctuation, and grammatical correctness. In later grades, conventions may refer to allocating separate ideas to separate paragraphs.

    Children of different ages and levels of development naturally will be more or less advanced in their performance within each trait. Spandel and her associates have listed behavioral descriptors at four levels of development:
    - *Exploring writers* are young writers who are experimenting with the whole enterprise of making meaning with graphic communication. Thus, within the trait of ideas and content, exploring writers might use pictures and scribbles to express ideas.
    - *Emerging writers* are still young writers, but they have advanced to the point at which they are starting to work the features of conventional writing into their graphic productions. Thus, within the trait of ideas and content, emerging writers may use pictures or both pictures and mock writing in such a way that a reader might be able to guess an approximate meaning.
    - *Developing writers,* through a mix of their own inventions and discoveries and overt teaching, can produce written messages that convey clear meaning, with the beginnings of formal organization and attention to some of the conventions of spelling and capitalization. Thus, within the trait of ideas and content, developing writers create stand-alone messages that are more readily decipherable. Their works show some attention to detail.
    - *Fluent/experienced writers* express meanings more eloquently in print and take advantage of many features of fluent writing within all six traits. Thus, within the trait of ideas and content, fluent writers create works that show advancing mastery of qualities of writing, including the ability to say things clearly and in fresh and interesting ways, honoring more and more of the conventions of writing.

- The length of each piece
- Organization: sticking to a topic and saying interesting things about it
- The appearance of new features, such as description or dialogue
- Attempts to write in a new genre, such as persuasion or description
- Attention to mechanics, such as spelling, punctuation, and handwriting

Before ending the conversation, ask the child to set goals—writing improvements to make in the next month. Write these down, or have the child write them, with a copy for yourself and a copy for the child. Provide regular reminders of the goals.

Ideas and Content:
Clear ideas. It makes sense.
The writer has narrowed the idea to a manageable topic.
Good information—from experience, imagination, or research.
Original and fresh perspective.
Details that capture a reader's interest. Makes ideas understandable. _____

Organization:
A snappy lead that gets the reader's attention. _____
Starts somewhere and goes somewhere. _____
The writer continually makes connections within the work. _____
Writing builds to a conclusion. _____
The writer creates a memorable resolution and conclusion.

Voice:
Sounds like a person wrote it.
Sounds like this particular writer.
Brings topic to life.
Makes the reader respond and care what happens.
The writer has energy and is involved. _____

Word Choice:
Words and phrases have power. _____
Word pictures are created. _____
Thought is crystal clear and precise. _____
Strong verbs and precise nouns. _____

Sentence Fluency:
Easy to read aloud.
Well-built sentences.
Varied sentence length. Some long sentences, some short.

Conventions:
Looks clean, edited, and proofread.
Free of distracting errors. _____
Easy to read. _____
No errors in spelling, punctuation, grammar and usage, capitalization, and indentation. _____

FIGURE 9.13

A Rubric for Assessing Writing:
Six Traits Writing Evaluation Sheet.

Involving Families in Their Children's Writing

FAMILY LITERACY

How can families become partners in their children's growth as writers?

Families can be partners in all stages of children's growth as writers. Research has shown that children who are drawn into family literacy activities, and especially into letter writing activities, make more progress as readers and writers (Clay, 1987).

Family Writing for Young Children

When children in kindergarten and first grade begin to explore the writing system, it helps if parents give them reasons and opportunities to practice their early writing, even when it bears only a slight resemblance to adult writing. As discussed in earlier chapters, children make progress both as readers and as writers if they are allowed to produce pretend versions of writing. Indeed, with a little training, it is possible to ensure that important concepts about print are discovered and practiced through early writing experiences, even scribbling and invented spelling. Families of younger children can invite children to write some of the following:

Greeting cards to relatives

Grocery lists

Captions on their drawings

Refrigerator notes to the rest of the family

You might need to explain to parents the importance of encouraging young children to write even before they have learned to do so conventionally. Many parents may worry that early untutored writing could reinforce incorrect habits. Assure them that this is not the case. However, you must then observe some safeguards in your classroom, such as making sure that the materials displayed for children to practice reading are written conventionally.

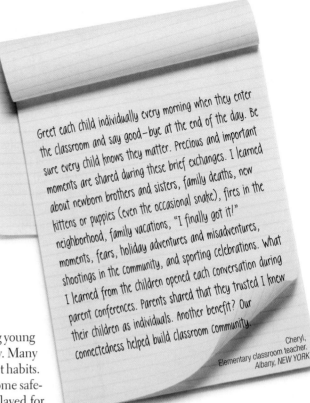

Greet each child individually every morning when they enter the classroom and say good-bye at the end of the day. Be sure every child knows they matter. Precious and important moments are shared during these brief exchanges. I learned about newborn brothers and sisters, family deaths, new kittens or puppies (even the occasional snake), fires in the neighborhood, family vacations, "I finally got it!" moments, fears, holiday adventures and misadventures, shootings in the community, and sporting celebrations. What I learned from the children opened each conversation during parent conferences. Parents shared that they trusted I knew their children as individuals. Another benefit? Our connectedness helped build classroom community.

Cheryl,
Elementary classroom teacher,
Albany, NEW YORK

Family Writing for Older Children

When children are able to spell words and write sentences, they should be encouraged to do meaningful writing at home. Writing at home might include the following:

- Writing up family stories to share on special occasions, as in family letters to relatives
- Letters to friends and relatives
- Writing to a safe circle of friends via a computer-based instant messaging service

Children will be inspired to write if they see family members writing. Some families make a custom of compiling and writing down family stories that occur during the year: the most outrageous camping trip, the funniest family event, and so on. These can be a fine addition to a family photograph album, and can be written by all—children included.

Children feel encouraged to write more when they receive letters—in one way or the other.

Using Technology in Teaching Writing

Why is technology particularly useful in the area of children's writing?

It is in the area of children's writing that technology plays one of its most useful roles in children's education. Technology—computers, e-mail, and the Internet—are a powerful invitation for children to write. Anyone who is a regular user of e-mail knows how much more writing is done when you can communicate with friends online. The same is true for children of all ages. But as Larry Cuban (2001) warns, in most cases, children use computers more frequently and more imaginatively at home than they do at school. This raises the specter of a technology gap, or **digital divide**, between families that can afford computers and the monthly fees levied by Internet service providers and the many families who cannot or do not spend the money on these things.

Communicating via Computers

Because communication via computers is still mostly done by typing on a keyboard, computers elicit a great deal of writing from children when they write to others via e-mail or instant messaging or in chat rooms. Children can communicate via computers in four main ways.

INDIVIDUAL E-MAIL ACCOUNTS.   Conventional e-mail allows users to read and send messages from and to people all over the world. E-mail systems save the messages that one receives and sends, and they enable the user—at the click of the mouse—to reply to messages, send messages to many people at once, and even to block senders of messages. Regular e-mail is not well suited for carrying on a conversation, however, because there may be delays of many minutes between the time a note is sent by one person and when it is received by another, and the reply might not come for hours or days.

INSTANT MESSAGING.   Instant messaging software is supplied by AOL, Microsoft, and others. It enables people to have nearly instantaneous conversations with a limited group of "buddies." Users typically sign up using a fictitious name—a fact that can, in some cases, invite people to write to others without the sensitivity they would normally maintain if their identities were known to each other. It is worthwhile to talk to students about the etiquette of chatting by instant messaging and in chat rooms (see Figure 9.14).

FIGURE 9.14

Etiquette for Electronic Conversations.

> 1. Let your parents know each time you go online. Tell them where you are going and with whom you are communicating. Let your parents participate in the conversations.
>
> 2. If anyone says something offensive to you online, log off and alert an adult—don't answer the message.
>
> 3. Don't write something online that you would not say to someone in person—in short, be polite.
>
> 4. Don't say unkind things about others online. Once they leave your computer, messages may "stay alive" and circulate to people other than those to whom you sent them.
>
> 5. Don't reveal personal contact information—not your last name, or your home address, or your telephone number. The person you are talking to might not be who you think that person is.
>
> 6. Limit the amount of time you spend in computer-based chats. Other people in your house may need to use the computer.

CHAT ROOMS.   Similar to instant messaging are Internet-based chat rooms, in which people may log in and exchange messages with many parties at once. Like instant messaging, chat rooms usually offer the option of signing in under a pseudonym. Chat rooms are sometimes moderated by someone whose job it is to screen out offensive messages. Children should be warned to avoid chat rooms that are not especially moderated to keep them safe for children.

ELECTRONIC MAILING LISTS.   Electronic mailing lists (also known by the trademark *LISTSERV*) are networks of users who sign up to receive messages from each other, usually focusing on a certain topic. There are lists for stamp collectors, kite flyers, fans of sports teams, fans of entertainers, and devotees of an infinite host of other topics. They can link students to communities of others who share unique interests.

PEN PALS AND OTHER EXCHANGES.   In the 1920s, an inspired French educator named Celestin Freinet (Temple, 1994) devised ways of having his elementary-grade students study geography and climate by corresponding with other students from around Europe and the world. Freinet's students asked about other children's surroundings, their weather, and their climate and how these affected their activities. Freinet's lessons were very popular with his students because investigating distant places by talking to the children who lived there was far more concrete, vivid, and engaging than reading dry facts from a book. Yet to pull off this innovative style of inquiry, Freinet's students used what computer savants today contemptuously call "snail mail." Their exchanges took weeks. With the use of e-mail and the Internet, pen pal networks have a global reach, and exchanges can be completed in a matter of days or even hours.

Today, many pen pal networks are available to students. Some central sources link individual children as well as whole classrooms in many countries around the world. Most of the sites have safety procedures, including moderators, to keep children out of contact with unseemly sorts, although caution is still in order. Two such sites are the Kids on the Web, at **www.zen.org/~brendan/kids-pen.html**, and ESD 105 at **www.esd105.wednet.edu/kp.html**.

Protecting Children from Harmful Material Online

Web sites, mailing lists, and chat rooms enable children to leave their own neighborhoods and communicate with others around the world who share the same interests. But this infinite mobility has a negative side. As psychologist James Garbarino (2000) points out, in some mailing lists and chat rooms, young people may find communities of a harmful sort. In an actual community, for example, a young person who has violent fantasies is not likely to find like-minded companions for encouragement, but in the virtual community of a chat room, this young person might find the support of others.

Parents should be reminded to monitor their children's e-mail and Internet use, just as teachers and librarians do when children are in school. Online services and software companies such as Norton and McAfee market programs that give families the ability to screen out whole categories of Web sites, such as those with prurient or violent content. Most e-mail software can be set to block undesirable e-mail messages, but only if the exact name or e-mail address of the sender is known.

Using Computers for Writing Reports

Computers show their greatest strength as learning aids when it comes to children writing papers. The ease with which young writers can add, delete, and move their words around makes computers the ideal support for the writing process described earlier in this chapter. Computers give children control over design capabilities that only layout artists could

The World of Reading

Teachers Become Writers

Laura Ingalls Wilder, author of the beloved *Little House on the Prairie* books, earned her teaching certificate when she was 15 and went right to work. Years later, she became a famous author of children's books. Many others have followed that route: Paul Janeszco, E. L. Konigsburg, Will Hobbs, and Pam Muñoz Ryan among them.

Why do teachers make good authors for young people? Because as any editor will tell you, it helps a great deal if an author really knows children—not idealized children, but real children—and understands their interests and their problems and how they talk and think.

Of course, knowing children is not enough. Writing and writing and rewriting are all required. But eventually, some guidance on professional writing is needed, such as the formats of different kinds of books, how plots are structured, and many tricks of the trade such as ways to prepare manuscripts and to approach publishers. For that kind of guidance, a very useful professional organization that is open to any aspiring writer for children is the Society of Children's Book Writers and Illustrators. Their Web site is **http://www.scbwi.org**. SCBWI has chapters in most of the United States and the Canadian provinces, as well as many foreign countries. Also, the Highlights Foundation, which is the publisher of *Highlights for Children*, Boyds Mills books, and Stenhouse Publishers, runs a summer school in Chautauqua, New York, that is lavishly supplied with some of the world's best children's authors, illustrators, and editors. Many aspiring authors get not only the insights they need, but some contacts who help them along through these and similar workshops. The address of the foundation is **http://www.highlightsfoundation.org/**

manage just a few years ago. Now they can arrange their writing in columns, experiment with different typefaces and even colors of fonts, and add artwork from software archives. All of this adds great appeal to the whole enterprise of writing.

With access to the Internet, children can download and paste into their papers photographs as well as text from a nearly infinite array of sources. Having control over so many variables expands children's creative potential, but it also sets them up to be scavengers of the fruits of other people's creativity unless teachers set clear guidelines for what constitutes original work. Strategies such as the I-Chart (see Chapter 8) are recommended when children are writing reports because the I-Chart format invites children to write a narrative of their investigation and then report their findings. Several online services are available to children for their review and to inform their research:

- Scholastic, Inc., has a Web site at **www.scholastic.com** that includes a Research Starters section. There, students can find illustrated presentations on a growing list of topics (e.g., Pilgrims, dinosaurs, Native American cultures) that are designed to whet their curiosity and give them enough information to begin inquiries that will take them beyond what is presented there.
- The Public Broadcasting Service offers a children's page (**www.pbskids.org**) (grades 4 and up) with links to interesting online articles.
- The National Geographic Society operates a Web site for children that is accessible through their main site at **www.nationalgeographic.com**.
- Classics for Young Children (**www.ucalgary.ca/~dkbrown/storclas.html**) is a large set of links to scores of complete works for children, many of them illustrated, that are in the public domain. The works include the E. Nesbit books (e.g., *The Treasure Seekers*), Frank Baum's *Wizard of Oz* books, Frances Hodgson Burnett's *The Secret Garden*, works by Mark Twain, and many others.

For Review

This chapter focused on both the process and products of writing. The process was described as one of interlocking, usually sequential activities: rehearsing, drafting, revising, editing, and publishing. Students as young as kindergarten age can learn to use some version of the writing process. They are helped to do so by a writing workshop, a regular period of class time set aside for students to receive focused lessons on one aspect of writing, do some writing, have conferences with the teacher and with each other, and share their works.

The products of writing are arranged into genres. Genres include expressive writing such as journals, stories, poems, expository writing, and persuasive essays. Suggestions were given for helping students write in each genre. Children sometimes need more explicit support than the writing workshop gives them. Different levels of support for children's writing include modeled writing, shared writing, interactive writing, guided writing, and independent writing. The special problems of struggling writers were also addressed, and it was suggested that strategies for writing be introduced to them through focused lessons and graphic organizers and be regularly practiced. Assessment is an important part of teaching children to write. Assessment should teach, by employing means that communicate clearly what the children are doing well and what needs work and by involving the children in assessing their own work.

Families have a role to play in supporting students' writing, and suggestions were given for families of younger children and older children. Instructional technology can play a valuable role in children's writing. More and more children in later elementary grades find it natural to communicate via e-mail or in chat rooms. Once the difficulty of keyboarding has been overcome, using the writing process to compose papers is ultimately easier on a computer than with a pencil. The variety of formatting possibilities on a computer is also a draw. That said, there are concerns about children's use of computers. Plenty of material is available on the Internet that is not suitable for children, and although schools have screening software, not all homes do. Also, although the Internet (and electronic encyclopedias) give report-writing students ready access to a wealth of material on virtually any subject, the challenge for teachers is to help students past merely downloading other people's material and teach them to use this information to inform their own reports.

For Your Journal

1. Try out the writing process for yourself with the assistance of a partner, although you can do this activity alone.

   - Make a list of five topics you might write about. These should be topics you might share with children in grades 1 though 5.

   - Ask yourself or have a partner ask you what interests you about each topic. Find your story!

   - Choose the topic that you most want to write about. Write it in the middle of a cluster. Brainstorm subtopics, and add them as satellites in the cluster.

   - Look over your cluster, and circle the details that seem most interesting to write about.

   - Write a draft of your paper. Write for eight minutes without stopping.

   - Read back over your paper, or have a partner read it, and consider areas you need to revise.

   - Write another draft of the paper, and incorporate the changes.

   - Now use the proofreading checklist to look over your paper.

   - Write your finished copy in your journal.

Once you have completed this process, reflect on what happened as you wrote. Did new ideas occur to you as you made your cluster? As you wrote your first draft, were you surprised at some of the ideas you came up with? Did the revision review lead you to helpful changes?

2. In helping children learn to write, where do you think the proper balance can be found between the need to encourage children to feel ownership for their writing and take initiative for their learning and the need to teach them to write better—that is, more coherently and correctly?

Taking It to the World

1. The writing process described in this chapter—rehearsing, drafting, revising, editing, and publishing—is often described as the way professional writers create. But is it? Find and interview at least two writers. If possible, look for writers of fiction and poetry as well as writers of nonfiction. Ask them what they do when they write. (*Hint:* Don't mention the writing process or talk about the steps. See whether they mention those themselves.) Compare your notes with those of your classmates. Do the writers do similar things as they write? Does the process they use seem to depend on whether they are writing fiction or nonfiction? Do their processes resemble the process described in this chapter?

2. The writing workshop described in this chapter is widely regarded in the educational literature as a valuable development. Many teachers use the workshop approach successfully and many children seem to have internalized the steps of the writing process, but maybe not as many as reading the literature might suggest. Visit an elementary school, and ask the teachers whether they use writing workshops with their children. If so, how often? What do they like about it? Does it work for all students? If not, what modifications must they use for the children who struggle? If they don't use the writing workshop, why don't they? What approach to writing instruction do they use?

Technology Connections

1. Visit the Web sites of Cyber Patrol (**www.cyberpatrol.com**) and Net Nanny (**www.netnanny.com**), and compare the services each company has to offer parents for protecting their children from gaining access to offensive sites. Which site would you recommend to parents? Why? Does either service offer the option of blocking undesirable e-mail messages?

2. Check out the online magazine for writing for and by children called Cyberkids (**www.cyberkids.com**). Investigate the Creative Works gallery. How might you be able to use this site to help you teach children to write?

Connect with Research

Review the following key words from the chapter, and then connect to Research Navigator (**www.researchnavigator.com**) through this book's Companion Website to conduct research on each of the various topics as they relate to reading and literacy education today.

active models
digital divide
dual-entry diary
genre
guided writing

independent writing
interactive writing
modeled writing
rubrics

shared writing
static models
writing process
writing workshop

Companion Website

To access chapter objectives, practice tests, weblinks, and flashcards, visit the Companion Website at www.ablongman.com/templeallchildren2e.

Go to Allyn & Bacon's MyLabSchool (**www.mylabschool.com**), enter Assignment ID RMV4 into the Assignment Finder. Watch the video, *Reading and Writing,* which provides an overview of strategies for making the connection between reading and writing for students, and shows an example of how a kindergarten teacher uses writing as a means of getting students to read.

Question: How would you explain the connection between reading and writing? You may also answer the questions at the end of the clip and e-mail your responses to your instructor.

chapter 10

What Is
Assessment?

Teacher Self-
Assessment

Terms Used
in Assessment

Assessing
Literacy

Differentiated
Instruction

What Do We
Need to Know
from Assessing
Children?

What Do We
Need to Know
About Beginning
Readers and
Beyond?

Assessing Literacy

Anticipation Guide

The following statements will stimulate your thinking about the topics covered in this chapter. Answer true or false in response to each statement. As you read and learn more about the topics in the statements, double-check your answers. See what interests you and prompts your curiosity toward more understanding.

———— ● Assessment of literacy is done at different times and for different purposes. At the beginning of the year screening assessment is done, followed by diagnostic assessment for those who need it. All during the year all students are subjected to monitoring assessment, and at the end of the year most face outcomes-based assessment.

———— ● High-stakes assessment has so alarmed and angered the American public that it probably won't be around by the time this book makes it into print.

———— ● The concepts of validity and reliability are not only of interest to researchers—teachers need to be concerned with the validity and reliability of the instruments they use.

———— ● Informal assessments are only given on weekends, preferably at a cookout with everybody dressed in old clothes.

———— ● An important piece of information yielded by assessment concerns children's independent, instructional, and frustration reading levels.

———— ● It is usually harder for a child to read words in the context of a meaningful passage than to read them off lists.

———— ● The online management and reporting of children's assessment data are becoming something of an industry in the United States.

———— ● All assessment should be done using scientifically tested instruments.

———— ● Readability measurement is an exact science. It is possible to pinpoint precisely the level of challenge any piece of text will pose to any reader.

———— ● Assessment is for children. There is no earthly reason why teachers should ever assess themselves.

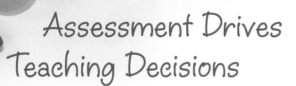

Assessment Drives Teaching Decisions

John Samuels teaches a diverse group of first graders at a small elementary school in a farming community. Of his twenty-seven students, seven speak Spanish at home. The parents of eight of the children (including two of the Spanish-speaking families) are scientists at a nearby agricultural experiment station. Some children are from families of farm workers, and others from families on public assistance. John believes very strongly that his job as a teacher is to help all of his children be as well-prepared for a happy and successful life as he can make them.

At the beginning of the year John, the school's reading teacher, and the three other first grade teachers in his school administer a screening test of early reading abilities to the entire first grade. They test the children's letter knowledge, their concept of word, their phonemic segmentation and phonics (through an invented spelling task), and their recognition of both environmental print and decodable words. The results for John's class are given in Table 10.1 on page 316.

John and the other three teachers look through all of the scores together. They decide that the top scoring readers in John's groups are probably beginning readers already. The middle group still needs a moderate amount of support in emergent literacy skills and concepts. The group with the lowest scores will need special intervention to help them profit from reading instruction during the year.

The first two weeks of the school year, John gives further diagnostic tests to his students. The children with the lowest scores have their concepts about print assessed as well as their awareness of phonemes in words. The early screening already showed him which letters of the alphabet each child still needs to recognize and be able to produce, and their other scores suggested that they will

FAMILY LITERACY

How is John partnering successfully with his student's families?

Assessment is an essential part of doing anything well, including the teaching of reading. The topic of assessment is getting more attention in reading instruction now than ever before. With the current emphasis on "research-based reading instruction," educators are paying more and more attention to how children are learning, what works and what doesn't, and why.

What Is Assessment?

Assessment means gathering, analyzing, and interpreting information to tell how well a student reads. Assessment covers everything from informal observations of a student's reading to the use of commercial tests. Assessment practices include:

- Deciding what we need to know about a child's or group of children's reading.
- Deciding what measures will tell us what we want to know.
- Gathering information.
- Interpreting the information.
- Making decisions on what to do next, based on the new information.

need a holistic introduction to reading, with lots of listening to read-alouds, lots of dictation and shared book reading, and shared writing. They will need the whole sequence of systematic phonics instruction.

But John is also a good "kidwatcher." He observes the children carefully as they participate in his early lessons. He is pleased to see them singing along to "Down By the Bay" and smiling as they clap along to the rhythm. He watches to see whom they interact with on the playground.

He has already visited with their families before school started. The parents want their children to learn, and they make it clear that they are counting on his suggestions for ways to help their children. Two of the mothers and one of the fathers is unemployed. They seem skeptical when John suggests that they might come into the classroom to help out, but John thinks at least the father and one of the mothers can be persuaded.

John finds time to read a simple book with each of the top- and middle-scoring children, and he keeps a running record of their abilities. He has learned to be a little skeptical of test scores, and he watches carefully to see if their performance in a real reading task lives up to what the test predicted. He is "roaming around the known," as Marie Clay puts it (1993). Soon he has found a reading level for each one and is ready to place them in their first group for guided reading.

As he makes running records of the middle-scoring children's reading, he finds levels of books they can read at the instructional level, too. He notes they have developed some sight vocabulary and are developing some phonics skills. They are not fluent readers—they read word by word, without inflection. He will see if he can match them up with tutors from the nearby college's service learning project.

The New York Times
nytimes.com

Themes of the Times

Expand your knowledge of the concepts discussed in this chapter by reading current and historical articles from the *New York Times* by visiting the **Themes of the Times** section of the Companion Website (www.ablongman .com/templeallchildren2e).

STRUGGLING READER

What is John doing to support his struggling students?

Why Do We Assess?

There are different purposes for assessment, and also different audiences for the information that assessment bring to light.

1. **We assess to guide our instruction.** We may assess to:
   - *Determine reading levels* (independent, instructional, and frustration) so we can place students in materials at the right level.
   - *Determine children's readiness or prior knowledge* before starting instruction. Many aspects of learning to read and write are developmental, and in order to give the right instruction, teachers need to know where learners are in their development. For example, as we saw in Chapter 4, children need to develop the ability to segment phonemes and also develop a concept of word before more advanced phonics lessons will make sense to them.
   - *Locate children's strengths and areas of need* to aim our instruction. In the previous chapters, we have covered many aspects of children's literacy development. Children need encouragement in all of them, and if there are a few or several aspects in which they are not progressing adequately, we need to locate those so we can of-

TABLE 10.1

Scores of First Graders on the Early Reading Screening Inventory

STUDENT	ALPHABET KNOWLEDGE (%)	CONCEPT OF WORD (%)	INVENTED SPELLING* (%)	WORD RECOGNITION (%)
High-scoring group				
Janice	100	100	92	80
Ephraim	92	100	88	75
Ignacio	98	100	90	80
Topaz	96	90	92	82
Middle-scoring group				
Peter	70	80	65	50
Carla	65	88	60	55
Laticia	68	80	70	60
Low-scoring group				
Juana	52	40	35	20
George	55	45	30	24
Alexia	40	40	20	10
Amanda	30	30	16	5

*Includes phonemic segmentation and early phonics.

fer specially tailored help. For example, a child may have learned many sight words, but have low reading fluency. We need to monitor that child's reading so we can identify the need to work on the student's fluency.

- *Identify children's literacy strategies* so we can strengthen them. For example, as we saw in Chapters 7 and 8, good readers preview texts and set purposes for reading to help them understand better. Does each child know how to do this?

2. **We assess to monitor the success of instructional approaches.** Approaches vary in their success with individual children, or with whole classrooms of children. We assess to:

- *Find out if a teaching approach or set of materials is working for a child.* For example, to build reading fluency, teachers may use "buddy reading" (see pages 177–178) or a computer program. But does the child know how to take advantage of these activities? Or in teaching word study, the teacher wants each child to study words that are right at his or her level of development of word knowledge. Is this the case? In guided reading, we want children to read some texts that are moderately challenging, and some texts that are easier. Is this the case for each child?

- *Find out what strategies seem best suited to whole groups of students.* Research shows that schools that are most effective in helping all children learn to read and write are those in which teachers monitor how well instruction is working, and then use this information as they work with other teachers to find ways to improve instruction (Cunningham & Allington, 1994; Taylor, et al., 1999). Teachers may monitor a host of factors, from classroom routines and management strategies, to teaching methods, to materials, to ways of working with instructional aides and parent volunteers, to ways of assessing children.

3. **We assess to give feedback to students and their parents.** Findings from assessments should be communicated to children and their parents, so both can work toward the children's success. We assess to:
   - *Show students what they are doing well and what they can do better* by communicating information in a way that helps them understand and purposefully reinforce those strategies they are using successfully, and that can point the way toward improvements.
   - *Help students set goals for better performance* and monitor their progress toward meeting those goals.
   - *Help parents understand how their children are performing* in learning to read and what the parents can do to help.

4. **We assess to make decisions on the placement of students in special instructional services.** All children in the United States are entitled by law to special education services as they need them, and they are also entitled to special support to learn the English language, if necessary. Parents may request that their children be screened for such services, but teachers may also identify students who need more support than what is likely to be available to them in the regular classroom. In either case, special screening is called for, including specialized tests that are normally administered by school psychologists. But the teacher's own observational records and assessment results play a useful role in these decisions.

5. **We assess to make sure all students are meeting state standards for learning.** The federal No Child Left Behind law that passed in 2002 mandated that every child in America be tested in reading from grades 3–8. The tests are developed by the individual states. Because the tests have considerable consequences, many teachers are giving more frequent assessments throughout the year to monitor their students' progress toward meeting the standards on which their state tests are based.

6. **We assess ourselves as teachers or as teachers-to-be.** We make sure our professional knowledge is up to date, and that our practices are serving our students as best they can. We assess our professional knowledge, both to keep ourselves current and to meet teaching licensing requirements.

Relax and enjoy the kids! Don't get so caught up in the content and the planning and the work, that you don't get to know the students.

Karen,
High School Mathematics
Cincinnati, OHIO

Approaches to Assessment

Let us look further at these and other kinds of assessment approaches that are used to measure and investigate children's reading and writing abilities.

NORM-REFERENCED TESTS.   Standardized or norm-referenced tests of reading compare children's performance with that of large numbers of other students. For example, tests such as the Stanford Achievement Test and the California Achievement Test report children's reading performance in comparison to other students at their grade level. The tests are given under rigorously controlled conditions so the results will be comparable. Norm-referenced tests are typically used, along with other information, to inform decisions about placing a child for special reading services. But these tests traditionally have lacked an obvious connection with any school curriculum, so it is difficult to tell what aspect of a school's instruction has contributed or failed to contribute to the children's performance.

STANDARDS-BASED TESTS.   Standards-based tests have come about in recent years as individual states have set standards for achievement in reading and other subject areas at each grade level, as they have been required to do by the federal No Child Left Behind Act (**http://www.ed.gov/admins/lead/account/saa.html#peerreview**). Standards vary from state to state, but in most states they are specific enough to guide teaching. In California, for example, first graders are expected to meet English language content standards, of which the following is a small sample:

Being a Professional Reading Teacher

Different Assessments for Different Phases of Instruction

Teachers use different kinds of assessments for different purposes at different points in the year. Schools with reading programs funded under the No Child Left Behind legislation as "Reading First" schools (**www.ed.gov/programs/readingfirst**) require four different types of assessment at four points during the year. Many other schools follow suit. The four are *screening assessment, diagnostic assessment, monitoring assessment,* and *outcomes-based assessment.*

SCREENING ASSESSMENT. Before instruction begins at the start of the year, teachers may administer screening measures to determine which children are at risk for reading difficulty and may need more support during the year. The screening instruments they use are as economical as possible, because they may be given to an entire class or an entire grade. So they typically examine only a few key aspects of literacy, just enough to identify the children who need extra attention.

DIAGNOSTIC ASSESSMENT. Another kind of assessment is used to identify more precisely a student's needs, so that the teacher can develop a teaching plan that is right for that child. If children have been identified by the screening tests as needing special help, the diagnostic instruments take up where the screening instruments left off. They not only tell that the child needs to know more letters of the alphabet but also which ones; not only that she is a struggling reader, but also that she is weak in comprehension, especially in making inferences. Individual diagnostic instruments may test specific skills, such as a test of phonemic segmentation or a test of reading fluency. Others are more comprehensive and test many areas of reading ability, such as an Informal Reading Inventory (see pages 339-341).

MONITORING ASSESSMENT. Sometimes called formative assessments because they occur while work is in progress, monitoring assessments are used once the teacher has a plan for instruction for a group of children to make sure the instruction is working and each child is making adequate progress. Monitoring assessments range from informal observations to formal probes. Reading First schools and many school districts may require that monitoring assessments use formalized instruments. If so, you must find an instrument with several alternative forms for each level. Informal assessments may consist of records of children's repeated reading scores, records of the numbers and levels of books read, and collected writing samples. Of course, teachers may observe other important behaviors that a test would miss: a child's favorite subjects, who her most productive workmates are, and her difficulties with concentration and how they are best handled.

Monitoring assessments are best done at regular intervals—every month or every quarter for most students, but more often for students who seem to have more difficulty learning. It is advisable that monitoring assessments be designed with the end-of-year assessments in mind. Because of No Child Left Behind, nearly all children in American public schools are now tested at the end of their third through their eighth years, so the monitoring assessments should see how much progress children are making toward meeting the standards embodied in those tests, while changes in instruction can still be made.

OUTCOMES-BASED ASSESSMENT. Outcomes-based tests are also referred to as grade-level reading standards-based assessments because the desired outcomes of a year's teaching are reflected in each state's learning standards. Yet another more general term, summative assessments, may be applied to them, because they come at the conclusion of or the summation of the period of learning that is being assessed. Standards-based assessments are used to test the skills that are named on the state's standards for learning in literacy. In most states, those skills include phonemic awareness, phonics, fluency, vocabulary, and comprehension because these are the areas emphasized in the No Child Left Behind Act.

READING

1.0 Word Analysis, Fluency, and Systematic Vocabulary Development

Students understand the basic features of reading. They select letter patterns and know how to translate them into spoken language by using phonics, syllabication, and word parts. They apply this knowledge to achieve fluent oral and silent reading.

Concepts About Print

1.1 Match oral words to printed words.
1.2 Identify the title and author of a reading selection.
1.3 Identify letters, words, and sentences.

Phonemic Awareness

1.4 Distinguish initial, medial, and final sounds in single-syllable words.

1.5 Distinguish long- and short-vowel sounds in orally stated, single-syllable words (e.g., *bit/bite*).

1.6 Create and state a series of rhyming words, including consonant blends.

1.7 Add, delete, or change target sounds to change words (e.g., change *cow* to *how*; *pan* to *an*).

1.8 Blend two to four phonemes into recognizable words (e.g., /c/ /a/ /t/ = *cat*; /f/ /l/ /a/ /t/ = *flat*).

1.9 Segment single-syllable words into their components (e.g., /c/ /a/ /t/ = *cat*; /s/ /p/ /l/ /a/ /t/ = *splat*; /r/ /i/ /ch/ = *rich*). . . .

Source: Reprinted by permission, California Department of Education.

Standards-based tests are meant to assess each student's performance on the standards set by the states. Students may be promoted to another grade or held back, depending on their performance, and schools may suffer sanctions if they do not make "adequate yearly progress." Standards-based tests are sometimes called **high-stakes testing**, because a child's performance on such a test can determine whether she or he is promoted to the next grade, and the performance of many children can decide if a school is achieving or underachieving (see the Standards and Literacy box).

Standards and Literacy

High-Stakes Testing

The U.S. Constitution left the governance of education up to the individual states, but with the passage of the No Child Left Behind Act in 2002 the federal government greatly increased its leverage over the states by mandating the requirement that states adopt standards-based education. As a result of this initiative, most states have set performance standards for children, and by the year 2006, most states developed tests for those standards. There is some variety from state to state in what children are expected to learn and what teachers are expected to teach. Some states have specified fairly explicitly what is expected, while others have left more room for the teachers' discretion.

The No Child Left Behind Act requires that schools report "disaggregated scores" for male, female, white, African American, Hispanic, Asian, Native American, limited English proficiency (LEP), special education, and economically disadvantaged students (those on free or reduced payment lunches). As President Bush has said, the legislation attempts to fight the "soft prejudice of low expectations." Talking about the different achievement rates of poor versus economically better off children, girls versus boys, and majority versus minority students is a beginning. But society must muster the will to do something about it.

Although the federal government has not required a single set of tests for use nationwide, connecting results with federal monies through the No Child Left Behind Act has placed great pressure on states and schools to comply. But that does not mean that everyone agrees with the standards movement. Richard Allington (2000), a prominent reading expert and leader in the International Reading Association, has noted two major omissions from the government's list of required areas of focus. One is the habit of reading. Allington argues that no amount of skills instruction is as effective as simply motivating children to read a lot, and children will not become proficient readers unless they read. The other is the absence of what Allington calls thoughtful reading: reading to solve problems, to generate ideas of one's own, to think critically, and to think interpretively. Allington points out that, although not required by the federal government, many state standards do include these two concerns. For example, New York State expects every student to read twenty-five books a year at grade level.

Another issue is what to do if children do not pass the state tests. In what has been called high-stakes testing, many states have ruled that children will not be promoted to the next grade, and that schools may be placed on deficiency lists—and parents will therefore be encouraged to transfer their children out of those schools or apply for publicly funded tutoring services—if enough pupils' scores fail to meet the standards. Many observers have complained that these are severe consequences to base on a one-time event such as an examination, and as of this writing there appears to be growing resistance to many of the mandates of the No Child Left Behind Act in many parts of the country. For example, Utah and Connecticut, two states with different demographics and levels of funding for education, have both threatened not to comply with the testing requirements of No Child Left Behind. A growing body of literature has exposed the legislation to serious critique (Peterson & West, 2003; Meier, 2004).

Nevertheless, from the time the legislation was passed, polls showed that a majority of parents support having standards and the tests that go with them (Public Agenda On-Line, 2002), and that support continues among a majority of families five years later (Public Agenda On-Line, 2006). Learning standards and some sort of standards-based testing are probably here to stay, and those who teach must be mindful of them.

CURRICULUM-BASED MEASUREMENT (CBM). As the term *high-stakes testing* implies, by the time a student takes a standards-based test, it is usually too late for the teacher to do anything more for the student that year. To make sure that children are making good progress toward meeting the standards measured on the high-stakes tests—and indeed, to better teach children to read—many educators are turning to the practice of **curriculum-based measurement** (Fuchs, Deno, & Mirkin, 1984; Shinn, 1989), a set of practices and instruments that have been borrowed from the special education field. These measures are normally based on the skills students are expected to acquire according to the state standards for learning, but they have the advantage of being given repeatedly—sometimes as often as weekly—throughout the school year so the teacher can still take corrective action as needed. Curriculum-based measurements are very brief samples of behavior, deliberately so because a teacher may have to test twenty-five or more children individually several times during the year. To test oral reading, for instance, a teacher may have a student read three passages aloud for one minute each and average the speed and accuracy of the reading. Nonetheless, even such brief measures of oral reading have been shown to predict students' later performance on different states' high-stakes standards-based tests. Although curriculum-based measures have many uses, among the most promising is they facilitate continuous monitoring of a student's performance in reading throughout the year, to ensure both the student's learning strategies and the teacher's instruction are working well.

Curriculum-based measurements may be designed by the teacher (see Jim Wright's guide on CBM at **http://www.jimwrightonline.com/pdfdocs/cbaManual.pdf**), or they may be purchased commercially. For grades 5–8, Timothy Rasinski and Nancy Padak (2005) offer a series of *Three-Minute Reading Assessments: Word Recognition, Fluency, and Comprehension*. Many states are using DIBELS, the Dynamic Indicators of Basic Early Literacy Skills, and studies have shown scores on DIBELS predict later performance on the standards-based tests of some states, including Arizona (Wilson, 2005), Florida (Buck & Torgesen, 2003), North Carolina (Barger, 2003), and Oregon (Shaw & Shaw, 2002).

DIBELS was created with public funds, and it is available for free on the Internet (at **http://dibels.uoregon.edu/index.php**). However, for a fee the providers of DIBELS offer an electronically based data management and reporting service that keeps track of each child's scores on each part of the test, follows the child's progress on each of several indicators over time, and makes available a number of verbal and graphic ways to display results.

The Developmental Reading Assessment (DRA) was developed by a commercial company. It, too, provides a range of assessments for screening, diagnosis, and monitoring. It also enables teachers to manage the test scores online and perform a number of tracking, comparing, and reporting functions—for a fee, of course. The Web address of DRA is **http://www.pearsonlearning.com/dra/**.

Some caveats are in order, however. The main advantage claimed for these brief measures is that they save time (Rasinski & Padak, 2005), and thus they afford teachers a feasible way to monitor children's progress toward meeting the states' or the locality's learning standards in reading. However, before serious educational decisions are made about a child—such as the placement of students in special educational services or whether a child should be promoted to the next grade—more extensive assessment procedures should be used.

INFORMAL READING INVENTORIES. Informal Reading Inventories (IRIs), developed 60 years ago by Emmett Betts (1946), are comprehensive measures of students' reading ability. IRIs are administered to individual children to measure their word recognition, fluency, comprehension, and overall reading levels. In contrast to standardized reading tests, IRIs have not been normed by elaborate field testing with hundreds or thousands of children. They are created from samples of grade-level texts, either taken from basal readers at ascending grade levels, or written by the test authors and matched to grade levels according to readability

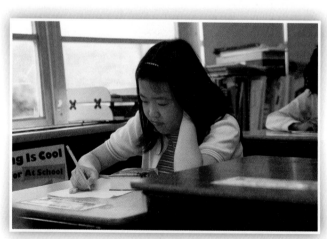

TECHNOLOGY

Research DIBELS on line and describe what you've found.

Thoughtful assessment procedures should be used before serious educational decisions are made about a student.

formulas. Hence they are called "informal" reading inventories. IRIs consist of lists of words and text passages of graduated levels of difficulty—usually from early first grade or *preprimer* through grade 8 or higher.

Teachers may create their own IRIs but many good ones are commercially available, including the *Qualitative Reading Inventory* (Leslie & Caldwell, 2005) and the *Classroom Reading Inventory* (Silvaroli & Wheelock, 2000). *The Developmental Literacy Inventory*, written by some of this book's authors (Temple, Crawford, & Gillet, in press), combines an Informal Reading Inventory with assessments of emergent literacy. (See Chapter 13, "Putting Effective Literacy Instruction into Practice: Grades 6 to 8," for further discussion of IRIs).

TEACH IT! 11

Phonemic Segmentation with Elkonin Boxes

THE READING MISCUE INVENTORY.   Also called the RMI or miscue analysis, the Reading Miscue Inventory (Goodman, Watson, & Burke, 1987) derives from the belief that reading errors should not be dismissed as matters of ignorance. Rather, like children's original utterances as they are learning to talk, reading errors are signs of children's efforts to understand, to find meaning, and to gain competence in written communication. Hence the term *miscue* is used instead of error: because if the child says something different from what is written in the text, the written word has *cued* a different response from the child than what was expected. According to the thinking behind the Reading Miscue Inventory, those cues can usually be categorized as having to do with the strings of letters on the page (*graphophonic cues*), the context provided by where the word occurs within the grammatical structure of the sentence or text (*syntactic cues*), or the context of the meaning of the passage (*semantic cues*).

To administer a Reading Miscue Inventory, the teacher chooses a moderately difficult text that is long enough to elicit at least 25 errors. The student's reading is tape-recorded for later analysis, during which each error is subjected to nine different questions to evaluate which sorts of cues the reader is using and how. Lessons are then developed to improve the child's reading based on the findings. The Reading Miscue Inventory is time-consuming to administer—fifteen to twenty minutes is required for the testing and another hour for the analysis—but many teachers value the information it yields.

RUNNING RECORDS.   Developed by Marie Clay (1993) to support her Reading Recovery Program, running records are teacher-made assessment devices administered to individual students to monitor their fluency, word recognition accuracy, and reading levels. Running records are partially based on the Reading Miscue Inventory (discussed previously), but are simpler to administer. Running records are usually carried out with younger readers in the first two grades, with whom they may be used every month or more frequently, both for diagnostic testing and for monitoring.

The teacher chooses simple texts that he or she suspects are at several difficulty levels for the child: one moderately challenging, one easy, and one more challenging. Clay suggests that an easy book be one that the child has read before with the teacher, and of which the child can read more than 95 percent of the words. A moderately challenging text would normally be one that the child had seen before but not studied with the teacher, and whose words the child can read with 90 to 95 percent accuracy. A difficult text would be one the child had not seen, and whose words the child could read with 80 to 89 percent accuracy.

The teacher's role is to observe carefully and record what the child says as she or he reads the book. It is best to construct a form for recording the student's performance, like the one shown in Figure 10.1, but in a pinch you may sit close enough to the child to see the words as they are read, and make notes on a piece of paper.

The running record shown in Figure 10.1 allows the teacher to observe the following:

- The error rate
- The self-correction rate
- The kinds of miscues (incorrect word identifications) that the child makes: visual, structural, or meaning-based
- Other behaviors, such as the direction in which the student reads, the number of repetitions of words, and so on

Name: _____ Date: _____

School: _____ Teacher: _____

Text Titles	Running Words Errors	Error Rate	Accuracy	Self-Correction Rate
Easy (100%–95%)		1:	%	1:
Instructional (94%–90%)		1:	%	1:
Hard (89% and lower)		1:	%	1:

Analysis of Errors and Self-Corrections
Information used or neglected [Meaning (M), Structure or Syntax (S), Visual (V)]

Easy: _____

_____

Instructional: _____

_____

Hard: _____

_____

Teacher Observations:				
Analysis of Errors and Self-Corrections				
Page	E	SC	Information used	
			E	SC
			MSV	MSV

FIGURE 10.1

Running Record Sheet.

Characterizing miscues as *visual, structural,* or *meaning-based* is intended to bring to light the kind of information a child is tracking in a text. Clay writes:

> **Meaning:** *Does the child use meaning (M)? If what he reads makes sense, even though it is inaccurate, then he is probably applying his knowledge of the world to his reading.*

> **Structure:** *Is what he said possible in an English sentence (S is for syntactically appropriate)? If it is, his oral language is probably influencing his responding. If it is not . . . [he] is paying close attention to detail, or to word by word reading. . . .*

> **Visual information:** *Does he use visual information (V) from the letters and words or the layout of print? [In a footnote, Clay adds, "Whether the child is relating visual information to sounds (phonological information) or to orthography (information about spelling) is a refinement of using visual information not distinguished in this analysis at this time."] (Clay, 1993, p. 31)*

A running record is a quick way to verify that a particular book is written at a child's instructional or independent reading level. It should be supplemented by other kinds of assessments when you want more detail on a child's word knowledge (see Chapter 5). Running records are used most often with beginning readers; however, when children reach a level of reading where both fluency and comprehension become issues—and teachers are rightly becoming concerned about both of these even with young readers—you will want to use measures for both fluency and comprehension. Many teachers follow a running record with a retelling task (i.e., the child is asked to retell what he or she just read, and the teacher may tick off items from a pre-prepared list of main ideas and details) (see the World of Reading box).

AUTHENTIC ASSESSMENT. Sheila Valencia and her colleagues (Valencia, Hiebert, & Afflerbach, 1993) popularized the idea of the *authentic assessment* of literacy. Authentic assessment addresses the problem that most assessment methods have students carry out contrived tasks that are not always representative of what they do in purposeful reading and writing. Contrived tasks may not yield the full picture, including what they have achieved, how they think about literacy, their interests and motivations, preferences, strategies, likes, and dislikes. Authentic assessment thus involves both *informal* and *structured observations* (sometimes called **kidwatching**) and *work-sampling,* including *portfolios.* Authentic assessment also includes the use of *rubrics.*

KIDWATCHING. Kidwatching is a term coined by influential literacy educator, Yetta Goodman (Goodman, 1985; Owocki and Goodman, 2002) to refer to a host of observations, ranging from observations quickly captured on stick-on notes, to home visits, to more formal assessments.

Kidwatching is informed. Teachers learn more from observing children in the daily life of the classroom if they know a good deal about language and literacy processes, as well as how children talk, read, think, investigate, and interact with each other and the world.

Kidwatching is nonjudgmental. Teachers record events or pieces of language as they occur, without filtering them through judgments. Planning what to do on the basis of the collected evidence will happen later, preferably after many different kinds of information have been collected. Here is an example of one kidwatcher's observation:

> *Notes on Erin (11/19) age 5½ in the library corner: Erin is turning the pages of* Fruits Good to Eat *in order, at a regular pace. She gets to the page with a pineapple on it, looks at it closely, turns to Robin, and asks, "Is this a pineapple?" Robin replies, "I think so, but let's ask Ms. B." They come to me. I ask Erin what she thinks, and she says, "I think so, but what does this say [pointing to the print]?" When I ask her what she thinks, she says, "I think it says pineapple because that's in the picture and there's a p." (Goodman, 2006)*

Note that this kind of written observation is also called an *anecdotal record.*

Kidwatching uses diverse sources of information. Goodman (2006) writes, "Kidwatchers use a variety of tools to document their observations, including informal conversations, formal interviews, check sheets, observation forms, field notes, portfolios, and home visits." Using many sources of information, including not only the teacher's observations

The Three-Cueing System

Both the Reading Miscue Inventory and running records highlight the importance of the **three-cueing system** in children's word recognition. The three-cueing system is the idea that children use visual (or graphophonic), structural (or syntactic), meaning-based (or semantic) information to recognize new words.

There is no doubt that readers use the surrounding context to help identify a word. For example, any time you administer an Informal Reading Inventory you expect students to recognize more words when the words appear in the context of meaningful passages than when they appear in isolation, such as on lists (see Table 10.2).

The argument arises over *when* the context matters. In the early days of the Reading Miscue Inventory, its advocates thought readers read words by sampling enough visual information from the text to create a sense of the meaning. Once they had a sense of the meaning, they needed only to sample the print to confirm or disconfirm what they thought the text must be saying. As long as they could assume what the text must be saying from the meaning that was forming in their heads, they had a reduced need to take in the visual information (the strings of letters) from the page. When it was unclear what the text was saying, they focused on more of the letters in the words.

But that view of reading aroused a chorus of criticisms. Penfetti (1985), for example, found that readers always read the words and the letters, and the most fluent comprehenders were the best at word recognition, because fluent word recognition freed up the brain's available attention for making sense of the text.

All of this matters because if you believe readers should rely heavily on context to read words, you are more likely to emphasize that approach as you help struggling readers. And if you believe that well-developed word identification skills, including decoding ability, are the key to successful reading, you are more likely to teach accordingly.

The National Reading Panel (2000) clearly endorsed the view that reading requires the reading of words, and not guessing words from context, and readers need to know the relations between letters and sounds to help them read words. Marilyn Adams (1998), a member of the National Reading Panel, has elsewhere expressed doubts about the idea of the three-cueing system, first because so many educators seem to follow it yet nobody is sure where it came from and, secondly, because the model doesn't underscore the primary importance of reading words or give much guidance to the teacher on what kind of correction is best if a child depends too much on one cueing system versus another.

Other educators strongly argue that the larger context of information should be kept in mind when teaching reading (see Margaret Moustafa's summary of these articles at http://instructional1 .calstatela.edu/mmousta/Research_on_Effective_Reading_ InstructionK-4.htm).

So when you pick up a Reading Miscue Inventory or a running record, or nod your head when you read an article about the three-cueing system, controversy may be lurking just around the corner.

TABLE 10.2

Scoring Word Recognition on an Informal Reading Inventory

	INDEPENDENT READING LEVEL	INSTRUCTIONAL READING LEVEL	FRUSTRATION READING LEVEL
Word Identification in Isolation	90% +	70%–89%	Below 70%
Word Identification in Context	97% +	90%–96%	Below 90%

but also the child's and the family's points of view, as well as more formal assessments, allows teachers to make small adjustments—and sometimes larger ones—to instruction and classroom procedures.

PORTFOLIOS.   Portfolios are collections of children's works gathered according to the objectives of the teacher's instruction. They may be maintained by the teacher as a way of keeping a diverse collection of artifacts related to a child's progress in learning to read and write. But usually they are maintained in collaboration with each child. The teacher and the child should decide in advance the sorts of items that should be kept in the portfolio. These might include

- Lists of books read
- A reading journal
- Repeated reading score sheets
- Written works chosen as indicative of the child's best work and range of work during a particular time period
- A list of topics for the child's writing
- Learning logs
- Running records

Periodically—at least once a month or once each marking period—the teacher schedules a conference or interview with the child. Ahead of the conversation, both the child and the teacher should look through the portfolio to find signs of progress and areas that need work. During their conversation, the child describes what he or she has learned during this period and sets goals for improvement during the next period. The teacher may ask questions to find out what things the child likes and doesn't like to read, what strategies he or she is using in reading, and aspects of the reading instruction that might be changed. The teacher makes suggestions to help the child learn.

RUBRICS.   According to Andrade (2002),

> A *rubric* is a scoring tool that lists the criteria for a piece of work, or "what counts" (for example, purpose, organization, details, voice, and mechanics are often what count in a piece of writing); it also articulates gradations of quality for each criterion, from excellent to poor.

Rubrics have the advantage of allowing teachers to observe and evaluate an authentic performance, such as a child's oral reading, or a piece of writing written for a real purpose other than testing. They also have the advantage of teaching. Especially when they are shared with a student before he or she carries out a ask, the rubrics tell the child how to do a task well.

It is so important to establish procedures and expectations from the first moment your students enter. Don't just cover the procedures once, but PRACTICE, PRACTICE, PRACTICE!! Doing this will make your classroom management easier and help your year to flow and allow you to focus on student learning!!

Jodi,
Fourth Grade Teacher
Cincinnati, OHIO

Rubrics may be already designed by educational experts, such as the Multidimensional Fluency Scale on page 339 in this chapter and the Six Traits rubric for evaluating writing discussed in Chapter 9. Rubrics may also be developed by teachers, or even by the students themselves. When students participate in designing a rubric, they may become more strategic in reading—that is, they have a better idea how they should try to perform.

It helps to think of a rubric like a chart. Each row names an important aspect of performance on a task, and in the boxes under each column are descriptions that range from unsatisfactory to satisfactory to excellent performance on that factor.

Terms Used in Testing

Students' performance on norm-referenced tests are usually reported three ways. First, they are given *raw scores*, which simply report the number or the percentage of items on the test they answered correctly. Raw scores mean little, however, without the understanding of how a particular child's score compares with those of other children the same age group.

Therefore, scores are presented in two additional ways. *Percentile scores* are based on a ninety-nine point scale, and they tell a child what percentage of the children in a comparison group received a lower score than his. *Stanine scores* may also be used to report performance on a test, especially when they are also used to eliminate the fine distinctions reported in percentiles that don't mean much. Stanine scores are reported in whole numbers on a nine-point scale. The spread of scores represented by each number is based on a normal curve of distribution. Scores of 4, 5, and 6 are average. Scores of 1, 2, and 3 are below average. Scores of 7, 8, and 9 are above average. **Grade-equivalent scores** are what they sound like: indications of what grade level material an average reader would read at an instructional or independent level based on her performance on this test. Thus if a fourth grader's grade equivalent score on a reading test is 7.5, that means he scored the way an average seventh grader would have scored on the material in that test. (But that doesn't mean the child is ready to be promoted to seventh grade; just because he read material on a test intended for fourth graders like an average seventh grader would doesn't mean that he will be able to read seventh grade materials like an average seventh grader.)

Tests are often described in terms of their validity and reliability. *Validity* refers to the extent that they measure what they claim to measure. Because all tests take a sample of a child's performance and claim to generalize from that sample to the child's more global level of performance, it is important to know if the test really does tell you what it says it does.

Educators often speak of different kinds of validity.

- **Content validity** is the degree to which a test measures what it says it does. If a test of reading comprehension asks students to answer questions about a passage after reading it, that test can be said to have content validity because answering questions is a reasonable demonstration of comprehension. But if the test asks students to locate all the words in a passage beginning with *B*, it would not have content validity as a test of comprehension.

- **Predictive validity,** also called *assessment-criterion relationship validity* (Linn & Gronlund, 2000), refers to the power of the test to predict the student's future performance on related tasks. Predictive validity is of great importance with screening assessments and monitoring assessments because a key purpose of those measures is to use students' present performance on early reading tasks to predict their future reading ability. Note, too, that the predictive validity of a test may depend on when—that is, with what age child—it is used. For example, a test of phoneme awareness given to five-year-olds is not a very good predictor of future reading performance (Snow, Burns, & Griffin, 1998). The same test given in first grade may have greater predictive validity because a greater number of six-year-olds versus five-year-olds display some phonemic awareness.

- **Reliability** has to do with the likelihood that the results of the test are stable and dependable: that is, if the same test were given to the same child by two different people, or on two different days, would the results be similar? The different ways reliability is thought of include:
  - *Test-retest reliability*, in which the same students are given the same test within a short interval, to see if the results are similar
  - *Split-half reliability*, in which samples of a student's performance on different items of the same test are compared with each other
  - *Inter-rater reliability*, in which an instrument such as a rubric is used by different raters to assess the same student, and the results are compared

The terms *validity* and *reliability* are usually applied to standardized tests, but they are worth considering regardless of the kind of assessment being done. The No Child Left Behind Act requires that assessments be scientifically validated, which often means that assessment instruments have demonstrated validity and reliability. But a caution is in order—many valuable ways of collecting and making judgments about children's reading and writing do not have demonstrated validity and reliability. Informal observation of students' reading is one; all types of Informal Reading Inventories are another.

What Do We Need to Know from Assessing Children?

We need to assess and monitor many things with respect to what children are learning about literacy.

Emergent Readers

Emergent readers are usually preschool, kindergarten, and first-grade children who are developing concepts about language and print and knowledge of the alphabetic writing system that form the foundation on which later reading is built. As we saw in Chapters 3 and 4, children develop all these at different rates and to different extents. Giving children special, finely tuned intervention early on can help many of them avoid reading failure and make progress as readers and writers. Assessment of children's early literacy is essential.

So what do we need to know? Effective early literacy assessments focus on:

- **Concepts about print and awareness of what books are and what they are for.** The more developed holistic sense children have of what literacy is about, the better they will be able to focus their attention to the details they must understand in order to read. Without an orienting sense of what literacy is and what books are for, early literacy instruction may be confusing for some children.

- **Awareness of sounds in language.** Writing represents spoken language, and in English, writing represents language at the level of words, onsets and rimes, and phonemes, as we saw in Chapter 3. The problem is that in speech, children can use language without thinking about it; but when they learn to read and write, children must be conscious of words, rimes, and phonemes. Those things must be real for young learners, because young learners will need to think hard about the relations between spoken units of spoken language and units of print.

- **Knowledge of the alphabet.** Children must know many letters of the alphabet to begin to develop the ability to read. Knowledge of the alphabet is an indicator of the amount of print exposure they have had (the more letters they know, the more print they are likely to have seen). But knowing letters is also important in itself because the more letters they know, the more successfully they can explore how print and speech go together. There is a difference between letter identification and letter retrieval. Because some disabled readers have difficulty naming letters quickly (Katzir & Pare-Blagoev, 2006), some assessments of early literacy include a timed letter identification task.

- **Knowledge of some words.** Virtually all children in America are exposed to print before they begin formal reading instruction. Many of them learn to identify some words: their own names, names of fast food restaurants, words from favorite book titles. The number of words they can identify while still prereaders is a sign of emergent literacy.

- **Listening comprehension.** Children need to have receptive language developed to the degree that they can follow books read aloud to them by the teacher and also comprehend texts themselves when they become readers. Some, but not all, emergent literacy assessment instruments include measures of listening comprehension.

- **Knowledge of letter-to-sound correspondences (phonics).** Children need to develop ideas about the relations between letters and sounds to learn to read. As we saw in the discussion of invented spelling (Chapter 4), most children don't wait to be taught. With even a little encouragement, however, they will begin to speculate

PHONICS and **PHONOLOGICAL AWARENESS**

Why is it important that children understand what literacy is about, and what books are for?

PHONICS and **PHONOLOGICAL AWARENESS**

When can children's understanding of letter-to-sound correspondences begin to be assessed?

actively on what those relationships are. Children's understanding of letter-to-sound correspondences can be assessed beginning in kindergarten and continuing through first grade. (Phonics knowledge will continue to be assessed in beginning readers and in older struggling readers.)

Contemporary assessment of early literacy, then, tracks the development of concepts about print, awareness of sounds, awareness of letters, knowledge of words, and (sometimes) listening comprehension. Note that we do not concern ourselves so much with children's ability to recognize colors or shapes, to repeat numbers back, or to distinguish a ringing bell from a chirping bird. Although some educators do concern themselves with general indicators like these of children's readiness to learn, when assessing early literacy it is best to focus on literacy-related factors because they more reliably predict children's future success as readers than the more general measures of learning readiness (Snow et al., 1998). Also, because teachers need to assess and monitor children's emergent literacy repeatedly during the school year, and the children must be assessed one at a time, they need to focus on aspects of emergent literacy that are most important. Note, too, that many factors, not just one, should be assessed. In practice, however, concepts about print tend to develop before the other factors do, so a teacher may stop assessing those concepts after children have shown that they have them and keep focusing on the other factors.

Measures of Emergent Literacy

Teacher-made measures of emergent literacy can be fashioned after the Early Reading Screening Inventory (Morris, 2000) and the Print Concepts Assessment (after Clay, 1999). The Early Reading Screening Inventory, as the name implies, has been widely used to identify young readers in early first grade who will need additional help to learn to read. Other emergent literacy assessment programs are in use around the United States, some of them promoted by individual states. The Phonological Awareness Literacy Survey (PALS) (**http://pals.virginia.edu/**) is provided to school districts in Virginia and is widely used elsewhere as both a screening and a monitoring tool. The Illinois Snapshot of Early Literacy is promoted by that state as a screening tool. The Texas Education Agency developed the Texas Primary Reading Inventory (**http://www.tpri.org/About/**), with versions for kindergarten through third grades, which can be administered as a screening, diagnosis, and monitoring tool.

At the University of Oregon, the Dynamic Indicators of Basic Literacy Skills (DIBELS) was developed with a federal grant and is available to teachers for free online. This test, which can be used as a screening, diagnosis, and a monitoring tool, begins with a preschool version that assesses initial sounds or *onset fluency*. At the kindergarten level are added tests of phonemic segmentation fluency, letter naming fluency, and nonsense word reading fluency. These continue through first grade, where an oral reading fluency measure is also added, and continues through third grade. These are called fluency tests because children's responses are timed, and the speed of the child's responses is noted in addition to accuracy (see **http://dibels.uoregon.edu/measures.php**).

"ROAMING AROUND THE KNOWN." How accurate are all of these measures? According to Snow et al. (1998), the correlations between the component measures listed earlier in this section and children's later success in learning to read are in the 30- to 50-percent range. Scores in this range suggest that the factors are important in reading, but there is a very real chance that a child will be more or less successful in learning to read than these tests predict. With these limitations in mind, prudent teachers avoid making important decisions about children's education on the basis of one of

Emergent readers can be young children who are developing a foundation upon which later reading is built.

these tests alone. Many use the practice of following the testing with "Roaming around the Known" (Clay, 1993): that is, taking the findings from the assessments as suggestions only, and teaching the child for several days to see how she or he responds to actual instruction—in other words, teaching with the idea that the assessments may very well be wrong.

What Do We Need to Know about Beginning Readers and Beyond?

Beginning readers are those who are starting to read words in connected text. Just as it is important to know that they have their emergent literacy concepts and abilities in place, it is also critical to know if each child is making progress in all aspects of beginning reading. These aspects include word recognition—including having a *sight vocabulary* stored in memory, *decoding skills* so that the child can read a word he didn't know before, and the ability to *use context* to help identify words. Their reading *fluency*—their accuracy, rate, and intonation—needs to develop apace as well. Their *vocabulary* should be growing by thousands of words each year, and they will need to learn vocabulary from reading. *Comprehension* is the ultimate goal of reading, and we want to know how this ability is growing, too. As we saw in Chapters 6 and 7, comprehension is a complex of many factors including having and using world knowledge, getting main ideas, making inferences, having metacognition or cognitive monitoring—that is, knowing if the text is making sense—and following the patterns of different kinds of fictional and informational texts to construct meaning. We also care about their attitudes toward reading and what kind of text and how much of it they read. But one measure that combines all of these factors is their reading levels.

Reading Levels: Independent, Instructional, Frustration

It is possible to measure students' *reading levels*, the levels of text they can read for different purposes. To talk about reading levels implies two things: that texts have levels of difficulty and that readers have levels of ability. To speak of levels of difficulty of texts implies that some are written on a first-grade level, some on a second-grade level, and so on. These levels of difficulty are referred to as **readability**, and we will say more about that later. When we speak of the reading levels of individual readers, it helps to ask what the reading task is: will they be studying a book in a group under the teacher's supervision, reading a textbook for homework, or reading for pleasure? Depending on the answers to those questions, it is proper to speak not of one reading level but three: the *independent level*, the *instructional level*, and the *frustration level*.

INDEPENDENT READING LEVEL. If the student is to read material on his or her own, without the support of a teacher or other more skilled readers, then the material should fall within the student's independent level of reading ability. In material written at the student's independent level, the student should encounter no more than three or four unknown words in a hundred and should enjoy nearly total comprehension.

Books that fall within students' independent level include books students choose to read for pleasure and textbooks they use independently for homework. Regardless of a student's grade placement, if the books are above the student's independent level, then the student should be given easier books or should be offered support for reading such as buddy reading, study guides, or tape-recorded text. Conversely, teachers sometimes have to prod students to read more challenging material that falls within their independent level.

INSTRUCTIONAL READING LEVEL.   In the classroom, teachers often work with students in material that is moderately challenging for them so they will learn from the supported practice. Material used for this purpose should fall within the student's instructional level of reading ability. Such material presents the student with unknown words at a rate of up to one in ten, and language and concepts that are not fully comprehended—at least not at first. The intention is that with guided practice in materials written at the instructional level, students will learn the unknown words and come to comprehend the once-challenging language and concepts. The instructional level corresponds to what Vygotsky (1976) called the *zone of proximal development*, the area of moderate challenge that is just at the threshold of a reader's growing abilities. It is here that teachers most often practice *scaffolded instruction*, providing temporary support, including teaching strategies that will help the student learn on his or her own in the future.

Again, a particular student's instructional level often falls above or below that student's grade placement level. Because of the value of working in moderately challenging materials when teaching a student to read, it is very important to locate a student's instructional level wherever it may fall.

FRUSTRATION READING LEVEL.   If the material is too challenging—that is, if it contains more than one unfamiliar word in ten, and language and concepts that substantially resist comprehension—the material is said to be written at the student's frustration level. The frustration level is not actually a reading level because students do not practice successful reading there. It is used rather to define the limits of a student's instructional level. Teachers can assign reading material during closely supervised instructional tasks that approach, but do not cross into, the frustration level.

As the name implies, frustration level text is so challenging to a student that the challenge of reading it is burdensome and disagreeable. Students may actually progress faster in learning to read and learning to spell when they are placed in instructional-level text, even though that is easier than frustration-level text.

Students' reading levels are often determined by administering an Informal Reading Inventory (IRI). When an IRI is used, it will normally tell you how many errors a student can make in each part to be independent, instructional, or frustrated at that level. If an IRI is not used, you can still get a rough idea of a student's reading level if you know the reading levels of several short texts. Have the child read a passage of at least 150 words. Mark each reading error as an *omission* (leaving out a word), a *substitution* (reading a word other than the word supplied in the text or misreading the word in the text), or an *insertion* (adding a word or words that were not in the text). Each counts as one error every time it occurs. *Proper names* that are misread count as one error, regardless how many times they are misread. *Reversals* (reading two words in the wrong order) count as one error. Repetitions do not count as errors, and neither do self-corrections or long pauses.

Using those criteria, here is how the scores are interpreted:

Independent level: 97 to 100 percent of the words are read correctly.

Instructional level: 90 to 96 percent of the words are read correctly.

Frustration level: Fewer than 90 percent of the words are read correctly.

These criteria are taken from Betts (1946).

READING LEVELS AND READABILITY.   Applying the concept of reading levels that was just presented, a teacher might test a particular third grade student and find that his independent level is second grade, his instructional level is third grade, and his frustration level is fourth grade. For this information to be useful to the teacher, we must assume that reading material is available that is written at the second, third, and fourth grade reading levels. This is a reasonably safe assumption, but there are some problems with it. Most importantly, we now know that whether a reader comprehends a particular text depends to some extent on what is already in the reader's head and not solely on what is in the text (Pearson & Anderson, 1985: Alexander, 2000). Two third grade readers may read a text about a game of basketball; even though they have equivalent reading abilities, if one happens to be a passionate player of the game, that student may understand the text better than the other student.

The determination that a text is written at a particular grade level is usually based on surface features of the text, such as the length of the sentences and the number of syllables in the words. The readability level might also be determined by trialing the text with a group of sample readers of different ages. Either way, a particular reader may have a harder or easier time reading a particular text, depending on that reader's background knowledge of, and interest in, the topic of the text.

Measuring Readability

In the 1940s an Austrian immigrant to the United States wrote a doctoral dissertation in which he developed a mathematical formula for estimating the readability level of written language. Soon Rudolph Flesch's formula and many others like it were being used to help publishers adjust the level of difficulty of their products, be they textbooks for children, newspapers and magazines for the general reader, or government publications aimed at special audiences such as farmers, cooks, or sanitation workers. Now readability formulas are available for most of the world's languages.

One of the simplest readability devices for English was developed by Edward Fry, now a retired professor of literacy at Rutgers University in the United States. Fry's procedure is to take three separate 100-word samples from a work to be studied, and to count the number of sentences to the tenth place, and to count the number of syllables in that sample. The sentence counts and syllable counts are averaged, and the results are plotted on the graph presented in Figure 10.2.

Fry's graph resembles other formulas in that it considers the length of sentences and the length of words as the variables that affect readability. The logic here is that longer sentences tend to be more grammatically complex, and more grammatically complex sentences are harder to read. Longer words tend to be more sophisticated, rarer, and encountered later in schooling. Combining the two measures of sentence length and word length yields a more reliable estimate of readability than one measure alone (see the Teach It! box).

Other readability formulas are Flesch-Kincaid (which is folded into most versions of Microsoft Word [go to Tools → Spelling and Grammar → Options → Check Readability Level]), Dale-Chall and SMOG ("simplified measure of gobbledygook").

What has rapidly become a widely used system for establishing readability level is the Lexile Framework (Lennon & Burdick, 2004). The Lexile system, developed with federal

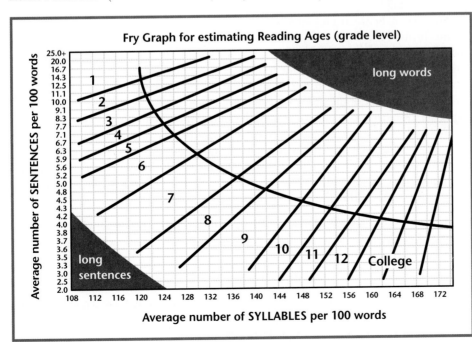

FIGURE 10.2

Fry Readability Graph.

Source: Edward Fry, "Fry Readability Graph" © 1977. Reprinted with permission of the McGraw Hill Companies.

TEACH IT!

Refer to your **Teach It!** booklet for further activities you can use to reinforce concepts discussed in this chapter.

The Fry Readability Graph

Try the Fry readability graph on a sample of this text. For a short exercise, instead of taking three 100-word passages and averaging the results, you can take just one 100-word passage. Count off 100 words, then count the number of syllables in that sample. Count the number of sentences to the tenth place. Plot the results on the graph. Are you surprised at the results? Try the readability graph on a children's book. Try it on an article from your daily newspaper. If you can, find a memorandum to parents from a local school and try it on that. Try it on the warranty statement of the next electronic item you buy, or on the user's agreement of the next software program you download.

If you are in a classroom, have students bring in some written materials that come in the mail at their house (with their parents' permission, of course!). Have them look at the fine print on an application for a credit card. Or have them go online and look up information on applying for U.S. citizenship through the U.S. Immigration and Naturalization Service. In pairs or triads, have them compute the readability levels.

What conclusions can you draw about the reading demands faced by citizens in your community? What levels of reading ability allow people to understand what kinds of communications? What are some of the consequences of having a low reading level?

funds by Metametrics, Inc., measures both readability of text and reading ability of readers. Readability measures are based on semantic (word-based) and syntactic (sentence-based) features of the text. The semantic score is calculated from the frequency or commonality of the words in the text and the length of the sentences. A computer program compares the words in a particular text to a dictionary that has a score for the frequency with which each word is typically encountered ("the" would be a common word; "Zoroastrianism" would be an uncommon one). The syntactic score is based on the average length of sentences in the text, and the two factors together yield a Lexile score of between 200 (for a very easy text) and 1,700 (for a very challenging one). The Lexile Framework is also used to assess a reader's ability to read a text. Using Lexile scores to match readers with books can be more accurate than establishing a child's reading ability in grade equivalents, and then matching the reading score with the readability score of a book. Students with a Lexile score of 300, for instance, would be expected to read with 75 percent comprehension a book with a Lexile score of 300. Information about the Lexile Framework is available online at **www.lexile.com**. Reading difficulty of text is now measured in grade equivalents, Lexiles, Reading Recovery levels, Fountas and Pinnell levels, and others (see Table 10.3).

Somewhere between a readability formula and a comprehension test is the cloze procedure (Taylor, 1953; Bormouth, 1968). The cloze procedure tests a reader's ability to read a particular text at the independent, instructional, and frustration levels. Thus if you are fairly sure of the difficulty level of the text, you can use the cloze procedure to get an idea of the reader's independent, instructional, and frustration levels. And if you are fairly sure of the reading ability of the group of people who take the test, you can use their performance on the cloze procedure to get an indication of the readability level of the text.

To conduct the cloze procedure, select a passage of more than 260 words. Leave the first sentence intact. Then go through and mark every fifth word thereafter until you reach fifty words marked. Then leave the sentence after the fiftieth word intact. Retype the passage, and replace every word you marked with a blanks of equal length. Have the students read the passage and fill in the blanks. Cloze tests are scored as follows:

The independent reading level = 60 percent and greater correct responses (30+ words)

The instructional reading level = between 40 and 59 percent correct responses (between 20 and 29 words)

The frustration level = fewer than 40 percent correct responses (fewer than 20 words)

More information about readability is available on the Internet. For a good introduction and links to other sites, you might begin with the article in Wikipedia, the free encyclopedia, at **http://en.wikipedia.org/wiki/Readability**.

TABLE 10.3

Comparing Readability Levels

Several different systems provide ratings of the difficulty levels of texts. Readability formulas such as the Fry, the Dale-Chall, and the Flesch-Kincaid report scores in terms of grade level equivalents. Most informal reading inventories report results as grade level equivalents, also. Recently, other systems have proliferated. In addition to Lexiles, which range between 200 and 1700, Reading Recovery (Clay, 1993), Fountas/Pinell (2005), and Developmental Reading Assessment or DRA (from Pearson Education **http://plgcatalog.pearson.com/program_mutliple.cfm?site_id=2&discipline_id=807&subarea_id=1000&program_id=23661**) provide fine gradations of difficulty for readers in the primary grades. This chart shows how scores from the different systems compare to each other.

GRADE LEVEL	INFORMAL READING INVENTORY SCORES	FOUNTAS/ PINNELL GUIDED READING LEVELS	READING RECOVERY LEVELS	LEXILES	DRA LEVELS
K		A	A, B		A
			1		1
		B	2		2
	Pre-primer 1	C	3		3
1.1	Pre-primer 2		4		4
	Pre-primer 3		5		
		D	6		6
			7		
1.2		E	8		8
			9		
	Primer	F	10		10
		G	11	200–299	
			12		12
			13		
	Grade 1	H	14		14
			15		
		I	16		16
2	Grade 2	J	18	300–399	20
		K	19		
		L	20	400–499	28
		M			
3	Grade 3	N	22	500–599	30
		O, P	24	600–699	34
					38
4	Grade 4	Q, R, S	26	700–799	40
5	Grade 5	T, U, V	28	800–899	44
6	Grade 6	W, X, Y	30	900–999	
7	Grade 7	Z	32	1000–1100	
8	Grade 8	Z	34		

Source: After Salt Lake City School District, 2006

Assessing Word Recognition

As we noted in Chapter 5, word recognition has several aspects to it:

- **Sight vocabulary.** These are the words a reader has stored in memory, that can be recognized instantly. Sight words are learned from reading. Words that may initially be decoded or figured out from context become sight words after repeated exposures.

PHONICS and **PHONOLOGICAL AWARENESS**

What's the difference between sight word reading and decoding?

- **Decoding ability.** Young readers frequently encounter words they do not have stored in memory. One way they can read them—which the National Reading Panel and the No Child Left Behind Act have indicated is the most important way—is to *decode* the word, or work out its identity by matching its letters and its sounds. Children differ in their ability to decode, and a task of assessment is to measure their ability to do it.

- **Identifying words from context.** When unrecognized words occur in meaningful texts, readers have two other ways besides decoding to figure out what they are. One is the syntax of the sentence. For example, if we read, "Give me the _____," we can be pretty sure that whatever fills that blank is a noun, or something that can function like a noun. But suppose the text said, "It was midnight. The safe cracker had opened the safe and taken the money. Just as he reached the door, the lights went on and a voice said, 'Stop. Now turn around slowly. Give me the _____.'" Now we would probably guess that the missing word was not only a noun, but *money*, because the meaning of the text limits our choices to that word. Both of these examples go under the name of *using context to support word identification*. However, Marie Clay's *running records* procedure keeps track of each kind of context support by distinguishing *structural cues* from *meaning-based cues*. Both of those are distinguished from *visual* or grapho-phonic cues.

Assessing Word Recognition and Phonics

There are several ways to assess word recognition. Assessments of reading fluency in the repeated reading task measure students' accuracy in word recognition. If you know the reading level of the book, and you know the student's accuracy score on at least a 100-word passage (the score, in percentages, is derived by dividing the number of errors by the total number of words), you can compute the student's level of word recognition in terms of grade-equivalents as follows:

Independent: 97–100 percent correct

Instructional: 90–96 percent correct

Frustration: Below 90 percent correct

Word recognition rates can also be measured by means of an Informal Reading Inventory. Many IRIs measure word recognition three ways. First, they give a measure of a child's *sight vocabulary*, the words a child has stored in memory and can recognize instantaneously. They do this by "flashing" (exposing very briefly between two index cards) words from a list (see the Assessment box on pages 336 and 337).

Second, they give a measure of a child's *decoding*. They do this by giving a long exposure of any words the child could not recognize instantly, and allowing the test administrator to compare the difference between the "flashed" and the "untimed" scores. The difference in favor of the untimed score shows the power of the child's decoding ability because it shows how many words he could not recognize instantly, but could sound out given the time to do so.

IRIs also give a measure of children's power to recognize words in context. The child reads aloud words from a text passage as the teacher listens carefully and records and scores the errors. The percentage scores of words correctly read in context are interpreted using the same criteria used in the fluency measure.

Assessing phonics knowledge can also be done by carefully observing the kinds of errors children make when they are recognizing words. In Chapter 5 we showed a system of categorizing errors that showed if a child's word reading was in the logographic, alphabetic, orthographic, or derivational stage.

Some tests, including DIBELS (the Dynamic Indicators of Basic Early Literacy Skills) and the Woodcock-Johnson-III Basic Reading Battery, assess phonics knowledge by testing children's reading of nonsense words, like *VAJ, KOL, NAK,* and the like. The advantage to having children read nonsense words is that we are assured they have never seen them be-

TEACH IT! 17

Analytic Phonics Lesson

fore, so the words must be read by pure decoding. The disadvantage is that, because they are nonsense words, the children don't have the normal self-correction to them that comes from arriving at a word they know in their speech. Another disadvantage is that some of the nonsense words do not conform to English orthography. For example, DIBELS uses *doj*, *ol*, and *huf*, even though there are no single-syllable words in English that are spelled that way.

Another test of phonics knowledge is done by means of children's spelling. The assessment inventories built into Kathy Ganske's (2000) *Word Journeys* have children spell challenging words, and then give teachers advice on (1) analyzing the spelling error to assign the child to a probable level of invented spelling and (2) pinpointing the aspect of phonics knowledge that the child needs to learn.

Assessing Reading Fluency

WRITING and READING CONNECTIONS

Why has reading fluency become an area of such intense interest to educators?

Reading fluency has moved from being a neglected skill (Allington, 1983) to an area of intense interest. In *Put Reading First*, Armbruster, Lehr, and Osborn (2001) define reading fluency this way:

> *Fluency is the ability to read a text accurately and quickly. When fluent readers read silently, they recognize words automatically. They group words quickly in ways that help them gain meaning from what they read. Fluent readers read aloud effortlessly and with expression. Their reading sounds natural, as if they are speaking.* (p. 22)

Assessing reading fluency is most simply measured by counting the number of words children read per minute minus the errors. This yields a measure called words correct per minute (WCPM), which is calculated using this formula:

$$\frac{(\text{Total words read, minus words read incorrectly}) \times 60}{\text{Reading time in seconds}} = \text{WCPM}$$

Thus, for example, if a third grade student reads 125 words in one minute but makes five reading errors, we would calculate her fluency rate of WCPM as:

$$\frac{(125 - 5) \times 60}{60} = \frac{120 \times 60}{60} = 120 \text{ WCPM}$$

According to Table 10.4 on page 333, this would be an acceptable reading rate for a mid-year third grader.

Reading fluency consists not only of speed and correctness, however, but also of reading with expression and with proper phrasing. Zutell and Rasinski (1991) developed the Multidimensional Fluency Scale (see Table 10.5 on page 339) to help teachers observe several dimensions of fluency at once. Those factors are expression and volume, phrasing, smoothness, and pace. The scale is a rubric to guide teachers' judgment. To carry out the procedure, the teacher selects a passage of at least 100 words that should be written at the students' grade level or a year below. The student reads the passage and the teacher tape records it. The teacher then plays the tape back and evaluates the student's reading for each of the factors of accuracy, phrasing, smoothness, and pace.

Assessing Vocabulary

Vocabulary development is recognized more and more as a critical variable in learning to read. But how do we know how many words a child knows? As we saw in Chapter 4, it depends on what we mean by "know." Does the child have a vague idea what the word means? Can the child understand the word when reading it or hearing it, but not when using it? Does the child know all of the meanings of it? These questions show what a complicated thing it is to **assess vocabulary**. Vocabulary has often been assessed as part of an IRI and

The word recognition inventory has two parts: a display list, which is shown to the child one word at a time, and a recording sheet for the child's answers.

To administer a word recognition inventory, you have two options. You can simply point to the words one at a time and have the child read them, putting a checkmark on the recording sheet for each word that is correctly identified. You may record what the child says when he or she misreads a word if you want to study those errors later. Count the number of words read correctly, and multiply by five points to yield a percentage score.

As an alternative, you can hold two index cards over the word and *briefly* expose the word (expose for about a quarter of a second) to the child. If he or she reads the word correctly, place a checkmark in the "flashed" column of the record sheet and go on to the next word. If the student fails to read the word correctly, record whatever he or she says in the "flashed" column and then open up the cards to expose the words. If she now reads the word correctly, place a checkmark in the "untimed" column; if not read correctly, record whatever the student says, or enter a zero if he or she says nothing. Calculate the scores for both columns by multiplying the words correctly identified by five points.

The scores can be used as follows to identify the child's independent, instructional, and frustration levels, as follows:

Independent level: 90 to 100 percent correct
Instructional level: 70 to 90 percent correct
Frustration level: Below 70 percent

Display List

cards	station
above	ought
library	idea
brave	coach
instead	type
dear	damp
press	elbow
popcorn	mystery
pretty	yourselves
monkey	midnight
feather	motorcycle
become	insect
grandfather	study
hair	easier
people	headache
kept	match
mountain	quit
pass	alive
seem	moment
anyway	range

Recording Sheet

	FLASHED	UNTIMED		FLASHED	UNTIMED
cards			station		
above			ought		
library			idea		
brave			coach		
instead			type		
dear			damp		
press			elbow		
popcorn			mystery		
pretty			yourselves		
monkey			midnight		
feather			motorcycle		
become			insect		
grandfather			study		
hair			easier		
people			headache		
kept			match		
mountain			quit		
pass			alive		
seem			moment		
anyway			range		
Total Errors:			**Total Errors:**		

0–2 errors = independent level
3–6 errors = instructional level
7+ errors = frustration level

Source: From C. Temple, A. Crawford, and J. Gillet (2007, in press). *Developmental Literacy Inventory: Reading and Spelling from Emergent to Mature Levels.* Published by Allyn and Bacon, Boston, MA. Copyright © 2008 by Pearson Education. Reprinted by permission of the publisher.

TABLE 10.4

Oral Reading Fluency Norms

GRADE	PERCENTILE	FALL WCPM*	WINTER WCPM*	SPRING WCPM*
2	75	82	106	124
	50	53	78	94
	25	23	46	65
3	75	107	123	142
	50	79	93	114
	25	65	70	87
4	75	125	133	143
	50	99	112	118
	25	72	89	92
5	75	126	143	151
	50	105	118	128
	25	77	93	100

*WCPM is words correct per minute.
The 50th percentile for upper grades is 125–150 WCPM.
Source: From Curriculum-Based Oral Reading Fluency Norms for Students in Grades 2 Through 5, by J. Hasbrouck and G. Tindal, 1992, *Teaching Exceptional Children, 24,* p. 42. Copyright 1992 by The Council for Exceptional Children. Reprinted with permission.

other reading tests. But with the advent of No Child Left Behind and Reading First, teachers are being called upon to assess children's vocabulary knowledge more systematically.

When states specify that teachers use scientifically based tests of vocabulary—that is, tests with proven validity and reliability—the choices are rather limited. A group commissioned by the U.S. Department of Education to approve assessment instruments for use with federally funded programs yielded a very limited list of approved instruments for assessing vocabulary at the points of screening, diagnosing, monitoring, and outcomes-based assessment.

According to the *Final Report: Analysis of Reading Assessment Instrument for K–3* (**http://idea.uoregon.edu/assessment/exec_summary.pdf**), one instrument, the *Peabody Picture Vocabulary Test-III*, was approved for all purposes for levels kindergarten through grade 3. This test costs $450. Other tests such as the *Expressive One-Word Picture Vocabulary Test*, the *One-Word Picture Vocabulary Test Revised*, the *Texas Primary Reading Inventory*, and the *Expressive Vocabulary Test* were approved for limited applications in certain grades. Recently, however, the U.S. General Accounting Office has questioned the propriety of some of the procedures the Department of Education uses to decide what materials and approaches are to be allowed for federal support.

Teachers who wish to construct their own vocabulary tests would do well to follow the advice of Barone, Hardman, and Taylor (2006) and construct devices that ask children to:

- Select the meanings from a set of possibilities when a target word is given.
- Select a target word from a set of possibilities when a meaning is given.
- Classify words into categories.
- Tell which word from a group of words does not belong.
- Use visual and contextual clues to understand difficult words in sentences.
- Choose the correct word meanings, an antonym, or a synonym from a set of possibilities.
- Show an understanding of root words, prefixes and suffixes, historical morphemes, or grammatical endings.
- Choose correct meanings for homophones (words that sound the same but have different meanings: *Read a book; a reed in a pond*) and homographs (words that are spelled the same but have different meanings: *Lead the singing; a lead pipe*).
- Complete a sentence with a correct word choice from alternatives.
- Demonstrate dictionary skills.

TEACH IT! 22

Repeated Reading

TABLE 10.5

Multidimensional Fluency Scale

	1	2	3	4
Expression and volume	Reads in a quiet voice as if to get the words out. The reading does not sound natural like talking to a friend.	Reads in a quiet voice. The reading sounds natural in part of the text, but the reading does not always sound like talking to a friend.	Reads with volume and expression. However, sometimes the reader slips into expressionless reading and does not sound like talking to a friend.	Reads with varied volume and expression. The reading sounds like talking to a friend with voice matching the interpretation of the passage.
Phrasing	Reads word-by-word in a monotone voice.	Reads in two- and three-word phrases, not adhering to punctuation, stress, and intonation.	Reads with a mixture of run-ons, mid-sentence pauses for breath, and some choppiness. There is reasonable stress and intonation.	Reads with good phrasing, adhering to punctuation, stress, and intonation.
Smoothness	Frequently hesitates while reading, sounds out words, and repeats words or phrases. The reader makes multiple attempts to read the same passage.	Reads with extended pauses or hesitations. The reader has many "rough spots."	Reads with occasional breaks in rhythm. The reader has difficulty with specific words and/or sentence structures.	Reads smoothly with some breaks, but self-corrects with difficult words and/or sentence structures.
Pace	Reads slowly and laboriously.	Reads moderately slowly.	Reads fast and slow throughout reading.	Reads at a conversational pace throughout the reading.

Source: Zutell and Rasinski (1991).

Assessing Comprehension

Reading comprehension consists of several abilities. Students' prior knowledge (sometimes called world knowledge) is needed to contextualize the new information they gain from the text. And students need to read actively, using their prior knowledge and clues from the text to set purposes and raise questions to answer while reading. They need the ability to find main ideas and supporting details and recall them later. They also need to be able to make inferences to construct meanings when ideas are not explicitly stated. They need to be able to follow the patterns of different kinds of texts, both fictional and informational, as guides to constructing meaning. And they need to keep building their inventory of vocabulary. They must do all this while reading aloud and silently.

That is a lot for a teacher to assess! In practice, when teachers want to observe this many factors, they often rely upon IRIs because they provide comprehensive measures.

Assessing Comprehension with an Informal Reading Inventory

IRIs allow teachers to **assess comprehension** by means of meaningful text passages written at ascending levels of difficulty. Questions are asked before and after the reading, and the child's behaviors are closely observed during reading.

Before reading a passage on an IRI, students may be asked a set of optional questions to ascertain what they know about the topic, to get an indication of the extent of their *prior knowledge* about the topic. Some examples, all taken from Temple, Crawford, and Gillet (in press), are in the following paragraphs.

After they have read the passage, students are asked a series of questions of different kinds. Some questions may also ask a student to summarize a main idea that has been stated in the text. For example, in a second-grade passage, the text says:

Jan lives in the city. The city has many big buildings. People work in some of the buildings. People shop in other buildings. Some buildings have apartments. . . . There are many cars, trucks, and buses in the city. They make a lot of noise. Many people walk on the street. Some people ride on the bus. There are many people on the bus.

The question asks: *What did this story say that it was like in the city?*

Some of the questions require the recall of important details. For example, the text says: *In Israel, the birthday girl or boy gets a beautiful crown of flowers. The mother places the royal crown on her child's head.* The question asks: *According to this passage, in what country does the birthday child wear a crown of flowers?*

Questions may require that readers make inferences to construct meaning where ideas are not stated explicitly. In narratives, some inferences require that the readers infer motives for behavior. For example, in a sixth-grade passage, the text says:

"Cast near the trunk. Watch out for the branches."
"I <u>know</u>, Dad," said Paco. But his first cast landed on top of the trunk. Without commenting, his father paddled the canoe to the other side of the dead tree, pried the lure from the bark, and gently tossed it into the water.

The question asks: *How did Paco feel about his father's advice? How do you know?*

When the text is informational, inference questions can require readers to derive an answer by applying logic to pieces of information that is given, although the answer to the question is not explicitly stated. For example, in a middle school level passage the text says:

Industries like the textile industry have had to shut down because of increased competition. They could no longer compete in the global economy. Increased competition often leads to lower prices for consumers. But lower prices can sometimes cause lower profits for industries.

The question asks: *From what the article said, do you think you pay more or less for a shirt now that we have a global economy?*

Questions may assess *vocabulary*, too. One kind of vocabulary knowledge is the knowledge of words and their meanings that is stored in memory. Another kind is the ability to infer word meanings from context. As an example of assessing words and meanings stored in memory in a second-grade passage, the text says, *Jan lives in the city. The city has many big buildings. People work in some of the buildings. People shop in other buildings.* The question asks, *When the text said "People shop in other buildings," what does "shop" mean?* As an example of assessing a child's ability to infer vocabulary meaning from context, in a fourth-grade passage the text says, *The wings quiver as they slice through the turbulent air.* The question asks: *In the sentence, "The wings quiver as they slice through the turbulent air," what does "turbulent" mean?* A student who did not already know that the word meant "stormy" or "stirred up" might infer the meaning from the context because it is obvious that *turbulent* refers to air that an airplane is flying through, and it is a condition that makes the wings of the airplane tremble.

For the purpose of scoring, correctly answered questions are counted as a percentage of the total number of questions the child is asked. The scores are interpreted as follows:

Independent reading level = 90 and greater percent correct responses

Instructional reading level = 70 to 89 percent correct responses

Frustration reading level = below 70 percent correct responses

Most IRIs contain both narrative and informational texts, so teachers can assess reader success in dealing with all of the factors just mentioned in different patterns or genres of text. For example, the inference question we saw before from the narrative passage about Paco fishing with his father relied upon the reader's prior knowledge of relationships between parent and child to make a successful inference. The inference question regarding the informational passage about globalization, however, requires the reader to consider information about a generalized situation (cheap labor brings down prices on consumer

"Word Conversations" for Primary Grades

Directed Reading-Thinking Activity (DRTA)

Anticipation Guide

Narrative 2nd Grade Level (2.2): Anita and the Airplane

Introduction: Teacher says: *"Can you imagine what it would be like to fly in a small airplane? Read to find out what happened when Anita went flying in her Uncle Albert's small airplane."*

Anita and the Airplane

Anita's Uncle Albert was a pilot. He had an airplane. "Why don't you come flying with me, Anita?" he asked.

"OK," she said. Little did she know what she was getting in for!

They were sitting in the tight cockpit. Uncle Albert looked at some dials and pulled some knobs. He said something into the radio. A voice came back on the radio. "You're clear for take-off," it said. The engine roared, and the airplane sped down the runway. Suddenly, trees looked like bushes. People looked like ants.

When they were high in the air, Uncle Albert showed Anita how to steer the plane. He showed her how to make it go left and right. He showed her how to make it climb and dip. Then he let Anita hold the steering wheel. She was flying!

Uncle Albert nodded, then he nodded again. Then he snored. His chin fell on his chest. Her uncle went to sleep!

"Wake up!" said Anita. But Uncle Albert just snored, so Anita flew the plane.

Uncle Albert suddenly opened his eyes. "Where are we? Oh, my goodness. I went to sleep," he said. "I shouldn't have done that."

Anita was glad he was awake. Uncle Albert saw the runway and made the plane go down. "Hold on tight," he said. They landed. And do you know what? It was the wrong airport!

Record the time at the end: _____.
231 Words in Passage   Errors in Oral Reading Accuracy: _____

Scoring Guide for Oral Reading
(Circle the boxes that correspond to the Student's Score)

	Oral Reading Accuracy
Independent level:	9 or fewer errors
Instructional level:	10 to 23 errors
Frustration level:	24 or more errors

FIGURE 10.3

Word Recognition in Context and Comprehension.

goods) and to draw a conclusion about the way it affects the reader personally (how much he will pay for a shirt).

IRIs also allow teachers to assess students' listening comprehension in contrast to their reading comprehension. In the case of developing readers, listening to a text is usually easier than reading it—the activity of recognizing written words and constructing understanding from them is less practiced than listening to speech and constructing meaning from it. In reading assessment, testing listening capacity offers an indication of readers' potential for comprehending a text, and may serve as a goal against which their reading comprehension of a text can be measured (see Figure 10.3).

Other Measures of Comprehension

IRIs afford a great deal of insight into a reader's comprehension, but they do so at a high cost of time required. Also, they must be administered to one child at a time, and to complete one with a child in third or fourth grade can take an hour. They are most useful for diagnostic testing, to identify strengths and weaknesses of a child's reading ability to guide instruction. Even when a full IRI is not administered, questions of the type just described can be made up by the teacher and used with any text passage, of course. Many teachers include a variety of questions like these during informal observations. For the more frequent testing that's used to monitor children's progress in learning to read, teachers rely on other, quicker means of assessing comprehension. These include oral retellings and fluency measures.

After a child has a read a passage, the teacher asks the child to give an *oral retelling*—that is, to retell the passage in his own words. The teacher then makes a mental calculation of how much of the information from the text the child retold. For a slightly more exact way of evaluating the retellings, teachers may use a retelling checklist, which is a list of pieces of information contained in the text, prepared in advance. The teacher checks off the pieces of information that the child retold, and then computes the score as a percentage of the whole list of items.

Another way of assessing reading comprehension is to use a structured observation procedure. The teacher sits alone with a child and has the child read a passage aloud. The teacher may ask the student questions before, during, and after the student reads. A checklist for guiding observations may then be used, such as the one shown in Chapter 7.

Fluency measures are sometimes used as a "proxy check" of comprehension. Fluency measures can be administered more quickly than actual comprehension measures because they involve no follow-up questions and answers. Also because fluency measures have been shown to predict growth in reading ability, including reading comprehension (Pinnell, et al., 1995), they are often used as monitoring assessments throughout the year.

Reading: Measuring Attitudes and Interest

It has long been noted, and was recently very eloquently affirmed (Allington, 2005), that children learn to read by reading. As we noted in Chapter 6, children differ enormously in the amount of reading they do, and as Stanovich (1992) has pointed out, those who read more benefit enormously in increased vocabulary, increased world knowledge, better spelling, and even greater measured intelligence. Somewhere between reading ability and the amount of reading that actually gets done is the will to read, a positive attitude toward reading, and a deep interest in books and reading. Where that motivation and interest is lacking, we have a problem. Teachers would do well to assess students' attitudes toward reading.

Surveys can look into children's general attitude toward reading. *The Elementary Reading Attitude Survey* (McKenna & Kear, 1990) is one widely used instrument that reveals how students are feeling about reading and reading instruction in general. This instrument can tell if a school or a classroom is succeeding in promoting an interest in reading among groups of children, as well as an individual child's attitude. It has also been used in research to track the attitudes toward reading of large groups of students over time.

Reading interest inventories are intended to find out individual students' interests and preferences, to help teachers and librarians match them up with books and learning experiences they will enjoy. A reading interest inventory from a librarian in Michigan is found in Figure 10.4.

Assessing Spelling Knowledge

Children's knowledge of spelling develops in two ways. One way is the level of words they can spell. For instance, we would expect a second-grade child to be able to spell *train, queer,* and *float,* but not *conceive* or *profitable,* while a sixth grader should be able to spell the harder words. Another way their spelling develops, as we saw in Chapter 3, is that they work

1. Do you like to read?
2. How much time do you spend reading?
3. What are some of the books you have read lately?
4. Do you have a library card? How often do you use it?
5. Do you ever get books from the school library?
6. About how many books do you own?
7. What are some books you would like to own?
8. Put a check mark next to the kind of reading you like best.
   (topics you might like to read about)

   _____history   _____travel   _____plays
   _____sports   _____science fiction   _____adventure
   _____romance   _____detective stories   _____war stories
   _____poetry   _____car stories   _____novels
   _____biography   _____supernatural stories _____astrology
   _____humor   _____folktales   _____how-to-do-it books
   _____mysteries   _____art   _____westerns

9. Do you like to read the newspaper?
10. If 'yes', place a check next to the part of the newspaper listed below you like to read.

    _____Advertisements   _____Entertainment   _____Columnists
    _____Headlines   _____Comic Strips   _____Political Stories
    _____Current Events   _____Sports   _____Editorials
    _____Others: (please list)

11. What are your favorite television programs?
12. How much time do you spend watching television?
13. What is your favorite magazine?
14. Do you have a hobby? If so, what is it?
15. What are the two best movies you have ever seen?
16. Who are your favorite entertainers and/or movie stars?
17. When you were little, did you enjoy having someone read aloud to you?
18. List topics, subjects, etc. which you might like to read about.
19. What does the word 'reading' mean to you?
20. Say anything else that you would like to say about reading.

Source: D. Hildebrant (2001), pp. 34–37.

FIGURE 10.4

Reading Interest Inventory.

their way through stages of spelling knowledge, and each stage is a way of thinking about the ways written words are structured.

USING WORDS FROM SPELLING TEXTBOOKS. Commercial spelling and language arts programs normally provide lists of words children are expected to learn every week. Those lists are arranged at difficulty levels according to their grades. Publishers use various means to level words, including surveys of children's writing and studies of the vocabularies of textbooks and trade books.

If you are using a spelling series, or if you are teaching grade-level-based spelling lists every week, it is important to find children's instructional level in spelling. The range of spelling abilities of a typical classroom of children is very wide. If students in a typical classroom were asked to spell words they had not yet been taught, their scores might range from less than 10 percent to more than 90 percent (Morris, Nelson, & Perney, 1986). But if the lowest scoring spellers were taught words at their instructional level of spelling instead of words at their grade-placement level, they might fill in the foundational spelling concepts that are taught at the lower grades and that they need for further learning—and in the long run actually make more progress learning to spell the harder words. This was exactly what Darrell Morris and his colleagues (Morris et al., 1995) found in an experimental study.

TABLE 10.6

Stages of Invented Spelling

STAGE	ALSO KNOWN AS	EXAMPLES	TYPICAL AGE
Prephonetic	Preliterate	*bumpy* = R4TSX	Preschool and kindergarten
Early phonemic	Early phonetic	*bumpy* = BP	Kindergarten and early first grade
Letter-name	Phonetic	*bumpy* = BOPE	Early to mid-first grade
Common patterns	Transitional, within-word pattern	*bumpy* = BUPPY	Late first to mid second grade
Syllable juncture		*batted* = BATID	Mid second grade through third grade
Derivational constancy	Conventional	*photograph* = FOTOGRAF	Fourth grade and above

Source: Bear, Invernizzi, Templeton, and Johnston (2000), Gentry (1981); Henderson (1990); Schlagal (1989); Temple, Nathan, Burris, and Temple (1993).

The instructional level of spelling is found by testing children on spelling words they have not been taught and finding the grade level of words where the children score from 50 percent to 75 percent (Henderson, 1990). To assess children's spelling ability for grade-level placement, construct a *spelling inventory*, consisting of twenty randomly chosen words from each grade level in grades 1 through 6, of the spelling program. (These lists are usually found as an appendix in the teacher's guide.) You can test a whole class by beginning with the words one year below grade level and calling out the words as the children spell them. Then call out the correct spellings, or display them on an overhead transparency, and have the children mark their own errors. Call out words from higher-level lists and have the children continue to spell words until they misspell 50 percent of the words. Children who score 50 percent spelling errors can stop. After you look over their papers, you can go back and privately ask some children to spell words from easier lists if they did not reach the instructional level on the first list you called.

ASSESSING SPELLING QUALITATIVELY. Students work their way through stages of spelling development that reflect how they think about the structure of words. Those stages are described in Table 10.6. The student's spelling level suggests ways that she or he can be taught to spell, as we saw in Chapter 9.

To assess a child's level of developmental spelling, you can administer a list of words that are arranged to elicit invented spellings at different levels. A typical list of such words is found in Figure 10.5.

Developmental spelling inventories with full explanations are available in *Words Their Way* (Bear et al., 2000), *Word Journeys* (Ganske, 2003), and *Developmental Literacy Inventory* (Temple, Crawford, & Gillet, in press). As all of these publications make clear, improving children's spelling knowledge improves their word knowledge, especially if they are taught to use what they learn in the context of writing and reading.

WRITING and READING CONNECTIONS

Why is children's spelling and word knowledge so important to their reading and writing development?

---

1. lit	6. peeked	11. spacious	16. physician
2. chap	7. sailed	12. design	17. biographical
3. rock	8. shove	13. brilliance	18. sympathetic
4. truck	9. sitter	14. traction	19. adjournment
5. lend	10. batted	15. doubting	20. collegial

Source: Temple, Crawford, and Gillet (in press). *Developmental Literacy.* Published by Allyn & Bacon, Boston, MA. Copyright © 2008 by Pearson Education. Reprinted by permission of the publisher.

FIGURE 10.5

Words to Elicit Different Levels of Invented Spelling.

Differentiated Instruction

Differentiated instruction begins with good assessment. *Screening assessment* indicates which students are where they are expected to be, which are above grade level, and which need additional support. *Diagnostic assessment* indicates how strong each student is in different aspects of reading and writing development. Based on diagnostic assessment, students will have different kinds of instruction designed for them. They will be assigned different levels of books for guided reading. They will be given different groups of words for word study and possibly will be placed in different points in the sequence of phonics instruction. The teacher will construct focused lessons on aspects of comprehension—on setting purposes for reading, summarizing, visualizing, making inferences, understanding vocabulary from context, learning new information, and interpreting the text. The students will be placed in groups that read different levels of text for fluency practice. They will be placed at their instructional level of spelling words to learn, even if that falls a year above or below their grade-placement level. The assessment picture will be rounded out by other information gained from interviews with the students to determine the topics they are interested in, the kind of reading they most prefer, the conditions they need to help them learn.

TEACH IT! 39
Shared Writing

TEACH IT! 42
The Writing Workshop

Once courses of instruction have been established for all students, they are given periodic *monitoring assessments*. Unlike the daily observations, these are more formalized and done on a schedule. The results may be shared with other teachers or with the reading specialist, and provide guidance for determining whether the present plan of instruction should be followed or if different strategies should be tried to improve a student's learning. In addition, the teacher should practice kidwatching by making a habit of selecting a small number of children every day, and asking how they are working, what exactly they are doing when they read and write, what they appear to be interested in, what kinds of tasks they are succeeding in, when they work best, and when they get off task, and in sum, how the teacher can help each one be successful in this class.

Late in the year come the outcomes-based assessments, which are based on the state learning standards for each grade level. This is a serious accountability event. While the daily informal assessments and the periodic monitoring assessments focus on children's development as readers, writers, and learners in general, these assessments also have one eye on the outcomes of instruction.

Teacher Self-Assessment

As new entrants to a profession, beginning teachers must have the professional knowledge they will need to be successful in the classroom. Experienced teachers, too, have the obligation as professionals to keep abreast of developments in the field of literacy and other domains of knowledge that impact their classroom and to continually perform **teacher self-assessment** activities.

Some years ago, Donald Schön (1983) developed the influential model of the *reflective practitioner*, a professional who is able to learn from experience and create his or her own practical knowledge and skill. This model is still useful today. Professors in your teacher education classes undoubtedly encourage you to observe as closely as you can individual children and whole classrooms, to sense patterns and find possibilities for action.

Becoming a reflective practitioner is not a solitary activity, however. As Taylor and Pearson (2005) noted, in "schools that beat the odds," where students outperform what is predicted for them, teachers come together to share information about their students, about teaching, and about what works in their schools.

Following is an example of a second-grade teacher's observation/assessment discussion with her team teachers:

> *I worked with Michele today. She is putting extra vowels in some words and leaving needed vowels out in others. Today, she spelled chin as CHIAN and cream as CREM; this is a pattern for her. I*

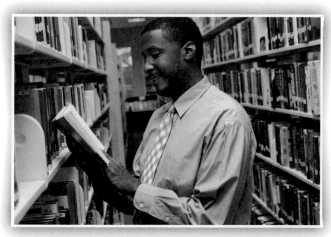

Both beginning and experienced teachers have the professional obligation of keeping abreast of developments in fields that impact their classrooms.

looked it up in a textbook, and this means that she is using but confusing vowel- and consonant-patterned words. Easy to see, but now what? She is on the verge of getting it but needs help. Here is what I am thinking. First of all, I don't think she can read the words she is trying to spell—chin and cream are not known words for her. I need to step back to a point at which she can succeed. What do you think? Give me some feedback.

This teacher received suggestions from the team on increasing assessments of Michele's understanding of the words she attempts to spell. They also suggested she give Michele more opportunities to write. Someone suggested word sorting by patterns—*chin, pin, tin, in*. They made a date for her to try some of these suggestions and report back to the group.

Teachers benefit from comparing and contrasting their ideas with those of others and from using multiple assessment measures. If the opportunity for collaboration does not exist in your building, you should create it with at least one other teacher. With teachers in your building, create regular meetings to talk shop before or after school, at planning times, or during working lunches.

Because of their many variables, teaching and learning are always in flux. Assessment helps to make order and sense of teaching and learning. For direction and planning, you will learn what children know on a daily basis. When physicians prescribe medication, they are following a routine that is grounded in research on groups of people. In addition, however, physicians tell patients, "Get back to me if this doesn't help within three days, and call me if you have any serious side effects." Modern medicine is wonderful, and much of its success depends on knowing what generally works and on the individual's responses. There is no silver bullet in the practice of medicine or the practice of education. However, we have good evidence on more successful medical and teaching practice that we must use to improve.

Professional organizations as well as state governments have something to say about the assessment of teachers, too. The International Reading Association (IRA) and the National Council for the Accreditation of Teacher Education (NCATE) jointly publish a set of *Standards for Reading Professionals* (2003) that outlines what a committee of reading educators believes teachers of reading should know. The standards are available online at **http://www.reading.org/resources/community/ncate_standards.html**.

The IRA/NCATE standards have been incorporated by many schools of education to guide their curricula, and they were also consulted in preparing this textbook. James Zarrillo has written a self-administered guide based on the standards entitled *Are You Prepared to Teach Reading?* (2007). It includes a sample written test at the end of the book.

For Review

Assessment is used in this chapter as a term to cover deciding what we need to know about children's learning, considering what means we will need to use to get the information and possibly designing our own, collecting the information, and interpreting the information to help us make instructional decisions to help the students.

With the federal No Child Left Behind Act and, particularly, with the Reading First program has come an intensified interest in assessment. Reading First requires that teachers assess children at four moments: for *screening*, for *diagnosis*, for *progress monitoring*, and to assess *outcomes*.

Several different kinds of assessment instruments are available to teachers. Standardized or norm-based tests compare children to other children; and standards-based tests look at their accomplishment of curricular standards. Curriculum-based measurement takes brief snapshots of learning, usually for monitoring purposes, and these are closely tied to the outcomes that are desired at the end of the year. Informal assessments such as the Informal Reading Inventory, the Reading Miscue Inventory, and running records reveal a rich array of information about children's reading. However, teachers need to pay attention to the validity (the extent to which the test measures what it claims to) and reliability (the extent to which the findings of the text are stable) of tests they use.

Assessments are done of various aspects of emergent literacy, including print concepts, language awareness, and letter knowledge. Once children can begin to read, we can assess reading levels (independent, instructional, and frustration) as well as their word recognition, fluency, vocabulary, and comprehension. The readability of the texts they read can be assessed by means of a readability formula or the cloze procedure. Their spelling and writing should be assessed, too. Finally, teachers and teachers-to-be should practice self-assessment, both to make sure they are acquiring professional knowledge and skills, and to keep advancing along with the growth of knowledge in the field of literacy.

For Your Journal

1. Now that you have read the chapter, return to the anticipation guide at the beginning. What differences are there in how you would answer those questions now?

2. Choose a grade that you would like to teach, or that you do teach. First describe what aspects of reading and writing you would want to test for in your screening and diagnostic assessments. Second, explain what instruments you would use and why.

3. Go online and find your state's standards for literacy at your chosen grade level. Read the information about the outcomes-based assessments given. Then, for each set of abilities and concepts that they list, describe the way you would monitor students' progress toward achieving those outcomes.

Taking It to the World

Now that you have read about the emphasis on accountability and the regimen of assessments that have been ushered in by the No Child Left Behind Act, go online with a search engine and look up "standards-based assessment" and "high-stakes testing." Be ready to see sparks fly! Who are the different groups posting things on the topic? What are they saying? Why are they saying it? Be sure to check at least one opinion poll, too, such as Public Agenda.

Technology Connections

Go online and look up the services that are offered by DIBELS (**http://dibels.uoregon.edu/**) and Developmental Reading Assessment (**http://www.pearsonlearning.com/dra/**). What exactly do they do for teachers and for schools? How do those services meet the mandates of the No Child Left Behind Act? Which services are required to meet the requirements of Reading First? How much do the services cost?

Connect with Research

Review the following key words from the chapter and then connect to the Research Navigator (**www.researchnavigator.com**) through this book's Companion Website. Look up the research on these terms and see what current research is saying about them.

assess comprehension	curriculum-based measurement	readability
assess vocabulary	grade-equivalent score	teacher self-assessment
assessing phonics	high-stakes testing	three-cueing system
assessing reading fluency	kidwatching	
assessment	phonemic awareness	

Companion Website

To access chapter objectives, practice tests, weblinks, and flashcards, visit the Companion Website at www.ablongman.com/templeallchildren2e.

Go to Allyn & Bacon's MyLabSchool (www.mylabschool.com), enter Assignment ID RMV4 into the Assignment Finder. Watch the video, *Assessing Writing,* in which your author, Charles Temple, discusses the connection between reading and writing. An eighth grade teacher also discusses how she can sometimes spot reading problems by evaluating a child's writing.

Question: How might a student's writing be an indicator of his or her reading abilities? You may also answer the questions at the end of the clip and e-mail your responses to your instructor.

chapter 11

Creating the
Learning Place

Assessment

Developing
Knowledge and
Skills

Putting
Effective Literacy
Instruction into
Practice:
Grades K to 2

Standards as
a Guide

Organizing for
Instruction

Reaching All
Children

Putting Effective Literacy Instruction into Practice: Grades K to 2

Anticipation Guide

The following statements will stimulate your thinking about the topics covered in this chapter. Answer true or false in response to each statement. As you read and learn more about the topics in the statements, double-check your answers. See what interests you and prompts your curiosity toward more understanding.

_____ ● Establishing a friendly and supportive psychological/social climate in the classroom should be a teacher's first concern in teaching early literacy.

_____ ● It is more important for children to learn to follow the teacher's rules than to manage their own behavior.

_____ ● Teachers are wise not to question their district's professional development program.

_____ ● The single most important way teachers can help children learn to read is to read to them.

_____ ● The "five-finger test" is a way of telling if a book is too difficult for children to read: If children miss five words on a page, the book is probably too hard.

_____ ● Children who are English language learners will not profit from reading instruction until they reach an advanced level of proficiency in English.

_____ ● Elkonin boxes are useful devices for teaching children phonemic segmentation.

_____ ● Once teachers have a masters degree, the classroom itself will provide all that is needed to continue to learn.

_____ ● Professional development is not available in local or state school districts.

Literacy Activities in a First-Grade Classroom

It is an early September morning, and nineteen first-grade children are reading and looking at books as their teacher, Ana Lopes, sets up for a lesson with a book entitled *Bread, Bread, Bread* (Morris, 1998). She read the book with the children twice the day before. This picture book has photos of people and their bread from all over the world, including Mexican tortillas, Indian nan, and French baguettes. Ms. Lopes stops to review her notes from the day before and rechecks a list of children who will not be participating in this particular lesson. She calls these children together and discusses two things they have been working on: the posters they are making for a science project and the new interest center the class created the week before. She tells the students that while she works with the other students in the class, they can work part of the time on their posters and part of the time in the interest center; or they can spend their entire time either in the center or working on their posters.

She allows each child to select his or her own activity.

Ms. Lopes then calls the remaining students into the group area and sets the big book on a stand. She says to the group, "You know we really enjoyed this book yesterday, so I thought we'd read it again. But first let's look at the pictures." The children look at the illustrations.

Ms. Lopes says, "Now, whisper something about this book to your neighbor. What did you like? Did you ever eat one of these breads?"

Ms. Lopes likes to use the whispering technique to provide varied and frequent opportunities for children to talk and interact. It ensures that everyone gets involved and prevents children from sitting with their hands in the air waiting for the teacher to call on them.

After the students have shared with each other for a minute, Ms. Lopes reads the big book to the children, pointing to each word as she reads and explaining that for each word spoken there is a letter

or unit of letters that make the word. She is teaching the *concept of word*. As reading proceeds, she stops a few times to spark discussions about the story or aspects of the writing. By doing this, she makes sure an instructional conversation takes place. She is teaching good reader behaviors and encouraging the readers to think and relate personally to books. She also shows the children that she is interested in what they think.

Ms. Lopes points out that some words in the story repeat again and again, such as "bread, bread, bread." She asks the students to find other words that repeat.

A child responds, "I see the word *eat.*"

"Excellent word watching!" Ms. Lopes responds. "Now let's see if we can spot the word *eat* repeated again."

As the literature responses proceed, Ms. Lopes explicitly draws the children into more focused reading by asking them to think about the book's words. As she points to various words, she wonders aloud, "I notice something about this word [pointing to the word *bread*]. What is the word?" The children say "bread," and Ms. Lopes points out other words beginning with *br-* and talks about blends and beginning letter sounds; then she

Now is truly the time for literacy for all. Becoming a global community and serving the rapidly changing student population necessitate changes in teaching practices and teachers' thinking. Because beginnings are so important, teachers of young children must provide the classroom contexts and instruction that support literacy learning. In the act of asks the children to pretend that they are making bread and eating it.

As the pretend play unfolds, Ms. Lopes quickly makes a list of words on the board, then passes out marker boards, erasers, and markers. She covers the board words with a sheet of paper and says, "When I say the word, you try to write its beginning letter on your marker boards and say the sound that the letter makes."

She encourages the children by telling them to take risks and reminding them that the exercise is just for practice. "It's okay if some letters are not quite right. If you can't make the letters, look at the alphabet on the wall. Let me know if you need help."

As the children write and whisper to one another, Ms. Lopes prompts them as necessary and observes and makes notes. Some begin to work independently, saying words, writing letters, and saying letter sounds. Ms. Lopes can see who is taking a chance, who seems able to work independently, who seems dependent, who seems to have a grasp of letter/sound relationships, and who seems lost. This segment ends with removing the paper covering the words on the board and

helping the children check their writing; children rewrite as needed.

She extends the lesson by showing the students a word wall containing some sight words from the bread book. "Do you see any words that have the same letter and sound as those you just worked with?" she asks.

The children point out some matches. Ms. Lopes then says and writes the words and letters under discussion on the board for all to see. She says, "There are some words that have a good letter/sound match and some that don't. We can call the words with a good match 'easy decode' words. For example, in the word *pot*, we can see and say /p/ for the sound *p* makes and the /ot/ for the sound that the letters *ot* make. We can match each letter or chunk of letters to the sounds we say and hear. If we can't see *and* hear a good letter/sound match we can call the words 'tricky.' The word *float* is a tricky word. We see the *fl* and hear and say /fl/; we see the letter *o* and hear and say /o/; and we can see the letter *t* and hear and say the /t/ sound. But we can't match all the letters in *float* to the sounds we hear and say because we see the letter *a* and don't hear the /a/ sound in

float, do we? So that makes it a 'tricky' word."

Ms. Lopes then asks them to find some "easy decode" words in the book.

The children work and talk with one another about words. Ms. Lopes then consolidates the lesson by reading the bread book once more, with the children taking the lead. She prompts, guides, and redirects as needed.

As Ms. Lopes teaches this lesson, she makes mental notes and jots down ideas about some children on a notepad. Her ongoing assessments are quick and valuable. She checks children's concept of word, word recognition, and competence with beginning letters and blends among other things. Later, she will take a few moments at her desk to write more notes about each child's progress and put the notes into the children's files.

gaining meaning from written language, children engage in a complex act of human cognition. In the making of a reader, cognition transacts with affective properties of the mind (interest, persistence, anxiety, curiosity, and courage) and results in the squiggles on a page coming alive with meaning.

Consider Your Options

Your career in teaching will be marked by ongoing professional development (PD). Improving literacy education in our schools is a lifelong undertaking. As you consider your options as a new teacher or a teacher changing jobs, take a good look at the kinds of PD that the school and district have to offer. Some districts have access to state-supported projects that offer high-quality PD. One example of this is found in Ohio. In 2000, this state established a high-quality PD project. This K–12 and Reading First project includes:

- Nine months of research-based core curriculum study for teachers guided by university/college literary specialists and field faculty.
- Regular meetings and school visits that build collaboration, trust, professional and personal support, and a learning place for teachers.
- A coaching component, based on the concept of "assisted performance" (Tharp & Gallimore, 1995).
- Opportunities to earn graduate credit at various participating universities and access to experiences that build leadership.
- An opportunity to earn a state Literacy Specialist Endorsement

Here are some paraphrased comments from primary grade teachers who have participated in the core curriculum:

- The discussions in our class are really valuable to me, especially as a first-year teacher. I've been able to get ideas and suggestions about my students and teaching. It is so reassuring to know that we can all support one another.
- I have learned a lot in this class. I know and now use multiple ways to teach children reading skills. I have enjoyed learning new things from the other members of the class too.
- Core gives you the opportunity to stay informed about best practices in literacy. But, perhaps, the most beneficial part is engaging in meaningful dialogues about your own and other's literacy practices.

For more information see **www.literacyspecialist.org**, and investigate PD through other resources available at **www.reading.org**.

YOUR PROFESSIONAL PORTFOLIO

- Including a statement of your philosophy about teaching beginning reading in your portfolio provides evidence of how you view children and reading and also provides a window on your writing abilities. Think about including a reflection about why you incorporated such a statement into your portfolio.
- Even if you intend to teach at a higher grade level, your portfolio will be greatly strengthened if you can incorporate some experiences in the levels from kindergarten to second grade. Because some older children are preliterate or not literate in English, providing evidence of your knowledge of emergent literacy and early reading can be important for any grade level. Lesson plans; thematic literature units; and lists of high-interest, low-vocabulary children's literature are among the artifacts you might think about including.

TEACHING RESOURCES If you are interested in teaching in the primary grades, a list of wordless books will be a very valuable resource. Children's librarians, sales staff in children's bookstores, other primary teachers, and even a search at **google.com** can help you locate these resources. The next step is to begin collecting the actual books. Try swap meets, thrift shops, friends whose children are older now, garage sales, and bookstore remainder tables. If you find two of the same title, buy both; trade with a friend later. Keep your receipts for these kinds of purchases; they are usually deductible for teachers when they file their income tax returns.

The goal of early-grade instruction is to nurture children emotionally and socially and to ensure their exposure to print, concepts about print, and the joy of reading and writing (IRA & NAEYC, 1998). Teachers need to support children's literacy skills learning and their belief in themselves. Effective teachers carefully craft their teaching so that children experience success. Because nothing succeeds like success, your students' success ensures your success. This chapter provides some new information and connects information with what you already know from reading this book or from your education classes.

Creating the Learning Place

What do we mean by a learning place? It's a place, a classroom, that is steeped in mutual respect and responsibility. Without these attributes, school becomes a place in which children and teachers fail to thrive. Chapter 2 provided good grounding in the importance of social/cultural contexts and community. Here we apply these concepts to early primary classrooms.

Young children come to school believing that they will learn to read and write. With eyes wide and minds open, children enter school so trusting; they trust in your expertise. However, some will be more anxious than others. In organizing and managing your classroom, you manifest your respect for your students. The effective and caring teacher in the early grades can make a tremendous difference in their lives. William Ayers (1993) notes that teaching requires sustained energy and dedication, which becomes self-sustaining when it is supported by certain attributes:

To create a literacy-rich classroom, it's important to include an array of books that appeal to all children's needs and interests.

- Strong principles
- A strong sense of responsibility for student learning and motivation
- A desire to search for personal strengths
- An enjoyment of interactions with students and an abiding compassion for them

As you consider ways in which you will create your classroom, think about disciplining. This is something that is uppermost in the minds of all teachers, especially beginning ones. What's the difference between disciplining and controlling children?

Before children come to school, you should have in mind ways in which you will help them learn to manage their own behaviors. For starters, generate a few simple classroom rules or guidelines, but be aware that for some children, it might be the first time they have experienced such structure. As you teach the children what is and is not appropriate behavior, be generous in showing them that you appreciate them and respect them. A simple thinking habit helps you do this—try to imagine what school is like for these little ones. Some may have had preschool, while others have not; some have traveled, known various people and places, others may have none of these experiences; some have sisters or brothers who have been to school, others have not.

It takes the first few of weeks of school to get acceptable behavior and routines established. Eventually, students learn to monitor their own behavior. This places appropriate responsibility on the child while you provide feedback, guidance, and support. As they learn, let them know that you have confidence in their ability to learn self-management. Contrast this teaching stance with that of disciplining and controlling children, which has aspects of punishment without guidance toward self-management.

From the beginning, talk with the children about what will happen during the day. It's a mystery to them! You might want to write a schedule on a chart for everyone to see; knowing what will happen creates comfort. Repeating the day's routine again and again, providing special attention as needed, and drawing the children into play and song activities will help calm anxiety, particularly for the youngest. By second grade, students will be more at ease with school routines. You might want to include students in your planning as a way of encouraging them to take on responsibility.

Providing special learning centers, such as reading areas or writing centers, is important in teaching small groups. But centers can be a problem if children are not taught to use them well. Two ways of teaching children proper behavior in the centers are as follows:

If I had one piece of advice for new teachers it would be, just stay patient. Your first year will be overwhelming, but give it time. The children are getting used to your presence, your teaching style, and your routine. . . . They are eager to read words. When they sit in the literacy area, they read the pictures and imagine that they are reading.

—Joel,
Head Start Teacher
BOSTON

- Role-play good center behavior and unacceptable center behavior. Provide plenty of practice and be open to repeating these roles as needed.
- Have children help in formulating rules for center behavior. Change, review, and improve center rules as needed.

Still, regardless of your teaching skills, children will have problems. A strategy that helps deal with conflicts is to establish an "I have a problem" writing place where children can write and draw about their problems. Set up a small table and chair in a part of the room

WRITING and READING CONNECTIONS

How can the teacher motivate young children to begin writing?

FIGURE 11.1

I Have a Problem
Note.

> Simon   5/12/02
> I have a problem.
>
> Today Bob pushed me into
> the lunch line and sed bad
> words. I told him to stop he din't
> stop

that offers some privacy, and put up a sign marked "Private." Provide writing materials and a "problems basket" where students can submit their writings and drawings to you. Assure the children that you will read all the messages in the basket and help them solve their problems. After you read the messages, individual children can read their notes with you and problem solving can take place. Figure 11.1 shows an example of the kind of message that might be written in an "I have a problem" note.

The literacy-rich classroom itself is a critical component of literacy success. The research of Hickman (1979), Morrow and Weinstein (1982), and Neuman and Rosko (1991) has shown that an abundance of high-quality books, classroom libraries, self-selection and ownership, the physical arrangements of the room, and children's construction of personal meanings contribute to a love of books. These things also support appreciation and preferences about genre, the habit of choosing to read more often, higher reading achievement, and intrinsic motivation (see the World of Reading box).

Developing Knowledge and Skills

As a primary teacher, you might ask, "What is the most important learning in the first years of school?" The answer is twofold. First, children must learn to love school and they must learn the basic skills of reading, writing, and spelling. Second, the teacher must learn and understand the developmental changes new readers experience. You have read a good deal about literacy development in previous chapters of this book, and if you become a K–2 teacher, the previous chapters and this one will serve your needs for years to come. Use it for teaching information and support or for your own family's enrichment!

Instruction in grades K–2 focuses not only on the five elements of **Reading First**—phonemic awareness, phonics, fluency, vocabulary, and reading comprehension—but also on oral language. Written language is grounded in oral language, and its development is supported by reading aloud, social interactions, and children's talk about work (lots of talk about work and classroom life!). A silent classroom creates barriers to learning. As children move through the stages of reading development, the goal is that they all arrive at silent reading and fluent oral reading by third grade. Some will gain these abilities by the end of first grade and many by the end of second grade. Children become better readers by (see Figures 11.2 and 11.3):

- Good guided reading instruction.
- Reading more challenging books.
- Becoming more aware of their own strategies.
- Taking more independent action based on their learning.

Quality Questioning

Good questioning on the part of a teacher promotes critical thinking in children and provides high-quality oral language teaching and practice. Open-ended questions require children to infer, reason, use language to express thought, and think deeply. Open-ended questions call forth more thinking and expressive oral language. Open-ended questions might include: Why do you think that? Why did the author of our story write about _____? What do you think will happen? What would you do? Can you tell me more about that? What is your prediction? Show how you can confirm that. Show us why you make that prediction. How do you think this problem can be resolved? Consider the following examples of open-ended questions and the child's answers:

Teacher	Child
What did the princess do to help?	She went off on her own to take care of the dragon.
Why did she do that?	She just did. Cause the prince wouldn't.
How could she do that?	She was brave, and she wasn't afraid.
How did the princess and prince dress?	Well, the prince was in nice prince clothes, but all the princess had was a dirty paper bag.
Why?	Because of the dragon. He burned up everything even her clothes.

Teacher	Child
What did the prince do?	He just stayed in the cave and said her clothes were a mess. And her hair too. That wasn't very nice.

Notice the vocabulary and textlike phrasing use: *brave, nice, prince, clothes.* Notice the length of the sentences and the clarity of thought, and consider the critical analysis that occurs in the child's last sentence. "That wasn't very nice." This child's responses demonstrate the use of inference.

Now consider this same discussion but with the teacher employing constrained, or closed, questions:

Teacher	Child
What happened to the princess?	She ran away.
The prince was no _____?	Help
Who was the prince afraid of?	The dragon.
What did the princess do to the dragon?	Made him tired.

Children can respond "correctly" to constrained/closed questions, yet totally miss the real meaning in the book. With practice, teachers learn open questioning. Some examples of open questions should be kept by your side as you teach. It is important to preread and know the children's literature you will use.

Name Will   Date may 14, 2001

What you read today The town mouse and county mouse

Word Strategies

1. List the strategies you used to figure out words when you were reading today.
   CHUNK, skip, sound.

2. Write down a sentence that had a word you had trouble with and underline the word.
   She had never seen such delicacies

3. Tell what you did to figure out what this word meant.
   I chunked the wiled out

FIGURE 11.2

Word Strategies.

> A good reader needs to now how to read. They need to pratis to be a grat reader. They need to skip it if they don't no it. They neen to make a gassand go bake and see if ther gas is rite. You shud read with a parint to see if you are nite with a wrde.
>
> I am Kathleen and I am a prity good reader

FIGURE 11.3A

I Am a Good Reader—Kathleen.

> A good reader sawnds out the werds. and per tends it is gess the coverd word. a good reader never geves up. a good reader read day and nite.

FIGURE 11.3B

I Am a Good Reader—Katie.

Helping children understand what they know and about good strategies builds metacognition and extends skills to all areas of their education and personal lives. These skills open up the world to children.

Why Does Reading Aloud Help?

Read to children (Adams, 1990). Through an analysis of the oral and written language of well-read-to young children, Victoria Purcell-Gates (1991) found that those children understood the vocabulary and structures of written language even before they learned to read. Thus, children who have had extensive read-aloud experiences before starting school have an important advantage.

In another study with low-income children who had not been well-read-to before starting school but then received extensive reading in kindergarten and first grade from their teachers, Purcell-Gates, McIntyre, and Freppon (1995) found that by the end of first grade, these children's knowledge of written language was comparable to that of upper-middle-class, well-read-to children. It is reasonable to infer that classroom read-alouds compensated for the children's limited reading experiences prior to school. Reading to young children is one of the most important things teachers can do. Teachers do make the difference.

PHONICS and PHONOLOGICAL AWARENESS

Why is it so important to teach phonics out of the context of children's needs?

Phonics Knowledge and Skills

As you know, phonics knowledge is necessary, but not solely sufficient, for learning to read. Effective reading instruction and assessment are based on well-established developmental stages of word recognition, writing, spelling, and vocabulary (Ganske, 2000). Phonics, how-

TEACH IT!

Refer to your **Teach It!** booklet for further activities you can use to reinforce concepts discussed in this chapter.

Phonics in the Context of Children's Needs

Daniel Woo is teaching a group of eighteen children in a transitional first grade. They have completed kindergarten, but are not yet ready for first grade. Most of the children struggled in kindergarten, and some are English language learners. Mr. Woo's school and its teachers recognize the need for an additional year of expert teaching before first grade to prevent later failure.

In the following lesson, Mr. Woo engages the children in explicit word study that is highly interactive and appealing to them. He has arranged for half of his class to go to music in the morning and half in the afternoon. In this way, Mr. Woo can provide more focused attention to specific children with similar needs in a smaller group. His needs-based lesson follows:

Mr. Woo asks the children to raise their left thumb if they are ready for word play. The children love word play and eagerly help one another find their left thumb.

He then asks the children to give him their "important" word, cautioning them that it must be a real word. This activity is similar to key vocabulary teaching. Mr. Woo says, "Tell us your word and new letters you want to try."

Taking turns, the children say their words and letters they want to substitute as the beginning letter. A child volunteers the word Lex (his dog's name) and the letters D and B.

Mr. Woo writes the word Lex on the board; then the children spell Dex and Bex. Mr. Woo then writes these words on the board. Next, he asks the children to work with the two words bat and big, and he writes the words on the board. He and the class change the beginning letters to make new real words, with the children leading the conversation.

Mr. Woo guides the instructional conversation, but makes every effort to "lead from behind." He employs scaffolding actions—warmth and responsiveness, coming to shared understandings with children, staying in their zone of proximal development—as he teaches.

For consolidation, he guides the children's participation in word learning practice. He chants, "If I know pig, I know jig." The children read this refrain with him from chart paper. The teacher and the children continue: "If I know day, I know play. If I know . . . ."

As an application and extension of the lesson, Mr. Woo distributes word cards that have the letter/sound patterns just taught and has the children engage in exclusive word learning practice in partner groups and individually.

As part of his ongoing assessment, Mr. Woo takes notes on several children after he has observed and interacted with them as they sort through the word cards. He makes a note to do a formal phonemic awareness test with three children he is worried about.

Contributed by Linda Headings, M.Ed.

ever, is an element of Reading First and plays an important role in balanced literacy instruction.

As much as a total of thirty minutes a day in the early grades may be spent on various kinds of phonics instruction. As was noted in earlier chapters, instruction within the context of reading or writing provides effective phonics learning opportunities. Children's writing and use of invented spelling is extremely important to phonics learning. A helpful view of phonics in context comes from Dahl and colleagues (2001, p. ix): "Phonics in context means: in the context of children's needs, in the context of children's developing language knowledge, [and] in the context of classroom reading and writing activities."

Phonemic awareness (PA) is a crucial kindergarten skill we've covered extensively. It is a skill stressed in Reading First. Young children must grasp the concept that words are made up of letters representing speech sounds and gain the ability to divide words into small units of sound. You have already read about many kinds of PA lessons. Another effective one that children enjoy is described in the Teach It! box on phonics in context.

Assessing PA is inseparable from teaching it. This is especially true when assessment takes place in ways that directly inform instruction. Assessment that also affords teaching opportunities is golden! Such a PA assessment is provided in the Assessment box.

Picture the teacher—he has observed his students during a rhyming word lesson and has decided to work with a few children who avoided participating or seemed lost during the activity. For a ten-to-fifteen-minute informal assessment, he gathers a selection of rhyming word cards (single syllable and consonant blend) including words from a lesson just taught: *table, able, chair, Blair, rag, bag, tag, goat, boat, float.*

The children sort the words into rhyming matches independently—they are seated spaced apart at a table. Having told the children he would make some notes, he watches for accurate matches, mistakes, signs of uncertainty, and signs of confidence. With a small group of four or five children, the teacher is able to make notes on each child. After this brief sort he asks the children to move together. Of course, the cards are slightly mixed up as they are slid across the table, but this gives the children another opportunity to quickly arrange their rhyming matches.

Beginning with accurate matches, the teacher asks why they are matches. He aims to guide children to identify rhyming patterns ("It's the ending letters!") and to encourage self-assessment. Through dialogue, the teacher and children discuss "good matches" and engage in "good fixes." This brings the assessment to a dynamic level; learners self-correct and feel accomplished. During this conversation the teacher affirms, repeats children's accurate reasoning, and corrects as needed. Some direct correcting is needed, but not very much because having begun with talk about accurate matches and why they are accurate, incorrect ones are more readily identified and fixed by the children.

Assessment notes are filed in children's folders as they return to their seats. Which is more informative, an assessment such as this or corrected worksheets? Which is a better use of teacher/student time? Which is more interesting to you as a professional reading teacher?

Organizing for Instruction

Nearly all young children benefit from and enjoy learning literacy with their peers. Young children approximate literate behaviors and reading and writing behaviors for some time before the behaviors become part of their repertoire. But not all children enter school with the same abilities. Some children have been in preschool for three or four years, while others may be experiencing school for the first time (Riley, 1996). Some might have disabilities, some might read independently, others might have literacy skills typical of a three-year-old, and for some, English might be a second language. Therefore, instruction must have breadth and great flexibility. In the early years in particular, teachers need to know what to expect in children's development, recognize differences, manage a broad range of development, and use research-based strategies that are designed for their children (see the Differentiated Instruction box).

Differentiate Instruction through Grouping and Planning

Grouping children and planning for instruction are major teaching strategies that are designed to address differences in children's learning. Traditional grouping, which identified students as high, medium, or low in ability, nearly guaranteed underachievement for many children and teachers. How could teachers be effective and still have the same children in the same low-ability group for nine months? For years? This concept is based on an invalid deficit learning model, and it invites a "blame the kid" attitude (Pressley et al., 2001, p. 233).

SIOP® Sheltered Instruction Observation Protocol*

Differentiated Instruction

A Rural Primary Classroom

Plans for a week of reading lessons in a Readers' Workshop. One lesson set supports children at several developmental levels, another provides for two interest groups, and another gives children opportunities to read their weekly "challenge" books. In teaching, focus on reading comprehension, fluency, and word recognition skills (vocabulary and phonics), as well as children's enjoyment.

For the guided reading groups, get multiple copies of the following books leveled by Reading Recovery:

- Books for more emergent readers:
  Wake up Dad (Randell, 1996c)
  At the Zoo (Peters, 1995)
  The Animals Went to Bed (Theodorou, 1996)
- Books for the solid beginning readers:
  Mrs. Wishy-Washy (Cowley, 1990)
  Baby Bear Goes Fishing (Randell, 1996a)
- Books for those farther along:
  Happy Birthday Sam (Hutchins, 1978)
  Henny Penny (Galdone, 1968)
  Leo the Late Bloomer (Krauss, 1987).

For interest groups, have several new books. For primary fiction include *Ace Lacewing: Bug Detective, Mr. Tuggle's Troubles,* and *Russell the Sheep.* For nonfiction include *Jose! Born to Dance, Brave Dogs, Gentle Dogs: How They Guard Sheep,* and *Recess at 20 Below.* During the week, children will have several opportunities to take turns reading these books alone and in pairs. As with all reading groups, attend to comprehension strategies and word recognition skills.

Have the children select challenge books from the classroom or school library. While you teach the guided reading group, instruct the students not in the group to read their self-selected books at their tables (or desks pushed together). Later in the day, meet and observe several readers. Something is always gained with the self-selected books, including new vocabulary and boosted motivation for the students to read. You gain too by learning what your students can do given varied and flexible opportunities to read with your guidance.

Research shows that once a child has been assigned to the low reading group, it is highly unlikely the child will ever be moved to a higher group (Hiebert, 1983; Good & Marshall, 1984). Children in low groups often have low self-esteem and receive instruction with fewer opportunities to think and work with meaning (Allington, 1983; Allington & McGill-Franzen, 1989; Eder, 1983). Observe the way Mariann Davis, a first-grade teacher, makes sure her children do not get locked solely into "ability groups."

The teacher's voice is in regular text, the children's is in brackets. It's Monday morning during roll call, each child reads her or his own name from large sentence strips the teacher holds up and then stands up.

Simon, what is your challenge book this week? [I'm going to do a science Frog and Toad book]. Hum, why? [Cause I want to read all those kinds of books]. Okay! Fisher, how about you? [A Stupid's book for me!] Yes, you do like those, I've seen you look at them in the library, what do you think? [They're funny, yep they are.] I see (smiling teacher). Now how about you Cody? [That new one, that's about trucks, I like trucks.] Yes you do, good selection. Maybe you can take it home to read to Shea, she likes trucks too. When we have our Reading Party be sure you have practiced some favorite part so you can read it to me, okay? [Okay.]

Reading Parties function as small group instruction; they are parties because all children are invited at various times throughout the week. The parties provide fun, reading instruction, and excellent opportunities for learning new vocabulary.

Two well known programs offer grouping ideas that are designed to help avoid the pitfalls of traditional grouping. Each approach makes a distinction between the organizational structures and the kind of instruction that goes on in them. Grouping strategies and other organizations for literacy instruction (e.g., writing time, word time, reading group time) are not prescriptions for effective teaching. Rather, what teachers do with children in specific blocks of time is what really matters.

DYNAMIC GROUPING. Fountas and Pinnell (2001) developed the concept of dynamic grouping as a way of providing targeted guided reading opportunities. Dynamic grouping involves the creation of several kinds of reading/writing groups that work together and receive instruction over the course of a school day. For example, dynamic groups provide for non–ability-based interest groups such as the Reading Party discussed earlier, peer tutoring and cooperative learning pairs, cross-grade buddies, and needs-based small groups (flexible and ability-based). In needs-based groups, children are moved regularly so that no child is stuck in any one group all year.

Guided Reading and the Four Blocks Approach

GUIDED READING AND FOUR BLOCKS. As described in Chapter 1, guided reading often takes place within a **four-blocks** language arts period. However, guided reading could take place in other approaches. For example, a wise and creative teacher can effectively guide children's reading using basal texts. This is because by definition guided reading creates "a context in which the teacher supports each reader's development of effective strategies for processing novel texts at increasingly challenging levels of difficulty" (Fountas & Pinnell, 1996).

Four blocks describes four specialized reading periods that address some of teachers' most challenging issues. No matter what reading program is used, all teachers are faced with the challenges of managing to teach a class of twenty to thirty students in ways that meet their needs and avoid having some children labeled and taught as "low-ability" students. Additionally, the question of how to manage grading young children looms large. Cunningham, Hall, and Sigmon (1999) and Cunningham, Hall, and Defree (1991) created a framework to address these questions and issues and to provide guidelines for organization, planning, teaching, and grading. (Grading is discussed later in this chapter.) The four blocks provide varied ample opportunities for primary grade children to learn and teachers to teach reading and writing.

The framework of four reading periods occurs during the school day and includes (1) guided reading, (2) self-selected reading, (3) working with words, and (4) writing. Within each block, specific structured activities take place. A major goal of four blocks is to give children a balance of reading, writing, and word instruction. Four-blocks planning provides what it takes for teachers to make each block as multileveled as possible. **Multileveled groups** include children with different needs and strengths (Cunningham et al., 1999). These four blocks contain key elements of instruction for all classrooms with dynamic or multileveled groups:

Shared Reading

- **Guided Reading.** For thirty to forty minutes, the teacher helps children learn children's literature and reading comprehension. The lesson focuses on developing prior knowledge, oral language, meaningful vocabulary, self-confidence, and motivation. Guided readings are periods in which the teacher, working with small groups, teaches reading concepts and skills. Within guided reading periods, children often engage in shared reading—the teacher reads to the children, the children read with the teacher in unison, or the children take turns reading. They read a big book or sets of the same little books. Following instruction, children read with their partners (often two children who read at somewhat different levels but who are compatible enough to read together). Next, the group comes together again to discuss major points in the book. The children or the teacher and the children usually write something about their reading.

- **Self-Selected Reading.** The goal of self-selected reading is to share different kinds of literature. The teacher leads read-alouds, encourages reading interests, provides instructional-level materials, and helps to build intrinsic motivation. Besides read-alouds, children read the books they select and then conference with the teacher individually to talk about books. This block lasts about thirty minutes.

- **Working with Words.** For about thirty minutes, the teacher and the children engage in various word-related activities, such as reading familiar words on the word walls and reading the new words added weekly (approximately five). The teacher asks the children to review the wall words and talks with them about the importance of these words (sight words, high-frequency words, and words in units of study such as favorite authors). Children write the words, say the words, look for patterns in words, and discuss and practice the words' spelling patterns. The teacher writes the words, showing how the letters and words are formed and pointing out word patterns (rhyming, blends, diagraphs, short/long vowel words, and so on, according to children's needs and strengths). The children practice making words and sorting words in a variety of ways.

- **Writing.** A minilesson, also occurring in a writing workshop, begins each writing period, which lasts forty-five to sixty minutes depending on how young children get along in an extended time period. Goals of this period focus on having every sentence make sense and using capital letters and punctuation to end a sentence. In addition, the writing block focuses on spelling. Children write during the minilesson on their own and with partners. This is an easy block to teach on multiple levels. Children engage in writing books, stories, and information pieces; illustrate their writing; and have conferences with the teacher for individual instruction. The word wall helps children to find words they need and to work on spelling. Writing time concludes with sharing writing in the author's chair. Be aware that different teachers use different formats and structures for writing workshops. What is important is that all writing workshops include the basic essentials, such as time to write, writing/spelling instruction, strong support, a warm and inviting work environment, and specific roles for teachers.

Cunningham et al. (1999) provide some basic guidelines to consider in using four-blocks teaching:

- Long-term planning for four-blocks teaching is organized around units of study (inquiry units) and the curriculum (literature, math, etc.). Short-term planning is laid out in weekly and daily descriptions.
- Oral language is not a specific part of the four blocks, but rather is integrated into all four blocks.
- Four-blocks teaching does not eliminate the need for interventions such as Reading Recovery; it is not an add-on and can be used with other approaches.
- Volunteers and paraprofessionals can be used to help support four-blocks teaching.
- The four blocks can be performed in any order that works in your classroom.

Lesson Structures

Because children need many and varied learning opportunities, teachers use various types of lessons to accomplish the desired outcomes in their classrooms. In all lessons, the teacher uses a before, during, and after structure. There is an introduction to the lesson, a period in which the heart of the lesson is conducted, and a conclusion, which is usually followed by an extension and application of what has been taught. Each type of lesson has structural aspects that help teachers meet their specific instructional needs. For example, some lessons are more comprehensive and include a strong focus on word study, while reading or writing is also taught. Other types of lessons include mini-lessons, teachable moments, and think-alouds.

MINI-LESSONS. Mini-lessons require fewer materials and are planned and taught fairly quickly. A mini-lesson is often taught at the beginning and focuses on one or two teaching points, such as self-monitoring one's comprehension and metacognition, providing the anticipation and focus of the lesson. The following is an example of a writing mini-lesson conducted by teacher Dr. Jill Dillard:

> Recess is over and the second graders are either reading or sitting at tables playing word games. Dr. Dillard asks the children to get ready for writing workshop.
>
> They gather around her and she talks with the children about yesterday's topic lesson, "I'm an expert." Several children generated new topics after that minilesson: Jarad selected a pet story; Sammie Ann selected a soccer story; and Kyle selected a story about his baseball team (see Figure 11.4).
>
> Dr. Dillard invites the children to talk to a neighbor about their writing topic. During this time, she circulates among the children prompting and encouraging.
>
> Dr. Dillard confirms the children's good ideas for stories and information writing and then asks the class whether they are ready to begin.
>
> With the children's consensus, she calls Monday's small writing group to meet with her to talk about their writing before Annie, the high school volunteer, arrives.

TEACHABLE MOMENTS. Teachable moments are lessons in which the teacher seizes on an incident or observation of something to reinforce a concept. For busy teachers, teachable moments are superior opportunities for providing individual instruction in the context of a child's need. The next example demonstrates how much a teacher can do in a very short time:

> First-grader Ransika is working in the writing center. As Mr. López walks by to check on him, he notices that Ransika is putting capital letters in the middle of some of his words. Mr. López intervenes immediately, asking Ransika if he is using capital letters.
>
> Ransika nods yes, and Mr. López reviews the morning talk about when to use capital letters.
>
> With a sheepish grin, Ransika realizes his errors and begins to erase. Mr. López nods approval and turns to help another child.

FIGURE 11.4A

I Am an Expert—Kyle.

FIGURE 11.4B

I Am an Expert—Sammie Ann.

With that interaction, Mr. López was able to reinforce the morning's lesson quickly and positively.

THINK-ALOUDS.   Think-alouds are lessons that demonstrate and model. They often show children how to think like a reader, writer, or speller. The following is an example of a reading comprehension think aloud:

> *Ms. Novacek rereads* Sheila Rae, the Brave *(Henkes, 1987) to her first and second graders in a multiage classroom. This book is a favorite, as is* Lilly's Purple Plastic Purse, *also by Henkes (1996). The children and Ms. Novacek discuss the topic of bravery, which the children think is the book's theme. For discussion among the children, Ms. Novacek has paired a slightly less experienced reader with a somewhat more experienced reader.*
>
> *Ms. Novacek's goal is to help the children work toward understanding a deeper meaning, one that has to be inferred. Henkes's books provide opportunities to teach children to infer meaning, and the implied meaning in* Sheila Rae, the Brave *is about sibling relationships.*
>
> *Ms. Novacek engages in the following think-aloud: "Class I've been thinking about this book and what Sheila Rae is like. I'm going to read a bit and keep thinking." Ms. Novacek reads and says, "I make a connection with Sheila Rae. When I was a child, I had a little brother, and I wasn't always nice to him. Sometimes I'd say mean things. What do you think about this?"*
>
> *The children discuss the idea, and Ms. Novacek picks up on their levels of understanding and carefully guides them to make inferences. She repeatedly talks about her own thinking and inferences.*

Routines That Teach

As was mentioned earlier, well-balanced daily schedules help young children to adapt more quickly and happily to the school day. Teachers incorporate a variety of strategies for implementing classroom routines. One strategy is to use a school script questionnaire and a teacher observation form, like those shown in Figures 11.5 and 11.6, to help children adjust to classroom routines and take ownership of them (Tattershaw & Prendeville, 1995). This strategy is particularly helpful with students who have difficulty adjusting or have learning difficulties. Students' completed questionnaires also can be used to teach classroom routines to new students who might enroll later in the year.

The following routines and lessons serve as examples of systematic routines that provide opportunities to work on important skills, such as word recognition and reading comprehension, in highly authentic situations.

Daily Routines in K–2 Classrooms

KINDERGARTEN ROUTINES.   A typical day in a kindergarten class would include many, if not all, of the following elements (Vukelich, Christie, & Enz, 2002, pages 45, 54–57):

TEACH IT! 41

Pillowcase or Me in a Box

- *Morning Greeting.* Engage in one-on-one conversations with the children, and use this time to observe how children talk with each other and which centers they self-select (e.g., reading center, writing center). This allows you to check for interest and avoidance.

- *Taking Attendance.* Use a creative technique to take attendance, such as singing a song that includes the children's names. Children sing along and learn one another's names. Use large name tags that children read and hang up on the attendance chart during the singing.

- *Shared Reading.* Read aloud to the children predictable books with repeated phrases. As the children become familiar with the words and phrases, have them join in. Read-alouds should occur several times in the course of a day. Figure 11.7 on page 369 provides a typical read-aloud lesson plan. This structure provides scaffolding.

School-Day Script Questionnaire

Child's name: _____ Date: _____

Teacher's name: _____

Ask the whole class to complete the questionnaire (or administer as an individual interview with a child). Tell the students that when a new student transfers into your class, some of them will be asked to use their questionnaires to help that new student learn about the class. Ask the students the questions and write their responses.

1. Tell me what happens when you come to school each day. What happens first . . . second . . . and so on?

2. Where do I usually stand when I want everyone to pay attention?

3. What do I say or do to get everyone's attention?

4. How do you know when I am changing to a different subject or activity? (For example, how can you tell that I am finished reviewing yesterday's work and will begin explaining something new?)

5. What are the rules in this class? What are the reasons for each rule?

6. What happens if someone breaks a rule?

7. How do you know what your homework will be each day? Do I write the assignment on the board or simply tell you what to do?

8. How do you remember what books or papers to take home so that you can do your homework?

9. Tell me about your homework time at home. Where do you do your homework? What do you do first, second, and so on?

10. How do you remember to bring your homework back to school?

FIGURE 11.5

School Script Questionnaire.

- *Shared Writing.* Model aspects of writing, such as letter formation, thinking about what to say, or using conventions such as periods and capital letters. Then have the children take turns writing letters and words. This provides high level scaffolding.

- *Writing Center.* Encourage use of the writing center where children can self-select and write on their own about topics of special interest to them (see Figure 11.8 on page 369).

- *Group Time.* Use group time to emphasize purposeful oral language. Demonstrate purposeful speaking, good listening, taking turns, and idea sharing. Use group time to discuss the daily schedule and center assignments. After center assignments have been made, assign a group of approximately six children to sharing time.

- *Sharing Time.* In smaller groups, children can be more at ease and engaged than they are when in larger groups. You also have opportunities to ask natural questions, such as "What happened next, Mark?" or "Does anyone have a question for Michael?" (Moffett & Wagner, 1983).

Beginnings are important, and good teachers teach children many things on the first day of school. The Teach It! box on pages 370–371 provides a model of how one teacher organizes her first day of kindergarten.

Script List

Child's name: _____ Date: _____

Teacher's name: _____

Please list the student's activities in the order that they occur on a typical school day. Write day-to-day variations, such as gym or library class, on the right side. This list will be used to assess and teach the child's knowledge of school activities and to select appropriate activity scripts for use in language assessment and intervention.

Typical School Day

_____

_____

_____

_____

_____

_____

_____

_____

_____

_____

_____

_____

_____

_____

_____

_____

_____

_____

Regular Variations

_____

_____

_____

_____

_____

_____

_____

_____

_____

_____

_____

_____

_____

_____

_____

_____

_____

_____

Source: From *Using Familiar Routines in Language Assessment and Intervention* by S. Tattershaw and J. Prendeville. Copyright © 1995. Permission granted by Sandra Tattershall.

The use of wall charts for things such as attendance and lunch schedules helps students learn to establish routines. How does this carry over to benefit children's learning?

Teacher Observations

Student's name: _____   Date: _____

Teacher's name: _____

Please use the following statements to guide your observations of the child on a typical school day. Write your comments after each statement.

1. The child seems to know the order of events in a typical class day.

   Yes   No   Comments: _____
   ☐   ☐   _____

2. The child looks in your direction when you are standing in your usual teaching spot.

   Yes   No   Comments: _____
   ☐   ☐   _____

3. The child responds appropriately and in a timely manner to your signals for attention.

   Yes   No   Comments: _____
   ☐   ☐   _____

4. The child can usually restate directions that you have given in his or her own words when asked to do so.

   Yes   No   Comments: _____
   ☐   ☐   _____

5. The child restates only the first part of directions.

   Yes   No   Comments: _____
   ☐   ☐   _____

6. The child restates only the last part of directions.

   Yes   No   Comments: _____
   ☐   ☐   _____

7. The child responds appropriately to your signals for transitions. (For example, the child puts away materials used for prior tasks, gets out materials for the new activity, or looks at you with apparent readiness for the new information or activity.)

   Yes   No   Comments: _____
   ☐   ☐   _____

8. The child seems to have difficulty leaving a project or task when you signal a transition.

   Yes   No   Comments: _____
   ☐   ☐   _____

9. The child seems to look at and follow peers' actions rather than respond independently to your signal for transitions.

   Yes   No   Comments: _____
   ☐   ☐   _____

10. The child's comments are appropriate for the topic under discussion.

    Yes   No   Comments: _____
    ☐   ☐   _____

11. The child seems able to understand and follow the rules and procedures of a game or classroom activity.

    Yes   No   Comments: _____
    ☐   ☐   _____

12. The child follows the class rules for behavior without reminders.

    Yes   No   Comments: _____
    ☐   ☐   _____

FIGURE 11.6

Teacher Observation Form.

Source: From *Using Familiar Routines in Language Assessment and Intervention* by S. Tattershaw and J. Prendeville. Copyright © 1995. Permission granted by Sandra Tattershaw.

Objectives: Engage children (through a shared reading).
Goals: Provide rich oral and written language experiences. Demonstrate the joy of reading.
Increase intrinsic motivation. (Guthrie & Wigfield, 2000)
Materials: Big book copy of The Wheels on The Bus (Kovalski, 1987), drawing paper, and crayons.

Demonstrate what is going to happen.

Immerse children in the literacy event by discussing illustrations.

Provide Word Study, and Guided Practice by reading the book, rereading children's favorite parts, building knowledge by singing and rereading.

Apply and Extend by having children draw their favorite part of the story.

Share several new little Wheels on the Bus books, invite children to read them as much as they wish.

Ongoing assessments: Write and file notes on level of participation, enjoyment, skills, and interest on the three to five children you select as focal for the week.

FIGURE 11.7

Reading Aloud Lesson Plan.

	Fisher Cook		
	David		
	Pirt Prtny		

FIGURE 11.8

Topics of Interest. Invitation to Fisher David Cook's Pirate Party!

FIRST-GRADE ROUTINES.   Routines that incorporated authentic reading and writing in kindergarten also work well with first and second graders. For example, taking attendance, lunch count, and accounting for jobs for the day require children to read and think. Wall charts that are used as tools in everyday teaching also serve children well. In early first grade, children need the support of illustrations and pictures to comprehend the reading they need to do. Later, these supports are removed as children become better able to read without them.

Each day, at some point during the day, all children engage in the following: guided reading, being read to, self-selected reading, peer or buddy reading, and writing. Read-alouds might begin to introduce some reading from information books such as topics on science or social studies. Far too often, the primary grade curriculum is strongly based on storybooks (fiction). Providing some reading of information books early helps prepare children for comprehension studies in later grades (Duke, 2000).

Establish learning centers where children can focus on particular reading and writing skills. Centers might include a writing area, an inquiry study area, a listening area with audio books, a computer area with options for self-selecting from two or three activities posted on the computers, a word work center, and, perhaps, an interest center. These centers, along with the teacher's guidance, provide vital reading experiences. Children should be rotated through the learning centers, and these assignments should be charted for the children to

TEACH IT!

Refer to your **Teach It!** booklet for further activities you can use to reinforce concepts discussed in this chapter.

First Day of Kindergarten

The following schedule was contributed by Linda Headings, M.Ed., a highly effective kindergarten and first-grade teacher.

HALF-DAY KINDERGARTEN SCHEDULE

Before the first day of school with all the children together, the children come to school in groups of about seven for one or two days until all have been transitioned into classroom life. Teacher Linda Headings welcomes the children and teaches them about centers and the number of children allowed in a center, how to work with the materials, and so on. She introduces a teacher-made attendance chart with all the children's names. Pictures of children taken on the transition days are mounted on the "Our Class" poster. Ms. Headings has used the first partial days to gather some personal information about each child from parents or from children's conversations in class.

GOALS: Begin (a) relationship building with children, (b) establishing daily routines, and (c) gathering data by observing children's interactions with environmental and class-created print and with read-alouds.

FIRST DAY OF KINDERGARTEN WITH ALL THE CHILDREN

Greeting: Greet children by name at eye level with a smile as they come in.

Remind children to put their belongings away in their cubby, to hang up their name on the attendance chart, and to sit on the group rug (use warmth, caring, and support).

Demonstrate and Immerse

REVIEW THE DAILY SCHEDULE: Tell children what is going to happen; be descriptive and lively while discussing group time, story time, taking a school tour, recess, center time, and time to go home. [*Use a schedule chart at children's eye level, and point to the words as you talk.*]

After reviewing the schedule, put it at the children's eye level for review. [*Going over the schedule often comforts an anxious child. The chart demonstrates that print carries meaning and that it carries important information.*]

Working with Words

ATTENDANCE AND READING: Hold up each child's name written on a large sentence strip. Have the child wave when his or her name is read so that the children can start to put the name with the face. As their name is called, children wave, and you make a personal connection—for example "Hi, Billy Jack. I hear you like animals."

Apply and Extend

- Do sorting activities with children's names. Use a magnetic board on an easel. Sort name strips by boys and girls. Note beginning letters in names.

---

see. They can check the chart for center assignments and go to work in them while you teach blocks of reading and writing.

The Teach It! box on pages 372–373 provides a model of how one teacher organizes her first day of first grade.

Teacher Linda Headings conducts a journal writing exercise with her students.

SECOND-GRADE ROUTINES. On the first day of second grade, you and the children might follow a schedule that is highly similar to the one used in first grade but with more advanced materials and activities. Just as in first grade, each day should include guided reading, being read to, self-selected reading, peer or buddy reading, writing, and word study/spelling. Table 11.1 models part of a weekly schedule for second grade that might be helpful. Creating such schedules helps to ensure that many varied learning opportunities are included daily.

Second-grade planning proceeds until all children are scheduled for a week of varied learning opportunities. The teacher's long-range plans need to be open to change and should include daily read-alouds, small-group reading, children's self-selected reading, spelling and word work, and at least twice-weekly comprehensive writing workshops with daily writing activities. You might also want to incorporate a

- Read *Dogger* by Shirley Hughes (1977). Introduce the main character, Alfie, and share that, "We will be reading other stories about Alfie the rest of the week." [*Teaches about authors.*]
- In small groups, invite sharing from the children of their favorite "lovey" brought from home. [*Show warmth and caring.*]

School tour: Review the locations of restrooms and the principal's office; talk about walking in line and using appropriate voices. Take children out to play on the playground for about fifteen minutes. If someone is having separation problems, delay playing outside. Work in a little recess when all the children are calm.

Center time: After returning to the classroom, review the names of the centers and their rules: (1) Only five children can be in a center at one time, and (2) children put their names on a waiting list so that everyone can have a turn. Demonstrate using waiting lists with role-play. [*Shows children the function and power of print.*] Review options if the waiting list is long. Role-play frequently. Dismiss the children from the group rug to the centers.

CENTERS AND MATERIALS:

- Writing center: Pencils, markers, note cards, name word cards, a variety of papers, etc.
- Reading center: Big books, manipulative charts, books on tape, bookshelf, magnetic letters, flannel board story
- Dramatic play center: Shoe store (correlation with buying new shoes for school), shoes, rulers, boxes, calculators, chairs, storage shelf, paper and pencil, receipts, a mirror (for looking at shoes)
- Math center: Blocks, Unifix cubes™, puzzles, sorting items, counting games
- Science center: Magnets, materials to experiment with, a scale, paper and pencils

As children use centers, monitor and observe who works well together, who engages, who likes to work by themselves, group dynamics, problem solving, who uses the waiting lists, and so on. Intervene as needed.

TRANSITIONS:

- Signify a transition by a bell or singing softly; ring the bell twice to signify clean-up.

End of day: In the whole-group meeting area, review the day, and explain something interesting that will be happening tomorrow. Close with the song *The More We Get Together* (Raffi, 1996), which has been written on a chart in advance. Point to the words as you sing. [*Demonstrate meaning and enjoyment of print.*]

DISMISS:

- Tell children to gather their gear and line up at the door when you call their names.
- Make a quick trip to the teachers' lounge, coffee break, and prepare for the afternoon group.

block of pleasure reading, perhaps every Monday, Wednesday, and Friday for twenty minutes right before the end of the day.

TABLE 11.1

Daily Schedule

OCTOBER	WEEK 1	GUIDED READING	BUDDY READING	INQUIRY CENTER
	Monday			
Daily read-alouds		Ben, Shealee, Sam, Tessa, Mark, Jenny	Books of choice (oral language practice)	Book research: work with frog facts (write findings)
	Tuesday			
Reading and writing		Joe, Michael, Dan, Angela	Listening center and read together	Report writing: science
Literature study		Janet, Nicki, Don		
		Helen, Jane, Chris, Mickey	Oral language practice	Author study (write and share)

Source: Adapted from Fountas and Pinnell (1996).

TEACH IT!

Refer to your **Teach It!** booklet for further activities you can use to reinforce concepts discussed in this chapter.

First Day of First Grade

Goals: Begin relationship building with children. Begin establishing daily routines. Begin gathering data by observing children's interaction with environmental and class-created print and with read-alouds.

Greeting: Greet children at the door at eye level; invite them to put their personal items on any table and come to sit on the gathering rug. Take attendance and lunch count. Children stand and point to their names on attendance chart and point to wording on lunch chart.

Opening: Introduce yourself by sharing objects that tell the children about you. Pull individual items out of a pillowcase, and share what they mean to you. Draw a web or graphic organizer of the pillowcase contents. [*This provides a visual introduction to webbing, organizing ideas, and storytelling and building relationships.*]

The quarters are for garage sales.

Graphic Organizer: Pillowcase

Tell the children that one of your favorite things to do on Saturday mornings, for example, is to go out to garage sales to find books for the classroom and to hunt for other treasures the class can use at bargain prices.

Welcome: Welcome children as a group by doing some sorting activities and writing them down on large pieces of white construction paper in front of the children. [*Introduce making a class big book.*] Use one page for each pair of children. [*Collaboration begins.*] Sorting examples that create the first class-made book are:

- Number of children in classroom enrolled along with number of boys and girls
- Number of children who walk, who ride the bus, who are dropped off
- Types and number of pets children own
- Favorite foods
- Favorite holiday

After selection of the sorting topics, the pairs of children dictate pages. After each page is written, read it together, pointing at each word. Observe who is attending and participating.

School tour of locations: Show children the bathrooms, lunchroom, office, nurse, music, gym, and art room.

Read aloud: Read *A Porcupine Named Fluffy* (Lester, 1986) [*The focus is on adjusting to a different place and making friends.*]

Work on book illustrations: Hand out to the class book pages from earlier in the morning for each pair of children to illustrate. [*This is collaboration in action.*] Talk about the size of illustrations and filling up the page so that the pictures can be seen from far away. Demonstrate by comparing the size of illustrations in a standard text to a big book's illustrations.

Classroom explorations: Following the book illustrations, allow children free exploration of the classroom. Items in the room for their explorations include puzzles, a variety of books, books on tape, Unifix cubes, magnets, pattern blocks, magnetic letters, checkers, art supplies, flannel board with story props, and some simple games.

Providing Appropriate Materials

Before the children come through the door on the first day of school, teachers have prepared the classroom for learning. They have also thought about the materials they will need to assist with that learning.

CLASSROOM LIBRARIES. Classroom libraries are essential in a literacy-rich classroom. Teachers and children use the book collection for lessons, pleasure reading, and inquiry work. Work with your school librarian to build your collection. In addition, join book clubs that offer good children's literature at reduced prices; leave no garage sale, yard sale, or library sale unexamined; find used bookstores; and contact the local public library to see if they have a program for obtaining children's books on a regular basis. Involve parents in helping find ways to obtain books. A good source for identifying books nominated as children's choices is *The Reading Teacher*, which can be accessed at **http://www.reading.org/ choices/**. When selecting books, provide a wide variety of reading materials, including informational materials such as brochures from stores, automobile sales offices, community

After children's exploration, clean up and line up for lunch by holding up the last name of each child. Observe and record impressions. Read as needed.

Lunch time.

After lunch read aloud *Tacky the Penguin* (Lester, 1993) [*Expand on the theme in* A Porcupine Named Fluffy.]

Journals: Introduce journal writing using the overhead projector. Illustrate a think-aloud writing of an idea. Write a bit on the topic idea. Tell the children that they will write in their journals. Encourage inventive spelling: "Spell words the way they sound to you. Don't worry about spelling, this is just practice." Ask all children to add an illustration to their writing until you are familiar with their spelling proficiency. (Collect written artifacts to check for writing, sketching, and illustration.)

Before children begin journal writing, divide them into two groups. Group 1 works on journals, and group 2 engages in buddy reading in the rug area. Use leveled books, kindergarten to late first grade, from the Wright Group or Rigby Books. Circulate among the two groups, observe, and talk with children about their work.

There are always lots of hesitations and questions when children start journals. Working with half the class helps keep order. Work in blocks of about twenty minutes and then have the children switch. Observe and record students who worked quickly, but shabbily, who procrastinated, who struggled, who went to the bathroom, and who seemed to love the writing process. As children finish their journals, they must check in with you to read their writing aloud. Observe and teach voice/print matching. Keep journal writing and reading to a time limit to regulate and work on pacing.

Science: The sink and float experiment.

Students sit in circle on the group rug with a large shallow tub of water. Ask the children what types of objects sink or float in water? [*Taps prior experiences and supports oral language.*] Pull out objects individually from a container.

Help the children hypothesize by predicting with thumbs up or down on what will happen when an object is placed in water. Assess. [*Watch for interactions. Who is in the lesson and who is out?*] Have small groups of children search the classroom to find one item they would like to test. Engage in the hypothesize/test cycle. Write group conclusions on chart paper. [*This is the first inquiry study.*]

Closing: Review the teacher-made attendance and lunch charts. Request that they hang up their names on the attendance chart and make their lunch request on the lunch chart before coming to the rug area the next morning.

Homework: Instructions to the children: To share their interests, bring some personal items to school tomorrow in a labeled bag. Six children will share each day. Two children share in the morning, two after lunch, and two at the end of the school day. [*This introduces sharing to the classroom community.*] Put the homework paper describing the project in the home/school correspondence folders.

Introduce correspondence folders: Discuss the folders with the children, and show them the basket where the folders are kept. The children are to bring their folders to school every day and place them in the basket first thing in the morning. Ask the children where they will put their folders at home. [*Use role-play.*]

Dismiss: Children line up to go home by responding to a riddle: "I'm holding the folder of a boy whose name begins with the sound of /*ch*/." Observe and record their responses.

The ideas and procedures presented on the first day of first grade are easily modified for second or third graders. Revise this first-grade summary after reviewing the developmental levels at which you find your students. For example, older children can collaborate on making the class-made book by doing some or most of the writing and illustrating. Children might also write and illustrate their own little books.

information centers, and the local police and fire departments. Add children's own works as they write and publish their books.

Leveled books. When you teach, review the leveled books your school has to offer. **Leveled books** are rated by a child's reading development stage, not by age or grade. Basal readers and other texts are often leveled only by grade. Often grade-level ratings are not sufficiently helpful. It is essential that texts be subjected to fine-grained leveling. Features that distinguish leveled books are level of syntax complexity (simple to more complex), number of words in sentences or on a page, accumulating vocabulary (number of high-frequency words and new words introduced), placement of words and sentences on a page, and level of support from illustrations. Fountas and Pinnell (1999, 2001) provide some criteria for book selection:

- Sentence complexity (length of sentence)
- Vocabulary (number of high-frequency words)
- Print features (length of book, illustrations, format of the book)

- Language features (similar to oral language, high-level written language)
- Content (children's special interest, universal themes)

Reading recovery leveled books are rated from A to Z, with levels A–C for kindergarten, D–E and F–H for first grade, and F–H and I–K for grade 2. Many children will be able to read above these levels, but the system provides a place to begin in selecting books. Here are some examples of books at each of these levels (Fountas & Pinnell, 1996).

A–C: *Wake Up Dad* (Randell, 1996), *At the Zoo* (Peters, 1995), *The Animals Went to Bed* (Theodorou, 1996).

D–E: *Mrs. Wishy-Washy* (1990), *Baby Bear Goes Fishing* (Randell, 1996).

F–H: *The Hungry Giant* (Cowley, 1998), *Just Cookie's Week, The Carrot Seed* (Krauss, 1989), *Ben's Tooth , Rosie at the Zoo* (Cowley,1985)

I–K: *Happy Birthday Sam* (Hutchins, 2001), *Henny Penny* (Galdone, 1968), *Leo the Late Bloomer* (Kraus, 1987), *Tidy Titch* (Hutchins, 1978), *Danny and the Dinosaur* (Hoff, 1999), *Henry and Midge, Kate the Great and the Pillowcase, Keep the Lights Burning Abbie* (Roop and Roop, 1985).

Assessing book levels. Some children need guidance when self-selecting books. The teacher might offer an array of books and ask the children to look them over and select from this array. The "five-finger test" offers one simple method: The child holds up fingers and thumb, reads the book, and turns down one finger for each word missed on a page. If the child gets to the thumb, the book is probably too difficult. However, children should read books they self-select regardless of level of difficulty—this builds interest! Children should not continue to read a book they do not like. There are far too many wonderful books available for that to happen. Be aware of easy books that might hold high appeal for struggling readers and diverse language learners so that they can experience success.

TECHNOLOGY

Why should we use great care in incorporating technology into the reading program?

TECHNOLOGY. Technology is necessary material in your classroom because today's students are comfortable with it. A number of programs can assist in the learning of basic literacy skills. Because of the fast-breaking changes in the Internet and products online, the new and improved programs become available very quickly. But many products are not as good as their hype. Use caution when selecting technology programs for your classroom. Here are some helpful resources to get you started:

- Australian Storytelling Guide (NSW) Inc. (**www.home.aone.net.au/stories/**) provides purposeful practice in storytelling and oral language, which is critical for K–2 children when they are learning to read (Roth, Speece, & Cooper, 2002). This storytelling site provides wonderful opportunities.
- Crayola.com (**www.crayola.com**) offers online stories, songs, and craft activities.
- Teacher Created Materials (**www.teachercreated.com**) offers a variety of word work activities and games.

Reaching All Children

LANGUAGE and DIVERSITY

How can we address the needs of English language learners?

There is little doubt that you will have English language learners and struggling readers during your teaching career. Teaching these children is one of your primary responsibilities. Previous chapters have provided information on these learners, and you will learn more in upcoming ones (especially Chapter 14). We focus here on the early grades.

English Language Learners

As with older students, young English language learners' English listening comprehension is more advanced than their ability to speak the new language, let alone read and write it. Much of the focus in the early years needs to be on oral language development, providing helpful teaching at every step. Helpful teaching includes the following:

- Warmth and acceptance of differences
- Reading the same book(s) in the English language learners' language and English
- Using parents and paraprofessionals, community volunteers, and anyone available in the school (all other support staff) to read and write with the children in their mother tongue
- Playing naming games of classroom objects in both languages
- Singing songs in two languages
- Making many positive and comforting experiences with cultural differences

Use snacks, dramatic play with culturally appropriate clothing, holiday and birthday celebrations, and units of study with home and family, friends, and visitors to demonstrate culturally interesting facts about the children's homelands. Volunteers that include parents and business and community people can really help if they know an English language learner's mother tongue.

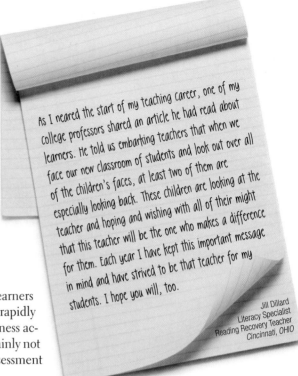

As I neared the start of my teaching career, one of my college professors shared an article he had read about learners. He told us embarking teachers that when we face our new classroom of students and look out over all of the children's faces, at least two of them are especially looking back. These children are looking at the teacher and hoping and wishing with all of their might that this teacher will be the one who makes a difference for them. Each year I have kept this important message in mind and have strived to be that teacher for my students. I hope you will, too.

Jill Dillard
Literacy Specialist
Reading Recovery Teacher
Cincinnati, OHIO

ENGLISH LANGUAGE LEARNERS IN KINDERGARTEN. For learners who come to school with some English literacy, learning will move more rapidly than those with little or none. A few might be ready for phonemic awareness activities in English by late kindergarten but probably not before—and certainly not before they reach an intermediate level in spoken English. For a quick assessment of the intermediate level perform the following process:

- Read a predictable storybook in English to a small group of children.
- See if they can respond well to most comprehension questions.
- If so, try some simple phonemic awareness picture sorts (see Chapters 1 and 5).
- If children are successful, continue instruction.
- If children are not successful, step back and continue oral language development, and perhaps try the language experience approach (see Chapters 5, 12, and 14).
- Repeat the cycle of teach, assess, and teach accordingly.

Few English language learners will reach the intermediate level at a young age unless they speak English (as well as their mother tongue) at home. As critical as effective, direct instruction is, other high-quality learning happens in the well-managed classroom, which is confirmed in a study by McCafferty and Iddings (2001). See how classroom organization provides for meaningful and frequent oral language practice in this next example:

- Picture two Hispanic kindergarten children, one more advanced in English than the other, seated in the housekeeping center.
- Nicole (the more experienced English language learner) is reading a very well-known storybook in English to Jorge (as assigned by the teacher).
- Nicole knows the story by heart, and despite the fact that this lesson is appropriate for these children, they soon become less and less engaged and eventually toss the book aside.
- Nicole then stands up and begins to pretend that she is preparing food for Jorge.
- She speaks in English as she makes a sandwich, and Jorge responds. He immediately joins in the pretend play.
- The two children engage in an extended English conversation in which Jorge actually speaks more English than Nicole!

Productive play episodes such as this are exactly what Jorge needs to gain the oral proficiency necessary for moving into written language instruction. "Real-life" pretend-play situations provide rich opportunities, and sometimes being "off task" can help! Productive play is most likely to occur when the teacher has made sure the children have sufficient English vocabulary and oral English as a second language (ESL) instruction. A simple discussion about favorite foods or places to go creates a fine opportunity for vocabulary

Using children's "favorites" in a LEA activity is a meaningful way to provide guided reading instruction to young children at the emergent or beginning phase of reading.

instruction in English. Children respond well to vocabulary words of personal significance to them, and book reading is a perfect place to teach vocabulary. Provide personal dictionaries (for home and school) in which children's favorite words may be kept. When your English language learners are ready for reading instruction, use **voice/print matching** with small groups and plenty of instructional conversations.

Children may be ready for phonemic awareness activities in their mother tongue, but not yet in English. (See Chapter 14 for a discussion on sheltered English and sheltered instruction observation protocol [SIOP].) Here is an example of an ESL lesson for intermediate English language learners who speak Spanish.

- Read a storybook in English that the children already know in their mother tongue (someone else might read the Spanish version). For example, *The Very Hungry Caterpillar* (Carle, 1987) is also available in a Spanish-language version entitled *La Oruga Muy Hambrienta* (Carle, 1994).

- Engage the children in an enjoyable conversation, and then reread the book using children's suggestions for their favorite parts and using rich, scaffolded discussion. With an English big book version or text on large chart paper, use voice/print matching and more discussion. Demonstrate how to identify a word, and help children identify words. To teach the concept of word, put your fingers and then their fingers at the beginning and end of a word. Make both book editions available for children's use in other explicit lessons and for self-selected use in pleasure reading and partner reading. The shared reading techniques described throughout this book help to extend this lesson. Use shared writing as well.

TEACH IT! 46

Language Experience with English Language Learners

ENGLISH LANGUAGE LEARNERS IN FIRST AND SECOND GRADES. Remember that some English language learners might enter your classroom having had no previous school experiences. As such, they are many months away from being ready for phonemic awareness activities in English. Their greatest need is for a strong emphasis on ESL lessons. Having developed English only at the level of basic interpersonal communication skills, a conversational level (Cummins, 1986, 1989), pronunciation difficulties often complicate letter/sound relationships and phonics learning.

As you will see in Chapter 14, many English language learners must learn to read first in English because of schools' limited resources to teach them more effectively or because of state or district policies. Unfortunately, they have probably not mastered English at an oral level sufficient to support academic instruction in English. The primary focus of your instruction therefore needs to be on word recognition and comprehension.

Phonics will be the English language learners' weakest modality for learning to read, even after they have learned to communicate orally in English. A phonetic approach is based on knowledge of the sound system, and English language learners probably speak English with a heavy accent, a very strong indicator that they have not yet mastered the sound system of English. Does this mean that you cannot teach these children to read until they master the purely phonetic approach? Not at all. Lessons discussed throughout this book provide varied and sound instruction for teaching these children. Here are some helpful hints:

- Focus on children's dictated texts (the language-experience approach [LEA]).
- Work with teacher- and children-selected sight words for practice.
- Focus on meaning, use word walls, sorting cards, word hunts and games (all described in previous chapters).
- Work on vocabulary. Your English language learners might know the word *big*, but not *huge* or *gigantic*, or *enormous*. (Use Chapter 6 to help you create sensible vocabulary instruction.)

Above all, involve the children, engage in conversations throughout the day—make it real for them!

Often, children making the transition from their mother tongue to English have periods of stuttering or other issues such as pronunciation and articulation. However, these periods do not necessarily signal a language disorder. In time, most of these children will improve. If they don't show improvement over time, seek help from school experts and work with parents who may not know where to turn. It is important to keep in mind that English language learners are no different than any other populations of children; and, just as with English speakers, a few may have problems with literacy learning (even in their mother tongue). However, the vast majority simply speak a language other than English and have many challenges to overcome.

Making a book available in your ESL students' mother tongue as well in English can help them make the connection between the languages.

Struggling Readers

Young children who do not show steady reading, writing, and spelling growth need careful evaluation and immediate intervention. The causes of delayed development may include a lack of early literacy experience or true lags in neurophysiological, psychological, and cognitive development.

Interventions such as reading recovery and the **Elkonin box** (Clay, 1985) provide support for struggling first graders. High-quality summer programs are also recommended. The Elkonin-box strategy focuses children's attention on letter/sound relationships. The routine goes as follows: The teacher might begin by asking a child to identify the problem word. When the child points to the word, the teacher writes the word.

How can Elkonin boxes provide extra support to struggling readers?

got

Then, together, they segment the word in chunks of letters and draw boxes around each letter chunk,

g	o	t

integrating a good deal of discussion about the letter/sound relationships along the way. A variation on this would be for the teacher to draw the boxes first and then coach the child to write the letters in the boxes as he or she works through the letter/sound relationships.

If the child cannot pronounce the word, the teacher provides support by saying the word first. To consolidate the lesson, the student and teacher write the word in a sentence and use it orally in a sentence.

The Elkonin box strategy fills several needs for children. For older children who still need help, the strategy clarifies segmenting and manipulating letter/sound relationships. The Elkonin box can also be used as a visual aid in working with multiple-syllable words. A more typical use of this strategy is to help young children who do not fully grasp phonemic awareness and who struggle in perceiving letter/sound relationships. Figure 11.9 provides an example of an accomplished teacher using this strategy with a struggling first-grader.

TEACH IT! 11

Phonemic Segmentation with Elkonin Boxes

Interventions

The earlier the intervention begins, the better the potential outcome. However, children in intervention programs are rarely able to function at grade level after the intervention stops (Bronfenbrenner, 1974; Spache, 1981). Gaskins (1998, p. 534) states that there is "more to [helping] delayed readers than good instruction." Here is a list of insights and

Elkonin Box Teacher and Child Conversation

Teacher: That was a wonderful job retelling that story. What would you like to write about that story?

Child: I want to say, "The crocodile got on."

T: That will be a fun sentence to write. [Here is where the teacher can encourage a more complex or a simpler sentence, depending on the needs of the child.] How would you begin the sentence, "The crocodile got on."?

C: With 'the.' I know 'the.'

T: I know you do! Write it on our book writing page. [The book writing page is the page where everything appears correct.]

Child writes the word 'The'.

T: I noticed you put a capital 'T'. Why did you do that?

C: 'Cause it starts the sentence.

T: You are just learning so much about writing! OK, say your sentence again.

C: The crocodile got on. I need crocodile.

T: Yes, let's see if we can work on that one together. What sounds do you hear in 'crocodile'?

C: Is it a 'c' or a 'k'?

T: What do you think?

C: 'c'

T: You got it! What else do you hear?

C: [*child stretches word*] 'r' and another 'c'

T: There is an 'r' and a 'c'; put the 'r' down and listen as I say the word. What do you hear before that other 'c'? [*Teacher stretches word*]

C: Oh! I hear an 'ah'. Ah, ah, octopus! 'O'!

T: You are really listening carefully for those sounds. OK, write o and the 'c' you heard. What does that much say?

C: The croc

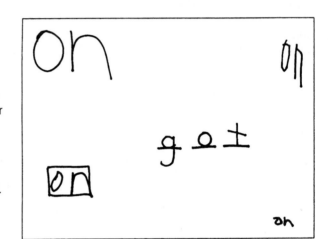

T: Yes, let's finish this word together [Teacher and student sound word together and collaborate on writing letters—student supplies all but the silent e, which the teacher adds] So now we have The crocodile; we need to finish the sentence. What did you want to say?

C: The crocodile got on. I need got.

T: I want you to work out got by yourself. I know you can do it! I'll tell you that 'got' has 3 sounds. [Teacher draws 3 lines on the try page; some teachers use boxes]

C: I know it starts with 'g'

T: Yes, sir! What do you hear next?

C: [*Stretches word*] A 't'!

T: 'T' is in that word! But where do you hear it? Say it again and listen.

C: 'Got'—it's at the end. 'Got'. Oh, I know! It's 'o' again! G-o-t

T: Wonderful work! I could just see your brain in action! Now, what do we need to finish your sentence?

C: The crocodile got on. We need on. a –n, right?

T: Let's think about it. You just told me crocodile had an 'o' for the 'ah' sound; and got had an 'o' for the 'ah' sound. So what do you think makes the first sound in ah-ah on?

C: 'o'!

Source: Contributed by Karen Morrow Durica.

FIGURE 11.9

Elkonin Box.

recommendations provided by Gaskins and the teachers at Benchmark School in Media, Pennsylvania:

- Engage in extensive reading instruction.
- Show respect and teach the children self-monitoring and self-directing.
- Hold the idea that all teachers can change is their own approach to children and that children change as a result of teacher and teaching change.
- Focus on academic and nonacademic roadblocks (issues with engagement, having a disposition for learning, self-esteem).
- Work with other teachers, school experts, outside services, and parents to plan goals and plot the most efficient route to achieve the goals.
- Realize that long-term intervention is critical; most delayed readers need help from kindergarten through middle school.

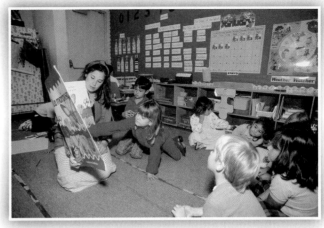

Using sound reading instruction with young at-risk readers can result in tremendous benefits years later.

At Benchmark, the teachers work with children's dispositions or characteristics, such as attentiveness, organization, and conscientiousness. Research indicates that accelerating reading ability was not sufficient for at-risk learners. They must also acquire a disposition for learning and other affective or cognitive abilities (Dahl & Freppon, 1995; Freppon, 1995).

Among the many instructional foci used at Benchmark, one of the most important is teaching the active search for meaning. Graphic organizers, rich discussion, and other techniques need to be used intensively over time with struggling readers. If a child receives intervention, the specialist's instruction and the teacher's instruction must be in accord (Gaskins, 1998). Children are often put even more at risk when the specialist teaches in one way and the classroom teacher in another. In addition, teachers can learn a great deal by communicating with school specialists. Cunningham and Allington (1999) suggest the following strategies for providing struggling readers with extra practice:

- Organize an after-lunch bunch in which you work with these children for ten or fifteen minutes reading easy books just for fun.
- Organize an easy reading time for ten or fifteen minutes after school using the same strategies with an after-lunch bunch.
- Create a classroom learning center and have at least thirty minutes, perhaps two fifteen-minute periods of the day, set aside for struggling readers to work in this center.
- Include in the learning center materials such as Legos™, puzzles, computer games, word board games, math and science manipulatives, Play-Doh™, chalk (slates), markers, pencils, stickers and stamps, children's magazines, and a TV connection for watching *Reading Rainbow* or other educational videos.

Another way to increase reading practice and build confidence is to provide opportunities for struggling children to read to others such as the school staff (cafeteria and custodial, too) and principal and earlier grades. Children will practice hard so they can be a "visiting reader." Here are some ways to accomplish this:

- Make arrangements with your fellow teachers and school staff.
- Make copies of a sheet that has a place for a date, place, child's signature, your signature, and other teachers/staff signatures.
- Guide the child to the appointed place/classroom for a signature and confirmation of the "visiting reader" appointment.
- Help your children select a good book to read aloud, and provide time for practice!

Nearly all children want to learn and enjoy learning. Most children begin school excited about learning, thinking that they can do everything. However, children who struggle can become defensive and appear to lose interest in learning. This stance can be well established even by first grade. Sometimes fear of failure can be traced to instruction that

Reading Applications

The standard addressed in this lesson was selected by the creator and writer of this lesson, classroom teacher, Heidi Varner, M.Ed. The overview of the lesson; its purposes, structure, and time; and how it address benchmark and indicators follows.

The Standard: *Reading Applications: Informational, Technical, and Persuasive Text*

Benchmarks: By the end of the K–3 program, the child will:

- Use text features and structures to make predictions, organize content, draw conclusions, and build text knowledge.
- Identify the central ideas and supporting details of informational text.
- Use visual aids as sources to gain additional information from text.
- Read and follow multiple-step written directions.

This lesson is designed as an introduction to a "Fall Outdoors" thematic unit in kindergarten. It weaves together good instruction and required standards. Choose an information text for using pictures to aid comprehension. Focus on the main ideas of the text, and probe children's background knowledge about fall outdoors. Share the book *Fall* (Hirschi, 1991) with the class, discussing the content and pictures throughout. This thirty-to-forty-minute lesson culminates with students illustrating, talking, and writing about what they learned from the book. The benchmark indicators addressed in the lesson are as follows:

Indicator 1: Use pictures and illustrations to aid comprehension.

Indicator 2: Identify the main idea of a selection that has been read aloud.

Resources/Materials:

Hirschi, R. (1991). *Fall*. New York: Cobblehill Books.

Blank paper or journals for students

Large chart paper for word wall

Markers and crayons

Before the Lesson: Demonstration and Immersion

Informally assesses students' background knowledge through a brief discussion of what students already know about fall.

T: "We are going to be talking about fall today. Who can tell me what fall makes you think about?" (Value all reasonable answers.)

T: "What kinds of things happen outdoors in nature during the fall? I will add some of your fall words to our chart." (Write words on large chart paper for word wall.) Accept all reasonable answers, making sure to direct children back to nature and the outdoors as needed. Write in full view of the children on a word wall individual fall words, grouping them according to plants, animals, and descriptive words/action words.

T: Before reading a book, discuss what good readers think about and what the book might be about. Children also look through the book for any pictures to see if they can find even more clues about what the book will be about. These things help good readers think about what they will find out in the book.

Introduce *Fall* by Ron Hirschi by previewing the book by sharing the photos, discussing them, and pointing out how some photos have words next to them to tell what they are.

T: "Is there anything else we can add to our word wall after looking at these photos?"

focused on right answers at the expense of making sense and using errors to increase learning. Some children engage in negative behaviors, such as refusing to turn in their homework, because of a deep fear that it will be incorrect or because of a family problem.

Children who are troubled might engage in behaviors that are self-destructive. These children need help, not blame. Children with struggles need the entire school system working for them. Beyond the risk of reading failure for students, their failures deeply hurt teachers, parents, and families (Dudley-Marling, 1990, 2000). Failure is suffering that no child, family, or teacher should have to experience.

During Reading: Guided Practice

Read the title, the author's name, and the photographer's name from the cover. Then read the title page and the dedication page.

T: "As we read the book, you will see the photos for a second time. Try to take a picture in your mind of what you see in order to help you remember the words you hear me read. Thinking about those pictures in your mind later will help you remember what the story is about."

The teacher guides the students:

T: "I wonder what this page will be about?" Ask for predictions from students (trees, yellow leaves, etc.). Read the page to see whether the predictions are confirmed. Acknowledge responses, and praise correct predictions and effort.

T: Read the next pages with the moon and spider web. "What do you think lilies, larkspurs, and shooting stars are?" Reread the first part of the sentence to show how the author gives us a clue: "The last flower petals fall. . . ."

T: Read the pages with the squirrel and turkey. "Why do you think the author uses the word treasure?" (It is important for squirrels and other animals and their survival during the winter.)

Continue this format of reading and discussing throughout the rest of the book.

After Reading: Application and Extension

T: -"Are there any other words we can add to our word wall now?"

T: -"One helpful way to remember what happens in a book is by thinking about the main idea of the book. The main idea is the big idea that can explain all about the whole book. We know that this book talks about plants." Show photo examples from the book. "We know that this book also describes animals." Show photo examples from the book. "These events take place during the fall. How could we say all of that in one sentence?" (Accept any reasonable responses, e.g., "This book is about what happens to plants and animals during the fall. This book is about the changes plants go through and the jobs that animals do during the fall.")

Assessment

T: "I will give each of you a piece of paper. I would like you to draw a picture that tells about something important from this book. Write a sentence that tells about this story as best you can. I will come around to ask you about your illustration and writing as you work."

Teacher action: Take a class chart for notes to keep a record of what children say about their illustrations. You will be able to determine whether or not children got the ideas in the text through analysis of their verbal description of their illustrations. Note children's writing—clarity of ideas, letter-sound relationships, spacing, and so on.

Student action: The students should use paper and markers or crayons to develop an illustration about the book. They should use inventive spelling to write about their illustration.

Reflection

After the lesson, take a few minutes to reflect on the lesson and write about it. What worked for you? What did not go well? How did students respond to various parts of the lesson? What parts of the lesson should you keep the same? What parts of the lesson could you change to improve?

Standards as a Guide

Despite the controversies surrounding standards-based education, **standards** can provide good guidance for schools and teachers. However, most standards call for an overwhelming number of student performance evaluations and can result in frustration. You might feel that you are expected to do everything, but you know you cannot. And you might feel as if you have no idea where to begin. Here are some recommendations for teaching in accord with standards (Caldwell, 2002):

- Don't agonize. Talk with colleagues, attend workshops and conferences, and take graduate classes that will help you find the insights you need. Let your administrator know that you need support. If you are interviewing for your first position, ask the administrator with whom you are interviewing about the support the school or district provides for teaching according to standards. Be proactive.

- Hold onto what you know is true and right. Keep your teaching in line with children's development. Find ways of consolidating standards and focusing on those that are most important for your students.

- Keep looking at the big picture and see what your standards really mean. Although stated in discrete pieces, standards cover overarching concepts that are critical to learning to read and learning from reading. Work with colleagues, and find ways to consolidate and group standards according to categories you relate to, add subcategories as you move along, and reread to consolidate.

- If the school or district mandates a basal or other reading program that you are expected to follow, work backward from the lesson you must teach to the skills and knowledge in the standards. You will find that you can match your lesson objectives with standards' benchmarks and grade-level indicators. When the instructional focus and materials are the teacher's decision, it might work well to read a group of consolidated benchmarks and indicators you have categorized and plan accordingly.

Caldwell (2002) advises connecting instruction and assessment according to standards. Each state and each school district provides a list of standards and benchmarks that outline the phonics and literacy instruction that are required. Look at these benchmarks and indicators, and think about how you want to teach them. Because you know how to teach and assess, you can link your instruction with standards, benchmarks, and indicators, and the matches will make sense. For example, the Standards and Literacy box on pages 380–381 illustrates a kindergarten lesson plan designed to teach to the following standard: Young children need to be able to identify an information text's central ideas and supporting details, be able to use visual aids, and follow multiple-step written directions.

Assessment

Imagine teaching with little knowledge of what children already know and what they have learned. For a long time, teachers depended on a yearly assessment, usually a normed test, that showed how children perform in comparison to others at the same grade level. Such mandated tests, and others required at the federal, state, and district levels can inform instruction. Of course, throughout history, good teachers have learned from their students and have used their own knowledge to assess the children, but not every teacher reached this level of competence. Today, however, change exists in the form of evidence-based assessment based on what children actually do in the classroom and our knowledge of literacy development. You already know a good deal about assessment from reading this far. Next we offer advice on grading and another procedure for assessing young children.

Grading

Because grading is a challenge and a trial, Cunningham and her colleagues note that the concept of grading young children in the typical sense is simply not realistic. Putting a number or letter grade on young children is not informative or helpful because children vary so much. In traditional grading, the struggling reader or English language learner will always receive lower grades (marking them as "not as good as others"), and the more experienced and fortunate children will always receive higher grades (marking them as "better than others"). Teachers work hard to communicate to parents and school administrators that grades should reflect effort and growth. What matters most in teaching is that children are developing and making progress. Avoid marking any child as a learner with static ability.

In *Classrooms That Work* (1999), Cunningham and Allington argue that education must change the way grades are determined. They too recommend that grades be based on effort and growth. The typical grading system tells children who struggle, "You are a failure." Many schools throughout the country do not assign letter grades to young primary children, focusing instead on their development. Even if you must work with a mandated traditional grading or report card system, you can maintain an encouraging attitude that is explicitly conveyed to children. Donald Graves (1983, p. 93) states, "Grading is a fact of life. It's the most difficult responsibility placed on teachers." He advises teachers to use grades to encourage children and to document well what children do in class.

Caldwell (2002) cites the limited format of report cards and suggests that teachers add to the report card in ways that show the children's growth and hard work. Here are some examples of this:

- Add a list of good comprehension strategies the child is working on and uses.
- Do the same for word learning.

To keep grading records such as these, divide the grade book into sections labeled with your teaching emphasis—for example, predicts in reading, connects self and the world to books, learning sight words. If you have a narrative report card, divide the report into categories, and keep information on all children in the same categories (reading comprehension, letter/sound relationships or phonics, spelling, etc.). In this way, you provide continuity in your report cards and even-handedness for all the children (Afflerbach, 1993).

Anecdotal Notes

Another tool that is vital for evaluating children's progress is teachers' anecdotal notes. Anecdotal notes are narrative notes written when observing a child or children (E. McIntyre, personal communication, September 10, 2005). They are descriptive (avoid a rush to judgment). They may pose questions ("Why is he doing that?") and hunches ("I wonder if he understands the flexibility of writing?"). Anecdotal notes are based on what is actually seen and heard. Taking anecdotal notes helps teachers ask good questions such as: Where is the child on meeting the first-grade standard benchmark indicator ____? Is the child engrossed in reading? Is she attending to print or dependent on pictures? Is the child anxious, distracted; if so, by what? Does the child ask for help; if so, from whom? Is the child benefiting from help? Can he successfully accomplish his work with help? What do I need to do?

Teachers take anecdotal notes to understand children's development and plan instruction and to demonstrate accountability when called upon. Teachers write about observable behaviors and insights and about what happens when they intervene, reteach, and provide high scaffolding. It is hard to imagine effective instruction without data gathered and analyzed through daily, informal notes. With knowledge of children's development in mind and the support of written developmental guidelines right beside them, effective teachers analyze anecdotal notes to gauge their students' progress or lack of it.

In addition, anecdotal notes can be written in ways that closely link to state standards (benchmarks and indicators). For example, a typical state benchmark states that young children must have alphabetic awareness. Teachers who write a portion of their anecdotal notes explicitly on children's demonstrations of this knowledge and skill will have very important information at their fingertips for report cards, parent meetings, and meetings with other school experts. Best of all, teachers have the information needed for planning and conducting future lessons. Build the habit of attending to standards and children's progress in daily note making. For example, a child might meet the criteria regularly, sometimes, or rarely. This, with a line or two of description about what the child is doing, creates reliable data when carried out consistently.

In the beginning it is often difficult to know what to write down in anecdotal records or to know what to do with the information. Carry a clipboard or pack of sticky notes with you so that you can write anecdotal notes throughout the day. Use your notes to look for patterns. For example, identify a child who never seems to know short or long vowel words, who wanders around the room, or who is consistently left out of social activities. Recognizing patterns is the first step in intervention.

Assessment Strategies

As you know, children must have some fundamental concepts to learn to read. The following discussion provides some ways to find out what your students know and thus what you may need to teach.

To learn to read and write, children must have the concept of **intentionality**, knowing that written language is a symbol system with linguistic meaning. Children who possess this concept know that written language provides understandable communication (Purcell-Gates, 1991). Without it, the child is lost in learning to read and write (Harste, Woodward, & Burke, 1984). This critical concept is easily taught once the teacher understands the children's needs. Assessment of intentionality should be done by using a combination of formal observations and anecdotal notes. A child may demonstrate by responses in the classroom that she or he realizes that written language carries meaning via the squiggles on the page, yet not exhibit this knowledge in an assessment situation. To determine children's concepts of intentionality, the following assessment might be helpful. You will need a tape recorder for this assessment.

> Ensure that the child is comfortable before you begin. Begin by explaining that the assessment will not be graded, nor will what the child does be on his or her report card. Assure the child that you are trying to learn how to be a better teacher and need the child's help. Playing with the tape recorder for a minute before and after assessing usually gets the interaction off to a good start and ensures comfort.
>
> Give the child a piece of paper on which appears this sentence (or any similar sentence): "A long time ago there was an old man." Note what the child says in response to the following questions:
>
> (i)   Is there something on this paper?
> (ii)   What do you think it is?
> (iii)   What do you think it could be for?
> (iv)   Why do you think it could be here?

If the child answers with "writing," "words," or "letters" but does not answer the other questions, probe with, "Have you ever seen writing (or words or letters) before? What do you think it was for? Why do you think we have writing?" You will likely need to ask only one or two questions to find out whether the child is grasping the concept of intentionality.

Finally, remember that no teacher should assess all the children alone. Teams of primary-grade teachers and other school experts can and should help you with assessing struggling readers and English language learners. Caldwell (2002) offers these suggestions for assessment management:

- Keep it manageable. Do not try to evaluate all children all the time.
- Evaluate children who struggle more often than you assess others (select a few focus children to concentrate on each week).
- Don't evaluate everything; focus on important things.

For Review

This chapter connects research-based information on children's learning with effective teaching from kindergarten through the second grade. It provides practical information for new and practicing teachers. Included are grading, four blocks (Cunningham et al., 1999), and guided reading and dynamic grouping (Fountas & Pinnell, 1996). Reading First, assessment, and other teaching information.

The use of standards as a guide in your teaching and assessing is presented with discussion on how you can work with standards. English language learners and struggling readers are focal topics.

A significant portion of this chapter is devoted to practice that develops the knowledge and skills of young children and your own! Discussion of routines that teach and "first day of school" illustrations provide concrete guidance. Organization and management of the classroom learning community include helping children learn to manage their own behavior, family, and community. Included also are discussions of materials, leveled books, and technology extensions.

For Your Journal

Look at the following notes, and write them in your journal. Then analyze each for its value as an anecdotal note. Indicate what makes it a good or a poor anecdotal note, and how you might write it to make it a more informative note.

1. Larry seemed miserable all day. He drew pictures and didn't attempt any scribbling, writing letters, or reading. I've seen this response for days and days. What's up? I need to talk with his parents and ask the school psychologists and my literacy specialists to sit in on some classes.

2. Victoria is driving me crazy. I think her mother is at the root of this. Mom works and is never home!

3. Nickie is so smart. She always knows the answers! If only I had more like her in my class. I remember her sister Donna, who was just as smart. That was a good year; I had a bunch of Donnas and Nickies!

4. Cody pretend-read *Frog and Toad* to me today; he uses a lot of textlike phrases and his own mix of oral language. This little guy maintains a story formation with a beginning, middle, and end. He even connected the real frog he had with Frog in the story!

Taking It to the World

Develop a home literacy project that will help make school life more authentic and draw families into the school community. For such a project, it is wise to connect homework activities with inquiry projects and to have culminating activities in the classroom to which parents and caregivers are invited. Identify an inquiry project that would provide an excellent forum for family member/caregiver involvement. Create questions the children could use for interviews, and plan for how they might be able to supplement the information with photos, toys, or perhaps articles of clothing. How would the children be able to tell their stories?

Technology Connections

1. Children in grades K–2 nearly always go through a period of intense interest in dinosaurs. Build on children's natural interest in dinosaurs and increase your teaching opportunities by using the following Web sites and books to enhance pleasure reading:

   - **www.enchantedlearning.com/subjects/dinosaurs** (an interactive child-friendly site with basic information about dinosaurs and extinction)

   - **www.fieldmuseum.org/sue** (a site dedicated to Sue, the largest tyrannosaurus rex yet discovered)

2. Nearly all teachers are concerned with motivation, and many experts believe that technology has motivational advantages over conventional teaching methods. Explore the following Web sites, and identify one that might work well with younger children (K–2). Add your views on why you think they would be useful.

   - **www.youthtrust.org**—then click on "e-mentoring" **www.itown.com/athens/mentor**

3. Try these Web sites for teaching practices:

   - Teaching Reading K–2 Workshop at **www.learner.org/resources/series175.html**

   - Teaching Reading K–2: A Library of Classroom Practices **www.learner.org/resources/series162.html**

Connect with Research

Review the following key words from the chapter and then connect to Research Navigator (**www.researchnavigator.com**) through this book's Companion Website to conduct a search into research on each of the various topics as they relate to reading and literacy education today.

Elkonin box	leveled books	Reading First
four blocks	multileveled groups	standards
intentionality	productive play	voice/print matching

Companion Website

To access chapter objectives, practice tests, weblinks, and flashcards, visit the Companion Website at www.ablongman.com/templeallchildren2e.

Go to Allyn & Bacon's MyLabSchool (www.mylabschool.com), enter Assignment ID RMV1 into the Assignment Finder. Watch the video, *An Interactive Writing Activity,* in which a kindergarten teacher demonstrates the reading skills her students are learning through writing activities.

Question: How are the students in the video applying what they're learning about phonics and spelling through this activity? You may also answer the questions at the end of the clip and e-mail your responses to your instructor

chapter 12

Developing Knowledge and Skills

Involving Family and Community

Instructional Planning Structures

Putting Effective Literacy Instruction into Practice: Grades 3 to 5

Organizing and Managing a Learning Community

Assessment: The Informal Reading Inventory

Differentiating Instruction in Grades 3 to 5

Transitioning English Language Learners

Putting Effective Literacy Instruction into Practice: Grades 3 to 5

Anticipation Guide

The following statements will stimulate your thinking about the topics of this chapter. Answer true or false in response to each statement. As you read and learn more about the topics in these statements, double-check your answers. See what interests you and prompts your curiosity toward more understanding.

_____ ● When children enter the third grade, there is little change from the first grade in the use of literature, in word recognition instruction, in reading in the content areas, and in writing.

_____ ● Teachers in grades 3 to 5 devote much less attention to phonemic awareness and phonics than those in grades K to 2.

_____ ● When children move from grades K to 2 to grades 3 to 5, the balance between oral reading and silent reading is about the same.

_____ ● As children reach higher grades, there is a greater range between their achievement levels, resulting in the need for careful grouping for instruction.

_____ ● The child's home can be the source of many family literacy activities.

_____ ● When children are reading orally for fluency, it is not possible to judge their comprehension.

_____ ● Formal assessment processes such as standardized testing do not provide information that is valuable in diagnosing the needs of individual students.

_____ ● Teaching English phonics to English language learners is the same as teaching it to native English speakers.

_____ ● Most children go through similar stages of spelling development.

_____ ● Computer technology is more useful in writing instruction than in reading instruction.

Literacy Activities in a Third-Grade Classroom

Chantell DeLaney is a third-grade teacher in a suburban classroom. Her twenty-seven students represent many different cultures and ethnic groups, but all are proficient in English. Today she has organized her students into three groups according to their levels of reading comprehension. One group reads slightly below grade level, another group reads at grade level, and some children read at fourth- and fifth-grade levels. Ms. DeLaney's children come together in these groups from time to time, but her overall approach to grouping for instruction is flexible, according to the children's needs and to the goals and standards she is addressing.

In today's lesson with a group of twelve children who are reading at grade level, Ms. DeLaney's plan reflects a three-stage structure: anticipation activities, building knowledge, and consolidation. She begins with two anticipation strategies. She first conducts a read-aloud of the story title and the first page of the story, asking the students questions about the illustration on the page, which she shows them from her copy of the book. She asks, "Based on the title and the illustration on this page, what prediction can you make about the story?"

Vinh says, "It's about a big animal. What is it?"

"Who knows?" asks Ms. DeLaney.

Theodore responds, "A hippopotamus!"

"How large is a hippopotamus?" asks Ms. DeLaney.

"Really big!" they shout.

She then introduces two new vocabulary words from the story, "huge" and "gigantic," with a t-graph, a graphic organizer.

For the part of the lesson in which the children build knowledge through reading, Ms. DeLaney uses two strategies that are often used in tandem: guided reading and chunking. She focuses the children's reading by asking a higher-order (comprehension-level) question before they read and by chunking the amount of reading they do after she asks the question, usually a single page, occasionally more than one page, or sometimes only a paragraph or two in difficult material. After she poses the purpose-setting question, the children read silently to find the

TEACH IT! **1**

Reading Aloud

As children move into grades 3 through 5, most have acquired a concept of print and can decode most of the words they encounter, especially when they are contextualized in connected text, are reading silently, are understanding what they read, and are expressing themselves in writing. The purpose of Chapter 12 is to weave together the major elements of a comprehensive and balanced reading program for implementation in self-contained classrooms in grades 3 through 5.

answer and then discuss what they have found out. Ms. DeLaney then proceeds to the next question and the next chunk. She uses the questions as a scaffolding strategy in a Directed Reading Activity (DRA). Placing the focus on the children's reading comprehension of what they read silently instead of only on accurate pronunciation and speed strengthens the children's abilities to understand what they are reading.

Ms. DeLaney's procedure is as follows: "Boys and girls, we are going to read a story about a girl who tries to hide from her mother the pet hippopotamus she found. Look in the table of contents for the story, turn to the first page, and close your book with your finger in the place. I am going to ask you a question before you read, and I want you to read to find the answer. How does Kamesha solve the problem of feeding her new pet so that her mother doesn't find out about it? Please read silently to find the answer."

The children read silently and, one by one, they raise their hands as they find the answer. Ms. DeLaney repeats the question and calls on Theodore, who responds correctly. She says, "That's correct, Theodore. Now, please read us the sentence that proves your answer." Other children offer their own opinions. She asks another question about the same page or chunk that they have just read, and they then move on to the next page, repeating this procedure for several pages.

In a consolidation activity after the children have read about half of the story, Ms. DeLaney asks them to retell the story so far in their own words, each child contributing part of the retelling. She asks, "How did our story begin?"

Tran contributes, "Kamesha found a huge hippopotamus at the park."

Nestor adds, "Her mother will be angry if she sees it."

"Why?" asks Ms. DeLaney.

"Because it will eat a lot of food," responds Nestor.

The children continue, negotiating with each other when there are disagreements or something is left out. Ms. DeLaney then asks the children to write two or three sentences predicting what Kamesha's mother will do when she discovers the hippopotamus. They can choose to read a library book or play one of the many reading games available to them as independent activities after they finish their writing. They will finish the story the next day but with only a brief review activity before the children continue reading.

The New York Times
nytimes.com
expect the worl.

Themes of the Times

Expand your knowledge of the concepts discussed in this chapter by reading current and historical articles from the *New York Times* by visiting the **Themes of the Times** section of the Companion Website (www.ablongman.com/templeallchildren2e).

Developing Knowledge and Skills

As you saw in earlier chapters, there is much variation in beginning reading programs for kindergarten and first and second grades. The range extends from scripted, direct instruction, one-size-fits-all programs of explicit phonics to literature-based programs in which shared reading of authentic connected text is a major activity, with phonemic awareness and phonics taught in the context of words the children have already learned to recognize. A basal reading program is also frequently employed; such programs are less scripted than formal code-emphasis programs but have more connected text for the children to read. Phonics elements and skills are systematically sequenced and presented explicitly. The text they read might be authentic in the case of anthologies of original versions of children's literature, but less so in the case of traditional basal readers, in which text is often manipulated to conform to various criteria.

Consolidating Primary-Grade Gains in Grade 3

Teachers in grades 3 to 5 must organize according to the experiences the children had in kindergarten and first and second grades and according to their degree of success there. Several very basic changes from children's initial reading experiences begin to appear in their reading instruction in the late second grade, continuing into the third grade. Individual differences among children not only continue to exist but also grow into even greater differences as some children have not been successful in kindergarten through second grade, most have been moderately successful, and others are leaping ahead in their abilities to process and benefit from both narrative and expository text. The result is an increased need for flexible grouping according to different needs, an increased need for a variety of instructional materials on several levels, and a need for more sensitive instructional strategies, especially for children who are not meeting standards for the grade level. Although this process might not always be under the control of the individual classroom teacher, the teacher should have the knowledge and skill necessary to develop such a program where that opportunity does exist or to adapt and augment the adopted program where possible.

USING CODE-EMPHASIS PRIMARY-GRADE PROGRAMS. A trend in some school districts is a reading program through which all children proceed at the same pace, regardless of differences in home language, proficiency in English, previous experiences or lack of experiences with print, knowledge of the sound system of English, availability of print in the home and community, and parent roles in providing emergent literacy experiences. Typically, these programs focus on phonemic awareness and explicit decoding skills, with text reading occurring in decodable text or fragments of text that are written specifically to provide regular practice in decoding. The major goal of such programs is for the children to achieve **automaticity**, which involves rapid and accurate pronunciation of words that follow phonic generalizations. Children may be discouraged from using cueing systems other than the graphophonic system. The obvious strength of such a program is seen in the formidable decoding skills of successful students when they attack regular words. But there are also problems with such a methodology:

- The focus of instruction is on accurate and rapid pronunciation, not on comprehension.
- Motivation is a frequent problem in that decodable text tends to be less interesting than authentic literature.
- Because of the systematic and sequential nature of instruction, children who fail to master some skills and elements have difficulty learning subsequent skills and elements that are based on previous teaching. Similarly, some children are already able to decode virtually any unknown words through skilled use of all cueing systems, but they are required to follow the program nonetheless.
- Many children have difficulty in the application of phonics generalizations to words that are not regular, especially if they lack experience in using other cueing systems as tools in the decoding of unknown words.
- Many English language learners must try to learn to decode in a language they do not understand and in which they have not mastered the sound system.

These children will benefit from additional emphases in their later reading instructional experiences:

- Extensive reading of authentic children's literature and expository text
- Instruction in the use of strategies from other cueing systems for when the children encounter new words that do not yield to analysis with regular phonics generalizations, such as using context clues, ignoring unknown words and reading on, using structural analysis skills, and questioning whether or not a word makes sense in the passage
- An increasing focus on silent reading as children gain proficiency in the middle grades, with questions to scaffold or guide that silent reading, followed by discussion

This situation was very much on Ms. DeLaney's mind when she planned her third-grade reading program. In grades 1 and 2, her children's teachers used a code-emphasis reading program that was characterized by explicit and systematic phonics in a very scripted, direct instruction approach.

To meet their comprehension needs, Ms. DeLaney selected a basal program that has particularly attractive and interesting literature. She continued to build their phonics and related word recognition skills from the program, but she drew those brief lessons out of the literature that the children were reading in the program in a process called "breaking the lockstep." She taught the components in the program but not always in the order in which they occurred in the teacher's manual.

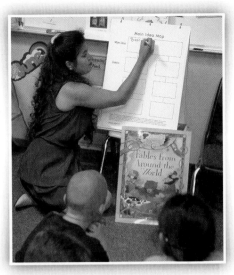

Whether you use a basal program or a literature-based program in your classroom, what is most important is making sure sound reading principles and instructional techniques are incorporated to meet the needs of your particular students.

USING BASAL PRIMARY-GRADE PROGRAMS. Basal reading programs tend to be broad and eclectic. Basal programs provide detailed teachers' manuals, often to the point of being scripted. Attention to phonemic awareness and phonics is usually ample. Instruction in the use of reading strategies, such as decoding, comprehension, and content reading skills, is provided in a sequence linked with the text to be read. Teachers often need to break the sequence by providing additional instruction related to a skill that is presented with a given story; this instruction might take several days. In the meantime, the children continue their reading of stories apart from this instruction, sometimes falling behind with respect to the skills presented with each story. A teacher might wisely decide to skip some direct skill development for children who have already demonstrated these abilities.

As children move into the middle grades from a basal reading program, you might choose the following options:

- Augment with multiple copies of trade books, apart from the basal reader or anthology.
- Provide scaffolding activities beyond those recommended in the basal reader when the children lack background knowledge about a story theme.
- Supplement skill development in decoding when gaps are encountered in the children's knowledge and skills, sometimes by reviewing word recognition lessons from previous levels of the program and sometimes by preparing new brief focused lessons.

USING LITERATURE-BASED PRIMARY-GRADE PROGRAMS. Some children might have had a less structured experience in the primary grades, such as those who have been in a language-experience approach or a literature-based program. Children who were in a literature-based program have often had extensive experiences with shared reading in the primary grades. Their texts are often group sets of authentic literature, for example, multiple copies of *The Very Hungry Caterpillar* (Carle, 1983), that a group of children works with for a week or two before moving on to another piece of literature. These books are often leveled, their difficulty having been assessed and taken into account before they are selected for use (Pinnell, Bridges, & Fountas, 1999).

Decoding skills are sometimes taught opportunistically rather than systematically. For example, teachers using this approach might notice several words in a piece of text that begin with the same sound/letter correspondence. It might be an element that the children have not examined formally, such as the consonant blend *spl*. The teacher develops a lesson on this sound/letter correspondence that has emerged from words the children have encountered in the story.

When you teach a group of children who have such an experiential background, there might be a need for a more systematic approach to word recognition to augment their earlier instruction and exposure to many types of comprehension scaffolding strategies.

Moving toward Independence in Grades 4 and 5

As children move further into the middle and upper grades, the same elements of the reading framework are in place, but the emphasis in each area and in the content changes. First, much more independent work takes place now that the children can read and write on their own. They still need support from the teacher, but they are much more self-sufficient.

Second, there is a diminished focus on skill development because the children have now mastered most of the word recognition skills they need to acquire. The focus on working with words in the four blocks is now more on vocabulary study than on letters and sounds, although occasional lessons are taught on letter/sound correspondences that are less regular or less frequently encountered, such as the silent consonants in *knee, write, pneumonia*, and *psychology* or prefixes of Greek origin, such as *poly-* and *biblio-*.

A third major change is that more instruction emphasizes reading in the content areas of the curriculum, with some lessons focusing as much on science or social studies as on reading. Writing activities are also broadening out from early narrative efforts into various aspects of expository writing, including persuasion and argumentation.

Building Fluency in Reading

PHONICS and **PHONOLOGICAL AWARENESS**

How can we further develop children's reading fluency in grades 3 to 5?

Although the reading **fluency** of many children is well established by the end of second grade, some children will benefit from continuing emphasis in this area. According to the report of the National Reading Panel (2000), children should read orally with appropriate timing, expressiveness, stress, and intonation. When necessary, fluency can be promoted through the following contextualized activities in grades 3 to 5:

- Providing daily self-selected reading of easy books at the children's independent levels
- Asking children to rehearse by reading to themselves before reading aloud
- Discouraging children from interrupting each other's oral reading with corrections
- Not being concerned about errors that do not change the meaning of the text and providing time for self-correction
- When correction is needed, focusing on comprehension by asking whether what was read incorrectly made sense
- Incorporating daily writing and encouraging invented spelling

TEACH IT! 22

Repeated Reading

Helping struggling readers to develop fluency in the middle grades is always a challenge because they already might be discouraged and they do not want to be perceived as needing to read easy books. Fielding and Roller (1992) suggest that the teacher can sometimes make more difficult books accessible to such children by doing the following:

- Having the children read to themselves first before reading aloud
- Providing paired reading opportunities in which a stronger reader supports a weaker reader (Caution: This can be overdone to the detriment of the more able reader.)
- Building background knowledge with easier books
- Having older troubled readers read easy books to younger children, which provides a good rationale for using less challenging materials at their independent reading levels
- Having children read the text in the mother tongue before reading orally in English (Crawford, 1993)

Finally, older children need extensive time for free-choice **sustained silent reading**, the self-selected reading aspect of the four blocks model. Worthy and Broaddus (2002) suggest beginning with about ten minutes each day, increasing to about thirty-five minutes each day as the children become capable of maintaining their attention and motivation for more time. Of course, the students need large numbers of high-interest books in a wide variety of genres.

Instructional Planning Structures

Throughout the book, you have seen and will see numerous strategies that support various aspects of reading instruction. Teachers must make decisions daily, and sometimes by the hour and minute, as to which strategies to use, when to use them, how to sequence them, why to use them, and even how many to use.

A major factor in planning reading instruction relates to the type of program being implemented. A highly scripted program requires little planning in the sense of organizing instruction, but it might be necessary to prepare charts and other materials to be used in the lesson from the manual. Basal programs are also highly organized with many activities, usually more activities than could be done during a typical lesson.

The task, then, is to plan the comprehensive reading program, assuming you have the latitude to combine elements and strategies from many sources to provide instruction that addresses the needs and interests of your students and the standards established for the school. When that latitude is limited or does not exist at all, the opportunity to address children's individual needs precisely is diminished.

Planning at the Daily Level

When planning daily reading lessons, consider the elements recommended in the four blocks approach in Chapter 1:

1. Demonstration of authentic acts of reading and writing in meaningful literacy activities
2. Attention to working with words and developing students' knowledge of the structure of written language
3. Guided practice in meaningful reading and writing so that the children internalize effective strategies
4. Carrying out independent activities in which they apply and extend their reading and writing abilities and develop lifelong habits of literacy.

State-adopted standards should also be reflected in lesson elements.

In grades 3 through 5, there will likely be more than one reading group in the classroom, sometimes three or four. Furthermore, one or more of those groups might be learning to read in Spanish or another language before moving into reading English later. The amount of needed planning can be daunting for a beginning teacher, but a year of teaching experience leads to efficiencies that facilitate the planning process.

Most lesson plans contain several common elements:

- One or more student objectives that emerge from student needs and standards
- Needed text and instructional materials
- An estimated amount of time planned for the lesson
- The body of the lesson:
- Anticipation activities to motivate and to activate or introduce needed background knowledge and vocabulary

- Reading activities to build knowledge for guiding and scaffolding the students' reading and comprehension of the text
- Consolidation activities, in which students apply new knowledge, often by writing
- A brief focused word study lesson, usually an element that is related to or emerging from the text to be read
- Assessment, often incorporated into a consolidation activity after reading, and also part of an ongoing process of observation and record keeping described in Chapter 11.

The Standards and Literacy box illustrates a lesson plan that might be designed to address some version of Little Red Riding Hood, a story that is familiar to most children. There are three objectives in the lesson, each emerging from one or more state standards—from the state of Massachusetts in this case. A description of materials that the teacher will need is provided along with an estimated amount of time scheduled for the lesson.

The body of the lesson contains the three elements that make up most reading lessons. The prereading *anticipation activities* are brief and simple because the story is well known to most children. The *activities to build knowledge* during reading are focused on higher-order questions. The children read silently to find information needed to answer the teacher's questions, and they occasionally read evidence aloud to support their responses. The postreading *consolidation activities* allow them to negotiate the story during the oral retelling. They enjoy the authentic writing activity at the end. They are writing to a real audience—the judge (their teacher)—and they have an authentic purpose for writing. They will enjoy reading the teacher's judgments about the culpability of the wolf. The assessment of the children's achievement during the lesson is also authentic because the teacher is observing their actual listening, reading, thinking, and writing behaviors.

This teacher has incorporated a brief focused lesson on phonics that reflects a need of the children and uses vocabulary from the story as a base for the phonics mini-lesson. In this case, the unvoiced final sound of /th/ is the focus of the lesson, and the teacher will check phonemic awareness, even though the children will undoubtedly have no problem with this aspect in the third grade. Then the teacher moves from the sound to words the children already know that end in the element, some of which come from the story they have read. Finally, the children combine their background knowledge about the sound and the letter and draw a conclusion about the sound in that position in new and unknown words. The focused lesson on phonics is brief and explicit, only about five minutes, but it is related to and emerging from the literature they have read. It is in the analytic or whole-part-whole mode.

As this lesson plan is examined in terms of the four block multimethod, multilevel approach described in Chapter 11 (Cunningham, Hall, & Sigmon, 2007), each of the four blocks—guided or directed reading, writing, self-selected reading, and working with words—is found. What is not readily seen in this example is the multilevel aspect of the four blocks approach. This could be accomplished by teaching the lesson to the entire class, making the text accessible to all students with multiple readings involving read-aloud, paired reading, and small flexible groups. There would be no problem in incorporating the writing and self-selected reading blocks of the approach, but the word study block might be less successfully applied in this example for grades 3 to 5. Some lower-achieving students might still not be comfortable with the unvoiced /th/ in the initial position, which they should probably know before moving on to that phoneme in the final position. And some children would have learned the sound/symbol correspondence of the final unvoiced /th/ years before.

PHONICS and **PHONOLOGICAL AWARENESS**

How can phonics instruction emerge naturally from children's reading?

TEACH IT! 15

Making and Breaking Words

TEACH IT! 9

Guided Reading and the Four Blocks Approach

Strategies to Integrate into Daily Lessons

A rich variety of instructional strategies we introduced in earlier chapters can be used as scaffolding strategies to support children's reading comprehension for use in reading lessons (see Table 12.1). Scaffolding is the temporary support provided by teachers when children are engaged in a task within Vygotsky's zone of proximal development. Bruner (1978) has described scaffolding as a temporary launching platform designed to support and encourage

Standards and Literacy

Sample Lesson Plan

Daily Lesson Plan: Third-Grade Level

LITTLE RED RIDING HOOD

Prepared to align with standards from the Massachusetts Language Arts Curriculum Framework, 2000.

Reading and Literature Strand

Standard 12: Students will identify, analyze, and apply knowledge of the structure, elements, and theme of a work of fiction and provide evidence from the text to support their understanding.

Objective: Students read silently and respond to inferential questions about the text.

Reading and Literature Strand

Standard 7: Students will understand the conventions of print and the relationship of letters and spelling patterns to the sounds of speech.

Objective: Students correctly pronounce the unvoiced consonant digraph /th/ in final position in new words (brief focused lesson).

Composition Strands

Standard 19: Writing. Students will write compositions, such as narratives, summaries, essays, letters, or directions, with a clear focus supported by logically related ideas and sufficient detail.

Standard 20: Consideration of Audience and Purpose: Students will write for different audiences and purposes.

Objective: Students write letters that present a coherent argument and in which writing conventions of spelling, punctuation, and grammar are grade-level appropriate.

Materials: Twelve copies of the story text —Little Red Riding Hood; easel and chart paper, markers

Time: Forty minutes

BODY OF LESSON PLAN

Anticipation reading activities: The teacher shows the book cover, and the children immediately recognize a familiar story. The teacher asks one or two students to share the beginning of the story before they begin reading. The teacher introduces two vocabulary words using the context of the sentences in which they occur: *hood* and *forest.*

Building knowledge through reading activities: guided silent reading, chunking, and discussion

Read the first two pages to find out how the author told you that Little Red Riding Hood was a disobedient girl.

How did you know that the wolf was hungry? Please read the sentence that proves your answer.

Let's read the next page to find out the effect on the wolf of his great hunger.

When Little Red Riding Hood returns home, what will her mother say to her? Why?

Read the next page to find out what kind of man the hunter was. How do you know that?

How do you know that this is a fantasy story?

BRIEF FOCUSED LESSON ON PHONICS ELEMENT

Step One: Students listen to words that contain the final unvoiced consonant /th/, such as *teeth* (the wolf's teeth from the story), *both,* and *bath.* The teacher asks how the words sound alike, as well as other questions that focus the children on the target sound.

Step Two: The teacher shows known words that contain the sound, asking how the words look alike. The teacher asks the students to focus on the letters that make up the sound and where they are.

Step Three: The teacher shows new words that contain the same element in the final position and asks the children to pronounce them. The teacher then asks the children to make a rule about the letters and the sound they have pronounced.

CONSOLIDATION READING ACTIVITIES

Oral retelling of the story: The children retell the story in their own words.

Writing activity: The teacher appoints each child to be an attorney for the wolf, who is in jail. Each child is to write a letter to the judge, asking for the release of the wolf. The teacher is the judge who will decide the wolf's fate in response to each letter. RAFT: Role is attorney; Audience is judge; Format is formal letter; Theme is getting the wolf out of jail (Buehl, 2001).

Read another fairy tale of your choice. Find two story elements that are similar to Little Red Riding Hood and two that are different and make notes about them. Be ready to talk about them tomorrow.

ASSESSMENT

Reading comprehension during reading: Success of the children in responding to inferential questions about the story and giving evidence for their answers.

Writing assignment: Coherence and persuasiveness of the argument to release the wolf; attention to the conventions of spelling, punctuation, and syntax.

Focused lesson on phonic element: Success of the children in decoding new words and correctly pronouncing the final sound of /th/ in them.

TABLE 12.1

Examples of Scaffolding Strategies to Support Reading Comprehension

ANTICIPATION ACTIVITIES BEFORE READING

Teacher read-aloud of beginning or selected parts of text

Discussion and predictions from book cover, title page, illustrations

Motivation by relating text to students' previous experiences

Think-pair-share

Quick-Write

Introduction of new vocabulary with semantic map, contextualized discussion

Activation or installation of background knowledge with semantic map, semantic feature analysis, advance organizer, shared discussion

ACTIVITIES TO BUILD KNOWLEDGE DURING READING

Guided or directed silent reading

Oral reading (generally limited to plays, dramatic activities, puppet shows, reading for expression, providing evidence)

Silent sustained reading

Think-aloud

Specific strategies, such as K-W-L, reader response, literature circles, the ReQuest procedure, reciprocal teaching, and questioning the author

CONSOLIDATION ACTIVITIES AFTER READING

Oral retelling

Written retelling

Review and elaboration of semantic map, semantic feature analysis from anticipation activities before reading

Writing workshop

Role-audience-format-theme (RAFT)

Reader's theater

Paired reading

Silent sustained reading

And more reading

And yet more reading

children's language development to higher levels of complexity. Pearson (1985) later described the temporary nature of scaffolding as the gradual release of responsibility. Good teachers intuitively use such scaffolding strategies to help children maintain their participation in learning activities (Crawford, 1994a).

Some strategies are appropriate as anticipation activities to prepare children for the reading they will do. Others might be helpful for building knowledge during their reading, supporting their comprehension, engaging them in the ideas they will encounter, and providing them with a structure to share their ideas with other students and the teacher. Others are most appropriate as consolidation activities to be completed at the conclusion of a lesson or even as homework. Some anticipation strategies, such as semantic mapping and semantic feature analysis, can be revisited as consolidation activities at the end of lessons for additions and revisions of initial predictions.

As you think about how these many strategies can be used in lessons, first consider that, as in choosing a meal in a cafeteria, you will take from each category the strategies that support your instruction, but not so many that the lesson becomes confused. Over the period of a year, you will likely use most or all of these strategies, but there is no need to use each one every week or even every month. As in all things, moderation is important. The most important activity in every lesson is the reading of connected text.

The recommended strategies that follow are those that will provide the underlying support, or scaffolding, needed for reading comprehension. It is the isolated skills development that you should consider carefully. Skill development should be viewed as an outcome of learning to read, not as its cause (Samuels, 1971; Smith, 1985). When a child's needs suggest that a directed skill lesson is needed, you can seek out an appropriate one in the teacher's editions and workbooks of traditional reading and language arts programs.

Finally, the structure of the following strategies has been applied to the narrative text in the chapter-opening vignette, but it can also be applied to expository text in science and social studies textbooks and related readings. Reading can be taught in many other subject areas of the curriculum.

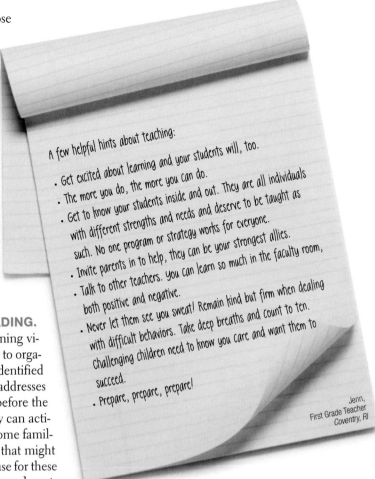

A few helpful hints about teaching:

- Get excited about learning and your students will, too.
- The more you do, the more you can do.
- Get to know your students inside and out. They are all individuals with different strengths and needs and deserve to be taught as such. No one program or strategy works for everyone.
- Invite parents in to help, they can be your strongest allies.
- Talk to other teachers. You can learn so much in the faculty room, both positive and negative.
- Never let them see you sweat! Remain kind but firm when dealing with difficult behaviors. Take deep breaths and count to ten. Challenging children need to know you care and want them to succeed.
- Prepare, prepare, prepare!

Jenn,
First Grade Teacher
Coventry, RI

ANTICIPATION STRATEGIES BEFORE READING.

An examination of Ms. DeLaney's lesson in the opening vignette makes it clear that she has given deep thought to organizing her instructional program in reading. She has identified the children's needs and has planned a program that addresses them carefully. She includes anticipation activities before the part of her lesson during which children read so they can activate background knowledge about the story and become familiar with the meanings of any new vocabulary words that might be needed. There are many strategies that she could use for these two purposes, but she uses only two to move the lesson along to the most important part: the reading.

Many strategies can be used to prepare children to read the text selected for a reading lesson. Two important factors affecting their readiness for reading are the background knowledge they bring to the task and vocabulary. Literature or expository text can be grouped into three levels of challenge with respect to these factors (see Table 12.2). The first category of text is not challenging because the background knowledge and vocabulary needed to understand are present in the culture and language of the children who will read it. In addition, the story might be in their oral tradition, or they might have been exposed to the story in a read-aloud or storytelling activity before their reading. In this case, you might elect to skip unneeded preparation activities that are provided in the teacher's manual of the typical basal reading program. When English language learners have read a story in the mother tongue in a parallel version of their reading program, the story might fall into this category.

The second category of text requires some activation of background knowledge and introduction of new vocabulary, and those anticipatory activities are usually provided for in the teacher's manual. If not, you can develop the needed activities, as Ms. DeLaney did.

The third category of text is very difficult because the children have little background knowledge about it, and new vocabulary is extensive and challenging. Although anticipatory activities are provided in the teacher's manual, you might decide that they are insufficient or inadequate. One option is to skip the story or text and move on to the next one. Another is to augment the anticipatory activities before reading, especially in areas of need for the children. How do you know in which of the three categories the text falls? That decision requires a professional judgment based on your knowledge of the children's strengths and needs and on analysis of the text before they begin reading.

All children have acquired background knowledge, but there is often a discontinuity between the background knowledge a child has and that assumed by the authors of instructional materials or literature used in the classroom. Crawford (1994a) indicates that the discontinuity between the assumption and the reality is deeper when the child comes from a

TABLE 12.2

Choosing Reading Texts Based on Readiness

READINESS CRITERIA

Text Level	Vocabulary	Background Knowledge	Teacher Action
easy 1 2 3 difficult	Present in daily culture	Present in daily culture	Preparatory activities may not be necessary
	Part of oral traditions	Part of oral traditions	
	Introduces some new vocabulary	Some activation of background knowledge	Some activities necessary to introduce new vocabulary
	Extensive new vocabulary	Little activation of background knowledge	Augment anticipation activities as necessary
	Very difficult		

TEACH IT! 21

Semantic Feature Analysis

language or culture different from that of the children for whom the materials are designed or intended—usually middle-class native English speakers. A story about a birthday leads a Mexican child to activate background knowledge about a piñata, whereas most children in the United States activate background knowledge about a party, a cake with candles, pin-the-tail-on-the-donkey, and gifts. Children from Senegal and Morocco do not think about birthdays at all because birthdays are not celebrated in their cultures. If children lack a schema or background knowledge for a birthday tradition presented in a literature selection representing a culture they do not know, then background knowledge must be activated or developed as a prereading activity. A very effective anticipation strategy for activating and developing background knowledge is **semantic feature analysis** (Pittelman et al., 1991). This strategy involves helping students build knowledge about a new topic by comparing it to knowledge about related topics about which students do have background knowledge. The Teach It! box illustrates this effective anticipation strategy.

READING STRATEGIES FOR BUILDING KNOWLEDGE DURING READING.
According to Smith (1985), children learn to read by reading. This fundamental idea should underlie your thinking about how children's time is best spent during reading instruction. Rather than having children study about reading by mastering skills, maximize the amount of reading they do. Some obvious counterproductive strategies are pencil-and-paper exercises. Another is the still-common practice of round-robin oral reading, in which each child takes a turn reading aloud to the group or class. This usually consists of having a child laboriously reading aloud a passage she or he has never before read, even silently, while the rest of the children in the group pretend to listen or read along. You might have memories of counting the children ahead of you in the first grade so that you could determine which paragraph you would read, although some wise teachers skipped around to prevent that strategy.

The child reading aloud focuses on pronunciation, not on understanding what is being read, and the other children are either bored or preparing to read when their turn comes. This practice is especially deceiving in regard to children who read in Spanish, for example. They can read orally with confidence in English, albeit with a Spanish accent and no comprehension. They are, in fact, pronouncing and not reading. Table 12.3 on page 402 identifies various reasons why round-robin reading should be kept to a minimum.

There are, however, some excellent uses for oral reading: reading a sentence aloud to provide evidence for a response to a question; reading poetry; reading roles in puppet shows and readers' theater; assessment; sharing writing; buddy reading or paired reading as a practice activity; read-aloud to parents, grandparents, or siblings; and improvement of fluency. Otherwise, valuable instructional time in grades 3 to 5 should be used for guided silent reading and comprehension development.

TEACH IT!

Refer to your **Teach It!** booklet for further activities you can use to reinforce concepts discussed in this chapter.

Semantic Feature Analysis

Students in a suburban school may have limited background knowledge about the falcon, the topic of expository text from a science book. Related areas about which students in a suburban school would already likely have background knowledge might be *parrot, chicken,* and *crow.* These topics are listed on the *x*-axis of a chart (the top) and generic elements that relate to parrots, chickens, crows, and falcons are listed on the *y*-axis (the left) (see the chart on the right). The teacher prepares the chart before the lesson and presents it on the chalkboard, a transparency, or a large piece of paper. Information about the falcon should be available in the text to be read. In a prereading group activity led by the teacher, the students discuss, marking a plus (+) where they know that a relationship is true, a minus (–) where they know that it is not true, and a question mark (?) where they do not have information or do not agree.

On the sample chart, the prereading predictions of a student group are listed and marked accordingly. The students then read the text on falcons, looking for information about elements from the chart.

At the conclusion of the reading, the students discuss the text and return to the semantic feature analysis chart as a consolidation activity. They discuss again, change incorrect predictions, providing evidence they have found in the text, and fill in areas where question marks were indicated.

Unlike some other text-based strategies, semantic feature analysis lends itself well to reading expository text in mathematics and the sciences. For example, a mathematics teacher might list the following elements in the left column: triangle, isosceles triangle, parallelogram, trapezoid, square, rectangle, right triangle, equilateral triangle, and circle. Across the top, the teacher might list such elements as parallel lines, nonparallel lines, straight lines, no straight lines, equal lines, pairs of equal lines, angles, equal angles, pairs of equal angles, and right angles.

Semantic Feature Analysis Chart
The Falcon

	parrot	chicken	crow	falcon
What color are they?				
Brilliant colors	+	–	–	?
Brown	–	+	–	?
Blue	–	–	–	–
Black	–	–	+	?
What do they eat?				
Meat	–	–	+	?
Fruit	+	–	+	?
Seeds	–	+	–	+
Where do they live?				
In the jungle	+	–	–	?
In the mountains	–	–	–	?
On the farm	–	+	+	–
In the desert	–	–	–	?
In the city	–	–	+	?

It is more difficult for teachers to provide extra support to English language learners because their need for it might be less obvious during the largely independent activity of reading silently. The need should be based on children's abilities to interact with the teacher and each other about what they have been reading—that is, their comprehension of what they have been reading.

Guiding children's reading with questions, a variation on DRA, provides valuable support in maintaining comprehension (Crawford, 1993). The teacher needs to precede the children's reading of a page or passage of a piece of literature by asking a higher-order question, that is, an open-ended question whose answer requires the child to use background knowledge and combine it with information from the selection to be read. An example of such a question is "Please read page 71 to find out why the main character is worried." Students will read page 71 to find the answer to the question; it focuses them on comprehension, not on production and accurate oral reading.

This questioning strategy brings key story concepts to children's attention as they read, and, perhaps more important, it provides moral support, interest, and motivation from someone who cares about them: the teacher. Children who cannot or will not read a lengthy

TABLE 12.3

Reasons for Minimizing Round-Robin Oral Reading

- It diminishes the amount of actual reading that children do.
- The focus is on pronunciation, not comprehension.
- Strong readers love to perform by reading orally, but they could read more, and faster, by reading silently.
- Poor readers hate to read aloud, disclosing their reading problems for the whole class to hear.
- Both children and teachers dislike listening to the agonizing efforts of poor readers.
- Although teachers can informally assess student outcomes during oral reading, a more systematic approach is needed (see the informal reading inventory discussed in this chapter).
- Teachers sometimes convert an oral reading lesson into a phonics lesson that interferes with comprehension.

selection alone might do so in chunks of a paragraph, or a page or two at a time within the security of a supportive teacher-directed group. These chunks are manageable and comprehensible sections, and questions can be used very effectively and naturally to accomplish this chunking. You can structure children's reading with questions that elicit predictions, with timely resolution of those predictions through discussion and any needed mediation.

Although there is considerable debate about the value of teaching reading comprehension skills through direct instruction, there are enough other reasons to guide silent reading with higher-order or comprehension-level questions. Table 12.4 provides some examples of poor low-level questions and strong higher-order questions. It takes no longer to formulate and ask a higher-order comprehension question than a low-level recall question before asking children to read to find the answer. Guided silent reading provides an opportunity for children to make inferences and predictions, identify cause-and-effect relationships, and apply other higher-order critical thinking skills when their comprehension is supported

TABLE 12.4

Examples of Different Levels of Questions from "Little Red Riding Hood"

LOW-LEVEL RECALL QUESTIONS

Tell what happened on the first page of the story.
Where did the wolf first see Little Red Riding Hood?
What color is Little Red Riding Hood's cape?
Where is Little Red Riding Hood taking the food basket?

HIGHER-ORDER COMPREHENSION QUESTIONS

How did the author tell you that Little Red Riding Hood was a disobedient girl?
How did you know that the wolf was hungry?
What was the effect on the wolf of his great hunger?
When Little Red Riding Hood returns home, what do you think her mother will say to her? Why?
Why did Little Red Riding Hood go to Grandmother's house by the forest road?
What kind of man was the hunter? How do you know that?
What advice would you give to Little Red Riding Hood for the future? Why?

(Crawford, 1993). This is seen in Ms. DeLaney's lesson in the chapter-opening vignette. Her students are now in the third grade, and they need to read silently with a focus on comprehension. But their abilities in this area are still limited, and she therefore scaffolded their comprehension by guiding their silent reading with carefully formulated higher-order questions. She also limited how much they read after each question to an amount they could understand and remember for the discussion that followed each chunk. Ms. DeLaney provided occasional opportunities for oral reading, as described in her lesson. She often asked children to read the sentence or sentences aloud that provided evidence for their responses to her higher-order questions.

CONSOLIDATION STRATEGIES AFTER READING.   Ms. DeLaney concluded her lesson with two consolidation activities. She integrated an **oral retelling** and a small authentic writing assignment into the closing part of the lesson—part to be done while she was with the group and the rest to be done after she left them. She collected the children's written predictions and later responded briefly in writing to the content of each one. If she noted a spelling error in a child's prediction, she used the word correctly in her response to that child. She also reviewed their papers for common problems, such as the correct use of the comma in a series. Instead of correcting that error, she would plan a minilesson on the element or detail for the next day. The children could then examine their own work and make needed changes or corrections.

Retelling is an excellent consolidation activity after reading. An oral retelling provides children with the opportunity to negotiate with each other about the meaning of the selection and requires them to listen very attentively to each other (Brown & Cambourne, 1990). Through this process, children can often incorporate new information gained through reading into existing background knowledge. They also observe that retelling promotes multiple readings of text as a part of the negotiation process. Koskinen et al. (1988) found that the verbal rehearsal that occurs in the retelling process also serves to improve the reading comprehension of less proficient readers. English language learners might elect to retell in their mother tongue what they read or heard in their second language (Crawford, 1993).

Retelling also provides a means for integrating writing into the program. Either through a cooperative learning process or through individual or paired writing, children can prepare a written retelling (Strickland & Feeley, 1985). As a result of their earlier discussion, the knowledge they gained through reading, and such prereading activities as semantic mapping and the examination of story grammar, children are better prepared to write a well-structured retelling. Like the demonstration that they provide during read-alouds, teachers should also model retelling with an actual example.

The most obvious consolidation activity after reading should not be overlooked: more reading. If you are successful in providing high-quality literature that children will choose to read and in supporting their comprehension, then you can expect gains in all areas of the language arts. Reading is more powerful than direct instruction in developing vocabulary, grammar, spelling, and reading comprehension, especially for English language learners. Provide extensive free voluntary reading with messages that are understood in low-anxiety situations. Good writing is promoted more by extensive reading than by writing (Krashen, 1985, 1993).

WRITING and READING CONNECTIONS

How can writing be incorporated into the consolidation activity of retelling?

Long-Term Planning Using Thematic Literature Units

The **thematic literature unit** is a very useful structure for organizing reading instruction around a topic that is of interest to children. It consists of a framework for organizing the work of several days or weeks (Zarrillo, 1994). This structure often parallels social studies units, such as "The Westward Movement," or science units, such as "Growing Up," and usually includes goals and objectives, activities, instructional materials, and assessment. The thematic literature unit provides an opportunity for you to integrate reading and writing across the curriculum because a part of the unit can incorporate expository text from social science, science, or other subject areas. You can augment the text in the classroom and library with text on the theme from the Internet as well.

A typical integrated thematic literature unit can be seen in Table 12.5. The teacher has assembled expository text, authentic literature, film, and other resources that reflect the theme of the unit, "Endangered Dolphins"; it therefore fits into the genre of critical literacy as well. There are two videos to initiate the unit and motivate students, one of news accounts of dolphin kills and another about dolphins in general. The unit includes expository text about dolphins and other sea mammals; multiple copies of trade books, including the Newbery Award–winning book *Island of the Blue Dolphins* (O'Dell, 1960); symbolic text to read on the sides of cans of tuna; related selections of text from the science textbook used in the classroom; and a book on drawing dolphins so that students can illustrate their written work. Over a period of about four weeks, the children will read the texts, building background knowledge and vocabulary related to the theme. Word attack skills and vocabulary will be devel-

TABLE 12.5

A Thematic Literature Unit on Endangered Dolphins

GOALS/OBJECTIVES*	ACTIVITIES	ASSESSMENT	TEXT SOURCES	INTERVAL†
Formulate questions about dolphins and their endangered status	View video	Quality of student questions generated	National Geographic's *Dolphins: The Wild Side* (VHS); news videos; cans of tuna	One day
Read with fluency	Paired reading	Accuracy of oral reading in primary level book	*In Dolphin Time* by Kathleen Dudzinski	Periodic over four weeks
Read silently with comprehension	Guided reading in small groups; discuss findings in literature circles	Observation; quality of discussion	*See and Explore Library: Whales, Dolphins, and Porpoises* by Mark Carwardine; other sources	Four days
Read silently with comprehension	Guided reading during science lesson	Observation; quality of discussion	Science textbook	Two days
Locate information on the Internet or in newspapers; interest groups formed to work together	Select theme to research: Poem about dolphins; Miami Dolphins football team; Greek myth about dolphins; Other themes of interest	Criteria: use of descriptors, refinement of descriptors, appropriateness of selected text	Google.com	Periodic over four weeks
Write informational and persuasive text about protecting endangered dolphins	RAFT (Role/Audience/Format/Theme) Word processing	Rubrics	*Dolphins: What They Can Teach Us* by Mary M. Cerullo	Three days following research activities
Illustrate informational writing accurately	Illustrate informational and persuasive writings	Relationship of illustrations to text written by students	*Drawing Whales and Dolphins* by Books Watermill	One day following writing activities
Read silently with comprehension	Silent sustained reading of self-selected narrative and expository books about dolphins and related ocean mammals	Motivation, conferences	*Island of the Blue Dolphins* by Scott O'Dell, *Dolphins at Daybreak* by Mary Pope Osborne, and other leveled books	Periodic over four weeks

*Goals and objectives reflect school district/state standards.
†Note: Days do not have to be consecutive.

oped in the context of their reading. Writing activities will also emerge from them, resulting in social action: student posters urging shoppers to buy only dolphin-safe tuna.

Critical literacy provides many opportunities for integrating across the curriculum within thematic units, involving not only literature, but also science, social studies, mathematics, and technology. It is also an excellent place to incorporate the writing process, especially persuasive writing. Powell, Cantrell, and Adams (2001) provide several assumptions that underlie critical literacy:

- Literacy instruction can never be neutral because of the decisions teachers make in planning every lesson.
- Critical literacy is a major element of a strong democratic system, requiring shared decision making in society.
- Literacy instruction can lead to transformative action.

Standards as a Guide

Most states and several professional organizations, including the International Reading Association and the National Council of Teachers of English, have developed standards for reading/language arts and other curriculum areas. These are most often expressed as expectations or minimal competencies to be attained by children, and they are sometimes tied quite specifically to grade levels. Recall that the Standards and Literacy box earlier in this chapter demonstrated how standards can be used to develop specific lesson objectives and a lesson plan.

Standards provide valuable focus on important elements of the reading/language arts curriculum. One unfortunate outcome of overreliance on standards for planning instruction, however, is a narrowing of and rigidity in the curriculum and a focus on teaching to the assessment tools that states, school districts, and schools use to assess the extent to which students have met those standards (Herman & Golan, 1993; Nolan, Haladyna, & Haas, 1992). There should always be room for the teacher's creativity and for taking advantage of the teachable moment that occurs when, for example, a child brings an injured bird into the classroom or when a tragedy such as September 11, 2001, occurs. The reading/language arts activities that emerge from such a moment will almost always address one or more important standards.

Assessment: The Informal Reading Inventory

Although there are already differences in achievement among children at each level from kindergarten to second grade, there is a much broader range of levels of proficiency in reading and writing in grades 3 through 5. Most states and school districts now conduct an annual or biannual assessment of children's reading achievement at several grade levels, but the data that those standardized tests yield are not designed for use in planning instruction for individual children. Teachers need to gather information about the individual strengths and needs of each child to plan instruction, select appropriate instructional materials, and group children.

In the chapter-opening vignette, Ms. DeLaney had divided her students into ability groups for that part of her instruction. According to results from the informal assessment she administered during the first week of school, the twenty-seven students in her classroom were reading at grade levels from second to fifth, with one group reading slightly below grade level, one group reading at grade level, and some children reading at the fourth- and fifth-grade levels. How did she assess to form those groups?

Perhaps the most widely used authentic assessment for reading is the **informal reading inventory (IRI)**, which is used to evaluate students' reading ability. The IRI allows the

Reading assessments can help identify a child's reading level as well as comprehension. How can a teacher use this information to plan for instruction?

teacher to determine children's individual needs. It consists of a series of graded passages, generally 100 to 200 words in length, with one or two passages for each grade level from 1 through 10. The levels of the passages are often determined by the level of the text from which they are taken, but these levels can be verified according to their levels on a gradient of leveled text. In addition, each passage is accompanied by four or more questions at the level of inferential comprehension, literal comprehension, and vocabulary.

Administering the Informal Reading Inventory

The IRI should be administered at the beginning of the school year, when the teacher is planning instruction, selecting textbooks and trade books for the class, and grouping children with similar needs. Because children are often grouped for instruction on the basis of the outcomes of the IRI, it is desirable to administer an IRI once or twice during the school year. Children have spurts of achievement gain, and groups that are formed at the beginning of the school year should not be so rigid that children never move from one to another. It might not be necessary to administer an IRI systematically to every child at the same time later in the year, as is done at the beginning of the year, but children should be reassessed when the teacher observes a change in achievement, whether positive or negative.

An IRI is an individual test, and a substantial investment of classroom time must be dedicated to the process of assessing each child, but it is time well spent. A skilled teacher can administer an IRI to an entire class within several hours, and the process goes faster with experience. Each child needs ten to fifteen minutes of uninterrupted time with the teacher. It is tempting to begin assessing the first day of school, but classes are often reorganized because of rapid changes in enrollment during the first week. Therefore, it might be wise to delay this process until enrollments in the school settle down late in the first week. You need to provide activities for the children who are waiting their turn for assessment and for those who are already finished. It is also important that children not be able to hear the assessment of their peers on this oral procedure. A paraprofessional or a parent volunteer can be invaluable in supporting the quiet environment needed during each child's IRI.

On the basis of widely accepted percentages of accuracy and comprehension, the teacher needs to decide what levels to administer, and the answer will be different for each child. Most teachers administer a grade level below their estimate for the child that is based on test scores and information on the cumulative record from the teacher of the previous year. For example, a third grader who was reading at grade level the year before would usually begin with an IRI passage on the second-grade level. The child should feel successful on the first passage. Children know when they have failed, and they are often reluctant to continue to another level, even if that level is lower—perhaps especially if that level is lower.

Explain to the child that he or she will be reading some passages out loud to you and will then respond to some questions about what has been read. The child then reads a passage aloud to you as you record the oral reading errors made by the child. Then take the passage back from the child and ask the questions that accompany it. On the basis of the child's performance, another passage will be administered, as described later.

Interpreting the Outcomes

As we saw in Chapter 10, the IRI yields four levels: frustration level, instructional level, independent level, and capacity level. The most important are the instructional and frustration levels. The instructional level is the level at which the teacher should target instruction and for which instructional materials should be selected. It corresponds to Vygotsky's zone of proximal development (Vygotsky, 1978).

In determining the instructional level of a child, the frustration level is determined at the same time. Children are asked to read and respond to questions from passages at various levels until they fail to meet criteria for **instructional level**, which are above 90 percent accuracy in oral reading and above 70 percent in comprehension. They should not have seen or read the passages before the assessment. The level at which the child fails to reach the criteria is the **frustration level**; the next level down—that is, the highest level where the criteria are met—is the instructional level. The percentages for accuracy are focused on a base score of 100 percent, each oral reading error resulting in the loss of one percentage point, for example, on a 100-word passage. The types of errors are as follows:

Mispronunciation: The student mispronounces a word, even if it is self-corrected.

Substitution: The student substitutes another word that makes sense in the passage.

Omission: The student leaves out a word.

Insertion: The student adds a word that is not in the original passage.

Reversal: The student reverses the order of letters, words, or clauses.

Repetition (regression): The student repeats words already read, sometimes an entire sentence.

Punctuation ignored: The student ignores punctuation.

Hesitation: The student hesitates for two seconds or more.

Teacher support: After five seconds, the teacher supplies the word.

The 70 percent criterion for comprehension is based on answering approximately three of four comprehension questions.

This complex process is best understood with an example. The teacher assessed a fourth-grade student who, according to the previous teacher and cumulative records, was reading at grade level last year. The teacher therefore administered a third-grade passage to begin, using the form shown in Figure 12.1 to record results. The child was successful

Age of student 9 Gender M Grade level 4 Home language English

Level administered	Accuracy	Comprehension
2	99%	100%
3	97%	75%
4	95%	75%
5	89%	25%
Frustration level***	5	
Instructional level*	4	
Independent level**	2	

  * Highest grade level with 95% accuracy, 75% comprehension
 ** Highest grade level with 99% accuracy, 100% comprehension
*** Next level more difficult than instructional level

FIGURE 12.1

Informal Reading Inventory (IRI) Results.

in reaching at least 90 percent accuracy and 75 percent comprehension, indicating that his instructional level was at least third grade. On the fourth-grade passage, he also met the criteria, but not at the fifth-grade level. The frustration level was at fifth grade, indicating that the instructional level was fourth grade because it was the highest level at which criteria were reached.

Figure 12.2 shows how the teacher evaluated the accuracy of oral reading on the third-grade passage. The accuracy percentage from Figure 12.1 was 97 percent, indicating the three oral reading errors that were subtracted from 100 percent. When a student commits a series of errors that are related, only a single error is counted. For example, if a student hesitates, mispronounces a word, then repeats the words that preceded it, and finally gives up on the word, only a single error is counted. This student, for example, was unable to pronounce *gift*, although he produced the sound of /j/, ordinarily a correct pronunciation of the /g/ followed by short /i/. He anticipated the problem with the word *gift* and repeated the phrase "to his son as a" preceding it and then hesitated before mispronouncing the sound of /j/. But the teacher counted only a single error because all were related to the problem with the word *gift*. The child ignored the period after *husband* and substituted *meet* for *greet*, a logical substitution that did not change the meaning of the sentence and that was consistent with the /ee/ in both words. In a process called *reading miscue inventory*, a skilled, experienced teacher can interpret children's errors and make valuable inferences about the children's strengths and needs (Goodman & Burke, 1972; Goodman, Watson, & Burke, 2005).

It is often possible to determine through observation that a student is reading at frustration level. The student exhibits some or all of the following behaviors: laborious word-for-word, or even letter-by-letter, reading with flat intonation; pointing behavior, especially when that is not observed in easier passages; squinting or moving the text very close to the eyes; and rocking back and forth, kicking the chair or table. Think about what your own physical behaviors would be if you were asked to read aloud from a quantitative chemistry text that you did not understand at all.

FIGURE 12.2

Example of Accuracy Scoring of IRI Passage.

Once upon a time there was a hunter and his wife who lived very well. Then a son was born to them.

One day the hunter caught a baby fox and brought it home to his son as a gift. The little fox was very

quick and smart. The boy liked him very much. His mother often left the boy and the fox together and went

to help her husband. When she returned, the little fox would run to meet her.
punctuation ignored

One day she returned home at noon. She was surprised because the little fox did not come to greet *meet*

her.

C 1. Describe the family in the story.

(The hunter, his wife, and his son)

C 2. Why did the little boy like the fox?

(He was quick and smart)

√ 3. What was the effect on the little boy's mother when the little fox didn't greet her?

(She was surprised)

C 4. What did the mother do with the little boy when she went to help her husband?

(She left him with the little fox)

The **independent reading level** is the level at which the child can read without support. It is generally one to three years lower than the instructional level. It is the highest level at which the child reads with 99 percent accuracy and 90 to 100 percent comprehension. In the example in Figure 12.1, the teacher had to drop to the second-grade level to determine the independent level. If the student had achieved less than 99 percent accuracy and 100 percent comprehension on the second-grade passage, the teacher would have dropped to a passage at the first-grade level.

Determining the independent level can dramatically increase the time it takes to administer and interpret an IRI, and the extra information might not be useful enough to warrant the additional time required. Essentially, it is important to know that children who select a library book to read independently will probably select an easier book than the one used in their reading group. This is the way it should be, because the teacher is providing extra scaffolding and support to children during the lessons that is not available during independent reading. Children with strong interests in a theme or topic might select books for independent reading at higher levels, but the extra motivation of a child reading about the butterflies he or she collects will compensate for the added difficulty.

This is also good information to convey to parents: When they help their children select books at the library or the bookstore, they should not steer the children to books at the same level as the textbooks they are using in the classroom. Children's independent reading should be done at a level at which they are very comfortable, reading for enjoyment and not struggling with decoding tasks or difficult vocabulary and concepts. Your own recreational reading as an adult is similar: You are likely to read more John Grisham than Marcel Proust.

Interpreting IRI Results for Linguistically Diverse Students

Most assessment strategies used with English speakers function well in other languages and also in English with English language learners. Some adaptations are indicated, however. For example, one element of evaluating oral reading accuracy in the informal reading inventory is the mispronunciation, each occurrence of which is counted as an oral reading error or miscue. When a mispronunciation error can be attributed to a conflict point with the mother tongue or dialect of English, and when it does not interfere with comprehension, a short *i* pronounced as a long *e*, for example, then an error would not be counted.

Kenneth Johnson (personal communication, 1977) provides a test sentence to illustrate this principle for the African American child whose mother tongue is African American Vernacular English. The sentence often elicits a mispronunciation that has the potential to interfere with comprehension. The child is asked to read the following sentence aloud: "As I passed the sign, I read it." In conformance with African American Vernacular English, the African American child sometimes pronounces *passed* as *pass*, dropping the *-ed* suffix that is also a past tense marker. If the child comprehends the marker, that is, understands that *passed* is in the past tense even though pronounced as in the present tense, then the child will pronounce *read* in the past tense. If not, the child will pronounce *read* in the present tense. According to Johnson, these children invariably correctly pronounce *read* in the past tense. In a study of teachers who administered IRIs to Spanish-speaking children, Lamberg, Rodríguez, and Tomas (1978) concluded that to avoid such problems, teachers need special training to use them with English language learners.

Other Informal Measures of Reading and Writing

As you saw in Chapter 10, there are many informal measures that teachers can use to assess their students' progress through the developmental processes of learning to read and

LANGUAGE and DIVERSITY

What is the effect of language and dialectical differences on the interpretation of oral reading errors in the informal reading inventory?

Using the IRI Capacity Level as a Measure of English Language Proficiency

Many commercial instruments are available for assessing English language proficiency. Most examine pronunciation, knowledge of syntax, vocabulary knowledge, and other discrete skills. Because state and federal funds are often involved for qualifying students, English language learners are usually assessed for redesignation as fluent English speakers in a very formalistic and legalistic process. The information gained from this type of assessment is less useful for instructional planning. To teach English language learners to read in English, teachers need to know how well they comprehend English.

According to A. Crawford (1982, 2000), teachers can use the reading capacity level, another level yielded by informal reading inventory, as a measure of listening comprehension that is a useful reflection of English language proficiency. They can use the IRI to make an informed decision about readiness for English language reading instruction in given materials by reading a selected passage aloud to the child. Crawford reported that children who read in the mother tongue and also respond correctly to 75 percent of compre-

hension-level questions about the material read to them in English usually have sufficient second-language proficiency to begin learning to read at the highest level at which they successfully respond to those questions.

For example, a second-grade teacher who believes that an English language learner may be ready for formal English reading instruction would read a passage of 100 to 200 words aloud to the child from the second-grade text used for teaching English reading in the classroom. Children who can respond correctly to three of four comprehension-level (not recall) questions about the text in English when it is read to them are providing evidence that they are ready to begin formal reading instruction in English at the second-grade level. This level is described as one of cognitive academic-language proficiency (CALP), explained in detail in Chapter 14. For those children learning to read in their mother tongue in a bilingual program, this is often at or near the grade level at which they are reading in that mother tongue. They will need all of the scaffolding support described in this chapter. The levels of their English vocabulary and syntax will in no way correspond to those of children who have been communicating in English since birth.

write. Chantell DeLaney, the teacher in the chapter-opening vignette, uses many of these measures daily. Although she makes effective use of the informal reading inventory periodically for all students, and when needed for individual students, she can observe the frustration level in her students' physical behaviors, as just described. She might note that some children rarely participate in discussion activities after silent reading, even with the support of the many scaffolding activities she provides. She takes careful notes about these observations and uses them in planning future instruction.

Each student in Ms. DeLaney's classroom has a portfolio of writing products. She urges them to add a sample of writing to their portfolios from their work each week. This can be used as a motivation tool when students are able to observe their progress as they page through the portfolio, week after week. It is also a valuable tool for use in parent conferences to document for parents their children's progress.

Transitioning English Language Learners

It is often during grade 3 that English language learners who have been in a mother tongue bilingual education reading program begin a process of transition to English language reading instruction. This may occur earlier or later for some children, depending on their age when they arrived. When children speak and understand English at an intermediate level, and when they are reading confidently in the mother tongue at least at a second- or third-

In most schools, one of the rites of spring is annual achievement testing. In these days of high-stakes testing, the results of these tests often have consequences in terms of children's academic prospects, school budgets, future curriculum planning, and even personnel changes within schools or districts. In short, they have become extremely important. In some schools, the curriculum has become focused on raising test scores at all costs. Aspects of the curriculum that are not directly related to testing outcomes, such as science, social studies, art, and music, are sometimes eliminated from the curriculum.

Normed referenced achievement tests permit schools and school districts to make comparisons of the reading performance of their children to those on a national level. Children often spend weeks practicing exercises presented in the format of these tests, usually multiple-choice items of word meaning and paragraph meaning. Unfortunately, the results of such tests are not very useful in making instructional decisions about individual students. They are designed for assessing groups of students, not individual students. You should be familiar with these kinds of tests. Possible test items might be as follows:

Word meaning (Circle the best answer):

After winning the grand prize of one thousand dollars, Emily was

a. sad   X **b.** ecstatic   **c.** pleased   **d.** bored

Paragraph meaning (Read the paragraph and select the best answer to the question):

Once upon a time there was a hunter and his wife who lived very well. Then a son was born to them. One day the hunter caught a baby fox and brought it home to his son as a gift. The little fox was very quick and smart. The boy liked him very much. His mother often left the boy and the fox together and went to help her husband. When she returned, the little fox would run to meet her. One day she returned home at noon. She was surprised because the little fox did not come to greet her.

What problem did the hunter's wife have?

    a. The little boy was quick and smart.
    b. The little boy didn't like the fox.
X c. The fox didn't greet the hunter's wife.
    d. The woman helped her husband.

grade level, they are ready to begin a formal transition to English, although they will have had many English language reading experiences before the formal transition. How can teachers help English language learners begin to make the transition into English language reading instruction?

Using the Language Experience Approach in English

In past years, it was commonly held that second-language learners should not begin learning to read and write at all in the second language until they had reached an intermediate level of fluency in speaking it. Teachers now recognize that informal processes of reading and writing in the second language can begin early in the English language acquisition process, especially for children who have developed literacy skills in the mother tongue. This early reading instruction is informal and incidental; it is not a formal English reading program. In addition, this incidental instruction should not be substituted for mother tongue instruction when it is possible to provide it.

LANGUAGE and DIVERSITY

How can English language learners learning to read in their mother tongue begin learning to read in English?

TEACH IT! 46

Language Experience
with English Language
Learners

TEACH IT! 13

Word Sorts

Bilingual teachers who teach reading in the mother tongue recognize that children's motivation to begin reading and writing in the English language is strong. Although it has already been noted that, where possible, it is most beneficial for children to learn to read and write first in the mother tongue, teachers can begin a cautious, early introduction to literacy in a second language to take advantage of that motivation. Although used mostly with young children, the language-experience approach (LEA) can also be used in grades beyond second grade when children are just beginning to learn to read in English or when older preliterate children need more time at the earliest stages of English reading, especially if they are unable to read in the mother tongue. Some migrant children or the children of refugees might never have been in school, even though they are ten or twelve years of age or older.

There are many LEA activities that can be adapted for English language learners. For example, multiple readings of the text are helpful to them (Crawford, Allen, & Hall, 1995). Using a copy of the text with some words left out and with empty spaces where words are missing, children can practice reading the text. This practice is known as an **oral cloze procedure**. Tell the children that some words are missing and ask whether they can predict what should be in the space. Reading the text with the children, the teacher pauses briefly when encountering a missing word, writing in the missing words as the children identify them.

Children may accumulate new words they learn, with these collections serving as their personal word files. After they have fifteen or twenty words, they can do sorting activities with their word files (Bear et al., 2000). Finding words that start with the same letter and sound is a way in which some children learn to associate letters and sounds, allowing them to learn best about letters and sounds from words they already know. They can look for words that are names of people, places, animals, colors, foods, and clothing.

If children are collecting the words they can read, they can try to build sentences with them. You might need to demonstrate before asking them to try it. Read their sentences to them if they cannot read them independently. Children can also try to reconstruct the same sentences they have used in their dictated texts.

One nonthreatening way to elicit text that reflects more mature syntax and vocabulary is an adaptation called the *collaborative chart story*. When children are dictating and beginning to read with confidence later in the process, ask them to negotiate their suggested text with the group. You can invite questions from other children about a suggested sentence, for example, by asking how they feel about the way it is stated and how effectively the vocabulary provided expresses what the group wants to say. When children who have dictated sentences with grammatical errors hear suggestions from other children about how it might be said in another way, they invariably agree to the change. The children do not view this collaboration as correction, but rather as reflecting the contributions they all make together in communicating with the audience that will read their text later. It is probably better to accept exactly what is dictated at the beginning of the LEA process so that children can see the direct links among what they say, what you write down, and what the group reads back later.

The language-experience approach can be used with students who are learning to read in English as their second language as a way to initiate students into print of interest and relevance to them (Dixon & Nessel, 1983; Moustafa & Penrose, 1985; Nessel & Jones, 1981). According to Crawford (1993), the language-experience approach also provides a means through which students can experience authentic literature in English that is above their ability to read and comprehend for themselves. After you tell or read a story aloud, the students can then dictate the story back, that is, retell it for you to record, although probably in a less complicated version than the original.

Beginning a language-experience approach activity with a piece of authentic literature will often result in a better structured dictation than the random list of sentences that often results from LEA dictations stimulated by an illustration, a manipulative, or other prompts. Peck (1989) suggests that listening to read-aloud stories helps children to develop a sense of story structure, which should be reflected in their dictated version, and it enhances their abilities to predict in this and other stories. The dictated text allows children to think, talk, read, and write about the piece of literature and to be exposed to its valuable cultural content. At the same time, they are actively interacting with it at a level of comprehension and of second-language proficiency appropriate for their stage of development.

Vocabulary Development

Reading is also a major factor in the vocabulary development of English language learners. Second-language acquisition and literacy in English can contribute mutually to each other's development for intermediate English language learners. In keeping with a meaning-based approach to teaching English language learners, Harmon (1998) provides an excellent contextualized strategy for vocabulary development. She provides two examples of how a teacher uses a new term and then elaborates and expands its meaning immediately:

What can you do to help your ESL students make the transition to English-language reading instruction?

> "Let's start <u>recounting</u> the events of the story. <u>Let's tell about the beginning, middle, and end.</u>"
> "This is an <u>excerpt—a small part.</u>"

In another strategy described by Nagy and colleagues (1993) and by Cummins and Corson (1997), Spanish-speaking students can use cognates they recognize from Spanish and English to support their reading comprehension in English. Words such as *general* are the same in spelling and meaning in both languages, and many other cognates are the same in meaning and similar in spelling, such as an example provided by Nagy and colleagues: *transform* in English and *transformar* in Spanish. But looking beyond their study, children must also be taught to be wary of such false cognates as *actual*, which means *nowadays* in Spanish, and *dime*, which means *give me*.

When children read, their lack of vocabulary knowledge is often an obstacle to comprehension. Because they may have insufficient academically related background knowledge and vocabulary development in the mother tongue that would accompany it, this can be an even greater problem for children who must read in their second language. Vocabulary is an aspect of background knowledge in prereading, but it is treated separately here to examine several concepts that relate more specifically to vocabulary.

One aspect of vocabulary development relates to the richness of language that surrounds children. It is well recognized that children become familiar with the meanings of words when those meanings are highly contextualized, not when they are studied in isolation as new vocabulary words. It follows, then, that a richer language environment should result in increased exposure to contextualized vocabulary and therefore to understanding of their meanings (Crawford, 1994b).

Schools often postpone or even eliminate instruction for at-risk children, however, in the very areas of the curriculum where new vocabulary words will be offered in the most highly contextualized ways—in science, social studies, art, music, health, and other areas of the curriculum. This is even more common for children who are learning in their second language. According to Crawford (1993), teachers must ensure that these areas of the curriculum are provided for all children, including English language learners, and that they are presented so that contextualized exposure to a rich vocabulary is promoted.

Another aspect of vocabulary is the issue of direct instruction. Although many vocabulary words will be acquired incidentally, some literature or content selections will contain a few vocabulary words that must be clearly grasped if the text is to be understood. There will be other words not known to the children that need not be addressed through direct instruction because they are not critical to understanding the selection or because they can be quickly analyzed through the context in which they appear.

Many of the strategies recommended for the activation or development of background knowledge constitute direct approaches to vocabulary instruction. Semantic mapping is one of these strategies, but its application should be limited to those key and conceptually difficult vocabulary terms that are more in the realm of background knowledge. Otherwise,

TEACH IT! 18

"Word Conversations" for Primary Grades

there will be little time left for reading following the completion of anticipation activities before reading.

Adapting Phonics and Decoding Strategies for English Language Learners

English language learners bring to the classroom phonemic awareness of sounds in the mother tongue. They should first learn phonics in the mother tongue out of the context of words they already recognize on sight, probably learned from their print environment and from language experience charts and big books. English language learners who learn phonics in the mother tongue generally have a much easier time learning phonics in English than do children who must learn phonics first in English. Some languages, such as Spanish and Korean, are very regular in their sound/letter relationships. Not only is phonics easier to learn, but children have more confidence in the process than do children who are learning to read in a language in which sound/letter relationships are not regular, such as English.

The language-experience approach and shared reading are holistic strategies for teaching reading. In these strategies, teachers do not begin with phonics. But learning about letters and sounds (phonics) is a part of learning to read in all methods, including these. In a developmental approach to teaching about letters and sounds, children should learn about reading first. They should dictate many LEA charts and read them, learning to read some 100 to 200 words on sight. They should have many shared book reading experiences, and then they are ready to learn about letters and sounds using words they already know in English.

The real dilemma for English language learners is when they must learn phonics in English first. Although they might have learned to speak and understand English, they still lack the phonemic awareness skills in English of a native speaker. For example, a native Spanish-speaking child will speak the forty-three sounds of English using the twenty-five sounds of Spanish. There are only five vowel sounds in Spanish, but fifteen in English. This accounts for the difficulty that Spanish-speaking children have in pronouncing short vowels in English, especially the schwa; they have similar difficulty in "reading" (correctly pronouncing) these sounds in a phonetic approach to reading. Although there are variations in the differences between other languages and English, similar difficulties arise for children who speak those languages. However, for children who learn phonics in their mother tongue, the process of learning English phonics is much easier because they have already figured out how the process works. The process transfers from the mother tongue, even if many of the sounds do not.

Finally, Sleeter and Grant (1999) remind teachers that they need to distinguish between mechanics and meaning when teaching students whose mother tongue is not English or standard American English. They concluded that teachers should not be bogged down in remediation whenever they encounter gaps in student learning that relate more to mechanics than to understanding.

Writing and Spelling

A major principle of a developmental view of literacy is the interdependence of listening, speaking, reading, and writing. Hudelson (1984) observed that English language learners address the four language processes as a totality, not as separate entities. According to Fitzgerald (1993), writing begins when children can draw, and there is no need to wait for reading. These ideas can be extended to English language learners, who should be encouraged to write in the second language early, especially if they have writing skills in their mother tongue. The errors they make should be viewed in the same way that errors in oral production are viewed: as a part of the natural processes of approximation and acquisition (Crawford, 1994a).

PHONICS and PHONOLOGICAL AWARENESS

What advantages may English language learners have in learning phonics in English if they first learn to read in the mother tongue?

WRITING and READING CONNECTIONS

How can we support the development of writing in English for English language learners?

For English language learners, writing can flow out of a variety of language acquisition activities, including the key vocabulary and language-experience approaches to reading and the consolidation strategy of written retellings after reading text. The structuring of their writing or their selection of vocabulary may be further supported through the use of semantic maps.

Spelling is another area in which instructional strategies must be adapted for English language learners. Consistent with the communicative approach principle of minimizing error correction and with the developmental nature of second language acquisition and literacy, described in Chapter 14, teachers of English language learners, like teachers of English speakers, should accept the invented spellings of their children as a very natural aspect of their developmental growth in writing. There are differences, however, in how English language learners will progress through some of the developmental stages of invented spelling.

In the letter name–alphabetic spelling stage of Bear et al. (2000), English language learners begin to approximate an alphabetic orthography and to conceptualize the alphabetic principle (see Chapter 5). They begin to demonstrate the relationship between sound and letter, and they sometimes use letter names as words. They begin to understand the left-to-right convention, and they may begin to segment words. Differences in the nature of invented spelling between languages will appear. The use of consonants tends to predominate over the use of vowels when children write in English as a mother tongue, for example, but vowels predominate over consonants when children write in Spanish as a mother tongue (Ferreiro & Rodríguez, 1994).

In the within-word pattern spelling stage of Bear and colleagues (2000), children have learned most basic rules of the orthographic system. They are aware of such word structures as prefixes, suffixes, contractions, compound words, and homonyms, and they continue to learn some less common spelling patterns and rules. It is at this stage that they begin to recognize when a word looks correct, a phenomenon that corresponds to the natural approach characteristic in which second-language learners begin to recognize when something sounds right or feels right. They are able to spell a large number of words automatically.

English language learners who are literate in another language will tend to move much more rapidly through developmental stages of spelling in their new second language of English than they did in their primary language. Nathenson-Mejia (1989) found that in their English writing, Spanish-speaking children in the beginning stages of English spelling made extensive use of Spanish pronunciation in their invented spellings in English. Edelsky (1982) made the same observation in a more generic sense. She adopted the positive point of view that children are applying some mother tongue writing skills to the second language rather than the negative point of view that it reflected interference from the first language on the second.

TEACH IT! 19

Semantic or Concept Web for Upper Grades

Scaffolding Strategies for Improving Reading Comprehension

Your own experiences in learning another language might remind you of the importance of reading for comprehension as opposed to word calling. Remember that comprehension and communication are the focus of reading and writing. There are many reading strategies that will help to ensure that children focus on comprehension instead of only on correct pronunciation.

The use of scaffolding strategies to support the comprehension of children in general is of great importance; but for English language learners, it is the difference between success and failure (Crawford, 1994a). Some English language learners have tended to be placed in perpetual compensatory or remedial programs in which teachers expect them to learn to read and write by acquiring isolated skills through interaction with incomplete fragments of language. These children rarely move successfully into the mainstream curriculum; more frequently, they leave these programs only when they complete their schooling—all too often as dropouts. Scaffolding strategies sometimes resemble most closely the enrichment activities that teachers of English language learners sometimes never have

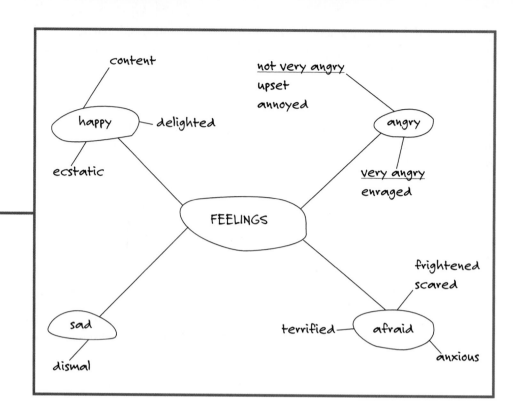

FIGURE 12.3

A Cumulative Semantic Map.

time for because they are busy teaching the isolated skills that the children seem to lack. Variations of two common comprehension strategies are especially effective in working with English language learners.

THE CUMULATIVE SEMANTIC MAP.   Ordinarily, a semantic map is used for activating background knowledge or introducing vocabulary as an anticipation activity before reading. It is developed and completed for one or two related lessons and not referred to subsequently. Teachers often find, however, that they are dealing with some language topics on repeated occasions. Therefore, it can be useful to return to a semantic map on such a topic, to add to it, and to contrast new additions with earlier ones. Crawford has identified this semantic mapping strategy as the **cumulative semantic map** (Crawford, 1994a).

Figure 12.3 shows a cumulative semantic map on the theme of feelings and emotions that has been augmented periodically during the first few weeks of school (Crawford, 2000). A teacher might introduce the new word *furious* from a piece of literature they are about to read and ask children where it should be added to the existing cumulative semantic map for words about feelings and emotions. At that point, the children can discuss how much anger the word *furious* implies, as compared to *miffed, enraged,* and *upset,* which had been added to the semantic map on earlier occasions. They add the new word *furious* to their cumulative semantic map. Many weeks later, the map has been elaborated, as seen in Figure 12.4, and, of course, this process continues through the school year.

When written on stick-on notes, the various words in a cumulative semantic map can be arranged and rearranged in ascending order of increasing anger as children negotiate the meanings with each other. Moustafa (1997) suggests placing words on cards for charts with cellophane tape across the top. The teacher can use the same piece of tape over and over by affixing the cards to a large wall chart made of plastic shower curtain material. This strategy can be adapted to the cumulative semantic map, which facilitates the moving of words from one place to another on the chart or in making room for a new word to be added.

In a writing assignment perhaps several months later, English language learners might refer back to the cumulative semantic map on the wall when they want to select just the right word to convey the degree of anger they have in mind (Crawford, 1994a). Discussing the choice of word with the teacher or with other children will be particularly helpful. When

Cumulative Semantic Map

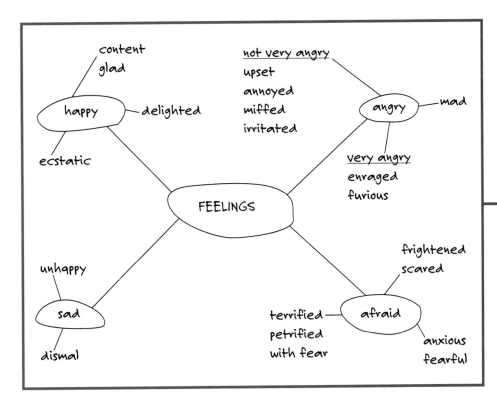

FIGURE 12.4

An Elaborated Cumulative Semantic Map.

children are ready to add yet another synonym for *angry* a week or a month later, they will have the opportunity to review other words or expressions for the same feeling, but within a context of known or somewhat familiar vocabulary. Teachers can view a well-developed cumulative semantic map as a "graphic thesaurus." Other suitable topics for cumulative semantic maps might include *see* (stare, peek, glare, etc.), *motion* (crawl, creep, dawdle, dash, poke along, lope, etc.), and *touch* (poke, tap, jab, stroke, etc.). Only the topics come from the teacher; the source of vocabulary is the literature the children are reading.

If your classroom has a word wall, this might be the place to attach several cumulative semantic maps that are used frequently. If there are so many that they do not all fit, several might be mounted on top of each other on the wall or an easel with a way of folding them up so the one in use during a lesson is visible. At the end of the school year, you might consider passing the cumulative semantic maps on to the children's teacher for the next grade, especially if most of the class will move to the new classroom intact as a group. Many teachers also save the children's portfolios for the children to pick up when they start the next school year. The children can take their portfolios to their new classroom and use them to introduce themselves to the new teacher.

READ-ALOUD ACTIVITIES. English language learners often benefit from read-aloud activities by the teacher, followed by discussion. Vocabulary is presented in context, and someone in the group will likely have some knowledge of most words. Other words may be analyzed by reviewing the illustrations in a story or an appropriate illustration, manipulative, or visual aid provided by the teacher. Because illustrations provide important visual information, paging through a selection and discussing the illustrations before reading provides an opportunity for presenting new vocabulary and for making predictions about the text.

Occasionally, you might find that presenting the entire selection as a read-aloud is needed before English language learners read themselves, especially in a particularly challenging piece. When a parallel version of a text is available in the children's mother tongue, you might choose to read it aloud before the children read later in the second language. Children in school are not bored or disturbed by several exposures to the same literature selection. The familiarity of a story that is an old friend becomes a real comfort. Familiarity

Teaching Connections

You have now seen the balanced literacy approach that is reflected in this book. How can your choices reflect balanced reading instruction in grades 3 to 5 as you address the problems that follow?

Grades 3 to 5

- How can you accommodate your reading program for the third-grade student who reads word by word without expression, unable to answer higher-order questions about the text read?
- Suppose that writing has not been the focus of instruction for your fifth-grade students in grades 1 to 4. How do you begin to incorporate it as an element of your fifth-grade program?

English Language Learners

- You have seen how some sounds in English are difficult for Spanish speakers. How would you go about determining which sounds in English are difficult for speakers of Korean?

- How do you decide when an English language learner is ready to begin formal instruction in English reading? What are the factors that you consider?

Your Portfolio

If you are interviewed for a middle-grade teaching position, you will likely be asked to describe how you would organize a reading/language arts program for the level. Your portfolio should include examples that you can show in response to that question: lesson plans that focus on reading comprehension; a thematic literature unit; student writing samples; and sample assessment tools, such as rubrics and observation criteria.

Teaching Resources

Children greatly increase their abilities to read with comprehension in grades 3 to 5. Their interest in reading authentic literature also grows. This is a good time to begin identifying literature for them. Look at lists of books such as Children's Choices from the International Reading Association (**www.reading.org**). Search on "children's book lists" at Amazon (**www.amazon.com**) for other examples. Then search for the books in the usual places.

---

with the background knowledge and structure of a story permits children to read with better comprehension and with fewer time-consuming visual cues, especially for children's early literacy experiences in English. The read-aloud activity also provides the teacher with the opportunity to demonstrate and model predicting, thinking about context, and other metacognitive strategies in a think-aloud during the teacher's oral reading.

Differentiating Instruction in Grades 3 to 5

By now, you have doubtless concluded that a one-size-fits-all approach to teaching children to read is most inappropriate. Each child needs instruction at an appropriate level, but, fortunately, usually many children have needs in common. Grouping children for instruction is a tricky proposition, but it addresses the need for appropriate instruction for all children. Some advocate for teaching the entire class at one time, a strategy that can be very effective in some areas of the curriculum. For example, placing students in small groups according to individual needs is not a common practice in the areas of science, social science, art, and music.

Whole-Class Instruction

When instruction in reading is consistently conducted with the whole class, it is often characteristic of highly scripted and sequenced direct instruction reading programs. The use of this type of approach implies that all children are the same and that a one-size-fits-all program is adequate for all. In reality, this means that every time a lesson is taught, it is just right for some children, too difficult for children who were unsuccessful in earlier lessons and did not attain prerequisite skills, and repetitious and boring for children who mastered the material weeks, months, or years before. Instruction should be planned to meet individual needs. This does not imply a separate lesson for each individual child, but it does permit children with similar strengths or needs to be grouped together for appropriate instruction. There are some reading/language arts activities that can be conducted with the entire class, such as a review of how to avoid run-on sentences in writing when almost all children show the need, teacher read-aloud activities, library visits, using a video of a story, conducting a poetry hour, and readers' theater (Burns, Roe, & Ross, 1999).

What are the potential benefits of grouping students for instruction?

Grouping: Why and Why Not?

Schools are sometimes tempted to group students homogeneously by reading ability on a classroom basis across an entire school. If there are five fourth-grade classes, why not place the students who are nonreaders in one classroom, those reading at grade level in another, those above grade level in yet another, and so on? The assumption is that each teacher will need to plan only a single reading lesson for the entire class. Teachers need to recognize that one result will often be racial, linguistic, and gender isolation. Another outcome is the classroom at each grade level with the lowest achieving children—twenty-five of thirty children are likely to be boys, and many of them will display behavior problems. English language learners often end up in the same class, despite their need to associate with native English speakers.

When all of these children with important needs are placed in the same classroom, the challenges for the teacher are extreme. The management of behavior in this classroom requires the most able and experienced teacher in the school, but all too often, this class is assigned to the newest teacher. The results can be negative attitudes, low self-esteem, and continuing low achievement. The classroom with the highest achievers will tend to have a preponderance of girls, along with much of the student leadership potential on the grade level. Although this classroom might seem to be an attractive assignment for most teachers, it is also a challenge.

There is really no such thing as a homogeneous group. Even children who have similar levels of achievement at the beginning of the school year will be very different from each other after a few months of instruction in which some gain more than others. In addition, teaching a reading lesson to a classroom-size group might not be the most effective way to provide effective instruction to them. If twenty children in a classroom are really reading at the same level and have similar strengths and needs, most experienced teachers would divide them into two groups and teach similar lessons to each smaller group to maximize individual attention.

In many countries, children are promoted from one grade to the next on the basis of their achievement, not their age. The tradition in the United States has been to promote on the basis of age because of research indicating that children do not benefit from being held back (Wheelock & Dorman, 1988). According to the Texas Education Agency (1996), being older than other students in your grade is a better predictor of future dropping out than underachievement is. In some states, attempts have been made to hold children back who do not reach a standard for their grade level, but most of these efforts are quickly abandoned when the numbers of children retained are much larger than was expected. The result is that children are usually grouped for instruction in reading to better address their different needs.

Grouping is most common in reading and mathematics. The higher the grade level, the greater is the need for grouping children as some fall behind and others forge ahead. In a first-grade classroom, as you have seen, most children are not reading, they are reading some, or they are reading well at a first-grade level. But in a fifth-grade classroom, the children might range from those not reading at all to some reading at a college level. Those who are not reading at all will tend to be children with severe reading disabilities or occasionally immigrant children without school experience or with very limited school experience.

Grouping children within the classroom can also have negative consequences. It does not matter what names the groups have; the children recognize that there are high groups and low groups, and they know which group they are in. This sends an unmistakable message to children in the "low" group. These expectations often become a self-fulfilling prophecy. Children in the "low" group in the first grade are all too often still there in the fifth grade.

Grouping Students without Tracking

The dilemma is how to meet individual cognitive and affective needs while avoiding the negative effects that can result from grouping by ability. Children need to receive reading instruction at their instructional levels, and so teachers must form groups that permit children to read at levels where they will be successful, interested, and engaged. Some fifth graders will be learning beginning reading concepts in the language-experience approach, and some in the same classroom will be reading and enjoying Shakespeare. It is difficult to put children from these two levels together when they are in guided reading lessons. There are two possible solutions to the dilemma, and they can be used at the same time: nonability-based groups and dynamic groups.

GROUPS NOT BASED ON ABILITY AND ACHIEVEMENT. The interest group is a grouping structure that is not based on ability and achievement, perhaps a group of children who are interested in fairy tales. They can all read fairy tales, even the same fairy tale in the same lesson, but from books written at different levels or from the same book but with different levels of teacher support. This allows students who are working at a lower level to work with students reading at higher levels from time to time so that they are able to say, "Sometimes I am in the same reading group as Janie." Interest groups might meet one day a week instead of every day, and they might meet for a month before dissolving so that students can form new and different interest groups. Fountas and Pinnell (1996) add other structures to introduce flexibility, including peer tutoring, cooperative learning pairs, and cross-grade buddies. In literature circles, children who have decided to read the same book, poem, or other text compare and share ideas about what they have read (Daniels, 1994).

STRUGGLING ◆ **READER**

How can dynamic grouping relieve the rigidity of grouping only by reading achievement?

DYNAMIC GROUPING. One other accommodation serves to loosen up the rigidity of grouping by achievement. Occasionally, the teacher should recognize that certain students need to work with a reading group other than their own for specific reasons. A bright but troubled and struggling reader might advance to a higher ability group to read a story for three days because the story will be of great interest to the student and because the student has much background knowledge about it. An otherwise high-achieving reader who has trouble decoding words with prefixes might join a lower-achieving group that happens to be working on that specific skill for a few days.

The ability grouping in Chantell DeLaney's third-grade classroom is what Fountas and Pinnell (1996, 2001) refer to as *dynamic grouping*, bringing students together for a period of time when, and for as long as, they have abilities and needs in common. The most capable students, reading at fourth- and fifth-grade levels in Ms. DeLaney's classroom, occasionally join the group working at the third-grade level, perhaps to learn or practice a needed word recognition skill or comprehension strategy. Often, however, they are working in individualized reading and on projects of interest, periodically meeting with Ms. DeLaney as a small group or conferencing with her.

Differentiated Instruction

Providing Trade Books at the Independent Reading Level

Self-selected reading is an element of the four blocks approach to reading (Cunningham et al., 2007) that requires differentiated instruction, just as the more obvious teacher-directed aspects of reading programs do. Most self-selected reading activities are carried out by children individually, occasionally in paired reading. How then can teachers differentiate instruction in this part of the program?

One of the most important strategies is to provide text in the form of trade books or other reading matter that is at each child's independent level. In our example in Figure 12.1 on page 407, we note that the student has an instructional level at the third-grade level, but an independent level at the second-grade level. This tells us that the teacher will provide formal and directed instruction at the instructional level, which is appropriate given the scaffolding support that the teacher will provide during the lessons: the introduction of new vocabulary, activating background knowledge, perhaps guiding reading with questions, and finally consolidation activities that allow the child to apply new knowledge.

But when the child selects a trade book to read for silent sustained reading (SSR) or self-selected reading, whether in the classroom or at home, that scaffolding support is often absent. The appropriate level of book then will usually be one or two grade levels lower for most children. By providing trade books for the classroom reading center at a variety of levels, a skilled teacher ensures that abundant books are available at the independent levels of all children.

But the teacher should also communicate the need for reading material at the independent level to parents. They will often provide books at home that are at the child's grade level, not the independent reading level. Librarians can help parents and children select books at an appropriate level for independent reading, and so can sales staff at specialized children's bookstores. At chain bookstores, however, parents may need guidance from the teacher about appropriate books. If motivation is high because a child has just received a computer and a book about how to use it, then a capable and highly motivated child might struggle and read successfully at the instructional level or even at the frustration level. But these are not the usual circumstances.

Teachers will find valuable information about the levels of hundreds, if not thousands, of trade books in Fountas and Pinnell's *Leveled Book List, K–8* (2005). Individual publishers of trade books also provide information about the levels of their books.

Echevarria, Vogt, and Short (2004) provide scaffolding suggestions to assist English language learners and other at-risk students in reading in the self-selected mode with books at the independent level. One recommendation is for the teacher to conduct a partial read-aloud of the piece of literature with the student or students who will read it. They can then pair up or work in small groups to continue through the material. Teachers can also scaffold by pointing out the text structure of what they are going to read—chronological in a biography or historical piece, for example.

Organizing and Managing a Learning Community

The lesson in the chapter-opening vignette seemed relatively simple and straightforward, but, of course, Ms. DeLaney doesn't just come in each morning and begin teaching. She has planned activities for students who are not working directly with her as she teaches small groups, she has arranged the furniture in the classroom, she has carefully selected instructional materials, she has scheduled precious instructional time, and she has made decisions about how to assess the outcomes of her teaching for the day.

Children's Identity and Motivation

In Ms. DeLaney's lesson on "Little Red Riding Hood," the focus was only on the group of children she was teaching. Over the period of a week, an observer in Ms. DeLaney's classroom sees a very complicated structure. She is usually working with one of several groups while the other two groups complete independent work, read trade books from the classroom library, write letters for the classroom postal system, work on projects in which reading and writing activities are integrated across the curriculum, use the classroom computers, and work in learning centers. There is much movement of students between groups, orchestrated by Ms. DeLaney as she assesses needs and asks students to join groups for a single lesson, a week, or even a month for activities to meet those needs.

A very important part of her planning involved the other two groups that were working independently while she was teaching the lesson to this group. The other large group that reads slightly below grade level needed much guidance and supervision. They had an independent assignment from the previous day's lesson to complete, but she also had learning centers that they could work in and a large variety of trade books at many levels for them to read. The group that was reading above the third-grade level required less direct supervision. Many of them were working on independent projects from social studies and science, and they were also deeply engrossed in library books that they were reading independently.

During Ms. DeLaney's guided reading lesson, there were intervals in which the children read silently for a few minutes. Ms. DeLaney took advantage of their focus and walked around the classroom to help children with questions. They knew that she would come around during the lesson and that they should not interrupt the group's work. In addition, she used her walks as a preventive classroom behavior management strategy, settling down children who were noisy or off task. But she always did this with a touch on the shoulder, a gentle tug on a pigtail, or a smile that said, "I caught you—back to work now." By the time the lesson group had finished the chunk they were reading, after just a minute or two, Ms. DeLaney was back with the group and seated, ready to continue with them until they read the next chunk of text.

On alternate Fridays, the children participate in an individualized reading program based on the many books Ms. DeLaney has accumulated for her extensive classroom library. They range from large-format picture books and simple stories to novels and nonfiction materials at upper grade and secondary levels. Self-selected silent sustained reading (SSR) characterizes the Friday program. As a good model for the children, Ms. DeLaney demonstrates how she reads for her own pleasure during part of the reading period, but she also spends much of her time conferencing with individual children about what they have been reading and encouraging them.

Managing Students and the Classroom for Learning

One important set of decisions for teachers in grades 3 through 5 concerns how to set up the classroom for instruction in reading and other subject areas. Some elements are inflexible, such as the positions of doors, windows, chalkboards, fixed cabinets, computer network connections, and the sink. But other elements indicate much about the philosophy of the program. Think about the difference between two university classrooms: one with chairs set up in straight rows facing the front, where a podium has been placed for the instructor, and another where there are round tables with chairs around them and no podium or front to the classroom.

One possible middle-grade classroom arrangement for reading/language arts instruction and also instruction in other areas of the curriculum would include the following:

- A U-shaped or kidney-shaped table for small-group lessons, with the teacher seated with back to the wall to be able to observe the entire classroom while teaching

- Movable individual children's desks that can be quickly and quietly rearranged when groups or activities change (two-student desks are only slightly less convenient)
- A library center with numerous trade books at many levels and places to sit, such as cushions on the floor, pillows in an old bathtub (for reading only), or a sofa (check the fire regulations)
- A computer center with at least two or three computers in the classroom
- The author's chair (Hanson & Graves, 1983), a very special chair in which children sit only when sharing their writing with others
- Other learning centers for individual or paired work, such as science, writing, or mathematics, with task cards that require children to read, write, and discuss
- A word wall above the writing center
- A listening center with earphones and a player for audiotapes, videotapes, and/or CD-ROMs
- Easels that can be moved from place to place, even for grades 3 to 5

Most teachers find it necessary to control or limit access to learning centers, which can often disrupt lessons. This can be done by doing the following:

- Limiting the number of students who can work in a center at the same time
- Limiting the amount of time each student can work in each center
- Assigning centers every day, with children rotating each day to a different one
- Occasionally informing children who misbehave when together that they cannot work in a center at the same time until they demonstrate more maturity

All of these controls have negative effects on children's spontaneity and their interests. Most teachers find that they can relax and even eliminate these controls over time, but they are very helpful early in the school year.

Selecting Appropriate Materials

There is a big difference between text used to teach reading at the primary-grade levels and at the fifth-grade level. It is partly in the quantity; fifth-grade students will be able to read more text during a reading lesson than primary-grade students will, but the difficulty of the material is also a major factor. It is easy to observe that text in basal readers at the third-grade level has fewer difficult words and more complex sentences than text has at the fifth-grade level. There is a difference between text included in basal readers and that in authentic literature. The biggest difference between authentic literature and basal reader stories or so-called decodable text is the variety of vocabulary that skilled authors use when they select the precise word needed to best express an idea. This increases the difficulty of the text but also the interest levels of the students (Crawford, 2000).

LEVELED BOOKS. After the teacher determines student reading levels using an informal reading inventory, it is then helpful to be able to identify the levels of textbooks and especially of trade books so that they can be matched to the children's levels. Many thousands of children's trade books have been leveled for the text gradient, a measure of text difficulty developed as a part of the reading recovery program (Fountas & Pinnell, 2001).

According to Fountas and Pinnell (2001), text difficulty is a function of the following factors:

- Book and print features, such as length, print, layout, illustrations, graphic features, and organizational aids
- Themes and ideas, such as interest, sophistication, and maturity
- Language and literary features, such as literary and figurative language and dialogue
- Vocabulary, such as multisyllabic words and content-related words
- Sentence complexity, including length, embedded clauses, and punctuation
- Content, including topics, organization, and special graphic features

- Text structure, including fiction (narrative literary devices such as flashbacks) and nonfiction (compare and contrast, cause and effect, description, temporal sequence, and problem/solution)

The resulting text gradient ranges from A (kindergarten) through Z (grades 7 and 8). Grade-level ranges for typical children are assigned to each letter, which allows teachers to select books that are in the so-called Goldilocks range—not too difficult, not too easy, but just right. They are also within Vygotsky's zone of proximal development. Fountas and Pinnell provide lists of thousands of leveled books in their many publications (Fountas & Pinnell, 1996, 1999, 2001, 2005; Pinnell & Fountas, 2001).

USING TECHNOLOGY IN GRADES 3 TO 5. Technology has the potential for creating many changes in the teaching of reading and language arts, some positive and some perhaps negative. Keep in mind, however, that the promise of instructional television and language laboratories to transform teaching never was realized (Griffith & Lynch-Brown, 2002). Possible roles for technology in grades 3 to 5 will be examined in two dimensions: reading and writing.

In reading. In the area of Web text reading, as contrasted to print text reading, Sutherland-Smith (2002) reported that students needed to use different reading strategies to acquire meaning from the two sources. She based this on student comments about the need to work fast on the Internet, in contrast to a more leisurely style of reading from books. She found that Web text reading was less linear, less hierarchical, and less sequential than print text reading. It was more interactive, allowing the reader to add, change, or move text, blurring the relationship between reader and writer. She described several strategies to help students in their Web text reading, all of which support the inquiry-based technology strategies already offered in Chapter 8:

- Encourage "snatch-and-grab" reading, scanning or reading superficially to find pertinent information and returning to it later if it survived the culling needed when large quantities of information are found
- Help students to focus on finding key words for searches as an important skill
- Encourage students to refine or delimit their problem or question so they are not overwhelmed with the amount of information they encounter
- Provide "sure-thing" links to students for their initial forays into the Internet
- Help students to differentiate between informative text and impressive visual images that might offer little information

In writing. A very effective use of technology in teaching writing in grades 3 to 5 is in the area of word processing. Several word processors are designed for children, including *The Amazing Writing Machine* from Broderbund and *The Student Writing Center for Windows* and the *Children's Publishing Center* from the Learning Company. In addition, *Bank Street Writer* III is a program that has been available in various versions for both Windows and Apple platforms for many years. Many teachers find that they can use Microsoft Word or the more simple word processing program included in Microsoft Works with children, teaching only the aspects of these complex programs that are needed for their writing. The appearance of the screen can be simplified by suppressing some of the toolbars and reducing the numbers of functions in those that remain to what is necessary for that grade level.

Finally, Wood (2000) has developed many interesting activities that incorporate the use of technology into the writing process:

TECHNOLOGY

How can technology enrich reading and writing instruction in grades 3 to 5?

WRITING and READING CONNECTIONS

How can teachers incorporate a simplified approach to word processing into the writing program?

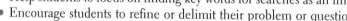

Computers can serve a number of purposes in the classroom. What do you think is the most common use of technology in the literacy classroom?

- Use the Web to publish student work; it is very exciting for children to see the results of their writing published on the Internet, perhaps with digital photos they have taken.
- Initiate e-mail exchanges between children in which they write to each other about topics of common interest; Wood provides an example of two boys comparing Quidditch teams (from the Harry Potter books) they have organized (in their imaginations), whose members are well-known American professional basketball players.
- Help children to establish their writing portfolios on their personal or class Web page.
- Encourage children to develop their own writer's voice. They might even want to pretend to be someone else to write in a new voice.

Involving Family and Community

FAMILY   LITERACY

How can teachers take advantage of home literacy opportunities to enhance reading instruction in the classroom?

Adults other than teachers play major roles at home and at school in supporting literacy instruction, even in the middle grades.

At Home

Authentic environmental print is a valuable resource that teachers can exploit in the home. Purcell-Gates, L'Allier, and Smith (1995) provide valuable print-embedded family literacy activities that are especially useful for children in grades 3 to 5 because they are authentic. Among them are the following:

- Daily living routines, such as shopping lists, reading recipes, and cooking together
- Entertainment, such as reading novels, storybooks, or television program descriptions
- School-related activity, such as homework or school assignments
- Interpersonal communication, such as notes on the refrigerator, e-mail
- Religion, including reading stories from the Bible, the Torah, the Koran, and other religious books treasured by the family
- Participating in information networks, such as sharing scores of sporting events, news of interest, and reactions to new films
- Work-related tasks, such as reading instructions, pay-stub information, and catalogs

Teachers often give students a consolidation or application activity to complete at home after their daily reading lesson. This activity may involve reading aloud to parents, siblings, or others who live in the home. When students are asked to read aloud, they should read something they have already read and practiced in the classroom. If they are to read something new, it should ordinarily be at their independent level, not at the instructional level (see the Differentiated Instruction box earlier in this chapter). When children struggle with reading aloud, potentially a very positive experience and one the teacher wants the child to have, it can turn into a negative experience with a well-meaning parent who tries to help by criticizing or by teaching a phonics lesson.

Similarly, the teacher might send the parents a note asking them to listen to the child read for ten minutes from an assigned book. The parent wants to do more and asks the child to read for thirty minutes from a more difficult book. Again, the well-meaning parent is trying to help the child, but fails to understand the importance of following the teacher's directions carefully.

At School

The presence of other adults in the classroom can be an important asset. Teacher assistants or instructional aides are paid paraprofessionals who may work all day or part of a day to support the teacher. They might range from a minimally educated community resident to a university student who is ready for student teaching. Paraprofessionals are particularly important in working with English language learners.

Another source of adult support in the classroom is the parent volunteer, who might also be a grandparent or other extended family member or caregiver. Tinajero and Nagel (1975) suggest that you need only invite participation. They recommend that you ensure in advance that parents have the needed skills to accomplish assigned tasks and that the activities you request are culturally appropriate. You might find it helpful to demonstrate for adult volunteers so their roles are clear. Adult volunteers can make many important contributions, including sharing information in oral discussions; tutoring; participating in journal activities by responding to children's entries; reading aloud to students, including in the mother tongue other than English, where appropriate; helping with homework assignments in after-school study; storytelling; and sharing life events, personal oral histories, and job experiences.

The reading program for most children changes as they proceed through the grades, with more emphasis on reading comprehension, silent reading, reading in the content areas of the curriculum, and writing in grades 3 through 5. There is still attention to phonics and other aspects of word recognition, but it occupies less time than it does in the primary grades. Developing fluency and automaticity may still receive some attention in the third grade.

The organizational structures for teaching reading are based on the four blocks framework that includes guided reading, working with words, self-selected reading, and writing. Teachers can use three typical stages of reading lessons for planning that reflects this framework: anticipation activities to build interest and connect students to background knowledge, guided reading activities to build knowledge through scaffolding students' reading and comprehension of text, and consolidation reading activities where students apply new knowledge and have opportunities for writing and self-selected reading. These stages are supplemented with mini-lessons focused on word study or another specific skill that usually have emerged from the text to be read in the lesson. Long-term planning can be systematized with thematic literature units that are often integrated with science and social studies instruction, even including critical literacy.

There is more variation in the reading levels of students in the middle grades than in the primary grades, and the need for grouping for instruction arises. Most useful is dynamic grouping that is flexible and includes multiple structures for instruction, including small ability groups, interest groups, buddy reading and cooperative learning pairs, peer tutoring, occasional whole-class instruction, and the frequent formation of temporary focused groups to address common weaknesses of students from all ability levels.

The informal reading inventory (IRI) is an important informal assessment tool for identifying students' reading levels. It is ordinarily administered during the first week or two of school and then as needed for individual students whose achievement changes, periodically through the school year. Formal assessment usually takes the form of standardized or normed reading achievement tests, whose results are interesting for school and district-level decision making, although less so for instructional decisions about individual students.

Most English language learners who have learned to read in the mother tongue are by now able to understand and speak English at an intermediate level. They are also often ready to begin a transition to English language reading in the third grade. Many scaffolding and support activities are particularly important for these students as they begin reading in their new second language, English.

You have now seen that students' abilities to understand text vary widely and students are grouped accordingly for some important comprehension instruction. Teachers must then be able to find textbooks, literature, and trade books that reflect those levels. Many thousands of books have been leveled on a gradient of difficulty, and teachers can quite accurately select books for students for whom they have assessment data. There is a growing role for the effective use of technology in the classroom in the middle grades. Children can do extensive reading on the Internet, but they must be prepared to deal with the immense amounts of information returned in the typical search. The introduction of new reading skills, such as identifying descriptors and criteria, scanning titles of returned references, and delimiting problems or assignments done on the Internet, will assist in their effectiveness. Children can make effective use of various types of word processors in the writing process at these grade levels.

Adults other than the teacher can make important contributions to students' progress in literacy. There are many activities that parents and caregivers can provide at home to complement efforts in the classroom. Teachers also need to take advantage of the services that other adults can provide in the classroom as paraprofessionals and volunteers.

For Your Journal

1. Using the lesson plan and the strategies illustrated in the chapter and the strategies you would like to incorporate from throughout this book, plan a similar lesson for the "Three Little Pigs," another story that most children know. Working with a partner should enrich your thinking as well as speed up completion of the task.

2. Identify a theme you could introduce to a class, such as "change." Visit the children's section of your local bookstore or public library, or look on a search engine for books, such as that at amazon.com. Try to find three trade books at about the same grade level that fit into the theme of your unit. Develop activities and assessment tools for integrating these books into the unit.

Taking It to the World

Now that you have moved into grades 3 to 5, you have found that most children have acquired a concept of print, they are able to decode many words they encounter, especially when they are contextualized in connected text, they are beginning to read silently, they are understanding what they read, and they are beginning to express themselves in writing. What changes from a second-grade reading program do you now expect to find in the use of literature, in word recognition instruction, in reading in the content areas, and in writing as children enter the third grade?

Write down one or two thoughts with respect to each of these elements of literacy, and compare notes with another student. Try to agree on a single list of how the focus on these elements might be different from working with K–2 students.

Technology Connections

1. Teachers can find reviews of software and books appropriate for the classroom by visiting The Kids Domain section of the The Kaboose Network at **www.kidsdomain.com**. Check out the latest review of a Broderbund's *Amazing Writing Machine* word processing program for children on the Internet at **www.kidsdomain.com/review/kdr/ awmachine.html**.

2. Using a search engine, such as Google (**www.google.com**), complete an Internet search for reviews on *Kid Pix, Reading Blasters, Bank Street Writer III*, and *Mattel Interactive Student Writing*. What do the reviews say about these technology products for children? How could they be used in grades 3 to 5?

3. Visit Education World's "Technology in the Classroom Center" online at **www .educationworld.com/a_tech**. Identify at least three technology products recommended by Education World's tech experts as appropriate for students in grades 3 to 5. What do the experts say about these products?

Review the following key words from the chapter and then connect to Research Navigator (**www.researchnavigator.com**) through this book's Companion Website to conduct a search into research on each of the various topics as they relate to reading and literacy education today.

automaticity	independent reading level	oral retelling
cumulative semantic map	informal reading inventory (IRI)	semantic feature analysis
fluency	instructional level	sustained silent reading
frustration level	oral cloze procedure	thematic literature unit

Companion Website

To access chapter objectives, practice tests, weblinks, and flashcards, visit the Companion Website at www.ablongman.com/templeallchildren2e.

Go to Allyn & Bacon's MyLabSchool (**www.mylabschool.com**), enter Assignment ID RMVG into the Assignment Finder. Watch the video, *Content Area Reading,* in which a third-grade teacher demonstrates teaching content area reading in a science curriculum.

Question: Why is it important to implement reading instruction in content area classrooms? You may also answer the questions at the end of the clip and e-mail your responses to your instructor.

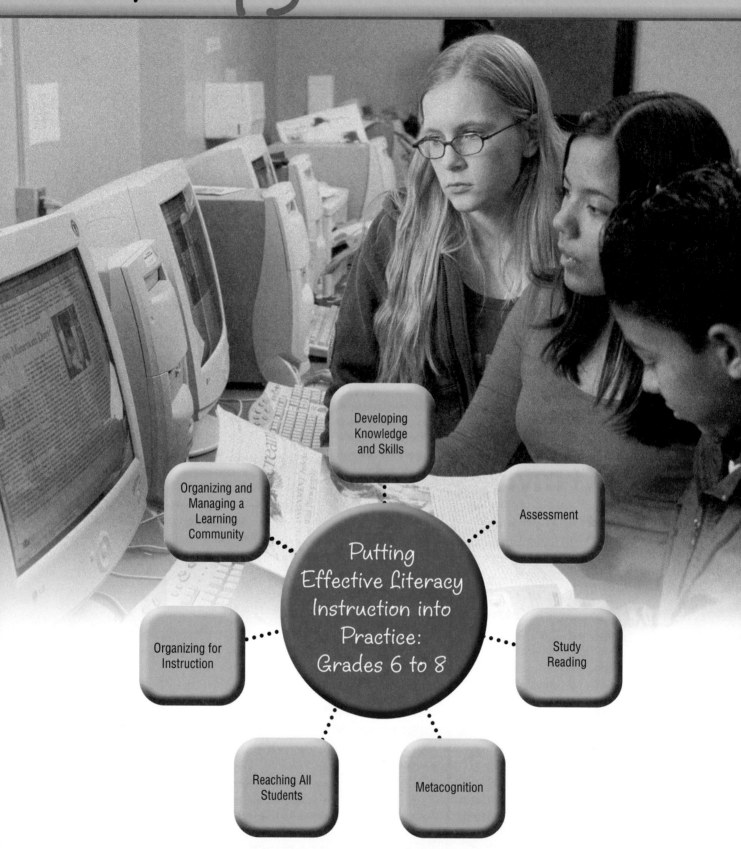

chapter 13

Developing Knowledge and Skills

Organizing and Managing a Learning Community

Assessment

Putting Effective Literacy Instruction into Practice: Grades 6 to 8

Organizing for Instruction

Study Reading

Reaching All Students

Metacognition

Putting Effective Literacy Instruction into Practice: Grades 6 to 8

Anticipation Guide

The following statements will stimulate your thinking about the topics of this chapter. Answer true or false in response to each statement. As you read and learn more about the topics in these statements, double-check your answers. See what interests you and prompts your curiosity toward more understanding.

_____ ● Schools can safely stop teaching reading by the time students reach the middle grades. Virtually all students will have learned to read adequately by then.

_____ ● Middle grade students should be assured daily opportunities to read because reading ability grows with practice.

_____ ● Having students post new words they have learned on a vocabulary bulletin board is effective because it helps for students to take ownership of their learning.

_____ ● "Possible Sentences" is a method of fitting punishments to crimes, and "Personal Clues" is a means of locating criminals.

_____ ● Reading aloud to students and encouraging them to listen to audiotapes is important because it provides an internal model of fluent reading.

_____ ● An Informal Reading Inventory reports students' reading ability on four levels.

_____ ● An important form of assessment is for the teacher to learn to look and listen carefully as students read.

_____ ● Part of a teacher's responsibility is to help students organize their time to afford more time for reading and studying.

_____ ● It is pointless to ask students to reflect on their strategies when they read because fluent readers are simply unaware of what they are doing.

_____ ● Teachers should be sure to give English language learners extra minilessons on reading materials before that material is discussed in class.

Integrated Reading Instruction in a Sixth-Grade Classroom

As part of an integrated unit on the Middle Ages, Rasheed Graham's sixth-grade students had the choice of reading *The Midwife's Apprentice* or *Catherine, Called Birdy.* Mr. Graham was concerned that some of the students might encounter difficulty with the setting and wanted to revisit a scene to emphasize its meaning and check for their understanding early on in the reading of one of the books. During Friday story share, Mr. Graham has students sit in a circle on the floor while he reads from what he considers a pivotal chapter in the *The Midwife's Apprentice* where the main character is shopping at a medieval market. The students follow along with the text as he reads aloud. Mr. Graham's goal is to make sure the students reflect on the significance of this section. While reading aloud, he stops to comment and ask the students for their thoughts on the content, and then he asks them to make predictions: "I thought you'd like to revisit this chapter because it seems like such a big moment for the main character. Let's see how we all interpreted this section. What do you all think about it? Let me read this part again while you follow along. The setup, as you recall, is that Beetle, the main character, has been directed by the midwife to buy some items at the market. Beetle has never been there before, and she is overwhelmed by all the new sights, smells, and sounds."

Mr. Graham reads from Chapter 5, then stops after reading, "She sniffed all the spices for free before buying nutmeg and pepper. The hangman was doing a brisk trade in murderer's wash water." To help the students develop the skill of reading for understanding, Mr. Graham has the students think critically about a sentence that might otherwise go unnoticed because of lack of understanding. He asks, "What do you think that means? It's not a beheading, but a hanging, so what do you think is going on?"

Jason speaks up, "'Murderers' wash water'? Isn't that just dirty bathing water? Why would anyone want that?"

"Does anyone have any ideas?"

"I guess it's like collecting things, you know, like stamps or rabbits feet," offers Tran.

Next, Mr. Graham reads a section in which the main character sees an ivory comb at a merchant's table. She loves the comb but has no money to buy it. Mr. Graham asks, "What do you think will happen? Will she use the money given her by the midwife to buy the comb or will something else transpire?"

Kayleigh states, "I hope she doesn't do that. If she does, the midwife will fire her, and she'll be worse off than she was before."

"I think she gonna steal it," calls out Deanna.

Mr. Graham continues to prod the students' thinking: "What makes you think that she would do that? Is there anything in her character that makes her out to be either a thief or irresponsible? Can you show that to me in the text?"

Here, Mr. Graham has asked students to match their predictions with the character's actual behavior so that they learn that predictions need to be linked to previous knowledge of events and actions. Then he continues reading and stops to help students focus on the key to this section: the development of the main character.

As for vocabulary, Mr. Graham checks to see how the students have dealt with some of the descriptive words and phrases the author had used in creating this scene. He first asks the students whether there are any particularly memorable descriptive phrases they liked. Then he focuses their attention on one that he found rich, asking them to turn to page 29 and read the paragraph silently, looking for the phrase he wrote on the board: "charming solemnity." Mr. Graham asks them what image that phrase evokes for them. Once they locate the phrase in the sentence, "Although, or perhaps because, she was new at the bargaining game, Beetle handled it with such charming solemnity that the merchant took a fancy to the skinny young thing and, with a broad wink, threw the comb with the cat into the pack with the flasks."

When there is no response, he asks them to try to define the meaning of the word *solemnity* as a reference to the way in which the main character bargained for spices: "Can anyone figure out what *solemnity* means? You might want to see if you can figure it out by reading it in the context of the paragraph."

One student offers, "Does it mean that she was nice to the merchant, maybe nicer than most people, especially the midwife?"

"That's a good guess," Mr. Graham says, "but what do you think the word actually means? Can we find the root word and work from there?"

He writes the word on the board as the students agree that the root word was *solemn*, but nobody seems able to define it. At that point, Mr. Graham suggests that a synonym is "serious, in a dignified manner." "Sometimes we think of the memorial services for those who died on 9-11 as very solemn," he says.

He then asks what the phrase would mean if we read "charming seriousness." "Why do you think this might be an appropriate way to describe Beetle?"

Jason responds, "Well, she probably was pretty scared doing this bargaining for the first time, and she knew she had to do well for the midwife, so she would probably have been pretty serious. 'Charming'? Well, the guy really seemed to like her, so she must have had some special way about her that he liked."

Jamaal adds, "Yes, and on page 31 it says that 'Beetle stood perfectly still. What a day. She had been winked at, complimented, given a gift, and now mistaken for the mysterious Alyce who could read.' So she must have been pretty interesting and attractive to others even though she didn't think so. 'Charming'!"

"Maybe she won't be so solemn the next time she goes to town!" pipes up Kara.

Mr. Graham is pleased that the discussion has returned to the word *solemn* and that it is attracting attention so it can become part of the words they would attend to later. He decides to keep *solemn* on the board and return to it later to build a larger set of associations for it with the students.

He also decides to take this phrase a step further and asks whether anyone can stand up and adopt a pose that would reflect "charming solemnity." Amid giggles, some hands come up, and Mr. Graham

asks one student to mime the phrase. "It worked!" Mr. Graham thinks to himself.

Mr. Graham had decided to do this lesson after careful consideration of the students' responses to the initial chapters of the story. He observed the students' responses in their journals and through his one-on-one discussions with three of the students. He quickly diagnosed their weaknesses in attending to and being able to use the descriptions of the setting and of Beetle. An initial check of students' vocabulary knowledge also had reinforced his need to guide students to the key terms, as they were generally unfamiliar with much of the language used by the author. Mr. Graham, therefore, planned this lesson (attending to details) with his students' learning needs in mind. As he guided their responses in this lesson, he made mental notes to himself, which he wrote in his student observation notebook later, about their participation during the lesson. For example, he noted the responses of both students who had elaborated on the meaning of "charming solemnity" by finding added information in the text. These were the kinds of uses of the text he was trying to scaffold.

Reading instruction is just as important in the middle grades as it is in the first grade. However, in recent years, there has been a declining emphasis on middle-level reading. Many schools have dropped the teaching of reading by the middle grades. This may be because of the great attention paid to content standards, and, also, many schools want to fit in more elective options for students. However, not teaching reading is shortsighted, because reading is part of learning across the curriculum and specific reading skills and strategies are needed in many different subject areas. Middle-level readers have increasing demands placed on them to become flexible and competent in reading a much broader range of materials than they had to read in earlier grades.

As students mature, the range of reading strategies they need expands as well. Both national and state standards include a range of areas of reading expected during the middle-school years. Most state standards specify levels of work that indicate that students are able to read in these ways. Some show examples of the levels of response that can be expected from competent students. Some states also include lists of the books that students should know and be able to discuss for each grade level. State Web sites often have examples of proficient student work. If you are unsure of what middle-grade students are capable of doing, these sources are good to use—and also to show students so that they can develop a realistic assessment of their own work in relation to what others are doing.

Adding to the complexity of reading instruction in the middle grades is the changing structure of this level of schooling. Many schools are organized into content departments, so students move from teacher to teacher, creating challenges in efforts to provide flexibility in time and integration of reading and writing with content-area learning. When students have multiple teachers and the curriculum becomes very content intense, aspects of good reading instruction often get overlooked. This chapter provides a framework for thinking about what needs to be taught and examines how different classrooms are organized so students have the opportunities to learn that they deserve. Recognizing the importance of reading for older students, the International Reading Association's Commission on Adolescent Reading (Moore et al., 1999) has published a document that lists seven reading rights of adolescents, as shown in Table 13.1.

TABLE 13.1

Reading Rights for Adolescents

1. Adolescents deserve access to a wide variety of reading materials that they can and want to read.

2. Adolescents deserve instruction that builds both the skill and desire to read increasingly complex materials.

3. Adolescents deserve assessments that show them their strengths as well as their needs and that guide their teachers to design instruction that will best help them grow as readers.

4. Adolescents deserve expert teachers who model and practice explicit instruction in reading comprehension and study strategies across the curriculum.

5. Adolescents deserve reading specialists who assist individual students having difficulty learning to read.

6. Adolescents deserve teachers who understand the complexities of individual adolescent readers, respect their differences, and respond to their characteristics.

7. Adolescents deserve homes, communities, and a nation that will support their efforts to achieve advanced levels and provide the support necessary for them to succeed.

Developing Knowledge and Skills

Given the wide range of reading development needed during the middle years, classroom instruction needs to be carefully structured so that all aspects of reading can be included. As a teacher, you need to ensure that you attend to each of these through the programs you develop. The following sections provide an overview of nine components to include in your reading program.

Daily Opportunities to Read

Reading is not a single activity, but one that is complex and that changes according to the situation, purpose, and type of text. For students to develop as flexible readers, they should be given a variety of purposeful reading opportunities each day. Each new type of text requires special attention, and the classroom teacher must supply assistance to students in approaching new materials. Teachers can remind students to adapt their reading strategies to their purposes and materials. Skimming headings and skipping from one chapter or section to another can be an appropriate strategy to use when reading for specific information. Reading and rereading may be the tactic to adopt when trying to understand and appreciate a poem. Some of the various purposes that students have for reading different texts include the following:

- Self-selected texts for personal enjoyment
- Texts for group discussions and sharing with others
- Content-area learning from textbook and resource materials, news magazines, newspapers, and electronic texts
- Experiences with poetry, humorous word plays, and cartoons
- Texts that enable students to perform tasks and follow directions
- Texts for specific problem-solving and learning activities

One of the most important kinds of reading is self-selected, independent reading. It is clear that students who read widely have a great advantage over students who do not read much or who never engage in self-selected reading. Cunningham and Stanovich's (1998) article, "What Reading Does for the Mind," makes a strong case for wide reading. The article summarizes data from various studies that show that relying on oral input to learn is just not adequate. An analysis of the vocabulary load of various books and television programs demonstrates that even preschool children's books have a more sophisticated range of vocabulary than adult television shows. Students will never encounter the words and concepts they need to succeed in a professional world if they do not read. When middle-level students read this information, many become convinced of the importance of their continued independent reading. It is through engagement in a great deal of reading that we encounter the concepts and forms of written discourse needed for life. We must keep reading!

Daily Reading at the Appropriate Instructional Level

Finding a balance between appropriately challenging reading materials and those that students can handle independently is part of each teacher's task. Students will improve in their reading when they have instructional-level materials that both challenge and reward them. If reading materials are too difficult, students cannot apply their skills to extend their proficiency. If materials are too easy, they do not need to apply their skills, so finding the instructional middle is essential. This is the zone in which students can develop as readers. Even so, situations in which the student must deal with materials that are too easy or too hard will still occur. Students need some easy materials so that they can gain pleasure from reading and move comfortably through texts.

In whole-class instruction, many students also will be faced with materials that are above their instructional level. In spite of these situations, support mechanisms are available and should be used to assist students. Some of these support mechanisms include the following:

- Prereading activation of knowledge and vocabulary under teacher or adult guidance, which might involve seeing videos to set the context and build knowledge
- Audiotapes of texts
- Use of buddy or partner reading
- Assistance from older or adult readers
- Adapted, easier texts on the same topic

Integrating Reading and Writing

Both reading and writing develop better when they are taught as companion tools for learning about and expressing ideas. Integrating units of content instruction with language arts skill development provides a rich context in which to help students learn. With more extensive units, teachers have time to develop students' background knowledge and to help them find their own questions and interests. Thus, the instruction can be personal and focused. Reading more deeply on a particular topic helps students to gain control of the ideas and learn the vocabulary and concepts more fully than a quick covering of curriculum often provides. As student knowledge of a topic increases, the student becomes more able to write about it with a sense of confidence and perspective. Examples of situations that encourage integration of curriculum and reading and writing together are included in this chapter, both in the opening vignette and later as we explore organizational options for teachers. Additional options include the following:

- Science fairs, history fairs, family history projects, and other events put on by a class, school, or larger organization that encourage projects for which students, working as individuals, pairs, or small groups, choose topics, conduct research, and create exhibits. All language arts are integrated when students engage in these types of inquiry and sharing.

- Addressing broad questions, as in the Great Books Program (Plecha, 1992) and the Paidea program (Adler, 1982), with groups coming together after reading to discuss key issues and topics raised. After rich discussions, students can write their own points of view on one of the questions raised. They might begin by using a graphic organizer to help them compare and contrast ideas raised or to identify a theme statement and then list examples and details that support their perspective.

- Inquiry projects in which students frame their own areas of inquiry around current problems and questions in the students' world and then go about answering their questions. Sharing the results of their inquiries becomes a shared, community event so students need to present their findings in visual, written, and oral formats (see the World of Reading box).

Strategies for Independent Reading

Various types of texts and tasks can provide models with which to teach specific strategic behaviors. To help students develop these strategies, you need to incorporate them in your planning for each part of the text lesson: before, during, and after the instruction as they *Anticipate, Build knowledge,* and *Consolidate* (ABC) what they learn. You need to explain how to use the strategies and the benefits that come from them. Then students can apply the specific strategies or make modifications that fit their own styles and preferences within the general ABC framework as they learn.

ANTICIPATING.   Students need to learn some simple strategies they can use before reading that will assist their learning. First, they need to learn the importance of establishing

The World of Reading

The Nation's Report Card

Since 1969, the National Center for Education Statistics (NCES) has assessed the educational progress of our nation's children in a variety of subjects, including reading, mathematics, science, writing, history, civics, geography, and the arts. Known officially as the National Assessment of Educational Progress (NAEP), and unofficially called "the Nation's Report Card," these periodic assessments have two major goals: To measure student achievement in the context of instructional experiences and to track change in achievement of fourth-, eighth-, and twelfth-grade students over time in selected content domains.

The degree of interest in education today is unparalleled in American history. More than ever before, parents, educators, and policymakers are concerned with whether America's children will have the knowledge and skills necessary to be productive members of our global society. NCES points out, however, that we can only know if our schools are succeeding in this task if the nation has impartial information about what students know and can do, whether their performance has improved or declined, and the ways they study and learn. The Nation's Report Card is intended to provide a common yardstick across all states and districts for evaluating student performance objectively and to monitor whether that performance changes over time.

Although the NAEP has been conducted at some level since 1969, the fall of 2003 marked a significant step in the assessment. While participation in NAEP is voluntary, the No Child Left Behind Act provides strong incentives for school districts and states to participate. Beginning with the fall 2003 assessment, any state receiving Title 1 grants from the federal government must participate in national and state assessments at least once every two years in reading and mathematics in grades 4 and 8. Therefore, 2003 marked the first year all 50 states participated, which included approximately 187,000 fourth graders and 155,000 eighth graders. For the reading assessment, students answered a combination of multiple-choice and constructed-response questions after reading three types of texts from typical grade-appropriate sources, representing different contexts for reading:

- Reading for literary experience
- Reading for information
- Reading to perform a task (grade 8)

Achievement is reported in two ways—scale scores and achievement levels. Scale score results report the distribution of achievement for groups and subgroups. Achievement levels catego-

rize student achievement as Basic, Proficient, and Advanced and are used to report results in terms of a set of standards for what students should know and be able to do. Under the No Child Left Behind Act, the goal is for all students to score as proficient in math and reading by 2014 or face sanctions.

Results from the 2003 NAEP for Reading indicate reading achievement remained relatively flat with little change from 1992 or 2002 in the average score for fourth graders and the score for eighth graders, decreasing one point from 2002. Eighth graders did show improvement over 1992 scores. However, although 63 percent of fourth graders and 74 percent of eighth graders read at or above basic level, 37 percent of fourth graders and 26 percent of eighth graders read at a below basic level.

In addition to the national test, part of the NAEP testing in 2003 was the second step in the Trial Urban District Assessment (TUDA) of Educational Progress, funded as part of the No Child Left Behind Act. The first TUDA, conducted by NAEP in 2002, examined reading and writing in five urban districts. In 2003, nine public urban districts (including the original five) participated in the TUDA in reading and mathematics at grades 4 and 8. Scores showed continued differences between ethnic groups and males and females, although these gaps indicated some narrowing. Results of the TUDA portion of the NAEP indicate all but one of the participating urban districts scored lower than the national average at both grades 4 and 8, with more students reading at a level below the national average.

NAEP is not without its critics as some see what was once considered a relatively neutral assessment now being used to assess individual state testing as well. Critics worry that linking results to federal funds will ultimately lead to a national curriculum and remove individualism from states. Some educators also feel that such a national assessment could be an "indictment" in some cases and put added pressure on individuals and school systems. Regarding the test results, then–Secretary of Education Rod Paige remarked, "we are moving in the right direction; but we are nowhere near satisfied with what we are trying to accomplish. We will not be satisfied until the achievement gap is completely closed and all students are reading at very high levels, at proficient levels."

For a complete review of the findings and to examine sample questions and evaluations, visit the Nation's Report Card online at **http://nces.ed.gov/nationsreportcard**.

Source: National Center for Education Statistics, National Assessment of Educational Progress (NAEP), 2003 Reading Assessment.

purposes for reading. Remind students repeatedly that they can read texts in different ways and that the manner in which they read a text should grow out of their purpose for reading. Review several purposes for reading:

- Wanting to skim a text or scan some kind of reading material to see what it contains
- Reading for enjoyment
- Reading to learn how to do something
- Reading to remember facts and ideas

Second, show students how to survey or preview the materials to determine both the external and internal features of the text. Explain to students that visual clues and signal words are features provided as aids make comprehension easier. External features include visual clues such as chapter and section headings, changes in typeface and font size, and illustrations and charts. Internal features include signal words that point to the text's structure. "Once upon a time," for example, signals the beginning of a fictional narrative. Words and phrases such as *consequently*, *therefore*, *because of*, and *as a result of* indicate the use of a cause-and-effect pattern.

Finally, students need to learn how to activate what is already known about the topic. Remind them that they will better understand what they read if they can connect it to what they already know both about the topic and about the way in which it is presented. Some ways to activate prior knowledge are the following:

- Brainstorming (Students can individually, in pairs, or in groups make lists of what they already know and then group these items into categories.)
- Writing out a list of questions they want answered
- Predicting what they expect will be in the text

BUILDING KNOWLEDGE. While reading, students add to what they know and deepen understanding as they construct meaning from the text ideas by doing the following:

- Making and confirming predictions
- Visualizing
- Summarizing and drawing inferences
- Generating questions
- Making connections
- Self-monitoring their progress
- Reflecting on an author's purposes and voice
- Checking accuracy of sources
- Comparing various texts on the same theme or topic

Ways of saving the ideas and images encountered in reading include using journals, bookmark notes, sticky notes, and graphic organizers. Writing and drawing require active thinking and processing and help to encode information in long-term memory as well as to create memory aids to help retrieve information later.

CONSOLIDATING NEW UNDERSTANDING. After students complete a text, they can review the whole and create a summary for themselves, generalize from the ideas, consider the text in relation to its purposes and content, make connections to other texts and their own experiences, participate in group sharing or writing experiences, identify themes and create interpretations of literary pieces (essential to the enjoyment and appreciation of literature), and reconstruct the major ideas of informational texts.

Engaging in Inquiry

Students also learn how to engage in inquiry projects and research. As they use their language skills in exploring new ideas, they have a real opportunity to make use of a wide variety of resources. Students engage their own thinking in both real and important pursuits. These applications of research and thinking abilities are not only made in language arts classes but across the curriculum. They need to develop their abilities to do the following:

- Ask good questions
- Seek appropriate sources of materials and evaluate their quality
- Synthesize ideas from multiple sources of information
- Use electronic media as a resource in learning, both in seeking information, organizing it, and in presenting ideas to others
- Create written, visual, or oral presentations to share findings

By the middle grades, instruction focuses on content area reading and helping students to develop a structured approach that will help them with formal school work.

At some point in the middle grades, schools introduce the more formal aspects of writing research papers and reports. This is where the teacher can provide a great deal of structure and guidance, because it is usually the first time such formal work has been required in which students need to show footnotes or references and develop a bibliography. Establish explicit guides for students and clear timetables for the work. You might have the students track their research and turn in weekly journal entries indicating what has been done during the time allocated so that you and the student ensure that things move forward. When there are questions or issues, conduct conferences with the students on their progress. This process of developing students' research skills is an example of where teachers can carefully scaffold the initial two components of good instruction: demonstration and immersion and attention to detail. Because the research takes so long to complete, you are preparing students for work they will be expected to do more independently in high school. Middle schools can help students to become more familiar with the research and writing process by giving added research opportunities with guided practice.

Strategies for Building Vocabulary

In the middle grades, students regularly encounter words in texts that they never hear in oral communication. Therefore, they must learn to attend to these new terms and have strategies to remember them. Vocabulary plays a crucial role in content learning because terms convey key concepts, and even familiar words often take on different and specific meanings. For example, consider the word *angle*; it means one thing in mathematics, in social studies it has another meaning, as in "what was the government's angle on the incident," and in general use it can be either a noun or verb (e.g., "the stream angled through the woods" or "he loved angling in the stream").

There are many ways in which teachers help students develop their language facility. A key to students' continuing vocabulary development in the middle grades is increasing their understanding of the ways in which words are formed and also how words enter English. When students become sensitive to identifying new words that they perceive as important, the chances of their being interested in words and retaining the ones they select are higher (Blachowicz & Fisher, 1996). Encouraging students to look for words outside of the classroom also is an important component in their developing sensitivity to words. Beck and McKeown (1983) found that the most significant component of their rich vocabulary instruction program was the word *wall*. Almost incidentally at first, one of the teachers made bulletin board space and encouraged students to post examples of the new words they were learning in class. This factor alone significantly improved the students' learning. Making vocabulary learning interesting and giving students ownership are two key ingredients of successful activities. As you plan your approach to vocabulary development, keep in mind several important components. Just playing games with words, for instance, is not enough. Nor is doing spelling and vocabulary worksheets. Table 13.2 identifies six basic elements of a good vocabulary program.

TABLE 13.2

Basic Elements of a Good Vocabulary Program

- The teacher models interest in language.
- Students engage in enjoyable word play.
- Students become attentive to new words and self-select words to learn.
- Students learn about the history and growth of English including the nature of words—affixes, combining forms, base words, and derivatives.
- Students develop basic strategies for learning and retaining new content-specific words.
- Students are involved in a great deal of reading that extends their knowledge.

TEACHER MODELING OF INTEREST IN LANGUAGE. By keeping a small set of books about language growth and development on your desk and reading about words periodically, you help to build students' inquisitiveness about language. Books by Richard Lederer and Bill Bryson are great sources for read-aloud pieces on language. The *Readers Digest's* regular vocabulary quiz is another easy resource that students (and teachers) enjoy taking and then exploring the definitions and uses of the terms. Jokes, too, often involve play with words and can be great starters for talk about language. Table 13.3 identifies some excellent books to keep as resources.

STUDENTS ENGAGE IN ENJOYABLE WORD PLAY. Middle-level students love to play with words and language. Music, clean rap word games, and jokes are wonderful ways they explore language. Even joke books should be considered for the classroom library. Comics are another favorite source of a very expansive vocabulary. The teacher can have great fun by introducing strange and unusual forms of words and together enjoying sesquipedalian words, portmanteau words, palindromes, and other strange word forms. Two great resources are *Superdupers: Really Funny Real Words* (Terban, 1989) and *A Cache of Jewels and Other Collective Nouns* (Heller, 1991).

SELF-SELECTION. Students do better in learning language when they have some control over and choice in what they learn. Studies of students' ability to self-select words they want and need to learn have shown that students are quite good at determining key terms when they are given practice and opportunities to discuss their selections with others (Blachowicz & Fisher, 1996). By first modeling how to notice unfamiliar words, the teacher helps students to realize that this is part of what good readers do regularly. The teacher should then provide opportunities for students to build vocabulary by recording words they find

TABLE 13.3

Valuable Language Resources

Bryson, B. *The Mother Tongue: English and How It Got That Way.* New York: Avon Books, 1990.

Bryson, B. *Made in America: An Informal History of the English Language in the United States.* New York: Avon, 1994.

Lederer, R. *Crazy English: The Ultimate Joy Ride Through Our Language.* New York: Simon & Schuster, 1998.

Lederer, R. *The Miracle of Language.* New York: Pocket Books, 1999.

Rheingold, H. *They Have a Word for It: A Lighthearted Lexicon of Untranslatable Words and Phrases.* Louisville, KY: Saraband Books, 2000.

interesting and new, trying to determine meaning from context and word parts, confirming hunches with dictionary or glossary checks, and then sharing their choices with others.

HISTORICAL DEVELOPMENT OF ENGLISH. The way our language has grown and changed is fascinating. William and Mary Morris's (1962) *Dictionary of Word and Phrase Origins* still is a great source of information about our language, as is Bartletts's (2003) *Dictionary of Americanisms*. Small sets of paperback books on language history give students the opportunity to read and discuss the English language together. The talk about words and language also reinforces the use of new words and words used in new ways.

Students in the middle grades need to have some structured study of words and language, too. At this stage, they should be learning how affixes work, how to use Greek and Latin combining forms, and how to connect derivations with base words. Content-area learning involves a great many specialized terms, so knowing how to look for specialized meanings of common words is also valuable. Table 13.4 provides a list of affixes of which students should become aware. Two useful books are *Techniques of Teaching Vocabulary* (1971) by O'Rourke and Bamman and the more recent *Words Their Way* by Bear et al. (2004).

Figurative language is also important to highlight and teach, especially for English language learners in need of help in understanding the many expressions of English. The elementary *Amelia Bedelia* books (Parish, 1966) and *The King Who Rained* (Gwynne, 1989) offer good strategies for introducing figurative language and helping students become aware of the challenge of our language for English language learners.

LEARNING AND RETAINING CONTENT-SPECIFIC VOCABULARY. Students' self-selection of words they want to learn is an important component of language growth. However, in content learning teachers don't want to leave to chance key terms that students need to make sense of the content. When content textbooks are used, a list of key terms can be developed from words suggested as important. Sometimes there is not a textbook program and standards are used to develop curriculum. In these cases, a helpful guide to checking students' vocabulary knowledge and selecting words for particular attention is Marzano's (2004) book on academic vocabulary. He includes lists of key terms taken from standards in all the academic areas and chunks them by grade levels. He also suggests several activities to help students learn the terms, including keeping a vocabulary journal and playing games with the key words periodically. Good strategies are needed to draw students' attention to specific words and their meanings in the particular context being studied. A few of these are listed below:

- *Chunking and categorizing words.* Students are given a list of key terms and asked to chunk them together in groups that fit. Once the groups are made, students are to give each chunk a label or category. In preparing for the activity, the first step is to create a list of the most important terms that students will encounter in their reading. Next the teacher ensures that there are at least two or three words that can be chunked together. If there are not, the teacher adds some words from the content that will help students build categories of related words.

- *Possible sentences.* Students are given a list of the key terms that will be in the text and need to be learned. Working with a partner or individually, they try to connect two or three of the words into a sentence. They write these sentences and later share their possible sentences, even though they might be unsure of the real meanings of the words. The activity raises students' awareness of words they will need to attend to as they read.

- *Exclusion brainstorming.* The teacher gives students a list of words that includes both words they will need for the content being studied and some that do not relate to the topic. The teacher asks the students to predict which words do not fit the content. This activity is fun because it shifts the purpose of the task from what students normally get while highlighting new words.

TABLE 13.4

Affixes

PREFIXES	MEANING	EXAMPLE
Un	not	*un*happy
In	not	*in*correct
Re	again	*re*pair, *re*move
Dis	not or away	*dis*agree, *dis*miss
Pre	before	*pre*school, *pre*pare
Ex	out	*ex*hale, *ex*port
Anti	against	*anti*freeze, *anti*war
Sub	under, below	*sub*way, *sub*marine
Super	over, more than	*super*sonic, *super*man
Com	together, with	*com*plete, *com*munity
Con		*con*nect
Col		*col*lection
Co		*co*operate
Cor		*cor*respond
Mid	in the middle	*mid*day, *mid*summer
Mis	wrong	*mis*behave, *mis*understand

NUMBER SUFFIXES	MEANING	EXAMPLE
Mono	one	*mono*tone
Uni	one	*uni*corn
Bi	two	*bi*cycle
Di	two	*di*alogue
Tri	three	*tri*cycle
Deca	ten	*deca*de
Centi	hundreth	*centi*pede
Cent	hundreth	*cent*ury

SUFFIXES	MEANING	EXAMPLE
s-es	plural	clock*s*
s-ing-ed	verb, time	sing, sin
er, est	comparison	late, lat*er*, lat*est*
ly	how done	quick, quick*ly*
ful	full of	peace*ful*
out	full of	fam*ous*
less	without	use*less*, sleep*less*
ist, ian	one skilled in	scient*ist*, physic*ian*
ness	state of being, having	sad*ness*, sick*ness*
ify, fy	to become, make	magn*ify*, de*ify*
en	make, cause, made of	soft*en*, wool*en*
able	can, able to, deserving	cap*able*, lov*able*
ible		poss*ible*, vis*ible*
tion	action, process	comple*tion*
ion		rebell*ion*
ish	have, quality of	fool*ish*, child*ish*
ment	state of, action	fulfill*ment*
ry, ery, ary	product or action of, place where	bak*ery*, pott*ery*
ize	make, made into	dramat*ize*
ism	practice of, act of	hero*ism*, vandal*ism*, patriot*ism*

Sources: From Dole, O'Rourke, & Curtis, *Vocabulary Building: A Process Approach.* Copyright © 1986. Reprinted by permission of Zaner-Bloser, Inc.

- *Predict-o-gram.* The teacher presents students with a list of words that come from the story they will read. The teacher asks the students to predict which words relate to the characters, setting, problem, or resolution. The teacher can use a graphic organizer with four blocks and space for students to write a prediction they make about the story content after completing the activity of categorizing the terms.

- *Vocabulary word cards.* Vocabulary word cards can be a fun and powerful way for students to build their vocabularies. They select the ten most important words from the unit of study and then create a 3×5 word card for each. On the front side of the card, they draw a picture to illustrate the meaning of the term. On the back side of the card, they write the word, the central definition, and added information to help them understand how to use the word. This might mean a sentence, some synonyms, or phrases in which the word might be found.

- *Personal clues.* The personal clue approach (Carr, 1985) is also an effective way to learn words in content areas. Words are grouped by the concept they are associated with or by the element or character in a piece of literature. Then students list attributes of the target words and think of one personal association that is the clue they will use to store the terms. For example, when learning *laconic*, one student wrote *terse* and *miserly* and associated them with Scrooge before Christmas. Then, on the second day, the student decided that from his study of American history, Calvin Coolidge was a better choice. On the third day, he added another clue: his New England uncle who hardly ever said more than three words. He had fun finding the right clue for *laconic*—but certainly wasn't laconic in his efforts (see the example in Figure 13.1).

- *Connect two.* Using the list of words being learned, students practice them by creating new and sometimes zany sentences that use either two or three of the new words. Doing this with a partner makes it more enjoyable for students because the sentences, which must respect the definitions of the words, can still be fun, and sharing makes it more enjoyable. Revisiting words is essential for retention.

TEACH IT! 20

Connect Two

Students also can use graphic organizers such as concept maps to help them learn new words. The organizer contains boxes or cells into which a question or concept is filled in. For example, a concept of *definition map* could include questions such as "What is it?" "What is it like?" "What are some examples?" and "What are some attributes?" After creating the web, students can keep expanding their webs—some draw pictures of the concept, some add antonyms, and others collect sentences in which the term is used—to help deepen their understanding of the term. (See Chapter 7 for examples of various graphic organizers.)

WIDE READING.   Doing a great deal of reading is a critical way for students to build their recognition of vocabulary and to learn the specific contexts in which words are appropriate. There is no substitute for reading. Studies have shown that direct teaching of specific words can account for only part of the growth in word knowledge needed to develop an adequate vocabulary (Beck & McKeown, 1983; Anderson & Nagy, 1991). When students enjoy reading and are attentive to language and vocabulary, they continue to build their awareness and ability to use an increasingly wide range of vocabulary terms.

In summary, you can guide students in their development of vocabulary sensitivity and curiosity by having them do the following:

- Keep personal records of words new to them or new uses of known words.
- Develop strategies for building meanings for these words.
- Use appropriate visual or graphic organizers to build and retain meanings.
- Practice using new terms in speaking and writing.
- Use resources, especially dictionaries, thesauruses, and glossaries.

> Character
> ⌐ Laconic
> ⌐ - terse
> ⌐ - miserly
> ⌐ personal clue:
>   Calvin Coolidge was so laconic—
>   but Uncle Ben is more so!

FIGURE 13.1

Personal Clue.

- Engage in word play by creating and enjoying jokes, word puzzles, poetry, and games such as *Scrabble*™ and *Pictionary*™.
- Understand how our language is evolving and how vocabulary grows and changes.
- Keep examples of new words and new usages (sports, pop music, and fashion are areas that keep inventing new words and usage that middle-grade students are interested in following).

Student Self-Reflection

In addition to self-monitoring, which refers to the active checking of one's own thinking while reading, students also become more confident readers when they learn to engage in reflection after the text has been completed. They learn to think about what they have just read and what is new or different. They also can reflect on their own active thinking processes and how well they have used their energies during reading. Questions such as "What did I learn?" "Was I using my energy wisely so I made best use of my time?" and "Did I use the best approach to the reading: visualizing, making a mental map of the test, outlining, or rephrasing as I read?" Adopting a reflective attitude encourages readers to take responsibility for their reading and to realize they can often do more to be effective readers. The teacher can encourage students to improve self-reflection by having them make marginal notes while reading and learning, discuss the process with peers and himself or herself, and keep a journal for self-reflections at the end of reading activities.

Another aspect of self-monitoring is learning to think about the process used in conducting research. Some teachers create guides for students to follow in forming and answering questions about their research: How did you begin your research process? How did you use your prior knowledge as a frame for deciding on what you would need to research? How did you compare and contrast different sources of information? Others have students keep journals of their research process and make notes of what they have done as they go. Another good way to increase students' self-reflection is to use the I-Search Paper model (Macrorie, 1988). In this model, students choose a topic and conduct research on it but focus most directly on how they go about the process rather than just focusing on the final paper. They reflect on how they went about their research, what caused problems for them, and what they would do the next time. The strategy creates a more reflective and powerful response to extended learning activities.

Opportunities to Model Fluent and Reflective Reading

The teacher can do a great deal to help students develop an internal model of what fluent reading is like by reading aloud to them on a regular basis. Selecting a variety of material to read helps students understand the beauty and depth of what can be communicated by writers. Contemporary students do not have many opportunities to engage in reflection about reading. Bringing in good audiotapes of texts being read can also help students begin to appreciate the sounds of written language read orally. For example, listening to books on tape such as James Joyce's *Dubliners* (1993) and Tony Hillerman reading his own mysteries helps students to gain an appreciation for the varieties of oral readers. This strategy can also help students to think of using their MP3 players and time spent in the car as potential time for listening to good books and poetry.

Reading aloud from interesting material also can be used to model critical thinking engaged in while reading. When reading to students, pay particular attention to reading with expression, asking questions as you read, and responding to the ideas in the text. Comments such as, "That was beautifully described—I can almost see it!," "Did I understand what the author just said?," "That doesn't sound possible to me," and "That reminds me of something else I just learned" are the kinds of reflections students need to use in their independent reading. Modeling such thinking encourages students to evaluate their own habits and can build new habits if they do not already have them. You can enhance the power of this thinking aloud by putting some of these thinking asides on the board or on strips hanging from the ceiling so that students are regularly reminded of them. Listening to you read aloud in this manner from a wide selection of texts provides students with many benefits, not the least of which are increased interest in print and sensitivity to vocabulary and language use. Think of the power of reading aloud in providing the following:

- A model of fluent reading
- A model of active and reflective reading
- A way to increase their store of knowledge about the world as well as their vocabulary

The amount of time you have with students will vary depending on how the school is organized. Read the Being a Professional Reading Teacher box and think about your preferences.

Fluency through Repetition

Rereading texts improves students' word knowledge, reading speed, and accuracy and deepens their understanding of that particular text. Effective methods for incorporating rereading and guided oral reading in the middle-level classroom, and thus promoting fluency, include the following:

- Rereading poems and short passages using techniques such as choral reading, two-part reading, and echo reading

Being a Professional Reading Teacher

Finding a Good Organization

Teaching reading in grades 6 to 8 is accomplished in varied ways depending on the school organizations. Some middle schools may have a separate reading teacher with major responsibility for teaching reading. However, some middle school organizations may have no designated reading period, with language arts and other content teachers assuming the responsibility of continuing the development of middle school students' reading abilities. In other communities these grades are part of elementary schools where teachers have self-contained classrooms, or they may be departmentalized for some subjects. Some have teams that teach together, with reading linked to social studies or science. Find out what instructional arrangements are used in your area schools. Think about how you would prefer teaching. If you are interested in these grades, investigate resources that are available for middle-level teaching. Reflect on what is important at this level and how reading instruction changes for young people at these grade levels.

Your Portfolio

Teaching in grades 6 to 8 requires special classroom management skills. Teaching preadolescent and adolescent young people can be a challenge. Write some reflections about how you have identified potential behavior problems related to adolescence and how you have solved them in your volunteer and/or paraprofessional experiences. These could be excerpted from entries in your daily journal.

Teacher Resources

Related to student behavior issues, make a list of books you might refer to students experiencing problems such as isolation from peers, gender confusion, a divorce at home, or other critical social problems that adolescents often face. You can find many valuable sources by searching on the term "bibliotherapy" at **www.google.com**.

As you read more, think about the following questions:

- Why is knowledge of the English language such an important part of reading programs at this level?
- How can teachers teaming together in integrated content units (for example, reading biographies and historical fiction in literature while studying American history) be beneficial to students in the sixth- to eighth-grade classrooms?
- How can the teacher scaffold reading comprehension for English language learners in grades 6 to 8?

- Readers' theater, a technique that involves students in rehearsing and reading aloud their interpretation of a character's lines in passages from a short story
- Self-timing drills, a procedure in which students time themselves or partners in reading and rereading short passages to increase their speed
- An introduction to a variety of new books and genres, giving students short amounts of time to skim through several to see which they like best

Assessment

Assessment is the starting point for good instruction. Students in the middle grades vary significantly in their reading abilities and interests, and, with the increasing range of reading genres and purposes that students this age must handle successfully, there is much teachers need to attend to. Throughout the year, the teacher's job is to monitor what all the students know and can do and to provide supportive instruction. Because this is a challenging task, it is also good to remember that the students themselves can be good assistants in the task of monitoring their knowledge and abilities. In fact, they should be made aware of their strengths and should participate in setting and monitoring their goals throughout the year.

Determining Reading Levels

As a result of the daily reading by students of materials in the classroom, the teacher should have a good idea of their development as readers and can guide them into reading appropriate materials. Determining students' instructional and independent reading levels can be done in a few ways.

INFORMAL READING INVENTORIES. If a reading series is available for use, one of the easiest ways is to use an Informal Reading Inventory (IRI) provided for the reading program. As you read in Chapter 12, the IRI contains a series of increasingly difficult reading passages; students are asked to read the passages and then to demonstrate their comprehension by answering a series of questions. If the IRI asks for oral reading of the passages, the guideline is generally that oral reading with 99 percent accuracy and 90 percent comprehension indicates independence with the material. The range for instruction (where your guidance as a teacher supports the reading) is 95 percent word accuracy and 75 percent comprehension. Less success with passages indicates that the material is really too difficult for students to be asked to read. In the language of reading assessment, those texts are at a frustration level for students. If the IRI involves only silent reading, then the students' comprehension responses are the focus. Usually, the kinds of questions that are included on the inventory try to tap some basic recall of main ideas of the text, some inferences that can be drawn, and some vocabulary knowledge. Be sure to look at the questions in advance. If you are not satisfied that they give you the information you need about particular students, go back and talk over the answers students gave for them and find out why the students responded as they did. Asking students to write a summary of a text is another good way to get information on how well students can follow the main structure and ideas of a passage they read. Then, with students for whom there are questions, some individual discussion about their reading and thinking can be useful. You will not need to have an individual diagnostic discussion with all the students but can focus on those about whom you have some concerns.

ADVANCED INFORMAL INVENTORY. As students mature, teachers also need to find out how well they can read information from more than one source, combine ideas, and learn to think critically about what they read. Teachers need to ask students to compare and contrast two different texts on some appropriate topic. A contemporary news story, two pieces of student writing with different perspectives, editorials in newspapers, and personal letters to the editor all make good content for student thinking. This will provide you with good data as you plan for having students do research (and use the Internet) and engage in extended projects. You can copy two short articles and create a few questions that require contrasting the pieces or ask students to write their opinion about the question addressed in the articles, citing references they find useful in the texts.

Another form of an advanced IRI is one that is specific for a content course. The teacher selects passages from the textbook or instructional materials that students read. Questions need to tap the range of reading comprehension tasks—from identifying key ideas, inferring relationships, understanding specific vocabulary meanings to reading visual information contained in charts, maps and graphs. This inventory can be completed in a group setting, so it saves much time for teachers.

LEVELED BOOKS. Many districts now have leveled the books they have available according to difficulty, taking into account a variety of features, including vocabulary and concept load, complexity of sentences and redundancy, and layout of the materials. If you have this resource available, you can select a representative set of books at a range of levels and ask students to read short sections. Then summarize what they have read or have them answer a few of your questions and find their instructional levels this way.

Classroom Fluency Measure

One of the easiest ways to begin to get information on your students' reading is to use the **classroom fluency measure** (Blachowicz, Sullivan, & Cieply, 2001). For this quick assessment, select a passage from the reading anthology you will be using or from other material that you will be asking students to read. Type the passage for your use, and number each line in the margin. Set up a time when you can work with each student individually, either when the class is doing silent reading or before and after school. As you work with each student, ask the student to read orally for one minute while you follow the reading and then ask the student to recall what he or she can from the passage. While the student reads, record any deviations the student makes from the text and subtract the errors from the total number of words read during the minute. By marking the student's location at the end of one minute, you can do this calculation easily after the student tells what he or she recalls from the text. After you have completed the fluency check on all students, you can create a class grid, arranging the students' scores from lowest to highest. This gives you a clear sense of the range within your class and helps you to determine which students you need to do more assessment with immediately and which you can observe in other ways to plan for future instruction.

Each year you become a better teacher and more comfortable in the job. In the six years I've been teaching I've learned so many new things but these are the three that make the most difference.

1. Never let on that you are about to lose it. When you feel like you want to explode, the worst thing to do is yell and scream and let the students know you've lost it because then it becomes like a game. They will continue just to see if they can get a rise out of you. There is nothing wrong with assigning a consequence after you've calmed down and really thought about it. These tend to be the better, more feasible consequences than the ones that slip out in anger.

2. Planning and organization are key. The more organized you are the easier your school year will be. There are a lot of issues that arise when implementing lessons (even curriculum lessons that appear easy to implement), so really plan and think out your lessons before teaching them.

3. Reflect, reflect, reflect.

Lisa
Fourth Grade Teacher
Pawtucket, RI

Strategy Knowledge

A third important component of students' reading that needs to be assessed early in the year is their awareness of the strategies they use to read successfully in different kinds of materials and for different purposes. One middle-grade teacher begins her year by asking students to fill out a survey of what their strategies are for reading (see Figure 13.2.) On it are examples of the kinds of reading tasks teachers in this departmentalized school expect of students. What the teacher and students learned by doing this survey one year was that the students were very "teacher and parent" dependent. Several students responded to the query about how to prepare for a social studies test that would be given on Friday by indicating that they would read over the chapter, maybe more than once, and then ask their mothers

FIGURE 13.2

Reading Strategies.

> **WHAT DO YOU KNOW ABOUT YOUR STRATEGIES FOR READING TO LEARN?**
>
> Your language arts teacher has set up a unit in which you will read novels in groups. Each night you will read one chapter. What strategies work best for you to help you enjoy and understand novels? What will you do?
>
> _____
>
> _____
>
> _____
>
> _____
>
> Your social studies teacher has assigned you a 25-page chapter on Monday. On Friday you will have a test on the material. You are on your own to read and learn. There are lots of headings and boldfaced vocabulary in the text. At the end of the chapter, there are many questions and activities. What will you do this week with this chapter? What is your plan?
>
> _____
>
> _____
>
> _____
>
> _____

to quiz them using the end of chapter questions. When asked how to figure out a difficult mathematics problem, again the response was to ask Mom. To develop students' awareness of what good readers do, discussing responses to this kind of survey can be a starting place.

Another approach is to ask students to indicate what they are aware of doing as they read a challenging short article. Inform students that they can use sticky notes if they want to while reading so they do not forget their thinking or strategies. When finished reading, each student should write a reflection on what he or she did before starting to read, what he or she was conscious of doing while reading, and what he or she did afterward. If students are frustrated by this task, it means that they are not yet fully conscious of what reading is as a strategic behavior and there is much for the teacher to do with them during the year to develop a vocabulary for and awareness of reading strategies.

Content Reading

Another area that is important for students who are developing reading abilities is their flexibility in reading a variety of different informational texts and in developing strategies for using that information. The teacher needs to know whether students can use the features of informational textbooks as well as glossaries and thesauruses and whether they can read and weave information from graphs, charts, tables, and pictures (with their captioned information) together with information in the narrative content. Do students use the physical layout of material they read to learn (see Chapter 8)?

Vocabulary and Concept Learning

As you listen to students read and respond to what they read, attend to their use of the language of the text materials. Ask them to define some of the key terms. You might want to be more formal initially and prepare a short vocabulary assessment for one of the first articles or stories you have students read with you in a guided reading setting. Vocabulary knowledge is so important to reading comprehension that you do not want to leave it to chance. You want an idea of students' vocabulary, and then you want to know whether they have learned and use any self-conscious strategies for adding words to their use vocabularies.

A quick way to find out how well students know the vocabulary of a particular novel, story, or informational text is to have them complete a Rate Your Knowledge chart (Blachowicz, 1986). Select eight to twelve key words that will be important for students to understand, and list them on a chart like the one shown in Figure 13.3. Give students choices to indicate their level of familiarity with the terms. Have students rate their own level of knowledge for each word. Asking students to define the words they mark as familiar can help to keep students from overestimating their knowledge.

You also want to know whether students have any self-conscious strategies for learning new words and phrases and whether they are interested in vocabulary. Asking a few questions (orally or in written form) about how students note new terms that they think are important and how they then go about learning the terms can stimulate some new ideas and help make some more focused on this aspect of reading and learning. For others, you might find out a lot about how they learn language and what rehearsal tools they have found useful (making cards, drawing pictures of terms, writing and using the terms orally, etc.). Some English language learners can provide good ideas for all students, growing out of their high need for vocabulary. Highlight their experiences if they are willing to share how they learn language. This is a good place for you to be a model and share your own vocabulary-

Put a check by the level of knowledge you have of each word. If you think you really know a term then either write a few words to define it or draw what it means.

Key Words	Unfamiliar	Have Seen	Know and Use	Definition/Drawing
Scavenge				
Scrawny				
Dung heap				
Midwife				
Apprentice				
Risk-taking				
Haggle				
Ointment				
Merchant				
Herbs				
Self-awareness				

FIGURE 13.3

Rate Your Knowledge.

learning strategies as a way of stimulating students' reflection and realization of the importance of being self-conscious learners.

Understanding Students' Interests

If students are going to develop as readers, they need to be reading regularly both in school and beyond. Therefore, you will be able to encourage students most effectively if you have some idea of what they are interested in reading and have an idea of their particular interests. This will allow you to help them combine these interests with new kinds of reading. For example, a student who is interested in snowboarding might find a magazine on the sport fascinating and develop an interest in deeper reading on this topic from articles in magazines. You can find out about students' interests by observing them as they interact with others, by engaging them in conversations, and by doing some journal writing with them about their own lives and what they read and do. At the beginning of the school year, simply asking your students to write about their two favorite books can help you get a feel for them as readers. There are several commercially available Interest Inventories that can also help you and the students identify areas for more reading and for ways you can involve librarians in helping locate appropriate and new materials for the class.

Developing a Diagnostic Eye and Ear

One of the most important forms of assessment is what you observe students doing during your ongoing classroom reading activities. During these activities, you will see students engaged with texts and responding to them in a variety of ways. Use all of these typical situations to observe carefully and make notes of what students show about their developing reading abilities. Experiment with ways to record information from these classroom events and build profiles of your students as readers. Many teachers keep a clipboard nearby and focus on two or three students a day, making notes about their engagement in discussions, their responses to specific questions, or their thinking aloud as they read with a group. Other teachers prefer looking at the whole class and recording evidence of students' thinking, no matter who seems to be revealing their strategies and understanding. Writing short sticky notes of these occurrences and noting the students' names on the notes permits you to add these sticky notes to a student folder where a variety of performance indicators are collected along with samples of written work. Another approach is to shadow a particular student for a day, a form of observation that helps a teacher to create a more complete sense of how the student reads across a variety of situations.

Study Reading

As students enter the middle school years, many find the shift in expectations quite startling. Instead of having teachers guide them through their assigned work, students are expected to know how to read and learn from assigned materials, to organize their own study time and come to class prepared, and to be able to study and learn a vast amount of information. There are several areas in which teachers need to guide students so they can be successful.

Scheduling Time to Study

Allocating time for study is an important aspect of learning for middle school students. This is a good time to provide students with weekly schedules and talk through ways to find regular study periods on weeknights and weekends. However, students often are not inclined to listen well to a teacher's recommendations. You can stress the need to study by calling on older peer models. Invite former students from high schools and universities to talk with your students about their study habits. Some students in class might have older siblings who can speak with authority about their strategies for learning. When middle-level students hear from older teens they respect, it becomes easier to guide them into more attentive reading and reflecting.

Students need to learn to keep a schedule for their study. You might ask visitors to bring their study plan books with them and show how important it is to develop a study schedule and keep records of assignments and time. Some of your own students might already have some form of study plan book or have parents who have given them planners. This can be a stimulus to help students review each week what they need to be working on and the time they will need to be prepared for all their assignments and projects.

Test Taking

Learning how to study for tests is important—and generally unknown to middle-level students. Take time to make a grid for different kinds of study and discuss with students strategies that are effective, particularly the advantages of spaced study and repeated rehearsal of new concepts and terms. Practice tests are becoming very familiar—almost too familiar—in states with high-stakes testing. However, making students aware of the nature of those experiences is important. Talk through with the students how they went about answering questions. How did the format of the test influence their strategy for taking the test? When did they read the questions—before or after reading the story or passage? Did they skim through the text if it was fairly long? How did they finally make the decision to answer the question as they did?

Introducing the **Question Answer Relation (QAR) strategy** (Raphael, 1986) at this point is a good way to help students understand the difference between typical classroom questions that are often of a higher thinking nature and those asked on standardized tests. The QAR approach divides questions into four types: those that can be answered by finding one piece of information (right there), those that require searching the text (think and search), those that require drawing on background knowledge to add to the text (author and you), and those that go beyond information in the text itself (on your own). Standardized tests given to thousands of students must include answers that are available in the text passages themselves. Therefore, according to the QAR terminology, there are no "on your own" questions. All questions have answers that can be found either in a specific location in the text (right there) or by combining bits of information from sections of the text (think and search).

Teacher Modeling

Another way to raise interest and awareness of the cognitive choices readers need to make as they read is to describe your own reading behaviors when you are learning. For example, you might describe how you study for a graduate course you are taking. Show students how you study, and get them to compare and contrast their own habits with yours. A key habit you can reinforce is the need to read the same text sections several times and make notes about what you consider to be important. Show students your own text markings or the sticky notes you insert at important points in a text.

Metacognition

Middle-level students are very pragmatic and seem to always want to know "Why do we need to do this?" They often lack the knowledge of what reading really involves and are unable to describe what they do. Middle-school students need to be better informed about what happens when they read and how they can become better readers. They need to develop **metacognition** about their learning, that is, an awareness of how they think. It involves three basic strategies: connecting new information to former knowledge; developing strategies for thinking; and planning, monitoring, and evaluating how they think (Dirkes, 1985). Activating metacognition can be done in a number of ways.

Active Reading

TEACH IT! 49

Visualization

Students' metacognitive awareness of what good readers do while reading should be developed at this level. Teachers often begin this process by engaging in thinking aloud when they read orally. Using books that have margin notations on them is also a good way to stimulate students' attention to the thinking that goes on when good readers interact with pieces of text. You might create your own examples by having older students mark up a story or essay that your class is going to read. Go over the notations, and discuss them with the students by asking, "Why do you think this note was made? What would have stimulated this comment? How would you have responded?" Comparing two or three different people's responses to the same article gives students a clearer idea of the wide variety of ways in which people engage with text. Then you can build a list of the kinds of engagements that others have made and begin to use these as thinking strategies for your class; that is, visualizing, connecting to another text or author, marking it as providing an answer to a question, arguing with the text, and so on (see the Standards and Literacy box).

Standards and Literacy

Creating Visual Images While Reading

Having noticed that many of her students rushed through their reading of fiction, the teacher questioned three students about what images were being created in their heads when they read. She got blank stares in response. Knowing that this was one of the objectives of the state standards, she decided that it was time to provide a focus on visualizing and imaging while reading.

A State Standards Literacy Plan

From Texas state standards: **Describe mental images that text descriptions evoke.**

TEACHER DECISION MAKING ABOUT THE LESSON

Focus of Instruction: Modeling imaging through a think-aloud process followed by students creating their own images as they read a short section of text.

Materials: The teacher creates an overhead transparency of a short paragraph that evokes images. The teacher makes copies of two paragraphs from a short story students can easily read that has good images.

Before the lesson: The teacher explains to the students that an important part of active reading is the creation of our own personal images—or seeing a movie in our mind. Some readers think of having a mind's eye that creates pictures from words on print.

Albert Einstein once said, "If I can't picture it, I can't understand it." A good way to ensure that you are comprehending when you read is to check to see whether you are creating mental pictures of what you read.

During the lesson: The teacher models the process by putting the paragraph on the transparency and uncovers the sentences one at a time. She thinks aloud about her own images as she reads each sentence. Then the teacher involves students in sharing any images they have. She writes down her own ideas on the transparency and does the same with the students' thoughts as they share.

The woman slowly emerged from the hollow.
In one hand she carried her good shoes.
She carefully protected the large, bulging bag she carried over her shoulder.

After this introduction to imaging, the teacher asks students to take the copies of the two paragraphs she had copied for them and read them silently, drawing or writing about the images that were created as they read. She then asks them to share these images with their partner. When this is completed, the class comes back together to reflect on their imaging.

After the lesson: The teacher asks that as the students read their novels that evening, they make notes in their journals of images that came to them as they read. They will share their own images the next day in class. She suggests that if students prefer, they can find pictures in magazines that reflect their images and create a collage of ideas from the reading.

Many good teachers use sticky notes as a way of helping students monitor and develop their thinking as they read. They pose the question, "What kinds of thinking do we do as we read?" To explore their own minds during engaged reading, each student can be given several sticky notes and instructed to use them when ideas, images, and questions come to them while reading. When the group (either the whole class or a small group) is finished reading, the students can compare their notes and begin to understand how different students think about the same text. These different responses can then be categorized, and students can talk about how they think. Extending this activity to explore how the same students read a different kind of text also helps the students extend their understanding of the impact of the text on reading and thinking.

A teacher's feedback and guidance can help students learn to assess their own development.

Self-Assessment

Once you have developed students' awareness of how to read and learn from text, they can then regularly include their own self-evaluations of the strategies they use in the work they do. You can do this by asking students at the end of class periods to fill out 3×5 cards on their class participation and work. You can alter the questions each day you hand out the cards with stems like these:

- What did you learn today?
- How did you learn best today?
- How was your class participation?
- What could you do better to help the class learn?
- What bothers you, or is still unclear?
- What was most interesting to you today?
- What would you like to learn more about?
- What questions do you have?

Begin the next class session by reviewing what the students wrote the day before. This simple process gives students a regular way to think about their learning and to know that the teacher is serious about taking advantage of class time to ensure learning. It also provides the teacher with important feedback on the success of the class sessions.

Learning Logs

Learning logs also give students a vehicle for ongoing self-reflection on their learning. At least weekly, students should be encouraged to review what they have learned that week, what questions they have, and how they have contributed to the class accomplishments. Key concepts and new vocabulary are also important to record in a learning log so that students stay focused on their primary purposes in school. This is serious business, yet it is very enjoyable when each student can keep a record of growth. Too often, students shift attention from learning to social acceptance at this age, and all the ways teachers can use to involve students in knowing and evaluating their own successes help to balance the intense peer focus these students feel.

Extended Unit Assessment

Units of instruction are another place where student self-reflection is important. Right from the start, students should have a record of what they know and the questions they want to have answered from their study. Keeping this record in the form of a K-W-L chart in

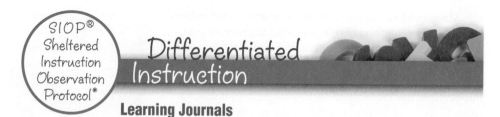

Differentiated Instruction

Learning Journals

Finding out what students know about the content being studied at the beginning of a unit or lesson is important. This is particularly urgent when there are students from a variety of linguistic and cultural groups in the classroom. Yet these are the students who are most hesitant to speak in class and to write out their ideas. An easy way to elicit some of what they know is to have students keep modified Learning Journals in which they record what they are learning on a regular basis. For English language learners, these journals can be places where they can draw and create diagrams and graphic organizers of their knowledge. Rather than insisting that students write in traditional formats, these more visual forms of representing ideas can give English language learners more confidence in activating what they know. A part of their journals can be dual-language lists of key terms. When teachers provide a list of important terms at the beginning of the unit, students can write these in their own journals in both English and their first language. For new terms, teachers can encourage students to copy visual illustrations of the terms from their textbooks or dictionaries or find visual representations they can photocopy.

students' notebooks means that it will be available when students have completed their units. One teacher had students also generate a possible table of contents for the insect report they knew they would write as a culmination to their integrated language arts/science insect study and make a semantic map of how those topics might be related. All of these pieces were kept in the students' notebooks throughout the unit. At the end of the unit, the teacher again asked students to look at their actual table of contents and compare it with the first one they had predicted would work. The teacher also had the students create a new semantic map and make a comparison with their first one. The teacher asked that the students respond in writing to some questions:

- What surprised you most about your learning?
- How did your first table of contents compare to your final one?
- What did you notice about your semantic maps?
- How do you feel about your learning?

One student responded, *"I can't believe how much I learned! I even thought spiders were insects when we started. I learned what that crunchy sound is when you step on an insect—it is the eco-skeleton. I also learned how to create a semantic map and show the relation of body parts and what insects can do."*

Students also can use personal notes like the sticky notes I-Chart (see Chapter 8) to evaluate their typical responses and thoughts while reading. When they compare their patterns with those of others in their class, they can begin to develop a broader sense of what reading can be and may consciously try to enhance their own thinking.

Portfolio Evaluation

Portfolios are great tools for student and teacher assessment at this level. These consist of personal collections of illustrative student work annotated to explain how they demonstrate learning or accomplishments. Students can collect examples of their own work that illustrate their best achievements and that also show the points they still need to take as goals. When you have students annotate or add note cards to the pieces in the portfolios, the students' self-reflection is deepened. Be careful to give guidelines and set parameters for portfolios, however, because they can easily get out of hand. Students love to sort and annotate their work and can spend hours creating covers for the portfolios. Space to save the portfolios is also an ongoing concern. So some clear guidelines about selecting a few pieces each quarter that illustrate both best work and work in progress can make the portfolio process integral to students' learning. Keeping a list of books and articles students have read with a short summary and evaluation can also become a lifetime habit. Students need visual records of what they are learning and reading, and the portfolio is a natural aid in helping them to celebrate the results of their efforts.

Reaching All Students

Each year that students grow and learn, they become more individual in their knowledge, skills, learning styles, and strengths and interests. Good teaching encourages and nurtures the particular talents and differences in students' learning, so we all must celebrate these increasing variations! Research on multiple intelligences has helped us to understand that variations are natural and need to be considered in organizing for instruction.

Your students will bring with them a wide range of cultural and linguistic abilities. Many students know more than one language and have had experiences in diverse cultural settings. You can enrich your own learning and provide great resources to the whole class by using these opportunities sensitively and well. Therefore, as a teacher, you have real challenges in creating classroom experiences that meet students where they are and challenge them as literacy learners.

Identify Strengths

A key to reaching all of your students is being a careful observer, or, to use the term coined by Yetta Goodman (1978), becoming a good kidwatcher. Each day you observe how your students come into your classroom; you can observe how they interact with their peers; you can listen to what they share; you can watch them as they read; and you can engage them in conversation. It takes just a few moments each day to become attuned to students. The effort is most valuable. Keeping a notebook page with bits of information gained from informal observations can help you to build a profile of each student that can be useful over time. Then, at an opportune moment, the particular strengths of a student can be called forth. For example, who is good with music and can help to plan the background pieces to accompany the presentations by the novel groups? Who is good at drawing and can illustrate the class book or movie reviews? Who is great at organizing on the computer and can catalogue the independent reading records? Who is a good oral reader or actor to help others visualize texts they are reading? Some of the less-adept readers and writers may have other strengths that will help them to learn more effectively and also contribute to the group in ways that can enhance their identity with literacy (see the Differentiated Instruction box).

Recognize Students' Cultures

Teachers can help to make all students feel a part of the classroom by ensuring that materials about their cultures and situations are available and by reading from some of these materials. Teachers can also sensitize students to the plights of immigrants and minority students by reading aloud from some stories that represent situations similar to those of students in the school. It is often from ignorance that young teens can seem callous and not caring. When they hear the stories of what others have had to experience, their sense of fairness and empathy can be expanded. Table 13.5 identifies some books that can be good for such read-alouds.

English language learners bring with them a wealth of knowledge about their own languages and often have the ability to contrast languages in ways that can be helpful to monolingual students in your classroom. Having bilingual or trilingual students in class can be

TABLE 13.5

Often Unrepresented Voices of Youth

Allison, A. *Hear These Voices: Youth at the Edge of the Millenium.* New York: Dutton Children's Books, 1999.

Bode, J. *New Kids in Town.* New York: Scholastic, 1989.

Na, A. *A Step from Heaven.* Asheville, NC: Front Street, 2001.

Rice, D. *Crazy Loco: Stories by David Rice.* New York: Dial Books, 2001.

Soto, G. *Baseball in April and Other Stories.* New York: Odyssey Books, 1990.

Walker, R. *Black, White and Jewish.* New York: Penguin, 2001.

a real asset. Help them to become comfortable talking about these differences in language and culture:

- When you are discussing characters in stories, ask them to reflect on how the same characters' actions would be perceived in their culture of origin. Discuss how the characters would have handled the same situations.

- Have them act out the behaviors of a character in a story as if the character were from their culture. Compare these with how the same character's actions are depicted by some other students.

- Analyze the language used. Would it be different if from another culture? For example, would characters express their emotions as they do in the story you are reading? How would they interact with strangers?

- When reading classic stories, ask whether students from other cultures have stories similar to those you are reading. Do they have the same story in translated form or is the story from their culture (e.g., *Arabian Nights, Aesop's Fables, Cinderella, The Nutcracker*)?

- Make lists of key vocabulary terms, and have students write the same words in their languages. These comparisons can often be the beginning point for discussion of where English has acquired its words.

- Graph the story structure of pieces you read with the class. Ask someone from another culture to show the structure of a typical tale from their culture. Are they the same? (For example, Athabaskan and Japanese tales often have a less-defined beginning and ending than Eurocentric tales do and can go on and on, leaving more to the reader to determine.)

- Read orally from news that reflects the world as represented by students in your school. Use maps so that the areas they come from become familiar to everyone. Use current events as the texts for some of the reading strategies you model. Often, students from abroad have a better sense of world events than do U.S. students, and their knowledge can be used to expand everyone's perspectives.

Adjusting Teaching for English Language Learners

When students are functioning in a second or third language, they need more time to process what they read and hear and more time to compose their own responses. Even when students have exited from bilingual programs, they have not had time to develop the depth of vocabulary and language usage required by middle school literature and content texts. The more the teacher can do to support their development of English, the better they will be able to engage fully in class activities and think deeply about content.

There are a few easy ways in which the teacher can support these students' learning within each area or theme. First, brainstorm the key terms you will be using, and check the students' familiarity with them. Create a glossary of the terms that are not known, and put these on a bookmark that students can keep with them while reading and studying. Second, as a way to introduce the writing of an author to students, have some parent volunteers tape-record the first part of a text (a novel or story or a chapter of informational material) so that the students can hear the language and begin to recognize the connections between the oral and written forms.

A third way to help English language learners participate fully is to give them some pre-experiences before the class begins a new area of study. You might hear this referred to as "jump-starting" their thinking and learning. For example, if you are going to have a unit on survival tales and will read some of Gary Paulsen's books, check out a videotape showing the setting of Canada and the northlands so that students can more easily visualize as they read. You might also find some easier books or magazine stories that introduce the same concepts that you will deal with in a novel or informational unit and let students take these home and learn from them before delving into the more difficult class texts. You also might be able to find easier versions of some of the stories you will have students read, and these can be used as advance organizers to prepare your English language learners for the complete version. Many readers do better with texts when they have a good idea of what the content is about; this is particularly the case for your English language learners. Help them to discover what works best for them, and then try to provide appropriate scaffolds for their learning.

Organizing for Instruction

Middle grades are just that—in the middle between self-contained elementary classrooms and high schools with their departmental structures. In some schools, grades 5 to 8 are treated much like the earlier elementary grades, in which one teacher has a single class with some special teachers perhaps providing elective courses in foreign language and music or computers for the students. Other schools create teams of students and teachers, so between 80 and 120 students are grouped together with four or five teachers, and the teams stay together for two or three years. Many middle school advocates have supported this model as a way to provide more guidance and create "home groups." Another variant is for students to have the same teacher for two or three subjects—usually language arts, reading, and social studies or a combined reading/language arts block. This core or combined teaching structure helps teachers to know their students more deeply, because they have fewer sections. Yet other schools are totally departmentalized with no groupings, so reading teachers teach four or five different groups of students each day. Any team teaching is done by individual teachers working together. Most new teachers have little say in how the school is organized. However, it is important that you know what kind of structure your school has in place because it provides the framework within which you have to teach.

There are several options for providing a range of reading opportunities that develop students' strategies and knowledge of reading, some of which are discussed in the following sections. The methods provided are certainly not exhaustive of how good instruction can be organized. Nor are they comprehensive.

Integrating Content Areas

As one reads about the kinds of reading strategies and skills that middle-grade students need to develop, the advantages of either teaming or having students for two or three subjects are clear. Students need to learn to read in many kinds of texts and for many purposes. They are more interested and engaged in developing these when they see the concrete and immediate use of them (Guthrie & Davis, 2003). For example, teaching students how to retain new and important vocabulary words is much easier if the teacher can show students how to do it when they need to master their history or science content. Helping them learn to read dense textbooks is easier when the teacher can use the students' own content textbooks. Middle graders are very pragmatic and concrete, and the more instruction is directly tied to needs, the more likely they are to attend and process the strategies.

There is so much that needs to be taught that teachers have come up with a wide variety of ways of organizing the curriculum to meet these wide-ranging aspects of reading. One of the basic issues to be faced is how to balance the reading of literature with reading in informational texts and helping students learn to use reading to learn. One good option is to divide the year into quarters and teach with fictional literature and poetry for two quarters; use a thematic focus for one quarter, involving students in reading and evaluating multiple sources; and spend another quarter on inquiry and research, linking with either science or social studies teachers so that students have both the content and process as high priorities. Within this quarter organization are many options for instruction.

Although a general organizational frame is structured around themes and units of instruction, there needs to be a continuing focus on students' independent reading and on their developing vocabulary interest and knowledge. The teacher needs to continue to provide a central model of good reading and show students how reading can be part of daily life. The teacher also needs to attend to the community climate and encourage a positive atmosphere associated with reading and learning; without attention to the students as individuals and as a community, much good instruction can be lost.

Teaching Literature

Most elementary students have been reading fiction and can anticipate the basic structures and techniques used in this kind of text. However, in the middle grades, several new genres are introduced, and they can pose problems for readers who are on automatic pilot much of the time in independent-level materials. Science fiction, fantasy, short stories, and stream-of-consciousness pieces are often new to these students. That said, with the current rage for *Harry Potter* and Tolkien's *Lord of the Rings* books, some fantasy texts are becoming better known even among younger students. Biography is another genre that is important to teach at this level because it provides a great link for students to the world at different periods of history and to people who have had important influences on the students' own development. Longer, narrative poetry is often given more attention in the middle grades, and students can be involved in dramatic play readings, choral reading, and readers' theater. Some teachers concentrate one unit on novel forms and a second on short stories, poetry, and drama. This is where the developmental continuum from fifth to eighth grades needs to be worked out among the reading and literature teachers so that students continue to learn more about literature each year. Teachers can develop their literature focus in at least three ways: using core novels and literature groups, literature circles, and readers' workshops.

CORE NOVEL AND LITERATURE GROUPS.   Use a core novel representing a genre you want to introduce with all students to begin the novel unit. Then have students select from four or five novels you have prearranged for their subsequent work in literature groups. By engaging all students in a single novel, you have a good context for introducing and modeling the concepts and strategies you think are important for students to be using independently later. With all students reading the same text, you can also help them develop good discussion skills and courteous behavior. Because a whole class is too large to hold engaging discussions most of the time, you can use a "fishbowl" technique and divide the class into two parts: Half the students sit in the center of the room and participate in oral discussion, and the other half sit around the outer part of the class and write their responses to the questions and flow of ideas and also monitor the participants' discussion behaviors. Use the same inner circle for the whole class period, or, if time permits, shift the roles halfway through the class period and give both groups the opportunity to participate both orally and in written form. By having the outer circle evaluate the participation of the inner circle, there is a good record of who has contributed and how the discussion proceeded. Students' written comments also serve as a good way to evaluate their own interpretation of the text and their response to the ideas discussed.

Supporting English language learners.   Using a single novel also helps students who are English language learners participate more fully in the class. Before the unit begins, a few students or parents can tape-record the novel or the first half of it so that English language learners can hear the sounds of the language and become familiar with the text. The teacher can also prepare special guides for these students so that they can follow the plot, know the characters, and think of questions ahead of class discussion. Some teachers have found that by giving English language learners mini-lessons before the general class sessions helps them to gain confidence in their understanding of the text so they can relax and enjoy the discussion of the text during the class periods. Finally, students gain confidence in their ability to contribute to class discussions when the teacher provides time for students to talk with partners before responding in the whole class or fishbowl. Pose a question for the group, then let students turn to their partners to think aloud about their responses, find the words and ways of expressing ideas in English, and get feedback that either modifies their ideas or confirms what they have said. Then open the conversation to the larger group. With this slight modification, many English language learners feel much more confident and comfortable participating in larger class groups. It is also a good model for all students: Think before speaking!

Connecting writing and reading.   While using a core novel with the whole class, you have the opportunity to model journal writing and use students' own responses to enhance the discussions. Students might need to learn how to respond to literature. Begin by showing your own journal entry for a part of the text the group is reading. Provide labels for the kinds of responses you make: connecting with the text (*this reminds me of . . .*), raising questions (*what does it matter if . . . ?*), visualizing (*I see . . . in my mind's eye*), responding emotionally (*I don't like ____ when . . .*), predicting (*I bet this problem will . . .*), and elaborating (*I know at this time in history there were often periods of . . .*). You might need to ask students to use two or three of the kinds of responses in their own journals so that they can develop the various ways of responding and then switch to other forms in the next entry. What you think is easy and automatic might be very uncomfortable for students. Rather than presuming a great deal, it is often better to start slowly and ensure that all students understand the tasks and intent of the journal experiences.

If students have a difficult time writing journal entries, they might do well to partner with another classmate and, between talk and writing, frame their joint responses to the text. You might find it useful to give students sticky notes to use while they are reading so that they don't lose the ideas that come to them while reading. Then they can return to those notes and elaborate on them as they write in their journals.

Journals can also serve as tools to help students focus on the features of the genre or other important elements of literature that you want to highlight. Students can keep a place in the journal where they record examples of specific literary elements, such as the setting in fantasy or futuristic elements in science fiction. They can also note special phrases or uses of language in the journal and share those later with other students. You can ask students to keep a section of their journals in which they can write new vocabulary items or new ways in which terms are used. If they record the pages on which the words occur, they can begin to see how authors often repeat the same vocabulary in different contexts. Adding drawings of the terms helps many students to enjoy this activity and remember the new words more easily.

LITERATURE CIRCLES.   Students tend to discuss books better when teachers are not leading the groups (Almasi, 1995; Hynds, 1997; Raphael & McMahon, 1994; Short & Kauffman, 1995). Many teachers prefer conducting their literature units by having students self-select the books they read and work in small discussion groups rather than in teacher-led discussions of the same novel. They do their teaching in mini-lessons at the beginning of

LANGUAGE and DIVERSITY

English sounds different than the written words may suggest. How can students hear correct academic English?

WRITING and READING CONNECTIONS

Argue for the importance of writing across units of instruction.

the class period so that all students can focus on the element the teacher highlights, but in their own texts, and then take on the role of active observers during book discussions led by the students. At times, teachers also serve as facilitators of the students' discussions, but they should not assume the role of "expert" at these times.

The nature of the mini-lessons that are used should derive from observations of the students as they are involved in reading and responding and by evaluating the written work of the students. The major framework that helps teachers to develop the foci for teaching comes also from the standards students should be able to meet.

For example, in Illinois, middle-grade students are expected to learn to "compare how authors and illustrators use text and art across materials to express ideas"—for example, foreshadowing, flashback, color, strong verbs, language that inspires (Illinois State Goal 1, middle/junior high). Knowing that expectation, a team of seventh-grade teachers developed a unit around the Middle Ages using novels and art representing that time period. They selected a set of novels including *The Ramsey Scallop* (Temple, 1994), *Catherine, Called Birdy* (Cushman, 1994), and the *The Midwife's Apprentice* (Cushman, 1995). They added materials that exemplified life in medieval Europe in other artistic forms: books about life in medieval Europe, including *Anno's Journey* (Mitsumasa, 1997), and *Castle* (McCauley, 1982); examples of tapestries from the collection at the Cloisters from the Metropolitan Museum for students to observe; and tapes of Gregorian chants. On the day the unit was introduced, the teachers played the music in the background, showed slides of the art, and talked about each of the novels. They then gave students time to look through each of the novels and make a decision about which books they wanted to read. Each student listed their first and second choices. From these lists, the teachers could help guide students to appropriate texts; some were much harder than others, and the teachers wanted all students to read somewhat challenging materials but not books they could not handle. During the unit, the teachers guided students to make comparisons about the artistic techniques used by artists in different media. Part of the journal guidelines for the students was to locate interesting examples of language used to create pictures of the times and compare that with other art. At specific points in the unit, the teachers also had students compare the plot and literary devices used by the different authors. In these and many other ways the teachers used the state standards and their own creative planning to develop a stimulating and enjoyable learning experience for the students.

Teachers varied the assignments they used to focus student learning. Because understanding point of view is another standard, some students were asked to keep a journal from the point of view of a character of their choice while reading. Students reading the same novel selected different characters so the impact of the plot and events on them could be recognized. Another group of students was asked to take particular scenes and rewrite them from a point of view different from that of the author. This proved a very interesting and challenging task. As a culmination, one group created a short readers' theater production for their novel that required students to take on the personas of the characters in the novel. In all these ways, the teachers focused the students' learning so that the maximum was gained for the time spent reading.

There are many advantages to having students in literature groups. First, the students' different reading abilities and interests can be accommodated much more easily this way, and all students can participate in the class activities. Assignments can be matched to the students' learning needs; not all able readers have developed the skills and strategies they need and can be focused through specific work. Using multiple texts permits teachers and students to make comparisons among authors and forms of art so authors' decisions and styles can be illustrated. Core vocabulary and concepts are generally repeated in various texts, so students gain a deeper understanding of the basic concepts and can develop better visual images of what they read. Students become resources for each other in very real ways when they are the authorities on particular texts. Speaking clearly, summarizing well, using good examples, and then listening to each other are very real communication skills that can be developed.

GUIDED READING AND READERS' WORKSHOPS. There is so much variety in the kinds of reading that students need to develop during the middle years that some group

TEACH IT! 29

Literature Circles

instruction by teachers is necessary. All students need to learn more about how textbooks are structured and the resources they contain. The differences in structures and discourse forms with which students must become familiar require teacher guidance. The various graphic aids and formats also need explanation and some direct attention. Then there is the issue of learning to do research and study independently. The middle years are when these become very important for students, and good schools provide a significant amount of time helping them learn to do research well and to construct reports and presentations. With the availability of computers, the use of the Web for collecting and evaluating information and the use of software for creating high-quality reports with digital pictures, imported pictures, and student-created diagrams and charts also need to be taught. For teachers who prefer doing most of their class work in fiction, this means that special segments of each week or a few weeks each quarter need to be devoted to informational reading and study.

How can students' assessments of each other's work help them to develop their comprehension and writing skills?

Some teachers prefer to structure a portion of their reading program around student-selected individual reading. Atwell (1998) has developed the **reading workshop** model, during which students all read individually in books of their own choosing and keep logs of their reading to use when they conference with the teacher. When students come together to discuss their reading, Atwell characterizes the conversations as a "dining room table" conversation about what each is reading. Although most of the time students read silently and write individual responses, the teacher brings students together periodically for mini-lessons in which aspects of literature or reading strategies can be explained. Later, students can apply these lesson foci when they engage in their own reading.

Depending on the amount of time the teacher has with students each day, the two components of a rich literacy program can be developed simultaneously or on alternating days and weeks. The two aspects can also be combined if teachers want to direct students' individual reading toward a particular theme or genre. For example, if the class is working on aspects of informational textbooks and scientific articles, then students could do their individual reading in books that include scientific essays, in magazines such as *Science* and *Scientific American* (or student magazines in the areas of science), and in biography. There are great texts that students can read and use to enlarge their horizons in this more guided reading workshop.

Expository Texts: Thematic Units

Most middle-level students enjoy exploring unanswered questions and making school relevant to their own lives. This is easier to do when a class is engaged in a focused group inquiry project or thematic unit of study. Because students are generally much less familiar with informational, expository texts than they are with fiction, providing a stimulating context for the study of such materials is very advantageous. By having the students read several texts on the same topic, you can more easily illustrate the various text structures that are used and can help students to determine the advantages and disadvantages of each. You can also provide activities in which students write using those same structures. Attention to the varieties of forms of informational writing is important, as is the need to make it interesting. Therefore, many teachers have found that developing units around interesting content permits better teaching and learning than other skill-focused instruction. This can be achieved either by creating units with content teachers (in departmental structures) or by integrating reading and content when you teach content and reading to the same students.

One model for integrated units developed by Michigan educators uses a key question as the focus for each unit, such as "Can the American dream be achieved?" In collecting the resources students will read, they use a planning grid to ensure that multiple perspectives

TEACH IT! 43
Descriptive Writing

THE AMERICAN DREAM UNIT OVERVIEW				

Thematic Statement: Personal goals and choices are influenced by our own values.

Focus Question: Is it still possible to achieve the American Dream?

Project: Persuasive Paper: Is the American dream still achievable for me?

Selection	Genre	Perspective	Diversity	Period
The Grapes of Wrath	novel/realistic fiction	negative	Lower-class Anglo-American	1930s
The Great Gatsby	novel/realistic fiction	negative	Upper-class Anglo-American	1920s
"I Have A Dream"	speech	positive	African American	1960s
"Maya Angelou"	poem	positive	African American	1990s
"An American Dream"	magazine	positive	European	1990s
"Charlie Two Shoes & the American Dream"	magazine	positive	Asian	1950s
"Is the American Dream Still Alive?"	magazine	positive	Mexican-American	1990s
"False Gold"	magazine	negative	Lower-class America	1990s

FIGURE 13.4

Thematic Unit Overview.

on the issues are presented and that a wide variety of literature, both fiction and nonfiction, is included. See the example in Figure 13.4 of the resources for one unit.

Essays and Biography

When teachers do not feel comfortable creating more extended units around themes or content topics, they can still provide guided instruction to help students handle informational reading. Contemporary magazines for middle school students contain much excellent writing and are good sources for reading development. *Cobblestones, Calliope, Faces, National Geographic World*, and *Boys' Life* magazines are great sources of articles. Collecting a variety of biographies, both long and short, is another way of providing texts that permit the teacher to guide students to reading more deeply in this genre. The different ways in which biographies are structured provide the opportunity to focus on organization and can be linked to students' writing of a biography later. Teachers can provide a good comparative study of how biographers represent the lives and accomplishments of well-known figures by structuring assignments so that students read and compare encyclopedia-type sketches and then read more in-depth book treatments of the same person. When more than one full-length biography is available, even more critical analysis is made possible, and students find it engaging. They easily become excited (and sometimes indignant) at how people are represented. Then good questions analyzing the author's purpose, context, and perspective are natural.

Drama and Choral Reading

One of the most interesting aspects of written language is hearing it read and performed orally. Middle-level students also love these kinds of activities. Some teachers allocate two to three weeks during the year for production of a play or choral reading and having students perform before audiences. These dramatic events can be part of science and social studies content as much as literature units. There are Web sites specifically devoted to readers' theater scripts for teacher use. This makes including this oral form of reading (and rereading for fluency) much easier for busy teachers.

For English language learners, opportunities to participate in rehearsed oral language productions or even oral reading of poetry helps to instill a sense of the sounds of English language that can last a lifetime. Regular opportunities to memorize or at least reread and rehearse language provides valuable patterns that English language learners can rely on and build from later.

Readers' Theater exercises can be incorporated into all areas of the curriculum; this is a popular technique with young people.

Organizing and Managing a Learning Community

As you plan instruction to include all that is important for middle-grade students to learn, consider some of the options suggested in Figure 13.5 for weekly programs. These can shift over the course of the semester; however, you need to use your time wisely, and attention to planning will always pay off. Note the allotted time for whole-group activities, small groups, and individual work and reflection.

Adolescents' Identity and Motivation

Reaching and teaching young adolescents takes special consideration. Students at this period in their lives are going through enormous changes; one day they might seem like they are adults and very much in control, and the next day the same students behave as if they are children, definitely in need of adult structure and guidance. Younger adolescents also feel tremendous pressures from their peers. They want to be accepted and part of the peer group of those they admire. Often, this drives them away from adults and family, and teachers have to build their trust to create open, safe classrooms where students will engage fully.

Adding to the normal developmental changes that middle-level students go through, our current culture inundates students with information and options—a sort of food court mentality. Everything students do involves choice, from what kind of milk to drink to which brand of French fries they want to eat. Even the cereals they eat in the morning might be their own selected favorites, chosen by no other family member. They become accustomed to having life tailored to their specific interests and preferences. This has real implications for their response to classroom activities. Choice needs to be a part of what is provided in terms of materials, groups, and learning activities. Children who are given choices outside of school expect them in school, too.

Young students live in a world that is ever changing and somewhat frightening to them. They look for classrooms that are safe and that respect their needs and interests. The teacher can do a great deal to make classrooms predictable and orderly simply by having clear routines and ways of engaging that students can anticipate. For instance, when students have

Monday	Tuesday	Wednesday	Thursday	Friday
Class focusing in whole group (10 min.) Share independent reading and viewing	Class focusing in whole group (5—10 min.) Teacher shares own reading	Class focusing in whole group (5—10 min.) Reflect on goals for week	Class focusing: teacher reads orally and thinks aloud—model use of target goal	Class focusing teacher/students share vocabulary
Teacher-guided lessons: reading and writing strategies attention to detail (30 min.+) & Small group and individual reading & writing activities: guided practice and independent work	Individual silent reading and writing (15—20 min.) & Partner/small group work (5—10 min.) Teacher conferences	Small group discussions (10—15 min.) and journal reflections Teacher observation of discussion—some participation Individual reading and writing (15 min.)	Teacher guided lessons: focus reading or vocabulary strategies (10—15 min.) Individual work reading, writing and research (10—15 min.)	Small group discussions (10—15 min.) journal reflections Individual work
Reflecting/ writing/planning ahead (5—10 min.)	Reflecting/ thinking ahead (5—10 min.)	Reflecting/ thinking ahead (5—10 min.)	Reflecting/ thinking ahead	Reflecting/ writing/ thinking ahead (1—10 min.)

FIGURE 13.5

Weekly Schedule.

several teachers each day, they often get confused about what kinds of participation each considers acceptable. Explaining how you want students to behave—when they have to raise their hands, when they can interrupt each other, when they can move around the room, and how they interact in small group activities helps many. Putting the rules on a chart that can be displayed regularly makes many others feel more comfortable. In addition, the clearer you make your expectations for the work students will do and how they will be evaluated, the more likely it is that students will relax and participate actively.

The humor, compassion, and idealism of young students are also wonderful attributes of this stage. They respond well to teachers who bring in humor, give them an opportunity to laugh, and encourage their fun sides. Many middle-grade students find meaning by being able to work with younger students, and some classes make it a regular practice to build buddy programs with primary classrooms so that the middle-level students serve as mentors and helpers for young children.

Finally, students at this stage need to see the relevance of the activities they are asked to do. The more learning can involve real inquiry about topics of concern to them, the more likely students are to become engaged. Beane (1991) even advocates that middle-school students together at the beginning of the school year determine the units that they study. Being clear about the goals and purposes of class activities and how they relate to the students is important. Establishing a safe climate where students can ask questions, engage in extended inquiry, and express their own ideas and conclusions is a foundation to their learning.

Beamon (2001) suggests that adolescents learn best when activities are interactive and purposeful and include meaningful engagement. The five circumstances that make this most likely are as follows:

1. Adolescents do something that makes sense in a larger context, such as confronting real-life issues and problems.
2. Their personal initiative and energy are moved into action through meaningful involvement with relevant and current content.
3. Their cognitive and affective capabilities are challenged, such as when connections are made between difficult content and its application to personal experience.
4. They can draw on a variety of resources in the learning environment, including personal experience, the local community, and the Internet.
5. Their knowledge and understanding are substantively broadened or deepened.

Selecting Appropriate Materials

Most new teachers start out the year having to use the materials that have already been selected—whether it is a reading anthology/basal series, a literature series, or a curriculum built around novels and thematic units of instruction. If there are classroom sets of novels, informational books, and magazines, these can be great resources for building a rich reading program. You want to make sure you can create a room that invites students in to reading and writing. One element of immersion is creating the right environment; the visual statement is a powerful one that all students notice. Having books and magazines is important, and ensuring that they are current and of interest is essential, as is displaying them attractively.

Assess what is available to you, and think of any holes that seem apparent. For example, check to see whether multiple levels of reading materials are available so that you can differentiate instruction for your students. Check to see whether fiction, poetry, plays, and readers' theater scripts are handy and that informational materials are in good supply. As you do your own inventory, also check with the school librarian and/or media specialist to see what resources they have for your use. And, of course, talk with the other teachers on your team or in your department so that you can be aware of all the collected materials that are available. Table 13.6 identifies some basic materials you will need to get started.

Given the current attention to state standards, a more focused curriculum is also quite likely. You will want to assess areas in which there are ample materials for your use when you want to go in-depth and do some lessons that provide attention to detail in practice materials. Some of these might be available for use on computers; make an inventory of all the resources you can locate.

Because it is important that students learn to think critically about their reading, check for ways in which you can help students read from a variety of resources on the same topic or theme. If you have an anthology to use for literature selections, locate two or three pieces that complement or contrast with the core text so you can go beyond a single selection. If you are linking to content areas like science and social studies, provide both fiction and nonfiction materials that will deepen the units of study and help you guide students into more sophisticated reading of these materials.

A wealth of resources is available for use with middle school learners. The following Web sites provide resources and links to literature discussions in which students can participate:

- The National Council for Social Studies provides a list of Notable Social Studies Books for Young People at **www.socialstudies.org/resources/notable/**.
- The National Science Teachers Association recommends a variety of resources, including books, at **www.nsta.org/recommends/**.

TABLE 13.6

Materials Checklist

- Range of core text materials at varying reading levels
- Variety of types of materials (short stories, novels, informational texts, magazines, newspapers)
- Resource materials (how our language grows and changes, language usage and vocabulary, thesaurus, dictionaries)
- Practice materials (print and electronic) including vocabulary supports
- Materials that provide contrasting points of view
- Professional materials for your use and students' use, as appropriate

- The International Reading Association provides lists of choice books compiled by teachers, young adults, and children at **www.reading.org/choices/**.
- Many books also contain book lists. Junko Yokota's book *Kaleidoscope* (National Council of Teachers of English, 2001) includes a booklist for grades K–8.
- Many local libraries have Web sites that provide links to online book clubs. Sometimes the libraries themselves sponsor book clubs. In many cases, libraries have partnered with the organization "Chapteraday," which has book clubs for teens as well as adults and covers a broad range of genres. Check out the following links to online book clubs: **http://www.chapteraday.com**, **http://www.surfnetkids.com/bookclubs .htm**, **www.planetbookclub.com**.

Assessing Reading Levels of Materials

Sometimes you may have a room full of materials, but you do not know whether they are appropriate for your students' reading development. You might want to do a quick fluency check to see how many of your students can handle the material easily. Sampling a few students who scored at the middle range, a few from the lower level, and a few from the upper level (as charted on your fluency scale) can give you a good idea of how you can use your material. One other easy way to check the match between any particular novel, text, or other material and your students is to develop a **cloze test** (Bormuth, 1968) and administer it to your students (see the Assessment box).

Involving Parents and the Community

Many parents of middle school students complain that their children no longer want to share with them what happens in school. One middle school decided to create a structure that would bring students and parents together. They initiated the Generations Literature Circle as a voluntary activity and then extended it to become a full part of school life. Parents and students agreed to read the same novel and come together for a book discussion and share their responses to the book. Both groups read and made notes about favorite passages, and both groups developed questions they wanted to ask others about the book. Parents were not to ask those questions of their own children but could offer them to the whole group. The book discussion replaced part of the parent conference night. It provided a good way for parents to understand the new forms of book discussion being used by the reading and language arts department. As they experimented with the discussions, one class had fun using the inner/outer circle idea. First the students formed the inner circle and discussed some aspects of the book under teacher facilitation. Then the parents took their turn and discussed the same issues. Both groups had a great time understanding a little better the responses of the other generation.

In the middle grades there is an increasingly wide variety of materials teachers can use to help students learn. One good tool to use to find out if the materials are within the reach of the students is the cloze procedure. It can be used with content textbooks, articles downloaded from the Internet, magazine articles, or any piece of text you consider using.

Cloze Assessment

To use the cloze test, take a passage of approximately 300 words from early in the text and retype it for your students, deleting every fifth word starting with the second sentence. Make sure that you have spaces of equal length for all the words that were left out and that the spaces are large enough that students can fill in what they think the author used. Then select one or two additional sections from later in the text if it is lengthy and do the same process.

Before giving the cloze test, model the procedure with your class because it might be unfamiliar to your students. Create a short sample from an article, leaving the first one or two sentences intact (see Figure 13.6). Then delete every fifth word until you have about five to ten spaces. Put the passage on the computer screen, on an overhead, or on the erasable board. Explain that you are going to try to fill in the exact words the author used, taking into account the style and total context of the piece. Let the students know that you are trying to determine whether the particular author has written in a way that matches their expectations and knowledge. Students might need another example that they can do independently or with a partner before completing the full cloze passage you have developed

(see Figure 13.7). If you use this second modeling, be sure that you take time to go over the answers and explain why particular choices are better than others.

Other Measures to Determine Levels

One of the most traditional ways to assess the difficulty level of materials is to use a formula that measures the difficulty of the words and the complexity of the sentences. Both the Dale-Chall (1948) Formula (for easy materials) and the Fry (1967) Readability Formula (appropriate through adult materials) use these indices of difficulty. Teachers can select a few passages from the text and determine their difficulty level; however, these formulas are general and provide only a rough estimate of difficulty for readers (see Chapter 10 for a review).

Use these tools just as rough starting places. Students' individual knowledge and interests influence how well they can understand texts they read. As students get older, the use of formulas becomes less predictive of the match between students and materials. Therefore, it is always good to check with students directly about their ability to understand materials. They can often provide clear feedback, and their ability to read and talk about what they read is the real measure we need. It is also true that the more students read on any topic, the more able they become to handle more difficult materials on the same topic. The same is true with authors; once students become familiar with an author's style, they can more easily independently handle more material by that particular author.

We have seen that the American colonists needed labor to build their fortunes and, in the process, build a nation. And we have seen their willingness to take that labor, by force, from Africans. But, African men and _____ did not willingly surrender _____ lives. The people who came _____ the boats were Africans, _____ by a strange tribe. _____ plantation owners did not _____ captives longing from freedom, _____ for ways to overthrow _____ who held them; they _____ slaves, people who would _____ without having to be _____ watched.

Taken from Now Is Your Time! By Walter Dean Myers (p. 36; HarperCollins, NY, 1991)

Exact words deleted: women, their from, captured, The, want, longing, looking, wanted, work, constantly

FIGURE 13.6

Cloze Passage.

When animal droppings and garbage and spoiled straw are piled up in a great heap, the rotting and moiling give forth heat. Usually no one gets close enough to notice because of the stench. But the girl noticed _____, on that frosty night, _____ deep into the warm, _____ muck, heedless of the _____. In any event, the _____ heap probably smelled little _____ than everything else in _____ life—the food scraps _____ from the kitchen yards, _____ stables and sties she _____ in when she could, _____ her own unwashed, unnourished, _____, and unlovely body.

Taken from The Midwife's Apprentice by Karen Cushman (p. 1; Clarion Books, NY, 1995)

Exact words deleted: and, burrowed, rotting, smell, dung, worse, her, scavenged, the, slept, and, unloved

FIGURE 13.7

Cloze Passage (Second Short Model).

Another exciting community reading event occurred when the mayor of Chicago declared that the whole city would read a book together. The book that was chosen was *To Kill a Mockingbird*. This book was already being used in many schools as part of the regular middle school literature/social studies curriculum, but for the special year, the middle school teachers in one K–8 building decided to involve the local school council members (the community school board) in a discussion of the book. During the first part of the evening, the council members sat in the inner circle and discussed their responses to the book while the eighth graders listened. Then it was the eighth graders' turn while the adults listened. What a memorable night! And what different perspectives were enabled!

For Review

Middle-level students are at a great stage of development—moving from childhood to maturity. They are eager and impatient to find themselves in the world, especially among their peers. Books and good instruction can provide great models and stimulate their best impulses. We as teachers have a great deal we can do to ensure that they develop into their best selves.

This chapter began by laying out the wide variety of literacy skills and strategies students need to develop in the middle grades. Particularly important changes occur at this point in schooling as teachers involve students more heavily in reading informational materials. Students need to become independent in their ability to apply appropriate strategies as they anticipate, build knowledge, and consolidate their learning. Vocabulary development is particularly important because students encounter so many words and concepts that are new to them. In the chapter, several activities that help students develop interest in and curiosity about words and strategies to retain new words for content learning and for their own personal vocabulary enhancement were described. Examples of good references to help teachers and students learn more about the rich nature of our language were also provided.

Because students in the middle grades possess a wide range of reading abilities, the section on assessment provided many avenues through which teachers can determine what students can do and what areas need more attention. These include using informal reading inventories, leveled books, fluency measures, and assessing awareness of text features, vocabulary, interests, and strategy knowledge.

Suggestions for how teachers can help students learn strategies for studying and retaining information from reading and develop their own self-monitoring of their learning were provided. The chapter stressed the value of writing and keeping portfolios as evidence of learning.

The importance of students engaging in reading on a regular basis is a theme that continues throughout the chapter. Specific ways to reach all students, including English language learners, were introduced. The chapter suggested ways to organize for instruction with literature and informational texts. These include integrating content learning and reading instruction through thematic units and teaching literature by using core novels and literature groups, literature circles, and guided reading with readers' workshop.

The final section dealt with ways to organize and manage a learning community by being sensitive to young adolescents and providing a rich array of materials that they can read with confidence and interest.

For Your Journal

1. What do you think is the optimal classroom environment in which to encourage and support middle-level students?

2. After reading about different ways to organize classroom instruction, take some time to reflect on which ideas and structures you think you could use most productively. What are the reasons that you selected one over another? Have you seen other ways of organizing that you prefer?

Taking It to the World

A pair of eighth-grade teachers added a new dimension to the study of the Bill of Rights by having their students conduct a mock court trial. The issue: A student is accused of humming during the national anthem, a violation of a rule. The teacher faces a loss of job and pension. During a month-long study of the issues, students assembled arguments and witnesses and then argued the case. Because one teacher's spouse is a lawyer, the students did get some assistance in determining exactly how they should argue both sides of the case. Class members served as lawyers, jury, clerks, and witnesses. The students got so involved in their research and legal work that the local newspaper heard about the trial and photographed the final session.

Look carefully at the U.S. Constitution's Bill of Rights. Brainstorm with a friend ways you could make a thematic study of the rights practical for your students. What issues in the community could be highlighted?

Technology Connections

1. Middle-level students love to share their ideas and find out what their peers think. Now it is possible for students to extend these discussions worldwide with some of the good sites that have been established for book discussions internationally. Search for some of the sites that help students to connect with their peers in other countries.

2. Visit the American Library Association (**www.ala.org**), and complete a search for materials for reluctant readers.

Connect with Research

Review the following key words from the chapter, and then connect to Research Navigator (**www.researchnavigator.com**) through this book's Companion Website to conduct a search into research on each of the various topics as they relate to reading and literacy education today.

classroom fluency measure portfolios
cloze test Question Answer Relation (QAR) strategy
metacognition reading workshop

Companion Website

To access chapter objectives, practice tests, weblinks, and flashcards, visit the Companion Website at www.ablongman.com/templeallchildren2e.

Where the classroom comes to life!

Go to Allyn & Bacon's MyLabSchool (www.mylabschool.com), enter Assignment ID RMV5 into the Assignment Finder. Watch the video, *Word Analysis Strategy,* in which your author Alan Crawford discusses how word analysis strategies such as context clues and cloze tests help students actively construct meaning. A teacher is shown using a cloze passage in class to become strategic in figuring out unknown meaning.

Question: What is a cloze procedure and how is it used to assess comprehension? You may also answer the questions at the end of the clip and e-mail your responses to your instructor.

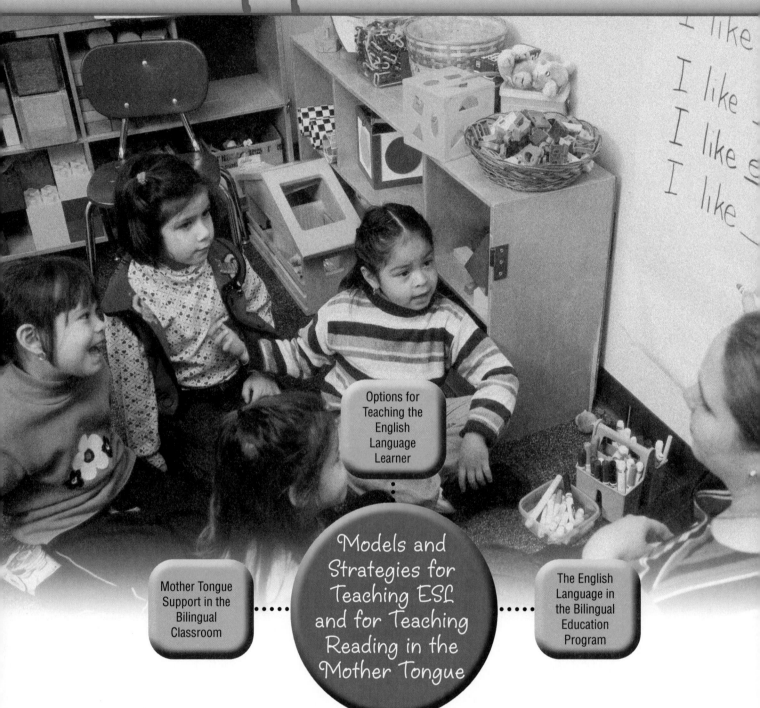

chapter 14

Models and
Strategies for
Teaching ESL
and for Teaching
Reading in the
Mother Tongue

Options for
Teaching the
English
Language
Learner

Mother Tongue
Support in the
Bilingual
Classroom

The English
Language in
the Bilingual
Education
Program

Options for
Teaching the
English
Language
Learner to Read

Models and Strategies for Teaching ESL and for Teaching Reading in the Mother Tongue: A Focus on Spanish

Anticipation Guide

The following statements will stimulate your thinking about the topics of this chapter. Answer true or false in response to each statement. As you read and learn more about the topics in these statements, double-check your answers. See what interests you and what prompts your curiosity toward more understanding.

_____ ● English language learners can learn English in one year.

_____ ● It is a waste of instructional time to teach a child to read in the child's mother tongue.

_____ ● Phonics is the most important component of reading for an English language learner.

_____ ● Children should always be grouped by level of English proficiency for English as a second language (ESL) lessons.

_____ ● Children who learn to read in Spanish have to start over when they learn to read in English.

_____ ● The teacher should always correct the grammatical errors of English language learners.

_____ ● Children who have learned to read in their mother tongue have little difficulty learning to read in English.

_____ ● English language learners should always respond in complete sentences.

_____ ● Some adolescent English language learners are not able to read in any language.

A Bilingual Teacher in a Bilingual Classroom

Ms. Ortega is a certified bilingual first-grade teacher. Her twenty-three students speak Spanish as their first language, and their English proficiency ranges from none to a few at a low-to-intermediate level. Her children are ready to learn to read in Spanish, and she is well prepared to teach them. The Spanish reading program she uses is parallel to the English language program used in other classrooms in her school, but it is not a direct translation. She also has a wealth of children's literature in Spanish.

Ms. Ortega begins her morning business in English. "Good morning, boys and girls." "Good morning, teacher," they respond, politely and respectfully addressing her by her title. After several weeks of school, the children can greet their teacher, respond to the roll and lunch count, and understand most classroom routines in English. Morning business is followed by a forty-minute ESL

TEACH IT! 10

Shared Reading

The children in Ms. Ortega's classroom are indeed fortunate. They are in a full bilingual program with a highly qualified teacher and with appropriate instructional materials. She addresses them in English in the parts of her program where they are ready to understand. She consistently devotes thirty to forty minutes of instructional time each day to ESL, focusing on listening with nonverbal or simple responses at the beginning, with more emphasis on production later.

Her Spanish reading program is analytic or whole-part-whole, with children learning about letter/sound correspondences in the context of words they already recognize. The plentiful authentic literature in her classroom provides for a strong focus on comprehension and motivation.

TEACH IT! 9

Shared Reading and the Four Blocks Approach

The vignette also displays how Ms. Ortega presents the elements of the four blocks framework described in Chapter 1: guided reading and writing, self-selected reading, and working with words (Cunningham, Hall, & Sigmon, 2007). She demonstrates reading to her students in the shared reading activities with big books. She works with words in the brief focused phonics lessons that emerge from meaningful reading and writing activities. She provides guided practice both in the shared reading of big books and in the dictation and reading back of dictated language-experience charts. The children extend their reading practice in reading shared books to each other and language-experience charts to family members. They will soon begin to write in Spanish as an outgrowth of their LEA activities.

The purpose of this chapter is to examine the teaching of reading in the mother tongue and also the teaching of ESL as it relates to the teaching of reading. The focus mother tongue language for the chapter is Spanish, the language most commonly encountered in lesson that is characterized by simple dramatized commands, questions, many gestures and smiles, and much laughter.

After recess, the children have whole-class shared reading activities in Spanish with big books. In smaller groups, they dictate language-experience chart stories in Spanish, read them, put the sentences in order, illustrate, read to each other, and play word games with vocabulary they have used. Independently and in pairs, they will take turns "reading" big books to each other and reading language-experience stories to family members at home.

Some of the children are beginning to associate sounds with letters they recognize, and Ms. Ortega has begun to teach brief focused phonics lessons related to elements that have emerged from their language-experience charts and for which they have demonstrated phonemic awareness in language play activities. They also work in the more structured Spanish reading program with anthologies of stories and some expository text. The program includes more systematic and explicit activities designed to introduce the relationships between sounds and letters in Spanish several weeks into the school year and after they have developed a basic sight vocabulary.

bilingual classrooms. The audience for the chapter is threefold: bilingual teachers who will teach reading and writing in a language other than English, teachers of English language learners whose mother tongue instruction will be conducted by a paraprofessional or other staff members under the teacher's supervision, and all teachers of English language learners who teach ESL.

Options for Teaching the English Language Learner

There are two basic categories of instructional programs for teaching English language learners. These categories are presented in terms of the generic K–8 school program for them; the specific questions of second language and reading instruction are treated later in the chapter.

Teach Them in English

English-only options for teaching English language learners exist in several forms and for many reasons. In some cases, the numbers of children who have a non–English language

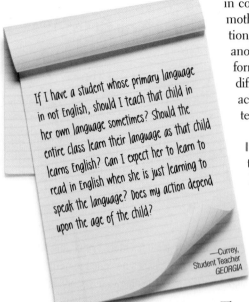

in common at a grade level are small, and it is not feasible to offer a program of mother tongue instruction. A lack of trained teachers and mother tongue instructional materials may exacerbate this situation. Political considerations constitute another reason for providing only English language instruction, such as in California and Arizona, where statewide ballot propositions largely discourage or make difficult the use of mother tongue instruction and mandate the use of what is characterized as structured immersion in English. But there are many limitations in teaching English language learners only in English, as you will see.

IMMERSION INSTRUCTION.   One approach to second-language acquisition is immersion, sometimes called structured immersion (see Figure 14.1). Immersion instructional programs are focused on intensive English instruction during the first year, although it is well documented that children need more than one year to master enough English to learn academic subjects and reading in English (Thomas & Collier, 1997).

ESL instruction is the most important element in an immersion approach to teaching English language learners. Their academic instruction in reading, mathematics, science, and social science is also conducted in English, although English language learners gain little from this instruction. They do not understand or speak English, nor can they read in English at a sufficient level of comprehension. In some cases, support in the mother tongue is provided by a paraprofessional or parent volunteer. For example, that adult might sit down with the English language learners to assist them in understanding a teacher's lesson taught earlier in English and in completing independent work.

What is often called a *submersion* approach is a variation on structured immersion, and it is truly a sink-or-swim approach. Although most educators do not advocate its use, the submersion approach is often observed as the default methodology in working with English language learners. Non-English-speaking children are simply thrown to the mercies of a teacher, classmates, and instructional materials in English, with no concessions to their language or cultural needs. This sometimes occurs for political reasons. It is sometimes simply a reflection of the school's inability to respond to the needs of a small number of children from a less common mother tongue who do not speak English.

Lambert (1975) contrasts additive and subtractive education programs for second-language learners. In an **additive program**, children add a new language and culture to the mother tongue and culture and its accompanying culture, along with a positive self-image. In a **subtractive program**, English and its accompanying culture are substituted for the mother tongue and culture, often leading to low self-esteem, leaving school, low academic achievement, and other negative consequences. Immersion programs are of the subtractive type.

Several major principles guide teachers' understanding of providing the best context for learning and for learning in a second language. Cummins (1986, 1989) describes two levels of language proficiency that demonstrate the need for high-level proficiency in the second language before academic instruction is provided in the second language. He describes **basic interpersonal communications skills (BICS)** as those that permit English language learners to carry on a simple conversation in the new second language, and they appear to be proficient. But a higher level of language proficiency, **cognitive academic language proficiency (CALP)**, is required for the student to learn to read in the second language or, for example, to learn the commutative principle of addition in mathematics. Cummins concludes that a threshold of language proficiency in the mother tongue must be reached for the student to attain academic proficiency in the mother tongue and later in a second language. This threshold is seldom met in programs of immersion in English.

STRUCTURES FOR PROVIDING ESL INSTRUCTION.   The most common pattern for providing English language instruction is that in which the teacher in the self-contained classroom provides all instruction, including ESL. Another common pattern is the pullout program, which is usually employed in elementary schools. ESL teachers have their own classrooms, and for periods of forty to sixty minutes, they pull children out of their self-

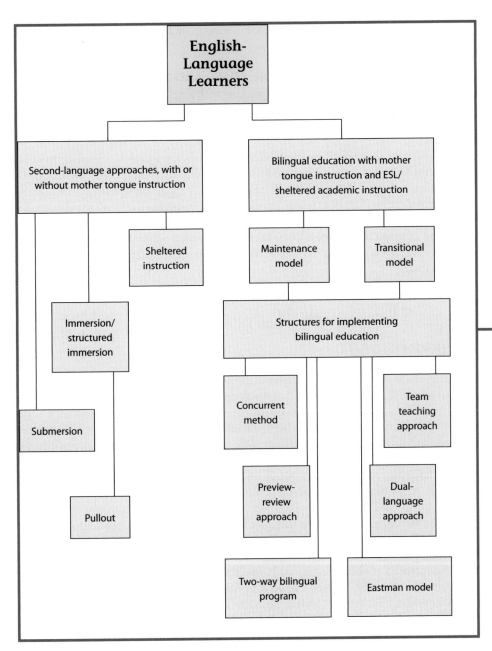

FIGURE 14.1

Model Program Structures for Meeting the Needs of English Language Learners.

contained classrooms for ESL instruction and then send them back. In semidepartmentalized and departmentalized intermediate or junior high schools, usually at the fifth- or sixth-grade level and above, one teacher might have responsibility for teaching ESL to all English language learners.

Unfortunately, not every teacher is well prepared—or perhaps prepared at all—to teach ESL. An advantage of a pullout program is that a specialist can be very effective in providing this important instruction and will usually have high-quality materials for this purpose.

The pullout approach also has several disadvantages. Children miss instruction in the regular classroom, depending on the hour during which they are absent. English language learners are singled out as "special" or "different" when they leave for ESL instruction, which often has negative consequences. Pullout programs are usually organized according to homogeneous groups in that the ESL teacher will pull beginners from several classrooms for a period of instruction, then intermediate learners from several classrooms, and so on. Even in the self-contained classroom, the teacher should consider teaching the English language learners as a single group, regardless of their proficiency. As you will see later in this chapter, there are advantages to having children at several levels of English language proficiency during ESL/language development lessons, including the presence of capable English speakers.

SHELTERED ENGLISH INSTRUCTION, SDAIE, AND SIOP. **Sheltered English instruction** is a very powerful approach for working with English language learners, but it is an intermediate approach. It is designed to follow an initial second-language acquisition program that takes students from non–English speaker status to that of intermediate speaker of English.

In California, sheltered instruction is called Specially Designed Academic Instruction in English (SDAIE). A more recent model of sheltered instruction is called the Sheltered Instruction Observation Protocol (SIOP) (Echevarria, Vogt, & Short, 2004).

It is therefore an important second-language component of all education programs for English language learners, whether they have been in bilingual education or in an English immersion program. It constitutes, however, a submersion approach when used, or misused, with beginning speakers of English. We examine sheltered English instruction later in this chapter.

Teach Them in the Language They Already Speak

The *Lau* v. *Nichols* decision (see Chapter 2) did not mandate bilingual education as a remedy, but school districts soon found that it was one of the few ways to ensure that English language learners had equal access to education, that is, education in their mother tongue while they learned English. In most bilingual education programs, children learn to read and write and also study the other subjects of the academic curriculum—mathematics, social science, and science—in their mother tongue. Simultaneously, they learn English as a second language, a process that typically takes two to five years or more (Thomas & Collier, 1997). As the result of a transition process called **positive transfer of skills**, children can then do in English what they have learned to do in the mother tongue (Cummins, 1981). The knowledge that English language learners have in the mother tongue, they will also have in English. Furthermore, once a child is able to read in the mother tongue, learning to read in English as a second language is a relatively smooth and effortless process— the child learns to read only once. When children do not have the opportunity to learn academic subjects in the mother tongue, they obviously fall behind in those subjects during the period of time they are learning English.

The underlying principles of bilingual education are as follows:

- Teach English language learners to understand and speak English as a second language.
- Teach the academic subjects, including reading and writing, in the mother tongue while the children are in the process of learning to understand and speak English.
- Transition the children from mother tongue academic instruction to English language instruction in a sheltered mode when they have an intermediate level of English.

Because of the lack of instructional materials and a lack of trained bilingual teachers in many languages, non–Spanish-language bilingual education programs are less common and usually limited in scope.

In *Preventing Reading Difficulties in Young Children*, Snow, Burns, and Griffin (1998) endorsed the efficacy of teaching children to read in the mother tongue wherever possible before teaching them to read in English. A major five-year developmental study conducted by Thomas and Collier (2002) provides additional evidence to support this point of view. Although many mother tongues were represented in their study of over 210,000 students in five school districts in Texas, Oregon, and Maine, most of the students were Spanish speaking. Thomas and Collier found that one-way or dual language bilingual enrichment programs that were 90:10 or 50:50 (the ratio of mother tongue instruction to English instruction) were the only programs in which students reached the fiftieth percentile in both languages and in which there were the fewest dropouts. Children whose parents refused bilingual education programs, insisting instead on English only, had much lower achievement. The strongest predictor of English language achievement in the study was the amount of formal mother tongue instruction. Thomas and Collier found that the highest achievement in bilingual education programs was associated with those that offered a natural learning environment in school, with rich oral and written language in both the mother tongue and English, problem solving, group student activities, media-rich learning, challenging thematic units, and use of the students' bilingual and bicultural knowledge to access new knowledge.

In a major meta-analysis of studies about the language and literacy development of language-minority students, The National Literacy Panel on Language-Minority Children and Youth published a report in 2006. Their conclusions paralleled those of the National Reading Panel (2000). First, they concluded that phonemic awareness, phonics, fluency, vocabulary, and text comprehension instruction were major factors in the development of literacy. They did, however, recommend that more focus be placed on working with particular phonemes that do not exist in their mother tongues.

Second, they found that although language-minority children were able to keep pace with their English-speaking classmates in the development of word recognition skills, they fell behind in comprehension and writing. They attributed this to the lower level of English language proficiency among these students.

Third, they concluded that children's oral proficiency and reading ability in the mother tongue can be used to facilitate the development of literacy in English as a result of the positive transfer of skills, a finding similar to that of Snow et al. in *Preventing Reading Difficulties* (1998) cited earlier.

Fourth, they concluded that there is a hierarchy of skills in English that must be attained before children can be successful in reading comprehension in English and that individual differences among children are a significant factor in this development. They further concluded that for language-minority children in special education programs, developing sight word reading and holistic learning strategies might be more effective in teaching them to read and write.

Fifth, they concluded that most assessment tools used with language-minority children are not effective in measuring their individual strengths and weaknesses. They also found little evidence of the effect of sociocultural variables on the development of literacy, except for the positive effect of home language experiences.

I'm worried about the self-esteem of my students. They need to develop English, but there is a danger of their losing the language and culture of their homes. How can I help them develop self-esteem so that they recognize the value of two languages and cultures?

—Leonora,
Preservice Teacher
Candidate
CALIFORNIA

TRANSITIONAL VERSUS MAINTENANCE MODELS OF BILINGUAL EDUCATION. There are two underlying philosophies about how to conduct programs of bilingual education: transitional and maintenance. In the more common **transitional model**, children learn English as a second language; learn their academic subjects, including reading and writing, in the mother tongue; and make the transition to English language academic instruction in a sheltered mode when they have reached an intermediate level of English, usually between the late second grade and early fourth grade. The major goal of the transitional program is to produce a monolingual, monoliterate, and monocultural child who temporarily uses the mother tongue as a vehicle for learning. Children in transitional bilingual programs usually continue their academic studies only in English after the onset of transition to English, although they sometimes receive continuing support in the mother tongue from a paraprofessional, as needed.

In the **maintenance model**, the process is the same up to the point of transition. After the children begin academic instruction in English, they continue to receive periodic lessons in the mother tongue in all subject areas. The major outcome of the maintenance program is a bilingual, biliterate, and bicultural child who is able to function easily and comfortably in two languages and cultures.

STRUCTURES FOR ORGANIZING PROGRAMS OF BILINGUAL EDUCATION
Within the transitional and maintenance models are several structures for grouping children and for assigning teachers and paraprofessionals that can be used in either model.

Concurrent approach.   One approach that is often used intuitively is called the *concurrent method.* The teacher says everything twice, once in the children's mother tongue and once in English, assuming there is only one non–English language in the classroom and the teacher is bilingual. When the teacher is not bilingual, a bilingual paraprofessional may fill that second role, basically serving as an interpreter. It is a time-efficient approach with an uncomplicated structure. It is also very ineffective. English language learners begin to tune out the English, which they cannot understand well or perhaps at all, and they listen only to their mother tongue. If they do learn some English as a part of the process, they learn it in terms of their mother tongue. The outcome is a compound bilingual child with two interdependent language systems. The result is a lifetime of unconscious translation from one language to another, a process that takes precious time, especially on examinations such as the SAT, the GRE, or the important high-stakes tests that are now required in many states. This approach also promotes code switching, the unconscious mixing of vocabulary and syntactical structures from two languages.

Team teaching.   The team-teaching approach is quite different. Two teachers, one bilingual, the other usually not, work together in the same classroom. They work independently; but when they teach, each teaches the entire class. The primary advantages of this approach are to provide outstanding language and cultural models to the children and to reduce the number of proficient bilingual teachers needed.

Dual language.   The dual-language model resembles the team-teaching model in that there are two teachers, one bilingual, the other usually not, but in separate classrooms. The monolingual English-speaking teacher teaches English as a second language and academic instruction in English for those in the two classrooms who are ready for it. The bilingual teacher teaches the academic subjects to the English language learners in the mother tongue and also teaches the other language, usually Spanish, as a second language.

The advantages of the dual-language model are that both teachers are working in a language of comfort to them and the children are learning English and their academic subjects from teachers who are good models. Unlike the concurrent method, they are not learning English in terms of the mother tongue but rather are developing as coordinate bilinguals with two independent language systems. The major disadvantage is that the English-speaking and non–English-speaking children are rarely working together because their needs are very different. It is important for English language learners to associate with English speakers because they learn English from those children as well as from their teacher. They can avoid the fossilization or stopping-in-place that can occur when children are separated from native and capable English-speaking peers. It also important for groups of children from different languages and cultures to associate with each other to avoid ethnic, linguistic, and cultural isolation.

Preview-review model.   The preview-review model is very complex, but it resolves some of the shortcomings of the other models. Two teachers work together as in the team-teaching and dual-language models: one bilingual, the other usually not. One teacher provides a preview of the lesson to the entire group in one language, and the other teacher then teaches the main body of the lesson to the entire group in the other language. Each teacher then reviews the main lesson with his or her language group after the main body of the lesson. The order of use of the languages is reversed in that subject area the next day. The children in whose language the main body of the lesson is not to be presented listen to a preview in their mother tongue. They also review the lesson in their mother tongue after the lesson is presented in their second language.

For example, two teachers, one bilingual and the other monolingual, teach a mathematics lesson. The bilingual teacher might conduct a ten-minute preview of the lesson in Spanish for all children. The monolingual teacher would then teach the core of the lesson to all of the children in English, probably for thirty to forty minutes. Both teachers would then review the lesson in English and Spanish, respectively, with children dominant in those languages for about ten to fifteen minutes. They would reverse the order the next day. The children always have the best possible model of both languages, and they are mixed for part of the lesson. The model also reduces the number of scarce bilingual teachers needed.

Eastman model. The Eastman model (Krashen & Biber, 1988) of the Los Angeles Unified School District also effectively alleviates the problem of isolating students from each other at the elementary level. Spanish-speaking students are organized for mother tongue instruction in reading, the language arts, and academic areas of the curriculum during the morning, along with a program of ESL. English-speaking students are similarly organized for reading and academic instruction in English in the morning. In the afternoon, Spanish-speaking students are mainstreamed with English-speaking students in art, music, and physical education, which are conducted in English. As Spanish-speaking students gain English proficiency after two or three years, they begin to receive sheltered academic instruction in English in the more concrete areas of the curriculum, such as mathematics and science. Social studies in English is introduced later.

Two-way bilingual education. The two-way bilingual education program has a different goal from mainstream bilingual education. It is used where two language groups of parents want their children to learn—and learn in—another language. Usually, one group of children will be native Spanish speakers learning English as a second language and academic subjects in Spanish. But another group of English-speaking students is in the classroom because their parents want them to learn Spanish and learn in Spanish. The program goal is additive in that each group learns the language and culture of the other group. The Eastman model is an effective organizational structure for conducting a two-way bilingual education program.

The English Language in the Bilingual Education Program

Teaching ESL is the underlying base of programs established to meet the academic needs of English language learners. It is the major element of the full bilingual education programs in which the mother tongue is used for academic instruction while children develop sufficient proficiency in English to benefit from academic instruction in English. And under No Child Left Behind requirements, it is the principal means of instruction.

Second-Language Acquisition

Whether or not children learn to read and write in their mother tongue, they clearly must learn to speak and understand English. In fact, it is not possible to address literacy for English language learners without considering the close links that must exist between the teaching of reading and writing and the teaching of ESL. Those links are rooted in the constructivist or whole-part-whole approaches that underlie effective practice in both.

At this point, we examine the contrast between constructivist and reductionist models of instruction. A constructivist view of instruction focuses on the construction of meaning, using what the child already knows and combining it with new knowledge, concepts, and skills to be integrated. It is learner centered and highly contextualized, important factors in working with the students from diverse backgrounds, who are often at risk of failure. The factor of background knowledge is well recognized as being a key to success in reading and writing, especially in reading comprehension. English language learners have no lack of background knowledge, but there is often a discontinuity between the background knowledge they have and that assumed by the texts they will use in learning to read and reading to learn. Within the constructivist view, language acquisition is embedded in function. Skills are taught in a meaningful context, not in a rigid, artificial, isolated, and fragmented way. There are several approaches to second-language instruction that reflect the constructivist view; they are in the communicative category.

The foundation for communicative approaches to second-language acquisition is based on concepts, theories, and hypotheses that have converged around the interaction of constructivist notions about making meaning, including Vygotsky's (1978) zone of proximal development, as described in Chapter 2. Conversely, **reductionist models**, or skills-based models, focus on the disassembly or fragmentation of curricular elements so that isolated skills and concepts can be mastered within a linear paradigm. Traditionally, most students have studied a second language, whether English or a foreign language, using such grammar-based approaches as the grammar-translation and audiolingual methods. These are reductionist or skills-based approaches that move learners from part to whole.

Most adults have personal experience with this type of approach. Perhaps you recall the grammar-translation approach from foreign language courses you took in secondary school and college. According to Chastain (1975), vocabulary was learned in terms of English from lists in which teachers paired words in the foreign language with their English counterparts. Grammar was also a major component of instruction. English was always the window through which the new second language was viewed and contrasted. Few students became functional in speaking and understanding the new second language. At best, they passed written tests of grammar, translated with difficulty, and read with halting comprehension (Crawford, 1994a).

The audiolingual approach has its roots in structural linguistics and behavioral psychology, resulting in a methodology based on a grammatical sequence, with mimicry and the memorization of pattern drills, but without the heavy grammatical analysis of the grammar-translation approach (Chastain, 1975). This approach is characterized by the unconscious mastery of sequenced grammatical forms, learning as the result of teaching patterned oral drills and an emphasis on correct oral production of grammatical forms in response to oral stimuli (Finocchiaro, 1974).

COMMUNICATIVE-BASED APPROACHES. The results of research have changed educators' conceptions of how a second language is acquired and how this acquisition is best promoted in the elementary and secondary classroom. There has been a major paradigm shift away from these grammar-based approaches to language learning and toward those called *communicative*, which are also consistent with meaning-based or constructivist approaches to literacy (Crawford 1994a, Crawford 2003).

Several important hypotheses underlie current practice in most communicative approaches to second-language acquisition (Krashen, 1982b). In his input hypothesis, Krashen concludes that growth in language occurs when learners receive comprehensible input, or input that contains vocabulary and structure at a slightly higher level than what they already understand. The input hypothesis reflects Vygotsky's zone of proximal development. The context of the input provides clues to maintain the integrity of the message. According to the input hypothesis, a grammatical sequence is not needed. The vocabulary and structures are provided and practiced as a natural part of the comprehensible input that the child receives, much as the process occurs with infants acquiring their mother tongue. Krashen (1981) relates the input hypothesis to the silent period, the interval before speech in either the mother tongue or second language in which the child listens to and develops an understanding of the language before beginning to produce language.

In his acquisition-learning hypothesis, Krashen highlights the difference between the infant's subconscious acquisition of the mother tongue and the conscious learning of a second language of the secondary student of French. Students acquire language subconsciously, with a feel for correctness. Learning a language, by contrast, is a conscious process that involves knowing grammatical rules. The infant, of course, is almost always successful in acquiring communicative competence, whereas the secondary school foreign language learner is usually not (Crawford, 1994a; Crawford, 2003).

According to Krashen's (1982b) natural order hypothesis, grammatical structures are acquired in a predictable sequence, with certain elements usually acquired before others. He concludes that the orders for first- and second-language acquisition are similar but not identical. He does not, however, conclude that sequencing the teaching of language according to this natural order or any grammatical sequence is either necessary or desirable.

Krashen's (1982b) related *monitor hypothesis* describes how the child's conscious monitor or editor serves to make corrections as language is produced in speaking or writing. Several conditions are necessary for the application of the monitor:

- Time to apply it, a situation that is not present in most ordinary oral discourse, especially in classroom settings
- A focus on the form or correctness of what is said, rather than on the content of the message
- Knowledge of the grammatical rule to be applied

These conditions serve to illustrate why so few children or adults learn to understand and speak a foreign language in a grammar-translation or audiolingual foreign language course in the secondary school or university.

In his affective filter hypothesis, Krashen (1982b) concludes that several affective variables are associated with success in second-language acquisition. These include high motivation, self-confidence and a positive self-image, and, most important, low anxiety in the learning environment. It is therefore important that teachers avoid high-pressure instruction and especially humiliation of students who are acquiring English.

OTHER BASIC PRINCIPLES.   Results from recent research have led to other major changes in educators' conceptions of how a second language is acquired and how this acquisition is best facilitated in the classroom, one of which is the obvious similarity between primary- and second-language acquisition. In both, primary- and second-language learners form an incomplete and incorrect interlanguage (Selinker, Swain, & Dumas, 1975), with most children moving through similar stages of development in this incomplete language.

The role of correction is also similar in both primary- and second-language acquisition. *Approximation* is a related process in which children imitate more proficient English speakers in all of dimensions of language, oral and written, and test hypotheses about it. Approximation underlies oral and written language in that children are acquiring new understandings and skills within the context of authentic wholes. Children demonstrate behaviors in which they approximate the language behavior of their English models, growing closer and closer to their levels of proficiency. In his view of successive approximation, Holdaway (1979) describes the process as one in which Vygotsky's adults and more capable peers, that is, teachers and proficient English-speaking students, use information in the output from children's responses to construct, adjust, and finally eliminate the scaffolding that facilitates progress in learning.

Terrell (1982) and Krashen and Terrell (1983) conclude that correction should viewed as a negative reinforcer that will raise the affective filter and the level of anxiety among English language learners. When errors do not interfere with comprehension, correcting them has no more place in the ESL program than it does when infants acquire their mother tongue. Caregivers might expand incorrect or incomplete forms, such as "me go" or "Kitty gots four feets," and say "Yes, you go" or "Yes, Kitty has four feet." There is little evidence, however, that this expansion has any positive effect. Errors are signs of immaturity, not incorrectness; they will disappear naturally as a part of approximation in the developmental process of language acquisition (Crawford, 1994a; Crawford, 2003).

These similarities between primary- and second-language acquisition are not consistent with either the grammar-translation or audiolingual approach. Children learning their first language do not rely on grammatical rules or on systematic acquisition of vocabulary. With its emphasis on early production instead of a silent period, on correct production instead of an acceptable though immature and incomplete interlanguage, and on grammatical sequence instead of function and communicative competence, the audiolingual approach bears little resemblance to the way primary or second languages are successfully acquired.

Finally, age is an important factor in second-language acquisition. Collier (1987) examined the relationship between the age of English language learners and their acquisition of a second language. She found that those who entered the second-language acquisition program at ages eight to eleven were the fastest achievers. Those who entered the program at ages five to seven were the lowest achievers, and they were one to three years behind children from eight to eleven years of age. Children who entered at twelve to fifteen years of age had the most difficulty acquiring the second language. She projected that they would need from six to eight years of classroom instruction to reach age-level norms in academic achievement.

Collier (1989) later analyzed other research on age and academic achievement in the second language and found that children who had academic instruction in the mother tongue generally required from four to seven years to reach national norms on standardized tests in reading, social studies, and science and as little as two years in mathematics and language arts, including spelling, punctuation, and grammar. She also found that children from ages eight to twelve who had at least two years of schooling in the mother tongue in their home country needed from five to seven years to reach the same levels of achievement in second-language reading, social studies, and science and two years in mathematics and language arts. Young children with no schooling in the mother tongue in either the home country or the new host country needed seven to ten years of instruction in reading, social studies, and science. Adolescent children with no ESL instruction and no opportunity for continued academic work in the mother tongue were projected, for the most part, to drop out of school before reaching national norms, whether or not they had a good academic background or interrupted schooling.

Instructional Strategies for Second-Language Acquisition

The implications of Krashen's hypotheses and of related similarities between first- and second-language acquisition are that approaches to second-language acquisition should do the following:

- Provide comprehensible input
- Focus on relevant and interesting topics instead of grammatical sequences
- Provide for a silent period without forcing early production
- Avoid correction
- Maintain a low level of anxiety

There are approaches to second-language acquisition that meet these criteria. The communicative approaches most appropriate for elementary and secondary classrooms are the total physical response method and the natural approach.

Using physical responses as a strategy of instruction in the bilingual classroom can help to reduce the anxiety ESL students might feel about the need to "perform."

THE TOTAL PHYSICAL RESPONSE METHOD. Asher's (1982) total physical response (TPR) method is an important communicative approach in the initial stages of second-language acquisition. The TPR method provides for comprehensible input, a silent period, and a focus on relevant content rather than on grammatical form. The focus of TPR is on physical responses to verbal commands such as "Stand up" and "Put your book on the desk." Because little emphasis is put on production, the level of anxiety is low.

Lessons can be given to small groups or an entire class. In the beginning, the teacher models one-word commands. This is done first with a few children to introduce new vocabulary and structures, then with the entire group, then with small groups of children, and finally with individual children. For example, the teacher says, "Sit," and then models by sitting down. Later, the teacher issues the command without modeling. As the children's levels of language increase, the teacher begins to use two- and three-word commands, such as "Stand up" and "Bring the book."

The children demonstrate their understanding by physically carrying out the commands. The order of commands is varied so that the children cannot anticipate which is next. Old commands are combined with new ones to provide for review. Whenever the children do not appear to comprehend, the teacher returns to modeling. After a silent period of approximately ten hours of listening to commands and physically responding to them, a child then typically reverses roles with the teacher and begins to give those same commands to other children. It is important for the teacher to maintain a playful mood during classroom activities.

The TPR approach can be extended to higher levels of proficiency by using the technique of nesting commands. The teacher might say the following:

Jamal, take the book to Svetlana, or close the door.
Noriko, if Jamal took the book to Svetlana, raise your hand.
If he closed the door, stand up.

A high level of understanding is necessary to carry out such commands, but no oral production is needed. Parents of young children will recognize that their infants can understand and carry out such commands long before they begin to speak themselves.

THE NATURAL APPROACH.   Terrell's (1977) original concept of the natural approach provided for three major characteristics:

- Classroom activities were focused on acquisition, that is, communication with a content focus leading to an unconscious absorption of language and a feel for correctness, but not an explicit knowledge of grammar.
- Oral errors were not directly corrected.
- Learners could respond in the target language, their mother tongue, or a mixture of the two.

Krashen and Terrell (1983) later added four principles that underlie the natural approach to language acquisition:

1. Comprehension precedes production, which leads to several teacher behaviors: teacher use of the target language, a focus on a topic of interest to the children, and maintenance of the children's comprehension.
2. Production emerges in stages ranging from nonverbal responses to complex discourse, with children able to speak when they are ready and speech errors not corrected unless they interfere with communication.
3. The curriculum consists of communicative goals, with topics of interest comprising the syllabus, not a grammatical sequence.
4. Activities must result in a low level of anxiety, a lowering of the children's affective filter, which the teacher accomplishes by establishing and maintaining a good rapport.

Terrell's (1981) natural approach is based on three stages of language development: preproduction (comprehension), early production, and emergence of speech.

Ms. Ortega, the teacher in the bilingual classroom in the chapter-opening vignette, uses the natural approach. The curriculum of her ESL program is made up of themes that are supported by large-format posters and charts, big books, and concrete objects in the classroom. She also uses the four blocks approach to organizing her reading program that is described in Chapters 1 and 11 (Cunningham et al., 2007), but her program is a five blocks approach. She has added ESL as an important fifth reading/language arts area of the curriculum.

The preproduction stage.   In the preproduction stage, topical, interesting, and relevant comprehensible input is provided by the teacher in a close parallel with Asher's TPR approach. The teacher speaks slowly, maintaining comprehension with gestures. Children may respond with physical behaviors, shaking or nodding their heads, pointing at pictures or objects, and saying yes or no. It is important that input is dynamic, lively, fun, and comprehensible. Crawford (1994a) provides an example in which the teacher uses a pet turtle and says,

> *This is a turtle. It is four years old. Is it green? Who wants to hold it? [Hand to child.] Who has the turtle? Does Tran have the turtle? Yes, he does. Does Rosa have the turtle? No, she doesn't.*

This basic input can be repeated with other objects in the classroom, such as large-format posters and illustrations (Crawford, 1994a). Crawford suggests that each child in the group be given a different illustration, and the teacher provides input:

> *Who has a picture of an airplane? Yes, Olaf, you do. Is the airplane large? Olaf, give your picture to Zipour. Who has a picture of a boat? Yes, Nicole has a picture of a boat.*

These examples include three primary preproduction techniques of using TPR strategies, TPR strategies accompanied by naming objects, and pictures.

The required responses include movement, pointing, nodding or shaking the head, and using the names of other children in the group. Remember that nodding the head for an affirmative response and shaking it for a negative one are not appropriate in all cultures; it is the converse in Albania, for example. Children might also have to learn these nonverbal behaviors. Because the emphasis at this stage is on listening comprehension, verbal responses in the mother tongue are also acceptable. This might be a problem if the teacher cannot understand the children's mother tongue, but children usually find a way to help the teacher understand.

Classroom props allow for relevant expansion of this and subsequent stages of the natural approach (Crawford, 1994a; 2003). Any manipulative or concrete object is helpful, including flannel boards and puppets. Large colorful illustrations, such as those in big books, are also very helpful. Sources of free color illustrations include calendars (outdated or otherwise), travel posters, large posters available from textbook and trade book publishers, and colorful illustrations in the annual reports of many large corporations, which are often available on request through announcements in major business magazines.

The early production stage. In the stage of early production, the child begins to produce one-word utterances, lists, and finally two-word answers, such as "big dog" and "in house." Some of the latter, such as "me want" and "no like," are grammatically incorrect or incomplete. According to Crawford (2003), teachers should view these responses as immature, not incorrect. In the presence of good models, these errors will disappear in time, just as they do among infants developing their mother tongue at home.

Several types of questions can be used to elicit one- and two-word responses that are within the reach of children as they move into the early production stage:

QUESTION FORMAT	ILLUSTRATIVE QUESTION
Yes/no	Do you like hamburgers?
Here/there	Where is the picture of the cat?
Either/or	Is this a pen or a key?
One word	How many dogs are there?
Two word	What fruits are in the picture?

As in the preproduction stage, these strategies should be integrated into activities that permit a variety of responses, ranging from physical responses from those not ready for production, to brief oral responses from those who are. As the children begin production, conversations should increasingly require one-word responses. Within the same conversation, the teacher can address questions calling for longer responses to those children who are ready. Teacher questions and commands here are in italics, and student responses are in brackets []:

> *Kjell, show us your picture. What is in Kjell's picture?* [A sandwich.] *Yes, it is a sandwich. What is on the sandwich?* [Ketchup.] *Is there an apple on the sandwich?* [No. Laughter.] *What else is on the sandwich?* [Meat, mayonnaise.] *How does it taste?* [Good.] *What do you like with a sandwich?* [Cookies. Soda.] *I like chips with mine.*

The emergence of speech stage. During the emergence of speech stage, children begin to produce structures that are richer in vocabulary, longer and more complex, and more correct. This production proceeds from three-word phrases to sentences, dialogue, extended discourse, and narrative, strategies that are also helpful in teaching standard American English to speakers of African American Vernacular English. At this stage, Terrell (1981) recommends such activities as games, group discussions, preference ranking, skits, art and music, radio, TV, pictures, filmstrips, readings, and filling out forms. An example of a chart that incorporates preference ranking is provided by Crawford (1994a) (see Figure 14.2).

After surveying the children about their preferences for pizza toppings and recording them, the teacher uses the survey results in Figure 14.2 to ask questions at different levels, each directed at a particular student and designed to elicit a response that reflects that student's stage of English-language development. Teacher questions below are in italics, and student responses in brackets []:

> *Does Sofik like pizza?* [Yes.] *What kind of meat does Sofik like?* [Sausage.] *How many like tomato on their pizza?* [Three, Margarita, Nguyen, and Petra.] *How much does Abdul like pizza?* [He doesn't like it.] *Which children like the same kind of pizza?* [Margarita and Petra.] *Is there a topping that no one likes?* [Yes.] *What is it?* [Anchovy.] *How do we know?* [Nobody wants anchovy.]

Not only is the chart a valuable source of comprehensible input, but the process of gathering the data for the chart is also. In addition, children begin to read each other's names and the words for popular foods in English.

Wordless picture books can also be used as a stimulus for the production of language at the emergence of speech stage. In an article that addresses struggling upper-grade readers, Ho (1999) describes strategies that will also be very effective for English language learners. After a brief book talk with the teacher, a small group of students creates a short text for a wordless book. One student member of the group records the text, although a paraprofessional or parent volunteer might fill this role when the students' writing abilities make this difficult. This is of even more value when two or three groups of students independently create their own text and then share it with the other groups.

SHELTERED ENGLISH INSTRUCTION FOR INTERMEDIATE-LEVEL ENGLISH SPEAKERS. When English language learners have reached an intermediate level of English proficiency, they are ready to move from academic instruction in the mother tongue to academic instruction in English by using sheltered English instruction, a mode that provides extensive support for comprehension. Sheltering strategies in the content areas of the curriculum add substantially to the knowledge and contextualized vocabulary that students need as a base for reading comprehension as they read and think in any language (Krashen, 1985). These strategies are consistent with the philosophy of communicative approaches to second-language acquisition, and they additionally provide access to academic areas of the curriculum in such a way that communication is maintained. Sheltered English strate-

Name	Favorite Pizzas					
	Cheese	Sausage	Pepperoni	Tomato	Anchovy	Mushroom
Margarita		X		X		X
Sofik		X				
Abdul						
Nguyen	X		X	X		
Petra		X		X		X

FIGURE 14.2

Second-Language Preference Ranking Chart.

gies are also very appropriate in providing support for teaching standard American English to speakers of African American Vernacular dialect. In California, sheltered English instruction is referred to as Specially Designed Academic Instruction in English, or SDAIE (CATESOL, 1992).

Cummins (1981) provides a set of intersecting continua that are very useful for conceptualizing the issue of balancing the complexity of curriculum content with demands on language proficiency (see Figure 14.3). The vertical continuum extends from cognitively undemanding to cognitively demanding—ranging, for example, from a conversation about what students ate for lunch on the cognitively undemanding side to a third-grade mathematics lesson about the distributive principle of multiplication on the cognitively demanding side.

Cummins' intersecting horizontal continuum extends from context embedded to context reduced, ranging, for example, from a science lesson on classification taught with concrete manipulatives on the context-embedded side to an abstract lecture/discussion about the principles of democracy on the context-reduced side. Sheltered instruction in English is most effective in subject areas of the curriculum that can be presented concretely, such as mathematics, science, art, music, and physical education. Although certain aspects of social studies can be taught concretely, such as geography and map skills, so many abstract concepts are taught that English-language instruction in this area might well be delayed until students acquire additional English proficiency, especially if expository text in English is an important source of knowledge for the children.

The purpose of a sheltered instruction approach to the core curriculum in English is to provide a focus on context-embedded activities, ensuring that comprehensible input is

	Cognitively undemanding	Cognitively demanding
Context enhanced	Art lesson Playing kickball Conversation about lunch Playing a board game Singing a song	Mathematics lesson using manipulatives Conducting a science experiment about evaporation Making a map of the schoolyard Watching the news on television
Context reduced	Beginning reading skills Talking on the telephone Listening to the news on the radio Reading a set of instructions	Responding to higher-order reading comprehension questions Participating in a debate on capital punishment Taking the SAT or the GRE

FIGURE 14.3

Classifying Cognitive Level and Contextual Support of Language and Content Activities According to Cummins' Framework.

Source: Based on Cummins (1981).

provided while treating increasingly cognitively demanding aspects of the core curriculum. The Los Angeles Unified School District (1985) prepared a set of English-language teaching strategies that provide the necessary scaffolding in content areas for intermediate English language learners. Among recommended strategies are that teachers do the following:

- Simplify input by speaking slowly and enunciating clearly.
- Use a controlled vocabulary within simple language structures.
- Where possible, use cognates and avoid the extensive use of idiomatic expressions.
- Use nonverbal language, including gestures, facial expressions, and dramatization.
- Use manipulatives and concrete materials, such as props, graphs, visuals, overhead transparencies, bulletin boards, maps, and realia.
- Maintain comprehension with gestures, dramatization, illustrations, and manipulatives.
- Check understanding by asking for confirmation of comprehension; by asking students to clarify, repeat, and expand; and by using a variety of questioning formats.

Teachers of English language learners can take two additional steps to ensure good communication with students as they teach: They should face the children when teaching, not the blackboard; and male teachers should ensure that moustaches are trimmed so children can see their upper lip.

Schifini (1985) recommends a focus on student-centered activities, especially at the secondary level, where lecturing and textbook use predominate. Richard-Amato and Snow (1992) provide valuable strategies for content-area teachers of English language learners. For mainstream teachers, they recommend providing a warm learning environment, recording lectures and talks on tape for later review, rewriting some key parts of text material at lower levels, asking native-English-speaking students to share notes with English language learners, and avoiding competitive grading until students have achieved sufficient English proficiency to compete successfully with native speakers.

It is clear that many of these strategies are nothing more than effective teaching practices, but their absence is very damaging to English language learners who are struggling to learn mathematics, science, and social studies in English when they have reached an intermediate level of English proficiency.

Several other strategies provide scaffolding for English language learners in specially designed academic instruction activities in English. The highly contextualized interactions that take place in cooperative learning can make the difference between what Krashen (1985, 1991) describes as submersion, or sink or swim, and sheltered instruction, the type of scaffolded subject-matter instruction just described. Cooperative learning is most effective when, in the words of Vygotsky, more capable peers—that is, stronger speakers of English—are included in groups with English language learners at various levels.

SHELTERED INSTRUCTION OBSERVATION PROTOCOL. The Sheltered Instruction Observation Protocol (SIOP) (Echevarria et al., 2004) is a carefully organized professional development model that incorporates strategies you have seen in this chapter and previous chapters:

- *Preparation*: lesson planning, content objectives, instructional materials
- *Building background*: integrating student background knowledge and developing academic vocabulary
- *Comprehensible input*: teacher speech presentation strategies and multimodal techniques
- *Strategies*: scaffolding instruction and promoting higher-order thinking skills
- *Interaction*: encouraging elaborated student speech and grouping students appropriately
- *Practice/Application*: activities to extend student learning of language and content
- *Lesson delivery*: delivering lessons that meet teaching objectives
- *Review/Assessment*: teacher review of key language and content concepts, assessment of student learning, and feedback to students

A SIOP lesson plan incorporates all of these elements. This model is designed for English language learners, but you can see how it would be very effective with speakers of

African American Vernacular English and with any student struggling with language and literacy. As a framework for planning and teaching effective lessons, it highlights best teaching practice for all children.

All of these sheltered strategies build background knowledge that supports the reading comprehension of English language learners as they begin to read expository text in their new second language. When instruction in the mother tongue precedes the sheltered instruction in English, their background knowledge is much richer.

Grammar as Part of the Curriculum?

According to Crawford (1994a), teachers who would advocate teaching the first-person present indicative tense to a seven-year-old English-speaking child in a primary school classroom would be incredulous at the suggestion that a parent teach the same concept to a three-year-old at home. Of course, both children can use the tense correctly, neither as the result of instruction. It is clear that the content of second-language acquisition programs should be based primarily on content, not on grammatical sequence.

A communicative second-language curriculum is usually organized around a set of topics to ensure the introduction of new vocabulary and concepts of interest and utility to the children. Needed language structures emerge and are acquired naturally within the context of topical lessons. Some communicative curricula include grammatical sequences as a subcategory.

Terrell (1981) suggests that the initial content should be limited to the following:

- Following commands for classroom management
- Names of objects in the classroom

- Colors and description words for those objects
- Words to describe people and family relationships
- Descriptions of children and their clothing; school areas and activities
- Names of objects in the school that are not in the classroom
- Foods, especially those eaten at school

Later in the acquisition process, topics of interest to children would include the children's families, their homes and neighborhoods, their favorite activities, and experiences they have had. They also enjoy discussing their preferences about food, colors, television programs and films, and other aspects of their lives.

Linking ESL Instruction and Literacy

There is a close link between literacy and the acquisition of a second language that becomes apparent when, as a part of the natural approach, Terrell (1981) recommends that key words be written on the chalkboard in the second language, especially for older children who are literate in their mother tongue. This corresponds to the key words to reading approach (Veatch, 1996; Veatch et al., 1979). In the early production stage of his natural approach, Terrell indicates that children may express themselves quite appropriately in one- or two-word utterances as they begin to acquire a second language. According to Crawford (1994a), it is altogether appropriate that they also begin to read key vocabulary that they have expressed for their teacher to write for them. They may later produce lists of related ideas, such as foods to eat at the school cafeteria, words that describe a favorite friend, or things to do after school. These topics and this output reflect the oral language common in the early production phase of Terrell's natural approach to language acquisition, output that is well suited for children to dictate for their teachers to record and for the children to read later.

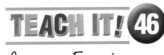

Language Experience with English Language Learners

Most bilingual teachers who teach reading in the mother tongue recognize that students' motivation to begin reading and writing in English early is strong. Although it is most beneficial for students to learn to read and write in the native language (Cummins, 1986, 1989; Krashen & Biber, 1988; Snow et al., 1998), where possible, teachers can begin an early introduction to literacy in English to take advantage of that motivation. The use of the key vocabulary and language-experience approaches should be done with caution to ensure that the second-language acquisition program does not evolve into an English literacy program presented before the student is ready. Being able to read and write in the mother tongue is always the most desirable base from which to establish literacy in English later because of the positive transfer of literacy skills to English.

As English proficiency increases, the key word approach to reading may give way to the language-experience approach described in Chapter 5. It is important that the teacher accept the language that the children use in their initial dictations. There will be incomplete sentences, missing words, and inappropriate vocabulary, but this represents the stage at which they are working in their new second language, and correction will only serve to dampen enthusiasm and diminish active participation.

As mentioned earlier, big books are an excellent source of large-format illustrations for ESL lessons. Later in the process, teachers will find that many children benefit from read-alouds in their new second language, especially when these are based on the background knowledge that children have already acquired as a result of lessons using the illustrations in these big books. The big books that are of most value will be very predictable and have repetitive elements.

Big Book Lesson

Other early second-language reading and writing activities that can emerge in the emergence of speech stage of the natural approach include the creation of vocabulary cards, with a word in English and an accompanying illustration from a magazine or by the student. These can be used for word games, including some that begin to focus on beginning sounds; this is especially productive for students who are already learning to read in the mother tongue. Children can also use their vocabulary cards for building word banks, student dictionaries, and word walls. Many children will be anxious to begin writing in their new second language. Simple poetry forms, such as the cinquain (see Chapter 9) and diamante, are useful structures for their initial attempts.

In their efforts to use the mother tongue of children in their classes, teachers sometimes provide cards with a vocabulary word in the mother tongue on one side and in English on the other. They also often provide bulletin boards in the two languages, and they often search out children's books with text in English on one side of the page and in the mother tongue on the other side. Although these efforts are laudable, such practices lead children to approach their new language of English through their mother tongue instead of directly. Vocabulary cards in English are a good practice, but a picture on the other side is a better choice than the word in the mother tongue. Teachers can and should provide bulletin boards in both languages, but not with both languages represented on the same bulletin board. For example, a science bulletin board can be provided in English on one side of the classroom, and the same bulletin board in the mother tongue can be placed on the other side of the room. Providing the same literature in English and the mother tongue has many advantages, but it is better provided in two separate books. Children will learn their new second language of English better if they do not approach it through the mother tongue.

Options for Teaching the English Language Learner to Read

There are two major options for teaching English language learners to read; these correspond to the two major categories of programs: English only and bilingual education.

In English

In an English-only instructional program, the children necessarily have to learn to read in English. This is not a positive approach, but it is often the only option when a mother tongue reading instruction program cannot be offered because of a very small number of children with a common non–English language, because of a lack of appropriate personnel and materials, or because of political considerations.

Assuming that an ESL program is offered beginning in kindergarten and extending into the primary grades, the English language learners should not be placed in a formal and systematic English reading program before they have any proficiency whatsoever in English. The reading program is not an appropriate place for beginning ESL instruction, which should instead focus on understanding and speaking. When reading in English is included at the beginning stages of instruction in listening comprehension and speaking English, the ESL program all too often evolves into a phonics- and text-based reading program instead of an ESL program, with very negative results in terms of both language acquisition and reading.

As children gain vocabulary in English in their ESL program, they will be interested in writing the words they learn, and they will begin to learn to read them, too, especially if they are learning to read in the mother tongue at the same time. A complete treatment of teaching the English language learner to read in English is provided in Chapters 11 and 12 in two dimensions: (1) the very positive process of teaching the English language learner who has first learned to read in the mother tongue and who has also reached the intermediate level of proficiency in understanding and speaking English and (2) the less desirable, but sometimes necessary, process of teaching an English language learner to read in English who has not learned to read in the mother tongue and/or who has not reached the intermediate level of English-language proficiency.

TEACH IT! 16

Word Wall Activities

Finally, some families will insist that their children learn to read and write only in English, even though the children do not speak or understand that language. Often, the parents themselves can express that desire only in the mother tongue. A few parents might even believe that the purpose of using the minority language for literacy is to maintain speakers of that language in an inferior social position. In this case, teachers need to demonstrate respect for the mother tongue, and they need to assure the children and their families that they will also have the opportunity to learn to speak, read, and write English. In addition, they need to reinforce the idea that children learn to read and write only once and that learning to read and write in another language later, such as English, is a relatively simple transfer process that is well supported in research, as seen later. Finally, teachers need to reinforce the idea that reading is *comprehension*, not just pronouncing or "reading" sounds. Nonetheless, some parents still insist on English only, and most schools accept that parental decision.

In the Mother Tongue

A fundamental precept of literacy for children who are English language learners is that they learn to read and write more rapidly and more effectively in their mother tongue than in a second language that they learn later. The first important and authoritative position taken on this issue was that of a UNESCO conference (UNESCO, 1953), in which it was concluded that children learn better to read in a new second language if they first learn to read in the mother tongue. This conclusion has been corroborated by many investigators in subsequent years. Saville and Troike (1971) reported that once a child has learned to read, transferring that ability to another language is not a difficult matter. Modiano (1968) found that Maya children in Mexico learned to read more rapidly in their mother tongue of Quiché than did Maya children who learned to read in their second language of Spanish. Subsequently, the first group read better in Spanish than those who first learned to read in Spanish. Through succeeding years, the evidence consistently indicates that children learn to read most effectively in their second language by first learning to read in their primary language (Cummins, 1986, 1989; Krashen & Biber, 1988; National Reading Panel Report, 2006; Snow et al., 1998; UNESCO, 1953).

How has our understanding of how English language learners learn changed in recent years?

Cummins' (1986, 1989) linguistic interdependence hypothesis indicates that what students learn in two languages is interdependent. This common underlying proficiency (CUP) (Cummins, 1981) forms the basis for positive transfer of skills. Children have knowledge and skills that they have learned in the mother tongue, and they can use them in the second language. They do not have to learn this knowledge and these skills again. In fact, it is axiomatic that children learn to read only once. They can transfer reading and writing skills to their new second language, just as adults do when they study a foreign language. Cummins indicates that CUP explains why children who have attended school in their country (and language) of origin tend to demonstrate higher achievement in English later than do children who lack that experience. These principles lead to the counterintuitive, but inescapable, conclusion that success in English-language proficiency is closely related to students' learning of reading, writing, and academic concepts in the mother tongue (Collier, 1989; J. Crawford, 1989; Cummins, 1989; Hudelson, 1987; Krashen, 1985; Krashen & Biber, 1988; Ramírez, 1991).

Language policy is a factor of great importance in literacy for children. Clearly, children learn to read and write most quickly and most effectively in the mother tongue. Many factors must be taken into consideration, however, before that decision is made (Crawford, 1995). For example, if skilled bilingual teachers are available, if children speak a minority language for which there is a well-developed written form, and if there are instructional materials in that language, the children can be given instruction in the mother tongue. If this is not the case, then the teacher can consider using the language-experience approach in English, as described in Chapter 5 and also later in this chapter.

If children speak a language for which there is not a well-developed written form, such as Hmong, then the children must be taught to speak and understand English and later to read and write in English, probably using the language-experience approach and simple predictable literature in English. If bilingual teachers are not available, then even the presence of instructional materials will not be sufficient to permit mother tongue instruction. The school can also prepare a literate speaker of the minority language as a paraprofessional who works under the supervision of a fully trained teacher who is not proficient in the mother tongue of the children.

In the case of a program of bilingual education, the children will have the opportunity to learn to read in the mother tongue, usually Spanish. If a Spanish-language bilingual program is provided for that population, children who speak another non–English language instead will likely be placed in an English-only approach.

In the case of Spanish and other languages that use the Latin or Roman alphabet, there is a close correspondence between literacy skills in English and these languages and therefore much transfer of skills from reading in the mother tongue to English:

TEACH IT! 14
Word Hunts

- The letters of the alphabet in Spanish are almost without exception identical to English, except for a few diacritical markings, such as the tilde (~) in Spanish.
- The left-to-right and top-to-bottom directionalities of the languages are the same.
- The concept of print and the alphabetic principle operate in the same way.
- Most consonant sounds and some vowel sounds are the same.
- There are significant similarities in vocabulary because of the many cognates that exist between English and Spanish, although a few are false cognates, such as *actual*, which means *real* in English and *present* or *current* in Spanish.
- Reading comprehension and organization skills are the same. When a child has learned to read in Spanish, these skills do not need to be learned a second time.

You can think of your own experiences in studying a foreign language. There were many new vocabulary words and grammatical elements to learn, but you did not have to learn to read and write again.

Teaching Children to Read in Spanish

Most English language learners in American schools speak Spanish at home, and almost all formal programs of bilingual education are conducted in Spanish (Fradd & Tikunoff, 1987). In most areas, it is only in Spanish that a wide range of instructional materials are available and that sufficient certified bilingual teachers are available to conduct such a program. Therefore, this section of the chapter is devoted to the teaching of reading in Spanish to these children.

As you have seen, the reading and writing processes in English and Spanish have a common alphabet and similar writing conventions. A major difference between English and Spanish is in the regularity of phoneme/grapheme relationships. In English, they are very irregular and inconsistent, especially with respect to the vowels; but in Spanish, they are very regular and consistent, especially with respect to the vowels.

Given this difference, one might expect that reading methodologies in Spanish would focus on phonics to take advantage of that regularity, and many do. But Latin American educators have found that children who learn to read using decoding as their only word recognition skill fall short in comprehension, just as occurs in English reading. Their reading is characterized as *silabeando*, that is, reading syllable by syllable. Their focus is on oral reading accuracy and speed, with little or no attention to comprehension or enjoyment. This is often observed in children who have learned to read in Spanish in Latin America.

A great variety of approaches for teaching reading in Spanish is available, just as there is in English. Table 14.1 summarizes those approaches.

TABLE 14.1

Major Approaches for Teaching Reading in Spanish

CATEGORY OF APPROACH	METHODOLOGY	CHARACTERISTICS	CITATION
Part-whole	Alphabetic (alfabético)	Letter names taught first; sequence of vowels, consonants, syllables, words, phrases, and sentences	Barbosa Heldt (1971)
	Phonetic (fonético)	Focus on sounds; sequence of vowels, consonants, syllables, words, phrases, and sentences	Barbosa Heldt (1971)
	Syllabic (silábico)	Focus on syllables; sequence of vowels, consonants, syllables, words, phrases, and sentences	Barbosa Heldt (1971)
	Onomatopoeic (onomatopéyico)	Focus on auditory associations between sounds of letters and natural sounds of the environment, such as the /s/ as the whistle of a fireworks rocket; sequence of vowels, consonants, syllables, words, phrases, and sentences	Barbosa Heldt (1971) Torres Quintero (1976)
Whole-part-whole	Everyday vocabulary (palabras normales)	An analytic approach in which words are broken into syllables, then into sounds, and then reassembled	Barbosa Heldt (1971) Rodríguez Fuenzalida (1982) Rébsamen (1949)
Global	Whole word (global)	Sequence of words and sentences, with little or no phonics	Barbosa Heldt (1971)
	Generated words (palabras generadoras)	Sequence of sight words, syllables, and sounds; use of these elements to create new words, phrases, and sentences	Hendrix (1952) Barbosa Heldt (1971)
Eclectic	Eclectic (ecléctico)	Combination of sight word development and phonics; typical of basal reader programs in English and Spanish	Barbosa Heldt (1971)
Constructivist	Whole language (lenguaje integral)	Focus on literature and authentic text; similar to whole-language focus in English; phonics taught implicitly and when need demonstrated (not explicit and systematic)	Freinet (1974) Solé (1992) Goodman (1989) Arellano Osuna (1992) Salmon (1995)

These approaches range from those that are highly synthetic to those that are whole-part-whole, even including what is characterized as constructivist or whole language in English. A balanced approach in the whole-part-whole tradition provides for a strong, well-rounded program that is characterized by the following:

- Extensive read-aloud activities to build background knowledge and vocabulary in the mother tongue
- Use of the key words to reading approach, the language-experience approach, and shared reading of authentic literature at the beginning stages to introduce the concept of print for children who do not have a rich print environment in the home
- Phonemic awareness activities emerging from vocabulary in children's background knowledge and from LEA charts and shared literature experiences
- An inductive whole-part-whole strategy for teaching phonics, with elements emerging from words the children have acquired in the activities just described
- Use of authentic literature in Spanish to serve as a basis for teaching reading comprehension
- Extensive and early opportunities for writing

Application of these strategies in Spanish is similar to that in English, with the exception of phonics, which is addressed later. These key instructional activities also represent the four blocks framework presented in Chapter 1 and, beyond the beginning stages of reading instruction, they should be augmented with the many highly effective strategies described throughout the book.

TEACH IT! 17
Analytic Phonics Lesson

METHODOLOGIES FOR TEACHING READING IN SPANISH. "He read slowly, spelling out each syllable and murmuring it quietly, as if with great relish, and when he'd

TEACH IT!

Refer to your **Teach It!** booklet for further activities you can use to reinforce concepts discussed in this chapter.

Inductive Phonics Lesson

In a simple three-step inductive lesson structure, the first step of auditory discrimination serves to verify students' phonological awareness of the sound stated in the objective of the lesson (see the figure on the next page). If the students are not successful in this first step, substitute phonological awareness activities for the second and third steps of the lesson, such as those described in Chapters 5 and 11. If the students are successful, as they usually will be in the first grade, proceed to the second stage of the lesson, which is to verify that the students can already read the sight words used in the first stage of the lesson and also indicate that they recognize the letter and its position in the words.

The third stage, that of associating the sound with the letter, is the key step in the lesson. The students who can correctly pronounce the letter or syllable indicated in the objective in unknown words in the association stage should be able to use that skill to recognize and pronounce that sound in the same position in other unknown words.

Many of the children will be able to state a rule or generalization when asked how they know how to pronounce the target sound in the unknown word. A six-year-old's rule might be a statement that he or she remembered other known words with that letter in the same position, thought about how it sounded in those words, and

pronounced it that way in the new word. The purpose of the extra stimulus question ("If that word is 'cola,' what is this word? 'Bala.'") is for the teacher to provide the part of the word that is not the subject of the lesson objective—only the initial syllable /*ba*/ is of interest.

This model lesson is inductive in that you ask questions that lead children to think about what they already know about sounds, letters, and words. You do not tell or explain. Many children will not be able to state a rule or generalization at the beginning of this type of inductive lesson, although most will be able to correctly pronounce the target element in the words. But after a number of lessons, increasing numbers of children will be able to formulate a rule. These generalizations will be remembered and applied more easily if they are derived by the children. If you provide them in a direct instruction activity, then the child must rely on memory to recall the rule later. When children learn to derive their own rules, they can transfer this ability to new unknown words. They can also transfer this generalized ability to English.

The instructional time required for the model lesson presented in the figure should be about five minutes, certainly less than ten minutes. Most instructional activities in beginning reading in Spanish should focus on comprehension through shared reading and, later, in small-group lessons in which children are reading in a directed or guided reading mode.

---

mastered the whole word, he would repeat it in one breath." In *The Old Man Who Read Love Stories*, a prize-winning novel written by a Chilean author about an elderly man who lives in the rain forest of Ecuador, Luis Sepúlveda (1989) has described very accurately the way too many Latin American children read as the result of the syllabic approach to reading instruction used in almost every country in the region. It is not uncommon to find the use of similar methodologies in the United States, often in the hands of bilingual teachers who themselves were educated in Latin America, perhaps even trained as teachers there. These approaches have many limitations when used in isolation; their best use would be as an ancillary word attack skill program to use with high-quality children's literature. But as in reading English, children who read in Spanish need to employ all cueing systems in support of their word recognition efforts, the semantic, syntactic, and pragmatic systems, as well as the graphophonic. See the Teach It! box for an example of a phonics lesson in Spanish.

PHONICS and PHONOLOGICAL AWARENESS

Why is the sequence of teaching word recognition skills in Spanish different from English?

ISSUES RELATED TO THE SOUND SYSTEMS OF SPANISH AND ENGLISH. The sequence in which Spanish phonics is introduced is different from that of English. It begins with vowel sounds because they are few in number and regular (see Table 14.2 on page 498). Consonants follow in an order that reflects their frequency and regularity. Few word recognition problems appear in reading in Spanish, but there are several difficult points in Spanish, as in English, in which one letter represents several sounds. These are often observed in the invented spelling of children, as seen in Figure 14.4 on page 499.

The invented spelling in the student's work presented in Figure 14.4 is very typical of children who write in Spanish, and it is also consistent with Gentry's phonetic stage (Gen-

Spanish lesson plan

Objetivo: pronunciar el sonido inicial de palabras nuevas que empiecen con la sílaba /ba/

Etapa de discriminación auditiva (verificar conciencia fonémica)

Les voy a decir tres palabras. Escuchen bien.

              bajo   baño   bate

¿Cómo se parecen? ¿Qué tienen en común?

¿En qué parte de cada palabra se encuentra este sonido?

Les voy a decir tres otras palabras. ¿Cuál no pertenece a este grupo?

           ballena   mesa   barra

¿Cuál es diferente? ¿Por qué? ¿Cómo es diferente? ¿En qué parte?

¿Qué otras cosas pueden ver en el salón que empiecen con el mismo sonido?

Etapa de discriminación visual

Vamos a leer tres palabras.

Levanta la mano si quieres leer la primera palabra.

          bajo, baño, bate   Muy bien, etc.

¿Cómo se parecen estas tres palabras?

¿En qué parte de las palabras se encuentra la letra?

Etapa de asociación

Ahora quiero que lean algunas palabras nuevas. ¿Quién quiere tratar de leer la primera palabra nueva? ¿Cómo sabías leerla?

        bala   base   barra   ballena

Si esa palabra dice "cola" ¿qué dice esta palabra? "Bala."

          cola

English version of Spanish lesson plan

Objective: pronounce the initial sound of new words that begin with the syllable /ba/

Auditory discrimination stage (confirm phonemic awareness)

I'm going to tell you three words. Listen to them carefully.

        (short) (bath) (bat)

How are they alike? What do they have in common?

In what part of each word do you hear this sound?

I'm going to tell you three more words. Which one doesn't belong with the others?

        (whale) (table) (bar)

Which is different? Why? How is it different? Which part is different?

What other things in the classroom can you see that begin with the same sound?

Visual discrimination stage

Let's read these three words.

Raise your hand if you want to read the first word.

        (short) (bath) (bat [baseball])

How do these three words look the same?

In what part of these words do you see that letter?

Association stage

Now we're going to read some new words. Who wants to read the first word? How did you know how to read it?

        bala   base   barra   ballena

If that word is "cola," what is this word? "Bala."

         cola

Inductive Phonics Lesson (Spanish/English)

try, 1981), where there is substitution of incorrect letters with similar or the same pronunciation. The word *castillo* is spelled *castio*, which yields the correct pronunciation of the word, but not the correct spelling. In the words *paresio* and *isieron*, the student substituted the letter *s* for *c*, again yielding the correct pronunciation of the word, but the wrong spelling. In addition, the silent *h* of *hicieron* was omitted. There is much confusion between the sounds of *b* and *v* in Spanish, both being pronounced similarly to the /b/ in English in the initial position and like /v/ in English when between vowels, resulting in the very typical substitution of *v* for *b* in *estava*.

Finally, there is a grammatical error that reflects a troublesome issue even for some adults. The conventions of Spanish require that the sequential repetition of a sound be avoided. Therefore, *y hicieron* should be written as *e hicieron* to avoid the repetition of the *y* (and) and the *hi* in *hicieron*, both of which carry the same sound (in English, *y* followed by *hi* would sound like two English long *e* sounds in succession).

TABLE 14.2

Sequence of Phonics Generalizations in Spanish

INITIAL SOUNDS	FINAL SOUNDS	WORD ENDINGS
a	a	os
e	e	as
i	o	diminutives
o	augmentatives	
u	d	verbs -ar
	l	verbs -er
m	n	verbs -ir
t	s	
l	r	Substitution of initial
p	z	consonants
n		
d	i	Substitution of final
s	u	elements
f		
r	**CONSONANT BLENDS**	Medial dipthongs
b		
g (soft)	br	Compound words
ll	cr	
c (hard)	dr	Verb endings
j	fr	
y	pr	Homonyms
h (mute)	tr	
ch	bl	Prefixes
z	cl	
qu	fl	Suffixes
g (hard)	gl	
c (soft)	pl	Homographs
gue, gui		
güe, güi		Grades of adjectives
x (medial)		
		Syllabication

Phonics lessons in Spanish should be drawn out of vocabulary from key words to reading lessons, language-experience approach lessons, and the shared reading experiences of children. The words used in the lessons should be within the children's sight vocabulary, moving from the whole (word) to the part (element to be taught) and back to whole (word) again. Because of the nature of Spanish, elements are frequently syllables in the form of CV (consonant/vowel).

INSTRUCTIONAL MATERIALS IN SPANISH. The variety of instructional materials for reading in Spanish is almost as rich as that in English. These include formal reading programs, authentic children's literature, and electronic resources, including the Internet.

Print resources. Most major publishers that provide an English reading program also offer a parallel program in Spanish. These programs would be fairly characterized as basal, although some have anthologies of original literature instead of contrived basal reader stories or decodable text. The best have children's literature from the Spanish-speaking world or children's stories written in Spanish by native Spanish-speaking authors. In both of these cases, the quality of Spanish language and the cultural appropriateness should be evaluated carefully.

FIGURE 14.4

Invented Spelling in Children's Writing in Spanish.

Most Spanish programs also contain authentic children's literature translated from English. It is important to consider carefully the quality of translation and the cultural appropriateness. The best programs also offer selections of authentic Spanish-language literature translated to English for their English versions, a demonstration of their respect for the literary traditions of both languages and cultures. A major strength of programs with parallel literature selections in two languages is that students who read a selection in the mother tongue as part of their mother tongue reading program have a powerful source of background knowledge when they later read an English version of the same story.

There is also a wealth of children's books and big books available in Spanish. The teacher who wishes to use authentic literature for a Spanish reading program instead of anthologies or basal readers will find the constantly expanding series of books on recommended children's literature in Spanish prepared by Schon (2000) to be an invaluable resource. In addition, she has published a compendium of children's books in Spanish with themes from around the world (Schon, 2001, 2002).

Electronic resources for English language learners and their teachers. As we discussed in Chapter 2, access to technology is a major issue for English language learners and other children in urban and rural environments characterized by poverty. But what resources can English language learners and their teachers access when technology is available?

Many Web sites can provide support to English language learners and their teachers, both in the areas of English language development and in Spanish. For example, an international school Web site registry provides the home pages of schools around the world that are interested in establishing relationships such as pen pal arrangements with other schools (Greenlaw, 2001). These have the advantage of allowing English language learners to correspond in their developing second language of English with students in other countries who are also studying English, probably as a foreign language. In addition, they may have opportunities to correspond in their shared mother tongues. This site registry is found at **http://web66.coled.umn.edu/schools.html.**

The Bilingual Writing Center is a useful word processing program for children in English and Spanish that is distributed by The Learning Company (Wepner, Valmont, & Thurlow, 2000). The teacher who conducts a search at **Google.com** or another search engine on the phrase "Bilingual Learning Center" will find references to many school districts that have valuable tips and information about how to use the Bilingual Writing Center on both Microsoft Windows and Macintosh computer systems.

TECHNOLOGY

What technology resources are available for English language learners?

In the area of ESL for teachers, the Internet TESLK Journal (**http://www.aitech.ac.jp/~iteslj/**) provides sample lessons and teaching ideas for teachers (Greenlaw, 2001). There are also articles and research papers, as well as other classroom activities.

Another valuable Web site for the teacher who is searching for outstanding children's literature in Spanish is the Barahona Center for the Study of Books in Spanish for Children and Adolescents, directed by Isabel Schon, who was cited earlier for her books on this topic. The center's Web site can be found at **http://www.csusm.edu/csb/**.

STRUGGLING **READER**

How can English language learners be helped by programs such as Reading Recovery?

TEACH IT! 46

Language Experience with English Language Learners

TEACH IT! 7

Modified Reading Recovery Lesson

Children Who Struggle Learning to Read in the Mother Tongue

Reading recovery has proven to be a very effective intervention strategy for children who experience reading difficulties in English (see Chapter 11). An authorized Spanish-language version of reading recovery, called *Descubriendo la Lectura*, has also been developed (Escamilla & Andrade, 1992). It follows the pattern of diagnosis and intervention of the original program, but in Spanish. Several adaptations to language and culture were necessary, including the need to locate children's literature in Spanish. The resulting program includes more than 300 books at twenty different levels of difficulty, about twenty books per level.

A Spanish diagnostic survey for the identification of students includes six observational tasks: (1) letter identification, (2) a word test, (3) concepts about print, (4) writing vocabulary, (5) dictation, and (6) running records of text reading. Procedures generally parallel those in the English language program, including the rereading of familiar books, a running record of the new book from the previous day, writing, rearranging a cutup story, and introducing a new book. The program is designed for first graders in the lowest 20 percent of the class after one year of reading instruction in the regular classroom.

In a national study of *Descubriendo la Lectura*, Escamilla et al. (1998) found that the program had a very positive outcome with Spanish-speaking second and third graders, more than 90 percent of students at each grade level scoring above average on Spanish text reading. On the SABE, a standardized achievement test in Spanish, more than 75 percent of students at each grade level met or exceeded the average score.

The World of Reading

My 24 First Graders Speak 14 Different Mother Tongues: What Can I Do?

An increasingly common scenario in American classrooms is the presence of children who speak many different home languages. A bilingual education program usually cannot be provided for most of them for the following reasons:

- The teacher is not proficient in more than one of the languages, if that.
- Reading materials are not available in the languages.
- It would not be feasible to provide reading instruction in several languages, even with a proficient teacher and adequate materials.
- There might not be enough children with a common language at a grade level to support a full bilingual education program.

When many children at a grade level have a common language and are scattered among several classrooms, it might be possible to gather all of them into a single classroom. This is especially desirable if there is a teacher who can teach them in their mother tongue or if a paraprofessional or parent volunteer can provide mother tongue support to lessons taught in English. Usually, these children will be taught only in English in an immersion program. Because English is the only language common to most, they acquire basic interpersonal communication skills rather quickly. Formal reading instruction is usually delayed, although children can work with key words and the language-experience approach early in the process of acquiring English. Shared big books also provide excellent comprehensible input in English, as well as an early introduction to the concept of print and much valuable background knowledge.

Differentiated Instruction

Teaching Older Children Who Are Preliterate

It is not uncommon for teachers of older English language learners from other countries to observe that a few lack literacy skills. Some have been in refugee camps without educational services, others have been working to contribute to family income, and still others have lived in very rural or isolated areas where attending school was not possible because of long distances and inadequate transportation. Many indigenous children from Latin America leave school because instruction is only provided in Spanish, which they might not speak or might not speak well. There are communities of speakers of Zapotec, Mixtec, Maya, Quechua, and many other indigenous languages living in the United States. Their Spanish might be very limited.

Other English language learners have had very limited school experience and left school, either for the reasons just cited, or occasionally because of the poor quality of education. According to Schifini (1996), many have large gaps in instruction in the primary grades, and they struggle as nonreaders in the higher grades. Schifini recommends several strategies for meeting the needs of these older preliterate English language learners:

- Develop a print-rich classroom environment that reflects student interests, including advertisements, brochures, bumper stickers, comics, drawings, magazines, murals, newspapers, photos, postcards, posters, recipes, and examples of their own work.
- Include native language print in the classroom environment.
- Use reading and writing workshop strategies and shared reading and literature studies.
- Use read-aloud activities for access to the core curriculum not available through reading.
- Use writing activities such as quick-writes to connect students to background knowledge.
- Provide shared book experiences with predictable and patterned books that are of standard textbook size and have mature story lines.
- Use collaborative chart stories, language-experience charts, and other forms of shared writing.

In their SIOP model, mentioned earlier in several chapters, Echevarria et al. (2004) recommend additional sheltered instruction strategies effective with preliterate older English language learners:

- Use graphic organizers, such as Venn diagrams, timelines, flow charts, and semantic maps, especially for reading in content areas of the curriculum.
- Use scaffolding techniques, such as paraphrasing or restating students' responses, and think-alouds.

Assessing the Oral Language Proficiency and Reading Proficiency of English Language Learners

Assessing the language and reading outcomes of English language learners is accomplished very much as is done for English speakers (Kameenui et al., 2001). A number of measures of English language proficiency are used for placement of students in bilingual education programs or programs for English language learners, depending on their levels of achievement (see Table 14.3). In general, they measure the language production of children in English, including vocabulary, syntactical complexity, and auditory discrimination/pronunciation. State and local school district authorities typically establish criteria for the reclassification or identification of children whose English proficiency has advanced sufficiently for mainstream placement in regular classroom programs of instruction, although usually with extra support from a paraprofessional or other speaker of the mother tongue at the beginning of the transition process.

TABLE 14.3

Assessment Measures for Spanish-Speaking English Learners

TYPE OF MEASURE	NAME OF MEASURE	SUBTESTS	ELEMENTS MEASURED	SOURCE OF MEASURE
English language Grades K–12	Basic Inventory of Natural Language (BINL)	N/A	Oral language production, language dominance, fluency, syntax, vocabulary, structural complexity	Checkpoint Systems
English-language development All LEP	California English Language Development Test (CELDT)	Listening and speaking Reading Writing	Oral language (one-on-one) Reading Writing	CTB/McGraw-Hill
English language Grades K–5	Language Assessment Scales (LAS)	N/A	Auditory discrimination, vocabulary, phoneme production, sentence comprehension, oral production of English and Spanish	CTB/McGraw-Hill
English language Grades K–12	Bilingual Syntax Measure (BSM)	N/A	Syntax, language dominance, second-language level, maintenance of first language	Psychological Corporation
English language (or other language) (observation rating scale) Grades 1–12	SOLOM	N/A	Comprehension, vocabulary, fluency, pronunciation, grammar	San Jose USD
Spanish reading (normed test) Grades 1–12	Aprenda: Prueba de Logros en Español,	Sonidos y letras	Phoneme matching, letter identification, letter/sound correspondence	Psychological Corporation
	Second Edition	Lectura de palabras	Word matching with picture, word identification	
		Lectura de oraciones	Sentence match with picture	
		Vocabulario	Synonym matching, defining words in context	
		Comprensión de lectura	Reading comprehension of riddles, modified close tests, comprehension questions	
Spanish reading (normed test) Grades K–3+	La Prueba de Realización, Second Edition	Reading	Matching written words, matching spoken words with written words, picture–word matching	Riverside Publishing
Spanish reading (normed test) Grades K–8	Comprehensive Tests of Basic Skills	Reading	Word attack, vocabulary, reading comprehension	CTB/McGraw-Hill
Spanish reading (normed test) Grades 1–8	Spanish Assessment of Basic Education (SABE), Second Edition, Level 1	Reading	Basic skills of reading, spelling, language skills	Hampton-Brown

There are also several widely used standardized or normed tests of Spanish reading proficiency that usually parallel similar tests in English (see Table 14.3). The results of these tests are often used to evaluate the progress of groups of children or the effectiveness of programs, but they are not very useful to teachers in identifying the levels of children for assignment to instructional groups or levels of textbooks.

In contrast, the informal reading inventory (IRI) serves the same function in Spanish as it does in English. It is an authentic measure of reading accuracy and comprehension, and the outcomes that it yields in Spanish, as in English, can be used to place children in reading groups and textbooks with some confidence (see Chapters 10 and 12 for a discussion of using the IRI in English). Some major publishers with Spanish-language reading programs provide IRIs for them.

Teachers can also construct their own IRIs by selecting passages from basal readers or anthologies to represent each grade level, just as is done in English. Teachers should verify the levels of the passages by using a readability graph for Spanish (Crawford, 1995) (see the Assessment box). As in constructing an IRI in English, the teacher should ensure that the content of each passage in Spanish corresponds to background and cultural knowledge that the child has in Spanish. With a passage selected for each grade level and four comprehension-level questions developed for each passage, the teacher can employ the same process and accuracy and comprehension criteria for Spanish as for English, as described in Chapters 10 and 12. The IRI in Spanish yields frustration, instructional, independent, and capacity levels, just as it does in English and with the same criteria.

Readability measures are often misused, and the teacher should be aware of their limitations. These measures assess only surface structure features of language, and they ignore the level of content and the background knowledge required of children. Teachers should carefully judge the content of passages they select for inclusion in IRIs for the children they will assess. Finally, teachers are often tempted to rewrite text, changing sentence length or vocabulary to raise or lower readability levels. This is a dangerous practice that should be avoided. A readability graph should be used only as a rough measure and never as a tool for writing to a level.

Mother Tongue Support in the Bilingual Classroom

Many teachers say, "I would like to teach my children to read in Spanish, but I don't speak Spanish." Monolingual classroom teachers who are unable to teach in their students' mother tongue might be able to use the services of a paraprofessional who can. Those paraprofessionals' services can extend from follow-up mother tongue support of lessons taught in English by the teacher to instruction provided in the mother tongue under the close and careful supervision of the teacher.

Vignette of a Nonbilingual Teacher and a Bilingual Paraprofessional in a Bilingual Classroom

There are twenty-six third-grade children in Room 14. Of the twenty-six native Spanish-speaking children, eleven have made the transition into English reading. Ten continue reading instruction in Spanish while receiving ESL instruction. They will make the transition to English reading within a few weeks or months as they become ready. Five new arrivals to the United States speak only Spanish.

Their teacher, Mr. Scott, is a certified elementary school teacher, but he does not speak Spanish. He is a very good teacher, and he provides all ESL and English reading instruction. But the Spanish reading program is conducted by Ms. Morales, a part-time paraprofessional and university student who plans to become a bilingual teacher. She is occasionally assisted by two Spanish-speaking parent volunteers who read to the children and tell stories from their childhood.

Today, Ms. Morales is teaching a reading lesson from an anthology of stories in Spanish, part of a reading program in English and Spanish that Mr. Scott is also using with the English-speaking students. Ms. Morales begins by introducing new vocabulary that students will encounter in the guided silent reading they will do in a few minutes. In addition, she helps them to construct a semantic map so that they can share background knowledge they have about the topic of the story: a young girl who lives in the Amazon forest of South America. She guides their silent reading with higher-order questions from the teacher manual and additional questions she has formulated herself. After today's lesson, during which they read the first half of the story, the children will write predictions about how the story might end when they complete it the next day. In the meantime, Mr.

TEACH IT! 18

Vocabulary or Semantic Web for Primary Grades

Scott is teaching a word analysis lesson to the English-speaking students on the other side of the room, which will be followed by a similar literature lesson from the English version of the same anthology that Ms. Morales uses in Spanish.

Mr. Scott meets daily with Ms. Morales to help her plan instruction, to answer questions about how to use the teacher's manual for the Spanish reading program, which is provided in both English and Spanish for his convenience, and to assess children's progress in Spanish reading. As they teach in parallel through the morning, he observes and monitors her activities. She also assists in parent conferences when needed.

Mr. Scott and Ms. Morales have molded themselves into a highly effective team, both making indispensable contributions to the language and reading development of the children in the classroom. She gains much from his long teaching experience as they plan instruction for the next day and, on a longer-term basis, for future days, weeks, and months. At the same time, he gains insights from the valuable background she has in the children's mother tongue and their culture.

Although the two are usually teaching parallel to each other, Mr. Scott is able to supervise Ms. Morales's work from his teaching station in the classroom, and he periodically walks around the classroom to encourage and reinforce the work of the children in both groups. Although he does not speak Spanish, he finds that he is able to understand much of what is occurring in her lessons.

The parallel structure of the English and Spanish anthologies from the third-grade reading program they use has many advantages. The teacher's manual for the Spanish part of the program has English and Spanish instructions on opposite sides of the teaching manual, so Mr. Scott can quickly determine the students' progress in their lessons. In addition, they will eventually read in English the stories they are now reading in Spanish. Their prior experience with the stories and the background knowledge developed will constitute an important part of scaffolding their comprehension as they move into reading in their new second language.

Supervising the Paraprofessional Who Teaches in the Mother Tongue

It is a challenging task for monolingual teachers to supervise the instructional activities of bilingual paraprofessionals. Teachers should first model for their paraprofessionals in English the teaching manner, approaches, and strategies that are to be employed in Spanish or another language. Teachers should then observe their paraprofessionals, assessing the effectiveness of their modeling. Even though teachers might not understand the paraprofessionals' words, the teachers' knowledge of what is being taught should support good communication. A major emphasis of teachers should be to impress on paraprofessionals the importance of building up the children's self-concepts and of avoiding harsh words, which can undo the effects of even excellent teaching.

At an operational level, there should be outstanding communication between the teacher and the paraprofessional. They should meet to plan before school in the morning and again before the paraprofessional leaves at the end of the day, discussing the activities of the day and planning for lessons to follow. Because the teacher and paraprofessional complement each other so well, the development of mutual respect between them is important. The teacher has skills and knowledge

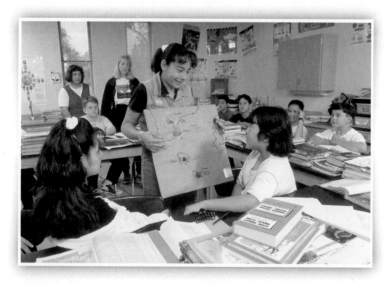

The help of bilingual classroom aides are extremely beneficial in the ESL/ELL classroom, but it is important that the teacher and the aides carefully coordinate their instruction so the messages to the students are consistent.

Number of syllables	1.0	1.5	2.0	2.5	3.0	3.5	4.0	4.5	5.0	5.5	6.0	6.5
220												4.3
218												3.8
216												3.3
214											5.3	2.8
212									9.7	7.2	4.8	2.3
210									9.2	6.7	4.3	1.9
208									8.7	6.3	3.8	1.4
206							13.1	10.7	8.2	5.8	3.4	1.0
204							12.6	10.2	7.8	5.3	2.9	
202							12.2	9.8	7.3	4.8	2.4	
200					16.6	14.1	11.7	9.2	6.8	4.4	1.9	
198					16.1	13.6	11.2	8.8	6.3	3.9		
196					15.6	13.2	10.7	8.3	5.8	3.4		
194					15.1	12.7	10.2	7.8	5.4	2.9		
192					14.6	12.2	9.8	7.3	4.5	2.4		
190			19.0	16.6	14.2	11.7	9.3	6.8				
188			18.6	16.1	13.7	11.2	8.8	6.4				
186	23.0	20.5	18.1	15.6	13.2	10.8	8.3	5.9				
184	22.5	20.0	17.6	15.2	12.7	10.3	7.8	5.4				
182	22.0	19.6	17.1	14.7	12.2	9.8	7.4	4.9				
180	21.5	19.1	16.6	14.2	11.8	9.3	6.9	4.5				
178	21.0	18.6	16.2	13.7	11.3	8.9	6.4	4.0				
176	20.6	18.1	15.7	13.3	10.8	8.4	5.9	3.5				
174	20.1	17.7	15.2	12.8								
172	19.6	17.2	14.7	12.3								
170	19.1	16.7	14.3	11.8								
168	18.7	16.2										

Number of sentences

Permission to copy with credit to the author.

Approximate level of readability

Instructions:

1. Count the first 100 words in the sample.
2. Count the number of sentences in the 100 words, rounding to the nearest tenth of a sentence.
3. Count the number of syllables in the 100 words.
4. Look for the number of syllables in the left column of the graph. Trace to the right to find the number of sentences. The number at the foot of that column is the approximate grade level of the passage.
5. If the text consists of more than a few pages, take samples from every three pages and compute the mean for each variable.
6. If the proportion of sentences to syllables for each 100 words does not appear on the graph, then the readability of the passage cannot be determined.

Crawford (1995)

Standards for English Language Learners

Some states have developed English-language development standards for English language learners. These are helpful in planning curriculum, instruction, and assessment for the ESL programs that these students need. California has one of the most fully developed sets of standards for this purpose (California State Board of Education, 1999). The California standards are organized into the following categories:

- Listening and speaking
- Reading: Word analysis
  Fluency and systematic vocabulary development
  Reading comprehension
- Writing: Strategies and applications
  Conventions
- Reading: Literary response and analysis

Standards in these categories are provided at beginning, intermediate, and advanced levels. They are designed to be used at K–12 levels but can be used as appropriate to the developmental level of the student. Some students may demonstrate that they have met advanced standards in the first grade, whereas a recent arrival may be just reaching beginning standards in the seventh grade. Here are examples of their standards:

Examples of English-Language Development Standards in Reading

Reading comprehension

Beginning level: Respond orally to stories read to the student, using physical actions and other means of nonverbal communication (e.g., matching objects, pointing to an answer, drawing pictures).

Intermediate level: Read and orally identify the main ideas and draw inferences about written text using detailed sentences.

Advanced level: Read and respond orally to familiar stories and other texts by answering factual comprehension questions about cause-and-effect relationships.

about teaching, and the paraprofessional contributes vital communication skills and cultural knowledge.

Many bilingual paraprofessionals are university students who are in varying stages of the teacher preparation programs. They are highly motivated to become teachers, they are proud of their abilities to manage two languages and two cultures, and they are anxious to assume leadership in their own classrooms as soon as possible. As they approach and then enter their own student teaching experience, many are able to teach parallel to the regular teacher with careful supervision.

Some paraprofessionals exhibit those same language and cultural skills, but they view their paraprofessional role as their final career goal. They are often members of the local community who might have minimal academic preparation and training as instructional aides. It is perhaps among the members of this group that teachers who do not share the language and culture with the paraprofessional must exercise their most careful judgment. Because they are not trained teachers, their strategies in interacting positively and constructively with children must be carefully monitored. Because the supervising teacher often does not understand what the paraprofessional is saying to the children, it will be important to note the tone of the paraprofessional's voice and the children's reactions.

Parent Volunteers

FAMILY   LITERACY

What is the role of parent and family volunteers in working with English language learners?

Parent volunteers can be an important support to the nonbilingual teacher in the bilingual classroom. An important aspect of preparation for literacy in the mother tongue and English later is oral language development in the mother tongue. Family resources in the form of stories from parents, grandparents, and extended family can make a major contribution to this part of the program. Teachers can invite these adults into the classroom to tell stories to the children that can be used as a source of content for language-experience stories, for example.

McQuillan and Tse (1998) describe strategies for extending these storytelling experiences into the English language. The narratives that teachers, parents, grandparents, and other sources use constitute comprehensible input in the hands of an expert storyteller. The children are exposed to rich vocabulary and their background knowledge on a variety of valuable topics is enriched.

McQuillan and Tse indicate that students begin to write and tell their own stories as their own language production flourishes. When stories are related in English, the children's second language, students should be allowed to listen to stories in that target language without concerns about understanding everything. They should focus on the main ideas. Four steps then follow: (1) telling a short and simple version of the story; (2) revising the story by retelling it with different characters or settings, extending the story beyond its original ending, and narrating the story from the point of view of another character; (3) the creation of a class story, which might involve considerable negotiation among the children; and (4) individual or small group creation of stories and books.

While McQuillan and Tse are most concerned about using the process to provide comprehensible input in English, the same strategies can be used to provide a stronger base of vocabulary and background knowledge in the mother tongue. In addition, this permits parents, grandparents, and other members of the extended family to play a valued role in the classroom. Finally, it validates and reinforces the value of the mother tongue and culture.

This chapter examined the teaching of reading in languages other than English and also the teaching of English as a second language (ESL), as it relates to the teaching of reading. The focus language for the chapter was Spanish, the language most commonly encountered in bilingual classrooms. The chapter addressed three audiences: bilingual teachers who are capable of teaching reading and writing in a language other than English, teachers of English language learners whose mother tongue instruction will be conducted by a paraprofessional or other staff members under the teacher's supervision, and teachers who are responsible for teaching ESL.

There are various structures and models for teaching English language learners. One major direction is English only, that is, teaching ESL and also teaching all academic subjects, including reading, only in English. This is popularly known as immersion or structured immersion, and no evidence indicates it is an effective approach. The alternative is known as bilingual education. It consists of an ESL program as in the other approach, but academic instruction is provided in the children's mother tongue during the two to three years that are required for learning English sufficiently to support academic instruction (CALP), as opposed to a conversational level (BICS). There is substantial research support for this approach, although its application is highly political.

ESL is the major component of both immersion and bilingual education approaches. There are many approaches and methods for teaching ESL, but the natural approach is well supported in the literature. It resembles most closely the language environment of the child learning the mother tongue, a process almost always successful. It is based on themes rather than on grammar. Its major features are the provision of comprehensible input, the avoidance of correction, the acceptance of immature language structures at the beginning, a silent period during which children respond with gestures instead of producing language, and the maintenance of a low anxiety level in the classroom.

The natural approach consists of three stages: preproduction (comprehension), early production, and emergence of speech. During the intermediate stage that follows, children are ready to begin academic instruction in English, but in a sheltered or supported mode.

Strategies for teaching English language learners to read in English are given in Chapters 11, 12, and 13. In this chapter, the focus was on teaching reading in the mother tongue other than English, using Spanish as the focus. Children learn to read only once. For children who learn to read in the mother tongue, there is a positive transfer of skills from mother tongue reading to the second language: English.

Learning to read in Spanish is not greatly different from learning to read in English. Teaching word recognition skills is easier in Spanish because of the regular correspondences between sounds and letters in Spanish, but it is slightly different because Spanish is a highly syllabic language. Children tend to learn syllables instead of the sounds of individual letters.

Teachers have no difficulty finding instructional materials in Spanish for all subject areas. Spanish reading is an especially rich area; most major publishers provide Spanish language reading programs that are parallel to their English language programs. In addition, there is ample children's literature in Spanish, some originating in Spanish and some in the form of translations from English. Because of a lack of materials in most other languages, it is uncommon to find reading programs except in Spanish, especially beyond the first or second grade.

Assessment in Spanish is similar to assessment in English, and many formal measures have Spanish language versions. Instructions were provided for locating or constructing an informal reading inventory (IRI) in Spanish. A Spanish language version of reading recovery, *Descubriendo la Lectura*, provides support to young children who are struggling.

Many teachers who do not speak their students' mother tongue find themselves in a bilingual classroom nonetheless. They are usually provided with a bilingual paraprofessional who conducts the mother tongue instruction under the teachers' supervision. It is important for them to develop a strong spirit of teamwork in which the paraprofessional benefits from the professional training and experience of the classroom teacher, who in turn benefits from the language and cultural skills of the paraprofessional.

Many technological resources are also available that support the teacher who is working with ESL and mother tongue reading instruction. There are Web sites that provide background information about teaching ESL and computer-based resources that children can access.

For Your Journal

Find a classmate who did not speak English on arrival at the school or spoke English as a second language but who speaks English now. Interview this person about his or her experiences in learning English and learning to read. If you have ever traveled to a foreign country and did not speak or read the language, what did you do to adjust? Discuss the feelings you might have had if you had experienced this as a child.

Taking It to the World

You should now have a very clear idea of the challenges facing English language learners in their new classrooms. If you were the parent of a six-year-old child and you were to move to Croatia, describe the language and reading program you would want for your child. What additional information would you need before making a final decision?

Technology Connections

1. AltaVista provides a primitive translation Web site where children can cut and paste text to be translated to and from English and Spanish, as well as French, Portuguese, German, and Italian. The resulting translations are only fair in quality, but it is an interesting and revealing exercise for children. Visit the site (**http://babelfish.altavista. digital.com/cgi-bin/translate?**), and experiment with it for yourself. How might you be able to use this site when teaching?

2. Little Explorer is a multilingual Web site with a picture dictionary and graphics and multiple language translations provided. The site also includes links to other related sites. Visit Little Explorer (**http://www.LittleExplorers.com**) and explore for yourself. Why might this site be a valuable resource in the multilingual classroom?

Connect with Research

Review the following key words from the chapter and then connect to Research Navigator (**http://www.researchnavigator.com**) through this book's Companion Website to conduct a search into research on each of the various topics as they relate to reading and literacy education today.

additive program
basic interpersonal communications skills (BICS)
cognitive academic language proficiency (CALP)
maintenance model
positive transfer of skills

reductionist models
sheltered English instruction
subtractive program
transitional model

Companion Website

To access chapter objectives, practice tests, weblinks, and flashcards, visit the Companion Website at www.ablongman.com/templeallchildren2e.

Go to Allyn & Bacon's MyLabSchool (**www.mylabschool.com**), enter Assignment ID ENV3 into the Assignment Finder. Watch the video, *An ESL Vocabulary Lesson,* in which a first grade teacher demonstrates ESL strategies for teaching vocabulary and word recognition.

Question: What do you know about methods for teaching language to students with limited English proficiency? You may also answer the questions at the end of the clip and e-mail your responses to your instructor.

Appendix

Standards for Reading Professionals: IRA and NCTE

Throughout this book, the impact of standards on the Literacy profession is discussed in various chapters and particularly in a special "Standards & Literacy" feature. Discussions are intended to promote an understanding of how standards affect curriculum and instruction throughout the country. Two sets of standards of particular interest to reading professionals are the International Reading Association's "Standards for Reading Professionals—Revised 2003" and the National Council of Teachers of English (NCTE) Standards for Language Arts. In this appendix, we will try to help you understand how the new International Reading Association standards have changed, as well as provide you with a listing of the NCTE Standards for Language Arts and a correlation of where the NCTE standards are addressed within *All Children Read.*

How Does *All Children Read* Correlate to the IRA Standards for Reading Professionals—Revised 2003?

In 2003, the Professional Standards and Ethics Committee of the International Reading Association issued new criteria for the development and training of new reading professionals. The focus of the new standards is on knowledge and skills and identifies what new reading professionals should "know and be able to do." The 2003 revised standards represent a fairly significant change from the 1998 version of the *Standards for Reading Professionals,* to which *All Children Read* correlates very carefully.

CHANGE 1: Greater focus on candidate performance, with the criteria being much more performance-based than ever before.

All Children Read: Every chapter contains numerous in-class examples and case studies, as well as ongoing assessment and special teaching strategies that provide you with all the tools necessary for teaching literacy skills to all students. Every chapter contains a special "Standards & Literacy" feature that discusses various state and national performance-based standards that address pertinent literacy skills and help you plan instruction.

CHANGE 2: Reduction in the number of core standards from sixteen to five:

- Foundational Knowledge
- Instructional Strategies and Curriculum Materials

- Assessment, Diagnosis, and Evaluation
- Creating a Literate Environment, and
- Professional Development

Each standard includes several elements that specify particular knowledge and skills relevant for each type of reading professional.

All Children Read: A full listing of the "Standards for Reading Professionals—Revised 2003" and where *All Children Read* correlates to these standards is included on the inside of the cover of this book. As you can see, *All Children Read* has been written to correlate tightly to the new IRA standards.

CHANGE 3: The complete IRA standards table identifies standards and elements for five reading professional categories.

Individuals in each of these categories have various degrees of responsibility for supporting and meeting the needs of all students and for interacting with colleagues in a school community to ensure that every student receives appropriate reading instruction. For a complete breakdown of the elements for each category of professional, visit IRA online at **www.reading.org/advocacy/standards/standards03_revised/index.html**.

THE PARAPROFESSIONAL

- Assists in classrooms and in after-school and summer programs
- Two-year postsecondary degree with an emphasis on human development and educational processes and a concentration on reading and reading instruction

THE CLASSROOM TEACHER

- Teaches reading and writing or literacy instruction in preschool, school, or adult education
- Undergraduate or graduate degree that includes a concentration in reading and reading instruction

THE READING SPECIALIST/LITERACY COACH

- Provides specialized reading and writing instruction, assessment, and diagnosis to students
- May serve as a professional resource, work with other professionals in planning programs, provide professional development opportunities at the local and state levels, and provide leadership in student advocacy
- Has previous teaching experience
- Master's degree with concentration in reading education

THE TEACHER EDUCATOR

- Provides instruction to candidates at the graduate and undergraduate levels
- Participates in scholarly activities
- Forges partnerships with other educational agencies to promote the advancement of literacy
- Minimum of three years' teaching experience including the teaching of reading
- Terminal degree that focuses on reading and reading instruction

THE ADMINISTRATOR

- Includes principals, superintendents, and reading curriculum specialists
- Recognizes and supports reading professionals as they plan, implement, and evaluate effective reading instruction
- Master's degree that includes a focus on reading and reading instruction and a concentration in instructional leadership and administration

All Children Read: A primary focus of the book is on the skill development of the first three categories of literacy professionals: paraprofessional, the classroom teacher, and the reading specialist/literacy coach. Throughout this book and in the special *Teach It!* booklet, you are provided with an abundance of strategies and activities that are ready to use in the classroom.

CHANGE 4: Inclusion of references to research that support each of the elements, an acknowledgment of the shift toward an emphasis on the use of research-based practices in schools.

All Children Read: All content and recommended strategies are rooted in the latest research and represent proven practices, from author Donna Ogle's own KWL to Ehri's work in linguistics.

CHANGE 5: A primary focus on the changing population demographic and the effect this has had on the cultural and linguistic diversity of today's classrooms.

All Children Read: Special ELL sections in every chapter and two unique chapters (Chapters 2 and 14) that examine the changing demographic of today's schools, the changing needs of these students, and special considerations for teaching in a culturally and linguistically diverse classroom and community. Use these chapters and activities to utilize the diversity of your children and their families in a way that empowers your instruction.

CHANGE 6: A much heavier emphasis on the use of technology for teaching children and preparing teachers to use technology effectively and efficiently.

All Children Read: The use of technology in the classroom and all aspects of daily living is growing rapidly, and you and your children need to learn to make good use of the technology available. This book contains numerous suggestions of technology options—ranging from educational programs to simple technology applications that can be used to encourage reading and writing. These suggestions appear in the written narrative of each chapter as well as within the special Technology Connections activities at the end of each chapter.

Source: Professional Standards and Ethics Committee, International Reading Association. (2003). Standards for reading professionals — revised 2003. Newark, DE: International Reading Association. Available: http://www.reading.org/advocacy/standards/standards03_revised/

How Does *All Children Read* correlate to the National Council of Teachers of English Standards for Language Arts?

Below is a listing of the NCTE Standards for the Assessment of Reading and Writing and a correlation of where those standards are addressed within *All Children Read*.

NCTE STANDARD	CHAPTER COVERAGE
1. Students read a wide range of print and non-print texts to build an understanding of texts, of themselves, and the culture of the United States and the world; to acquire new information; to respond to the needs and demands of society and the workplace; and for personal fulfillment. Among these texts are fiction and nonfiction, classic and contemporary works.	2, 6, 7
2. Students read a wide range of literature from many periods in many genres to build an understanding of the many dimensions (e.g., philosophical, ethical, aesthetic) of human experience.	1, 2, 5, 6, 7
3. Students apply a wide range of strategies to comprehend, interpret, evaluate, and appreciate texts. They draw on their prior experience, their interactions with other readers and writers, their knowledge of word meaning and of other texts, their word identification strategies, and their understanding of textual features (e.g., sound-letter correspondence, sentence structure, context, graphics).	2–12
4. Students adjust their use of spoken, written, and visual language (e.g., conventions, style, vocabulary) to communicate effectively with a variety of audiences and for different purposes.	3–5, 8–12
5. Students employ a wide range of strategies as they write and use different writing process elements appropriately to communicate with different audiences for a variety of purposes.	3, 4, 8, 11
6. Students apply knowledge of language structure, language conventions (e.g., spelling and punctuation), media techniques, figurative language, and genre, to create, critique, and discuss print and non-print texts.	3, 4, 9–11
7. Students conduct research on issues and interests by generating ideas and questions, and by posing problems. They gather, evaluate, and synthesize data from a variety of sources (e.g., print and non-print texts, artifacts, people) to communicate their discoveries in ways that suit their purpose and audience.	6, 7, 10, 11
8. Students use a variety of technological and informational resources (e.g., libraries, databases, computer networks, video) to gather and synthesize information and to create and communicate knowledge.	All chapters
9. Students develop an understanding of and respect for diversity in language use, patterns, and dialects across cultures, ethnic groups, geographic regions, and social roles.	2, 3, 5, 9, 10, 12
10. Students whose first language is not English make use of their first language to develop competency in the English language arts and to develop understanding of content across the curriculum.	2, 4–12
11. Students participate as knowledgeable, reflective, creative, and critical members of a variety of literacy communities.	All chapters
12. Students use spoken, written, and visual language to accomplish their own purposes (e.g., for learning, enjoyment, persuasion, and the exchange of information).	2–12

References

Achilles, C. M. (1999). *Let's put kids first, finally: Getting class size right*. Thousand Oaks, CA: Corwin Press.

Adams, M. J. (1990). *Beginning to read: Thinking and learning about print*. Cambridge, MA: MIT Press.

Adams, M. J. (1998). The three cuing system. In J. Osborne & F. Lehr (Eds.), *Literacy for all: Issues in teaching and learning*. New York: Guilford Press.

Adler, M. (1982). The Paideia proposal: Rediscovering the essence of education. *American School Board Journal, 169*(7), 17–20.

Afflerbach, P. (1993). Report cards and reading. *The Reading Teacher, 46*, 458–465.

Aitchison, J. (1987). *Words in the mind*. Oxford, England: Blackwell.

Alexander, P. (1998). The nature of disciplinary and domain learning: The knowledge, interest and strategic dimensions of learning from subject matter text. In C. Hynd (Ed.), *Learning from text across conceptual domains*. Mahwah, NJ: Erbaum.

Alexander, P. A. (2000). Learning from text: A multidimensional and developmental perspective. In M. Kamil, P. B. Mosenthal, P. D. Pearson, & R. Barr (Eds.), *Handbook of reading research, volume III*. Hillsdale, NJ: Erlbaum.

Alexander, P., Jetton, T. L., Kulikowich, J. M., & Woehler, C. (1994). Contrasting instructional and structural importance: The seductive effect of teacher questions. *Journal of Reading Behavior, 26*, 19–45.

Allard, H. (1977). *Miss Nelson is missing!* Illustrated by J. Marshall. Boston: Houghton Mifflin.

Allington, R. (1983). Fluency: The neglected reading goal. *The Reading Teacher, 36*(6), 556–561.

Allington, R. (2005). *What really matters for struggling readers*. Boston: Allyn and Bacon.

Allington, R. L. (1983). The reading instruction provided to readers of differing reading ability. *Elementary School Journal, 83*, 549–558.

Allington, R. L. (1997). Overselling phonics. *Reading Today, 14*, 15.

Allington, R. L. (2001). *What really matters for struggling readers: Designing research-based programs*. New York: Longman.

Allington, R. L., & Johnson, P. H. (2002). *Reading to learn: Lessons from exemplary fourth-grade classrooms*. New York: Guilford Press.

Allington, R. L., & McGill-Franzen, A. (1989). School response to reading failure: Instruction for chapter one and special education students in grades two, four, and eight. *Elementary School Journal, 89*(5), 529–542.

Almasi, J. F. (1995). The nature of fourth graders' socio-cognitive conflicts in peer-led and teacher-led discussions of literature. *Reading Research Quarterly, 30*(3), 314–351.

Anderson, R. C., & Nagy, W. E. (1991). Word meanings. In R. Barr, M. L. Kamil, P. B. Mosenthal, & P. D. Pearson (Eds.), *Handbook of reading research*, (Vol. 2). New York: Longman.

Anderson, R. C., & Nagy, W. E. (1992). The vocabulary conundrum. *American Educator, 16*, 14–18, 44–47.

Anderson, R. C., & Pearson, P. D. (1984). A schema-theoretic view of basic processes in reading. In P. D. Pearson (Ed.), *Handbook of reading research*. New York: Longman.

Anderson, R. C., Wilson, P., & Fielding, L. (1988). Growth in reading and how children spend their time outside of school. *Reading Research Quarterly, 23*, 285–303.

Andrade, H. G. (1997). Understanding rubrics. *Educational Leadership, 54*(4). Retrieved July 22, 2006, from http://www.middleweb.com/rubricsHG.html

Andrade, H. G. (2002). *Understanding rubrics*. http://learnweb.harvard.edu/ALPS/thinking/docs/rubricar.htm

Archambault, J., & Martin, B. Jr. (1989). *White dynamite and the curly kid*. Illustrated by Ted Rand. New York: Henry Holt.

Arellano Osuna, A. (1992). *El lenguaje integral: Una alternativa para la educación*. Mérida, Venezuela: Editorial Venezolana.

Armbruster, B. B., Lehr, F., & Osborn, J. (2001). *Put reading first: The research building blocks for teaching children to read. Kindergarten through grade 3*. Washington, DC: National Institute for Literacy.

Asher, J. J. (1982). The total physical response approach. In R. W. Blair (Ed.), *Innovative approaches to language teaching* (pp. 54–66). Rowley, MA: Newbury House.

Ashton-Warner, S. (1963). *Teacher*. New York: Simon & Schuster.

Atwell, N. (1987). *In the middle*. Portsmouth, NH: Heinemann.

Atwell, N. (1998). *In the middle: Writing, reading and learning with adolescents* (2nd ed.). Portsmouth, NH: Boynton/Cook.

Austin, J. L. (1962). *How to do things with words.* Oxford, England: Oxford University Press.

Avi. (1994). *Nothing but the truth: A documentary novel.* Thorndike, ME: Thorndike Press.

Ayers, W. (1993). *To teach.* New York: Teachers College Press.

Baker, L., Serpell, R., & Sonnenschein, S. (1995). Opportunities for literacy learning in the homes of urban preschoolers. In L. M. Morrow (Ed.), *Family literacy: Connections in schools and communities* (pp. 236–252). Newark, DE: International Reading Association.

Banks, J. A. (2003). *Teaching strategies for ethnic studies.* Boston: Allyn and Bacon.

Barbosa Heldt, A. (1971). *Cómo han aprendido a leer y a escribir los mexicanos.* Mexico City, Mexico: Editorial Pax México, Librería Carlos Cesarmán.

Barger, J. (2003). *Comparing the DIBELS Oral Reading Fluency indicator and the North Carolina end of grade reading assessment* (Tech. Rep.). Asheville: North Carolina Teacher Academy.

Barker, C. (2006). How many syllables does English have? Retrieved from http://ling.ucsd.edu/%7Ebarker/Syllables/index.txt

Barone, D. (1992). That reminds me of . . .: Using dialogue journals with young readers. In C. Temple & P. Collins (Eds.), *Stories and readers: New perspectives on literature in the elementary classroom.* Norwood, MA: Christopher-Gordon.

Barone, D., Hardman, D., & Taylor, J. (2006). *Reading first in the classroom.* New York: Pearson.

Barthes, R. (1974). *S/Z.* New York: Hill and Wang.

Bartlett, J. R. (2003). *Dictionary of Americanisms.* Hoboken, NJ: John Wiley & Sons.

Baumann, J., Kameenui, E., & Ash, G. (2003). Research on vocabulary instruction: Voltaire redux. In J. Flood, D. Lapp, J. Squire, & J. Jensen (Eds.), *Handbook of research on teaching the English language arts* (2nd ed.). Mahwah, NJ: Erlbaum.

Beamon, G. W. (2001). *Teaching with adolescent learning in mind.* Arlington Heights, IL: Skylight Professional Development.

Beane, J. (1991, October). The middle school: The natural home of integrated curriculum. *Educational Leadership, 49*(2), 9–13.

Beane, J. (2002). Beyond self-interest: A democratic core curriculum. *Educational Leadership, 59,* 25–28.

Bear, D. R., Invernizzi, M., Templeton, S., & Johnston, F. (2004). *Words their way: Word study for phonics, vocabulary, and spelling instruction.* Upper Saddle River, NJ: Merrill.

Beck, I, Kucan, L., & McKeown, M. (2002). *Bringing words to life.* New York: Guilford.

Beck, I. L., & McKeown, M. G. (1983). Learning words well—a program to enhance vocabulary and comprehension. *The Reading Teacher, 36,* 622–625.

Beck, I. L., McKeown, M. G., & Kucan, L. (2002). *Bringing words to life: Robust vocabulary instruction.* New York: Guilford Press.

Beck, I. L., McKeown, M. G., Hamilton, R. L., & Kucan, L. (1997). *Questioning the author: An approach for enhancing student engagement with text.* Newark, DE: International Reading Association.

Becker, H. J. (2000). Who's wired and who's not: Children's access to and use of computer technology. *Children and Computer Technology, 10,* 44–75.

Berthoff, A. (1981a). *The making of meaning.* Upper Montclair, NJ: Boynton/Cook.

Berthoff, A. (1981b). *The web of meaning.* Portsmouth, NH: Boynton/Cook.

Bettelheim, B. (1975). *The uses of enchantment.* New York: Vintage.

Betts, A. E. (1946). *Foundations of reading instruction, with emphasis on differentiated guidance.* Chicago: American Book Company.

Biklen, D. (1981). Should "The Ugly Duckling" be banned? In D. Biklen & L. Bailey (Eds.), *Rudely stamp'd.* New York: University Press of America.

Blachowicz, C. L. Z. (1986). Making connections: Alternatives to the vocabulary notebook. *Journal of Reading, 29,* 643–649.

Blachowicz, C. L. Z., Sullivan, D., & Cieply, C. (2001). Fluency snapshots: A quick screening tool for your classroom. *Reading Psychology, 22*(2), 95–109.

Blachowicz, C. L. Z., & Fisher, P. (2000). Vocabulary instruction. In M. L. Kamil., P. Mosenthal, P. D. Pearson, & R. Barr (Eds.), *Handbook of reading research* (Vol. 3). New York: Longman.

Blachowicz, C. L. Z., & Fisher, P. (2006). *Teaching vocabulary in all classrooms* (3rd ed.). New York: Prentice Hall.

Blachowicz, C., & Fisher, P. (1996). *Teaching vocabulary in all classrooms.* Englewood Cliffs, NJ: Prentice Hall.

Bleich, D. (1978). *Subjective criticism.* Baltimore: Johns Hopkins University.

Block, C. C., & Pressley, M. (Eds.). (2001). *Comprehension instruction: Research-based best practices.* New York: Guilford.

Bond, G. L., & Dykstra, R. (1967). The cooperative research program in first-grade reading instruction. *Reading Research Quarterly, 2,* 5–142.

Bormuth, J. R. (1968, Autumn). Cloze test readability: Criterion reference scores. *Journal of Educational Measurement, 5*(3), 189–196.

Bos C. S., & Anders, P. L. (1989). Developing higher level thinking skills through interactive teaching. *Journal of Reading, Writing, and Learning Disabilities International, 4*(4), 259–274.

Bos, C., & Anders, P. (1990, Winter). Effects of interactive vocabulary instruction on the vocabulary learning and reading comprehension of junior-high learning disabled students. *Learning Disability Quarterly, 13*(1), 31–42.

Bradley, L., & Bryant, P. (1985). *Rhyme and reason in reading and spelling.* Ann Arbor: University of Michigan Press.

Britton, J. (1970). *Language and learning.* Harmondsworth, England: Penguin Books.

Bromley, K. (1999). Key components of sound writing instruction. In L. Gambrell, L. Mandell Morrow, S. B. Neuman, & M. Pressley (Eds.), *Best practices in literacy instruction* (pp. 152–174). New York: Guilford Press.

Brooks, W. (2006). Reading representations of themselves: Urban youth use culture and African American textual features to develop literary understandings. *Reading Research Quarterly, 41*(3), 372–392.

Brooks, W. M. (2005). Reading linguistic features: Middle school students' response to the African American literary tradition. In B. Hammond, M. E. Rhodes Hoover, & McPhail, I. P. (Eds.), *Teaching African American learners to read* (pp. 253–263). Newark, DE: International Reading Association.

Brown, H., & Cambourne, B. (1990). *Read and retell: A strategy for the whole-language/natural learning classroom.* Portsmouth, NH: Heinemann.

Brown, M. (1949). *The important book.* New York: Harper.

Brown, R. (1955). *Words and things.* Garden City, NY: Basic Books.

Browne, N., & Keeley, S. (2000). *Asking the right questions: A guide to critical thinking.* New York: Prentice Hall.

Bruner, J. (1978). The role of dialogue in language acquisition. In A. Sinclair, R. J. Jarvella, & W. M. Levelt (Eds.), *The child's conception of language* (pp. 241–256). New York: Springer-Verlag.

Bruner, J., & Ninio, A. (1978, February). The achievement and antecedents of labeling. *Journal of Child Language 5,* 1, pp. 1–15.

Buck, J., & Torgesen, J. (2003). *The relationship between performance on a measure of oral reading fluency and performance on the Florida Comprehensive Assessment Test* (FCRR Tech. Rep. #1). Tallahassee, FL: Florida Center for Reading Research.

Buehl, D. (2001). *Classroom strategies for interactive learning* (2nd ed.). Newark, DE: International Reading Association.

Burnett, F. H. (1996). *Little Lord Fauntleroy.* New York: Puffin. (Original work published 1906)

Burns, P. C., Roe, B. D., & Ross, E. P. (1999). *Teaching reading in today's elementary schools.* Boston: Houghton Mifflin.

Butler, A., & Turbill, J. (1985). *Towards a reading-writing classroom.* Portsmouth, NH: Heinemann.

Caldwell, J. S. (2002). *Reading assessment: A primer for teachers and tutors.* New York: Guilford Press.

California Commission on Teacher Credentialing. (2001). *Standards of quality and effectiveness for professional teacher preparation programs.* Sacramento, CA: California Department of Education Web site at www.ctc.ca.gov/SB2042/SB2042_info.html.

California State Board of Education. (1997). *English language arts content standards for California public schools: Kindergarten through grade twelve.* Sacramento, CA: Author.

California State Board of Education. (1999). *English language development standards.* Sacramento: Author.

Calkins, L. (1996). *The art of teaching writing.* Portsmouth, NH: Heinemann.

Calkins, L. M. (1986). *The art of teaching writing.* Portsmouth, NH: Heinemann.

Campbell, J. (1968). *The hero with a thousand faces.* New Haven, CT: Bolingen Press, 1968.

Carle, E. (1987). *The very hungry caterpillar.* New York: Philomel Books.

Carle, E. (1994). *La oruga muy hambrienta.* New York: Philomel Books.

Carlisle, J. F. (2000). Awareness of the structure and meaning of morphologically complex words: Impact on reading. *Reading and Writing: An Interdisciplinary Journal, 12,* 169–190.

Carlisle, J. F., & Stone, C. A. (2005). Exploring the role of morphemes in word reading. *Reading Research Quarterly, 40,* 428–449.

Carlo, M. S., August, D., McLaughlin, B., Snow, C. E., Dressler, C., Lippman, D. N., Lively, T. J., & White, C. E. (2004). Closing the gap: Addressing the vocabulary needs of English-Language learners in bilingual and mainstream classrooms. *Reading Research Quarterly, 39*(2), 188–215.

Carr, E. M. (1985). The vocabulary overview guide: A metacognitive strategy to improve vocabulary, comprehension and retention. *Journal of Reading, 28,* 684–689.

Carr, E. M., & Ogle, D. (1987). K-W-L Plus: A strategy for comprehension and summarization. *Journal of Reading, 30,* 626–631.

Carroll, L. (1992). *Alice in wonderland.* Hertfordshire, England: Wordsworth Classic. (Original work published 1875)

Castañeda v. *Pickard,* 648 F.2d 989, 5th Circuit (1981).

CATESOL. (1992). *Position statement on specially-designed academic instruction in English (sheltered instruction).* Orinda: California Teachers of English to Speakers of Other Languages.

Caverly, D. C., Mandeville, T. F., & Nicholson, S. A. (1995). PLAN: A study reading strategy for informational text. *Journal of Adolescent and Adult Literacy, 39,* 190–199.

Chall, J. (1967). *Learning to read: The great debate* (Rev. ed.). New York: McGraw-Hill.

Chall, J., & Dale, E. (1995). *Manual for the new Dale-Chall Readability: An appraisal of research and application.* Cambridge, MA: Brookline Books.

Chastain, K. (1975). *Developing second-language skills: From theory to practice.* Chicago: Rand McNally.

Chomsky, C. (1971). Write first, read later. *Childhood Education, 47*(6) 296–299.

Chomsky, N., & Halle, M. (1970). *The sound pattern of English.* New York: Macmillan.

Clay, M. M. (1975). *What did I write?* Portsmouth, NH: Heinemann.

Clay, M. M. (1985). *The early detection of reading difficulties: A diagnostic survey with recovery procedures.* Portsmouth, NH: Heinemann.

Clay, M. M. (1987). *Writing begins at home: Preparing children for writing before they go to school.* Portsmouth, NH: Heinemann.

Clay, M. M. (1993). *An observational survey of early literacy achievement.* Portsmouth, NH: Heinemann.

Clay, M. M. (1993). *Reading recovery: A guidebook for teachers in training.* Portsmouth, NH: Heinemann.

Cleary, B. (1997). *Ramona and her father.* New York: Harper Trophy.

Clymer, T. (1996, November). The utility of phonic generalizations in the primary grades. *The Reading Teacher, 50,* 3, pp. 182–187.

Cole, S. (2001). *Allosaurus!: The life and death of Big Al.* New York: Dutton Children's Books.

Coleman, J. S., Campbell, E. Q., Hobson, C. J., McPartland, J., Mood, A. M., Weinfeld, F. D., & York, R. L. (1966). *Equality of educational opportunity.* Washington, DC: U.S. Government Printing Office.

Collier, V. P. (1987). Age and rate of acquisition of second language for academic purposes. *TESOL Quarterly, 21,* 617–641.

Collier, V. P. (1989). How long? A synthesis of research on academic achievement in a second language. *TESOL Quarterly, 23,* 509–539.

Collins, J. L. (1998). *Strategies for struggling writers.* New York: Guilford Press.

Conrad, P. (1992). *Pedro's journal.* New York: Scholastic.

Cowhey, M. (2006). *Black ants and Buddhists.* Portland, ME: Stenhouse.

Cowley, J. (1985). *Rosie at the zoo.* Melbourne: Nelson.

Cowley, J. (1990). *Mrs. Wishy Washy.* San Diego: Wright Group.

Cowley, J. (1998). *The hungry giant.* Othell, WA: Wright Group.

Crawford, A. N. (1982). From Spanish reading to English reading: The transition process. In M. P. Douglass (Ed.), *Claremont reading conference yearbook* (pp. 159–165). Claremont, CA: Claremont Reading Conference.

Crawford, A. N. (1993). Literature, integrated language arts, and the language minority child: A focus on meaning. In A. Carrasquillo & C. Hedley (Eds.), *Whole language and the bilingual learner* (pp. 61–75). Norwood, NJ: Ablex.

Crawford, A. N. (1994a). Communicative approaches to second language acquisition: From oral language development into the core curriculum and L₂ literacy. In C. F. Leyba (Ed.), *Schooling and language minority students: A theoretical framework* (2nd ed., pp. 79–121). Los Angeles: California State University, Los Angeles, Evaluation, Dissemination and Assessment Center.

Crawford, A. N. (1994b). Estrategias para promover la comprensión lectora en estudiantes de alto riesgo. *Lectura y Vida, 15*(1), 21–27.

Crawford, A. N. (1995). Language policy, second language learning, and literacy. In A. N. Crawford (Ed.), *A practical guidebook for adult literacy programmes in developing nations* (pp. 9–16). Paris: UNESCO.

Crawford, A. N. (2000). Strategies for teaching reading and writing to English language learners. In J. W. Gillet, C. Temple, A. N. Crawford, S. R. Mathews, & J. P. Young (Eds.), *Understanding reading problems: Assessment and instruction* (pp. 416–453). New York: Longman.

Crawford, A. N. (2003). Communicative approaches to second language acquisition: The bridge to second language literacy. In G. García (Ed.), *English learners: Reaching the highest level of English literacy* (pp. 152–181). Newark, DE: International Reading Association.

Crawford, A. N., Allen, R. V., & Hall, M. (1995). The language experience approach In A. N. Crawford (Ed.), *A practical guidebook for adult literacy programs in developing nations* (pp. 17–46). Paris: UNESCO.

Crawford, A., Saul, W., Mathews, S., & MaKinster, J. (2005). *Lessons from the thinking classroom.* New York: IDEA.

Crawford, J. (1989). *Bilingual education: History, politics, theory and practice.* Trenton, NJ: Crane.

Cuban, L. (2001). *Oversold and underused: Computers in classrooms.* Cambridge: Harvard University Press.

Cummins, J. (1980). The construct of language proficiency in bilingual education. In J. E. Alatis (Ed.), *Georgetown University roundtable on languages and linguistics* (pp. 76–93). Washington, DC: Georgetown University Press.

Cummins, J. (1981). The role of primary language development in promoting educational success for language minority students. In California State Department of Education (Ed.), *Schooling and language minority students: A theoretical framework* (pp. 3–49). Los Angeles: California State University, Los Angeles, Evaluation, Dissemination and Assessment Center.

Cummins, J. (1986). Empowering minority students: A framework for intervention. *Harvard Educational Review, 56,* 18–36.

Cummins, J. (1989). *Empowering minority students.* Sacramento: California Association for Bilingual Education.

Cummins, J., & Corson, D. (1997). *Bilingual education.* Amsterdam: Kluwer.

Cunningham, A. E., & Stanovich, K. E. (1997). Early reading acquisition and its relation to reading experience and ability 10 years later. *Developmental Psychology, 33*(6), 934–945.

Cunningham, A. E., & Stanovich, K. E. (1998, Spring-Summer). What reading does for the mind. *The American Educator,* pp. 8–17.

Cunningham, P. M. (1995). *Phonics they use: Words for reading and writing* (2nd ed.). New York: HarperCollins.

Cunningham, P. M., & Allington, R. L. (1999). *Classrooms that work: They can all read and write* (2nd ed.). Reading, MA: Addison-Wesley.

Cunningham, P. M., Hall, D. P., & Defree, M. (1991). Non-ability grouped, multileveled instruction: A year in a first-grade classroom. *The Reading Teacher, 44,* 566–571.

Cunningham, P. M., Hall, D. P., & Sigmon, C. M. (2007). *The teacher's guide to the four blocks.* Greensboro, NC: Carson-Dellosa.

Curtis, C. P. (2000). *Bud, not buddy.* New York: Yearling.

Dahl, K. L., & Freppon, P. A. (1992). *Learning to read and write in inner-city schools: A comparison of children's sense-making in skills-based and whole language classrooms.* Final report to the Office of Educational Research and Improvement. (Grant No. G008720229). Washington, DC: U.S. Department of Education.

Dahl, K. L., & Freppon, P. A. (1995). A comparison of inner-city children's interpretations of reading and writing instruction in the early grades in skills-based and whole language classrooms. *Reading Research Quarterly, 30*(1), 50–74.

Dahl, K. L., Scharer, P. L., Lawson, L. L., & Grogan, P. R. (2001). *Rethinking phonics: Making the best teaching decisions.* Portsmouth, NH: Heinemann.

Dahl, R. (1998). *Danny, the champion of the world.* Illustrated by Quentin Blake. New York: Puffin.

Dale, E. (1965). Vocabulary measurement: Techniques and major findings. *Elementary English, 42,* 82–88.

Damico, J. S. (1991). Descriptive assessment of communicative ability in limited English proficient students. In E. Hamayan & J. S. Damico (Eds.), *Limiting bias in the assessment of bilingual students* (pp. 157–218). Austin, TX: PRO-ED.

Daniels, H. (1994). *Literature circles: Voice and choice in one student-centered classroom.* York, ME: Stenhouse.

Daniels, H. (2001). *Literature circles: Voice and choice in book clubs and reading groups.* Augusta, ME: Stenhouse.

Daniels, H. (2002). *Literature circles: Voice and choice in book clubs & reading groups* (2nd ed.). Markham, Ontario: Pembroke.

Davis, F. B. (1944). Fundamental factors of comprehension in reading. *Psychometrica, 9,* 195–197.

Davis, F. B. (1968). Research in comprehension in reading. *Reading Research Quarterly, 3,* 499–454.

Delpit, L. (1990). Language diversity and learning. In S. Hynds & D. Rubin (Eds.), *Perspectives on talk and learning* (pp. 247–266). Urbana, IL: NCTE.

Delpit, L. (1991). The silenced dialogue: Power and pedagogy in educating other people's children. In M. Minami and B. Kennedy (Eds.), *Language issues in literacy and bilingual/multicultural education.* Cambridge, MA: Harvard Educational Review.

Delpit, L. (1995). *Other people's children: Cultural conflict in the classroom.* New York: New York Press.

Delpit, L. (1996). Skills and other dilemmas of a progressive black educator. In L. Delpit (Ed.), *Other people's children.* New York: New Press.

Dewey, J. (1913). *Interest and effort in education*. Boston: Riverside.

Diana v. State Board of Education of California, Action No. C-7037RFP (N. D. Cal. Jan. 7, 1970 & June 18, 1973).

Dirkes, M. A. (1985). Metacognition: Students in charge of their thinking. *Roeper Review*, 8(2), 96–100.

Dixon, C. N., & Nessel, D. (1983). *Language experience approach to reading and writing: LEA for ESL*. Hayward, CA: Alemany Press.

Donahue, P. L., Finnegan, R. J., Lutkus, A. D., Allen, N. L., & Campbell, J. R. (2001). *The nation's report card: Fourth-grade reading 2000*. (NCES 2001-499). Washington, DC: U.S. Department of Education, National Center for Education Statistics.

Doty, W. (1986). *Mythography: The study of myths and rituals*. Tuscaloosa: University of Alabama Press.

Droop, M., & Verhoeven, L. (2003). Language proficiency and reading ability in first and second language learners. *Reading Research Quarterly*, 38, 78–103.

Dudley-Marling, C. (1990). *When school is a struggle*. Richmond Hill, Ontario: Scholastic.

Dudley-Marling, C. (2000). *A family affair: When school troubles come home*. Portsmouth, NH: Heinemann.

Duffy, G. G., & Roehler, L. R. (1989). Why strategy instruction is so difficult and what we need to do about it. In C. B. McCormick, G. Miller, & M. Pressley (Eds.), *Cognitive strategy research: From basic research to educational applications*. New York: Springer-Verlag.

Duffy-Hester, A. (1999). Teaching struggling readers in elementary school classrooms: A review of classroom reading programs and principles for instruction. *The Reading Teacher, 52*, 480–495.

Duke, N. K. (2000). 3–6 minutes per day: The scarcity of informational texts in first grade. *Reading Research Quarterly*, 35(2), 202–224.

Duke, N. K., & Pearson, P. (2002). Effective practices for developing reading comprehension. In Alan E. Farstrup & S. Jay Samuels (Eds.), *What research has to say about reading instruction* (3rd ed., pp. 205–242). Newark, DE: International Reading Association, Inc.

Durkin, D. (1978–1979). What classroom observations reveal about reading comprehension instruction. *Reading Research Quarterly*, 15, 481–433.

Echevarria, J., Vogt, M. E., & Short, D. J. (2004). *Making content comprehensible for English language learners: The SIOP model* (2nd ed.). Boston: Allyn and Bacon.

Economic Policy Institute. *The State of Working America 2006/2007*. http://www.stateofworkingamerica.org/swa06_ch08_international.pdf

Edelsky, C. (1982). Writing in a bilingual program: The relation of L_1 and L_2 texts. *TESOL Quarterly, 16*, 211–228.

Eder, D. (1983). Ability grouping and students' academic self-concepts: A case study. *Elementary School Journal, 84*(2), 149–161.

Eeds, M., & Wells, D. (1989). Grand conversations: An exploration of meaning construction in literature discussion groups. *Research in the Teaching of English*, 23, 4–29.

Ehrenreich, B. (2001). *Nickled and dimed: On (not) getting by in America*. New York: Owl Books.

Ehri, L. C. (1991). Development of the ability to read words. In R. Barr, M. Kamil, P. B. Mosenthal, & P. D. Pearson (Eds.), *Handbook of reading research* (Vol. 2). New York: Longman.

Ehri, L. C. (1997a). Learning to read and learning to spell are one and the same, almost. In C. Perfetti, L. Rieben, & M. Fayol (Eds.), *Learning to spell* (pp. 237–269). Hillsdale, NJ: Erlbaum.

Ehri, L. C. (1997b). *The development of children's ability to read words*. Paper presented at the convention of the International Reading Association, Atlanta, GA.

Elley, W. (1992). *How in the world do students read?* The Hague: The International Association for the Evaluation of Educational Achievement.

Elley, W. (1996). *The IEA study of reading literacy*. Oxford, England: Pergamon.

Escamilla, K., & Andrade, A. (1992). Descubriendo la lectura: An application of *Reading Recovery* in Spanish. *Education and Urban Society*, 24, 212–226.

Escamilla, K., Loera, M., Ruiz, O., & Rodriguez, Y. (1998). An examination of sustaining effects in *Descubriendo la Lectura* programs. *Literacy Teaching and Learning*, 3, 59–81.

Federal Register. (2006). Title I—Improving the Academic Achievement of the Disadvantaged; Final Rule. 34 CFR Part 200, September 13, 2006. Washington, DC: Department of Education.

Ferreiro, E., & Rodríguez, B. (1994). *Las condiciones de alfabetización en medio rural*. México: CINVESTAV.

Ferreiro, E., & Tebersoky, A. (1982). *Literacy before schooling*. Portsmouth: Heinemann.

Fielding, L., & Roller, C. (1992). Making difficult books accessible and easy books acceptable. *The Reading Teacher*, 45, 678–685.

Finocchiaro, M. (1974). *English as a second language: From theory to practice*. New York: Regents.

Firth, V. (1985). Beneath the surface of developmental dyslexia. In K. E. Patterson, J. C. Marshall, & M. Coltheart (Eds.), *Surface dyslexia* (pp.310–330). London: Erlbaum.

Fisher, P., Blachowicz, C., & Smith, J. (1991). Vocabulary learning in literature discussion groups. In J. Zutell & S. McCormick (Eds.), *Learner factors/Teacher factors: Issues in literacy research and instruction* (pp. 201–209). Fortieth yearbook of the National Reading Conference. Chicago: National Reading Conference.

Fitzgerald, J. (1993). Literacy and students who are learning English as a second language. *The Reading Teacher, 46,* 638–647.

Fitzgerald, J. (1995). English-as-a-second-language reading instruction in the United States: A research review. *Journal of Reading Behavior, 27,* 115–152.

Flesch, R. (1956). *Why Johnny can't read.* New York: Popular library.

Folse, K. S., (2004). *Vocabulary myths: Applying second language research to classroom teaching.* Ann Arbor, MI: University of Michigan.

Foorman, B. R., & Mehta, P. (2002, November). *Definitions of fluency: Conceptual and methodological challenges.* PowerPoint presentation at A Focus on Fluency Forum, San Francisco, CA. Retrieved from www.prel.org/programs/rel/fluency/Foorman.ppt

Fountas, I. C., & Pinnell, G. S. (1996). *Guided reading: Good first teaching for all children.* Portsmouth, NH: Heinemann.

Fountas, I. C., & Pinnell, G. S. (1999). *Matching books to readers: Using leveled books in guided reading, K–3.* Portsmouth, NH: Heinemann.

Fountas, I. C., & Pinnell, G. S. (2001). *Guiding readers and writers: Grades 3–6.* Portsmouth, NH: Heinemann.

Fountas, I., & Pinnell, G. S. (2005). *The Fountas & Pinnell leveled book list, K-8, 2006–2008 Edition.* Portsmouth, NH: Heinemann.

Fox, M., & Mullins, P. (1992). *Hattie and the fox.* Chicago: Scott Foresman.

Fradd, S. H., & Tikunoff, W. J. (Eds.). (1987). *Bilingual and bilingual special education: An administrator's guide.* Boston: Little, Brown.

Frazier, D. (2000). *Miss Alaineus: A vocabulary disaster.* San Diego: Harcourt.

Freeman, D. (1978). *Corduroy.* New York: Viking Junior.

Freinet, C. (1974). *El método natural de lectura.* Barcelona, Spain: Editorial Laia.

Freppon, P. A. (1995). Low-income children's literacy interpretations in a skills-based and a whole-language classroom. *Journal of Reading Behavior, 27*(4), 505–533.

Frith, U. (1985). Beneath the surface of developmental dyslexia. In K. E. Patterson, J. C. Marshall, & M. Coltheart (Eds.), *Surface dyslexia* (pp. 310–330). London: Erlbaum.

Fry, E. (1967). Fry's readability graph: Clarifications, validity, and extension to level 17. *Journal of Reading, 21,* 242–252.

Fuchs, L. S., Deno, S. L., & Mirkin, P. K. (1984, Summer). The effects of frequent curriculum-based measurement and evaluation on pedagogy, student achievement, and student awareness of learning. *American Educational Research Journal, 21*(2), pp. 449–460.

Galdone, P. (1968). *Henny Penny.* New York: Scholastic.

Ganske, K. (2003). *Word journeys.* New York: Guilford Press.

Garbarino, J. (2000). *The lost boys: Why our sons turn violent and how we can save them.* New York: Anchor Books.

García, E. E. (2005). *Teaching and learning in two languages: Bilingualism and schooling in the United States.* New York: Teachers College Press.

Garcia, E. (1991, Autumn). Factors influencing the English reading test performance of Spanish-speaking Hispanic children. *Reading Research Quarterly, 26*(4), 371–392.

Gardner, H. (1980). *Artful scribbles.* New York: Basic Books.

Gaskins, I. W. (1998). There's more to teaching at-risk and delayed readers than good reading instruction. *The Reading Teacher, 51,* 534–547.

Gee, J. P. (1999). *An introduction to discourse analysis: Theory and method.* New York: Routledge.

Gee, J. P. (2001). A sociocultural perspective on literacy development. In S. B. Neuman & D. K. Dickinson (Eds.), *Handbook of early literacy research.* New York: Guilford Press.

Gelman, R., & Greeno, J. G. (1989). On the nature of competence: Principles for understanding in a domain. In L. Resnick (Ed.), *Knowing, learning, and instruction: Essays in honor of Robert Glaser.* Hillsdale, NJ: Erlbaum.

Gentry, J. R. (1981). Learning to spell developmentally. *The Reading Teacher, 34,* 378–381.

Gentry, J. R. (1989). *Spel . . . is a four-letter word.* Portsmouth: Heinemann.

Gersten, R. (1998). Recent advances in instructional research for students with learning disabilities: An overview. *Learning Disabilities Research and Practice, 13*(3), 162–170.

Gersten, R., & Baker, S. (2000). What we know about effective instructional practices for English-language learners. *Exceptional Children, 66,* 454–470.

Gibson, E., & Levin, H. (1975). *The psychology of reading.* Cambridge, MA: MIT Press.

Gill, J. T. (1992). The relationship between word recognition and spelling. In S. Templeton & D. Bear (Eds.), *Development of orthographic knowledge and the foundations of literacy: A memorial fesschrift for Edmund H. Henderson.* Hillsdale, NJ: Erlbaum.

Gillet, J. W., & Kita, M. J. (1980). Words, kids and categories. In E. H. Henderson & J. Beers (Eds.), *Developmental and cognitive aspects of learning to spell: A reflection of word knowledge* (pp. 36–45). Newark, DE: International Reading Association.

Gillet, J. W., & Temple, C. (1978, December). Developing word knowledge: A cognitive view. *Reading World, 18*(2), 132–140.

Gillet, J. W., Temple, C., & Crawford, A. (2004). *Understanding reading problems* (6th ed.). Boston: Allyn and Bacon.

Gillet, J. W., Temple, C., & Crawford, A. (2007, in press). *Understanding reading problems* (7th ed.). Boston: Allyn and Bacon.

Gleitman, L. R., & Rozin, P. (1973). Teaching reading by use of a syllabary. *Reading Research Quarterly, 8*, 4 (Summer, 1973), pp. 447–483.

Goatley, V. J., Brock, C. H., & Raphael, T. E. (1995). Diverse learners participating in regular education "book clubs." *Reading Research Quarterly, 30*(3), 352–380.

Goldman, S. R., & Rakestraw, Jr., J. A. (2000). Structural aspects of constructing meaning from text. In M. L. Kamil, P. Mosenthal, P. D. Pearson, & R. Barr (Eds.), *Handbook of reading research* (Vol. 3, pp. 311–335). Mahwah, NJ: Erlbaum.

Gollnick, D. M., & Chinn, P. C. (1998). *Multicultural education in a pluralistic society*. Upper Saddle River, NJ: Merrill.

Gomes de Matos, F. (2002). Teaching peace-promoting vocabulary: A new frontier. *Glosas Didacticas, 8*. Retrieved eg. March 25, 2006 from http://sedll.org/doces/publicaciones/glosas/n8/resena3.html

Good, T., & Marshall, S. (1984). Do students learn more in heterogeneous or homogeneous groups? In P. L. Peterson, L. C. Wilkinson, & M. Hallinan (Eds.), *The social context of instruction*. New York: Academic.

Goodman, K. S. (1967). Reading: A psycholinguistic guessing game. *Journal of the Reading Specialist, 6*, 126–135.

Goodman, K. S. (1986). *What's whole in whole language?* Portsmouth, NH: Heinemann.

Goodman, K. S. (1989). *Lenguaje integral*. Mérida, Venezuela: Editorial Venezolana.

Goodman, Y. (1978). Kid watching: An alternative to testing. *National Elementary Principal, 57*, 4, 41–45.

Goodman, Y. M. (2006). *Kidwatching*. Retrieved July 22, 2006, from www.reading.org/downloads/publications/books/bk558-27-Goodman_Kidwatching.pdf

Goodman, Y. M., & Burke, C. L. (1972). *Reading miscue inventory: Procedure for diagnosis and evaluation*. New York: Macmillan.

Goodman, Y. M., Watson, D. J., & Burke, C. L. (2005). *Reading miscue inventory: From evaluation to instruction*. Katonah, NY: Richard C. Owen.

Goswami, U. (2000). Phonological and lexical processes. In M. Kamil, P. Mosenthal, P. D. Pearson, & R. Barr (Eds.), *Handbook of reading research* (Vol. 3). New York: Longman.

Graves, D. H. (1982). *Writing: Students and teachers at work*. Portsmouth, NH: Heinemann.

Graves, D. H. (1983). *Writing: Teachers and children at work*. Exeter, NH: Heinemann Educational Books, 1983.

Graves, M. (2006). *The vocabulary book: Learning and instruction*. Champaign, IL: NCTE.

Greenlaw, W. (2001). *English language arts and reading on the Internet*. Columbus, OH: Merrill Prentice Hall.

Griffith, P. L., & Lynch-Brown, C. (2002). Owning technology. *The Reading Teacher, 55*, 614–615.

Guthrie, J. T., & Davis, M. H. (2003). Motivating struggling readers in middle school through an engagement model of classroom practice. *Reading & Writing Quarterly, 19*, 59–185.

Gwynne, F. (1988). *A chocolate moose for dinner*. New York: Aladdin.

Gwynne, F. (2006). *The king who rained*. New York: Aladdin Paperbacks.

Haggard, M. R. (1986). Vocabulary self-selection strategy: An active approach to word learning. In E. K. Dishner, T. Bean, J. Readance, & D. Moore. *Reading in the content areas*. Dubuque, IA: Kendall-Hunt.

Hall, E. T. (1983). *The dance of life*. New York: Doubleday.

Hall, S. L., & Moats, L. C. (1999). *Straight talk about reading*. Lincolnwood, IL: Contemporary Books.

Halle, T., Kurtz-Costes, B., & Mahoney, J. (1997). Family influences on school achievement in low-income African American children. *Journal of Educational Psychology, 89*, 527–537.

Halliday, M. A. K. (1975). *Learning how to mean*. London: Edward Arnold.

Hanson, J., & Graves, D. (1983). The author's chair. *Language Arts, 60*, 176–183.

Harmon, J. M. (1998). Vocabulary teaching and learning in a seventh-grade literature-based classroom. *Journal of Adolescent & Adult Literacy, 41*, 518–529.

Harris, K., & Graham, S. (1996). *Making the writing process work: Strategies for composition and self-regulation*. Cambridge, MA: Brookline Books.

Harris-Wright, K. (2005). Building blocks for literacy development: Oral language. In B. Hammond, M. E. Rhodes Hoover, & I. P. McPhail (Eds.), *Teaching African American learners to read* (pp. 189–199). Newark, DE: International Reading Association.

Harste, J., Woodward, J., & Burke, C. (1984). *Language stories and literacy lessons*. Portsmouth, NH: Heinemann.

Hart, B., & Risley, T. R. (1995). *Meaningful differences in the everyday experiences of young American children*. Baltimore: Brookes.

Harter, M. (2000). *A framework for reading for information*. Workshop presented at Reading Leadership Institute, National-Louis University, June 2000.

Harvey, S., & Goudvis. (2000). *Strategies that work: Teaching comprehension to enhance understanding*. Markham, Ontario: Pembroke Publishing.

Heath, S. B. (1983). *Ways with words: Language, life, and work in communities and classrooms*. Cambridge, England: Cambridge University Press.

Heath, S. B. (1986). Sociocultural contexts of language development. In *Beyond language: Social and cultural factors in schooling language minority students* (pp. 143–182). Sacramento: Bilingual Education Office, California State Department of Education.

Heller, R. (1991.) *A cache of jewels and other collective nouns*. New York: Putnam Juvenile.

Henderson, E. H. (1995). *Teaching spelling*. Boston: Houghton Mifflin.

Hendrix, C. (1952). *Cómo enseñar a leer por el método global*. Buenos Aires, Argentina: Editorial Kapelusz.

Henkes, K. (1987). *Sheila Rae the brave*. New York: Greenwillow.

Henkes, K. (1996). *Lilly's purple plastic purse*. New York: Greenwillow.

Henkes, K. (2006). *Lilly's big day*. New York: HarperCollins Children's Books.

Herman, J. L., & Golan, S. (1993). The effects of standardized testing on teaching and schools. *Educational Measurement: Issues and Practice, 12*, 20–25, 41–42.

Hickman, J. (1979). *Response to literature in a school environment*. Unpublished doctoral dissertation, Ohio State University, Columbus.

Hickman, J. (1981). A new perspective on response to literature. *Research in the Teaching of English, 15*, 343–354.

Hickman, J. (1992). What comes naturally. In C. Temple & P. Collins (Eds.), *Stories and readers*. Norwood, MA: Christopher-Gordon.

Hiebert, E. H. (1983). An examination of ability grouping for reading instruction. *Reading Research Quarterly, 18*, 161–171.

Hill, R., Carjuzaa, J., Aramburo, D., & Baca, L. (1993). Culturally and linguistically diverse teachers in special education: Repairing or redesigning the leaky pipeline. *Teacher Education and Special Education, 16*, 258–269.

Hintze, J. M., Ryan, A. L., & Stoner, G. (2003). Concurrent validity and diagnostic accuracy of the Dynamic Indicators of Basic Early Literacy Skills (DIBELS) and the Comprehensive Test of Phonological Processing. *School Psychology Review, 32*(4), 541–556.

Hirsch, E. D., Jr. (1981). *The philosophy of composition*. Chicago: University of Chicago.

Hirschi, R. (1991). *Fall*. New York: Cobblehill Books.

Ho, D. B. (1999). Using wordless picture books to support struggling sixth grade readers and writers. *The California Reader, 32*, 9–11.

Hoban, R. (1995). *Bedtime for Frances*. Illustrated by Garth Williams. New York: HarperTrophy.

Hoberman, M. A. (2000). *The eeensy weensy spider*. Boston: Little, Brown.

Hoff, S. (1999). *Danny and the dinosaur*. New York: Harper-Festival.

Hoff-Ginsburg, E. (1998). *What explains the SES-related difference in children's vocabularies and what does that reveal about the process of word learning?* Paper presented at the Boston University Conference on Language Development, Boston, November 6–8.

Hoffman, J. V. (1992). Critical reading/thinking across the curriculum: Using I-Charts to support learning. *Language Arts, 69*, 121–127.

Holdaway, D. (1979). *Foundations of literacy*. Portsmouth, NH: Heinemann.

Hollie, S. (2005). Acknowledging the language of African American students: Instruction that works. In B. Hammond, M. E. Rhodes Hoover, & I. P. McPhail (Eds.), *Teaching African American learners to read* (pp. 173–188). Newark, DE: International Reading Association.

Hudelson, S. (1984). Kan yu ret an rayt en Ingles: Children become literate in English as a second language. *TESOL Quarterly, 18*, 221–238.

Hudelson, S. (1987). The role of native language literacy in the education of language minority children. *Language Arts, 64*, 827–840.

Huey, E. B. (1908). *The psychology and pedagogy of reading*. Cambridge, MA: MIT Press.

Hughes, S. (1977). *Dogger*. London: Reds Fox.

Hutchins, P. (1978). *Happy birthday Sam*. New York: Greenwillow.

Hutchins, P. (1994). *Tidy tich*. New York: Mulberry Books.

Hutchins, P. (1995). *Don't forget the bacon!* New York: Scholastic. (Original work published 1976)

Hynds, S. (1997). *On the brink: Negotiating literature and life with adolescents*. New York: Teachers College Press.

Individuals with Disabilities Education Act 1997 (Reauthorization). (1997). 20 U.S.C. 1400 et seq.

Individuals with Disabilities Education Improvement Act of 2004. (IDEA).

International Reading Association & National Association for the Education of Young Children. (1998, July). Learning to read and write: Developmentally appropriate practices for young children: A joint position statement of the International Reading Association (IRA) and National Association for the Education of Young Children (NAEYC). Newark, DE and Washington, DC: Authors.

International Reading Association and the National Council for the Accreditation of Teacher Education. (2006). *Standards for reading professionals*. Newark, DE: Author.

International Reading Association. (2001). *Second-language literacy instruction: A position statement of the International Reading Association*. Newark, DE: Author.

Iser, W. (1974). *The implied reader*. Baltimore: Johns Hopkins University Press.

Iser, W. (1978). *The act of reading*. Baltimore: Johns Hopkins University Press.

Ivey, G., & Broaddus, K. (2001). "Just plain reading:" A survey of what makes students want to read in middle school classrooms. *Reading Research Quarterly, 36,* 350–371.

Jeffers, O. (2005). *Lost and found*. New York: Philomel.

Johnson, J., Aruma, A. M., & Ott, A. (2006). Reality check 2006: Is support for standards and testing fading? Public Agenda. Retrieved from http://www.publicagenda.org/research/research_reports_details.cfm?list=100

Johnson, K. R., & Simons, H. D. (1974). Teaching reading to children who speak Black English. In *MetroVoices (Teacher's edition)*. Beverly Hills, CA: Benziger.

Johnson-Coleman, L. (2001, May). *Keep on keepin' on: Motivation for the young and young at heart*. Keynote address presented at the annual conference of the International Reading Association, New Orleans, LA.

Johnston, R., & Watson, J. (1997). Developing reading, spelling, and phonemic awareness skills in primary school children. *Reading, 31,* 37–40.

Juel, C. (1988). Learning to read and write: A longitudinal study of 54 children from first through fourth grades. *Journal of Educational Psychology, 80,* 415–447.

Kagan, S. (1997). *Cooperative learning*. San Clemente, CA: Kagan.

Kameenui, E. J. (1998). The rhetoric of all, the reality of some, and the unmistakable smell of mortality. In J. Osborn & F. Lehr (Eds.), *Literacy for all: Issues in teaching and learning*. New York: Guilford Press.

Kameenui, E., Simmons, D., Cornachione, C., Thompson-Hoffman, S., Ginsburg, A., Marcy, E., Mittleman, J., Irwin, J., & Baker, M. (2001). *A practical guide to reading assessments*. Washington, DC: U.S. Department of Education.

Katz, L., & Feldman, L. B. (1981). Linguistic coding in word recognition: Comparisons between a deep and a shallow orthography. *Journal of Experimental Psychology of Learning and Memory Cognition, 9*(1) (January 1983), pp. 157–166.

Katzir, T., & Pare-Blagoev, J. (2006). Applying cognitive neuroscience research to education: The case of literacy. *Educational Psychologist 41*(1), 53–74.

Kawakami-Arakaki, A. J., Oshiro, M. E., & Farran, D. C. (1988). *Research to practice: Integrating reading and writing in a kindergarten curriculum*. Champaign, IL: University of Illinois at Urbana-Champaign—Center for the Study of Reading.

Klenk, L., & Kibby, M. W. (2000). Re-mediating reading difficulties: Appraising the past, reconciling the present, constructing the future. In M. L. Kamil, P. B. Mosenthal, P. D. Pearson, & R. Barr (Eds.), *Handbook of reading research* (Vol. 3, pp. 545–562). Mahwah, NJ: Erlbaum.

Koskinen, P. S., & Blum, I. H. (1986). Paired repeated reading: A classroom strategy for developing fluent reading. *The Reading Teacher, 40,* 70–75.

Koskinen, P. S., Gambrell, L. B., Kapinus, B. A., & Heathington, B. S. (1988). Retelling: A strategy for enhancing students' reading comprehension. *The Reading Teacher, 41,* 892–896.

Krashen, S. D. (1981). Bilingual education and second language acquisition theory. In California State Department of Education (Ed.), *Schooling and language minority students: A theoretical framework* (pp. 51–79). Sacramento: California State Department of Education, Office of Bilingual Bicultural Education.

Krashen, S. D. (1982). *Principles and practice in second language acquisition*. New York: Pergamon Press.

Krashen, S. D. (1985). *Inquiries and insights: Second language teaching, immersion and bilingual education, literacy*. Hayward, CA: Alemany Press.

Krashen, S. D. (1991). *Bilingual education: A focus on current research*. Washington, DC: National Clearinghouse for Bilingual Education.

Krashen, S. D. (1993). *The power of reading: Insights from the research*. Greenwood Village, CO: Libraries Unlimited.

Krashen, S. D. (1997). Conflicting claims concerning computers: A comment on Hinkson (1996). *The California Reader, 30,* 16–17.

Krashen, S. D., & Biber, D. (1988). *On course: Bilingual education's success in California*. Sacramento: California Association for Bilingual Education.

Krashen, S. D., & Terrell, T. D. (1983). *The natural approach: Language acquisition in the classroom.* New York: Pergamon/Alemany.

Kraus, R. (1987). *Leo the late bloomer.* New York: Simon & Schuster.

Kraus, R. (1989). *The carrot seed.* New York: Harper & Row.

Kuhn, M. R., & Stahl, S. A. (2003). Fluency: A review of developmental and remedial practices. *Journal of Educational Psychology, 95,* 3–21.

Labbo, L. D., & Teale, W. H. (1990). Cross age reading: A strategy for helping poor readers. *The Reading Teacher, 43,* 363–369.

LaBerge, D., & Samuels, S. J. (1974). Toward a theory of automatic information processing in reading. *Cognitive Psychology, 6,* 293–323.

Labov, W. (1970). *The study of non-standard English.* Champaign, IL: NCTE.

Labov, W. (1972). *Language in the inner city: Studies in Black English vernacular.* Philadelphia: University of Pennsylvania Press.

Ladson-Billings, G. (1994). *The dreamkeepers: Successful teachers of African American children.* San Francisco: Jossey-Bass.

Lamberg, W. J., Rodríguez, L., & Tomas, D. A. (1978). Training in identifying oral reading departures from text which can be explained as Spanish-English phonological differences. *The Bilingual Review/La Revista Bilingue, 5,* 65–75.

Lambert, W. E. (1975). Culture and language as factors in learning and education. In A. Wolfgang (Ed.), *Education of immigrant students.* Toronto: O.I.S.E.

Lampman, E. S. (2001). *The shy stegosaurus of Cricket Creek.* Keller, TX: Purple House Press.

Landrum, J. (2001). Selecting intermediate novels that feature characters with disabilities. *The Reading Teacher, 55,* 252–258.

Langer, J. (1995). *Envisioning literature.* New York: Teachers College Press.

Lau v. Nichols, 414 US 563 (1974).

Lehr, F., Osborn, J., & Hiebert, E. (2006). *A focus on vocabulary.* Honolulu: Pacific Resources for Education and Learning.

Lehr, S. (1988). Children's developing sense of theme as a response to literature. *Reading Research Quarterly, 23,* 337–357.

Lennon, C., & Burdick, H. (2004). *The Lexile Framework as an approach for reading measurement and success.* Durham, NC: MetaMetrics.

Leslie, L., & Caldwell, J. (2005). *Qualitative reading inventory* (4th ed.). Boston: Allyn and Bacon.

Lester, H. (1986). *A porcupine named fluffy.* Boston: Houghton Mifflin.

Lester, H. (1993). *Tacky the penguin.* Boston: Houghton Mifflin.

Levi Strauss, C. (1970). *Structural anthropology.* Garden City, NY: Basic Books.

Linn, R. L., & Gronlund, N. E. (1999). *Measurement and assessment in teaching.* New York: Prentice Hall.

Loban, W. (1976). *Language development: Kindergarten through twelfth grade.* Urbana, IL: National Council of Teachers of English.

Los Angeles Unified School District. (1985). *Strategies for sheltered English instruction.* Los Angeles: Author.

Luke, A., & Freebody, P. (1999). A map of possible practices: Further notes on the four resources model. *Practically Primary, 4,* 2.

Luria, A. R. (1976). *Cognitive development: Its cultural and social foundations.* Cambridge, MA: Harvard University Press.

Mann, V. A., Tobin, P., & Wilson, R. (1987). Measuring phonological awareness through the invented spellings of kindergarten children. *Merrill-Palmer Quarterly, 33,* 365–391.

Manzo, A. V. (1969). The ReQuest procedure. *Journal of Reading, 13,* 123–126.

Marsh, G., Friedman, M., Welch, V., & Desberg, P. (1981). A cognitive-developmental theory of reading acquisition. In G. MacKinnon & T. Waller (Eds.), *Reading research advances in theory and practice,* volume 3. New York: Academic Press.

Marshall, E. (1994). *Fox and his friends.* Illustrated by James Marshall. New York: Puffin.

Martinez, M., & Roser, N. (1991). Children's responses to literature. In J. Flood, J. Jensen, J. Lapp, & J. Squire (Eds.), *Handbook of research in teaching the English language arts.* New York: Macmillan.

Martinez, M., Roser, N., & Strecker, S. (1999). "I never thought I could be a star": A readers theatre ticket to reading fluency. *The Reading Teacher, 52,* 326–334.

Marzano, R. J. (2004). *Building background knowledge for academic achievement: Research on what works in schools.* Alexandria, VA: ASCD.

McCafferty, S. G., & Iddings, C. (2001). *Carnival: Putting a round peg in a square hole.* Paper presented at the meeting of the National Reading Conference, San Antonio, TX.

McCartney, K. (1984). Effect of quality of day care environment on children's language development. *Developmental Psychology, 20,* 244–260.

McCutcheon, M. (2000). *Descriptionary: A thematic dictionary* (2nd ed.). New York: Checkmark Books.

McGee, L. M., & Richgels, D. J. (2003). *Literacy's beginnings: Supporting young readers and writers* (3rd ed.). Boston: Allyn and Bacon.

McKeown, M. G., & Beck, I. L. (1988). http://www.indiana.edu/~eric_rec/ieo/digests/d126bib.html *Remedial and Special Education*, 9(1), 42–46.

McKissack, P. C. (1997). *Ma Dear's aprons*. New York: Alladin.

McLaughlin, M., & Vogt, M. (1996). *Portfolios in teacher education*. Newark, DE: International Reading Association.

McPhail, E. P. (2005). On literacy and liberation: The African American experience. In B. Hammond, M. E. Rhodes Hoover, & I. P. McPhail (Eds.), *Teaching African American learners to read* (pp. 9–23). Newark, DE: International Reading Association.

McQuillan, J., & Tse, L. (1998). What's the story? Using the narrative approach in beginning language classrooms. *TESOL Journal*, 7, 18–23.

McTighe, J., & Lyman, F. T. (1988). Cueing thinking in the classroom: The promise of theory-embedded tools. *Educational Leadership*, 45, 18–24.

Mehan, J. (1979). *Learning lessons*. Cambridge, MA: Harvard University Press.

Meier, D. (2004). *Many children left behind: How the No Child Left Behind Act is damaging our children and our schools*. New York: Beacon Press.

Moffett, J. (1976). *Teaching the universe of discourse*. New York: Holt, Rinehart & Winston.

Moore, D. W. (1996). Contexts for literacy in secondary schools. In D. J. Leu, C. K. Kinzer, & K. A. Hinchman (Eds.), *Literacies for the 21st century: Research and practice* (45th Yearbook of the National Reading Conference, pp. 15–46). Chicago: National Reading Conference.

Moore, D. W., Alvermann, D. E., & Hinchman, K. A. (2000). *Struggling adolescent readers: A collection of teaching strategies*. Newark, DE: International Reading Association.

Moore, D. W., Bean, T., Berdyshaw, D., & Lycis, J. (1999). *Adolescent literacy: A position statement for the commission on adolescent literacy of the International Reading Association*. Newark, DE: International Reading Association.

Morais, J., & Alegria, J. (1987). The relationships between segmental analysis and alphabetic literacy: An interactive view. *Cahiers de Psychologie Cognitive*.

Morris, A. & Hevman, K. (1989). *Bread, bread, bread*. New York: HarperCollins.

Morris, D. (1992). What constitutes at-risk: Screening children for first grade reading intervention. *Best Practices in School Speech-Language Pathology*, 2.

Morris, R. D. (2006). *The Howard Street tutoring manual*. New York: Guilford Press.

Morris, R. D., Blanton, L., Blanton, W. E., Nowacek, J., & Perney, J. (1995, November). Teaching low-achieving spellers at their "instructional level." *Elementary School Journal*, 96(2), 163–177.

Morris, R. D., Nelson, L., & Perney, J. (1986). Exploring the concept of "spelling instructional level" through the analysis of error types. *Elementary School Journal*, 87, 181–200.

Morris, W. (1962). *Dictionary of word and phrase origins*. New York: Harper & Row.

Morrow, L., & Weinstein, C. S. (1982). Increasing children's use of literature through program and physical design changes. *The Elementary School Journal*, 83, 131–137.

Moskal, M. K., & Blachowicz, C. (2006). *Partnering for fluency*. New York: Guilford Press.

Moustafa, M. (1997). *Beyond traditional phonics*. Portsmouth, NH: Heinemann.

Moustafa, M., & Penrose, J. (1985). Comprehensible input PLUS the language experience approach: Reading instruction for limited English speaking students. *The Reading Teacher*, 38, 640–647.

Munsch, R. (1992). *The paper bag princess*. Toronto: Annick Press.

Murray, D. (1985). *A writer teaches writing*. Boston: Houghton Mifflin.

NAEYC. (1998). *Learning to read and write: Developmentally appropriate practices for young children*. A joint position statement of the International Reading Association (IRA) and National Association for the Education of Young Children (NAEYC). *Young Children*, 23(4), 30–46.

Nagy, W. E., Anderson, R. C., & Herman, P. A. (1987). Learning word meanings from context during normal reading. *American Educational Research Journal*, 24, 237–270.

Nagy, W. E., Anderson, R., Schommer, M., Scott, J., & Stallman, A. (1989). Morphological families and word recognition. *Reading Research Quarterly*, 24, 262–282.

Nagy, W. E., et al. (1985). http://www.indiana.edu/~eric_rec/ieo/digests/d126bib.html? (Technical Report No. 347). Urbana, IL: Center for the Study of Reading.

Nagy, W. E., García, G. E., Durgunoglu, A. Y., & Hancin-Bhatt, B. (1993). Spanish-English bilingual students' use of cognates in English reading. *Journal of Reading Behavior*, 25, 241–259.

Nagy, W., & Anderson, R. C. (1984). How many words are there in printed school English? *Reading Research Quarterly*, 19, 304–330.

Nagy, W. E., & Scott, J. A. (2000). Vocabulary processes. In M. L. Kamil., P. Mosenthal, P. D. Pearson, & R. Barr (Eds.), *Handbook of reading research* (Vol. 3). New York: Longman.

Nathan, R., Temple, F., Juntunen, K., & Temple, C. (1988). *Classroom strategies that work: An elementary teacher's guide to process writing.* Portsmouth, NH: Heinemann.

Nathenson-Mejia, S. (1989). Writing in a second language: Negotiating meaning through invented spelling. *Language Arts, 66,* 516–526.

Nation, I. S. P. (2001). *Learning vocabulary in another language.* New York: Cambridge University Press.

National Center for Education Statistics (NCES). (1993). *Adult literacy in America: A first look at the National Adult Literacy Survey.* Washington, DC: U.S. Department of Education.

National Center for Education Statistics (NCES). (1994). *National assessment of educational progress.* Washington, DC: U.S. Department of Education.

National Center for Education Statistics. (1999). *Digest of education statistics, 1998.* Washington, DC: U.S. Department of Education.

National Center for Education Statistics. (1999). *The condition of education.* Washington, DC: U.S. Government Printing Office. Available at http://nces.ed.gov/programs/coe/

National Center for Education Statistics. (2000). *Elementary and secondary education: An international perspective.* Washington, DC: U.S. Department of Education. Retrieved from http://nces.ed.gov/ pubs2000/2000033.pdf

National Council for the Accreditation of Teacher Education. (2000). *Standards for reading.* Retrieved from www.ncate.org/standard/m_stds.htm

National Geographic World. Washington, DC: National Geographic.

National Literacy Panel on Language–Minority Children and Youth. (2006). *Developing literacy in second–language learners: Report of the National Literacy Panel on Language–Minority Children and Youth* (D. August and T. Shanahan, Eds.). Mahwah, NJ: Erlbaum.

National Reading Panel Web site. (2003). *Reports.* Retrieved from http://www.nationalreadingpanel.org

National Reading Panel. (2000, December). *Teaching children to read: An evidence-based assessment of the scientific research literature on reading and its implications for reading instruction.* (Reports of the Subgroups). Washington, DC: National Institute of Child Health and Human Development, National Institutes of Health.

NCELA (National Clearinghouse for English Language Acquisition and Language Instruction Educational Programs). (2006). U.S. Department of Education. Introduction to Language Instruction Educational Programs. Retrieved July 19, 2006, from http://www.ncela.gwu.edu/about/lieps/.

NEA [National Education Association]. (2004). *NCLB: The intersection of access and outcomes.* Washington, DC: National Education Association.

Nessel, D. D., & Jones, M. B. (1981). *The language-experience approach to reading.* New York: Teachers College Press.

Neuman, S., & Rosko, K. (1991). The influence of literacy-enriched play centers on preschoolers' conceptions of the functions of print. In J. Christie (Ed.), *Play and early literacy development* (pp. 167–187). Albany: State University of New York Press.

Neuman, S. B., & Celano, D. (2001). Access to print in low-income and middle-income communities: An ecological study of four neighborhoods. *Reading Research Quarterly, 56,* 8–28.

Neuman, S. B., & Celano, D. (2006, April/May/June). The knowledge gap: Implications of leveling the playing field for low-income and middle-income children. *Reading Research Quarterly, 41*(2), 176–201.

Neuman, S. B., & Dickinson, D. K. (2003). *Handbook of early literacy, volume 1.* New York: Guilford.

New York State Education Department. (2002). *English language arts resource guide.* Albany, NY: Author. Retrieved from at http://www.emsc.nysed.gov/ciai/ela/pub/elals.pdf

Newport, E. L., Gleitman, H., & Gleitman, L. (1977). Mother, I'd rather do it myself: Some effects and non-effects of maternal speech style. In C. E. Snow & A. Ferguson (Eds.), *Talking to children: Language input and acquisition.* Cambridge, England: Cambridge University Press.

Nolan, S. B., Haladyna, T. M., & Haas, N. S. (1992). Uses and abuses of achievement test scores. *Educational Measurement: Issues and Practice, 11,* 9–15.

O'Leary, D. (2002). 2002 *widening achievement gap.* Tucson: League of Latin American Citizens (LULAC).

O'Rourke, J., & Bamman, H. A. (1971). *Techniques of teaching vocabulary.* Menlo Park, CA: Benjamin/Cummings Publishing Company

Office of Economic and Community Development. (2001). *The OECD programme for international student assessment.* New York: Author.

Office of English Language Acquisition (OELA). (2004). Retrieved July 19, 2006, from http://www.ed.gov/print/programs/sfgp/index.html

Ogle, D. (1986). K-W-L: A teaching model that develops active reading of expository text. *Reading Teacher, 40,* 564–570.

Ogle, D. (1991). The know, want to know, learn strategy. In N. Muth (Ed.), *Children's comprehension of text: Research and practice* (pp. 22–23). Newark, DE: International Reading Association.

Ogle, D. (2000). Make it visual: A picture is worth a thousand words. In M. McLaughlin & M. Vogt (Eds.), *Creativity and innovation in content area teaching.* Norwood, MA: Christopher-Gordon.

Ogle, D., & Blachowicz, C. (2001). Beyond literature circles: Helping students comprehend informational texts. In C. C. Block & M. Pressley (Eds.), *Comprehension instruction: Research-based best practices.* New York: Guilford Press.

Olson, M. W., & Gee, T. C. (1988). A review of story grammar research. *Childhood Education, 64*(4), 302–306.

Organisation for Economic Co-operation and Development. (1995). *Employment outlook.* Paris: Author.

Organization of Economic and Community Development. (2000). *Program for international student assessment.* New York: The United Nations. Retrieved from http://www.pisa.oecd.org/

Osborn, J., Lehr, F., & Hiebert, E. H. (2003). *A focus on fluency.* Honolulu: Pacific Resources for Education and Learning. Retrieved from http://www.prel.org

Owocki, G., & Goodman, Y. (2002). *Kidwatching: Documenting children's literacy development.* Portsmouth, NH: Heinemann.

Palincsar, A. S., & Brown, A. L. (1986). Interactive teaching to promote independent learning from text. *The Reading Teacher, 39,* 771–777.

Parrish, P. (1992). *Amelia Bedelia.* Illustrated by Fritz Siebel. New York: HarperCollins.

Paterson, K. (1994). *Lyddie.* New York: Puffin.

Patterson, E. (1984). *Language, letters, and learning.* Lecture at Hobart and William Smith Colleges, Geneva, NY.

Pearson, P. D. (1985). Changing the face of reading comprehension instruction. *The Reading Teacher, 38,* 724–738.

Pearson, P. D., & Anderson, R. C. (1985). A schema theoretic view of the learning to read process. In P. D. Pearson, R. Barr, & P. Mosenthal (Eds.), *Handbook of reading research: Volume 1.* New York: MacMillan.

Peck, J. (1989). Using storytelling to promote language and literacy development. *The Reading Teacher, 43,* 138–141.

Pellegrini, A. D., & Galda, L. (2000). Children's pretend play and literacy. In D. S. Strickland & L. M. Morrow (Eds.), *Beginning reading and writing, language and literacy series.* Newark, DE: International Reading Association.

Pennycook, A. (1985). Actions speak louder than words: Paralanguage, communication, and education. *TESOL Quarterly, 19,* 259–282.

Perfetti, C. A. (1986). Cognitive and linguistic components of reading ability. In B. Foorman & A. Siegel (Eds.), *Acquisition of reading skills, cultural constraints and cognitive universals* (pp. 11–40). Hillsdale, NJ: Erlbaum.

Perfetti, C. A. (1992). *Reading ability.* New York: Oxford University Press.

Peters, C. (1995). *At the zoo.* Boston: Houghton Mifflin.

Peterson, P. E., & West, M. R. (Eds.). (2003). *No child left behind?: The politics and practice of school accountability.* New York: Brookings Institution Press.

Pilkey, D. (2000). *Captain Underpants boxed set.* New York: Scholastic.

Pinker, S. (1994). *The language instinct.* New York: Harper-Perennial.

Pinnell, G. S., & Fountas, I. (1998). *Word matters.* Portsmouth, NH: Heinemann.

Pinnell, G. S., & Fountas, I. C. (2001). *Leveled books for readers, grades 3–6.* Portsmouth, NH: Heinemann.

Pinnell, G. S., Bridges, L. B., & Fountas, I. C. (1999). *Matching books to readers: Using leveled books in guided reading.* Portsmouth, NH: Heinemann.

Pinnell, G. S., Pikulski, J. J., Wixson, K. K., Campbell, J. R., Gough, P. B., & Beatty, A. S. (1995). *Listening to children read aloud: Oral fluency.* Washington, DC: National Center for Education Statistics, U.S. Department of Education.

Pittelman, S. D., Heimlich, J. E., Berglund, R. L., & French M. P. (1991). *Semantic feature analysis: Classroom applications.* Newark, DE: International Reading Association.

Plecha, J. (1992). Shared inquiry: The Great Books method of interpretive reading and discussion. In D. Temple & P. Collins (Eds.), *Stories and readers: New perspectives on literature, the elementary classroom* (pp. 103–114). Norwood, MA: Christopher-Gordon.

Powell, R., Cantrell, S. C., & Adams, S. (2001). Saving Black Mountain: The promise of critical literacy in a multicultural democracy. *The Reading Teacher, 54,* 772–781.

Preece, A. (1998, July 1). Personal Communication. Sinaia, Romania.

Pressley, M. (1999). Self-regulated comprehension processing and its development through instruction. In L. B. Gambrell, L. M. Morrow, S. B. Neuman, & M. Pressley (Eds.), *Best practices in literacy instruction.* New York: Guilford Press.

Pressley, M. (2000). "What should comprehension instruction be the instruction of?" In M. L. Kamil, P. B. Mosenthal, P. D. Pearson, & R. Barr (Eds.), *Handbook of reading research* (Vol. 3, pp. 545–562). Mahwah, NJ: Erlbaum.

Pressley, M. (2002). Metacognition and self-regulated comprehension. In A. E. Farstrup & S. J. Samuels (Eds.), *What research has to say about reading instruction* (pp. 291–309). Newark, DE: International Reading Association.

Pressley, M., & Afflerbach, P. (1995). *Verbal protocols of reading: The nature of constructively responsive reading*. Hillsdale, NJ: Erlbaum.

Pressley, M., Allington, R. L., Wharton-McDonald, R., Block, C. C., & Morrow, L. M. (Eds.). (2001). *Learning to read: Lessons from exemplary first-grade classrooms*. New York: Guilford Press.

Pressley, M., Rankin, J., & Yokoi, L. (1996). A survey of instructional practices of primary teachers nominated as effective in promoting literacy. *Elementary School Journal, 96,* 363–384.

Pressley, M., Wharton-McDonald, R., Mistretta, J., & Echevarria, M. (1998). The nature of literacy instruction in ten grade 4/5 classrooms in upstate New York. *Scientific Studies of Reading, 2,* 159–191.

Public Agenda On-Line. (2002). *Reality check, 2002.* New York: Public Agenda Retrieved from at http://www.publicagenda.org/specials/rcheck2002/reality.htm

Purcell-Gates, V. (1991). Ability of well-read-to kindergartners to decontextualise/ recontextualise experience into a written-narrative register. *Language and Education: An International Journal, 5*(3), 177–188.

Purcell-Gates, V. (1995). *Other people's words: The cycle of low literacy.* Cambridge, MA: Harvard University Press.

Purcell-Gates, V., L'Allier, S., & Smith, D. (1995). Literacy at the Harts' and the Larsons': Diversity among poor inner city families. *The Reading Teacher, 48,* 572–578.

Purcell-Gates, V., McIntyre, E., & Freppon, P. A. (1995). Learning written storybook language in school: A comparison of low-SES children in skills-based and whole language classrooms. *American Educational Research Journal, 32*(3), 659–685.

Raffi. (1996). The more we get together. *Raffi Sampler.* [CD]. Cambridge, MA: Rounder Records.

Ramírez, J. D. (1991). *Final report: Longitudinal study of structured English immersion strategy, early-exit and late-exit bilingual education programs.* NTIS, 300-87-0156. Washington, DC: U.S. Department of Education.

Randell, B. (1996a). *Baby bear goes fishing.* Crystal Lake, IL: Rigby.

Randell, B. (1996b). *Ben's tooth.* Crystal Lake, IL: Rigby.

Randell, B. (1996c). *Wake up, Dad.* Crystal Lake, IL: Rigby.

Raphael, T. E. (1986). Teaching question answer relationships, revisited. *The Reading Teacher, 39*(6), 516–522.

Raphael, T. E. (1998). Balanced instruction and the role of classroom discourse. In J. Osborn & F. Lehr (Eds.), *Literacy*

for all: Issues in teaching and learning. New York: Guilford Press.

Raphael, T. E., & McMahon, S. I. (1994). Book club: An alternative framework for reading instruction. *The Reading Teacher, 48,* 102–117.

Raphael, T. E., Goatley, V., McMahon, S., & Woodman, D. (1995). Teaching literacy through student book clubs. In N. Roser & M. Martinez (Eds.), *Book talk and beyond: Children and teachers respond to literature* (pp. 66–79). Newark, DE: International Reading Association.

Rasinski, T. V. (2003). *The fluent reader: Oral strategies for building word recognition, fluency, and comprehension.* New York: Scholastic.

Rasinski, T., & Padak, N. (2005). Three-minute reading assessments: Word recognition, fluency, and comprehension. New York: Scholastic.

Rasinski, T., Blachowicz, C., & Lems, K. (Eds.). (2005). *Fluency instruction: Research-based best practices.* New York: Guilford Press.

Read, C. (1975). *Children's categorization of speech sounds in English* (Research Report No. 17). Urbana, IL: National Council of Teachers of English.

Rébsamen, E. C. (1949). *La enseñanza de la escritura y lectura en el primer año escolar: Guía metodológica.* Paris: Librería de la Vda de Ch. Bouret.

Reichle, E. D., & Perfetti, C. A. (2003). Morphology in word identification: A word experience model that accounts for morpheme frequency effects. *Scientific Studies of Reading, 7,* 219–237.

Richard-Amato, P., & Snow, M. A. (1992). *The multicultural classroom: Readings for content content area teachers.* New York: Longman.

Rickford, R. R., & Rickford, A. E. (1995). Dialect readers revisited. *Linguistics and Education, 7,* 107–128.

Riley, J. (1996). *The teaching of reading.* London: Paul Chapman.

Rodríguez Fuenzalida, E. (1982). *Metodologías de alfabetización en América Latina.* Pátzcuaro, Michoacán, México: UNESCO/CREFAL.

Roop, P., & Roop, C. (1985). *Keep the lights burning, Abbie.* Minneapolis: Carolrhoda Books.

Rosen, M. (2003). *We're going on a bear hunt.* Illustrated by H. Oxenbury. New York: Alladin.

Rosenblatt, L. (1978). *The reader, the text, and the poem.* Carbondale: Southern Illinois University Press.

Roth, R., Speece, D. H., & Cooper, D. H. (2002). A longitudinal analysis of the connection between oral language and early reading. *Journal of Educational Reasearch, 95,* 259–272.

Routman, R. (1996). *Literacy at the crossroads: Crucial talk about reading, writing, and other teaching dilemmas.* Portsmouth, NH: Heinemann.

Rowe, M. B. (1974). Wait-time and rewards as instructional variables: Their influence on language, logic and fate control: Part one—Wait time. *Journal of Research in Science Teaching, 11*(2), 81–94.

Rylant, C. (1987). *Henry and Mudge.* New York: Simon & Schuster.

Sachar, L. (1998). *Holes.* New York: Farrar, Strauss, & Giroux.

Sainsbury, M. (2001). *The 2001 IEA progress in international reading literacy study.* Paper presented at the 12th European Conference on Reading. Dublin, July.

Salmon, K. (1995). *Lenguaje integral: Una alternativa para la enseñanza-aprendizaje de la lecto-escritura.* Quito, Ecuador: Abrapalabra Editores.

Samuels, S. J. (1971). Letter-name versus letter-sound knowledge in learning to read. *The Reading Teacher, 24,* 604–608.

Samuels, S. J. (1979). The method of repeated readings. *The Reading Teacher, 34*(4), 403–408.

Samuels, S. J., & Farstrup, A. E. (Eds.). (2006). *What research has to say about fluency instruction.* Newark, DE: International Reading Association.

Sanacore, J. (2004). Genuine caring and literacy learning for African American children. *The Reading Teacher, 57*(8), 744–753.

Saville, M. R., & Troike, R. C. (1971). *A handbook of bilingual education.* Washington, DC: Teachers of English to Speakers of Other Languages.

Scarcella, R. (1990). *Teaching language minority students in multicultural classrooms.* New York: Longman.

Schifini, A. (1985). *Sheltered English: Content area instruction for limited English proficient students.* Los Angeles: Los Angeles County Office of Education.

Schifini, A. (1996). Reading instruction for the pre-literate and struggling older student. *NABE News, 20,* 5–6, 20, 30.

Schön, D. (1983). *The reflective practitioner: How professionals think in action.* New York: Basic Books.

Schon, I. (2000). *Recommended books in Spanish for children and young adults, 1996–1999.* Lanham, MD: Scarecrow Press.

Schon, I. (2001). Los niños y el mundo: Children's books in Spanish from around the world. *The Reading Teacher, 54,* 692–698.

Schon, I. (2002). From Pulgarcito to Shakespeare. *Language, 2,* 28–30.

Schon, I. (2004). *Recommended books in Spanish for children and young adults, 2000 through 2004.* Lanham, MD: Scarecrow Press.

Schon, I., & Corona Berkin, S. (1996). *Introducción a la literatura infantil y juvenil.* Newark, DE: International Reading Association.

Schwartz, A. (1982). *The cat's elbow and other secret languages.* New York: Farrar, Straus and Giroux.

Schwartz, R. M., & Taffy, R. (1985). Retrieved from http://www.indiana.edu/~eric_rec/ieo/digests/d126bib.html. *Reading Teacher, 39*(2), 198–205.

Scieszka, J. (2001). *Balone (Henry P.).* Illustrated by Lane Smith. New York: Viking Junior.

Scragg, D. G. (1974). *A history of English spelling.* New York: Barnes & Noble.

Selinker, L., Swain, M., & Dumas, G. (1975). The interlanguage hypothesis extended to children. *Language Learning, 25,* 129–152.

Sepúlveda, L. (1989). *The old man who read love stories.* New York: Harcourt Brace.

Shanahan, T. (2002). *A sin of the second kind: The neglect of fluency instruction and what we can do about it.* PowerPoint presentation at A Focus on Fluency Forum, San Francisco, CA. Available at www.prel.org/programs/rel/fluency/Shanahan.ppt

Sharmat, C. (1972). *Nate the Great and the Pillowcase.* New York: Dell Random House.

Shaw, R., & Shaw, D. (2002). *DIBELS Oral Reading Fluency-based indicators of third grade reading skills for Colorado State Assessment Program (CSAP)* (Tech. Rep.) Eugene, OR: University of Oregon.

Shaywitz, S. E., Escobar, M. D., Shaywitz, B. A., Fletcher, J. M., & Makuch, J. R. (1992). Evidence that dyslexia may represent the lower tail of a normal distribution of reading ability. *New England Journal of Medicine, 326,* 145–150.

Shinn, M. R. (Ed.). (1989). *Curriculum-based measurement: Assessing special children.* New York: Guilford.

Short, K., & Kauffman, G. (1995). So what do I do? The role of the teacher in literature circles. In N. Roser & M. Martinez (Eds.), *Book talk and beyond: Children and teachers respond to literature* (pp. 140–149). Newark, DE: International Reading Association.

Short, K., Harste, J., & Burke, C. (1996). *Creating classrooms for authors and inquirers.* Portsmouth, NH: Heinemann.

Silvaroli, N., & Wheelock, W. (2000). *Classroom reading inventory*. Columbus, OH: Merrill.

Simon, S. (1955). *Sharks*. New York: HarperCollins.

Simpkins, G., Holt, G., & Simpkins, C. (1974). *Bridge: A cross-culture reading program*. Boston: Houghton Mifflin.

Sims, R. (1982). *Shadow and substance: Afro-American experience in contemporary children's fiction*. Champaign, IL. NCTE.

Sleeter, C. E., & Grant, C. A. (1999). *Making choices for multicultural education*. Upper Saddle River, NJ: Merrill.

Smith, C. B. (1997). Vocabulary instruction and reading comprehension. *ERIC Digest*. ERIC Clearinghouse on Reading English and Communication #126.

Smith, F. (1973). *Psycholinguistics and reading*. New York: Holt, Rinehart & Winston.

Smith, F. (1985). *Reading without nonsense*. New York: Teachers College Press.

Smith, F. (1986). *Keynote address: How education backed the wrong horse*. Presented at the meeting of the California Reading Association, Fresno.

Smith, M. C. (2000). The real-world reading practices of adults. *Journal of Literary Research, 32*(1), 25–32.

Snow, C. E., Burns, M. S., & Griffin, P. (Eds.). (1998). *Preventing reading difficulties in young children*. Committee on the Prevention of Reading Difficulties in Young Children. Commission on Behavioral and Social Sciences and Education, National Research Council. Washington, DC: National Academy Press.

Snow, C. E., Griffin, P., & Burns, M. S. (2005). *Knowledge to support the teaching of reading: Preparing teachers for a changing world*. San Francisco: Jossey-Bass.

Snow, C. E., Tabors, P. O., & Dickenson, D. K. (2001). Language development in the preschool years. In D. K. Dickinson & P. O. Tabors (Eds.), *Beginning literacy with language*. Baltimore: Brookes.

Souriau, E. (1955). *Les deux cent milles situations dramatiques*. Paris: Flamarion.

Spache, G. (1981). *Diagnosing and correcting reading disabilities* (2nd ed.). Boston: Allyn and Bacon.

Spandel, V. (1996). *Seeing with new eyes*. Portland, OR: Northwest Regional Educational Laboratory.

Spandel, V. (2000). *Creating writers through 6-Trait writing assessment and instruction* (3rd ed.). Boston: Allyn and Bacon.

Spinelli, J. (1990a). *Maniac Magee*. Boston: Little, Brown.

Spinelli, J. (1990b). *Maniac Magee*. New York: Scholastic. Large-print version from Library Reproduction Service, ISBN 0-590-45203-7.

Stahl, S. A., & Fairbanks, M. (1986). The effects of vocabulary instruction: A model-based meta-analysis. *Review of Educational Research, 56*, 76–110.

Stanovich, K. E. (1986). Matthew effects in reading: Some consequences of individual differences in the acquisition of literacy. *Reading Research Quarterly, 21*, 360–407.

Stanovich, K. E. (1992). Are we overselling literacy? In C. Temple & P. Collins (Eds.), *Stories and readers*. Norwood, MA: Christopher Gordon.

Stanovich, K. E., & Siegel, L. S. (1994). Phenotypic performance profiles of children with reading disabilities: A regression-based test of the phonological core variable-difference model. *Journal of Educational Psychology, 86*, 24–53.

Stauffer, R. (1975). *The language experience approach to the teaching of reading*. New York: Harper.

Steele, J. L., & Meredith, K. E. (1997). *Critical thinking*. New York: Open Society Institute.

Stein, N. L., & Glenn, C. F. (1979). An analysis of story comprehension in elementary school children. In R. O. Freedle (Ed.), *New directions in discourse processing: Vol. 2. Advances in discourse processes* (pp. 53–120). Norwood, NJ: Ablex.

Sternberg, R., & Powell, J. (1983). Comprehending verbal comprehension. *American Psychologist, 38*, 878–893.

Stoll, D. R. (Ed.). (1977). *Magazines for kids and teens*. Newark, DE: International Reading Association.

Strickland, D. S. (1991). Cooperative, collaborative learning for children and teachers (emerging readers and writers). *Reading Teacher, 44*, 600–602.

Strickland, D. S. (1998). *Teaching phonics today: A primer for educators*. Newark, DE: International Reading Association.

Sulzby, E. (1985). Kindergarteners as writers and readers. In M. Farr (Ed.), *Advances in writing research: Vol. 1. Children's early writing development* (pp. 127–199). Norwood, NJ: Ablex.

Suro, R., & Singer, A. (2002). *Latino growth in metropolitan America: Changing patterns, new locations*. Washington, DC: Brookings.

Sutherland, L. M. (2005). Black adolescent girls' use of literacy practices to negotiate boundaries of ascribed identity. *Journal of Literacy Research, 37*(3), 365–406.

Sutherland-Smith, W. (2002). Weaving the literacy web: Changes in reading from page to screen. *The Reading Teacher, 55*, 662–669.

Sutton-Smith, B. (1981). *The folk stories of children*. New York Olympic Marketing.

Szymborski, J. A. (1995). Retrieved from http://www.indiana.edu/~eric_rec/ieo/digests/d126bib.html. M.A. Project, Kean College of New Jersey.

Tattershaw, S., & Prendeville, J. (1995). *Using familiar routines in language assessment and intervention.* San Antonio, TX: Communication Skill Builders.

Taylor, B., Pearson, P. D., Clark, K., & Walpole, S. (1999). *Beating the odds in teaching all children to read.* Ann Arbor, MI: CIERA. http://www.ciera.org/library/reports/inquiry-1/1-010/1-010.pdf

Taylor, B. M., & Pearson, P. D. (2005). Using study groups and reading assessment data to improve reading instruction within a school. In S. Paris & S. A. Stahl (Eds.), *Children's reading comprehension and assessment* (pp. 237–255). Mahwah, NJ: Erlbaum.

Taylor, B. M., Graves, M. F., & Ven Den Broek, P. (Eds.). (2000). *Reading for meaning: Fostering comprehension in the middle grades.* New York: Teachers College Press.

Taylor, M. (1997). *Roll of thunder, hear my cry.* New York: Puffin.

Taylor, W. L. (1953). Cloze procedure: A new device for measuring readability. *Journalism Quarterly, 45,* 415–433.

Teaching the English language arts: A sample standards-based lesson plan. (2002). In *Orientation to K–12 English language arts standards.* Unpublished work (available from Literacy Specialists Project Office, John Carroll University, 20700 North Park Boulevard. University Heights, OH 44118).

Teale, W. H., & Sulzby, E. (1987). Literacy acquisition in early childhood: The roles of access and mediation in storybook reading. In D. Wagner (Ed.), *The future of literacy in a changing world* (pp. 111–130). New York: Pergamon Press.

Temple C., & MaKinster (2005). *Intervening for literacy.* Boston: Allyn and Bacon.

Temple, C. (1994). The "global method" of Celestin Freinet: Whole language in a European setting? *The Reading Teacher 48,* 1 (September, 1994) pp. 86–89.

Temple, C., Crawford, A., & Gillet, J. (in press). *Developmental literacy inventory: Reading and spelling from emergent to mature levels.* Boston: Allyn and Bacon. *instruction.* Washington, DC: National Institute of Child Health and Human Development.

Temple, C., Martinez, M., Yokota, J., & Naylor, A. (2002). *Children's books in children's hands* (2nd ed.). Boston: Allyn and Bacon.

Temple, C., Nathan, R., Burris, N., & Temple, F. (1992). *The beginnings of writing* (3rd ed.). Boston: Allyn and Bacon.

Temple, F. (1992). *Tiger soup.* New York: Orchard.

Temple, F. (1995). *Tonight, by sea.* New York: Harper Trophy.

Temple, F. (1996). *The Beduin's gazelle.* New York: Orchard.

Templeton, S. (1991). Teaching and learning the English spelling system: Reconceptualizing method and purpose. *Elementary School Journal, 92,* 183–199.

Templeton, S., & Morris, D. (2000). Spelling: Reconceptualizing spelling development and instruction. In M. Kamil, P. B. Mosenthal, P. D. Pearson, & R. Barr (Eds.), *Handbook of reading research* (Vol. 3, pp. 525–539). Mahwah, NJ: Erlbaum.

Terban, M. (1989). *Superdupers: Really funny real words.* New York: Clarion.

Terman, L. (1916). *The measurement of intelligence.* Stanford, CA: Stanford University Press.

Terrell, T. D. (1977). A natural approach to second language acquisition and learning. *Modern Language Journal, 6,* 325–337.

Terrell, T. D. (1981). The natural approach in bilingual education. In California State Department of Education (Ed.), *School and language minority students: A theoretical framework* (pp. 117–146). California State University, Los Angeles, Los Angeles: Evaluation, Dissemination and Assessment Center.

Terrell, T. D. (1982). The natural approach to language teaching: An update. *Modern Language Journal, 66,* 121–122.

TESOL. (1997). *Policy statement of the TESOL board on African American vernacular English.* Arlington, VA: Center for Applied Linguistics.

Texas Education Agency. (1996). *Comprehensive bienniel report on Texas public schools: A report to the 75th Texas legislature.* Austin: Author.

Texas Education Agency. (1998). *Texas essential knowledge and skills for English language arts and reading: Subchapter A. Elementary.* Austin: Author. Available at www.tea.state.tx.us/rules/tac/chapter110/ch110a.html#110.1

Theodorou, R. (1996). *The animals went to bed.* Crystal Lake, IL: Rigby.

Thomas, W. P., & Collier, V. (1997). *School effectiveness for language minority students.* Washington, DC: National Clearinghouse for Bilingual Education.

Thomas, W. P., & Collier, V. P. (2002). *A national study of school effectiveness for language minority students' long-term academic achievement final report: Project 1.1.* Santa Cruz, CA: Center for Research on Education, Diversity and Excellence.

Tomlinson, C. A. (2000). Differentiation of instruction in the elementary grades. Champaign, IL: ERIC Clearinghouse on Elementary and Early Childhood Education. http://ceep.crc.uiuc.edu/eecearchive/digests/2000/tomlin00.pdf

Tompkins, G. (2000). *Teaching writing: Balancing process and product.* Columbus, OH: Merrill.

Topping, K. J. (1987). Paired reading: A powerful technique for parent use. *The Reading Teacher, 40,* 608–614.

Torres Quintero, G. (1976). *Método onomatopéyico.* Mexico City: Editorial Patria.

Trieman, R. (1985). Onsets and rimes as units of spoken syllables: Evidence from children. *Journal of Experimental Child Psychology, 39,* 161–181.

Trout, B. (1993, November). Little dogies, lay down. *Highlights for Children.*

U.S. Census Bureau. (2000). *U.S. Census 2000.* Washington, DC: U.S. Department of Commerce.

U.S. Department of Education. (2001). *No child left behind.* Retrieved from Retrieved from http://www.ed.gov/offices/OESE/esea/

U.S. Department of Education. (2002). *Guidance for the Reading First program.* Washington, DC: U.S. Department of Education, Office of Elementary and Secondary Education. Retrieved from http://www.ed.gov/programs/readingfirst/guidance.doc

U.S. Department of Education. (2003). *The facts about . . . reading achievement.* Retrieved from http://www.nclb.gov/start/facts/reading.html

U.S. Department of Education. *Reading first.* http://www.ed.gov/programs/readingfirst/index.html

UNESCO. (1953). *The use of vernacular languages in education.* Paris: UNESCO.

University of Wisconsin–Eau Claire. (2000). *Hmong population research project.* Retrieved August 3, 2001, from www.uwec.edu/Academic/Econ/HmongResearch/HPopulation.htm

Urrea, L. A. (1996). *By the lake of sleeping children: The secret life of the Mexican border.* New York: Anchor Books.

Vacca, R., & Vacca, J. (1986). *Content area reading.* Boston: Allyn and Bacon.

Vacca, R., & Vacca, J. (1996). *Content area reading* (5th ed.). New York: HarperCollins.

Valencia, S., Hiebert, E. & Afflerbach, P. (1993). *Authentic reading assessment: Practices and possibilities.* Newark, DE: International Reading Association.

Van Buren, T. (n.d.). Six Trait writing evaluation sheet. Retrieved from http://coe.west.asu.edu/students/tvanburen/sixtreval.htm

Vander Meer, C. D., Lentz, F. E., & Stollar, S. (2005). *The relationship between oral reading fluency and Ohio Proficiency Testing in Reading* (Tech. Rep.). Eugene: University of Oregon.

Vaughn, J., & Estes, T. (1986). *Reading and reasoning beyond the primary grades.* Boston: Allyn and Bacon.

Veatch, J. (1996). From the vantage of retirement. *The Reading Teacher, 49,* 510–516.

Veatch, J., Sawicki, F., Elliott, G., Flake, E., & Blakey, J. (1979). *Key words to reading: The language experience approach begins.* Columbus, OH: Merrill.

Vellutino, F. R. (1979). *Dyslexia: Theory and research.* Cambridge: MIT Press.

Vellutino, F. R., & Scanlon, D. M. (2001). Emergent literacy skills, early instruction, and individual differences as determinants of difficulties in learning to read: The case for early intervention. In S. B. Newman & D. K. Dickinson (Eds.), *Handbook of early literacy research.* New York: Guilford Press.

Vellutino, F. R., Scanlon, D. M., Sipay, E. R., Small, S. G., Pratt, A., Chen, R., & Denckla, M. B. (1996). Cognitive profiles of difficult-to-remediate and readily remediated poor readers: Early intervention as a vehicle for distinguishing between cognitive and experiential deficits as a basic cause of specific reading disability. *Journal of Educational Psychology, 88,* 601–638.

Verhoeven, L. (1990, Spring). Acquisition of reading in a second language. *Reading Research Quarterly, 25*(2), 90–114.

Vernon-Feagans, L., Hammer, C. S., Miccio, A., & Manlove, E. (2001). Early language and literacy skills in low-income African American and Hispanic children. In D. K. Dickenson & S. B. Newman (Eds.), *Handbook of early literacy research.* New York: Guilford.

Virginia State Department of Education. (2002). *English standards of learning for Virginia public schools.* Richmond, VA: Author. Retrieved from http://www.pen.k12.va.us/VDOE/Superintendent/Sols/2002/EnglishK-12.doc

Vogt, M. E. (2000). Content learning for students needing modifications: An issue of access. In M. McLaughlin & M. E. Vogt (Eds.), *Creativity and innovation in content area teaching* (pp. 329–351). Norwood, MA: Christopher-Gordon.

Vukelich, C., Christie, J., & Enz, B. (2002). *Helping young children learn language and literacy.* Boston: Allyn and Bacon.

Vygotsky, L. S. (1978). *Mind in society: The development of higher psychological processes.* Cambridge, MA: Harvard University Press.

Vygotsky, L. S. (1986). *Thought and language.* Cambridge, MA: MIT Press. Retrieved from http://www.publicagenda.org/research/research_reports_details.cfm?list=100

Walsh, D., Price, G., & Gillingham M., (1988). The critical but transitory importance of letter naming. *Reading Research Quarterly, 23*(1), 108–122.

Washington, J. A., & Craig, H. K. (1999, January). Performances of at-risk, African American preschoolers on the

Peabody Picture Vocabulary Test-III. *Language, Speech, and Hearing Services in Schools, 30,* 75–82.

Webb, S. (2000). *My season with penguins.* Boston: Houghton Mifflin.

Wepner, W. B., Valmont, W. J., & Thurlow, R. (Eds.). (2000). *Linking literacy and technology: A guide for K–8 classrooms.* Newark, DE: International Reading Association.

Wheelock, A., & Dorman, G. (1988). *Before it's too late: Dropout prevention in the middle grades.* Boston: Massachusetts Advocacy Center and Chapel Hill Center for Early Adolescence.

Whipple, G. (Ed.). (1925). *The twenty-fourth yearbook of the National Society for the Study of Education: Report of the National Committee on Reading.* Bloomington, IN: Public School Publishing.

White, E. B. (1980). *Charlotte's web.* New York: Harper Trophy. (Original work published 1952)

Whitehurst, G. J. (1994). *Dialogic reading for parents: Headstart, K, and pre-K* (available from G. J. Whitehurst, State University of New York at Stony Brook, Stony Brook, NY 11794–2500).

Whitehurst, G. J., & Lonigan, C. J. (2001). Emergent literacy: From pre-readers to readers. In S. B. Neuman & D. K. Dickinson (Eds.), *Handbook of early literacy research.* New York: Guilford Press.

Whorf, B. L. (1964). *Language, thought, and reality.* (J. B. Carroll, Ed.). Cambridge, MA: MIT Press.

Williams, S. (1991). Classroom use of African American Language: Educational tool or social weapon? In C. Sleeter (Ed.), *Empowering through multicultural education* (pp. 199–215). New York: State University of New York.

Willms, J. D. (1999). *International adult literacy survey: Inequalities in literacy skills among youth in Canada and the United States.* Ottawa, Ontario: Ministry of Industry.

Wilson, J. (2005). *The relationship of Dynamic Indicators of Basic Early Literacy Skills (DIBELS) Oral Reading Fluency to performance on Arizona Instrument to Measure Standards (AIMS).* Tempe, AZ: Tempe School District No. 3.

Wilson, P. (1992). Among non-readers. In C. Temple & P. Collins (Eds.), *Stories and readers.* Norwood, MA: Christopher-Gordon.

Winner, E. (1982). *Invented worlds: A psychology of the arts.* Cambridge, MA: Harvard University Press.

Wise, W. (2000). *Dinosaurs forever.* New York: Dial Books for Young Readers.

Wong-Fillmore, L., & Snow, C. (2000). *What teachers need to know about language.* Washington, DC: U.S. Department of Education, OERI.

Wood, J. M. (2000). *A marriage waiting to happen: Computers and process writing.* Newton, MA: Education Development Center.

Woodward, V., Harste, J., & Burke, C. (1984). *Language stories and literacy lessons.* Portsmouth, NH: Heinemann.

Worthy, J., & Broaddus, K. (2002). Fluency beyond the primary grades: From group performance to silent, independent reading. *The Reading Teacher, 55,* 334–343.

Wylie, R. E., & Durrell, D. D. (1970). Teaching vowels through phonograms. *Elementary English Journal, 47,* 787–791.

Yolen, J. (1997). *Sleeping ugly.* New York: Puffin.

Zarillo, J. (2006). *Are you prepared to teach reading?* New York: Prentice Hall.

Zarrillo, J. (1994). *Multicultural literature, multicultural teaching: Units for the elementary grades.* Fort Worth, TX: Harcourt Brace.

Zutell, J. (1999). Sorting it out through word sorts. In I. C. Fountas & G. S. Pinnell (Eds.), *Voices on word matters* (pp. 103–113). Portsmouth, NH: Heinemann.

Zutell, J., & Rasinski, T. (1991). Training teachers to attend to their students' oral reading fluency. *Theory into Practice, 30,* 212–217. Paperstar Book.

Name Index

Subject Index

Board games, 152
Book baggies, 131
Book clubs, 37, 218
Books
    big books, 126–127, 142–143, 491
    classroom-produced, 129–130
    emergent literacy and, 126–130
    leveled book selection, 373–374, 423–424
    little books, 126–129
Boys, as troubled readers, 61, 62, 64
Brainstorming, 213, 285, 441, 442
Buddy reading, 38, 177–178, 215, 362
Budget issues, availability of books and materials, 62
Building knowledge phase, ABC model, 213–216, 250

California Achievement Test, 317
California State English-Language Arts Standards, 45
California Young Readers Medal, 39
Calkins, Lucy, 293
CALP (cognitive academic-language proficiency), 184, 410, 476
Campbell, Joseph, 227
Casteñeda v. Pickard, 51
Casual register, 94
Cause-and-effect chart, 298–299
Cause/effect idea organization, 255
Caxton, William, 88
Center for Applied Linguistics , 25
Ceremonial register, 93
Chants, 119, 122–124, 148–149
Chapteraday, 466
Chapter graphic organizers, 253, 254
Character clusters, 224, 226
Character maps, 224–225, 226
Characters, contrasts between, 229
Charts and posters, classroom, 116–117
Chat rooms, 306
Children's Publishing Center, 424
Chomsky, Carol, 77
Chomsky, Noam, 77, 97
Choral reading, 143, 180–181, 463
Chunking, 441
Cinquains, 297–298, 492
Classics for Young Children, 308
Classroom fluency measure, 447
Classrooms
    environment of, 36
    grades 3–5, 421–422
    for learners of informational materials, 273
    libraries in, 36, 116
    for nurturing emergent literacy, 116–117
    organization and management of, 421–425
Classrooms That Work, 383
Clay, Marie, 109, 110–111, 321, 334
Cloze procedure, 331–332, 412, 467
Clusters, 285, 298
Code-emphasis primary-grade programs, 392–393
Cognitive academic-language proficiency (CALP), 184, 410, 476
Cognitive schemes, 9
Coleman Report, 55
Collaboration, in writing, 285–286
Committee on the Prevention of Reading Difficulties in Young Children, 16, 19
Communication, writing as, 288
Communicative approach to second language acquisition, 482

Community, 34–42, 42–44, 468
Comparison/contrast idea organization, 255
Compound words, 86, 155–156
Comprehension, fiction. See also Assessment
    aesthetic stance, 206
    anticipation, 212–214
    building knowledge, 214–216
    consolidation, 216–228
    critical literacy, 207–208
    defined, 7
    as an element in balanced literacy, 19
    elements of, 8–9
    fiction, 204
    reader response theory, 205–207
    scaffolding, 211–212
    schema theory of, 15, 205, 206
    story grammar and, 92
    strategies and skills for, 208–211
    understanding, 204
    vocabulary and, 89, 169, 183, 209
Comprehension, informational texts. See also Assessment
    ABC model, 245
    classrooms for learning and, 273–274
    importance of background knowledge, 245–246
    instructional priorities, 244
    knowledge standards and high-stakes assessment, 243–244
    nature of informational materials, 251–258
    research and, 272–273
    strategies for, 259–271
    student engagement, 249–250
    teachers and, 244, 246–249
Computers
    in the classroom, 37
    equity and access to, 63–64
    grades 3–5 and, 424–425
    informational texts and, 274
    teaching writing and, 305–308
Concatenation, 210
Concept books, 130
Concept ladders, 193–194
Concept maps, 188, 189, 258, 443
Concept of word, 108
Concurrent method of bilingual education, 480
Conferences, writing, 286–287, 290
Connect two approach, 443
Connotations, 183
Consolidation phase, ABC model, 216–229, 250
Consonant blends, 76
Consonant digraphs, 76
Consonants, 75–77, 80, 83
Constructivist view of instruction, 205, 481–482
Content questions, 268–271
Content validity, 326
Content words, 187
Context, 158–160, 334. See also Social contexts
Conventions, writing, 284
Cooperative learning, 65, 213, 362
Coretta Scott King Award, 173
Correction, in second-language acquisition, 483
Counting books, 130
Crayola.com, 374
Critical literacy, 10, 65, 207–208, 405
Critical reading, defined, 7
Cross-cultural issues, international, 4, 16, 60
CROWD (dialogic reading), 119–120

Trial Urban District Assessment (TUDA), 437
Tutoring, 57, 168
Two-way bilingual education, 481

Validity, 326
Value line, 221–222
Venn diagrams, 298, 299
Videotapes, parent communication and, 42
Visual and graphic information, 254–255
Visualizing, 209, 452
Vocab-o-gram, 192–193
Vocabulary
  academic learning and, 184
  assessing, 190, 338
  comprehension and, 183, 209, 245–246, 257–259
  defined, 182–183
  development of, 186–188
  and the diluted curriculum, 65
  diverse students and, 183
  as an element in balanced literacy, 19
  importance of, 89–90
  kindergarten to grade 2, 191–195, 363
  knowledge levels, 90
  middle grade students and, 439–444
  online sources for, 196
  and reading aloud, 185–186
  relationships among term and word parts, 189, 191
  teaching, 184–185, 188–189
  thought and language and, 185
  tiers of, 90
Voice choirs, 180
Voice/print matching, 376
Volunteers, 168, 426
Vowel reduction, 80–81
Vowels, 74–75, 80, 84
Vygotsky's zone of proximal development, 330, 396, 407, 424, 482

Wait-time, 48
Webbed questions, 193, 194
Web text reading, 424
Whisper reading, 149–150
Whole-class instruction, 418–419, 436. See also Instructional reading levels
Whole-language movement, 14–15
Whole-part-whole teaching, 142
Whole-word reading versus phonics, 14
Whorf, Benjamin, 185
Wiggle Works, 154
Wikipedia, 332

Woodcock-Johnson-III Basic Reading Battery, 334–335
Word banks, 144
Word cards, 190, 191, 443
Word conversation, 214
Word games, 186
Word hunts, 153, 154, 158
Word journals, 156
Word Journeys, 335, 344
Word knowledge, 82. See also Word recognition
Word origins, 88–89, 441
Word play, 440
Word processing, 424
Word recognition
  and the alphabetic reader (grades 1–2), 145–150
  assessment, 333–335
  as a component of reading ability, 7–8
  and the derivational reader (grades 3–4+), 155–161
  differentiated instruction for, 142–145
  and the orthographic reader (grades 2–3, 3–5), 150–155
  stages in children's development of, 140–142
  vocabulary and, 89, 169
Word recognition inventory, 336–337
Words, concept of, 108
Word sorts, 150, 152–154
Words Their Way, 344
Word wall chants, 148–149
Word walls, 146, 156, 158, 417
Word wheels, 145
Work sampling, 304, 323
Writing. See also Four Blocks approach
  assessment of, 300–304
  and emergent literacy, 125–126
  genres, 293–300
  importance of, 283
  involving families, 304–305
  in kindergarten to grade 2, 363
  levels of support for, 290–293
  in middle grades, 436
  prerequisites for, 283–284
  research and, 272–273
  sample writing lesson, 126
  technology and, 305–308
Writing corners, 37
Writing process approach, 14–15, 285–290
Writing workshops, 12, 125, 287–290

Zarrillo, James, 346
Zone of proximal development, 47, 330, 396, 407, 424, 482

Text and Photo Credits

TEXT CREDITS

Page 41, "The End" by A. A. Milne from *Now We Are Six* by A. A. Milne, copyright 1927 by E. P. Dutton renewed © 1955 by A. A. Milne. Used with permission of www.penguin..com

Page 45, From *Maniac Magee* by Jerry Spinelli. Copyright © 1990 by Jerry Spinelli. By permission of Little, Brown, and Co.

Page 121 From Temple, Charles A. et al. *Intervening for Literacy: The Joy of Reading to Young Children*, 1/e. Published by Allyn & Bacon, Boston, MA. Copyright © 2005 by Pearson Education. Reprinted by permission of the publisher.

PHOTO CREDITS

P. xl, 2, Ellen B. Senisi; p. 4, Michael Newman/PhotoEdit; p. 12, Ron Chapple/Taxi/Getty Images; p. 15, Nancy Sheehan Photography; p. 23, Stephanie Maze/Corbis/Bettmann; p. 30, 32, Gary Conner/PhotoEdit; p. 47, Ellen B. Senisi; p. 52, Michael Newman/PhotoEdit; p. 57, Bill Aron/PhotoEdit; p. 63, Nancy Sheehan Photography; p. 70, 72, Ellen B. Senisi/The Image Works; p. 89, Nancy Sheehan Photography; p. 97, Richard Hutchings/PhotoEdit; p. 104, 106, Ellen B. Senisi; p. 108, Lindfors Photography; p. 116, Lindfors Photography; p. 127, Ellen B. Senisi; p. 132, Ellen B. Senisi; p. 136, 138, Ellen B. Senisi; p. 143, David Mager/Pearson Learning Photo Studio; p. 156, Lindfors Photography; p. 166, 168, Ellen B. Senisi; p. 173, Lindfors Photography; p. 177, Ellen B. Senisi; p. 191, Will Faller; p. 200, 202, Robin Sachs/PhotoEdit; p. 213, Mary Kate Denny/Stone/Getty Images; p. 224, Mary Kate Denny/PhotoEdit; p. 238, 240, Lindfors Photography; p. 245, Ellen B. Senisi/The Image Works; p. 271, Mary Kate Denny/PhotoEdit; p. 278, 280, Ellen B. Senisi/The Image Works; p. 293, Lindfors Photography; p. 305 (left), Ellen B. Senisi/The Image Works; 305 (right), Ellen B. Senisi; p. 312, 314, Ellen B. Senisi; p. 320, Lindfors Photography; p. 328, David Mager/Pearson Learning Photo Studio; p. 346, Corbis Royalty Free; p. 350, 352, Lindfors Photography; p. 355, Lindfors Photography; p. 376, Lindfors Photography; p. 377, Lindfors Photography; p. 379, Ulrike Welsch/PhotoEdit; p. 388, 390, Bob Daemmrich/The Image Works; p. 393, David Young-Wolff/PhotoEdit; p. 406, Lindfors Photography; p. 413, Michael Newman/PhotoEdit; p. 419, Mary Kate Denny/PhotoEdit; p. 424, Brian Smith; p. 426, Paul Conklin/PhotoEdit; p. 430, 432, Michael Newman/PhotoEdit; p. 439, Myrleen Ferguson Cate/PhotoEdit; p. 453, Will Hart/PhotoEdit; p. 461, Will Hart/PhotoEdit; p. 463, Paul Conklin/PhotoEdit; p. 468, Chip Henderson/Stone/Getty Images; p. 472, 474, Lindfors Photography; p. 484, Paul Conklin/PhotoEdit; p. 493, Michael Newman/PhotoEdit; p. 504, Will Hart